INSID

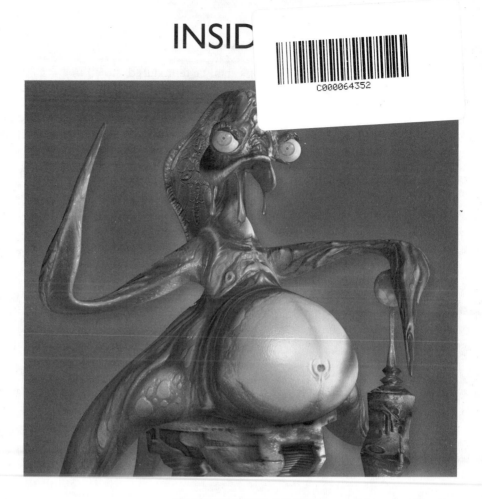

CONSULTING EDITOR
Kim Lee

New Riders

201 West 103rd Street, Indianapolis, Indiana 46290

Inside 3ds max 4

International Standard Book Number: 0-7357-1094-5

Library of Congress Catalog Card Number: 00-111151

Printed in the United States of America

First Printing: August 2001

05 04 03 02 01   7 6 5 4 3 2 1

Interpretation of the printing code: The rightmost double-digit number is the year of the book's printing; the rightmost single-digit number is the number of the book's printing. For example, the printing code 01-1 shows that the first printing of the book occurred in 2001.

Trademarks

Warning and Disclaimer

Publisher
David Dwyer

Associate Publisher
Al Valvano

Executive Editor
Steve Weiss

Product Marketing Manager
Kathy Malmloff

Managing Editor
Sarah Kearns

Acquisitions Editor
Linda Anne Bump

Development Editor
Audrey Doyle

Project Editor
Michael Thurston

Copy Editors
Nancy Albright
Krista Hansing

Technical Editor
Paul J. Baccash

Cover Designer
Aren Howell

Cover Art
Kim Lee
Mike O'Rourke

Compositor
Kim Scott

Proofreader
Marcia Deboy

Indexer
Brad Herriman

Media Specialist
Jay Payne

Contents at a Glance

Table of Contents

Part II Production Workflow

Part III   Modeling

7   Non-Organic Modeling for Broadcast/Film   187

8   Non-Organic Modeling for Games/Interactive Applications 215

9   Organic/Character Modeling Using the Patch Method for Broadcast/Film   245

10   Organic/Character Modeling Using the Box Method for Broadcast/Film   305

11   Organic/Character Modeling for Games/Interactive Applications   339

Part IV   Rigging

12   Non-Organic Model Rigging for Broadcast/Film Applications   381

About the Contributors

Kim Lee is a freelance animator/technical director based in New York City. A former senior animator at Curious Pictures, Kim has worked with many New York-based production houses, including Pitch Productions, Nick Digital, Spontaneous Combustion, and Shooting Gallery. He is also a freelance demo artist/trainer for Discreet, and is recognized as one of the top trainers for 3ds max and combustion. In his position as a leading Discreet Training Specialist, he has trained artists and instructors in both Europe and North America at companies as diverse as IBM, Electronic Arts, and MTV. He co-authored *3D Studio 2.5 Effects Magic* (New Riders) and teaches part-time at the Pratt Institute's Continuing Education program. One of his passions is creating independent 3D shorts such as "Pool Tools," produced with Boris Ustaev, which was the demo reel signature piece for Discreet's booth at SIGGRAPH '99. He also owns Worlds Away Productions, a small boutique production company focused on broadcast and 3D Web content.

Brian Austin is co-founder, along with Boris Ustaev, of orisian, a production/funding studio based in New York City. Formerly an animator at Spontaneous Combustion, a New York-based digital studio specializing in creating visual effects and design for the advertising, broadcast, and film industries, Brian's animation talents have earned him a Grammy nomination, plus two Telly Awards. His icon/interface design can be found on Reuters risk management software. Before turning to the commercial world, Brian worked as a fine artist; he has been in many shows, including, most recently, PS1 Contemporary Arts Center (1999) and Exit Art (1997) in New York City. His artwork is in the collection of the Museum of Modern Art and C.W. Post College. In 1996, he developed and organized a group installation and public symposium at the Nexus Contemporary Art Center in Atlanta. He has created Off-Broadway theatre sets and exhibition design. Brian holds a Bachelor of Fine Arts in painting from the School of Visual Arts in New York, and studied architecture and animation at Pratt University, NYU, and Parsons School of Design.

Doug Barnard is presently employed at Illusion Inc. as an art director, designing the next generation of virtual-reality entertainment. In the evenings, he teaches 3ds max 4 at the DH Institute of Media Arts in Santa Monica, California. He has been a freelance digital artist/consultant for clients such as Sony Music, MCA, the Disney Channel, Krislin Entertainment, and Activision. At the bleeding edge of technology, he is an alpha/beta tester for Discreet's 3ds max, character studio, and combustion. His published writing credits include chapters in *Inside 3D Studio MAX 2, 3,* and *4* and chapters in Discreet's courseware for 3ds max 3 and 4 and character studio 2 and 3. He spends his off-hours scheming on ways to build a boat and cruise off to be a digital artist in paradise.

Neil Blevins has been an artist since approximately the age of three. However, he entered the 3D arena about six years ago using POVRRay, 3D Studio DOS, and finally max when it was first released. He is actively part of the 3D community, answering questions on the Discreet Web board (`http://www.support.discreet.com`), writing tutorials, and displaying art at his Web site (`http://www.neilblevins.com`). After graduating from Concordia University with a degree in Design Art, Neil started working at the all-powerful Blur Studio in Venice, California, making content for video games, film, and television (commercials and broadcast). He has recently expanded his areas of interest to include scripting. Visit `http://www.blur.com/blurmaxscripts` for close to 100 scripts available for free download.

Ian Christie is currently a senior technical director at Industrial Light & Magic, the largest and oldest visual effects facility and one of the pioneers of computer graphics, where he has contributed to films such as *Deep Impact*, *Star Wars Episode One*, and *The Mummy Returns*. His path to ILM has been varied. After studying photography at Rochester Institute of Technology, Ian moved to New York City where he worked on projects from Broadway plays to magazine illustrations. His experimentation with incorporating computer graphic elements into his photographic work led Ian to the Pratt Institute Computer Graphics graduate program. From Pratt, Ian joined Curious Pictures as an animator. He moved to ILM in 1997. Ian lives in San Francisco with his wife, designer Terri Bogaards, and their two cats.

Brandon Davis is a technical animator at renegade animation house, Blur Studio, where he is most commonly viewed as an essential Quake rocketmagnet. His credits include annoying people at lunch with stories of his days as a paratrooper.

Diana Diriwaechter was born and raised in Zurich, Switzerland. Educated in the U.S., she graduated from the Savannah College of Art and Design. For several years, Diana worked as a computer animator for the post-production company Spontaneous Combustion, servicing such clients as AT&T, Estee Lauder, and the Sci-Fi Channel. Currently, Diana works as a freelance 3D artist in the New York City area. Her clients include HBO and PBS. She also teaches 3ds max classes at New York University. You can reach Diana at `ddiriwa@hotmail.com`.

Max Ehrlich works as a freelancer in the New York City area creating pieces for broadcast television. He has a background in graphic design. Max has taught computer animation at universities in New York and Atlanta. When he is not working, he enjoys driving his 1962 Ford Fairlane on long road trips.

Sean Feely is currently an artist at Pentagon Studios. While writing this book he was a 3D artist at Ronin Entertainment, working on game environments for the PC and Xbox. Before joining Ronin, he worked for Atlandia Design as a visual supervisor for its Real-Time Urban Simulation databases and pre-rendered architectural fly-throughs.

Mike Hall started his career in 3D at a young age by animating flying logos on a painfully slow Video Toaster system at a local public access TV station in Colorado. Dreaming of greener pastures and faster CPU cycles, he soon weasled his way into the game industry, where he worked for the next three years on a fantasy game for the PC. He is currently hard at work at Ronin Games as lead artist on a secret title for the Xbox. He spends his free time obsessively mastering lawn bowling. His next project to be done in max 4 is a 3D music video for a song about glue.

Adam Holmes is a CG specialist at Discreet, the creators of 3ds max, combustion, and other special effects/editing software. He tests and works with the latest tools for creating digital media content. Prior to joining Discreet, Adam worked for three years as a lighting and FX animator at Big Idea Productions on the popular video series "Veggie Tales". A graduate of Columbia College in Chicago, Adam's other creative interests include photography and producing documentaries and short films. He is a tribal member of the Choctaw Nation of Oklahoma, the third largest Indian Nation in the U.S., and wishes to acknowledge his relatives and ancestors for their creative inspiration and guidance.

Mike O'Rourke, a Discreet employee, is the lead product designer for gMax, the gaming version of 3ds max that is expected to be available in late 2001. The same gaming experiences that have helped Mike develop this new application, through which gamers can develop their own characters, has helped him to fine-tune his skills in modeling and rigging for game distribution.

Boris Ustaev is co-founder, along with Brian Austin, of orisian, a production/funding studio based in New York City, where he focuses on animated children's programming. Formerly an animator at Spontaneous Combustion, Boris has been praised as using his highly developed traditional art skills to breathe life into computer-generated characters. Prior to joining Spontaneous Combustion, Boris served as a computer graphic specialist at Discreet. In addition to serving as a demonstration artist for 3ds max, Mental Ray, combustion, and character studio, Boris provided artistic and technical assistance to production studios and was heavily involved in the production of *Lost in Space*. He also did freelance animation for Curious Pictures, Spontaneous Combustion, and Pitch. A well-rounded animator, Boris also was a partner/lead animator at Pixel Generation, doing character design and animation for in-house game development. While a student at the School of Visual Arts in New York City, Boris provided the animation of the Nick at Nite character for Curious Pictures, and served numerous clients including Crest, Wendy's, Dr. Pepper, and Cap'n Crunch.

Joseph Yoo is a freelance animator from New York City who has worked on projects for clients including Nickelodeon Jr., Charmin, HBO, Audi, and Tech TV. He also has created game cinematics for Electronic Arts. He has taught workshops in New York, 3D courses at Pratt Institute in Manhattan, and classes in San Francisco. He currently resides in the Bay Area.

About the Tech Editor

Paul J. Baccash began his career as a production manager for a prominent Web design firm, and found his true passion in 3D design and animation. He quickly shifted industries to embark on this newfound niche. Paul is currently a freelance artist in New York. With his extensive Web design background, Paul has directed himself toward 3D application for the Web, but also dabbles in broadcast media as well as 3D gaming and CD-ROM designs, to name a few. Paul is also a partner at Clique Design Group LLC, a Web design company servicing the northeast. Paul has been successful in offering his clients interactive 3D designs for their sites, maximizing their Web presence and ability to have more of an impact on their target market. Paul can be reached at pbaccash@cliquedesign.com or cliquedesign@home.com.

Dedication

Max Ehrlich would like to dedicate his chapters to his wife Tabitha and their two cats, who did not complain too much while he neglected his family duties in order to complete his part of the book.

Jerril Yoo would like to dedicate his chapters to his family, who have been really supportive.

Acknowledgments

Kim Lee would like to first thank all of the authors for their professionalism and dedication to this project. Also many thanks to Linda Bump, Audrey Doyle, and Paul Baccash for helping to maintain the integrity of this book. He would also like to extend his gratitude to Michael Thurston and Jay Payne for their work on putting together the CD-ROM.

Kim would personally like to thank his family for their support, Kristen for her immense patience, Frank Delise for his advice and support, Phil Miller for his insights on being an editor, Kells Elmquist for the AA insights, Boo and Mars for their inspired performance and professionalism as actors, Rob Ruotolo and Anthony for the lights and assistance with the shoot, and Luis and Rich for their help in keeping it real with the UT stress management sessions.

Diana Diriwaechter wishes to thank Adam Burr for all his encouragement and creative criticism; Brian Austin for being such a great co-author; Kim Lee for his advice; Ellen, Thomas, her brother Rainer, and Elizabeth for their eternal support.

Sean Feely would like to thank and acknowledge Wendy Horwitch for introducing him to computer graphics.

Adam Holmes wishes to acknowledge his relatives and ancestors for their creative inspiration and guidance.

Boris Ustaev extends special thanks to his wife Stella Ustaev.

A Message from New Riders

As the reader of this book, you are our most important critic and commentator. We value your opinion and want to know what we're doing right, what we could do better, in what areas you'd like to see us publish, and any other words of wisdom you're willing to pass our way.

As Executive Editor at New Riders, I welcome your comments. You can fax, email, or write me directly to let me know what you did or didn't like about this book—as well as what we can do to make our books better. When you write, please be sure to include this book's title, ISBN, and author, as well as your name and phone or fax number. I will carefully review your comments and share them with the authors and editors who worked on the book.

Please note that I cannot help you with technical problems related to the topic of this book, and that due to the high volume of email I receive, I might not be able to reply to every message. Thanks.

Email: steve.weiss@newriders.com

Mail: Steve Weiss
         Executive Editor
         New Riders Publishing
         201 West 103rd Street
         Indianapolis, IN 46290 USA

Visit Our Web Site: www.newriders.com

On our Web site, you'll find information about our other books, the authors we partner with, book updates and file downloads, promotions, discussion boards for online interaction with other users and with technology experts, and a calendar of trade shows and other professional events with which we'll be involved. We hope to see you around.

Email Us from Our Web Site

Go to www.newriders.com and click on the Contact Us link if you

- Have comments or questions about this book.

- Want to report errors that you have found in this book.

- Have a book proposal or are interested in writing for New Riders.

- Would like us to send you one of our author kits.

- Are an expert in a computer topic or technology and are interested in being a reviewer or technical editor.

- Want to find a distributor for our titles in your area.

- Are an educator/instructor who wants to preview New Riders books for classroom use. In the body/comments area, include your name, school, department, address, phone number, office days/hours, text currently in use, and enrollment in your department, along with your request for either desk/examination copies or additional information.

Call Us or Fax Us

You can reach us toll-free at (800) 571-5840 + 0 (ask for New Riders). If outside the U.S., please call 1-317-581-3500 and ask for New Riders. If you prefer, you can fax us at 1-317-581-4663, Attention: New Riders.

Technical Support for This Book

Although we encourage entry-level users to get as much as they can out of our books, keep in mind that our books are written assuming a non-beginner level of user-knowledge of the technology. This assumption is reflected in the brevity and shorthand nature of some of the tutorials.

New Riders will continually work to create clearly written, thoroughly tested and reviewed technology books of the highest educational caliber and creative design. We value our customers more than anything—that's why we're in this business—but we cannot guarantee to each of the thousands of you who buy and use our books that we will be able to work individually with you through tutorials or content with which you may have questions. We urge readers who need help in working through exercises or other material in our books—and who need this assistance immediately—to use as many of the resources that our technology and technical communities can provide, especially the many online user groups and list servers available.

Introduction

Hello, fellow artists, and welcome to this installment of the Inside series. It occurs to me as I write this introduction that introductions are certainly in order for this book in particular. For one thing, Discreet has changed the name of its flagship 3D application from 3D Studio MAX to a much shorter 3ds max for this fourth and latest incarnation. Thank you, Discreet—the shorter, sleeker name befits the faster, more streamlined version of the tool that so many of us work with.

But there are many more introductions to be made. With this new edition of *Inside 3ds max 4*, New Riders Publishing decided to make some big changes, starting with a new editor—or, rather, consulting editor.

When New Riders first contacted me about being involved in this project, they said they wanted a fresh, new approach to the series that would appeal specifically to intermediate and advanced users. Having read many of the past volumes as well as other works on the subject, I suggested that we put together a book that not only covered the many new features in 3ds max 4 but also focused on real-world use of the tool in production. I stressed that if it were up to me, I would want to read only books by authors who worked full-time in their respective industries as hands-on artists and technical directors. I felt that if this book was to target intermediate and advanced artists, it had to be written by professionals in the field who work day in and day out with the tool in production. These artists could bring a much-needed insight to the subject that results only from working in a production environment. Although this had, in fact, been done to some degree in previous books, many of my peers and I felt that there was a need for a book authored entirely by production artists focusing directly on addressing the issues of the production world.

I also felt that the book should try to mirror as closely as was feasible a real-world production workflow (or pipeline, for those of you who like catch phrases), which led to the suggestion of a title change from *Inside 3ds max 4* to *In-Production 3ds max 4*. Finally, I felt that the book needed to focus on two of the main industries using max—namely, broadcast/film and games/interactive. To my surprise, the response from New Riders was, "Okay, get started." (They said "no" to the title change—oh well, four out of five ain't bad.) Thus began one of the most challenging yet rewarding projects I have had the opportunity to work on.

Introducing a New Focus

So why did we structure the book the way we did? Having taught at both the undergraduate and continuing education levels—and having been a member of the Discreet Training Specialist (DTS) team—I realize that, for many advanced students and professionals in the field, books on this topic are a major resource for the ever-expanding technical knowledge required by today's computer graphics community. Unfortunately for many readers, myself included, all too often the texts available to the public present tutorials and instruction that, although perhaps technically and theoretically sound, are not practically applicable in a production environment. Being active in the broadcast industry, I, as well as many of my colleagues, have been frustrated by the seemingly constant stream of new animators who have been taught impractical 3D techniques and are unclear on how a full production is completed. Therefore, the decision was made to model the structure of the book after the process of the production world.

We also decided to cater to the intermediate to advanced users, for whom there seem to be far fewer useful texts. However, this book is not meant to be a substitute for the manuals that ship with the program. I urge any beginning users to first read the 3ds max 4 user manuals that ship with the product, followed by *3ds max 4 Fundamentals* available from New Riders.

With that decided, we realized that to keep the integrity of the work high while keeping the project at a manageable size—and also to meet any hope of a timely completion—we needed to narrow our user focus. It was decided that by concentrating on both the broadcast/film and games/interactive industries, we would be able to provide useful information and insights to not only users in those respective fields, but also hopefully to users in many other industries, such as architecture and design, that could benefit from the techniques covered.

Introducing Some New Authors

Then came the hard part. We found ourselves in a Catch-22 situation that I am sure is familiar to anyone in the education field. We wanted to put together a writing team of respected and accomplished artists working in production who could represent the high-end users of their field. But, of course, the people we were looking for had the least amount of time available because they were busy with production projects.

We wanted to pull together a team of artists spread all over the United States and have them write a book that required them to share files and work as if they were all artists at the same production company. It became obvious that this was going to be a tremendous undertaking—and something that, to my knowledge, had never been done before. Thankfully, despite their busy, often insane, schedules, we were able to put together a team of professionals who were not only really good at what they do, but, more importantly, also excited to take part in this ambitious endeavor.

The next question to be answered was what project the authors should write about. Having so many artists from different companies as authors precluded the idea of using any recently created projects from the real world, such as commercials, films, or games. So, two new projects had to be devised: one for games and interactive projects, and one for broadcast and film.

The project for broadcast and film involves integrating a character and a prop into a live-action video scene. The backplate footage was shot interlaced on DV. Although it's certainly not the highest-end format for people working in broadcast or film, it was attractive for two reasons. First, it simulates a worst-case scenario for the kind of material that an artist might be handed in production. Second, it is a commonly available format that most readers can conceivably have access to for their own projects. (I imagine that not many users have access to HD cams or film cameras and scanners.) The project takes the reader through the entire production process, from building a character and a vehicle prop to texturing, rigging, lighting, camera matching, rendering, and compositing, with some MAXScript, particle, and animation insights thrown in to round things out. On the gaming side, you will be using different techniques to build, texture, and rig a character, as well as light environments. Production insights will be included for issues such as game-engine exporting.

We realized early on that there would be no way to cover every possible type of project that an artist might encounter and still address issues to the depth that we wanted to. Therefore, you will not find specific chapters on creating space scenes, water scenes, natural disasters, car commercials, or the next greatest real-time strategy game. However, all the concepts and techniques here can definitely play a role in any of these examples.

The authors have aimed to cover the many new features of 3ds max 4 within the context of a real project. Within these pages, you will find many topics that other publications have merely touched on or even ignored. However, you might find that certain other topics or techniques have been seemingly left out. The reason for this is simple: The first mandate given to all the authors was, "If you don't use it, don't write it." Although there are numerous solutions to a given problem in a tool such as 3ds max 4, some are impractical or lack flexibility. This book provides techniques that the authoring artists have found to be the best practical solutions in a production environment. Of course, they are by no means the only solutions in this ever-changing and evolving field of 3D animation. Hopefully these insights will plant the seeds for newer and even better techniques.

How to Use This Book

Because of the nature of the projects covered in this book, many of the topics and exercises can be taxing to your computer. A few recommended hardware minimums should be considered. Although these are merely suggestions, readers with under-powered systems might experience slower-than-desired performance when working in chapters that "push the hardware," so to speak. Generally, the requirements out-lined in the 3ds max 4 installation guide documentation represent a minimum desired configuration.

Suggested hardware configuration includes the following:

- Dual Pentium III processors, 500MHz or faster

- 256MB of RAM

- OpenGL or DirectX accelerated graphics adapter (optionally, a graphics adapter based on the newer Nvidia chipsets that support pixel shading will take advantage of new features covered in Chapter 2, "Changes in Modeling and Materials.")

- Network card installed or loopback adapter drivers installed for standalone machines

- TCP/IP network protocol installed

Before you read through this book and proceed with the exercises, you should be aware of a few things regarding the locations of files on the included CD. Chapter folders for each of the book's chapters on the CD contain all pertinent files referred to by the authors. Readers should especially note that there are color JPEG versions of all the figure files printed in the book. These should be referred to often because it might be difficult to tell what is going on from a grayscale print. This is especially true for chapters dealing with textures, lighting, rendering, and compositing. Any AVI animation files referred to in a chapter can be found in the respective chapter folder on the CD.

In the case of the backplate footage for the broadcast/film project in Chapter 19, "Camera Matching," and Chapter 26, "Compositing and Finishing in Combustion," we have included the sequential targa image files only once because of storage issues. Because we will be referring to this footage in multiple chapters, you will need to refer to the Footage folder on the CD to find the proper files. It is also strongly suggested that you copy this backplate footage to your local hard drive, to improve performance in max when accessing these files.

This book was written using version 4.02 of 3ds max. For users running the original version of 3ds max 4, it is suggested that you update your max installation to version 4.02. This free update is available from the Discreet Web site, at www.discreet.com. The newer point release of 3ds max 4 might be available by the time you read this, and hopefully it will fix bugs or inconsistencies experienced when we authored this book.

As is the case with any undertaking of this nature, New Riders and myself are interested in any suggestions or constructive criticisms that you might have regarding its usefulness to you.

During a conversation on making a living as a 3D artist, a colleague once said to me, "Don't forget, this is commerce, not art." This phrase has encapsulated for me the constant struggle between creating quality 3D animations and getting a project done on time and on budget—it's a struggle faced by working 3D artists everywhere. On behalf of myself, the authors, and the team at New Riders, I hope that you find some useful techniques in this book that will improve your abilities as a 3D artist and that maybe, just maybe, will help you reach that sweet spot between commerce and art.

Kim Lee

Part I

What's New

Chapter 1

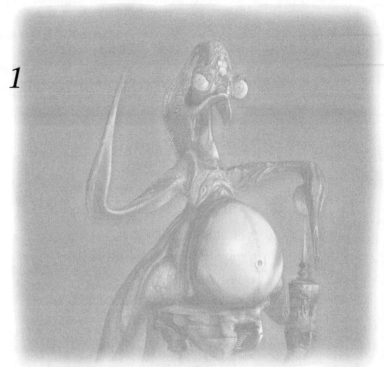

Changes in the Interface

by Kim Lee

Much like the previous version, 3ds max 4

benefits from a design philosophy focused

on customizability. Enhancements to the

general user interface are significant,

enabling artists to optimize workflow in almost any way they please. This chapter focuses on these enhancements and possible configurations that users might find helpful.

Changes to the interface include the following:

- Resizable viewport panels
- An expandable Command panel
- A redesigned Stack View display
- Redesigned drop-down menus
- Improved Transform type-in fields
- New Quad menus
- New manipulators
- An enhanced track bar
- Enhanced playback controls and time configuration
- Improved interactive rotation
- New Visual MAXScript

Resizable Viewport Panels

The user-resizable viewport panels are one of the smaller yet immensely useful feature enhancements. By simply clicking and dragging the viewport borders, the user can increase the size of a particular viewport or viewports while simultaneously decreasing the size of the remaining viewports. Viewport sizing can be reset by right-clicking anywhere on the viewport borders and then selecting the Reset Views button that appears. This provides greater freedom to focus on particular details in a given view without needing to configure a custom viewport layout.

Expandable Command Panel

The existing capability to work with the Command column in either free-floating or docked configurations has been taken even further with 3ds max 4. The user now has the ability to horizontally expand the Command column to better accommodate modifiers or objects with a previously unwieldy number of rollouts (see Figure 1.1). The benefits of this capability can be seen especially with objects such as particle arrays, editable meshes, editable polys, and editable patches, to name a few.

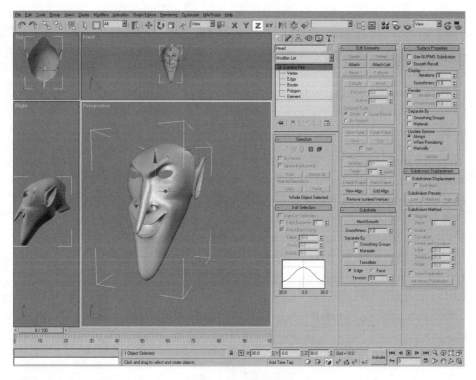

Figure 1.1   The Command column expanded horizontally to three columns.

Working in conjunction with this horizontal expandability is the capability to reorder the rollups displayed in the Command column. Simply click and drag the rollup's title bar to a new location that will be highlighted by a horizontal blue line. This can speed up accessing frequently used rollouts, especially when the Command column is not expanded horizontally.

Note

The rollup order is not associated with a particular object. Therefore, if you change the order of the editable poly rollups while working with a given object, they will remain in that order any time you access the editable poly controls, regardless of the object selected. To change back to the default order, you must right-click in the Command column and select the last option, Reset Rollup Order.

Redesigned Stack View Display

Another major change related to the Command panel focuses on workflow with the Modifier Stack. The workflow for applying modifiers has been enhanced, and, by default, the modifier buttons of version 3 have been replaced by a very long drop-down list of modifiers (see Figure 1.2). This list has been organized by modifier sets, which can be a little disorienting, even for seasoned artists. One of the reasons for this disorientation is that, when the Modifier List is organized by category (the default), the modifiers are not listed in alphabetical order.

Luckily, users have some options. If you right-click over the Modifier List drop-down, you are presented with options to configure modifier sets, list display options, and list preconfigured sets. Choosing the first option, Configure Modifier Sets, lets you set up custom modifier sets, much like in version 3. Show Buttons enables you to work with an interface more like version 3 (see Figure 1.3). Show All Sets in List displays the modifiers organized by sets (see Figure 1.4). Turning off this last option is my personal preference, but, of the course, the choice is yours.

Figure 1.2
Modifiers displayed as a list organized by sets.

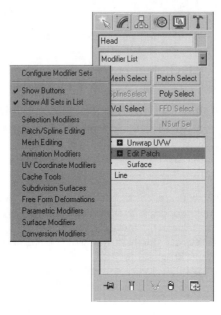

Figure 1.3   The right-click menu for controlling the modifier
               list display.

After the modifiers have been applied, users will find that the interface for working with the Modifier Stack has been redesigned.

The new Modifier Display window is organized into multiple columns starting with the Enabled column (see Figure 1.5). To the far left of the modifier entry name is a light bulb icon representing the active or inactive state of the modifier entry, similar to layer visibility controls in many popular compositing and editing packages. Note that base entries, such as an editable mesh, do not have an associated light bulb icon because they cannot be turned on or off. Additionally, you will find that by right-clicking in the Stack View display, users have the option of turning a modifier on or off in either the viewports or the renderer independently, which can prove very useful for calculation-intensive modifiers.

To the right of the light bulb icon is an expand/collapse toggle button that uses either a + or – icon, depending on its current state. This icon controls whether the modifier display will show the sub-objects of a Modifier Stack entry and will allow the user to switch to a given Sub-Object (gizmo) level, all from within the Modifier Display window. This makes it much easier to navigate from the various Sub-Object levels of different stack entries and is the reason why the Sub-Object button has been removed.

To the right of the expand/collapse icon is the name of the Modifier Stack entry. The last column in the display shows an icon that denotes whether the given modifier is operating at the Object or Sub-Object level. This makes it much easier to quickly see what is going on in long, complex modifier stacks.

With all these additions, it is easy to see that an expanded modifier stack can quickly grow very long. To account for this, you will find that below the buttons that lie beneath the Modifier Stack View display is a black horizontal line that enables you to vertically size the Stack View.

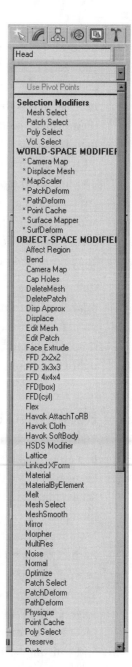

Figure 1.4
The Modifier List sorted alphabetically with Show All Sets in List turned off.

Users familiar with version 3 and earlier will notice the removal of the Edit Stack button, which had previously allowed access to functions such as cutting, copying, pasting, and renaming modifiers, as well as collapsing the stack. You now can access this functionality by right-clicking in the Stack View display (see Figure 1.6). To change the order of the modifiers in the stack, simply drag and drop modifiers. This capability is not limited to the given object's stack. You can now drag and drop modifiers from the Stack View display to different objects in a viewport. To copy a modifier, you simply drag and drop from the stack to an object. To make an instance copy, you must hold the Ctrl key while dragging and dropping. To move a modifier, hold Shift while dragging and dropping.

Collapsing the stack is achieved now by choosing the appropriate option from the right-click menu of the Stack View display. To selectively collapse to a particular modifier, you can simply highlight the modifier and choose Collapse To from the right-click menu.

Redesigned Drop-Down Menus

Many of the existing drop-down menus have been reorganized in a more intelligent manner, and new drop-down menus have been added to the main menu bar. The Track View and Schematic View menus have been combined under the common entry of Graph Editors. In the case of the new Create and Modifier menus, they provide redundant access to tools found in the Command column, which is useful for users who prefer to work in Expert mode or do not like the Command column. The Animation menu contains new features such as the new IK solvers, Wire Parameters, and Add Custom Attribute, while also including creation tools for the new bones and Point objects and constraints. The Tools menus now include entries for the LightLister and Isolate macroscripts that were buried in the Tab panel in version 3. The Tab panel is off, by default, in version 4, but it can be activated by right-clicking in the main toolbar

Figure 1.5
New layout of the Modifier Display window.

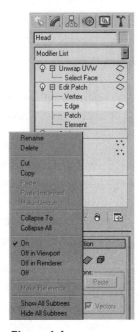

Figure 1.6
Right-clicking on the Stack View display produces a function menu.

and selecting Tab Panel. The Rendering menu has been given entries for the new ActiveShade feature as well.

The Customize menu has seen much change in this version, starting with the Customize UI entry. Selecting this option presents a newly organized tabbed window that includes entries that were previously found in the Preference window, such as keyboard hotkey setup and UI color setup (see Figure 1.7).

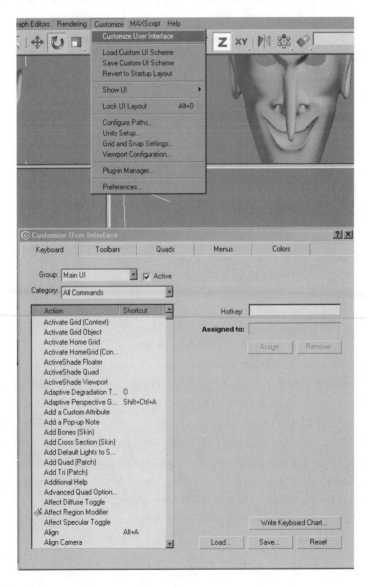

Figure 1.7   The Customize User Interface window.

But three new entries here greatly extend the customization capabilities. The Quads tab enables the user to configure the new Quad menus that are covered later in this chapter. The Menus tab allows for the customization of the main menu bar with any combination of commands or command sets. The Toolbars entry has been relocated from the old Customize UI entry of version 3 and essentially does what it did before, with a less cluttered interface. The button-editing tools found in the old version have been moved to a floating dialog window that is accessed by right-clicking a toolbar button and selecting Edit Button Appearance (see Figure 1.8). A notable addition that is not immediately obvious is that user-defined macroscripts can be configured as entries for Quads, toolbars, and menus, allowing proprietary tools to be included seamlessly anywhere in the interface.

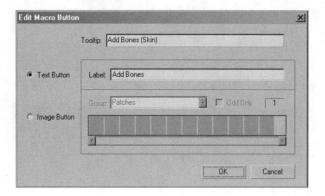

Figure 1.8   The Edit Macro Button dialog box.

Also new to the Customize menu is the Plug-in Manager (see Figure 1.9). The Plug-in Manager is similar to the Summary Info feature found in the File menu, in that it gives the user a list of the loaded plug-ins. But it goes far beyond that in functionality by enabling the user to dynamically load or defer specific plug-ins without needing to restart max. Loaded plug-ins appear in the list with a green circle next to them, while deferred ones (ones not loaded into memory) appear with a yellow circle. The user can tag any number of entries by right-clicking in the main window and thus can select large groups of plug-ins to be deferred or loaded quickly. The user also has the capability in this window to load plug-ins, no matter where they reside on disk, independent of the paths determined in the Configure Paths dialog box.

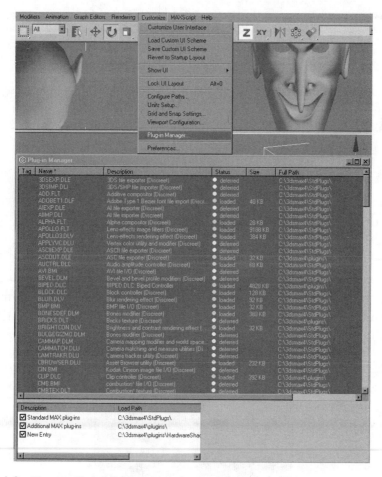

Figure 1.9   The new Plug-in Manager window.

Improved Transform Type-In

The Transform readouts located below the viewport area have thankfully been enhanced to accept input via a spinner control or by manual type-in, negating the need to open the old Transform Type-In dialog boxes from previous versions of max (see Figure 1.10). The X, Y, and Z type-in fields are context-sensitive to whatever transform tool is selected. A new button to the left of this area enables the user to toggle between Absolute and Relative transform modes.

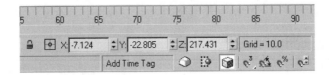

Figure 1.10   Transform Type-In fields now accept input.

New Quad Menus

The viewport right-click menus have been totally redesigned and replaced with a new Quad menu system whose design seems inspired by similar implementations in some other popular 3D packages. Now when right-clicking in a viewport or on an object, a system of context-sensitive popup menus appears. These menus are arranged around a square base, with a maximum of four menus available at the root level. Quad menus enable the user to access the last used command from a particular quad by clicking on the appropriate yellow quad box at the center of the menu. This allows for faster execution of commonly used commands (see Figure 1.11).

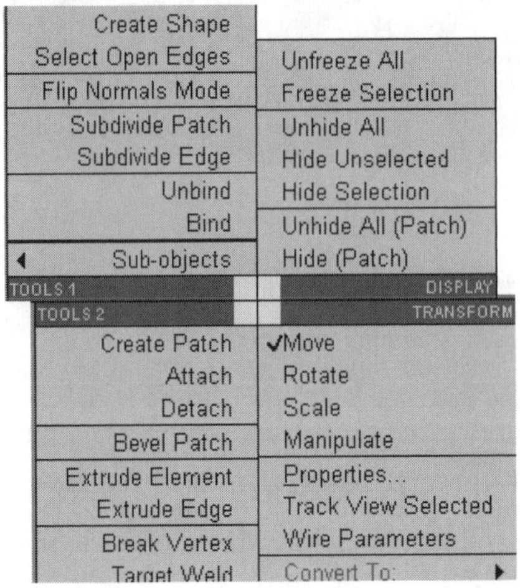

Figure 1.11   The new right-click Quad menu.

Quad menus can be customized to a particular user's needs by selecting Customize User Interface/Quads from the Customize drop-down menu. From this window, users can create new Quad menus as well as assign these menus to hotkeys. This means that, in addition to the default right-click quad, a user can have as many custom Quad menus as desired. Quad menus can be configured to open one at a time as the mouse is scrolled over the center yellow quad boxes, or all at once. As stated earlier even macroscripts can be assigned as quad entries, and custom quads can be saved and loaded.

The Advanced Options window is accessed by pressing the Advanced Options button in the Quads tab of the Customize User Interface window. This window presents controls that allow for full size, font, and color configuration of the menus, as well as settings for menu behaviors when opening and when near the edge of the screen. An interesting feature made possible under Windows 2000 is the capability to set the opacity level of the Quad menus, thus allowing the user to still see the objects that lie behind the menu. This can be adjusted with the Opacity Amount spinner. Also note that the Vertical Margins spinner will control the overall size of the Quad menus.

Proficient use of the Quad menus can significantly increase an artist's productivity, especially for those who prefer an uncluttered interface. For example, polygon-modeling tools could be assigned to a Quad menu that is triggered by a given hotkey, while patch tools or such could be assigned to yet another Quad menu.

New Manipulators

In the main toolbar located just to the right of the select/transform tools is a new button called Select and Manipulate. This button gives the user access to manipulators that are similar in nature to the gizmo sub-objects of modifiers—they enable the user to change certain object parameter values interactively in the viewport.

Not all primitives and extended primitives have manipulators associated with them. Generally only spherical or cylindrical shapes with a radius parameter have manipulators such as sphere, geosphere, cylinder, capsule, oil tank, and the ever-present teapot, to name a few. Spline shapes such as the circle, Ngon, and arc have manipulators as well. Manipulators can also control spotlight hotspots and falloff cones, the new HI-IK solver's swivel angles, the Reactor Controller's influence, reaction state and reaction value, and UVW Map modifier coordinate and tile parameters. Object manipulators appear as green gizmos in the viewport (see Figure 1.12).

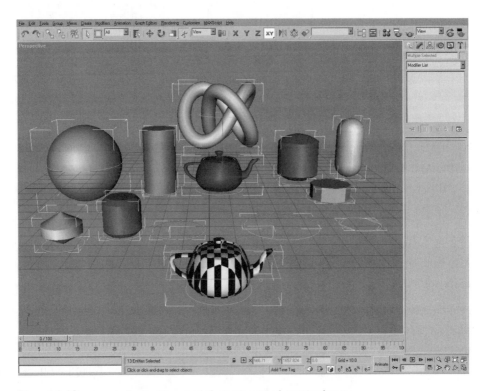

Figure 1.12   Assorted primitives and their associated manipulators.

Although implementation of manipulators in these areas can be helpful, manipulators are perhaps most beneficial and powerful when they're used in conjunction with the new Helper Manipulator objects found in the Create/Helpers tab of the Command panel (see Figure 1.13). These new slider, cone angle, and plane angle objects enable the user to easily create custom user-interface objects in the viewport. These objects can be connected, or wired, to control almost any parameter in max with the new Wire Parameter feature or the much-improved Reactor Controller.

Enhanced Track Bar

The mini-track bar located below the time slider has been significantly enhanced. Keyframes are now displayed as colored rectangles, while the current keyframe indicator appears as a semi-transparent overlaid blue rectangle. Note that this transparency is available only under Windows 2000.

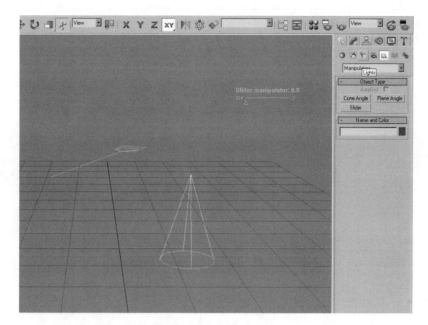

Figure 1.13   The three new Helper Manipulator objects.

The user also now can adjust the start frame and end frame of a sequence without having to go into the Time Configuration window. Holding down the Alt and Ctrl keys while clicking and dragging in the timeline results in different functions, depending on the mouse button used. For instance, Ctrl+Alt+left mouse button drag lets the user change the start frame, while Ctrl+Alt+right mouse button drag changes the end frame. Ctrl+Alt+middle mouse button drag pans the timeline. This is very useful for working quickly with small chunks of long animation. For example, a user can have a 400-frame animation but can set the start frame to 0 and the end frame to 20, effectively creating a 20-frame window view of the larger animation. Then by using the Alt+Ctrl+middle mouse button drag capability, the animator can easily pan this window and not have to deal with the clutter of keyframes from the entire animation.

Additionally, the track bar has been given some new configuration options, which can be accessed by right-clicking the timeline (see Figure 1.14). For instance, Show Selection Ranges displays a range bar when keys are selected in the timeline. This range bar enables the user to scale and shift ranges of keys in the track bar without having to open a Track view.

Show Sound Track displays the waveform of any sound file loaded into the scene file. As in previous versions, users must load sound files from the Track View window by right-clicking the Sound entry and choosing Properties (see Figure 1.15). On a related note, sound files will no longer loop when the animation frame range is longer than the duration of the sound file.

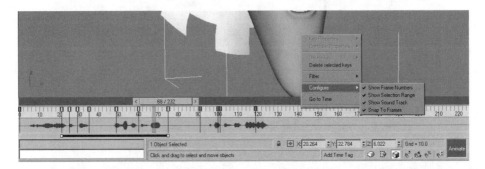

Figure 1.14   New configuration options for the track bar.

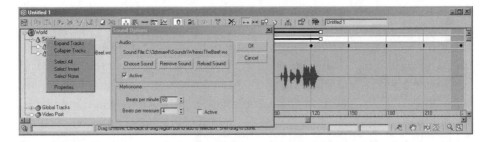

Figure 1.15   Adding a sound file from the Track View window.

Enhanced Playback Controls and Time Configuration

The Play button in the Playback Control area now has two fly-out modes that can be accessed by left-clicking and holding down the Play button.

The main Play button works as before, but the second option that appears as a white Play button plays only animation on selected objects. This can greatly improve playback speed and allows the animator to concentrate on only the object or objects being worked on at the moment. There are also some new options in the Time Configuration window. This window is accessed by either right-clicking any of the transport buttons or left-clicking the Time Configuration window. With the Real Time playback option unchecked, the user now has the ability to loop or not loop playback, as well as play the animation forward, backward, or ping-pong (see Figure 1.16).

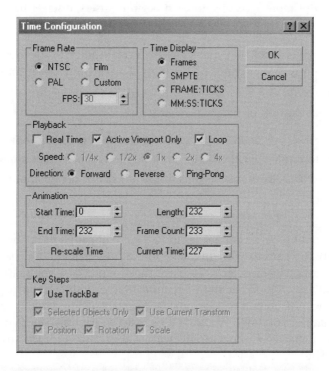

Figure 1.16   New options in the Time Configuration window.

Improved Interactive Rotation

Typically in past versions of max, interpolation between rotational keys has been essentially linear (that is, if two rotation keys exist for a given object, the computer will rotate the object in the direction of least rotation). So, for example, if an object were rotated 190° clockwise with only two keyframes set to define the motion, max would most likely rotate the object 170° counterclockwise. This annoying problem that usually cropped up after the first key had been fixed when using the default TCB rotation controller or the Euler (pronounced *oyler*) XYZ controller.

New Visual MAXScript

Although MAXScript has been a part of max since version 2 and is a relatively easy scripting language to learn, many users have not explored its capabilities. Even with the addition of the macroscript recording feature, many of these users—from beginners to advanced—might have felt slightly intimidated by the idea of scripting. To make MAXScript more accessible to even beginner users, discreet has added Visual MAXScript.

Visual MAXScript is a tool that enables users to create and edit the user interfaces of their scripts quickly and easily with a minimum of hand coding. Although it will not magically write scripts for you, it will speed up the process of adding interface objects, such as buttons or sliders, to your scripts.

The following exercise illustrates this new feature and its use by showing you step-by-step how to create a custom script for a fictitious project. For a more complete explanation of MAXScript, please consult the 3ds max 4 documentation.

Exercise 1.1   Recording MAXScript Code

Say you're working on a commercial for a soup company where the client wants hundreds of soup cans dancing in place. You decide that the can characters could be created with cylinder objects. To make them dance, you could apply a Stretch modifier and a Bend modifier and then animate the parameters of these modifiers. However, it will be quite a tedious process to create a cylinder and apply the two modifiers hundreds of times. Wouldn't it be easier to have a script that could create a finished can character automatically, with slider controls for the stretch amount and bend angle?

For users who have no scripting experience, this might seem complicated, but it really only requires that you remember one MAXScript command and one rule of scripting.

1. In the Command panel, click the Utilities tab and select MAXScript.

   The MAXScript rollout will appear in the Command panel.

Note

There are actually three ways to access MAXScript functionality: At the lower-left corner of the UI, from the MAXScript drop-down menu, and from the Utilities panel.

2. Click the Open Listener button and the Listener window appears. You will be looking at only the MacroRecorder feature of the Listener window.

3. If you see only a white text area with the text "Welcome to MAXScript," click the horizontal gray bar just below the drop-down menus to expand the MacroRecorder area of the Listener (see Figure 1.17).

   The MacroRecorder records whatever the user does in the max UI and displays it in its MAXScript form in this pink MacroRecorder area.

Figure 1.17   The MAXScript Listener with expanded MacroRecorder panel.

 Warning

Not all commands executed in the UI are capable of being MacroRecorded. As you begin to write more complex scripts, you will need to consult the MAXScript documentation for commands that are not recordable.

4. Click the MacroRecorder drop-down menu and check Enable to enable the MacroRecorder. Check to make sure that your recorder options are set to Selection-Relative Scene Object Names, Relative Transforms Operations, and Selection-Relative Sub-Object Sets. See Figure 1.18.

5. Move the Listener window to the side so that you can see the Perspective viewport. If you resize the window, make sure you can still see the pink MacroRecorder area.

6. From the Create panel, create a cylinder primitive in the Perspective view with a radius of around **20** and a height of approximately **60**. The actual measurements are not critical. Notice that the MacroRecorder has recorded the appropriate MAXScript code for you. See Figure 1.19.

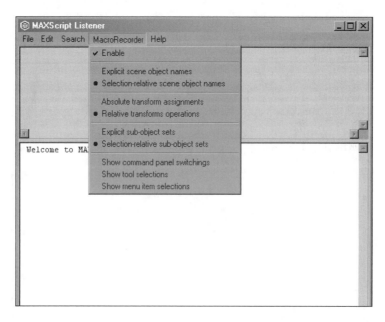

Figure 1.18   MacroRecorder options.

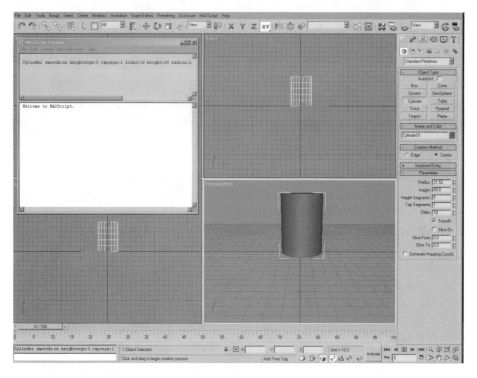

Figure 1.19   MAXScript code recorded for creation of cylinder.

7. Go to the Modifiers tab and apply a Stretch modifier to the cylinder, followed by a Bend modifier.

    You should see two new lines of code recorded in the MacroRecorder reflecting these additions.

8. Click the Stretch modifier in the cylinder's stack and adjust the Stretch spinner. It really doesn't matter what you change it to.

    You're doing this only so that the MacroRecorder can record the command for adjusting the stretch. You should see two more lines of code added reflecting this step. See Figure 1.20.

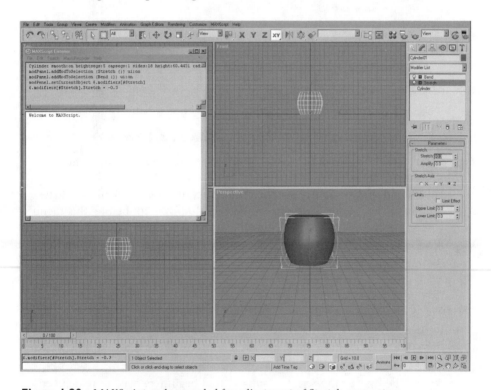

Figure 1.20   MAXScript code recorded for adjustment of Stretch parameter.

9. Click the Bend modifier in the cylinder's stack and adjust the Angle spinner.

    Again, you're doing this only to record the proper command. You should see another two lines of code recorded. See Figure 1.21.

10. In the MAXScript Listener window, disable the MacroRecorder. You have all the code you need to create your custom script.

11. Click again on the Utilities panel and take another look at the MAXScript rollout.

Figure 1.21   Final two lines of code recorded after adjusting Bend Angle parameter.

You should now be able to see the drop-down menu called Utilities at the bottom of the rollout. If you have never used MAXScript before, this menu will probably have no entries. You will be creating something called a Utility MAXScript, which, when complete, will be available to the user from this drop-down menu.

Exercise 1.2   Creating a Script and an Interface

1. In the MAXScript Listener window, choose New Script from the File drop-down menu. Place the New Script window to the right of the Listener window.

   Now comes the 1 MAXScript command that beginners need to remember. This will be the only code that you actually write in your script.

2. In the New Script window, type the following line of code:

   ```
   Utility canscript "Can Creator"
   ```

3. At the end of the line, press Enter.

   Utility is a MAXScript command that defines this as a utility script. canscript may be any arbitrarily chosen name for the script, which will be its internal MAXScript name. The last part of the command is the name of the script that you want the end user to see. This, too, can be pretty much anything you want.

Next, you'll need to know one of the rules of scripting, and that is the idea of blocks of code. Typically, scripts are organized into blocks of code, which is a way of organizing multiple commands into manageable groups. We will need to first create an empty block.

4. Assuming that the cursor is on the line below your first line of code, type an open parenthesis. Press Enter twice and then type a closed parenthesis. Your script should look something like this:

```
Utility canscript "Can Creator"
        (

        )
```

5. Now put the cursor on the empty line between the two parentheses and choose Edit Rollout from the Edit drop-down menu. You should see the Visual MAXScript window appear. See Figure 1.22.

   The first thing you need to do is vertically expand your main workspace located on the left side of the Visual MAXScript window.

6. Simply drag down on the small black square at the bottom of the currently minimized workspace.

   Now you can start creating interface objects.

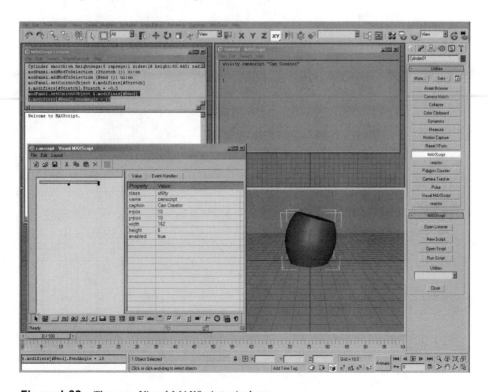

Figure 1.22   The new Visual MAXScript window.

7. Along the bottom of the Visual MAXScript window are the available interface items. Click the Create a New Button icon (third from the left) and then click-drag a rectangle of the desired size in the main workspace. See Figure 1.23.

8. Using the same procedure, create two slider objects below the button. These should look similar to Figure 1.24.

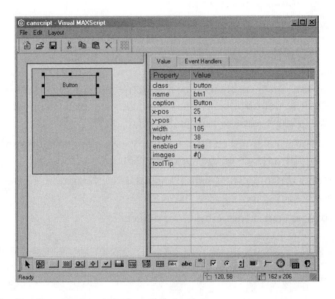

Figure 1.23   Creating a button interface object.

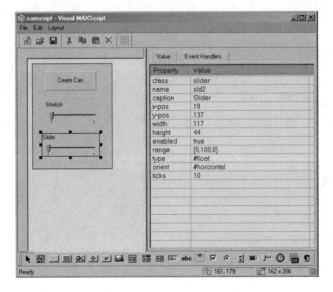

Figure 1.24   Creating slider interface objects.

Now that you have your interface created, you need to set some properties and give them functionality.

Exercise 1.3   Setup Properties and Events

1. Click the button that we created and look at the right side of the Visual MAXScript editor window. Notice that there are two tabs, Value and Event Handlers. Make sure that Value is the selected tab and then click the Name field in the Property column to edit its value.

   This is the internal MAXScript name of the interface item. Name it **canbutton**.

2. Change the Caption property value to **Create Can**. This is what the button text will appear as to the user.

3. Click the Event Handlers tab. There is only one type of event associated to a button, and that is pressed. Click Pressed and the Edit Event Handler window appears. See Figure 1.25.

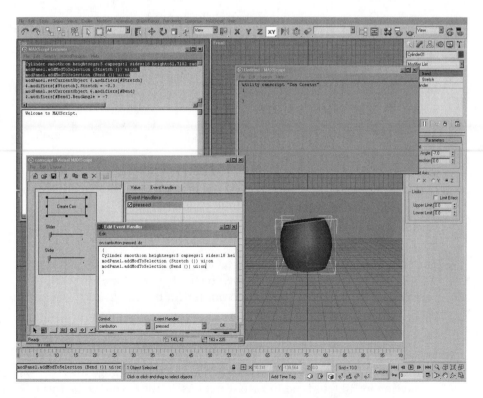

Figure 1.25   Copying code for the Button Event Handler window.

Notice that Visual MAXScript has already added the code for handling this event at the top of the window. It should read "on canbutton pressed do." Now you need to create an empty block like you did earlier.

4. Create an open and close parenthesis in the white text area.

Now you can go back to the MAXScript Listener window and copy and paste the proper code for creating your can character.

5. Highlight the first three lines of code that the MacroRecorder recorded, and then press Ctrl+C or select Copy from the Edit menu. Place the cursor in the empty line between the parenthesis in the Event Handler window, and press Ctrl+V to paste the three lines of code in your empty block. Now click OK and you're done with the button (see Figure 1.25).

6. Select the first slider, and then click the Value tab to show its properties. Change the name to **stretchslider**, and change the caption to **Stretch**. You also need to define a range for the slider, so change the three range values to read **–1, 1, 0.** This sets the minimum to –1, the maximum to 1, and the default value to 0.

7. Click the Event Handlers tab and then click Changed.

You need to set up functionality only for when the value of the slider changes. Using the same procedure as in Steps 5 and 6, copy only the fifth line of code from the MacroRecorder window. It should read something like this:

```
$.modifiers[#Stretch].Stretch = -0.3
```

The number at the end will probably be different than this, but it doesn't matter because you will be deleting it anyway.

You don't want the stretch value to be –0.3 every time you move the slider, of course. You want the value to reflect the movement of the actual slider. To do this, you need to make a small edit to your code.

8. Change the number that follows the equals sign to read `stretchslider.value`. See Figure 1.26.

This takes the value of your slider object and pipes it into the Stretch modifier's Stretch parameter. Be careful when typing in the values; MAXScript is very picky about spelling. Click OK to finish with this slider.

Finally, you need to set up the second spinner that will control the bend of the can.

9. Repeating the process of Steps 7 through 9, change the name of the slider to **bendslider** and change the caption to **Bend**. Also set the range to **–180, 180, 0,** allowing for 180° of bend in both directions. In the Event Handler window for the Changed event, copy the last line of code from the MacroRecorder window and change the number at the end to read `bendslider.value`. See Figure 1.27.

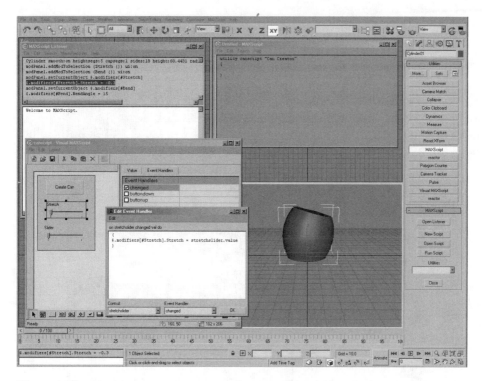

Figure 1.26   Changing the Event Handler code for the Stretch slider.

10. After all event editing has been completed, click the Save icon or choose Save from the File menu. You will see a whole bunch of code added to your previously empty script window (see Figure 1.28). Now you can close the Visual MAXScript window.

11. In your newly written script window, choose Save from the File menu and give the script a name. To run the script, choose Evaluate All from the File menu, or press Ctrl+E.

    You should see the script entry Can Creator show up in the Utilities drop-down menu. You've done it.

12. To make sure that everything works, delete the original can that you created. You can also close all the MAXScript windows. In the MAXScript Utilities panel, select Can Creator from the drop-down menu.

    When you press the Create Can button, the script will toss you into the Modifiers panel. You can see here that both the Stretch modifier and the Bend modifier have been correctly applied to the cylinder.

13. Go back to the Utilities panel and play around with the Stretch and Bend sliders. As long as you typed all names correctly, everything should work.

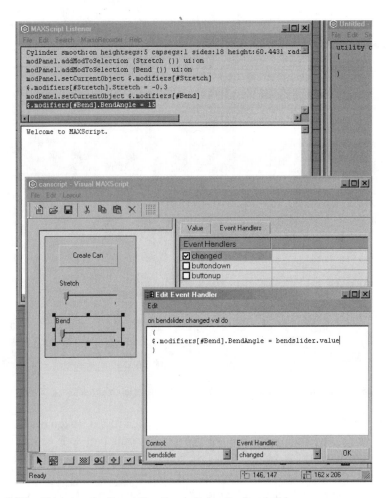

Figure 1.27   Changing the Event Handler code for the Bend slider.

You can also load the script Can_Creator.ms from the accompanying CD-ROM to compare your results. Ultimately, you should be able to see how Visual MAXScript can speed the creation of scripts no matter what level your scripting skills are.

```
utility canscript "Can Creator" width:162 height:206
(
    button canbutton "Create Can" pos:[25,14] width:105 height:38
    slider stretchslider "Stretch" pos:[26,73] width:111 height:44 range
    slider bendslider "Bend" pos:[19,137] width:117 height:44 range:[-18

    on canbutton pressed  do
    (
    Cylinder smooth:on heightsegs:5 capsegs:1 sides:18 height:60.4431 re
    modPanel.addModToSelection (Stretch ()) ui:on
    modPanel.addModToSelection (Bend ()) ui:on
    )

    on stretchslider changed val do
    (
    $.modifiers[#Stretch].Stretch = stretchslider.value
    )

    on bendslider changed val do
    (
    $.modifiers[#Bend].BendAngle = bendslider.value
    )
)
```

Figure 1.28   The final MAXScript code.

Summary

As you have seen, the 3ds max 4 user interface has received quite a few enhancements and new features. Although no single feature will completely change the way an artist works, when taken as a whole, these improvements can significantly speed the process of getting art out of your head and onto the screen.

Chapter 2

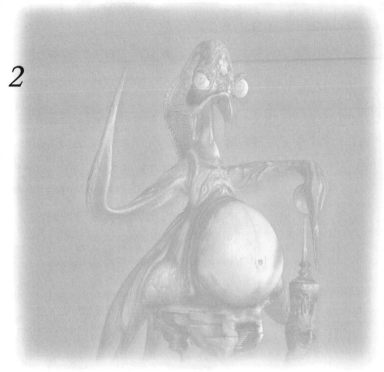

Changes in Modeling and Materials

by Kim Lee

In addition to the improvements and additions made to the user interface, many enhancements were made to the modeling and material tools of 3ds max 4.

Topics covered in this chapter include the following:

- Modeling tools
  - Mesh modeling with the editable mesh
  - Meshsmooth
  - Poly modeling with the editable poly
  - Hierarchical Subdivision Surface Modeling (HSDS Modifier)
  - Spline and Bezier Patch modeling
  - The Multi-Res modifier
- Changes in materials and mapping
  - Vertex data
  - Multi/Sub-Object materials
  - Viewing of multiple maps in viewports
  - Opacity map/alpha transparency
  - Pixel Shader/Hardware Shaders
  - Asset Browser

Modeling Tools

Many improvements have been made in the area of modeling in this latest version of 3ds max, with a strong focus on its existing areas of strength, specifically polygon-based and patch-based geometry. NURBS (Non-Uniform Relational Bézier Spline) functionality, which has traditionally not been one of 3ds max's strong points, has not been changed or enhanced in this version of max. This, and the fact that most 3ds max power users agree that the current implementation of NURBS is more often than not an impractical or unusable modeling solution, is why we will not be covering NURBS in this book. Readers interested in finding out more about using NURBS in 3ds max 4 are urged to consult the manuals or read *Inside 3D Studio Max 3*, also available from New Riders.

Mesh Modeling with the Editable Mesh

Changes to the Editable Mesh object type—and, hence, the Edit Mesh modifier—have focused on the area of game development. New options have been added to the Surface Properties rollup for vertex, face, polygon, and element sub-objects.

Users may now assign an illumination color and an alpha value at the aforementioned Sub-Object levels, which can be used by certain game engines for vertex lighting and transparency. Additionally, at the Vertex Sub-Object level, users can select vertices by Vertex Illumination value as well as by Vertex Color value (see Figure 2.1).

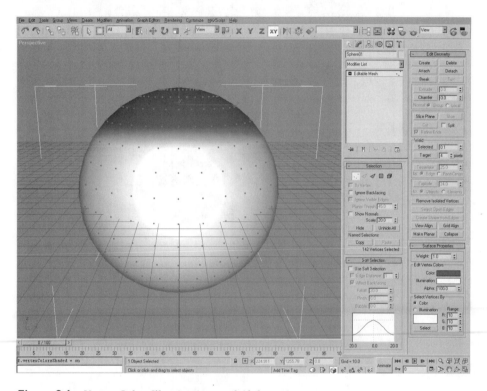

Figure 2.1   Vertex Color, Illumination, and Alpha assignment.

To see the effect of these new vertex value assignments in the viewport, you must open the Properties window of the object. Then, in the Display Properties section, check the check box for Vertex Color and press the Shaded button to the right. The drop-down menu enables you to select which Vertex channel to view: Color, Illumination, or Alpha (see Figure 2.2). Only one may be displayed in the viewport at a time. Note that to see vertex colors in a final render, you must place a Vertex Color Map in the Diffuse Map Channel of the object's material.

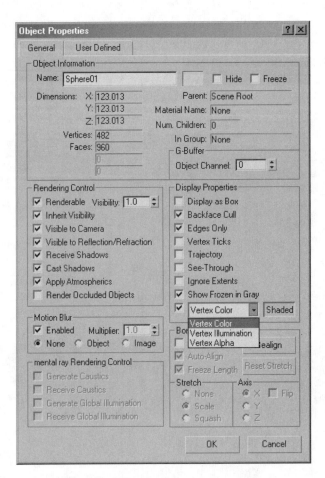

Figure 2.2   Vertex Color, Illumination, and Alpha display properties.

Poly Modeling with the Editable Poly

The Polymesh object type is a new geometry type that shares many similarities with editable mesh. Polymeshes, however, give the user much more control over the specific topology of a model. Developed initially to answer the rising needs of artists in the game development industry, this new feature provides modeling tools useful to artists in all the 3D disciplines.

The primary advantage of the polymesh to artists is that it does not create invisible edges and thus will not insert extra vertices when using cut or slice functions. As an example, create a cylinder and make a copy to the right of the original. Convert the left cylinder to an editable mesh and the right one to an editable poly. Using the

Cut tool at the Edge Sub-Object mode of the mesh cylinder cut across the top of the cylinder from one side to the other, without cutting through the exact center. Now do the same to the polymesh cylinder. In the properties of both objects, turn on Vertex Ticks in the Display Properties section. Notice how the mesh cylinder has extra vertices, while the polymesh version is clean (see Figure 2.3).

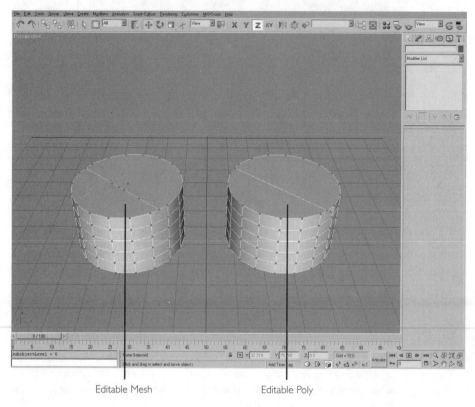

Editable Mesh   Editable Poly

Figure 2.3   Editable mesh versus editable poly.

The second major advantage over working with an editable mesh is that polymesh models tend to subdivide cleaner and more predictably when using modifiers such as Meshsmooth. This can be seen clearly when you extrude a polygon and apply a Meshsmooth modifier to the two models from the previous example, as shown in Figure 2.4.

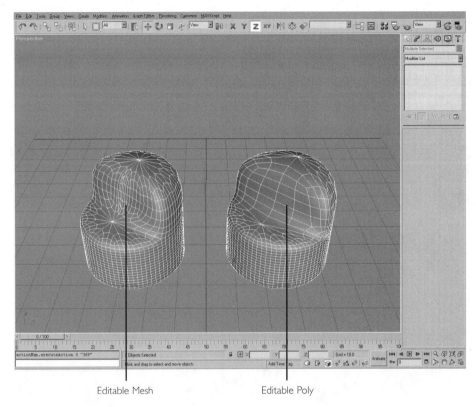

Editable Mesh   Editable Poly

Figure 2.4   Subdivision comparison of an editable mesh and an editable poly.

 Note

Traditionally, many max artists have used the terms "poly" and "mesh" interchangeably to describe polygon-based geometry. Now that 3ds max 4 has made a definite distinction between what a mesh is and what a polymesh is, it is very important when reading this book that you do not confuse the two terms.

An editable poly works much the same way as an editable mesh, except that its geometry does not limit the artist to working with triangular faces and all the problems that go with it, especially in the area of low poly modeling. Polymesh geometry is based instead on true polygons in that the number of vertices that can make up a polygon is not limited to three (see Figure 2.5). Just like editable mesh, editable poly has a companion modifier called Select Poly that enables users to add a sub-object selection entry in the stack. Because many of the functions of the editable poly are identical to those of the editable mesh, this chapter covers only new functionality.

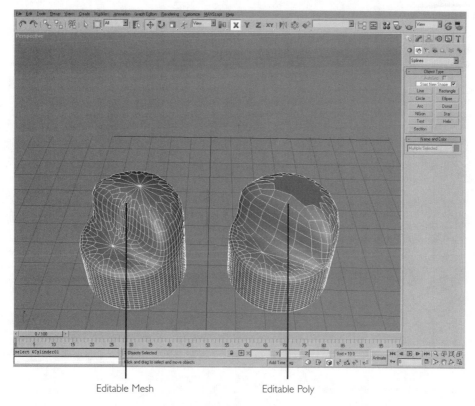

Editable Mesh   Editable Poly

Figure 2.5   Notice that the top of the editable poly object on the right is one polygon.

To convert an object of some other geometry type to a poly object, simply select the object and right-click to bring up the Quad menu. Choose Convert from the lower-right quad and then select Convert to Editable Poly.

The first thing you will notice with the editable poly is that the sub-object selection choices differ from an editable mesh. There is no face sub-object because faces are defined by three vertices, and, in a polymesh, a face—or, rather, a polygon—must be defined by at least four vertices. You will also notice that there is now a border sub-object represented by what looks like a kidney shape. Borders are essentially the edges of a hole in an object. If you deleted a group of neighboring polygons, the Border sub-object tool would let you select the edge of the resulting hole (see Figure 2.6).

The new Subdivide rollout enables the artist to apply Meshsmooth subdivision to a model at both the Object and the Sub-Object levels without needing to add multiple modifiers to the stack (see Figure 2.7). At the Sub-Object level, this allows users to add detail to select areas of the model as necessary, while granting immediate control over the newly created geometry components (vertices, edges, polygons).

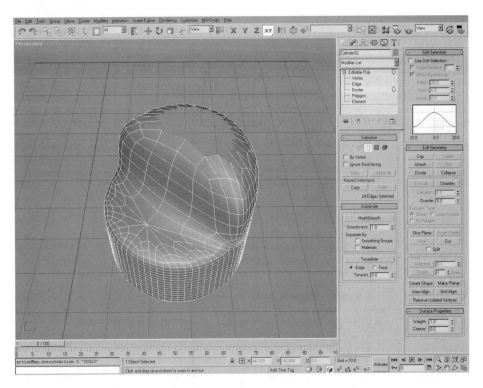

Figure 2.6   Selecting a Border sub-object.

Although this is much faster than having to apply a mesh select to select some polygons followed by a Meshsmooth modifier to subdivide the selection and then an Edit Mesh modifier to move the newly created vertices, the new capabilities also sacrifice a certain amount of flexibility. Because all the geometry subdivision and component translation happens within the editable poly entry of the Modifier Stack, there is no way to back-track through the modeling process if changes need to be made. You will be limited by the number of undo levels available, or you will need to save many iterations of the model, which, for the record, is generally a good idea anyway.

By breaking the modeling process down into individual Modifier Stack events, you can always go back and change, for example, which polygons you want to use Meshsmooth on. But in some cases when the artist knows exactly what he needs to build, the addition of subdivision tools within the Editable Poly object will certainly speed up the modeling process.

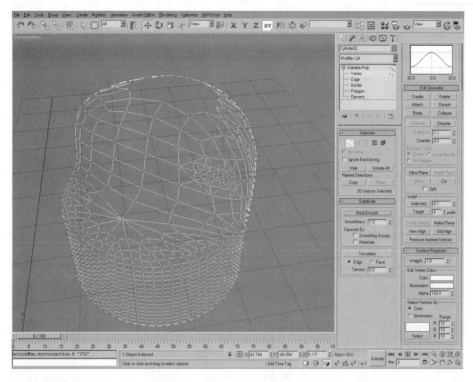

Figure 2.7   Applying Meshsmooth on selected vertices from the Subdivide rollout.

The Surface Properties rollout provides tools for using Non-Uniform Rational Meshsmooth (NURMS) subdivision at the Object level of the model. This rollout displays different parameters, depending on what Sub-Object or Object level is chosen (see Figure 2.8).

At the Object level, it enables you to toggle on or off the application of NURMS subdivision and surface smoothing. These controls are identical to those found when using NURMS subdivision in the Meshsmooth modifier. Users can set the number of iterations of subdivision and smoothness individually for both display and rendering. This will control the overall effect of the subdivision.

At the Vertex Sub-Object level, a weight parameter will be available to control the influence of a selected vertex on the applied NURMS subdivision.

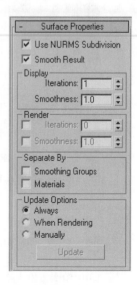

Figure 2.8
The Surface Properties rollout.

At the Edge and Border Sub-Object levels, two controls are available. The Weight parameter works similarly to that of the vertex's and generally results in a gentle pulling or pushing effect. The new Crease parameter, as you've no doubt guessed, results in a much more well-defined, sharp crease. It is interesting to note that the resulting crease appears to effectively override any smoothing group settings for the adjoining polygons. Therefore, if all the polygons of a model were assigned to smoothing group 1, applying a crease would visually override smoothing across the selected edge while leaving the original smoothing group settings unaffected.

At the Polygon and Element Sub-Object levels, the Extrude and Bevel functions have been given a new Extrusion Type option. When used on a selection of polygons that share edges, the By Polygon option enables the user to extrude or bevel multiple polygons individually along their respective normals (see Figure 2.9).

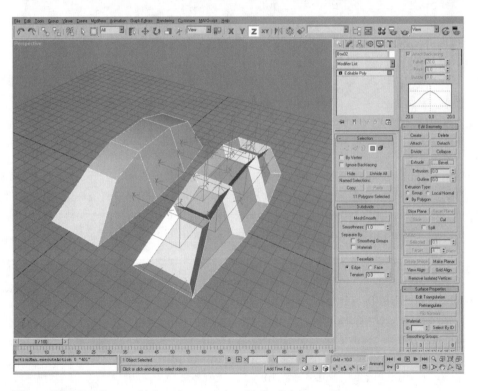

Figure 2.9   Beveling multiple polygons using the By Polygon option.

Controls also have been added to increase user control of surface triangulation. Some users might think that the inclusion of these controls contradicts the idea of the polymesh; after all, the polymesh does not use triangular faces. Although this is indeed true, you must remember that for the purposes of rendering, whether it be to the viewport or a final render, the computer must at some point work with triangular faces. This is true for all geometry types in max, including patches and NURBS surfaces.

Usually the computer will handle this conversion under the hood, so to speak, but many times leaving this up to the computer will not result in an aesthetically pleasing result. Hence the need for these controls.

Edit Triangulation, when activated, presents the user with a display of the triangular edges that will be used for rendering purposes. Users can select a point on the polygon, at which point a dotted line will extend from the picked point to the cursor. The user must then click on an alternate vertex to complete the edge, at which time max will adjust triangulation of the rest of the polygon to accommodate the user's choice. The advantage of this tool is less apparent on more simple co-planar polygons, but when used on non–co-planar polygons comprised of larger edge counts, it can become invaluable and can help the user avoid having to build new faces manually, as in past versions of max (see Figure 2.10).

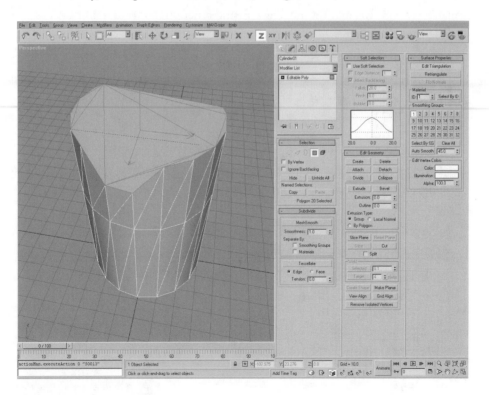

Figure 2.10   Triangulation tools in an editable poly.

Retriangulate lets max to do its best-guess triangulation on the surface. Note that using this will remove any manual triangulation that you might have already done, so it's best to try this option first.

Flip Normals operates as in editable mesh, but users should remember that in a polymesh, this option is available only for element sub-objects, not for polygons.

As in the editable mesh, the editable poly has the same vertex illumination and alpha assignment capabilities.

Meshsmooth

The Meshsmooth modifier in 3ds max 4 has been improved in two major areas. In the area of workflow, a new rollout called Local Control has been added. This rollout contains controls that enable the user to edit vertices and edges from within the Meshsmooth modifier without having to jump to an Edit Mesh modifier somewhere else in the stack. When working with vertex sub-objects from within Meshsmooth, users have access to weight controls. (Note that weight controls work only when using the NURMS subdivision algorithm.) At the Edge Sub-Object level, controls are available for both weight and the new creasing function (see Figure 2.11).

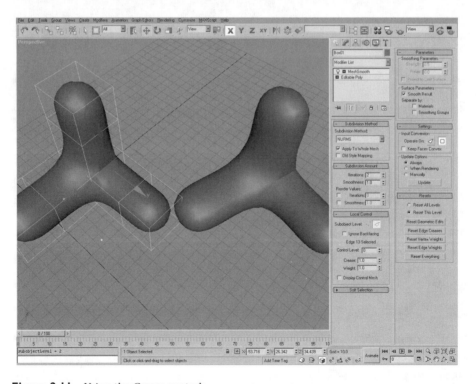

Figure 2.11   Using the Crease controls.

Although this level of control is useful on its own, the real power of the improved Meshsmooth modifier is seen when used in conjunction with the Control Level spinner. The Control Level enables the user to navigate up and down through the iteration levels of the Meshsmooth, thus allowing for direct manipulation of vertices and edges at any point of the subdivision process.

Take, for example, a cube. By applying a Meshsmooth modifier, the user could set the iteration level to 3, creating a smooth spherical model comprised of 386 vertices. Changing local control to 1, the user could then work with any of the 26 vertices that would be available if the iteration controls were set to 1. Any changes made to the model by transforming any of those 26 vertices would affect the surface generated by subsequent iteration levels (see Figure 2.12). The equivalent workflow to achieve the same result in the previous version of max would require adding a Meshsmooth modifier to the stack for each subdivision iteration required, and placing an Edit Mesh modifier between each to allow for manipulation of the vertices and edges at each iteration. Although this would add the capability to perform face and polygon operations (such as extrudes and bevels) at every iteration, for times when only vertex and edge manipulation is required, the Local Control feature provides a much faster and neater way of working.

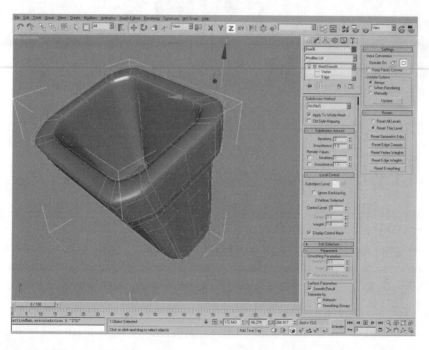

Figure 2.12   Adjusting two vertices at control level 0 will affect vertices at all other control levels.

The other major area of improvement is in the area of mapping. max 4 introduces a new default method for handling the subdivision of an object-mapping coordinate that fixes the stretching and slipping effects experienced in the previous version. For compatibility purposes, users can elect to use the old style of mapping used in Max 3 by checking the check box called, strangely enough, Old Style Mapping (see Figure 2.13.)

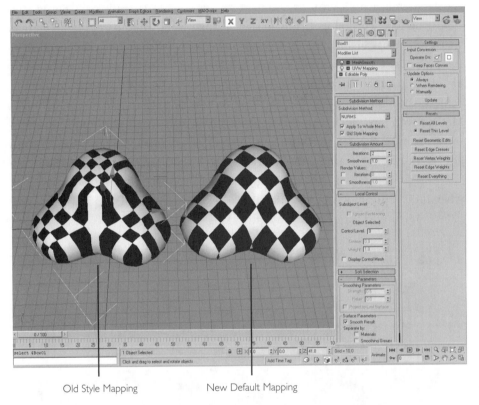

Old Style Mapping   New Default Mapping

Figure 2.13   Comparison of old-style mapping and the new improved default mapping.

Hierarchical Subdivision Surface Modeling (HSDS Modifier)

max 4 introduces a new method of subdivision modeling called HSDS. Subdivision surfaces have become quite the buzzword in the 3D community lately, and, as with all issues of this nature, it is important to distinguish the reality from the hype.

Discreet's implementation of this technology, HSDS, stands for Hierarchical Subdivision Surface. Per its name, the hierarchical nature of the surface means that as modifications are made at a lower, less subdivided level, they are passed up the hierarchy to higher, more subdivided levels that will reflect the cumulative modifications.

Therefore, if an artist has modeled a wart on the nose of a character at the fourth level of subdivision, moving the vertices of the nose at the first level will move the wart along with the nose. We will first take a look at the parameters of the HSDS modifier and then compare it to the other modeling techniques available.

The first thing to realize is that for every level of subdivision, the HSDS modifier creates a lattice-like grid around the object that the vertices of the object will conform to. This is much like the way an FFD works, except that the lattice or grid created by HSDS conforms much more closely to the topology of the model. It is the sub-objects of this grid that users will manipulate within the HSDS modifier, not the sub-objects of the actual model. Users should also note that, based on parameter settings, the vertices of the actual model might, to varying degrees, not exactly match the positions of the HSDS grid vertices. An understanding of this is important for achieving predictable results using HSDS. Another thing to keep in mind is that the output of the HSDS modifier is a mesh-based model; in other words, it uses triangular faces. If you want to continue working with a polymesh object, you must convert the object to a polymesh.

In the HSDS Parameters rollout, four Sub-Object levels are available. Subdivision cannot be applied unless a selection is made at one of the Sub-Object levels (see Figure 2.14).

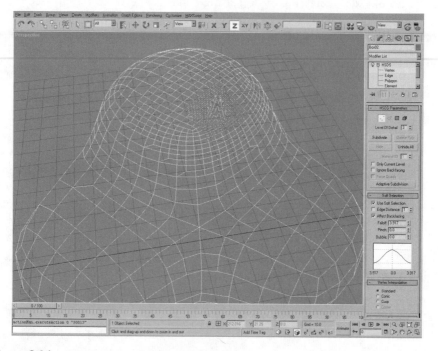

Figure 2.14   Adjusting LOD 3 using HSDS modifier.

The Level of Detail spinner allows for navigation up and down the hierarchy or sub-division levels, with 0 representing the base level. The Subdivide button will perform one subdivision on the selected sub-object region. Delete Poly is fairly self-explanatory and is available only at the Polygon and Element Sub-Object levels. Note that to use Delete Poly, the polygon must share all its edges with other polygons. Hence, you cannot use Delete Poly on the polygons around the perimeter of a plane. Hide and Unhide All also work only at the Polygon/Element Sub-Object levels and are good for speeding up interactivity when working at higher levels of detail.

The check box called Only Current Level enables the user to quickly hide the parts of the model not influenced by the current level of detail. Like the Hide feature, this can greatly improve the interactivity speed because it will dynamically hide different portions of the model as the user navigates up and down the levels. Ignore Backfacing works the same way that it does everywhere else in the program. The Force Quads check box forces the HSDS modifier to output a quad-based surface. This parameter should be set before any editing or subdividing is done because changing this setting resets the modifier and erases any work done.

The Adaptive Subdivision button enables you to select presets or user-defined parameters for globally increasing or decreasing detail of the HSDS output (see Figure 2.15). This feature should be used after all work in the HSDS modifier is complete. Be careful when using Adaptive Subdivision to increase detail because your model can get very heavy very fast, much like working with Meshsmooth.

Figure 2.15   The Adaptive Subdivision window.

When you press the Adaptive Submissions button, a window appears bearing the same name. The first three presets, Low, Medium, and High, provide differing levels of detail reduction or addition; the fourth preset, Custom, gives you more control of the process. When increasing detail, the Max Level of Detail (LOD) spinner defines how many times HSDS can subdivide the existing model. The Length parameter defines the maximum allowed length of an edge after subdivision. Therefore, a lower length value results in a denser, more detailed model. The Angle spinner works much the same way but defines the maximum angle allowed between two adjoining edges. So, as with the Length control, lower Angle settings result in a denser, more subdivided model.

The Vertex Interpolation rollout gives the user control over how closely the vertices of the model will conform to those of the HSDS grid. In practical use, these options act like vertex-weighting presets. Vertices using Standard interpolation will match the HSDS grid the least, while Cusp will force the closest match. The Corner option is available only for geometry with open edges where a vertex is shared by three or less polygons, such as around the edge of a hole or the outer edge of a plane (see Figure 2.16).

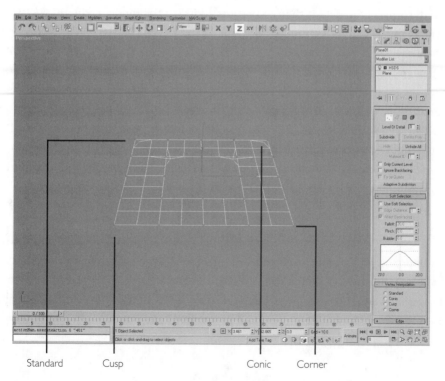

Standard   Cusp   Conic   Corner

Figure 2.16 The different types of vertex interpolation in the HSDS Modifier.

Finally, the Edge rollout contains the Crease control, as covered earlier with an editable poly. The Crease control is available only when in Edge Sub-Object mode.

FAQs About HSDS

With the addition of the new Polymesh geometry type, the HSDS modifier, and the enhancements made to the Meshsmooth modifier, it can be quite confusing trying to decide which method to use. After all, the concept of subdivision surfaces is really not something new to max users: It has been available in the form of the Meshsmooth modifier. For many users who have become comfortable and proficient using techniques based on the Meshsmooth modifier and the Editable Mesh geometry type, some obvious questions need to be answered.

Q: Why HSDS? I can already perform subdivisions at the Sub-Object and Object level with vertex weighting using combinations of editable mesh, edit mesh, select mesh, and Meshsmooth.

A: HSDS is not meant to replace techniques based on these existing tools. Rather, it is meant to enhance them. HSDS is best used as a finishing tool to add small details to models, such as wrinkles on a face. This is due largely to the fact that HSDS will not dynamically update if the geometry is added to the model earlier in the stack, such as in the case of extruding polygons at the Editable Mesh level. In this case, where the vertex count of an object has changed, any subdivisions made with HSDS will be lost and will require HSDS to be deleted from the stack and reapplied. It does have some advantages over Meshsmooth in that it can output cleaner quad-based models. Using NURMS in Meshsmooth on a selected area of a model results in a subdivided area with triangular faces around its perimeter. Also, it is possible to selectively subdivide specific areas at the Sub-Object level at any level of detail (iteration) from within one HSDS modifier. To do the same with Meshsmooth would require a larger Modifier Stack with many Meshsmooth and Select Mesh modifiers.

Q: Why use an editable poly instead of an editable mesh?

A: Any artist working on low-polygon applications such as game and interactive development will benefit from the lack of hidden edges inherent to polymeshes. Therefore, cutting and slicing will not result in the creation of extra vertices, while the retriangulation tools address the resulting need to control the eventual triangulation necessary for both real-time and prerendered output.

Another benefit of the polymesh that is not immediately apparent is seen when it is used as a base for the various subdivision modifiers. Polymeshes subdivide in a much cleaner, more predictable manner than triangle-based meshes. Also, unlike editable mesh, the editable poly allows for sub-object and object subdivision all within one modifier.

Spline and Bezier Patch Modeling

Spline and Bezier Patch modeling has been another major area of focus in this release of max. This technique typically incorporates the creation of a spline framework onto which a patch surface is created. Improvements have been made in most of the tools commonly used in this process.

Editable Spline

The foundation of spline/patch modeling in max is the editable spline. Although not new, many enhancements have been made to this object type to make its workflow more consistent with that of the editable mesh, poly, and patch objects while also extending the existing capabilities.

Looking first at its functionality in the Modifier Stack, the Show End Result button is now "sticky." In other words, it will now remain depressed after being turned on so that users can work within the Editable Spline modifier while seeing the final surface resulting from a Surface modifier applied later in the stack.

The General rollout has been removed and its functionality has been split between two new rollouts. The first, Rendering, contains controls allowing the spline to be rendered as geometry. Users now have the option of setting the number of sides to be generated at render time and the angle at which those faces are aligned around the spline. For example, if the user wants a spline to render as a four-sided cable and have it lie flat on the floor, the Angle button will allow for rotation of the rendered cross-section. The capability to display Render Mesh is a huge timesaver, allowing the artist to adjust the parameters of the renderable spline without having to constantly render while tweaking. An option is also available to use the viewport rendering setting for the final render (see Figure 2.17).

The second offshoot of the old General rollout is the Interpolation rollout that now contains controls for the spline detail between vertices.

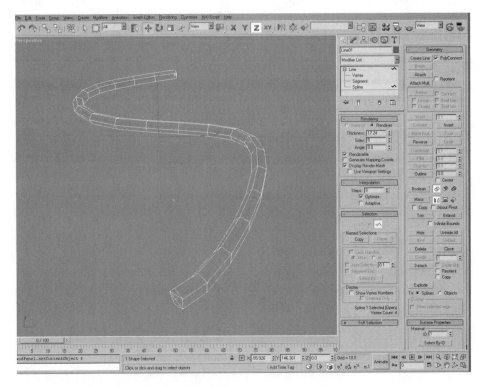

Figure 2.17   New rollouts for editable spline and Line objects, showing spline as renderable in the viewport.

The Selection rollout now contains two new options that make editing Surface Tools–style frameworks much easier. When in Vertex Sub-Object mode, users can now turn on Segment End to accurately select specific vertices. A common situation when modeling with splines is that vertices of different splines will occupy the same 3D space as a result of snapping. Segment End enables the user to select the desired vertex by clicking the corresponding segment. Holding down the Ctrl key enables the user to add to the selection. The Select By button enables the user to select all the vertices of a previously selected spline or segment. To use this feature the user must first select either a segment or a spline at the appropriate Sub-Object level and then switch to the Vertex Sub-Object level, click Select By, and choose the desired method.

Soft Selections have been added to the editable spline, making workflow more consistent with that of the editable geometry types. Although its controls are the same as previous versions, use of Soft Selection with spline objects requires some additional care. When used on spline frameworks commonly used for Surface Tools, users should be aware that at the Segment and Spline Sub-Object levels, toggling on Edge Distance can produce unpredictable results.

The Geometry rollout also contains some new features. A new feature common to both Object and Sub-Object levels is the PolyConnect check box. When creating new splines using the Create Line function, the first drawn vertex will weld to the end vertex of an existing spline by default if the user starts the new line over the existing spline's end vertex. This is often undesirable, so the user now has the ability to toggle this function with the PolyConnect check box.

A general rule of thumb is to use Edge Distance only on vertex sub-objects of an editable spline comprised of many interconnected cross-sections.

The Refine function has also been enhanced, giving the user the option to either refine or connect when clicking directly on an existing vertex. This is useful for artists who prefer to create new splines by first clicking the vertices to be connected and then clicking the Create Line button. When the user turns on Refine and clicks directly on an existing vertex (typically using the Snap Vertex To function), a dialog box pops up, presenting a choice of either Refine or Connect.

Editable Patch

Many of the same enhancements made to editable spline and editable mesh have also been made to editable patch. The Show End Result button is now sticky and Soft Selections have been added.

As discussed earlier with editable mesh, users may now assign an illumination color and an alpha value at Sub-Object levels of an editable patch. Additionally, at the Vertex Sub-Object level, users can select vertices by vertex illumination value as well as by vertex color value.

A new feature unique to editable patch is the inclusion of Relax Mesh controls. In previous versions of max, this functionality was available only in the form of the Relax modifier, which proved invaluable as a finishing tool for patch-based models. However, the Relax modifier was not patch-friendly; it took in a patch-based model and output a mesh-based model. Although the current version of max has addressed this problem with the Relax modifier, a variant of Relax has made its way into the editable patch.

The effect of using either of these tools is significantly different. Using the built-in Relax function produces results more akin to using a Meshsmooth modifier with an editable mesh. The patch surface will become increasingly smoothed and rounded, while the original spline vertices and handles will remain in their original positions, effectively forming a control lattice for the patch surface. When combined with traditional box-modeling techniques using the Extrude and Bevel tools, organic patch-based models can be easily built using a workflow that artists working with mesh- and polymesh-based geometry will be familiar with (see Figure 2.18).

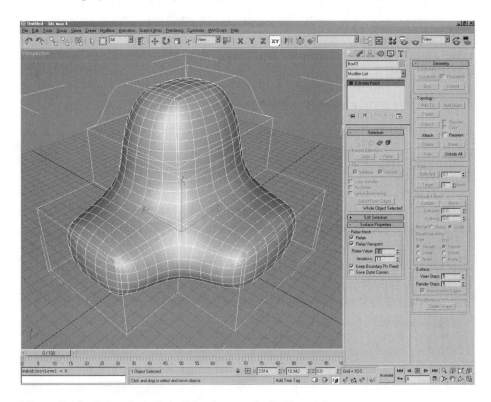

Figure 2.18   Using the built-in Relax feature of editable patch.

Texture mapping for patches is perhaps one of the areas of biggest improvement. In the past, one of the biggest headaches for artists was in applying bitmaps correctly to patch-based models due to the linear interpolation of a patch's UV coordinates. max 4 introduces the capability to work with curved UVW coordinate space based on Vertex Bezier handles. What this means to artists is that bitmap-based textures will no longer distort unpredictably across patches. Complimenting this is the newly updated UVW Unwrap modifier that allows for manipulation of Bezier handles to fine-tune mapping of patch models.

Much of the advanced functionality already available in editable mesh has now been incorporated into editable patch. The following is a summary of these migrated tools:

- Selected patches display as shaded in the viewports
- Select Edges and Patches by Vertex
- Ignore Backfacing
- Select Open Edges
- Break Vertex and Edge
- Target Weld
- Weld Selected Edges
- Create Shape
- Create Patch
- Normal Control for patches, including Flip, Unify, and Flip Normal Mode

Patch-Compliant Modifiers

As of 3ds max 4, the following modifiers will not convert a patch-based model to a mesh. This is not a complete list of all patch-compliant modifiers; it includes just those that have been updated in max 4.

- Patch Select
- Delete Patch
- Relax
- Material
- UVW Map
- UVW Unwrap
- Volume Select
- Normal
- Smooth

Multi-Res Modifier

The new Multi-Res modifier is used to down-res models, or, in other words, to lower the vertex count of the model that it is applied to. The Multi-Res modifier is a better solution than the old Optimize modifier because it is faster and affords the artist more control of what parts of a model will be decimated (down-resed). Usually artists working in gaming, Internet, or even broadcast and film prefer to build models expressly optimized for low-poly applications. However, many times it is more practical to decimate existing high-res models because of time, money, or manpower issues.

The modifier consists of one rollout containing spinner controls for adjusting the vertex resolution by either a percentage of the original count or an absolute vertex count value. Before adjusting these spinners, the user must first click the Generate button, which will generate the version of the model that will be decimated. Bear in mind that as long as the Multi-Res modifier is not collapsed, any adjustment of Multi-Res parameters is nondestructive, so you will always be able to get back to your original vertex count. The model of the Jester face in Figure 2.19 shows three Multi-Res versions at different resolutions. Note how well the overall shape integrity of the model is maintained, even at nearly 18% of its original vertex count.

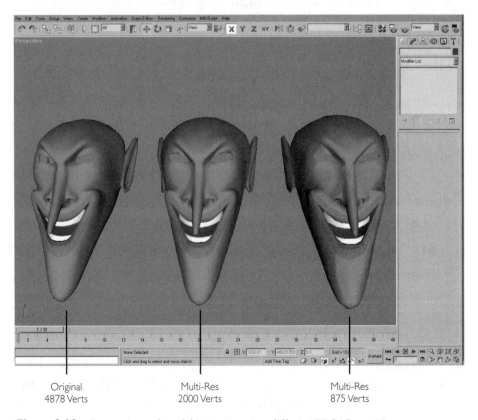

Original	Multi-Res	Multi-Res
4878 Verts	2000 Verts	875 Verts

Figure 2.19 Comparison of model integrity using different Multi-Res settings.

The Generation Parameters group contains controls for fine-tuning and controlling the decimation process. Note that you will need to click the Generate button for these controls to take effect. Vertex Merging should be turned on when the model being decimated consists of different elements. This is the case when a model has been created by using the Attach command (such as is found in editable mesh) to attach different models into one, without welding together vertices of each element. When Vertex Merging is active, the Merge Threshold spinner will control how close vertices from different elements need to be to each other to be merged. If you want to merge only vertices from different elements that are coincident (occupying the same 3D coordinates in space), you can leave the spinner at 0.0.

The Boundary Metric toggle forces Multi-Res to try to preserve the boundaries between Material IDs. This is useful when dealing with single-mesh models that have Multi/Sub-Object materials applied.

The Maintain Base Vertices check box is used in conjunction with Multi-Res Vertex Sub-Object selections. Whatever vertices you select when in the Vertex Sub-Object mode of the Multi-Res modifier will be preserved, while all other parts of the model are decimated. This is useful in allowing the artist to select the portions of the model that need to maintain detail.

As of version 4.02 of 3ds max 4, the Multiple Normals Per Vertex check box and its associated Crease Angle spinner do not have any noticeable affect on the decimation process. Similarly, the Within Mesh toggle option used with the Vertex Merging feature described earlier has no apparent affect either.

Changes in Materials and Mapping

One of the major focuses in 3D Studio Max 3 was to bring the level of tools for high-end rendering up to par with that of other state-of-the-art 3D packages. max 4 introduced an incredible amount of improvements in the areas of materials, lighting, and rendering. Although much of the focus of improvement in version 4 is in the areas of modeling and animation, there are still some significant enhancements to the tools for working with materials. Although many of these new capabilities were specifically intended to address game/interactive industry issues, they should prove quite useful to artists working in all areas of 3D animation.

Multi/Sub-Object Material

This material type has undergone a big makeover, allowing for much more flexibility in workflow (see Figure 2.20).

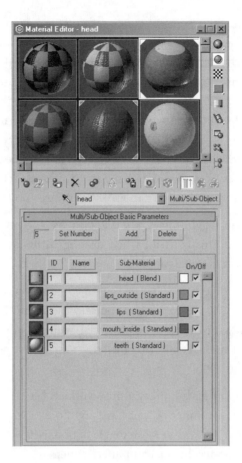

Figure 2.20   Redesigned Multi/Sub-Object material.

Two new buttons, Add and Delete, have been added to compliment the existing Set Number button. Changes made with Set Number can now be undone, and the Delete button allows users to selectively choose which material to delete. To delete a material, users must click the small sample sphere that appears to the left of the ID number to select the material.

The ID column enables users to change the Material ID number at any time. Clicking the ID button above the column sorts the list by ascending ID number order.

The Name column enables users to enter a custom name for the sub-material that is separate from the actual name of the sub-material used, and the Name button above the column sorts the list by name. This is useful, for instance, when the user puts a material called Leather into a sub-material slot for a character and wants to call it Pants in the Multi/Sub-Object material.

The Sub-Material button in the list gives the user access to the actual material controls; the Sub-Material button above the column enables the user to sort the list by sub-material name.

The Color swatch lets the user select a diffuse color for the sub-material. The On/Off Toggle is relatively self-explanatory: It makes a sub-material render black when turned off.

Viewing of Multiple Maps in Viewports

One of the most impressive changes to material and mapping workflow has been in the way the viewport displays maps. 3ds max 4 now enables users to see more than one map of a material at a time in the viewports (see Figure 2.21). This enables artists to more accurately build materials that use procedural maps such as mix or noise with bitmaps assigned as their components. This functionality is accessed by pressing the Show Map in Viewport button at the Parent level of the material. Previously, the Show Map in Viewport button worked only at the child/map level of a material. This functionality is available only when using Open GL or Direct X display drivers. Viewing multiple maps in viewports will not work using the Software Z-Buffer display drivers (HEIDI).

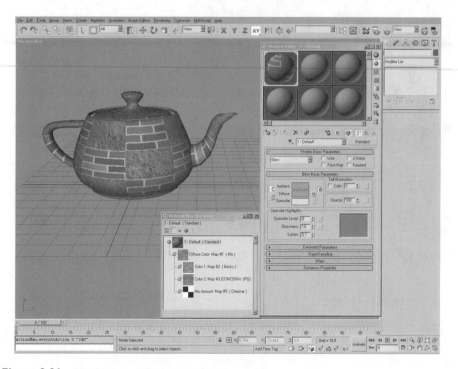

Figure 2.21   Displaying multiple maps in viewports.

Note

If you turn on Show Map in Viewport and the multiple maps are not displayed, try refreshing the viewport by pressing the Refresh hotkey (the number 1 key on the main keyboard, not the numeric pad).

Opacity Map/Alpha Transparency

Complimenting the capability to see multiple maps in the viewport is the capability to display opacity maps in the viewports (see Figure 2.22). This capability is automatic when the Show Map in Viewport button is turned on at a material's parent level, as discussed previously. Again, if the viewport does not display the opacity map, you might need to manually refresh the viewport.

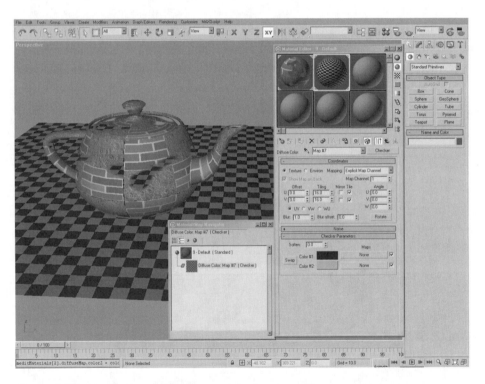

Figure 2.22   Displaying transparency maps in the viewport.

3D Procedural Maps

The viewports can also now display all 3D procedural maps except Particle Age and Particle Mblur (see Figure 2.23). Although this is a welcome improvement, be aware that viewport display is not all that accurate relative to the final render. One thing that can be done to improve scale accuracy when displaying these map types is to adjust the 3D Map Scale value in the Material Editor Options window. To do this, right-click any sample sphere in the Material Editor and choose Options. Within the Options window, adjust the 3D Maps Scale value to match the scale of the object. For instance, if a sphere has a radius of 50, change the 3D Maps Scale value from 100 to 50.

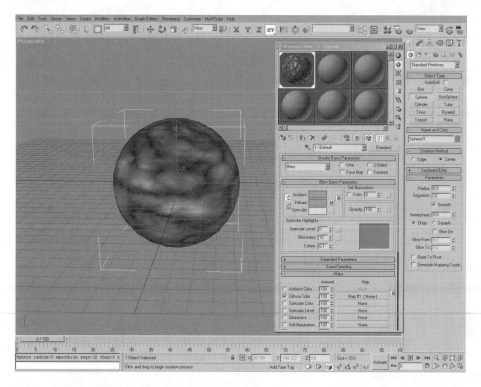

Figure 2.23   Displaying procedural maps in viewports.

Vertex Data

The new Vertex Data type discussed earlier, which includes vertex illumination, vertex alpha, and vertex color, can be displayed in the viewports also. To do this, go to the Properties window of the object by right-clicking the object and selecting Properties from the lower-right Quad menu. Toggle on the last check box in the Display properties group next to the drop-down menu of vertex shading choices. The Shaded button to the right controls whether max displays the object as a shaded surface or as if it were self-illuminated (see Figure 2.24).

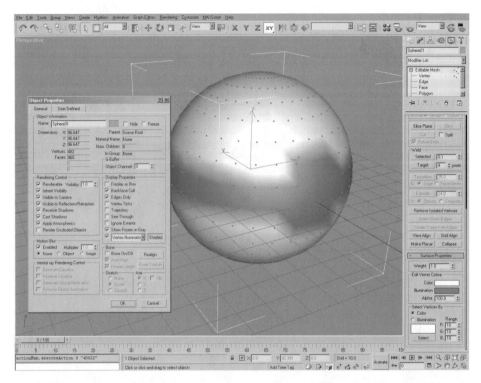

Figure 2.24   Turning on the Vertex Illumination display property to see vertex illumination in viewports.

 Note

To see vertex colors in a final render, you must place a Vertex Color Map in the Diffuse Map Channel of the object's material.

Pixel Shader/Hardware Shaders

A new map type is available for users who are running 3ds max 4 with a video card that supports hardware pixel shading. Currently, the most popular of these cards use chipsets from Nvidia. If you are running one of these cards, you must first be using the Direct X display drivers and then you must configure max to load the proper plug-in.

Go to the Customize menu and select Configure Paths. Select the Plug-Ins tab, and click the Add button. Select the directory called HardwareShaders, found in the Plug-In directory. Next select the Bitmaps tab and add the same path that you just added for plug-ins so that the plug-in will be capable of finding the maps that it requires. Close max 4 and then restart the program. Now when you open the Material Editor and add a map to a channel such as Diffuse, you will see a new Pixel Shader map in the list (see Figure 2.25).

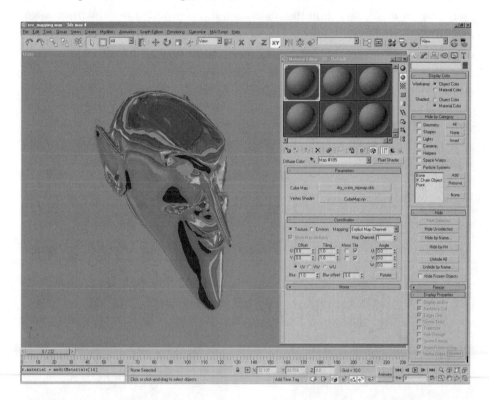

Figure 2.25   Hardware Pixel Shader applied to Jester head.

Select Pixel Shader as the reflection map, turn on the Show Map In Viewport button, and apply the material to an object. You should see a very fast viewport rendering of the object with a high-quality reflection mapped onto it that updates in real time as you arc-rotate the view. Note that this feature is intended to benefit primarily artists in the games development industry because it will not affect final renders. The intention of this plug-in is to allow game developers to accurately preview work that is intended to run on game platforms such as Microsoft's Xbox.

Asset Browser

The Asset Manager has been renamed as the Asset Browser, and for a good reason. The Asset Browser now enables users to manage and browse bitmaps and geometry from any location on the Internet, as well as from the local machine and network.

When users drag max files from the Asset Browser to a viewport, a menu will be displayed enabling users to merge the file, Xref, or open the file. Users can configure this by going to the File menu of the Asset Browser and choosing Preferences. When users drag geometry files from the Internet to the viewport, a new Internet download window will appear displaying the source URL, the connection status, and two download progress bars. A check box in this window is labeled Place Objects When Download Completes. If this is checked, max 4 gives the user the capability to click on the desired position of the new object in the viewport (see Figure 2.26).

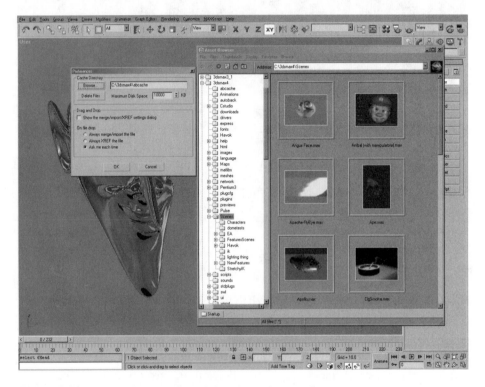

Figure 2.26   Preferences for drag and drop from the Asset Browser.

Summary

As you have seen, functionality across the different geometry types has been made more consistent. Artists now have multiple solutions available for subdividing surfaces. Functionality has been added to allow artists to more accurately preview their work when applying materials, which should help improve productivity.

Chapter 3

Changes in Animation

by Kim Lee

This chapter looks at new or improved tools available for animating in 3ds max 4. These tools enable the user to do everything from building complex working mechanisms, such as engines, to setting up easy-to-use interfaces for animating fully articulated characters.

Tools covered in this chapter include the following:

- Bones
- IK
- Constraints
- Skin
- Flex
- Point Cache
- Reactor
- Wire Parameter
- Havok dynamics
- Explicit Set Key
- Spring controller

Character Animation Overview

Perhaps the most noticeable area of improvement in 3ds max 4 is in its character-animation tools. This is especially true for its bone and IK systems, which have been totally rewritten from the ground up in this release.

As a quick overview, essentially three tools are commonly used to set up or rig a character model for animation. The first is the bone system, which is used to create a skeleton for the character. The second is a combination of inverse kinematics (IK) and forward kinematics (FK) chains that the animator will interact with to drive the motion of the bones. Last is the skinning tool, also known as enveloping, which gives the user control over how the character model will deform to follow the motion of the bones.

These three tools are generally used to set up the basic rig of a character and connect the model to the rig. After doing this, it is often necessary to create custom controls for the character to facilitate easier manipulation of what can become a very complex rig. These controls can be set up for anything from facial expressions to finger motion. The new Wire Parameter and Reactor features make this possible.

Depending on the animation, there might also be an additional stage required to create secondary animation such as the jiggle of an alien's antennae or the flow of loose clothing on a character. Tools to achieve this include the Flex Modifier, the Spring controller, and the Reactor plug-in, which is available separately from Discreet.

Although we will be explaining the use of these tools in the context of character animation, the reader should consider that there are an infinite number of other applications that they could be applied to.

Bones

The new bones system in max 4 gives the user unique capabilities to work faster and smarter with state-of-the art tools. The bones system in previous versions of max were significantly less than perfect when attempting anything but the simplest tasks, so when Discreet decided to focus version 4 on the issues important to character animation, it started from square one. High on the list of requirements was the need for the new system to be flexible but also intuitive.

Bones are essentially a hierarchy of linked joints. For example, consider a typical human arm, which is comprised of three joints: the shoulder, elbow, and wrist joints. These are connected by a representation of two physical bones: the upper-arm and forearm bones. In max 4—and most other 3D packages, for that matter—a *bone object* is a joint that represents a pivot point for the bone object. The visual representation of the actual bone length is drawn from this base joint to the next child joint in the hierarchy. The important thing to remember when working with bones is that the position and orientation of the joints is much more important than how the bone between them is represented. A big change from the old bones system in max is that, in the new system, bones represent the parent joint, not the child joint. For example, in Max 3, if you rotated the length of bone between the shoulder and the elbow, you were really rotating the elbow. In max 4, if you do the same thing, you rotate the arm from the shoulder, which is much more intuitive (see Figure 3.1).

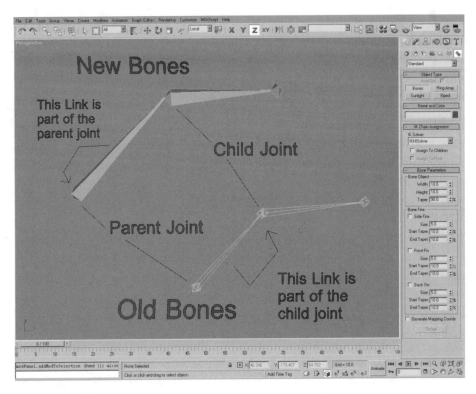

Figure 3.1   Comparison of the new bones system and the old bones system.

Creating Bones in max 4

Bones can be created in max 4 by going to the Creation tab of the Command panel and selecting the System button and then Bones. The first rollout in the Command panel when creating bones is the IK Chain Assignment rollout (see Figure 3.2).

 Note

As you will see later in this chapter, the bones are not assigned by default to IK controllers. Instead, they are assigned IK Solvers as a separate operation after creation of the bone chain(s). However, this rollout enables the user to automatically assign an IK Solver to the bones upon creation. The three types of IK Solvers available will be discussed in detail later in this chapter. Although this can be a faster approach for experienced users, it is not a typical workflow because, more often, the application of IK Solvers to a bone chain requires a certain level of experimentation to arrive at the perfect setup for a given character.

To start creating bones, go to the Create panel, click the Systems tab, and select Bones. Left-click in the viewport to place the first joint. Note that the first bone will be created after you release the left mouse button on the initial click. In other words, you do not left-click, hold, drag, and release to draw your bones. Each successive left-click places the base joint of a bone.

Now as you click to create each joint, the previous (parent) joint is rotated to face the new child joint automatically. This is a big improvement over the old bones system that did not orient the bones as you drew them, requiring users to build bones that followed the world axis and then later rotate them into the proper position. You must right-click to finish drawing a system of bones, at which point a final extra bone is created. This bone is necessary for calculating the orientation of its parent bone/joint (see Figure 3.3).

To draw branching bones systems like those found in a character's pelvis area, begin drawing a new chain by left-clicking an existing bone. Alternatively, you can simply use the Link tool in the toolbar to link the parent bone of a hierarchy to another bone of a different chain. The only difference is that no visible bone object will be drawn to represent the link.

Adjusting Bone Objects

One of the first things users will notice after creating a chain of bones is that quite a few controls are now available in the Modifiers panel for adjusting the geometric representation of the bone objects. This is because bone objects in max 4 are now actual geometry, not just a 2D wire-frame representation of the bone. 3ds max 4 can allow for skeletons to be built that more closely represent the actual volume of the character that the bones are controlling. This alleviates the animator from

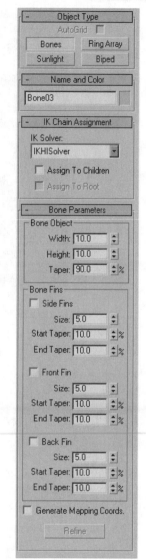

Figure 3.2
The new Bones Creation panel rollouts.

having to rely on seeing the actual geometry of the character model, which in some cases can be a very computationally heavy affair that usually slows down the program's interactivity speed. Correctly created bones, in effect, can become a sort of proxy for the actual character geometry (see Figure 3.2).

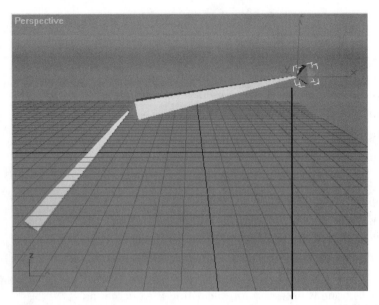

Automatically created bone at end of chain

Figure 3.3   Extra bone created automatically when user right-clicks to finish chain.

Bone Parameters Rollout

The Bone Parameters rollout presents controls for the width, height, and taper of the bone object, which enables the user to set the bone's volume. The Bone Fins section gives the user the option of creating one or more fins on the bone.

Fins

Fins are a new feature of bones that are useful as visual aids to the animator in determining the orientation of bones. Say, for example, that you created the tail of an extremely detailed, geometrically heavy dragon and were in the midst of animating it as it flailed and twisted around. It would be rather difficult to visualize whether the tail had twisted without displaying the model and thus slowing down your productivity. But by using fins, it would be extremely easy to see and keep track of the amount of twist being animated (see Figure 3.4).

To activate the fins of a bone, simply check the appropriate Fin check box and adjust the size, start taper, and end taper controls to create the desired shape. The Generate Mapping Coordinates check box is provided to enable users to texture-map the bones. This can be useful for rendering test animations quickly, again using the bones as a proxy for the actual model.

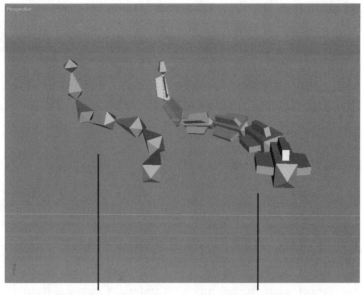

No fins, uniform size, difficult to   Fins turned on, size adjusted, easier
see twisting and volume   to see twisting and volume

Figure 3.4   Benefits of the new bones' fins and sizing features.

Refine Button

The Refine button is useful if you decide that, after creating a bone system, you need the chain to be comprised of more bone segments. To use this feature, go to the Modifiers panel and then select a bone that you want to refine in the viewport. Click the Refine button and then click the point along the length of the bone where you would want another joint to appear. This can save quite a bit of time re-creating skeletons when experimenting with the best placement of bones for a particular model.

Note

As mentioned before, the new bone objects in max 4 are actual geometry and thus possess all the benefits of geometry objects in max. More specifically, they can be edited as geometry by collapsing them to either a mesh, a poly, a or patch object, and they can be edited with all the associated editing tools, such as Edit Mesh. They can also be modified by using any of the modifiers available. So, for example, there would be no reason a user couldn't decide to make a model based on a bone system that was edited using common box-modeling techniques and then subdivided using Meshsmooth.

Squash and Stretch

One of the more impressive new features added to bones is the capability to configure a bone's squash and stretch scaling, which is necessary to achieve the traditional squash and stretch character motion ubiquitous in Disney and Warner Brothers–style animations. This functionality is supported by the IK Solvers as well as the Skin modifier, enabling users to easily set up these kinds of characters.

Applying Bone-Like Properties

Another important distinction to make is that, as of version 4, any object can be used as a bone and can be given bone-like properties. Although this is partially because the IK Solver's functionality has been separated from the base properties of bones, certain properties unique to bones are also available as properties for all other objects, if the user desires. The advanced properties that make bone objects bones are available via the Object Properties window.

To access these properties, right-click an object and select Properties from the lower-right quad. In the lower-right corner of the Object Properties window, you will see Bone properties, where you can tell the object to act as a bone by checking Bone On/Off (see Figure 3.5). This enables two capabilities.

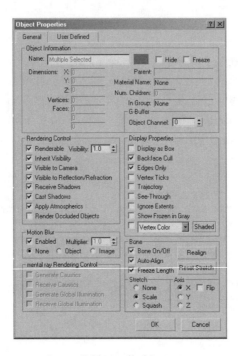

Figure 3.5   New Bone properties available to all objects.

Display Bone Links

First, it enables the user to display bone links in addition to or in place of the original geometry. To do this, go to the Display tab of the Command column and open the Link Display rollout. Checking the Display Links box represents the geometry with bone links; checking the Link Replaces Object box hides the original geometry and shows only the bone links (see Figure 3.6). Note that the links displayed in this manner are of the old max bones type. This means that the pivot point of the original geometry is represented by a 2D (nonshaded) diamond object. The triangular links drawn between these joints are part of the child joint. Therefore, using the earlier example of an arm, rotating the forearm link would actually rotate the wrist joint, not the elbow joint. This can be confusing, considering that the new max bones view the link as part of the parent joint.

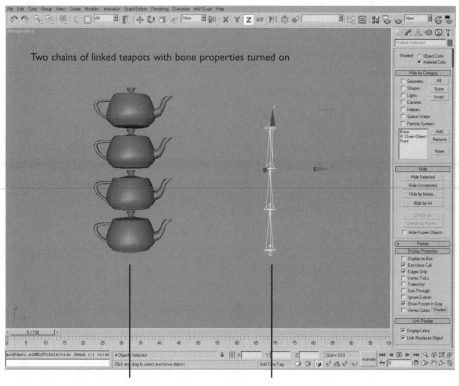

Displayed as normal   Displayed as links and link replaces object

Figure 3.6   Displaying linked objects as links.

Bone Scaling and Alignment

Checking Bone On/Off in the Object Properties window also enables the bone scaling and bone alignment functions.

Auto-Align Check Box

For instance, the Auto-Align check box (in the Object Properties window, and on by default) automatically rotates the joint of the selected link to align with the next child joint in the hierarchy if the user uses the Move tool to reposition the child joint. If this check box is turned off and the next child joint is repositioned using the Move tool, the selected joint's axis might not be aligned correctly to allow for predictable rotations. Also note that by turning off Auto Align, the Freeze Length option is turned off, enabling the user to change the length of the child bone. The Realign button enables the user to manually force joint alignment.

Freeze Length Check Box

The Freeze Length check box (also in the Object Properties window, and on by default) enables the user to freeze or unfreeze the length of the selected bone link when the child bone is moved. This box must be unchecked to allow for any of the different types of stretch. Be aware that it is not the links drawn that get affected by the different Stretch setting, but rather the original geometry that will either scale or stretch. Therefore, to see the effect of choosing None, Scale, or Stretch, the user should not turn on Link Replaces Object, as discussed previously. The Axis controls enable the user to choose the axis along which the object will stretch. The Reset Stretch button returns the link to its original scale.

 Note

All the Bone controls found in the Object Properties window also affect the actual max 4 bone objects discussed earlier.

Inverse Kinematics (IK)

As stated earlier, bone hierarchies are typically used in conjunction with inverse kinematics (IK) chains. The IK systems in previous versions of max have typically been problematic, but, thankfully, with version 4 this has been totally rewritten and now is one of the most advanced IK systems available commercially.

A Review of IK

Before delving into what makes the new IK system so good, it's important to review exactly what an IK system is, what it should do, and what terminology is used. Be aware that because of the technically advanced nature of this topic, you should first thoroughly read all the IK chapters of the manual for more detailed explanations of terminology and functionality. In the spirit of the entire book, this chapter is meant to provide practical insights into the application of these tools. Additionally, the chapters on model rigging in Part IV, "Rigging," provide more hands-on coverage of the IK system.

Forward Kinematics Versus Inverse Kinematics

To understand an IK system, you should first examine a *forward kinematics (FK)* system. FK is a method by which animators can pose nodes of a hierarchy like a skeleton.

A *node* is more of a concept than an actual object, and it is a generic term used in the computer animation industry to refer to anything from an object in a 3D program to a bitmap in a complex material-shader tree. For the purposes of this chapter, a node represents any object in or out of a hierarchy, such as a leg bone or a point helper or a sphere.

In an FK setup, the general rule is that a parent node in a hierarchy drives the motion of any child node. For example, if you moved your forearm (parent), your wrist (child) would go along for the ride. But, if you moved the wrist node, the forearm would remain where it was. Animating using the FK method is much like posing action figures: When you pose the limbs (children) of the figure, you can move the torso (parent) of the figure and all the limbs keep their positions relative to the parent.

This is an easy, intuitive way to animate things, such as the arms of a walking character, because the animator has to worry only about the motion of the arms relative to the parent, not relative to world space. Also, you should note that when you animate using FK, rotation keys are set for each joint that is rotated for a particular pose. However, when the arms of the character need to hold on to something inanimate in the world, such as the railing of a staircase, it becomes apparent that FK is not the best method to use.

By contrast, *IK* is a method of animation in which the child node drives the motion of a parent node(s).

Using the arm example, if you moved the wrist using IK, the computer would calculate how to move and rotate the other parent nodes of the arm to arrive at the
desired pose. This process is known as solving for an IK solution.

Typically, a few more elements are necessary to work with an IK chain. The position
of the wrist in the previous example would represent the position of what is know
as an end effector. The end effector is an IK node that represents the end result of
an IK solution. Additionally, another object, called the goal, represents the desired
position of the end effector. Generally, animators manipulate the goal object only
to ultimately position the wrist because the IK Solver always tries to match the position of the end effector to the goal (see Figure 3.7). In some cases, however, the user
might move the goal to a position that is impossible for the end effector to match
because of such limitations as arm joint rotations or simply a too-short length of the
arm.

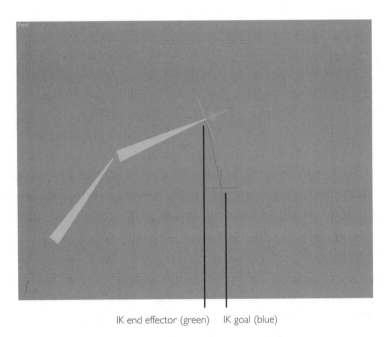

IK end effector (green)   IK goal (blue)

Figure 3.7   The IK goal object and IK end effector object.

One of the big advantages of working with the IK method is that end effectors can
be planted. That is, if you move the wrist goal to a position on a staircase railing
and then move the torso of the character, the wrist will stay in place on the railing
as the arm joints automatically change to facilitate the position of the wrist and the
new position of the body. Achieving something like this using FK is much more

tedious and labor-intensive. Also, in contrast to FK, animating the goal objects in an IK chain, by default, sets positional keys for the goal objects and does not set rotational keys on the joints of the IK chain.

So, it appears that, depending on the task at hand, both methods have their advantages and disadvantages. Typical solutions in the past have included using FK on the upper torso of a character and IK on the legs. Although this method can be useful for many animations, what happens if the character is required to walk on its hands? Even more complex setups have been used in other 3D packages, such as creating one full FK skeleton, one full IK skeleton, and a third skeleton that can be animated to blend the two. The ideal solution is to have a system in which you could switch back and forth between FK and IK as needed. Among other things, this is one of the major advantages to the new IK system in 3ds max 4, as you will see shortly.

IK Solvers in 3ds max 4

In 3ds max 4, IK Solvers are implemented as a new type of animation controller and thus can be applied to any hierarchy of objects, not just bone objects. These solvers are modular in the sense that third-party developers can write their own custom solvers for use inside max 4. Three IK Solvers are built into max 4, as outlined next (see Figure 3.8).

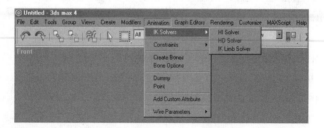

Figure 3.8   The three types of IK Solvers.

History Independent (HI)

This new IK Solver overcomes many of the problems of the IK system of previous releases. *History independent* simply means that the solver does not have to rely on what happens in previous frames to calculate an IK solution. Therefore, interactivity does not slow down as the animator works on later frames of a long animation. This solver can be used on any number of bones in a chain. This is generally considered the best choice of IK Solver for working with complex characters or on long sequences.

History Dependent (HD)

This is essentially a repackaged version of the old IK system of Max 3. Because of its history-dependent nature, it is not a good choice for long animation sequences because interactivity speed will slow as the animation progresses. However, it does allow for sliding joints, such as joints of a hydraulic piston; the HI Solver can do only sliding joints in FK mode. Note that if you use an HD Solver, you will be manipulating end effectors directly because there will be no goal object.

IK Limb Solver

This solver is similar to the HI Solver: It is history-independent but is meant to work only on two bone chains. It shares all the same parameters and rollouts of the HI-IK Solver. It was created specifically for human-like limbs such as arms, in which the upper arm/shoulder joint would be the first bone, the forearm/elbow joint would be the second bone, and the wrist joint would be the location of the end effector.

Although you could assume that this is really three bones, the IK Limb Solver solves for only rotations on the shoulder and elbow joints. Another important difference is that the first joint of the chain (shoulder) must have three degrees of freedom (X, Y, Z) while the second joint (elbow) can have only one. Finally, the IK Limb Solver was included as part of Discreet's Open Source Initiative and was designed to be exported directly to a game engine.

HI Solver and IK Limb Solver Parameters

This section takes a look at the actual parameters of the new HI Solver and IK Limb Solver, and examines their uses. The HD Solver will not be covered because it has not changed since the previous release.

Unlike most objects in 3ds max 4, the parameters of the new IK Solvers are manipulated not from the Modify panel, but from the Motion panel of the Command column (see Figure 3.9). As such, it is important to note that from within the Assign Controller rollout, three main parameters can be animated and controlled by controller types: Swivel Angle, IK Goal, and Enabled. One of the advantages of this is that multiple controllers can be combined to control a given parameter. So, for example, the IK goal position could be assigned a

Figure 3.9
IK Solver parameter rollouts in the Motion panel.

Position List controller comprised of any number of XYZ position controllers. This would enable the artist to essentially layer animation in passes, with each pass of animation stored in each successive XYZ position controller of the list. This would mimic the functionality of the Layer feature found in a character studio biped.

The IK Solver Rollout

The IK Solver rollout enables the user to do much more than merely choose which of the two new IK Solvers to use. The Enabled button works as an animateable toggle that enables the animator to switch between working in FK and working in IK. This is possible because when either the HI or the IK Limb Solver is applied to a chain, an FK controller is automatically applied beneath them. This FK controller remains effectively dormant as long as the Enabled button is engaged, giving the IK controller control over the chain. However, when the Enabled button is released, the IK controller is temporarily turned off, giving the FK controller control of the motion of the chain.

The IK for FK Pose Check Box

The IK for FK Pose check box is available for use only when the Enabled button is disengaged. The reason for using IK for FK Pose is to allow max to set rotational keys for each joint of the given chain, while still allowing the animator to work quickly by moving the IK goal to position the end effector.

This becomes immensely useful, for example, if the animator is trying to achieve an arching arm motion but wants to set only two keys by moving the IK goal. Normally when using IK, the goal object moves linearly from the first key to the second key, resulting in the wrist moving in a straight line between the keys. With IK for FK Pose engaged, the same keys would result in a more realistic arching motion of the arm, in which the end effector would move away from the goal during frames between the keys but would start and end matching the position of the goal.

IK/FK Snap

IK/FK Snap is typically not needed during first passes of animation if the Auto Snap check box is turned on. This is because max 4 automatically snaps the IK goal to match the position of the end effector whenever the Enabled button is turned on or off. However, when going back over previously animated sequences, as is often the case during the course of animation, it becomes noticeably useful in avoiding unwanted jumps or pops in motion when switching between FK and IK. It is at these points that the goal object often will not match the exact position of the end effector, requiring the user to manually snap it into place.

Pick Start Joint and Pick End Joint

The Pick Start Joint and Pick End Joint buttons are most useful when the user is still trying to determine the best placement of IK chains in the hierarchy. These buttons enable the user to change the number of bones in the IK chain and generally are more useful when using the HI Solver, which is not limited to the number of bones in a chain.

IK Solver Properties Rollout

The IK Solver Properties rollout contains all controls for manipulation of the IK Solver Plane and the accuracy and smoothness of the IK solution.

 Note

For a complete explanation of IK Solver Planes, review the white paper on Swivel Angle of the HI-IK Solver found in the max 4 help files by choosing the Index tab and typing **whitepaper.**

Besides manually adjusting the Swivel Angle manipulator in the viewports (see Chapter 1, "Changes in the Interface"), the Swivel Angle spinner can be used as one of three methods to control the swivel angle of an IK chain. The third method involves the use of a separate target object, which is selected by clicking the Pick Target button and selecting any object in the scene. This last option is useful when you want to have some other object drive the swivel angle.

Manipulation of a chain's swivel angle generally results in the twisting of the bones in the chain. This twist will occur around the axis of the IK chain, which is indicated by a white line drawn between the parent joint and the end joint of the chain when the goal object is selected. The choice of either IK goal or Start Joint for the IK Solver parent space is useful when multiple IK chains are used to control a chain of bones. Using the example of an insect-like leg, by setting the IK chain's main leg's parent space to Start Joint and the foot's parent space to IK goal, the main leg can be twisted without affecting the swivel angle or twist of the foot. However, if the foot's parent space is set to Start Joint, the foot's swivel angle/twist would change as the main leg's swivel angle changed.

Threshold

The Threshold area of the IK Solver Properties rollout provides two controls that affect the precision of the IK solution. The only one that actually works with the built-in HI Solver and IK Limb Solver is the Position parameter because position keys are being set on the goal object. The Rotation parameter is provided in case a solver is written by a third-party developer to take advantage of the rotation threshold. This number represents how close the end effector needs to match the position of the goal for the IK solution to be considered solved. Therefore, the lower the number used, the better. Note that this parameter is scale-sensitive: Depending on the size of your scene, you might need vastly different values to obtain accurate results.

Iterations Parameter

The Iterations parameter found in the Solutions group determines how many times max 4 will try to solve for a close match between the end effector and the goal. A common problem requiring the adjustment of these controls occurs when a character's leg has been animated to be planted on the ground, and the resulting animation shows unwanted jittering or jumpiness in the foot. Assuming that the problem does not lie in the function curves of the goal animation, the first thing to do is to increase the iteration's value. There are no magic numbers to use; values as high as 200 have been used in certain cases. Next, you might need to lower the value for Position Threshold.

IK Display Options

The IK Display Options rollout contains all controls for displaying the IK gizmos in the viewport. This is where you can force an IK Solver to display even when the associated goal is not selected. This is also where the user can choose to see the end effector gizmo, which, by default, is hidden because the user will be moving the goal gizmo to animate. It is sometimes useful, however, to display the end effector, especially when troubleshooting jittery motion using the Threshold and Iteration parameters, as described earlier.

Although these rollouts just examined constitute all the control parameters for an HI-IK Solver, a few more parameters located elsewhere in the interface are important factors in calculating an IK solution. These parameters can be accessed by pressing the IK button in the Hierarchies tab of the Command column. Here you will find the Sliding Joint and Rotational Joint rollouts. This is where the user can set up ranges of motion allowed for particular joints, as well as constrain motion along specific axes.

Parameters inside the Sliding Joint rollout are used by the HI-IK Solver only when the solver is toggled to FK mode. While in IK mode, these parameters are not considered in solving motion for the end effector. Typically, it is a better idea to use the HD-IK Solver when dealing with sliding joints required by things such as pistons or collapsing telescopes. These parameters work identically to the ones in the previous versions of max. One often-overlooked function, however, is that if you click on the Text label of the From or To parameters, the selected bone temporarily moves to the appropriate limit position. This is useful for checking limits in the viewport.

The Rotational Joints rollout provides check boxes for enabling or disabling motion of a joint around each of the three axes. When the Limited check box is toggled on, the From and To parameters for that axis are calculated by the HI-IK Solver. Again, like the Sliding Joint rollout, if a user clicks on either of the From or To labels, the selected bone will rotate to that limit temporarily. The Preferred Angle parameter is used by the new IK Solvers to determine which direction the joint should rotate when the goal is animated. This parameter is especially necessary to check whether the user has built a hierarchy that is perfectly straight, as can be the case when creating bones with the Snap To grid function on. If a hierarchy is drawn with a slight bend at a joint, the preferred angle will default to whatever that joint's angle was when the IK Solver was applied. The effect of this parameter is painfully clear if the knees of a character bend in the wrong direction.

Constraints

Constraints are a new feature of max 4 that work in a manner similar to that of controllers. In fact, the introduction of constraints could be considered a splitting of the traditional controllers into two groups. One interesting observation is that what max users have traditionally defined as controllers has been more widely defined as constraints by most other 3D software packages. Although this is a seemingly insignificant reason to rename certain controllers to constraints, it is actually a more accurate way to think of the application of these tools. It is also helpful for users of other 3D packages in learning the workflow of max 4.

Constraints can be thought of as a subcategory of controllers that rely on another object to function properly. Although controllers such as TCB rotation, Bezier Position, and Position Motion Capture all require direct input from the animator to produce keys on their respective animation tracks, constraints do not. For example, if a position constraint is applied to a sphere and uses a box as the constraint input, the sphere's motion will be driven not by position keys set on the position constraint track, but rather by the motion of the box that might have a Bezier Position controller assigned to it.

Constraints can be applied to an object by selecting an object and then making a selection from the Constraints menu found in the new Animation drop-down menu. One point of potential confusion for users is that the seven new constraints in max 4 can also be found mixed into the lists of controllers that are available in the Assign Controller window of the Motion panel and the Track view (see Figure 3.10).

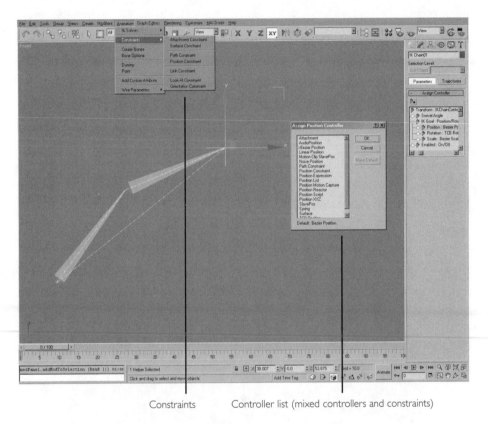

Constraints   Controller list (mixed controllers and constraints)

Figure 3.10   Constraints and controllers.

Most of the new constraints serve the same function as they did in previous versions of max, where they were called controllers. However, four of them (Position, Path, Look-At, and Orientation) now give the user the option to choose more than one object to constrain to. This enables the user to animate the weight of each constraint individually. The following is a brief outline of the new functionality of these constraints, with suggestions for applying them in your work. Note that often you will need to combine various constraints to achieve the desired result.

Attach Constraint

This constraint operates just as it did when it was called the Attachment controller. This constraint is useful for attaching an object to the surface of another. It differs from the Link tool in that the Attach constraint attaches the pivot point of the selected object to the actual surface of the target object instead of the target object's pivot point.

The obvious advantage to this is that the Attach constraint honors any geometry deformations resulting from modifiers or space warps. An obvious use for this constraint would be to attach buttons, medals, or other accessories to the deforming geometry of a character's clothes.

One unfortunate side effect that users might encounter in using this constraint is an unwanted 180° flipping when the attach face of the target object rotates more than 90° in world space. This can be seen easily seen in the example of a teapot with an Attach constraint used for the top of a bending cylinder. If the cylinder is bent beyond 90°, the teapot will flip 180° on its local Z-axis (see Figure 3.11).

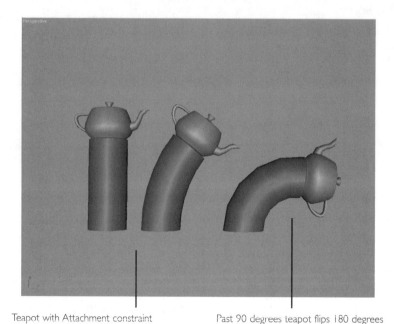

Teapot with Attachment constraint   Past 90 degrees teapot flips 180 degrees
to top of bending cylinder

Figure 3.11   Attach constraint flipping.

The workaround to this problem involves using a third object, such as a point object, and an Orientation constraint. The user should make sure that the Align to Surface check box is turned off in the Attach Constraint panel. Then the point object should have a Euler XYZ controller assigned to Rotation. Using the Wire Parameter feature (covered later in this chapter), wire the cylinder's bend angle to the Y rotation of the point object. You will need to add the command **degtorad** (degrees to radians) before the word *angle* in the Expression box of the Wire Parameter window to correctly translate the bend angle value to rotational degrees. Finally, apply an Orientation constraint to the teapot and use the point object as the target.

Link Constraint

This constraint replaces the old Link Control controller and enables the user to animate the parenting of the object. This is useful when an object needs to be the child of different objects at various points of an animation.

A good example is a baseball being caught and then thrown. The baseball would start out linked to the world and then, where it contacts the baseball glove, it would be linked to the glove object. Then, when the throwing hand grabs the ball, it would be linked to the hand object. Finally, at the point of release it would be linked to the world again.

Surface Constraint

This constraint constrains the position of the selected object to any parametric surface. Unfortunately, in many cases this constraint is much too limited for practical use. One reason is that the object types that can be used as target surfaces are limited. For example, although you can constrain an object to a Quad or NURBS patch, it will work correctly on only one patch in a model made of many Quad or NURBS patches. Also, the Surface constraint will not work on an object whose surface has been changed with modifiers.

A better solution in many cases is to use the Attach constraint, which works with all types of geometry and still allows the location of attachment to be animated. However, the Surface constraint is useful if you need to attach an object to an animated NURBS surface.

Path Constraint

The Path constraint works essentially the same way as the old Path controller, with some useful additions. Users can now pick multiple target paths and animate a weight value for each path.

Two new check boxes are also available. By default, the Path constraint will no longer allow the object to move back to the beginning of the path when it reaches the end. Turning on the Loop check box overrides that. Also, the Relative check box enables the user to maintain the original position of the object relative to the path that effectively lets you offset the object from the actual path object (see Figure 3.12).

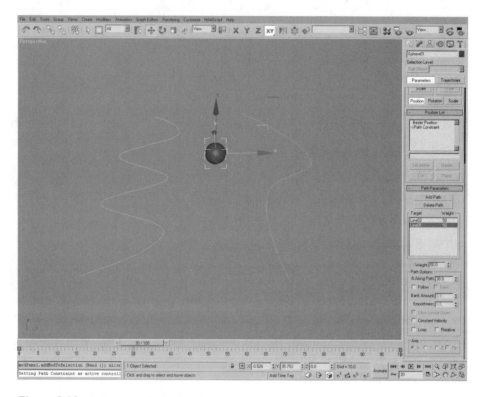

Figure 3.12   Sphere constrained to two paths.

One possible use of the new weighting functionality is to have two paths for a camera—one smooth and the other with noise applied. By animating the weighting of each path, the animator could make the camera shake at specific points without having to set up multiple noise controllers for the camera in the Track view.

Position Constraint

This new constraint enables the user to constrain the position of the object to one or more target objects with individual weighting control for each. This is useful for automatically keeping an object between two or more objects without having to use an expression controller (see Figure 3.13).

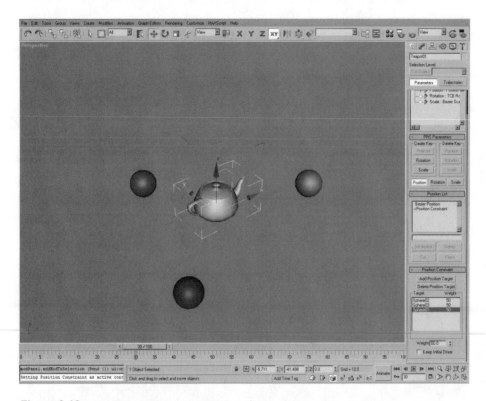

Figure 3.13   Teapot position constrained to three spheres.

Adding a Bezier Position controller after the Position constraint enables the user to animate the offset of the object from the target object. This constraint can also be used in place of the Link constraint to animate an object being picked up or released.

Look-At Constraint

A much more powerful and useful incarnation of the old Look-At controller, this constraint also enables the user to constrain the object to multiple target objects with weighting control for each (see Figure 3.14). The Keep Initial Offset button keeps the object from changing its current orientation when the Look-At constraint is applied. However, the Set Orientation button enables the user to adjust the global rotational offset of the object at any time.

Also, controls are now available to select an upnode and upnode axis for the object. The upnode is necessary to control the roll of the constrained object in much the same way that the Swivel Angle control works in an IK chain. Using the world as the upnode can result in unwanted flipping if the Look-At target is moving around in all three axes. It is often better to select an actual target object as an upnode to reduce occurrences of this flipping. This enables you to use the upnode object to control the roll of the constrained object.

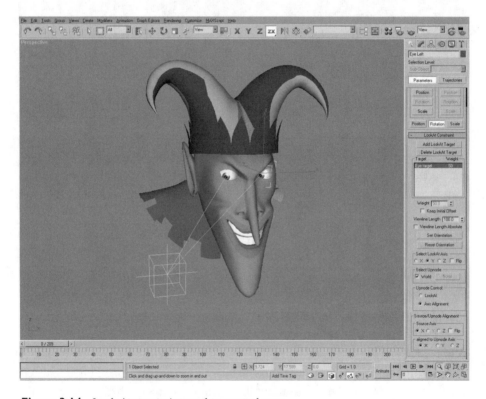

Figure 3.14   Look-At constraint used to control eyes.

When doing this, bear in mind that the Source Axis selection refers to the constrained object's local axis, and the Aligned to Upnode Axis refers to the local axis of the object that has been selected as an upnode. Because of this, it is usually a good idea to work in the local reference coordinate system.

One limitation for advanced users is that the Look-At constraint does not make its axis rotation values' output available for the purposes of driving another object's Orientation constraint or for use with the Wire Parameter. This necessitates collapsing or baking of keyframes for the constrained object's rotation track, either manually in the trajectories section of the Motion panel or through MAXScript. Of course, this would need to be done after the animation resulting from the Look-At constraint is finalized.

With this said, the Look-At constraint is quite useful for setting up eye controls for characters as well as automatically aiming gun turrets at a target and animating which of multiple targets to aim at.

Orientation Constraint

This last constraint allows the rotation of the constrained object to be controlled by one or more target objects. The Transform Rule group contains two choices—Local → Local, and World → World—whose effects are more apparent when the constrained object is linked to another object.

When set to Local → Local, the constrained object inherits rotation from its parent object. Then, if the target object(s) is rotated, that rotation value is added locally to the constrained object's inherited rotation. When the Transform Rule is set to World → World, the constrained object does not inherit any rotation from its parent and obtains rotation input only from the target object(s).

This constraint can be used to help correct flipping problems with the Attach constraint (mentioned previously). It could also be used to make stationary rotation controls for other objects that are moving around a scene, such as the head of a motorcycle rider whose motorcycle is constrained to a winding path.

Skin

This chapter has examined almost all the elements necessary to set up animation for characters, with one important exception. It's necessary to somehow connect the character model to the bone/IK skeleton and allow it to deform as the skeleton is animated. This process, which is known commonly as enveloping or skinning, can be achieved by using the Skin modifier.

Although it's not a new feature, significant enhancements have been made to Skin since the previous version of max. Obvious comparisons have and will be made to the two alternative plug-in solutions available—namely, character studio's Physique modifier (available from Discreet) and Bones Pro (available from Digimation), which have traditionally been the tools of choice for top max artists.

Although these plug-ins provide artists with more refined tools and maximum flexibility, the new enhancements to the Skin modifier make it a viable option for all but the most demanding tasks. In addition, it ships with 3ds max 4, so it's essentially free.

Among the many improvements made to the Skin modifier are the capability to see envelope influences in shaded viewports, the addition of Bone Exclusion Lists, the addition of Angle Deformers, and the capability to load and save envelopes. Skin's interactivity speed, already fast in Max 3, has been increased even more in this latest version.

Parameters Rollout

Upon applying the Skin modifier to your character model, the first thing you will see in the Modifier panel is the Parameters rollout (see Figure 3.15). Here the user selects what objects will be used as bones for the model by clicking the Add Bone button and selecting the appropriate objects from the Select Bones window.

Pressing the Edit Envelopes button or selecting the envelope sub-object from the Stack View display enables you to edit the size and placement of each bone's envelope in the same manner as the previous version. It is now possible, however, to see the influence of these envelopes in the viewports while in Smooth + Highlights mode. The area of the model that is under the influence of a particular envelope is displayed as a color gradient from red to yellow to blue, similar to a thermal view showing hot and cold areas. Red (hot) signifies areas under maximum influence, while blue (cold) signifies areas of no influence; the various shades of yellow in between signify the falloff of this influence (see Figure 3.15).

Controls for editing the size and location of envelopes remain the same as in version 3. Individual cross-sections and points can be either moved and resized in the viewports or adjusted with the Radius spinner. Absolute or Relative modes can be selected in the Envelope Properties group, which determines how vertex weighting will occur relative to the envelopes.

The first of the new parameters, Squash, is also located in this group. Squash is a multiplier value that works in conjunction with the bone properties Scale and Squash when the corresponding bone's Freeze Length toggle is off. This Squash parameter enables you to either exaggerate or under emphasize the squashing or scaling effect.

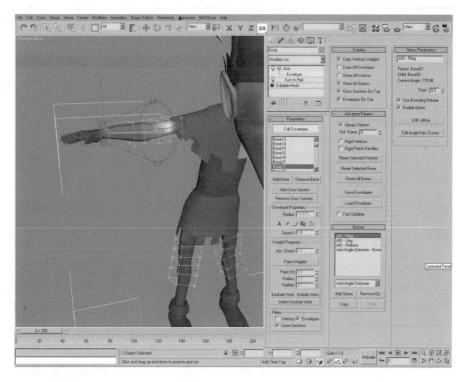

Figure 3.15   Skin Modifier rollouts.

Three new buttons are available in the Weight Properties group. Exclude Verts enables you to selectively exclude vertices from the influence of a given envelope, while pressing the Include Verts button results in the opposite effect. The Select Exclude Verts button selects all vertices that are currently excluded from the influence of the selected envelope.

The functionality provided by these new buttons is especially useful when adjusting vertex weighting on areas such as fingers and toes, where the envelopes of many bones often overlap. Note that use of these buttons requires the vertices' filter, which is off by default, to be activated so that the user can select individual vertices of the skinned model.

Note

Users should be aware of a few things when weighting individual vertices. Although the Paint Weights feature can be useful on simple models or as a first rough weighting pass, it is often not precise enough for very demanding tasks. It might be necessary to use if Relative Weighting mode has been selected and small problem areas need to be fixed. Although it's more tedious, a manual approach using the Absolute Effect spinner while in Absolute mode can be more effective.

Display Rollout

The Display rollout contains controls that enable the user to display or hide the various sub-objects of the Skin modifier. This can become invaluable when working with complex bone hierarchies to eliminate unnecessary clutter in the viewports.

Advanced Parameters Rollout

The Advanced Parameters rollout contains tools for saving and loading envelopes as well as reconfiguring bones relative to the model. The first two controls work in tandem.

For instance, the Ref. Frame spinner enables the user to choose which frame should be used by Skin to determine the reference position for the bones and the model. This value defaults to 0, so typically you would start your animation at frame 1 so as to leave frame 0 untouched. Although this common approach works well, sometimes it is necessary to adjust the orientation of the bones relative to the mode. It is often easier to resize and reorient a bone structure to facilitate a good enveloping setup than it is to try to manually compensate for incorrectly placed and oriented bones.

Because the relative relationship between the bones and the model has already been established upon applying the Skin modifier, you would need some way to disable the current relationship and define a new one. This is where the Always Deform check box comes into play. By unchecking this option, the Skin modifier temporarily ignores the current relationship defined at the reference frame. The user then can adjust the bones relative to the model without the model reacting, and then can reactivate the Always Deform function to let Skin use the new relationship.

The Rigid Vertices check box is primarily used in game-development applications when the game engine dictates that vertices cannot have weight distributed across multiple bones. For non–game-development applications, this could be useful for skinning a one-piece model of a robot or a suit of armor, in which blended deformations are not desired.

The Rigid Handles check box is used when skinning bezier patch-based models and causes a vertex's associated bezier handles to be weighted with the same value as the vertex. This can often ease the skinning process for patch models.

The three Reset buttons enable the user to remove any custom vertex weight values assigned and revert back to the initial weight values. These are useful when experimenting with weight values, and they enable the user to revert quickly back to the weight values assigned by envelope placement.

The Load and Save Envelopes buttons are welcome additions to the Skin modifier, enabling artists to try different enveloping solutions for a model or even apply envelopes from other models. This can be useful in a production environment where changes might be made to the model after artists have already started the skinning process. This would keep artists from losing hours of work reskinning the newer model.

The last control in this rollout, the Fast Updates check box, turns off weighted deformations in the viewports, thus speeding up interactivity. This is usually useful after the model has been successfully skinned and is being animated.

Gizmos Rollout

Perhaps the most interesting new feature added to the Skin modifier is located in the Gizmos rollout. Angle deformers enable the user to define specific types of localized deformations to the skinned model based on the rotation angle of a given bone.

Joint and Bulge Angle Deformers

Angle deformers are a significant addition when you consider the difficulty of enveloping characters. Traditionally, artists have had to come up with a "perfect" enveloping setup that allows the animator to pose the character in an infinite number of extremes while preventing the model from breaking or deforming incorrectly. Anyone who has tried to do this on character models of even reasonable complexity levels will realize that this is a practically impossible pursuit.

Usually one of two things happens. If the project has a generous schedule that allows for R&D, perhaps the artists can achieve that elusive perfect enveloping solution. However, if the project has a tight deadline, which is usually the case, sometimes the solution is to have multiple copies of the same character with different envelope solutions applied. This is often an acceptable workaround, considering that most shots in broadcast or film are relatively short, which limits the variety of motion that a character might need to perform between cuts. This way, an enveloping solution can be optimized for the needed action. It is this constant quandary that the angle deformers address. Instead of preventing all possible skinning artifacts in a character, the angle deformers enable the user to selectively fix bad deformations when and where they occur. Therefore, if a character has a bad deformation artifact only when its arm rotates to 120°, the artist can use an angle deformer to compensate for it every time the arm rotates to that angle (see Figure 3.16).

Joint Angle Deformer

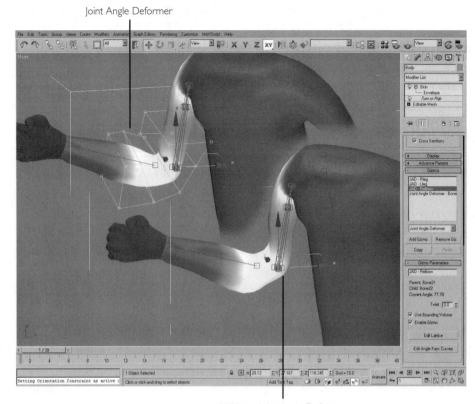

Without Joint Angle Deformer

Figure 3.16   Effect with and without a Joint Angle Deformer.

The Joint and Bulge Angle Deformers create a deformable lattice for the user to manipulate. The points on this lattice are not animated based on time, but rather, on the rotation state of a given joint.

Following are the three different types of angle deformers:

- Joint Angle Deformer can be used to affect vertices that are influenced by both the child and parent envelopes of a given joint. It is typically used to adjust the way a model creases at a particular joint. This deformer creates a lattice around the selected vertices.

- Bulge Angle Deformer can be used to affect only vertices that are influenced by the parent envelopes of a given joint. It is typically used to create a muscle-bulge effect on the parent side of a particular joint. Like the Joint Angle Deformer, it creates a lattice around the selected vertices (see Figure 3.17).

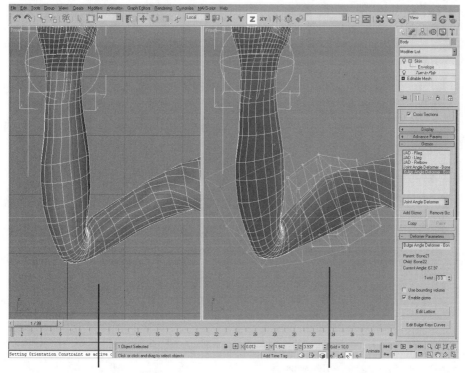

No Bulge Angle Deformer   Bulge Angle Deformer applied

Figure 3.17   Bulge Angle Deformer.

- Morph Angle Deformer is similar to a Joint Angle Deformer, in that it can affect vertices belonging to both parent and child sides of a given joint. This is useful when the lattices of the Joint and Bulge Deformers do not give the user enough control to create the desired deformation. This deformer uses custom-made morph targets to define what deformations will occur (see Figure 3.18).

The proper workflow in using any of the angle deformers is to first be in Edit Envelopes mode, and then select the appropriate bone/envelope. Make sure that the Vertex filter is checked on, and select the appropriate vertices. Choose an angle deformer from the drop-down list, and then click the Add Gizmo button. A deformer gizmo will appear, either as a yellow lattice (Joint and Bulge Angle Deformers) or as yellow vertices (Morph Angle Deformer).

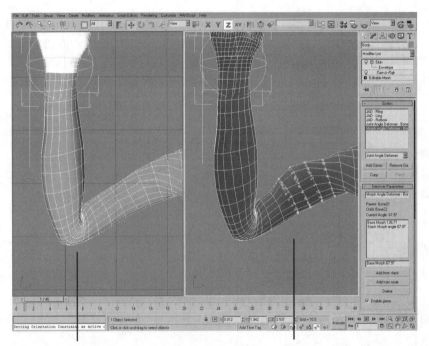

No Morph Angle Deformer   Morph Angle Deformer applied to selected vertices

Figure 3.18   Morph Angle Deformer.

Note

If there is already animation on the skeleton, the user should apply the deformers at a frame where the unadjusted model is deforming correctly so that the deformer has a correct base state to start from. Then, either by scrubbing to a problem frame or by positioning the bones into a problem pose, the user should adjust the gizmo.

Note

You should keep a couple of things in mind when first creating either the Joint or the Bulge Angle Deformer. You should realize that the orientation of the resulting lattice is based on the local orientation of the parent bone. This explains why a lattice created for a perfectly straight selection of vertices on a cylinder or arm might appear incorrectly angled. Depending on the orientation of the bone hierarchy, you might want to use the Twist control to orient the lattice more appropriately.

Also, for artists who must routinely start the enveloping process before character models have been finalized, the Use Bounding Volume check box should be turned on. This allows the vertex count and model shape to change without requiring re-creation of the deformer. Be aware that this should be applied *only* to the Bulge and Joint Angle Deformers, which are lattice-based. The Morph Angle Deformer is subject to the same vertex count limitations as all morphing operations are.

In the case of the Joint and Bulge Deformers, the user adjusts the points of the lattice by first clicking the Edit Lattice button located in the Gizmo Parameters rollout and then adjusting the lattice points. There is no need for the Animate button to be on because the positions of the points are being keyed to the rotation angle of the bone, not the frame. This adjustment can be repeated for every problem pose. This process is analogous to creating morph shapes of the lattice and associating each shape with a target angle.

When satisfied that all problem angles have been addressed, the user then may optionally click on the Edit Angle Keys Curve button. This button allows for the adjustment of the Ease curve for every lattice point that was adjusted. It provides total control over the rate at which each lattice shape "morphs" into the others. The Joint Graph window that appears displays a function curve representation of the transformation rate for each shape, with the horizontal axis representing degrees measured 0° to 360°, and the vertical axis representing relative position (see Figure 3.19).

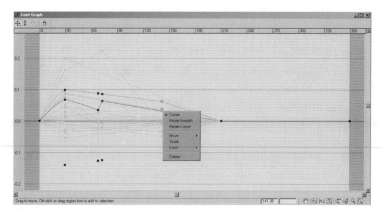

Figure 3.19   Joint Graph window.

Because many curves can be represented in this window, it is important to understand how to discern which curves affect which lattice point. Curves for currently selected points are displayed in color, while unselected points appear grayed out. For each selected point, three curves are associated with it. Red, green, and blue curves each represent the respective local X, Y, and Z positions of the point. If the user is careful during the initial creation of lattice shapes at the proper rotation angles, it usually is not necessary to adjust the curve points horizontally. However, if the keys of a lattice shape need to be associated with a different angle, it is easy enough to do this by moving the keys laterally. Typically it is not necessary to move the curve points vertically because the result is easier to achieve by simply repositioning the appropriate lattice point in the viewport while the bone is at the proper angle.

The most common task of the Joint Graph is the adjustment of curve tangents. By right-clicking a point or selection of points, the user can choose from one of three tangent types: corner, bezier-smooth, or bezier-corner. By default, all points are set to corner tangent type and thus produce linear transformations as the bone angle rotates through its range of motion.

If desired, the user can also create angle keys directly in the Joint Graph either by clicking the Add Point button in the Joint Graph toolbar or by right-clicking the Joint Graph window and selecting either Insert/Corner or Insert/Bezier. All other transform and window navigation operations of the Joint Graph are identical to those of the Track view.

Morph Angle Deformer

Although the workflow described previously is identical for both Joint and Bulge Angle deformers, working with the Morph Angle Deformer is a bit different. Theoretically, the Morph Angle Deformer is applied, again while the selected joint is in a neutral state. Then, as before, after rotating the joint to a problem angle, the user assigns a target morph shape to the current angle. However, in this case, the morph shape is not of a lattice, but of the actual model geometry.

The target shape can be acquired in one of two ways: either from a separate node—usually a copy of the original model that has been adjusted—or from the state of the current model as it exists at the top of the Modifier Stack. This second choice can be confusing, so a short explanation is in order.

Because the Modifier Stack represents a kind of history of the procedures performed (modifiers) on objects in max to arrive at a final state, you can utilize the last state, represented by whatever modifier is at the top or end of the stack, as a sort of temporary morph target. For the purposes of the Morph Angle Deformer, one of the Edit modifiers (edit mesh, edit patch, and so on) is typically used to enable the user to sculpt a proper morph target shape that compensates for the given bone angle.

After a Morph Angle Deformer gizmo is created, a Base Morph target is automatically created using the current shape of the model and the current bone angle. If the user wants to acquire the morph target from the stack, an appropriate Edit modifier must be first added to the end of the stack and then used to modify the model into the proper shape. Then, when the user clicks the Add From Stack button, max takes a virtual snapshot and uses that as the Morph Angle target for the current angle. However, because the Edit modifier still resides at the top of the stack, it must be deleted to avoid the resultant double transform of the affected vertices. This process may be repeated for as many morph angles are needed.

If the user decides to acquire the morph target from a separate node, the Snapshot tool must be used to make a Mesh Snapshot of the model while posed in the problem pose. Following this, the user would create an appropriate morph target by using the usual editing techniques. Finally, after creating a morph target that fixes the original problem pose, the user would press the Add From Node button and then select the newly modified copy of the model.

Although it's more complex in workflow, the Morph Angle Deformer presents the most flexibility of all three deformer types. One unfortunate limitation, however, is that it is not possible to edit the Ease curves controlling the morph transformations that default to linear. This restricts the user's ability to control the speed at which the various morph targets transition from one to the other.

Flex Modifier

The Flex modifier has seen some big changes since its introduction in Max 3. This modifier, which is primarily used to create simulated soft-body secondary animation, has been beefed up with complex spring-system options and the capability to work in conjunction with space warps and deflector objects. This gives Flex the capability to more accurately maintain object volumes while creating more realistic motions driven by things such as wind and gravity. The capability to also work with deflectors enables the user to simulate collisions between soft-body objects and solid objects.

Flex can be used in two general ways: to add jiggly motion to parts of an object and to simulate soft-body dynamics on an entire object. An important thing to keep in mind for readers unfamiliar with procedural animation tools such as Flex is that getting the desired results often requires quite a bit of experimentation. Working with Flex can often become a "tweak-fest," with the user trying a seemingly endless combination of parameter values before arriving at acceptable results. This section tries to shed some light on the practical effect of the various parameters, but every case will be different depending on variables such as object scale and relative speed. With this in mind, the next section examines the many parameters of this modifier, as seen in Figure 3.20.

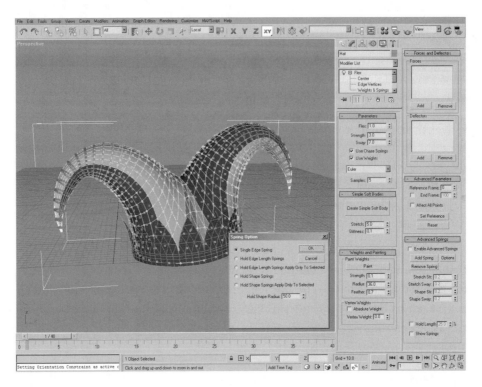

Figure 3.20   Flex modifier.

Flex Spinner

The first rollout, called Parameters, presents the most basic of the parameters. The Flex spinner represents the amount of flex effect that you want to mix in. This value works almost like a multiplier value: A value of 1 results in a normal amount of flex applied. Values less than 1 decrease the effect, and values above increase it.

Strength

The next parameter, Strength, can be confusing because of its name. This value does not refer to the strength of the flex effect, as it would appear to. Instead, it refers to the strength of chase springs. Chase springs are used primarily when the user wants to add things such as jiggly antennas or fatty areas of a character. The chase springs try to return the object to its original shape, so a lower value actually results in the flexed object regaining its original shape slower. A larger value results in a faster, "tighter" jiggle.

Sway

The Sway parameter is even more misleading. The sway amount actually refers to how long it takes for the flexed object to come to rest. However, this time larger values decrease it while lower values increase it. Using a lower value, such as 0.1, results in faster flexing that continues for a long time, while using a higher value, such as 100, results in a very slow lagging of the flexed portion of the model that comes to rest sooner.

Use Chase Springs

The check box labeled Use Chase Springs is used to enable or disable the object's chase springs. This would be disabled when trying to simulate a soft-body object being dropped or draping cloth. Turning off Use Chase Springs allows the flexed portions of the object to be completely subject to forces such as gravity or wind.

Use Weights

The next check box, labeled Use Weights, is used to enable or disable individual vertex weighting. For the jiggle effect on fatty areas of a character, you would usually want Use Weights to be enabled. By turning off Use Weights, the flex affects the object as a whole, which is necessary when using forces and deflectors to create a dynamics simulation.

The drop-down list that follows gives the user a choice of three algorithms for Flex to use in its calculations. Generally, Euler is the fastest and least stable and accurate, while Midpoint and Runge-Kutta4 are progressively slower but more stable and accurate. A reasonable workflow would be to start with Euler and progress to the other algorithms as necessary.

The Samples value represents the number of times per frame that the Flex simulation is calculated. Use higher values when you encounter random glitches, such as the all-too-common "exploding" object.

Simple Soft Bodies

The next rollout, Simple Soft Bodies, contains a simplified set of parameters for working with springs. The Create Simple Soft Body button generates springs for the selected object automatically. This tool can provide a good starting point when trying to simulate soft-body dynamics with forces and deflectors. However, because of its automatic nature, it is a good idea to use it on simple geometry. For use with complex, high–poly-count models, you should probably apply Flex to an FFD space warp that is bound to the actual model and use controls in the Advanced Springs rollout to create springs.

The Stretch and Stiffness parameters are used together to control the springs created by the Create Simple Soft Body button. Two kinds of springs are created with Flex. Edge springs are created along existing geometry edges and allow for control of edge stretch (length) and sway (angle). Shape springs are created between vertices of geometry where there are no existing edges. For example, a Shape spring is often created between vertices that lie on opposite sides of a model. The combination of Edge and Shape springs is used to maintain an object's volume. To better understand what the Stretch and Stiffness parameters do, the next section jumps ahead and looks at the Advanced Springs rollout.

Advanced Springs Rollout

For each of the two types of springs, there are two values controlling their behavior. Each has a Strength value that controls the length of the spring. Higher Strength values maintain the original length, while lower values allow more variation of length.

The second value, Sway, controls the angle between springs. Think of this like a control for the amount of bend allowed. Higher Sway values maintain the original angle, while lower values allow more variance. Looking back at the Stretch and Stiffness parameters, the Stretch parameter controls the Stretch Strength and Stretch Sway values, while the Stiffness parameter controls the Shape Strength and Stretch Sway values. If the user needs to control each of the four parameters independently, the Enable Advanced Springs check box must be checked in the Advanced Springs rollout. If this is done, the Stretch and Stiffness controls no longer are used. In many cases, it is probably easiest to start by adjusting the Stretch and Stiffness values to get the Spring values close, and then enable the Advanced Spring controls to fine-tune the simulation.

Weights and Painting Rollout

The Weights and Painting rollout contains controls for applying custom vertex weight values for Flex. It is important to remember that the more weight a vertex is given, the less it flexes. Therefore, you will need to remove weight for areas that need to jiggle more.

To use these tools, you must first be in Weights and Springs Sub-Object mode. Select one or more vertices. The Weight Painting tool works identically to the one used in the Skin modifier. Paint a relative Strength value onto the vertices in a cumulative manner. If the Strength value is negative, you are removing weight. Alternatively, you may keep a positive value in the Strength spinner and then hold the Alt key while painting to paint the inverse value. The Radius and Feather parameters control the size of the brush and the falloff of the weight value painted.

Use of the Absolute Weight toggle and the Vertex Weight spinner can be a bit confusing. First, you must have vertices selected while in Weights and Springs Sub-Object mode. Then, to apply the same value to all select vertices, turn on Absolute Weight and adjust the spinner to the desired value. If you want to offset the current weight values of the selected vertices, adjust the Vertex Weight spinner with Absolute Weight turned off.

Forces and Deflectors Rollout

The Forces and Deflectors rollout contains two lists for the respective space warp types. This is where the user can either add or remove Force and Deflector objects from being calculated by Flex.

Advanced Parameters Rollout

The Advanced Parameters rollout enables the user to determine start (reference) and end frames for the Flex calculations. The Affect All Points check box forces Flex to affect the entire object and ignore any sub-object selections before it in the Modifier Stack. The Reference button is used to update the viewport and is useful when adjusting the Center sub-object. Reset simply resets all the weights of the vertices to their defaults, which is often useful when experimenting with custom weight values that prove unsuccessful.

The Advanced Springs Rollout

The Advanced Springs rollout provides controls to create individual springs as well as more flexible (no pun intended) parameter control over them. To use the controls in this rollout, the user must first turn on the Enable Advanced Springs check box and be in Weights and Springs Sub-Object mode. It is also a good idea to turn on the Show Springs option at the bottom of the rollout. Then, before clicking the Add Springs button, click the Options button. This brings up a window of five choices that determine what type of spring(s) to create and where:

- Hold Edge Length Springs creates edge springs along all edges that are shared by the selected vertices.

- Hold Edge Length Springs Apply Only to Selected creates edge springs only along edges that lie between select vertices.

- Hold Shape Springs works in conjunction with the Hold Shape Radius spinner. Shape springs are created from the selected vertices to all other vertices that lie within the defined radius. Users should be careful when using this option, especially on complex geometry.

- Hold Shape Springs Apply Only to Selected creates shape springs only between selected vertices.

- Hold Shape Radius defines a threshold of distance from the selected vertices and is used to determine where shape springs can be created.

Note

Single Edge Spring works only if two vertices are selected. The two vertices do not need to be neighboring or connected by an existing edge.

Below this window are diagnostic displays of Average, Maximum, and Minimum Edge Length for the selected object. These displays should be used to correctly set the Hold Shape Radius parameter.

Note

It is widely agreed that, for all but the simplest cases, it is a far better idea to manually create springs using these controls than to let the computer do it automatically with the Create Simple Soft Body button covered earlier. The automatic process usually creates far too many springs for practical applications and often causes Flex calculations to slow to a standstill. It is a good idea to manually create just a few springs first and then add springs as needed until you get a better feel for the number and type of springs needed for particular tasks.

After you have made selections in the Spring Option window, you must select vertices in the viewport to apply the desired springs to. Then press the Add Spring button to actually apply the springs. If you need to delete incorrect or unneeded springs, select the vertices that are connected by the spring(s) and then press the Remove Spring button.

When springs have been created, you must adjust the four Spring parameters. Although this can often be a bit of a crap shoot, the Flex modifier makes a suggestion for a Strength setting that is often a good starting point for experimentation. The Hold Length parameter represents a percentage of the original length of a spring. By enabling this value, spring lengths will be forced to not exceed the entered length percentage. This can be a good way to control flex lengths in some cases, but it is important to remember that this clipping effect is performed after the normal Flex calculations. This means that the length of a spring—and, therefore, the shape of the object, can be different after calculating the Hold Length than it was when the normal Flex calculations were made. This can cause problems if your object is colliding with deflectors.

Although the Flex modifier is much more powerful now, it is probably not the best solution for anything more than simple tasks, such as flowing flags, jiggly stomachs or ears, and the occasional simple dynamics simulation involving only a few simple objects. A better solution for more complex dynamics-intensive scenes is the reactor plug-in (not to be confused with the Reactor controller). A limited version of the plug-in is included with max 4, and this is a much more powerful tool specifically designed for dynamics simulations. Unfortunately, it is beyond the scope of this book to cover the nuances of this plug-in. For more information, read the plug-in documentation.

Point Cache Modifier

The Point Cache modifier enables the user to create a cache file on disk that stores all the cumulative vertex transform information of an object. It essentially bakes or collapses any animated deformations made earlier in the Modifier Stack and saves it to disk for later playback.

When a cache file is saved, it is possible to disable the modifiers earlier in the stack so that, instead of calculating stack deformations on-the-fly for every frame, max can simply play back the collapsed vertex animation. This is useful for speeding up viewport playback on objects with complex, calculation-intensive deformations applied, such as those encountered when using the Flex modifier. This helps the animator preview deformations in the viewport in real time. It is also helpful when settings to modifiers such as Flex are finalized and the artists know that the animation on the object will not be changing. This way, the animator can concentrate on other aspects of the scene without having interactivity slowed by the now point-cached object. Additionally, it can be used to apply the same animation to copies of the object. By adjusting the start times for every object, more complex crowd-like motion can be quickly applied to a scene.

There are two flavors of the Point Cache modifier: object space and world space. If your object is not being deformed by a space warp binding, you can simply use the object space version. However, if you have any space warp bindings in the object's stack, you should use the world space version. The two versions operate identically and have the same parameters, as seen in Figure 3.21.

Operation of the modifier is relatively simple. The Start Time value enables the user to choose the frame at which the cache begins playback. This value is expressed as a floating-point number (decimal) for subframe accuracy while Frame: ticks is used to display time.

The Use Relative Offsets check box enables the user to exaggerate the original motion of the object. This is used in conjunction with the Strength parameter to add the recorded vertex motion to the motion calculated by the object's modifiers. This is usually used with the modifiers that are below the Point Cache turned on.

The Strength parameter controls the amount of recorded motion to be added. A value of 1 adds the exact recorded motion to the modifier-calculated motion, resulting in a doubling effect. Values from 0 to 1 lessen the amount of motion added, values above 1 increase the amount, and negative values add reversed motion. A value of –1 effectively cancels out all motion, and values below –1 result in a reversal effect.

Figure 3.21
Point Cache modifier.

Usually, the first step is to click the Record button. A file window is displayed, enabling the user to pick a name and destination for the cache file. The cache file records the frames determined with the Start and End Time values. The Samples parameter is used to calculate subframe motion that is important for correctly calculating motion blur. The Set Cache button is used to load previously recorded motions onto the object. After recording the cache file, users usually click the Disable Modifiers Below button to play back the motion as it was recorded. However, for exaggeration effects as covered previously, this might not be desirable. Typically this modifier is used with characters that use the Skin and Flex modifiers because real-time calculations often inhibit acceptable playback in the viewports.

Wire Parameter

This is one of the most powerful new tools introduced in 3ds max 4, and it can be beneficial to users working in all industries. Wire Parameter enables the user to wire, or connect, the value of any animateable parameter of any object to any other animateable parameter of any other object. This is commonly used in conjunction with the new Manipulator helper objects and the Add Custom Attribute feature to create custom animation controls, but the applications are unlimited. Both one-way and two-way connections are allowed, giving the user the ability to create complex connections between many parameters.

The Wire Parameter tools are accessed either by right-clicking an object and selecting Wire Parameter from the lower-right Quad menu (see Figure 3.22), or by selecting Wire Parameter from the Animation drop-down menu. A nested pop-up menu appears in the viewport, prompting the user to select from the available parameters for the object. Upon selecting a parameter, a dashed line appears (similar to using the Link tool). At this point the user should left-click the second object. A second pop-up menu appears, listing the available parameters for the second object. When the user selects this second parameter, the Wire Parameter dialog box opens.

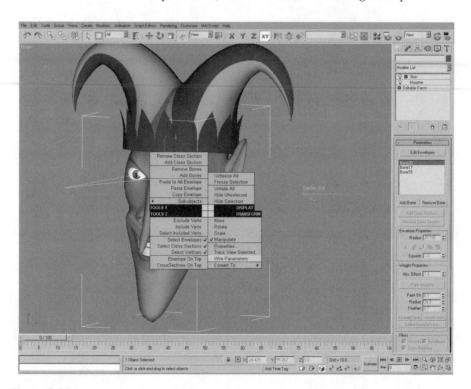

Figure 3.22   Choosing Wire Parameter from the right-click Quad menu.

The Wire Parameter dialog box displays two object tree lists, one for each of the chosen parameters. It really doesn't matter which side a particular object is displayed in because the connection direction can be selected. Above both lists are two buttons. The Show All Tracks button enables the user to jump to the top of the object list and allows for navigation of all the scene object's parameters. The Find Next Parameter button, with the binocular icon, is used to jump to the next wired parameter. This is useful for finding pairs of parameters if the user needs to edit existing connections.

Between the two lists are three arrow buttons that are used to determine the connection direction. The first one, Bidirectional, allows for the two-way connection of parameters when changing either parameter will affect the other (see Figure 3.23). The left arrow sets up a one-way connection in which the parameter displayed in the list on the right controls the parameter displayed in the list on the left. The right arrow produces the opposite effect. After selecting one of the direction buttons, the user must click the Connect button to apply the connection. The Disconnect button breaks any existing connection between the selected parameters.

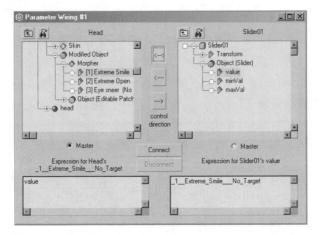

Figure 3.23   Parameter Wiring dialog window showing a two-way wire between a morph target and a slider manipulator.

Below both lists is a radio button labeled Master. Although there can be only one Master parameter in each wired pair, this designation is really important only for controlling which of the parameters receives the automatically created subcontroller when using a bidirectional connection. This is further explained in the max 4 documentation, but, in virtually all cases, this designation is not really important.

At the bottom of the dialog box, below each list, is an Expression window. This is where the user may optionally add an expression for one or both of the parameters when a one-to-one value connection is not desired. For example, if the user wants the radius of a cylinder to always equal half the height of a box in a two-way connection, the cylinder's expression window would read `height/2` while the box's expression window would read `radius*2`.

It is important to remember that the connections made using the Wire Parameter feature are direct, constant connections. In the previous example, as the box height value changes, the cylinder radius will change, no matter what the value, to infinity. When this is not the desired effect and limited or variable relationships between parameters are needed, the Reactor controller could provide a better solution.

Reactor Controller

The Reactor controller provides a powerful tool in creating custom, variable relationships between any parameter in max. Unlike using Wire Parameter, which creates constant direct connections between parameter values, the Reactor controller enables the user to set up finite relationships by defining parameter states, in which different parameter states (values) can result in various parameter reactions.

For example, say that you want the height of a jet to affect the needle of an altimeter that had a range of 0 to 10,000 feet. Two reactions could be set up. One reaction with the jet at a height of 0 would result in the needle pointed at 0 feet. The second reaction would be defined with the jet at a height of 10,000 feet and the needle pointed at 10,000 feet. However, if the jet was animated beyond 10,000 feet, the needle would appear to be maxed out and pinned at a reading of 10,000 feet, no matter how much higher the jet went.

Reactor controllers exist in five forms: Position Reactor, Rotation Reactor, Scale Reactor, Point3 Reactor, and Float Reactor. Which Reactor controller you use depends upon the type of parameter you are trying to apply it to. When you attempt to change a controller for a given parameter, the proper form of reactor will be listed in the controller list.

How Reactors Work

To understand how Reactor controllers work, you will set up a Reactor controller to control the pouring of tea from a teapot based on the teapot's rotation. This way, the animator could merely animate the teapot without having to worry about set-ting separate keys to control the pouring of the tea.

Exercise 3.1   Setting Up an Automatic Tea Pour with the Reactor Controller

1. To begin, open the file teapot_reactor.max from the CD.

 Note

This file contains a teapot and a superspray particle system that has already been posi-tioned and linked to the teapot. The settings for the superspray have been set up to shoot a constant stream of tea for the length of the animation.

The superspray particle system has been set up so that the release of tea can be con-trolled by one parameter, the birthrate. This is the parameter that will be assigned a Reactor controller. If you want to apply the Reactor controller to one of the transform tracks position, rotation, scale) of an object, just go to the Motions panel of the Command panel and open the Assign Controller rollout. Then, by clicking one of the three Transform channels followed by the Assign Controller button, the Controller list can be displayed, allowing the application of the Reactor controller. However, because you want to apply Reactor to the Birthrate parameter in this example, you must use Track view.

2. Select the superspray object in the viewport, right-click, and choose Track View Selected from the lower-right Quad menu.

This opens a Track view with the superspray object displayed.

3. In Track view, navigate to the Birthrate parameter track, located under Object (Superspray). Select the Birthrate parameter name, and then click the Assign Controller button located in the Track view toolbar. Choose Float Reactor from the list of controllers (see Figure 3.24).

The Reactor Parameters window opens, waiting for you to tell it what to react to.

4. Click the React To button and select the teapot in the viewport.

A pop-up menu listing all the parameters of the teapot is displayed.

5. Select Transform/Rotation so that the rotation of the teapot triggers the tea to pour (see Figure 3.25).

 Note

Optionally, users might want to apply a Euler XYZ rotation controller to the teapot rotation track to allow for more precise control. For the purposes of this example, however, the default TCB controller will be fine.

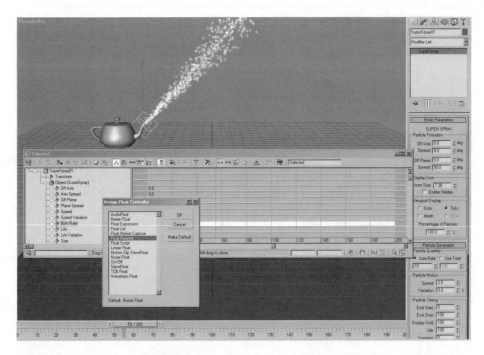

Figure 3.24   Applying a Float Reactor to the Superspray Birthrate parameter.

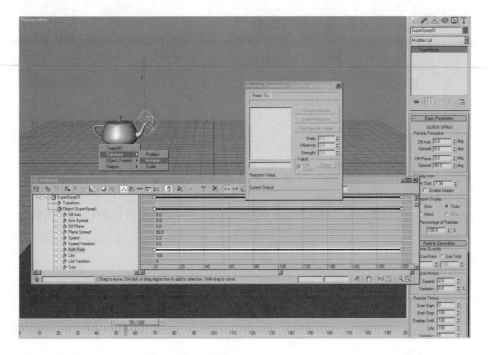

Figure 3.25   Select the teapot's Rotation transform as the birthrate's React To parameter.

After this, the Reactor controller creates the first reaction using the current rotation of the teapot and a value of 0 for the State parameter, which represents the birthrate value.

6. In the field below the Reaction list, rename Reaction01 to **No Tea**.

Now you need to create a few more reactions for the Birthrate parameter to react to.

7. Rotate the teapot 25° clockwise, and then click the Create Reaction button.

This adds a new entry to the reaction list.

8. Do not change the State value, which should still be 0, but do click the Set Reaction Value button to define a reaction that represents the last point of rotation before tea will start pouring. Rename this reaction **Still No Tea**, as seen in Figure 3.26.

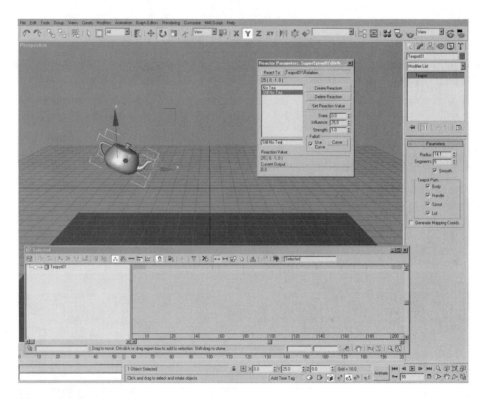

Figure 3.26   Setting up the second reaction.

9. Next, rotate the teapot another 5° clockwise. Click the Create Reaction button again, but this time change the State parameter to **1** and then click Set Reaction Value.

This defines the point of rotation at which tea will start to pour (see Figure 3.27).

10. Rename this reaction **Tea Trickle**.

11. Finally, rotate the teapot another 45°. Like before, click the Create Reaction button and change the State parameter to **10**; and then click the Set Reaction Value button.

This defines the point of rotation where the flow of tea will be at its greatest. Note that no matter how much more the teapot is rotated, the Birthrate will be maxed out at 10. You can get only so much tea through that spout.

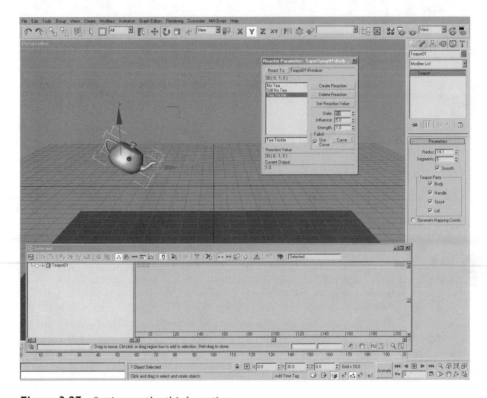

Figure 3.27   Setting up the third reaction.

12. Rename this last reaction **Max Tea** (see Figure 3.28).

Now you may animate a few back-and-forth rotations for the teapot. Experiment with different amounts of rotation for each keyframe. You should see tea being automatically poured when you rotate the teapot enough.

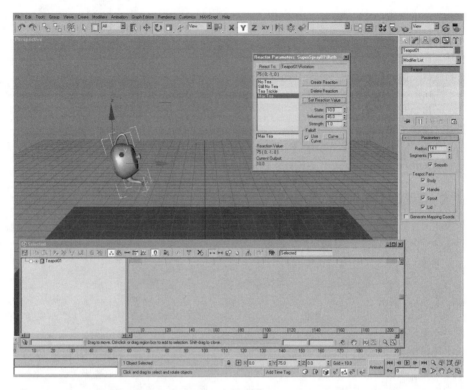

Figure 3.28   Setting up the final reaction.

Note

This file was set up to work from only frames 0 to 100. If you want to animate a longer animation, you will need to extend the Range Bar of the Birthrate track, which represents the frame range for which the Reactor controller will be used. You also will need to change the Emit Stop and Display Until parameters in the Particle Generation rollout of the Superspray to tell the particles to pour and be displayed beyond frame 100. Some other things that you can try are to assign a Reactor controller to the speed parameter of the Superspray so that the farther you rotate the teapot, the faster the flow of tea is.

Although this example shows how to use the Reactor controller to control specific parameters, it can easily handle general transforms. The only difference is in how you define the state of a reaction.

For example, if you want the position of a sphere to react to the scale of a cylinder, you would apply the Reactor controller to the Position track of the sphere and then choose the Cylinder/Scale track as the React To object. Just like before, the first reaction will already be created. Change the scale of the cylinder and then click the Edit Reaction State button. This enables you to change the position of the sphere.

Finally, you would press the Set Reaction State button to associate this new sphere position with the current cylinder scale. Normally, without pressing the Edit Reaction State button, you would not be able to manually move the sphere because the Reactor controller is in total control of its position.

Further fine-tuning is possible using the Influence, Strength, and Falloff Curve controls (see Figure 3.29). Depending on the type of reaction being used, the Influence parameter reflects a distance in world units, a rotation in degrees, or a floating-point value. This number represents an influence range for the selected reaction and determines how gradually or quickly one reaction will transition to the next. Larger values will overlap the influence ranges, causing a more gradual transition, while lower values will shrink the range, causing the reactions to seem to snap from one to the other. In most cases, you will probably want overlapping influence ranges. In such a case, the Strength parameter can be used to apply more or less weight to specific reactions.

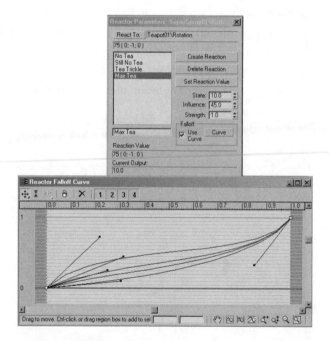

Figure 3.29   The Reactor Falloff Curve window.

Finally, the Falloff area enables you to use either a Spinner value to determine falloff speed or a function curve. It is usually more intuitive to use the Curve option, and it also allows much more flexibility.

Explicit Set Key

When animating, many animators prefer to use the Position XYZ, Euler XYZ, and Scale XYZ controllers in place of the default Bezier Position, TCB Rotation, and Bezier Scale controllers. This is because it usually allows them more flexibility and precision because separate tracks are used for each axis of motion. However, a long-standing complaint among users, many of whom were familiar with the workflow of 3D software such as Softimage, was that max created keys on all three axis tracks automatically, even when the user wanted a key to be placed only on one axis.

In response to this need, 3ds max 4 now enables users to set explicit keys on specific transform axes. This functionality, however, is not accessible in the default user interface. It must be configured in the Customize User Interface dialog box and assigned to either hotkeys, custom Quad menus, custom toolbar buttons, or drop-down menu items. The commands to create explicit keys are found in the Category drop-down menu under Keyframe Tools (see Figure 3.30). The Animate button does not need to be active to use this command, but it is important to understand exactly how these commands are achieving their results. When a key is set using a Create Explicit Key command, it deletes any existing keys on the other two axes at the current frame. Therefore, to create keys on two of the three axes at a particular frame, you must use the appropriate Delete Key command for the unwanted axis.

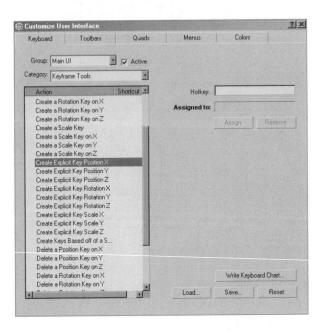

Figure 3.30   Accessing the Explicit Key commands for hotkey assignment.

Spring Controller

The new Spring controller is used to apply secondary lag motion to the selected object based on either its own animated motion or the motion of another object(s). It is different from the effect achieved using the Flex modifier in that the Spring controller works only at the object level and will not distort the geometry of the object. It can be useful to add a sense of weight and momentum to solid objects or to apply realistic momentum effects to things such as cameras or lights.

To apply the Spring controller, select an object and go to the Motions panel. In the Assign Controller rollout, select the Position track and click the Assign Controller button. Pick Spring controller from the list. A Spring Properties window appears (see Figure 3.31).

The Mass parameter controls the exaggeration of the spring effect, with larger values resulting in more exaggerated motion.

The Drag parameter can be set between 0, for a more springy effect, and 10, for a less springy effect.

Like many of the constraints examined earlier, the Spring controller can have multiple objects assigned to it, allowing the object to be connected to many objects with virtual springs. Each spring object assigned is listed in the spring list along with its associated Tension and Dampening settings. The Tension value controls how stiff a spring is between the object and the spring object. Lower values result in a slower, more lagged effect. The Dampening parameter works much like the Drag parameter, with larger values resulting in fewer bounces. The Relative and Absolute modes control how the Tension and Dampening spinners work. The Relative mode adds the spinner amount to the existing value. Typically, it is more predictable to keep this set to Absolute, at least until you feel comfortable with how the values will affect your animation.

Figure 3.31
The Spring controller properties window.

Forces Limits and Precision Rollout

The Forces Limits and Precision rollout contains controls that enable you to add the effects of Forces-type space warps to your spring calculations. This enables the use of forces such as wind or gravity to simulate the effect of the environment on your objects. The Add and Remove buttons obviously add or remove the chosen space warps to the External Forces list.

Calculations Parameters

The second part of this rollout, Calculation Parameters, controls the overall spring calculations. It enables the user to choose a start frame for the effect of the Spring controller as well as the accuracy of the spring calculations. Increasing the Iterations value improves the accuracy of the spring motion and should be used when troubleshooting erratic results. The XYZ Effect spinners enable you to apply a global limiting or amplifying of the spring effect along individual world axes.

Remember that the Spring controller can serve many purposes beyond the obvious applications of making an object seem to have mass or momentum. For example, it could be used when the Flex modifier proves too quirky or unpredictable for practical use. If you are animating something like a hanging chain or rope from a crane, you could create a spline and Link Xform its last vertex to a dummy that has the Spring controller applied. The Spring controller could then have the arm of the crane added to the Springs list, which would allow the movement of the crane to drive the dummy motion, which drives the spline deformation. In addition, dummies with Spring controller applied could have IK goals linked to them, giving the IK chains spring-like motion. Of course, these are only a couple possibilities.

New Space Warps

Two new space warps have been added to the existing lineup. The Vortex space warp is used to create black hole or whirlpool effects such as water spiraling down a drain. This is a welcome addition because the Motor space warp of previous versions was not as suited for tasks such as these (see Figure 3.32).

Also new is the Drag space warp, which is used to slow the velocity of particles or objects using the Flex modifier or Spring controller. Using the Drag space warp, users can finally apply a more realistic slowing effect to objects and particles, simulating the drag of either wind or friction with another object (see Figure 3.33).

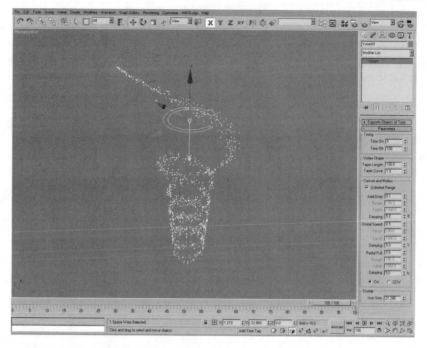

Figure 3.32   The new Vortex space warp.

Figure 3.33   The new Drag space warp.

Summary

That about wraps up the new animation features in 3ds max 4. As you've seen, many powerful new tools are available to make animating easier, especially for character-animation applications. Bear in mind that the real power of many of these tools is tapped only when you start using them in conjunction with other tools. As always, the rule of thumb is to experiment with combining features to solve a particular problem. There will always be multiple ways to achieve the results you seek—you just need to try them all out to see which one works best for your situation.

Chapter 4

Changes in Rendering

by Kim Lee

Although the release of 3D Studio Max 3 marked the most significant improvements in the areas of rendering quality with its enhancements of lights, materials, and the rendering engine, there are some useful rendering additions in 3ds max 4.

Generally, the new tools are focused on making the improvements made in release 3 more accessible and useful by streamlining workflow during the material, lighting, and rendering phases of a project.

Topics covered in this chapter include the following:

- New Multi-Pass effects, including Depth of Field and Motion Blur
- New ActiveShade
- New Exposure control
- New Render Elements functionality
- Enhanced network rendering

New Multi-Pass Effects

3ds max 4 introduces a new implementation of two commonly needed effects: Motion Blur and Depth of Field. These fall under the new category of Multi-Pass effects because of the method in which they are created. When they are used, max renders multiple passes and blends them together to produce the finished frame, hence the name. One of the advantages of the Multi-Pass effects is that they can be rendered in the viewports with hardware acceleration rather than using only the software renderer. This enables the user to make accurate adjustments to Motion Blur and Depth of Field settings without having to go through the usual render and tweak process.

Using these effects requiress the use of a camera, and the controls for these Multi-Pass effects are found in the camera's Modifier panel in the Parameters rollout (see Figure 4.1).

By enabling the Multi-Pass effects, the user has a choice of one of two effects in the drop-down menu: Motion Blur or Depth of Field. The Preview button is enabled when the Camera view is the Active viewport. It enables the user to preview the selected effect in the Camera viewport. Whether max uses hardware acceleration to create the preview in the viewport depends on which display driver is being used by max. You select the display driver by selecting Preferences from the Customize drop-down menu and clicking the Viewports tab. At the lower-right corner of the Viewport Preferences dialog box are choices for selecting drivers and settings. If OpenGL or D3D is chosen, the preview will use hardware acceleration.

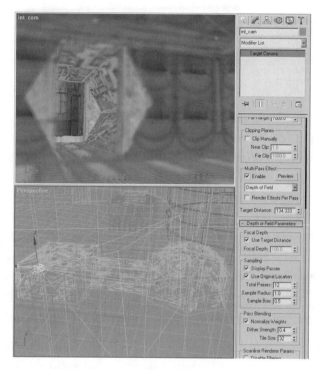

Figure 4.1 The camera's Multi-Pass effect controls in the Modifier panel.

The check box for Render Effects Per Pass is used to control the rendering of Render effects in concert with the Multi-Pass effects. Typically Render effects, found in the Render menu under Effects, are post effects that are applied after a frame has been rendered. When the check box is checked, the Render effect is applied to each pass of the Multi-Pass effect. As a result the Render effect is affected by the Multi-Pass effect.

For example, if a Glow Lens effect is applied to a moving sphere and is rendered from a camera that has the Motion Blur Multi-Pass effect enabled, the glow will be rendered on each pass of the motion blur, effectively blurring both the sphere and its glow. Depending on the Render effects used, this can result in long render times. However, if the Render Effects Per Pass check box is disabled, the Render effect will be rendered only after all the passes of the Multi-Pass effect are completed. Using the previous example, this would result in an unblurred glow effect composited over a motion-blurred sphere. Although this is certainly faster as far as render times are concerned, it can produce unrealistic results depending on the Render effects used.

Depth of Field

The Depth of Field Multi-Pass effect does a much better job of simulating camera depth of field than the solution provided by the Render effects feature. The Render effects version, which was introduced in 3D Studio Max 3, was really capable of producing only limited multiplane depth of field effects and was not very good at producing a gradual blurring effect between in-focus and out-of-focus areas. With the new Depth of Field effect, the camera is offset in a star pattern centered on its actual position while targeted on the original point in space, and the resulting images are blended together. This produces a smooth transition from parts of the scene that are in focus and those that are not.

Tip

Depth of Field relies on a focal point, which can be located at the camera's Target Distance or based on a Focal Depth parameter. Generally, for the most control and predictable results, users should opt to check the Use Target Distance check box. This enables the user to base the focal distance on the position of a target camera's target object or, in the case of a free camera, the Target Distance spinner.

The Sampling group contains controls that affect the quality and amount of the Depth of Field blurring. Turn off Display Passes to avoid seeing every render pass at render time. For most purposes it is unnecessary to turn off the Use Original Location toggle unless you don't want one of the passes to be blended with the offset renders. The Total Passes spinner should be raised for smoother blur results, especially if higher Sample Radius values are used. Be aware, however, that this value controls how many times a frame needs to be rendered, resulting in potentially long render times.

The Sample Radius value determines the outer radius of the star points where the camera will be offset. The higher this value is, the more pronounced and exaggerated the Depth of Field effect will be. The Sample Bias control determines the magnitude of the star pattern used (see Figure 4.2). At a setting of 1, all points of the star have the same radius, effectively making it more of a circle pattern. At a setting of 0.5, the radius of the inner star points is half of the Sample radius (outer). At a setting of 0, the inner star points have a radius of 0, placing them in the same position as the original camera position. This last setting is unadvised because it wastes half of the render passes by rendering the same image.

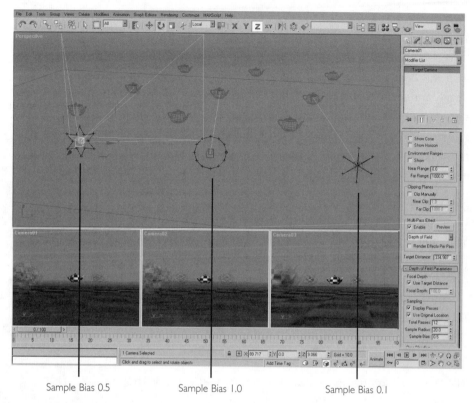

Sample Bias 0.5   Sample Bias 1.0   Sample Bias 0.1

Figure 4.2   Examples of three Sample Bias settings and their respective results.

The Pass Blending group contains controls that determine how the multiple rendered passes will be dithered together when executing a final (software) render. These controls have no effect on viewport previews. For most users, Normalize Weights should be kept on unless a grainier result is desired. The Dither Strength parameter should be kept relatively low to avoid grainy results. Typically, the results of changing the tile size are subtle and are dependent on the combination of parameters used in the effect.

Finally, the Scanline Renderer Params group contains toggles for disabling filtering and anti-aliasing in the final render. These are typically used to speed up render time for test renders and are turned back on for final renders. Like the Pass Blending controls, these controls do not affect viewport previews.

Motion Blur

The Motion Blur Multi-Pass effect represents a third alternative to the existing object, image, and scene motion-blurring techniques already present in max 4. As with the Depth of Field Multi-Pass effect, one of the chief advantages over object, image, and scene motion blur is that the Motion Blur Multi-Pass effect can be accurately previewed in the viewport without executing a final (software) render. Additionally, users should note that although the Multi-Pass Motion Blur effect is most similar to Scene Motion Blur in its underlying method, the Multi-Pass version allows for bias control, which is explained here.

Many of the controls for the Motion Blur effect are the same as those for the Depth of Field effect (see Figure 4.3). In the Sampling group, turn off Display Passes to avoid seeing each pass as it renders during a final render. The Total Passes spinner determines how many renders (samples) will be blended together to produce the final motion blurred image. Increasing this value produces smoother results at the expense of render time and is recommended when higher duration values are used.

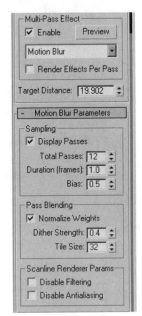

Figure 4.3
Controls for the Multi-Pass Motion Blur effect.

The Duration spinner is measured in frames and controls the chunk of time over which the total passes will be rendered. The Duration value is split evenly before and after the current frame, so a setting of 1 results in a chunk of time starting a half frame before the current frame and ending a half frame after the current frame. Higher Duration values produce more exaggerated Motion Blur effects and, depending on the relative speed of motion in your animation, will probably require a higher Total Passes value.

The Sample Bias enables the user to control the weighting of the motion blur to either before or after the current frame (see Figure 4.4). At a lower value closer to 0, more of the total passes will be rendered before the current frame; the motion blur will appear ahead of the object's position or leading edge, in this case. With a higher value closer to 1, the motion blur will appear to trail behind the object.

Sample Bias 0.25

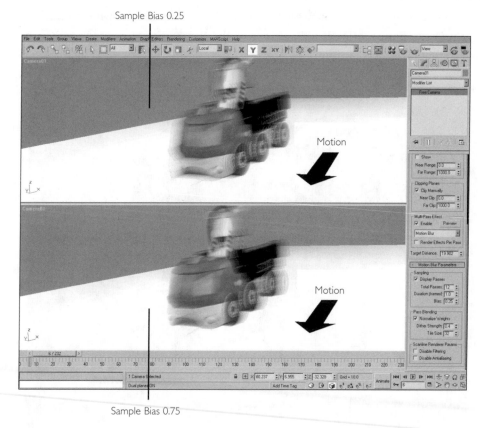

Sample Bias 0.75

Figure 4.4   With the Sample Bias, users can control the weighting of motion blur to either before or after the current frame.

The remaining controls for Pass Blending and Scanline Rendering parameters are identical in operation to those covered previously for Depth of Field.

New ActiveShade

3ds max 4 introduces ActiveShade, a new, faster way to provide the artist with feedback when working with lighting and materials (see Figure 4.5).

This functionality can be accessed in three ways. The ActiveShade feature can be accessed from the Rendering drop-down menu as a free-floating ActiveShade floater, or it can be docked to a viewport as an ActiveShade viewport. The ActiveShade floater function is also located at the far right of the max 4 toolbar. The third way to create an ActiveShade window is through the Render Scene dialog box. Click

Render Scene in either the max 4 toolbar or the Rendering drop-down menu, select ActiveShade from the lower-right corner of the Render Scene window, and then click the ActiveShade button.

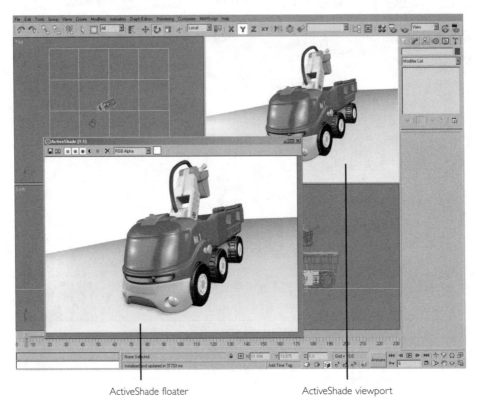

ActiveShade floater   ActiveShade viewport

Figure 4.5   The new ActiveShade at work in 3ds max 4. Note that the ActiveShade viewport and floater cannot be used simultaneously.

When executing a normal software final render in max, many of the parameters that are calculated do not change when adjusting lights or materials. Rather than calculate the same unchanging parameters every time the user makes a lighting or material change, ActiveShade calculates these parameters once initially and caches the results for subsequent renders. This can dramatically decrease render time and subsequently increases artist interactivity. Of course, to achieve this, certain assumptions have been made by the software developer about exactly which parameters will be cached in the pursuit of faster render times. A complete list of what is and what isn't cached or prerendered is available in the printed and online manuals. Depending on the adjustments made, the user might need to force an ActiveShade initialization to see the effect of the change made (see Figure 4.6).

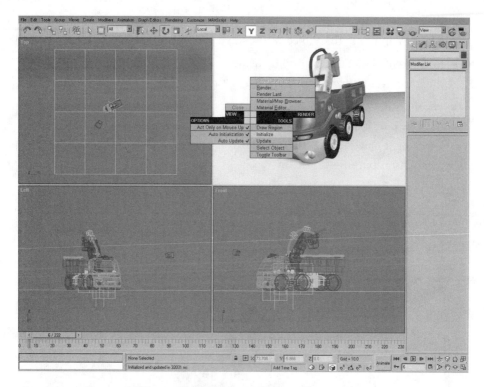

Figure 4.6   ActiveShade initialization forces max to re-render the image.

Here are some of the more commonly encountered situations that require a manual initialization:

- Turning on or off shadow casting for a light
- Changing any shadow parameters, such as Sample Range or Bias
- Moving an object other than lights

 Note

Users should bear in mind that although the ActiveShade feature can be a boon to productivity, its results are not completely identical to a final software render.

Remember a couple of time-savers when working with ActiveShade:

- When using an ActiveShade viewport, you can drag and drop materials directly to the object in the ActiveShade viewport.
- When working with complex scenes, you can right-click in the ActiveShade window (both floater and viewport) and choose Select Object from the

lower-right quad. Then select an object from within the ActiveShade window, and only that object will be updated when making changes.

- Interactivity can be improved by using the Draw Regions function located in the lower-right quad or the right Quad menu.

- When using an ActiveShade window docked to the viewport, remember that the viewport toolbar is still available by choosing Toggle Toolbar from the lower-right Quad menu. This enables you to save or clone the image for comparison purposes.

Tip

ActiveShade will not operate on a full-screen toggled viewport (W), but it will work if the user drags the desired viewport borders to the maximum size (see Figure 4.7).

Drag viewport border for larger ActiveShade window

Figure 4.7   The desired viewport borders dragged to the maximum size.

New Exposure Control

The new Exposure control gives the user the capability to affect the output of final software renders through the use of a physical light model based on a candela multiplier. *Candelas* are an industry-standard measure of light used throughout the film and architecture industries; one candela represents the approximate light output of one candle. This multiplier is applied to the multiplier of each light in a scene as well as to self-illumination and reflections/refractions created with the raytrace map or material. Exposure control will not affect reflections/refractions created with the Reflect/Refract or Flat Mirror maps.

The Exposure controls can be accessed from within the Environment dialog box located in the Rendering drop-down menu (see Figure 4.8). By selecting Automatic Exposure Control, an automatic histogram is created and applied to the final rendered image. The result is a significantly more contrasted image that, in the case of very dark scenes, can give certain lighting effects more punch.

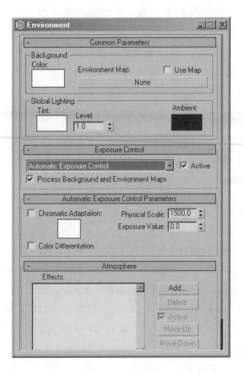

Figure 4.8   The Exposure controls, accessed from within the Environment dialog box in the Rendering drop-down menu.

Only four parameters are used to control the Automatic Exposure feature. The Physical Scale parameter is used as a multiplier measured in candelas; it can serve to either dim or brighten a scene. However, it is possible to reach a Physical Scale value above which the scene will not get any brighter. Exposure Value serves to either raise or lower the overall brightness of the final render, resulting in the effect of either an under- or overexposed image. Both of these parameters are animateable, enabling the user to create gradual exposure change effects.

The Chromatic Adaptation toggle enables the user to select a color with the provided color picker that will be used as a basis for adjusting all colors of the final render. This is intended to be used as a sort of color correction for colored casts from lights in a scene. For example, if a scene has a slight blue cast on the specular highlights in the scene, that blue-tinted highlight color can be selected and all the colors of the scene will be adjusted to make that color appear as white in the final render.

The Color Differentiation feature is intended to replicate the eye's incapability to differentiate colors in very dim lighting situations. The resulting effect is that extremely dim colors are rendered as tones of gray. This effect becomes apparent only when the Physical Scale value is set to around 25 or below, or if an extremely low light multiplier value is used.

Note

Although these Automatic Exposure controls can be useful for users who plan to use 3ds max 4 as their sole image creation/manipulation tool, the resulting effects can be achieved more practically using Discreet's combustion, flame, inferno, or some other comparable compositing package. The advantage to using a separate compositing package to achieve these results is increased control and flexibility.

New Render Elements Functionality

The Render Elements feature is a much-needed tool for easing the integration of 3ds max 4 render output with compositing tools such as Discreet's combustion, flame, or inferno, as well as packages such as Adobe After Effects, Eyeon Software's Digital Fusion, or Nothing Real's Shake. The reality of production environments today is that a 3D package rarely exists in a vacuum. After the 3D elements are rendered, even for scenes comprised entirely of 3D elements, it is desirable to do final adjustments or tweaks in a 2D compositing package. This process is covered more extensively in Chapter 5, "Workflow in the Broadcast/Film Environment," and Chapter 26, "Compositing and Finishing in Combustion."

In previous versions of max, it was necessary to create multiple versions of the same file to render different element passes for compositing purposes. This process could potentially take hours to set up, depending on the complexity of the scene and the number of elements required. By using Render Elements, the user can simply choose which individual elements are needed and press Render. The separation of the elements is now automatic.

The Render Elements rollout is accessed from within the Render Scene window (see Figure 4.9). By default the Elements Active toggle is on in addition to the Display Elements toggle, which results in each element being displayed in its own independent virtual frame buffer and also being saved to disk. All that needs to be done to render elements to disk is to add the desired elements via the Add button. The resulting Render Elements dialog box presents the various element types in a list. Unfortunately, the user cannot select multiple element types at the same time, but must click the Add button and select from the list for each element required.

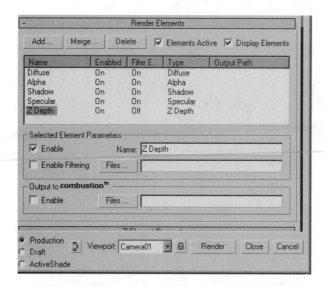

Figure 4.9   The Render Elements rollout, accessed from within the Render Scene window.

A complete list of the different available element types and descriptions is available in the max 4 documentation, but following is a description of the ones that require more involved setup:

- **Blend.** This element is used to combine two or more of the eight existing element types into one element layer. Click the check boxes for the desired element in the Blend Elements Parameters rollout to create the required element combination.

- **Z Depth.** This element requires the correct adjustment of two parameters in the Z Element Parameters rollout. The Z Depth element represents the depth of a given pixel in the scene. This can be confusing for some beginners because 3ds max typically associates the world Z-axis of a scene as height or up. The Z Depth element, however, abides by the industry standard of referring to the depth into the frame as Z.

  The Z Depth element represents the depth of pixels in shades of gray, so there are practical limits on how much depth can be accurately represented with a limited number of gray shades. The Z Min (white) parameter represents the closest point in from the camera plane that should be represented, and the Z Max (black) parameter represents the farthest point from the camera plane that should be represented in the Z Depth element.

  An interesting possibility for scenes that are too deep in the Z-axis to represent accurately with the limited grayscale is to render multiple Z Depth elements with different Z Min and Z Max settings. One unfortunate limitation that users should be aware of is that the Z Max setting has a maximum setting of 10,000, which limits the actual scene depth that will be represented in the Z Depth element.

The Merge button enables the user to merge Render Elements lists from another max scene file. This can be used to avoid having to re-create long Render Elements lists that an artist might use repeatedly.

Below the actual Render Elements list window is the Selected Element Parameters group. Here the user can enable or disable an element as well as turn on or off anti-aliasing for individual elements. The name of the element can be renamed in the Name field, and the output path can be designated. To save time, the user can first set the overall output filename and path in the Render Output group of the Common Parameters rollout. If this is done before adding elements, the individual element filenames and paths will automatically be filled in, using the filename created in the Render Output group as a prefix base. The type of element will be tagged onto the end of the filename.

When using Render Elements, the user also has the option of outputting a combustion workspace file. Of course, this requires the combustion software package that is available separately from Discreet. If this feature is enabled, max will create a CWS file that contains the rendered elements, which saves further time in setting up the compositing phase of the project. Users who plan to use this feature should bear in mind that certain file types are not supported under combustion—namely, EPS, FLC, FLI, and CEL files.

Enhanced Network Rendering

3ds max has always had very strong built-in network-rendering capabilities, and, in this latest version, it has been rewritten to allow greater flexibility and speed. Users are urged to read the network-rendering documentation provided in the printed and online manuals for a more complete explanation of a network rendering setup. This book covers only significant changes in functionality and workflow, and assumes a basic level of understanding regarding TCP/IP networks.

In its simplest form, network rendering is comprised of two components: a Manager and a Server. The Manager distributes the rendering tasks to the Server, which does the actual rendering. A computer is designated Manager or Server, or, in some cases, both, by launching either the Managerapp.exe or Serverapp.exe programs, located in the root 3DSMax4 directory by default. For users who want to run these programs as services under Windows NT/2000, services versions of these programs have been provided.

For all practical purposes, the number of machines that can be used for network rendering from one license of 3ds max 4 is unlimited. But even if you do not have access to multiple machines, network rendering can be used to queue multiple jobs on a single machine. This requires that the user install the TCP/IP loopback adapter software that is built into Windows 2000/NT but that is not installed by default. Refer to your operating system documentation for more information.

Running as a Service Versus Running as an Application

The first thing that should be decided is whether to run the Manager and Server applications as normal executables or as NT services. One of the advantages of running them as services is that they will always be resident in memory and ready to render as soon as the computer finishes booting. This might be important for medium- to larger-size facilities that have many machines. In these cases it could become a timely ordeal to go to every machine and start the Server application when it is needed for rendering. To avoid having a user's machine suddenly start rendering a render job while in the middle of working on something else, the service could be configured to load only under a particular login name by using the

Hardware Profiles functionality built into Windows 2000/NT. Refer to the Windows 2000/NT documentation for more information. Users could be instructed to log off when they leave for the day and log in as a specific user name such as render so that as soon as the user leaves, his or her machine will become available for rendering duty.

The downside to running the Server or Manager apps as services is that there will be less diagnostic information available onscreen in case rendering problems arise. This is because the service will not display the log window that is displayed when Manager or Server is run as a program.

Most users will probably be fine running these apps as programs. This has the advantage of easily making a machine available or unavailable for rendering duty in a manner that most users are most comfortable with, without having to disable or enable NT services. A certain amount of automation is also available if a user chooses to go with this process because the ManagerApp.exe or ServerApp.exe programs can be added to the startup folder for dedicated render farm machines or for specific user accounts, much like the example process outlined in the previous paragraph. We will concentrate on the program version of the Manager and Server apps.

The Network Rendering Manager

The first thing that needs to be done is to pick a machine that will fill the role of network rendering Manager. Bear in mind that this machine will be handling network traffic to and from all the Server machines and will be storing a copy of the max scene files that get queued for network rendering, as well as potentially any map files required by that file. This means that the Manager should have a reasonable amount of free disk space on a fast hard drive and, depending on the amount of rendering traffic expected, should not be used for some other I/O-intensive tasks such as burning CD-ROMs. Also, depending on how large of a render farm you plan to deploy, the type of operating system license could become an issue.

Upon launching the max Network Manager program for the first time, the Network Manager General Properties dialog box opens (see Figure 4.10).

The TCP/IP section enables the user to change the Manager and Server ports, which are used to communicate between machines. This probably needs to be changed only if some other networking software has already used the default port numbers. If these port numbers are changed, they will need to be changed on every machine involved in network rendering.

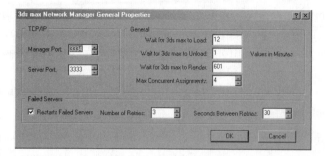

Figure 4.10   The Network Manager General Properties dialog box.

The General section enables the user to tailor the Timeout setting for network rendering. The time values for the Wait for 3DS max to Load, Wait for 3DS max to Unload, and Wait for 3DS max to Render are now shown in minutes instead of seconds, as in Max 3. These determine how long the network-rendering software will wait before flagging a particular machine as failed. The Wait for 3ds max to Render spinner is new and is useful in cases in which a Server encounters a problem and "hangs" on a render. These numbers must be adjusted depending on the complexity of the scene files being rendered and the speed of the network. Larger files or scenes that require longer render times necessitate increasing these values. No changes have been made to the Failed Servers section.

The 3ds max Network Rendering Manager window is comprised primarily of a large log window that gives various levels of diagnostic and status information (see Figure 4.11).

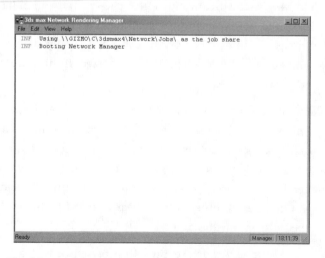

Figure 4.11   The 3ds max Network Rendering Manager window.

The File menu contains two options: Close and Shutdown. Users familiar with network rendering in the previous version of max should note that choosing the Close option or clicking the X button in the upper-right corner of the window does not stop the application from running. The application stays resident and active in memory, and merely minimizes. To actually end the process, you must choose the Shutdown option.

The Edit menu contains another two choices: General Settings and Log Settings. The General Settings window is identical to the window that is presented the first time you start Manager, as described in the previous paragraph. Log Settings contains choices for what types of status and diagnostic data to either display in the Manager Log window or save to a log file. Typically users who are not experiencing network-rendering problems will not need to turn on all these options.

The View menu presents choices for displaying the status bar at the bottom of the Manager window, choosing the font size, and determining whether to autoscroll the log list in the display.

The Network Rendering Server

After a network Manager has been launched, one or more machines may be designated as Servers. Depending on the size of the files being rendered, almost any reasonably capable machine may be used as a Server.

The only real practical issues involved in a machine's capability to be a useful Server are how much RAM is installed, how much free space is on the local hard drive, and how big of a swap file (virtual memory) is configured. This is important because there must be enough combined memory available between both physical RAM and virtual memory to fit the entire scene file being rendered. If this is not the case, you might experience Server failures.

Other considerations are the number and speed of the processors in the Server. In some cases, it might be impractical to use a slower machine in conjunction with many faster machines. For example, when rendering a scene file (render job) with a very low frame count, a significantly slower machine could actually delay the completion of the render job, especially on jobs in which the time to render a frame is more than 15–30 minutes. Another issue to bear in mind is the operating system license used, especially on the Manager.

Upon first launching the Serverapp.exe, the user is presented with a Network Server General Properties window (see Figure 4.12). The TCP/IP section contains settings for the Manager port and Server port, which must match those of the Manager, as described in the previous section.

By default, the Automatic Search check box will be on and the user will have the option of entering the Subnet Mask. The Subnet Mask is an IP number that is used to find the machine running the network rendering Manager software. This IP number usually defaults to 255.255.255.240 on most systems, but, at certain facilities, it could be different. If you are not sure of the proper Subnet Mask, contact your network administrator.

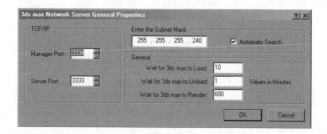

Figure 4.12   The Network Server General Properties window.

Be aware that if you are running the network rendering Manager software on more than one machine, Automatic Search will use the first Manager that it finds. Thus, it probably is best to turn off Automatic Search. With Automatic Search disabled, you are prompted to enter either a Manager name or an IP address. You would do this typically in two situations:

- If you plan to run multiple Managers on a network with static IPs in which every machine has a nonchanging IP number, you will need to enter either the name of the machine running Manager or its IP address.

- If you need to deploy network rendering on a network that employs DHCP, where a given machine's IP address might change every time it is rebooted, you must enter the Manager's name. This works because the network-rendering software records the Network Interface Card (NIC) number of each machine and can use that along with its machine name to locate a given computer.

The General section contains settings identical to those of the Manager software for configuring time thresholds (measured in minutes) for network jobs to load, unload, and render.

When the Server software is launched, users are presented with a Server window that looks similar to that of the Manager software. Functionally, all the menus operate identically to those of the Manager window.

Sending a Job to the Render Farm

When at least one Manager and one Server have been configured and launched, you may begin to utilize the network-rendering features of 3ds max 4.

Begin by loading the scene file to be rendered. Click the Render Scene button in either the toolbar or the Rendering drop-down menu, and check the Net Render check box. Next, click the Files button in the Render Output group.

Warning

It is vitally important that you use care in entering the name and path for the rendered image files. You must remember that the path entered must be accessible from all the Server machines. Although it is possible to map the destination machine and drive to the same drive letter on all render Servers, this is usually not practical on anything but the smallest home networks.

Instead, it is a better idea to get used to using the Universal Naming Convention (UNC) format for assigning destination paths. Under Windows 2000/NT, this can be easily done after clicking the Files button. In the Save In drop-down menu, select My Network Places. In the resulting file list, choose Entire Network, followed by Microsoft Windows Network. Depending on your network's topology, choose the proper workgroup or domain. Finally, select the machine name followed by the drive name and destination folder. This all assumes, of course, that you have turned on Sharing for the desired drive. Optionally, you can merely type the full UNC path in the File Name field. Getting into a habit of using the UNC format in place of the drive letters common to most Windows users can help you avoid much frustration. Often render jobs are submitted to the Network Render queue with the intention of rendering overnight for a presentation the next day; however, all the render Servers might fail 10 minutes after the artist leaves the office if they can't find the path specified.

Network Job Assignment Window

After the proper UNC path and filename have been entered and all the desired rendering settings have been made, you can click the Render button. The main max interface will minimize, and a new Network Job Assignment will appear (see Figure 4.13). Enter a desired job name, preferably one that is somewhat descriptive, especially in facilities where many artists are rendering jobs. Ideally, a naming convention should be established for larger projects to avoid having a co-worker accidentally cancel your render job. The + button enables you to automatically increment the job name, which can be especially useful when rendering multiple test renders of the same scene.

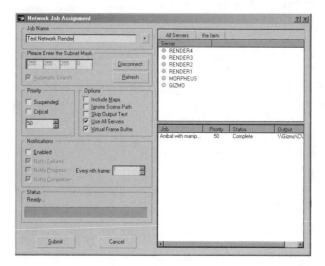

Figure 4.13   The new Network Job Assignment window.

As in the Server window, the Automatic Search button is enabled by default and prompts the user for a Subnet Mask number. These settings depend on how your network is configured, as described earlier. After the proper settings have been entered, click the Connect button to connect to the Manager machine.

The Priority section enables you to assign a priority level to your render job. The Suspended toggle is useful when you want to send multiple jobs to the queue before initiating rendering, especially when you are running both Manager and Server on a single machine for queuing purposes. The Critical setting is useful in situations when you need to have a render job rendered immediately while other jobs are currently being rendered. Out of consideration for your fellow artists, you should probably not get in a habit of using this unless it is absolutely necessary because it halts rendering on all other jobs until the critical job is complete.

The Priority spinner enables you to employ a system of numerical job priority, with lower numbers having higher priority. This can be especially useful if it's integrated into a project workflow with certain scenes or shots designated a particular priority number so that the individual artists can concentrate on the artwork instead of the project schedule.

The Options group gives the user control over five toggles, two of which are new. Ignore Scene Path enables the user to force Server machines to retrieve the render job file from the Manager machine via TCP/IP. Turning this on can be useful when 10 or more Servers are deployed and the Manager machine is running Windows

2000 Professional or NT4 Workstation due to a maximum connection limitation in those operating systems.

Skip Output Test enables the user to bypass the default test that max runs to check whether all Servers can access the designated file output path. In most cases you should leave this unchecked so that if a Server fails the test, you will be notified immediately with an error message in the Server window.

Although it's not new, the Virtual Frame Buffer check box determines whether each Server will display the current frame being rendered. Because the Virtual Frame Buffer uses memory that would otherwise be used for rendering, you might want to turn this off, especially when rendering at high resolutions or when your Server machines have limited memory installed.

The right half of the Network Job Assignment window displays a list of Servers and Server groups at the top and a job list at the bottom. Server status is shown by a colored circle. Green signifies available, yellow means busy, red denotes a failed Server, and gray means that the Server is unavailable. Right-clicking the Server list area produces a menu of options for displaying all or partial Server details and for creating a custom Server group. Creating Server groups can be useful for assigning certain groups of Servers to particular jobs. The Properties option is available when clicking the name of a Server; it displays useful information, including available drive space, memory, and number of processors.

Finally, when all settings have been made, click the Submit button to send the job to the queue. At this point, the user must use the Queue Manager software to change job settings and manage queue order.

The Queue Manager

The Queue Manager enables the user to change the order of jobs in the queue, as well as cancel, suspend, delete, or change render settings of jobs (see Figure 4.14). This is also where you can remove or add Servers from jobs or apply schedules to them. Finally, the Queue Manager provides useful information for checking the status of render jobs as well as troubleshooting problematic jobs.

The Manager menu contains four new options. Request Queue Control enables users to remotely request read/write control from the user currently running the controlling Queue Manager. Request Client List displays a list of all machines running Queue Manager, as well as which one has read/write access. These two features should be a relief to artists working at larger facilities who previously had to run around an entire office to find the machine with read/write access. Turning off Auto Refresh forces the user to manually refresh the state of the queue. Turning this off can be useful if you are using either the Frames Summary list or the Log display to troubleshoot a render. Shut Down Manager enables the user to remotely shut down the Manager software as long as it is not being run as a service.

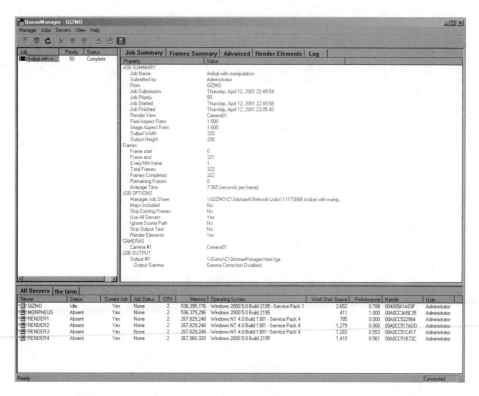

Figure 4.14   The Queue Manager enables the user to change the order of jobs in the queue, as well as cancel, suspend, delete, or change render settings of jobs.

The Jobs menu contains three new options. Edit Settings enables the user to access the Job Settings dialog box for the highlighted job and make changes to it. Generally, if this is done, it is a good idea to use the Restart Job option if the job has been partially rendered. Change Priority enables you to change the current job level, when needed.

The Servers menu has four new options. Assign to Selected Jobs and Remove from Selected Jobs enables the user to either assign or remove multiple highlighted Servers from multiple highlighted jobs with a single click. Show Job Servers Only is useful for finding out which Servers are assigned to the highlighted job. All Server Details displays, strangely enough, all Server information in the Server list.

No other function of the Queue Manager has changed. For further explanation of features in the Queue Manager, users are urged to consult the printed or online documentation.

Summary

Many of the new rendering features introduced in 3ds max 4 grew out of the specific needs expressed by the broadcast and film industries. Features such as Render Elements lend themselves to workflows that include a compositing phase, which might not be as commonly practiced outside of broadcast and film. However, the benefits of these tools are by no means limited to artists in a particular market. Artists working in any industry, including architecture, design, and interactive fields, might find that they can achieve faster and more flexible results by adopting techniques such as compositing render elements. Other features that we have covered, including ActiveShade, Multi-Pass effect, and network rendering, can increase productivity for artists across the board in almost every type of work.

Part II

Production
Workflow

Chapter 5

Workflow in the Broadcast/Film Environment

by Kim Lee

One of the most important elements in the success of a project is the planning stage. Although this has been echoed around the industry, it cannot be stressed enough. Proper planning can make or break a project, but there are many phases of the planning stage. The most commonly covered areas are usually the story, design, and storyboard phases, but it doesn't end there.

To support the conceptual planning aspect, there needs to be a solid execution plan. How many artists will be involved? How many technical directors will be involved? Will they all be located in the same building, or will they work remotely? How will the work be delegated? And how can the tools available in 3ds max 4 be used to facilitate all this?

All these and many other questions must be answered in a manner that will get the project done on time and on budget. A good workflow, or pipeline, can be just as challenging to create as the artwork that it facilitates. As we explore this chapter, you will see the differences and similarities of the broadcast and film industries while examining important aspects of building a successful pipeline with 3ds max 4.

Note

It is important to note that all the issues covered in this chapter were addressed during the course of producing this book. As you read this book, it is important to realize that it was purposely organized and executed to mirror actual production workflow. Granted, many alterations were made to the pipeline to compensate for the fact that all the authors were trying to do three things at once.

For one, we were doing two actual productions—one for games/interactive and one for broadcast/film. These two project tracks were intended to be executed just like any other production job, in which certain artists could not begin work until others had completed theirs. On top of that, we had to write a book documenting and hopefully giving some insight on the individual phases. Of course, this could sometimes be done only after the actual production work was completed. Third, we all had to work at our day jobs, which entailed, for almost everyone involved, production work. Another unique hurdle was that the authors were spread from New York to California, making artist collaboration difficult. These are just some of the reasons why some liberties were taken in the workflow used to complete the projects in this book.

Before we look at specific workflow suggestions, we should examine the many elements of the problem we are trying to solve. These elements, which we'll discuss in this chapter, include the following:

- The Project/the elements
- The Artists
  - Geography
  - Schedule

- Approvals
- Changes
  - The tools

The Project/The Elements

The first step in creating a successful workflow is to examine the project and establish a list of the necessary elements. Artists from both the broadcast and the film industries might be faced with totally different artistic and technical challenges with each new project. One client might need digital set extensions involving camera tracking, while another might need hundreds of digital characters and clothing. No matter what the scenario is, someone must sit down and go over every shot and determine what elements are needed and how they should best be created.

Typically this decision-making process will be a collaborative effort including a director, producer(s), and visual effects supervisor(s). In cases involving a smaller production staff, the role of the visual effects supervisor will be filled by either the project lead, the technical director, or the lead artist—and, in some cases, all of these. Regardless of the number of people or their titles, the important thing is that individuals strong in a combination of both artistic and technical skills be involved to consider both the artistic integrity of the finished product and the feasibility of the methods employed to achieve them. Although the methods by which a particular element is realized might change over the course of actual production, it is important at this point to determine which, if any, of the elements required are impractical to achieve in their current form.

Sometimes the results of these meetings will require a rewrite of the script, a change in the storyboards, or a reworking of preproduction designs. Ultimately, after every aspect of the project has been analyzed and agreed upon, a shot-by-shot list should be compiled detailing the element requirements. It is at this time that the individual(s) fulfilling the role of visual effects supervisor must decide what talent and tools are needed to do the job.

The Artists

Regardless of what the marketing departments at software and hardware companies say, the quality of the final work does not come down to the tool but rather to the talent of the artists. Ultimately, it is the artists that drive the industry, and perhaps the hardest part of putting together a successful production workflow is finding the right artists. Regardless of whether the artists are on staff or freelance, their individual skills and talents should complement the type of work needed.

Essentially, artists can be put into one of two categories: those who have a strong interest and, hopefully talent, in multiple disciplines, making them a kind of jack of all trades; and those who prefer to specialize in only one or two areas. The type and size of the production company will obviously have an influence over which type of artists are available. Generally the two most apparent production strategies favor the two types of artist. Larger production companies, most apparent in film, seem to favor the specialized/departmentalized approach with many specialized artists working only on specific pieces of a project. One of the higher-profile examples of this is Industrial Light & Magic, where 3D modelers do nothing but model and character animators do nothing but animate. The results of this approach certainly speak for themselves.

However, the other approach, which is certainly proven viable by smaller companies every day, involves a workflow in which artists might need to wear multiple hats on a project. These artists might model, texture, and rig a character, while another might handle lighting, particles, and rendering. Ultimately, many factors influence the approach that best fits the project, including budget, schedule, and, last but certainly not least, available talent.

Geography

In many cases, the particular mix of talent deemed necessary for the success of a project might not be readily at hand, in house, in state, or even in country. Ideally, most projects would certainly benefit from having their entire team located under one roof. In fact, for many projects, the immediacy of having artists available for spur-of-the-moment creative meetings with directors, project leaders, and art directors is a must. The added benefits of synergy between artists are another strong reason for having the talent all working in-house.

However, the influence of the Internet and the increasing access to high bandwidth for many companies and artists cannot be denied. Depending on the specifics of the project, allowing artists to work remotely can definitely be a viable and possibly economical option. Assuming a fast enough Internet connection on both sides, some factors that will influence the decision between onsite and remote include the following:

- Is the artist a known quantity?
- Has the artist worked with this team or production company before?

- How well is the artist able to communicate with and receive direction from the director?

- How closely will the remote artist(s) need to work with others in house?

- If the artists are specializing in a certain area, will there need to be a lot of back-and-forth adjustments to files between artists? For example, a character rigger might experience a significant number of back-and-forth adjustments as the rigs are tested by the animator, so working remotely could slow production unacceptably. On the other hand, if a cinematic full-motion video (FMV) sequence is needed for the opening of a game, the artist(s) might not be closely tied to the actual game production at all; in that case, the remote approach could definitely work.

- What is the balance between schedule and budget? It might be significantly cheaper to let someone work remotely without the burden of transportation and lodging costs that might be necessary to bring that talent on site. Of course, this must be balanced with any possible adverse effect to the project schedule.

Ultimately, it will come down to the comfort level of the director/producer in the ability, speed, and professionalism of the given artist.

If a remote approach is needed, certain obvious infrastructure issues will need to be implemented onsite. These include possible FTP site setup, a project Web site for artists, strict naming conventions, and availability to the artist of any third-party or proprietary tools or plug-ins needed for the project. Another obvious but often-overlooked issue is whether the remote artist is using the same exact version of the software.

Schedule

Working out a realistic project schedule is obviously of paramount importance, followed closely by actually adhering to the schedule during production. In setting up a schedule, many variables must be taken into consideration. The first is to understand the eight different phases required in 3D production. Typically these are as follows:

- Layout/previs
- Modeling
- Texturing/mapping
- Rigging/animation setup

- Animation
- Lighting
- Rendering
- Compositing

Note

It is important to note that it is typical for the approval process to be closely tied to these phases. This is covered in the next section.

Now is probably a good time to point out just how dependant all the phases are on the others, not just in a schedule sense. None of these phases can operate in a vacuum without taking into consideration the technical issues of the others. For example, how a modeler builds a model will influence the ease or difficulty of the texturing/mapping phase and the rigging phase. Additionally, artists rigging a character must work closely with the animators to produce a rig that is easy to animate and capable of the action required. Lighting will affect the look of textures, and how a shot is rendered will affect how smooth the compositing phase proceeds.

For some of these phases (modeling, texturing/mapping, animation, and lighting), it is obvious, even for intermediate users, from their names what kind of work is involved. Let's look at a few of the phases that readers new to production might be unfamiliar with.

Layout/Previs

During the layout/previs (or previsualization) phase, the project will be blocked out in 3D. This is often done using very low-resolution models, often barely more than primitives. It is here that the director can see any potential timing or staging problems before full-blown production commences. Animation during this phase is typically very rough and basic. Optionally, if the project requires the integration of CG elements with live-action backplates, as in this book, this phase also might require camera matchmoving to execute the actual layout/previs. Otherwise, in an all CG shot, lighting issues and camera issues such as lens and animation can be worked out quickly, relative to the action being previsualized.

Rigging/Animation Setup

The rigging phase is more common to 3D character work but can also include other types of animation setup. Typically this phase will be handled by artists in the role of technical director (TD). A character TD will usually be charged with creating the skeletons and IK setups for a character, along with any custom animation controls required by the animators. Using 3ds max 4, this would include creating complex IK hierarchies, creating manipulators or custom attribute controls, skinning/enveloping the character model, writing custom scripts (possibly using Visual MAXScript), and setting up morph controls for facial animation. Optionally, this might also include setting up any clothing or hair controls. For noncharacter work this phase could include setting up any mechanical hierarchies and controls, particle systems, and any other custom scripts necessary for the other phases of the project.

Rendering

The rendering phase in production is usually a bit more involved than merely clicking the Render button. Artists or TDs will usually need to have a good understanding of the compositing process to set up render passes or elements that are needed by the compositors. Often the same individuals who handle the lighting phase might be involved in the rendering phase. This is also the phase in which individuals known commonly as render wranglers will oversee any distributed rendering on a render farm using 3ds max 4's Network Rendering features.

For the gaming industry today, in which most of the 3D work is destined to be rendered by a real-time gaming engine on a client's computer, this phase can be replaced with (or renamed) Export to Game Engine. Often this is handled by programmers rather than 3D artists.

Compositing

Finally, the compositing phase is where it all comes together. This is where the final look of the work is tweaked. Traditionally, this work is done using 2D compositing packages such as Discreet's combustion, flame, or inferno, or in other popular third-party compositing packages such as Adobe's After Effects, Eyeon Software's Digital Fusion, or Nothing Real's Shake. Recently, however, the industry has begun to incorporate new tools that enable compositors to maintain much of the flexibility of the 3D realm while working with 2D image files. This functionality is most obviously seen with the integration features found between 3ds max 4 and combustion. Regardless of which platform a project is composited on, the compositing phase allows for faster and more flexible tweaking of the final look than would be afforded by re-rendering in 3D. Ultimately, it is a workflow step that is popular not only for large production companies, but also for individuals working on a smaller scale.

This phase, along with the modeling, texturing/mapping, animation, and lighting phases, is not new to the process of creating 3D animation. However, it is important to understand that to complete a project within the confines of schedules typical to 3D production, it is often necessary to have a schedule set up in which the different phases can overlap. The example schedule spreadsheet shown in Figure 5.1 illustrates this overlap.

	Week 1	Week 2	Week 3	Week 4	Week 5	Week 6	Week 7	Week 8	
					Example 3d Schedule Overview				
Scene #									
	modeling	modeling							
	character modeling	character modeling							
		texture/mapping	texture/mapping	texture/mapping					
1		Rigging/Setup	Rigging/Setup						
			animation	animation					
				character animation	character animation	character animation			
			fx	fx	fx				
					lighting	lighting			
						Rendering	Rendering		
							Compositing	Compositing	

Figure 5.1   Example schedule spreadsheet.

Notice that the modeling phase has been further divided into two areas of expertise, character modeling and (general) modeling, and that a similar division has been made to the animation phase. Regardless of how you need to categorize the different parts of the process, the important thing to do is to organize it in a way to keep the workload as even as possible given the number of artists on the project. This example schedule assumes that multiple models need to be built over the course of two weeks. The artists working on modeling can begin work on another scene after the second week of production. Meanwhile, texture/mapping artists and riggers/TDs can begin working on models that have been completed after the first week.

It is easy to see how this kind of schedule would be suitable for a production company based on the specialization model of distributed labor. However, this can also work for shops that employ artists that are proficient in multiple disciplines. The only difference is that more careful planning will be necessary to make sure that the schedules for a particular artist's strengths are not in conflict. For example, you could easily have the same artist fill the roles of texture artist and lighting artist. Of course, this schedule is only a rough guideline because every production will necessitate a custom approach. The three ingredients that are key to producing a similar workable, realistic schedule are listed here:

- Knowing how many artists are available and what their strengths are
- Being able to make realistic estimates of how long a given task will take to complete
- Not forgetting about the client approval process

The first point should be relatively easy to put together. The second is probably the hardest, especially when dealing with reasonably unseasoned production artists. However, this can be difficult for even seasoned pros when faced with design/technical issues that they do not have extensive experience with. Sometimes there is just no way to accurately estimate how long something will take until you try to do it. This is why the research and development (R&D) phase exists. Not all projects will have enough time or budget for an R&D phase, but if you find yourself blessed with one, use it wisely.

Either way, you should remember to ask yourself a few basic things and make some assumptions when trying to estimate time needed for a given task:

- How fast/proficient are you or the artist?
- How familiar are you with the technology (when dealing with new techniques such as new plug-ins or hardware)?
- Assume that the software *will* crash.
- Assume that you *will* find bugs or shortcomings in the software that you were unaware of.

I realize that these last two points might seem a bit pessimistic or even humorous, but, as the saying goes, "That's the nature of the beast." That's the reason for writing this book. Although many workarounds are covered in this book based on artists learning what works the hard way, you will no doubt discover issues not covered within these pages that will require an adjustment of your production schedule, hopefully in a positive sense.

Approvals

The client approval process can sometimes prove to be the slowest phase of a production and must be accounted for early. Although it's not always the case, clients are often uneducated in the realities of 3D production. In their defense, it really isn't their problem; it's ours. However, it is important early in the planning stage to implement a strict approval process and set ground rules covering how many and what kind of changes can be made at a given phase of production. Obviously, it is preferable to get final approvals or client sign-offs on 3D models while still in the modeling phase of the schedule rather than during the rendering phase.

However, there must also be a limit set for how many times a client may request changes at a given stage, especially if the client is new to the 3D production process.

Often, if left to their own devices, clients can ask an artist to tweak a model or a scene for so long that it starts to eat into the time allotted for other scenes or phases. In the end it is usually the artist who pays, finding him or herself working around the clock to make up for misspent time. Other times the production company will be forced to hire extra artists near the end of production to get the project out the door. Although this scenario seems ubiquitous in everything from film work to games, an awareness of the issue can certainly lessen the impact on the project.

Changes

If there is any one truth shared in life and in working in 3D, it is that the only constant is change. There will *always* be changes to your work, no matter how well-crafted you believe your work might be. Although we are hopefully all artists at heart, and whether we are working on a game, Web site, commercial, movie, architectural walkthrough, or product display, remember the phrase quoted at the end of this book's Introduction: "This is commerce, not art." We will undoubtedly all become personally attached to whatever piece we are working on, but remember that we are being paid (hopefully) to please a client. And because, in theory, "the customer is always right," your workflow, like the artist's, must be designed to facilitate and adapt to changes at any point of the project.

Luckily for us the underlying architecture of the 3ds max 4 software is reasonably flexible and capable of allowing the artist to make changes earlier in the pipeline without losing all later work. This can be achieved with hopefully minimal suffering on the part of the artist through careful technical planning and use of certain features of the software.

However, there certainly are varying degrees of feasibility when it comes to making changes. Obviously, it is impractical to change the design of a character if the existing character models have made it all the way to the final animation stage. Knowledge of what changes are feasible given the software and workflow is necessary in preparing or briefing a client early on as to what can be changed and when it can be changed. Of course, this is tied closely to the topic on approvals covered earlier.

The Tools

Because this is primarily a book focused on the technical/tool side of the process, we will be looking at some of the ways to take advantage of certain features of max that will facilitate a good workflow. Bear in mind that the following suggestions might not be ideal for your particular project, but they will hopefully inspire alternate approaches that might be more suitable.

Assuming a workflow pipeline in which many artists will need to access files created or modified by others, here are some guidelines taken in the order of a generic production, starting first with general advice common to all phases.

General

- Agree on a standard file-naming convention and centralized storage location.
- Take the time to name objects in a file intelligently and consistently, whether it is a model, a texture, a light, a bone, or a glow effect.
- Get in a habit of saving incrementally. This can be done easily with the plus (+) button located in the Save As dialog box.
- If you're unsure of the results of a procedure that you plan to perform, use the Hold feature often. The Hold feature is located in the Edit drop-down menu. Remember that executing a Hold will actually save your scene to a temporary file that gets overwritten every time you use it. However, even if max crashes, you can retrieve your last Hold file by using the Fetch feature.
- Learn some basic MAXScript. It's not hard, it will make your life easier, and it just might open a whole new world for you.
- Whenever possible, create selection sets for models, rigs, lights, and so on. This makes hiding and unhiding things much easier, which will speed up productivity.
- Use the Pop-Up Notes feature to include important comments for other artists that will appear when they open your file. This is especially important if you need to hand your work off to someone else to complete.

Layout/Previs

- If time permits, always do a previs.
- Create the previs as accurately as possible in terms of timing, camera moves, and overall action. Don't overwork the previs. It's more important to see if the overall pacing of a scene is correct at this stage than it is to see if a character is bending its knees correctly.
- If possible, build the previs to the same scale as the real scene is intended to be built. This way you might be able to swap in models and animation using

the previs file as a base, and therefore avoid totally rebuilding everything that was worked out in the previs.

Modeling

- Whenever possible, avoid collapsing an object's Modifier Stack. This will maintain the object's history and allow for easier changes. Of course, at some points you must collapse the stack. Therefore, you will need to save incremental files so that you can get back to any stage of the modeling process, if necessary. In many cases you will ultimately want to collapse the Modifier Stack to cut down on CPU/memory overhead for phases such as rigging or texturing. In this case, save a separate uncollapsed version of the model for safe keeping.

- Set up hotkeys or custom Quad menus to speed up productivity.

- Agree upon a standard scene scale, especially if many artists will be building models for the same project.

- If Xrefs will be used in production, use the master model to make low-res proxy versions to speed the animation process.

Texturing/Mapping

- If at all possible, use individual modifiers to assign Material IDs to sub-object selections and to apply mapping coordinates. This enables you to easily go back and make changes without having to dig into one editable mesh, poly, or patch entry. It also makes your work transferable because the modifiers can be copied to other objects. This is especially useful if the animation phase needs to begin before the texture/mapping phase is completed.

- When picking bitmap files for use in a material, consider whether others will be opening the file and whether they will be able to access the same map paths. If centralized storage is configured in your production environment, try to use UNC paths so that every machine can see the same path.

- Name materials and maps intelligently.

- Create material libraries to facilitate the use of your materials in other scene files.

Rigging/Animation Setup

- Get in a habit of giving bones unique names and/or a prefix for the particular character. For example, if your character is called Jester, name your bones jester-bone01, jester-bone02, and so on. This way, if the character needs to be merged into another file with other characters, you can avoid same-name conflicts and the confusion that goes with it. Make sure to do the same for any helper or manipulator objects used.

- If you know that your rig will be merged into other files, be aware that, when using constraints, the object you are constraining to will be merged even if it is not selected in the object merge list. This can cause problems, especially if you are constraining an object to part of another rig. You might want to create a temporary proxy object for your constraints for merging purposes.

- Talk to the animators at length to get a good idea of what kind of motion they will need the rig to be capable of. Be prepared to cater to their needs. Remember that the most complex rig is useless if the animator cannot use it easily. The best rigs/setups hide the complex technical aspect from the animators and let them just worry about the art of animation, not the technology.

Animation

- If applicable, use the capabilities of controller lists to allow animation to be added in layers. This will make trying out alternate animation performances easier without having to change existing keyframes.

- Use the RAM Player whenever possible to compare and examine animations. It's much more flexible than the Media Player that comes with Windows 2000/NT.

- When feasible, use the Xref features of max to include externally referenced models in your scene. Although this feature does work with the Skin modifier now, typically using Xrefs involves bringing in prop objects that will not be deformed. Remember that you can use the proxy feature of Xrefs to animate with the low-res version of the models, which will speed things up especially in heavy scene files.

Lighting

- Name lights intelligently, especially when you know that they might be merged into other scene files.

- If possible, work closely with the texture/mapping artists and the rendering artists.

Rendering

- Use UNC paths wherever possible, especially when using network rendering.

- Whenever it will speed up production, render out separate passes (elements) for compositing purposes. If something can be done faster on the compositing side, then do it, especially if you think that changes or tweaks are likely.

- If you really want or need to use a post effect from the max side, such as a glow, render it as a separate pass also.

Compositing

- Make sure to sit down with the artists who will be doing the compositing and make a checklist for yourself of everything the artists will need. Do not take anything for granted. A few of the things that you should not forget to discuss are Alpha Channels, frame rates and counts, pixel aspect ratios and frame resolution, image file formats, and compression types, if applicable.

- Don't use the compositing phase as a crutch for 3D. Just because a project will be implementing a compositing phase doesn't mean that the 3D artists can get sloppy or lazy. Only so much can be tweaked or fixed in compositing. Remember that compositing is supposed to add the icing to the cake, not fix the baking stage.

Summary

These are just a few guidelines that are important to consider. As you progress through the production portions of this book, you will see some of these points discussed in greater detail. Ultimately, the success of a given pipeline will increase as the artist gains experience and discovers what techniques work better, faster, and are more reliable.

Chapter 6

Workflow in the Games/Interactive Environment

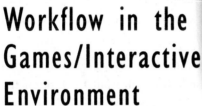

by Mike O'Rourke

Video game development hasn't been around for very long. Everyday people are innovating, adjusting, and rethinking the process to make a more efficient team. Many similarities exist between developing a game and developing for film/broadcast. Planning is equally important in both industries, and many of the issues that the film and broadcast industry deals with are also felt in the game industry. For an in-depth discussion of this, see Chapter 5, "Workflow in the Broadcast/Film Environment."

However, there are many differences between the film/broadcast industry and the game industry. One of the most obvious is the platform that each industry is developing for. For instance, the broadcast and film industries have been around for decades and have established format standards. When you are working on something for NTSC or PAL, you know the spec, and you are probably aware of its many pitfalls and the workarounds that have been established to work with the format. Also, the delivery format and performance are a known quantity that is pretty much standard for your current and future audiences.

In the game industry, there's an entirely new platform out every year, offering better technology and new opportunity. Of course, artists will want to work on the newest systems right away because they offer the most features and the most avenues for innovation. There can be problems with this, though. Often the new features need to be implemented by programmers before the artist can even touch them.

Therefore, a decision needs to be made about which platform to develop for, keeping in mind that you can develop for multiple platforms at the same time. As soon as a platform is chosen, the next step is to start thinking about the technology that the team will use. Will a new engine be written? Will an old one be updated? Or will one be licensed from another company? These issues are crucial because they can affect everyone on the team. For instance, if an engine is licensed, the programmers might have saved some time by not having to write an engine from scratch. But now they are working with someone else's code, and if they want to make core changes, it might not be easy—or even possible—in some cases.

For the artist, buying an engine can be quite nice. You will know very early whether you can use an application such as 3ds max 4 to make the levels, whether the characters can have weighted skinning or whether they must be segmented, and what general limitations you'll have to work with. When an artist knows the limitations, he can work within and around them with confidence.

This chapter covers the following:

- The different roles in a game team
- The game artist's workflow
- Game-specific tools in max 4

The Artist's Role on a Game-Development Team

The first thing that needs to be said is this: Every game development project can be—and usually is—set up completely differently. There isn't a formula yet for a groundbreaking A+ Title game-development machine. The team is defined by its members and what each of them brings to the table. In the next section, you'll go through the standard setup for a game-development team. Keep in mind that these are guidelines and that many game-development teams are set up differently.

The Lead Artist/Art Director

The *lead artist/art director* is typically an artist who has been working in the 3D industry—usually games—and who can produce art and also manage the artists underneath. Unfortunately, this often turns into a pipe dream because many artists aren't great managers, and vice versa. It's an interesting position, though, because it can be so many different things.

For instance, this person might just be the glue among the artists, helping them keep a common vision. Depending on the individual's managerial skills, the role might be less art-intensive and instead might require more scheduling and project maintenance. On the other hand, a lead artist/art director might do very little management, instead focusing on more art-intensive items.

Senior/Advanced Artist

The *senior artist* is an artist with experience who has been working in the industry for a couple of years and typically has worked on a few titles. The senior artist often is a person who can hold his own, be self-reliant when need be, and just get the job done in general. There isn't much "hand holding" required.

One of the interesting things about being an artist in the game industry is that technology is changing so fast that it forces the senior artist to be aware of what is happening technologically on a daily basis. Getting your art to be the way you want it to be in the game is not necessarily an easy and obvious thing to do. The senior artist is typically the person who can get the art done and then get it to work in the game the way that it should.

Junior/Intern Artist

The role of junior artist can be many things. It can be that of an unpaid intern who does Photoshop actions all day, or it can be an entry-level, full-time position with the team. The junior artist typically requires guidance to get the job done, which brings up a few issues. The people who know how to accomplish the task that the junior artist is trying to complete are typically senior artists. It must make sense, in terms of both time and money, to take the senior artist away from his tasks to help a junior artist.

Of course, some junior artists are talented people who don't have a flashy portfolio and a lot of industry experience. Instead, they've been pounding away on a cheap, three-year-old CPU with old software and are actually very talented. Given the chance and the hardware, they can produce excellent work. This is the starting point for many people entering the game industry, and the position you take scales based on your experience and history.

Roles: Who Does What?

Staying with the theme that every team can be set up differently, it's hard to define the roles of each artist in a game-development team. The following is a typical situation:

- Producer
  - Assistant producer
- Programmer
  - Lead
  - Senior
  - Junior
- Designer
  - Lead
  - Senior
  - Junior

- Artist
  - Lead
  - Senior
  - Junior
- Sound and other departments

This is a typical layout of a game-development team. Keep in mind that artists might be level designers and that some producers are wanna-be artists.

In general, the team is the producer's responsibility. The producer overlooks all aspects of the game's creation, with the help of assistant producers. Underneath this management level are the three main divisions: programming, art, and design.

Communication among these different divisions is crucial and can often be the source of problems in a game-development environment. If the artists aren't aware of relevant code changes, they can potentially create content that won't work properly in the game. If the programmers aren't aware of what the artists are capable of, they might make the wrong assumptions about how an artist might make something look in the game. For an artist, it's important to know as much as possible about programming, without actually getting in the way.

Game Artist's Workflow

Many steps are involved in the typical workflow of game production. Depending on the team and the situation, the workflow might be a predefined guideline or might be more free flow and open to change. Whichever method is used, most artists will follow some generic steps.

Concept/Brainstorming

In the first stage, ideas are brought to the table, concepts are drawn, and some models are made. Brainstorming sessions and concept creation determines the look and feel of the game. Artists might work closely with designers to understand the game concept, which then helps them develop an art feel that matches the game design. The conceptual process can go in so many ways: It can be a very free-form process, or it can be a rigid process that takes several weeks or months to develop certain art guidelines for the game.

Modeling

During the modeling phase, models can be created based on the conceptuals. These conceptuals can be either hand-drawn or created with one of many other types of media, such as Super Sculpey. Whatever method the artist prefers, it is at this stage that the look and feel of certain elements are determined. Some artists prefer modeling in 3D right away without a concept, while some prefer the aid of a conceptual drawing during the modeling process.

It takes a broad range of skills to tackle the task of modeling for games. Roles range from level creation to character animation. Levels are usually huge and can be quite complicated. The level creator needs to take special care to spend the polygons wisely and to set up the scene so that it is manageable. Typically, a level is one file that the artist will be working with for days or months. When an artist comes to work in the morning (or evening, in some cases), the level needs to be organized and manageable.

Characters and other moving things, on the other hand, need to be modeled with animation in mind. If the character can only be 1000 polygons, for example, those polygons need to be spent not only on the details and the form, but also on the areas of the model that are deforming the most or that need to stretch. Knees, elbows, and the groin area are the common problem spots for low-polygon characters as far as animation is concerned.

Another important aspect of character modeling is knowing what is important and what isn't. If the title is a fast-paced action shooter, in which all the characters are running at mach speed, it might not make sense to spend a whole lot of detail on a character's mustache. It's important to know the target platform that you are developing for so that you make the most relevant, optimized content possible.

Texturing

After a model is completed, and often during the modeling process itself, the model needs to be textured. Texturing is a two-step process of texture mapping and texture creation.

Texture mapping is the process of applying mapping coordinates to the model. In other words, this is how the texture will be "wrapped" around the model. *Texture creation* is the process of creating the texture, either from scratch or by piecing together existing elements in a program such as Adobe Photoshop. Often the texture creator, or "skinner," doesn't alter the model. He uses the model to view the texture that he is working on, but he doesn't actually apply the mapping coordinates himself. On the other hand, some artists will do the whole process themselves, without the assistance of another artist.

Texturing is important for video games. Because the polygon count is limited, a lot of detail needs to be done at the texture level. If a texture is done right, it could fool the viewer into thinking that something is modeled, when it's actually just drawn in on the texture.

Rigging/Animation Setup

After the model is completed, it is ready to be set up for animation. At this stage, bones or one of many other techniques are used to set up the character so that it can be animated in the best possible way.

3ds max 4 has really been improved in this area by providing several solutions for rigging characters. The new inverse kinematics (IK) and constraint system enables the artist to create bone systems in any shape and then to set them up to be animated nicely with IK and constraints. The Skin modifier has gotten several improvements also. Gizmos enable you to handle problem spots such as armpits and other joints by using angle deformers. On top of these powerful tools, character studio 3 provides another character animation option.

Character studio consists of Biped—a customizable premade bipedal skeletal system—and Physique—a deformation modifier. Biped has many new features, including the capability to animate pivot points on the fingers and feet. Physique has gotten a much-needed speed improvement, as well. And, on top of all this, character studio 3 includes Crowd, a fully customizable and scriptable crowd control system.

Animation for games can be quite different from what you might see in a film/broadcast environment. For example, many games need the character to be animated walking in place. The game engine handles the actual movement of the whole model while the "walk" animation is being played. It is important for the animator to know how the character moves in the game engine to make the animations look correct. The animation process eventually turns into a combination of animation tweaking and then exporting to check the animation in game.

Exporting/Testing

After a model has been created and animated, if necessary, it then must be exported to the game engine. This is done in a variety of ways. Sometimes games will support a common format such as .3ds. More often a game will have its own format. In the case of Quake3Arena from Id Software, the models are in the .md3 file format. This is the format that stores polygonal data. You can export to this format with a plug-in. After you have exported the file, you need to view it either in-game or with one of many model viewers available on the Web. At this point, you might decide that an animation needs to be adjusted. Often this turns into a workflow: check animations, tweak animations, check again, tweak again, and so on.

Many settings can be set in 3ds max 4 so that what you are doing in max more closely resembles what is going on in the game. This can save you the hassle of going back and forth many times. One example of this is controller types. In certain games, the animation system supports only linear controllers. So, instead of animating something with Bezier curves, you might switch all the controller types to linear because that is what they will be by the time you have gotten the animation in-game.

The animator is typically the person who will export character models because usually some tweaking must be done, and the animator has the most control over the model and animation at that point. Level designers are in a similar situation export-wise, although, because of the sheer size of some levels, the process of exporting can take much longer than that of a character.

The Tools

This next section looks at several things that can help in the game development process. Obviously, this book covers many of max 4's features in great detail. Here you'll learn about the little things that can make a big difference in the day-to-day use of max 4.

Setting Up max to Work for You

You can customize max in many ways so that it works just the way you like it. This next section covers some of the things that you can change with preferences and discusses max's highly customizable UI.

Keyboard Shortcuts

Using keyboard shortcuts will help you work faster. If you find yourself going to a button a lot, try to set it to a keyboard shortcut. Do this by going into Customize/Customize UI. Click the Keyboard tab. By clicking the resulting buttons, you can make all your assignments.

Viewport Rendering

You can do a lot to improve what you see in the viewports in 3ds max 4. To start, you'll look at the viewport settings and adjust a few video card settings.

- **Texture size**. This setting determines what resolution the textures will be set to in the viewports. The higher the setting, the better it will look, but be sure that your video card can handle it. The Match Settings button sets the viewport resolution as close to the bitmap's size as possible. It's best to use the Match Settings button unless you are working within certain restrictions or your video card doesn't perform well.

- **Mip mapping**. By setting this to Linear, max enables mip mapping. This process is much like Level of Detail (LOD) models for materials. As the object gets farther away from the viewer, its texture gets knocked down in resolution.

Customizing the UI

3ds max starts up with a default interface. This is a good overall UI to work with, but you may want to make your UI more specific to the task that you have to complete. 3ds max 4 gives you the ability to customize the UI to your liking, from drop-down menus and toolbars, to colors and icons. You can change pretty much everything in the UI to make it just the way you like.

- **Changing menus**. Go into the Customize UI window by choosing Customize/Customize UI from the main menu bar. This window enables you to customize a lot of 3ds max 4. When you've figured out which tools you are using most frequently, go ahead and customize your UI so that you get to the tools the way you want to. These possibilities include menus, Quad menus, toolbars, and keyboard shortcuts.

- **Quad menus**. Quad menus are extremely useful, especially when they've been customized to fit your needs. For instance, imagine that you have your Move, Rotate, and Scale modes set to some keyboard shortcuts. You don't need this same functionality in two places, unless you prefer to, so you can delete those tools from the Quad menu and replace them with something that you use a lot. You can also go a step further and customize the way the Quad menus look and behave in the Quad menu settings. Explore the possibilities of customizing the UI—it can make using max a whole lot easier over the long run.

- **Colors**. Almost every color that you see in 3ds max 4's UI is customizable. Explore changing these colors to create an environment you are comfortable working in. If you are working with max for long periods of time, you might consider adjusting the colors to be a bit easier on your eyes by choosing some softer color tones.

- **Transparency and saturation**. You also can change the transparency and saturation of the icons in the UI by locating the Icons item in the Customize UI/Colors window and adjusting the values.

Modeling

When creating something like a character or a world element, you might want to keep a couple of things in mind. Often, in a game a lot of details in a model go unnoticed because of the speed of character movement or because of lighting. This is a fact of life in many action games because the goal of the game could be to move as fast as possible and destroy everything. The one thing that does get seen in that situation is the overall form of the model. This is easiest to visualize by analyzing a model's silhouette.

Tip

To view a model's silhouette, make a new material and make its diffuse color black. Turn all the shininess parameters down to 0, and change the background color to a light color by going into Render/Environment in the main menu. Now rotate around your model and watch for details that stand out. Also watch for bland areas. If the character has a strong silhouette, it will stand out well in the game environment.

Detail: Animation Relevance

When modeling for games, it is very important that considerations are made for the animation phase. When you're modeling things that will be animated, think about where the detail is most useful. The armpit and crotch are typical areas for this type of detail. Because the leg joint will be deforming around the crotch area, detail needs to be put in the proper place to allow for smooth deformation.

Because the artist is restricted to a certain polygon limit, decisions need to be made regarding where to put details in the model. In the case of a character, the artist might be tempted to spend a lot of polygons to make the face look great or to model individual fingers on the character's hands. If this character is going to be shot close-up, maybe for a real-time cinematic, then those are good areas to spend extra polygons on. However, if the character is for a fast-action first-person shooter, it might be best to spend the polygons for details in other spots or to just leave off the details for speed considerations.

Tip

This is a really obvious tip. If you are working on something that is symmetrical, such as a face or a torso of a character, you can model one side and then mirror and weld to make the other side. The tricky part is welding all the vertices after you have mirrored the model. This is done by selecting all the points that are along the seam of the model and then adjusting the Weld Threshold to match the distance of the weld. Press the Weld Selected button when you're done. The best way to do this is to start with a small number and work up. If there are no vertices with that threshold, a Warning dialog box will appear. Adjust the setting a little higher, and try again. This Weld Threshold number might be very large or quite small, depending on the scale of your object.

Smoothing Groups

Many gaming engines support smoothing groups. By using the smoothing groups in max 4, you can make certain areas seem to blend into each other by giving them a common smoothing group. When two polygons are next to each other and share the same smoothing group, the shading will make them look smooth across the two faces.

Tip

To adjust smoothing groups, simply apply an Edit Mesh modifier or collapse the object into an editable mesh. Now go into Sub-Object/Face or Sub-Object/Polygon mode and select some polygons. All the way at the bottom of the Edit Mesh modifier is a large box of numbers. These are the smoothing groups. By pressing a numbered button, you assign that smoothing group number to those polygons. Those selected polygons will appear to be smooth. You can also use smoothing groups to make creases by not putting the same smoothing groups on two neighboring polygons.

STL Check Modifier

The STL Check modifier is an excellent way to check a low-poly model for defects. The STL Check modifier lets you check for a few common problems, most notably double-sided faces. Sometimes during the modeling process, you create a face on both sides using the same vertices. This is an easy mistake to make, and sometimes it is intentionally done for a certain effect.

The STL Check modifier gives you a quick and easy way to check for this. Just put the modifier on your model and select the appropriate option that you want to check for; the modifier will find out how many errors are in that particular model.

Also, if you choose to have the STL Check modifier select the offending faces or edges, you just need to put an Edit Mesh modifier on top of the STL Check and go into the appropriate Sub-Object mode. The offending faces or edges will be selected for you automatically.

Patches for Games

Although many game engines might not support real-time patches, there is something to be said for the flexibility that patch modeling gives an artist when creating game content. Even if the game doesn't support the patch in real time, you can use patches to model; and then just convert to polygons when you want to export. If you will need to make several LODs, patch surfaces give you the ability to adjust the tesselation steps, enabling you to make several steps instantly, which you can then convert to polygons for export.

MultiRes Modifier

The MultiRes modifier is an excellent way to reduce the polygon count in your model without terrorizing your texture mapping. Simply put the MultiRes modifier on a mesh and type in the amount of polygons that you want it to be. Press the Generate button, and MultiRes generates a mesh with the appropriate amount of polygons.

Texturing

Texturing can be really tricky. Chapter 18, "Materials/Shaders and Mapping for Games/Interactive Applications," covers mapping techniques for games. Here are a couple of quick things that you can keep in mind while texturing.

First, think about what is going to be seen the most. If you are making a character whose face matters a lot, you should spend some extra texture coordinate space on that area. If the face isn't important, shrink it down in texture space. Go through the model and see if some features could use less texture space—or could use more.

Another thing that can be tricky in regard to mapping is dealing with texture distortion. When polygons are mapped from an angle, there can be texture stretching. This occurs when some polygons are skewed in texture space. This is typically a bad thing and should be avoided at all costs. Texture coordinates are easily viewed with the Unwrap UVW modifier.

Tip

Putting a checker map on a model makes it clear where there is texture distortion. When a checker map is applied, you can adjust texture coordinates using the checkers as a guide for stretching and distortion. You want to make sure that the checkers are not weird shapes, but are as square as possible. The checkers might rotate a bit and might be different sizes between areas, but this is common. If you want everything even, then you have a perfect guide to work with. Otherwise, it's just a really easy method to check for texture distortion.

Rigging

Many new features in max 4 enable you to rig characters in many ways. Manipulators can be created and wired to a certain parameter, such as a bone rotation, with Parameter Wiring. This is easy for an artist to set up because the process is very straightforward. In Chapter 15, "Organic/Character Model Rigging for Games/Interactive Applications," you learn how to create and use manipulators and Parameter Wiring for a game character.

One of the biggest new features for max 4 is the new IK system. Not only has a new solver—the History Independent (HI) Solver—been introduced, but the workflow also has changed. Creating IK setups is as easy as picking a bone, selecting the IK type from the drop-down menu, and picking the end of the chain. Manipulators are then available to control the swivel angle of an IK chain, or an object can be selected to have the chain point to it. This is especially handy for use with a character's knees and elbows. To further control complex rigs, constraints enable you to constrain an object's transformations in many different ways. In max 4, constraints are applied much like the IK chains, by simply selecting them from the main menu drop-down lists, under Animation.

The bones system is new as well. The bones are customizable geometry that can be resized to fit your model, and wings and fins can be added to further shape the bone. The great thing about the rigging system in max 4 is that any object within reason can be used for a bone and can have IK applied to it. Splines, dummies, and mesh objects are all available to use in a rig.

Animation

You should keep in mind many things when animating a character for a game. One thing that is especially important is how the character is handled in-game. If the character's movement is a defined speed, get that value converted by working with a programmer, perhaps, so that you know how far the character is traveling in-game.

With this type of information, you can make the animations fit the environment better by reducing sliding in the character's animations. Sliding occurs when the animation is not timed properly with the actual game movement. For instance, if a character moves forward at 20 units per second, the animation for that character's walk cycle should be timed to move at this same speed. If the legs move too slow or too fast, it will look like the character is ice skating. This is just one scenario in which extra precaution should be taken when animating for games.

Export Considerations

When it comes time to export to the engine, being organized can be a real time-saver. Exporting can be a painful process if you are getting unexpected results, and a lot of trouble shooting can be involved. If you have not already done so, set up a clear and easy-to-understand folder structure on your hard drive to organize all your assets. Whether you do it by object type, by project, or by the guidelines of the engine you are working with, make sure that you don't have random files hanging around, and be clear where the files that you are currently working with are stored.

The process or workflow that you will use to export varies depending on the game that you are working on. Typically, if you are exporting a model or a character, you will use a plug-in that enables you to export using the File/Export menu item. Other developers might make it a Max Utility or a modifier. A lot of exporters are MAXScripts, as well. This enables you to put them into the UI in many different ways: through a button, a keyboard shortcut, a Quad item, or a regular menu item. Whichever method you use, that export will create a file (or multiple files) that needs to be saved in the right place to work properly. This is where a nice clean folder structure comes in handy.

Summary

The games industry is changing so fast that it requires artists to be able to respond to changes quickly. The games portion of this book shows a lot of tools that the games artist can use to ultimately become more flexible. There is an art to making 300 polygons come to life and actually resemble something believable. This polygon count number has grown and will keep growing in the future, and the games artist needs to be ready to take advantage of these types of assets, along with entirely new technology, as it becomes available.

Part III

Modeling

Chapter 7

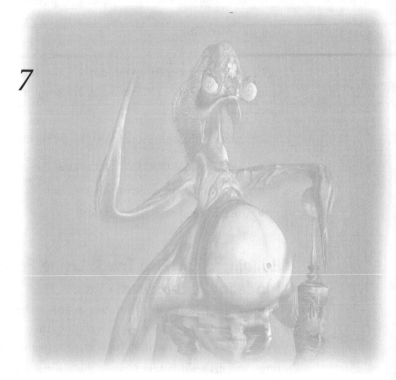

Non-Organic Modeling for Broadcast/Film

by Joseph Yoo

This chapter covers non-organic model-

ing. Non-organic models are not charac-

ters or other organic life forms, such as

plants or trees. Usually non-organic

models are objects such as buildings, cars, and other manmade things within an environment. Non-organic models are commonly used in broadcast for product modeling.

Specifically, you'll learn how to do the following:

- Use polygonal modeling techniques
- Use the Free Form Deformer modifier
- Use edit mesh and Meshsmooth

Building a Toy Fire Truck Using Polygonal Modeling Techniques

You will use polygonal techniques in this chapter to create a model of a toy fire truck. To make this a bit more interesting, there is only one Perspective view for the reference photo of the model toy. Perspective warps the appearance of the proportions and makes it harder to determine the dimensions of the truck. You will have to get the proportions for relative measurements off the Perspective view.

Exercise 7.1   Creating the Truck Body

1. Start by creating a box with **3** length, **3** width, and **3** height segments.

2. Go to Edit/Clone and make a copy of the box to use as reference.

   You will modify the original, which will update the reference with the Meshsmooth modifier.

3. Apply a wireframe texture to it (F3) and a Meshsmooth modifier. You can access this tool by going to the Modifier panel, selecting the More button and then selecting Meshsmooth from the list of available modifiers. By default, the iteration level is set to **0**, so go to a value of **2**, as seen in Figure 7.1.

   One of the best places to start the modeling process for box modeling is from the Profile view (see Figure 7.2), which is where you will start for this exercise. You can also work in another orthogonal view, such as the Top or Front views.

   You will build the truck's parts to a rough point and then build the other parts of the truck. Then you'll go back to modeling the specific details of the truck. This is useful so that you don't overwork an area and then have to change it when you have moved to another object. So, for this exercise, you will begin by sculpting out the front cab's curve for the negative space for the wheels. You will do this using by modifying the area with Edit Mesh modifiers and with a Free Form Deformer (FFD) modifier. You will then pull up the vertices and modify them to make a curve for the wheels.

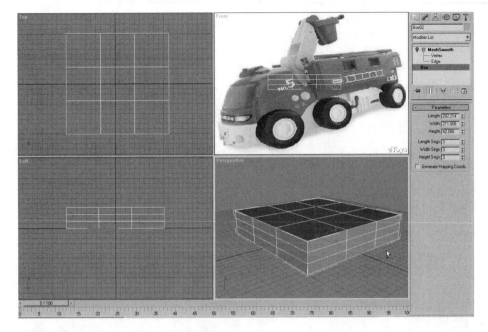

Figure 7.1   Start by using a box with segment 3×3×3.

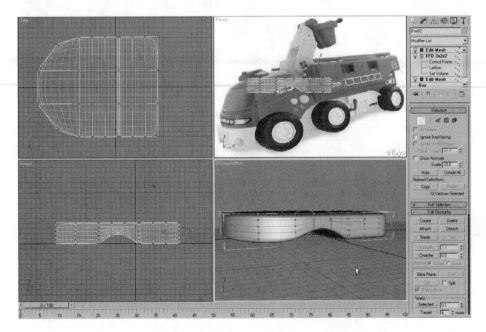

Figure 7.2   Here modeling has been done in the Profile view and then a bit more in the Top view, using the Perspective window to check the work.

4. Start to work on the top part of the cab: Select all the top faces and extrude them. The extrusion is found in the Face level of an edit mesh. The number of extrusions is determined by the corresponding number of control edges.

5. As you extrude them, in the Top view apply scaling operations to create the ridge in the front of the cab, as seen in Figure 7.3. These scaling operations to taper the top portion of the cab will be best seen in the Perspective window, where you can see the changes in real time.

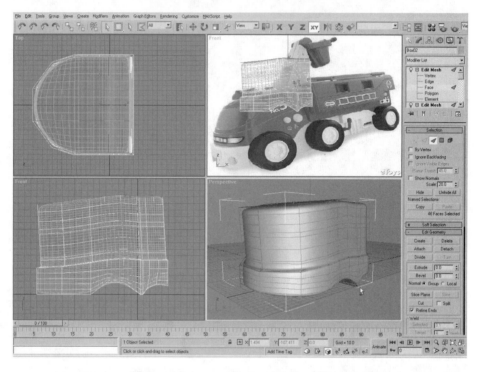

Figure 7.3   Here you have extruded the faces several times. Notice that there is enough detail for the window and the details in the top of the cab.

Note

If you have moved the vertices on the face that needs to be extruded, this will cause errors with the extrusion. These errors will happen even if you move the vertices in a direction co-planar to the face. To avoid this, be careful about which vertices you are moving, and place a Slice modifier behind the faces to be extruded. Then select the faces to be extruded and select the Make Planar option.

6. The top of the cab needs to be rounded. This can be done with several modifiers, including edit mesh and FFD.

Using multiple modifiers and Sub-Object Level modifiers will help you get the results you want. However, be sure to constantly check all the views while you are modeling so that you are modeling in three dimensions (see Figure 7.4).

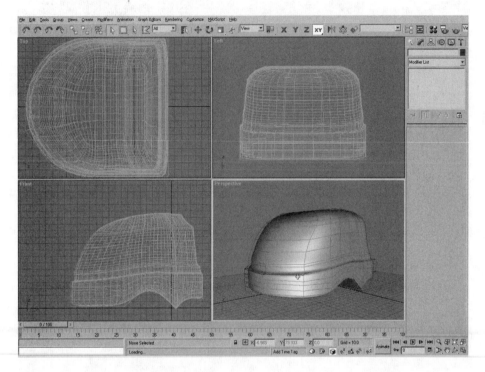

Figure 7.4   It is very easy to overwork an area in one orthographic perspective and then have to make more changes in all other views.

7. Using Figure 7.5 as reference, make visible the edges that will make up the window of the front cab. Do this on both sides of the truck.

The next step is to create the wheels.

8. Start creating one wheel by using a chamfered cylinder.

Chamfered cylinders are additional parametric polygons that max has under the Create tab, under Extended Primitives. Chamfer creates a rounded edge so that the lighting is not so harsh where the edges meet. Because they are parametric, they can later be modified interactively to get the desired smooth value on the edge of the cylinder.

Create the chamfered cylinder with **1** height segment, **4** filet segments, and **33** sides. (See Figure 7.6.)

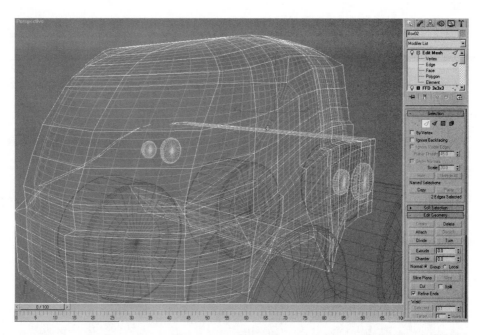

Figure 7.5 Making edges visible or invisible affects how the model is shaded. It is very important during model construction that you are aware of which edges are visible and which are hidden because this can drastically affect the rendering.

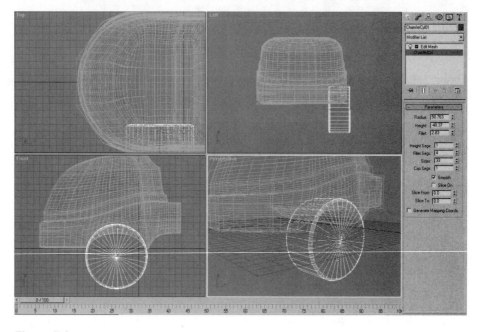

Figure 7.6 Here you create the wheel.

9. Select the faces on the outer side of the wheel. Using the Spinner setting of the extrusion in the Face sub-object, spin any amount and then spin down to 0 and release the spinner.

The extrude of 0 creates a duplicate face that can't really be seen until the selected faces are scaled back.

Note

The zero extrusion techniques must be used with caution. You want to remember that you have done this operation, so perform a scalar operation that reveals that you have a zero extrusion. Even though it's not visible, the doubling of faces can cause confusion with rendering problems and seams.

10. Without deselecting these faces, scale them in Profile view and repeat Steps 9 and 10 once more. Use Figure 7.7 as a reference.

This will give you enough detail to add depth to the wheel instead of having a simple cylinder.

11. Now copy the wheel object as an instance and place the wheels where they belong on one side of the vehicle only.

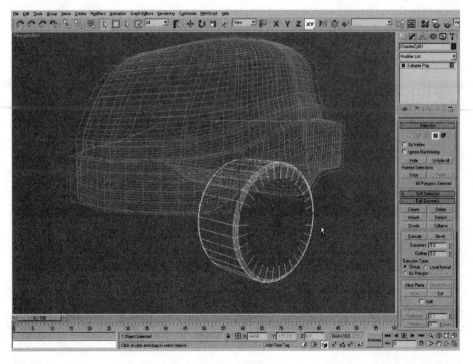

Figure 7.7 Here is the result of the initial zero extrusion, which adds detail to the side of the wheel.

Note

An *instance* is a duplicate of the original geometry that maintains a direct connection to the original. Thus, if the original is modified, the instance updates to reflect this. If you modify the instance, the original matches any modifications done to the instance. Reference modeling works on the basis that the reference gets any modifications from the original, but the original model gets no modification information from the reference. Referencing and instancing also free up the machine from heavy computation.

12. Create the circular details on the side of the cab with chamfered cylinders. Create one chamfered cylinder, and place it in Profile view near the rear of the cab.

13. Mirror all the newly created objects, as seen in Figure 7.8.

14. Create a box that will be the rear of the fire truck, as seen in Figure 7.9.

15. Select the top two rows of faces on both sides of the rear part of the truck, and extrude the shapes. Shape the top of the extrusions as you extrude them so that they resemble the rear portion of the truck's windows, which come out from the base of the side of the truck.

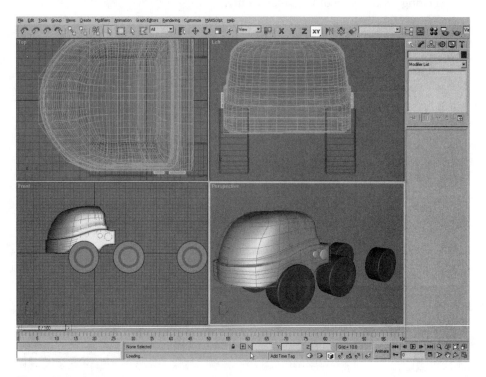

Figure 7.8   Mirror the geometry. Make sure that you are working in the correct coordinate space if you have not created all the initial geometry in the middle of the origin.

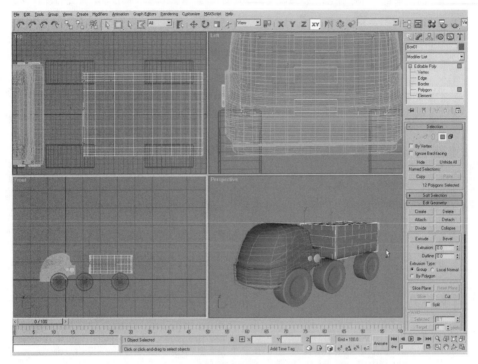

Figure 7.9   Here you can see the beginnings of the volume of the truck being flushed out. You have not yet worked on the details because you want to get the truck's proportions right before adding the details. This saves you from having to tweak the details because your volumes are wrong.

16. Select the front faces of the truck. Extrude these faces to add the canopy area in the front of the truck. Use a Slice modifier (under the Modifier tab under More/Slice) to create a row of edges that will create a rigid edge to the corner when the Meshsmooth is applied. Use Figure 7.10 as a reference.

17. Add an Edit Mesh modifier and select the faces that will correspond to the windows of the rear of the fire truck. Extrude the faces and shape the top of the extrusions, as you did in Step 15. Figure 7.11 shows the result.

    Next you will do a negative extrusion on this face selection. You will see that when the Meshsmooth is applied at the end of the stack, the windows' extrusion will have no definition and will be too undefined. You can see the difference when you add a Slice modifier to create some more definition in the corners of the window. Figure 7.12 shows only one Slice modifier. To get the other corners to look more defined, you will need to add three more Slice modifiers.

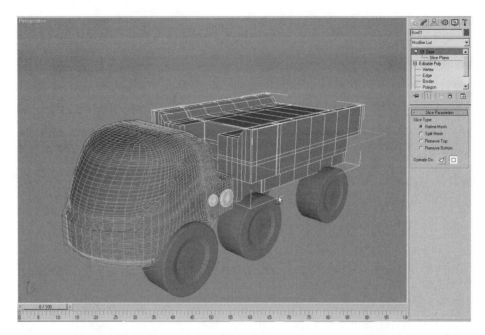

Figure 7.10   Here you see the relative placement of the slice. Careful placement of Slice modifiers during reference modeling can create sharp corners with the normally round Meshsmooth technique.

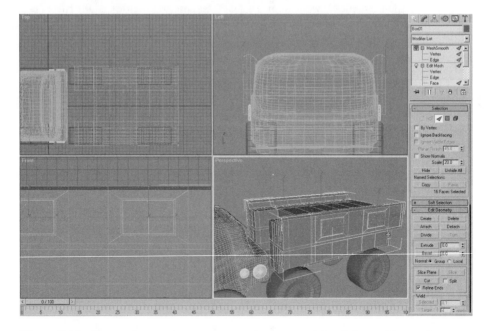

Figure 7.11   The resulting negative extrusions have created detail that will be used to create negative cavities for windows.

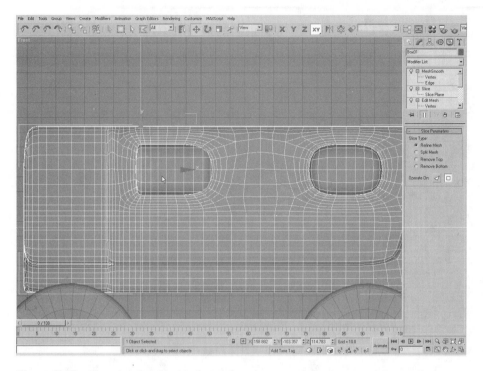

Figure 7.12   Here the slice has hardened the edge around the corners of the window.

18. Add three more Slice modifiers by right-clicking the Slice modifier and selecting Copy. This option copies the modifier. Then right-click the top modifier in the Modifier Stack and select Paste. This places the copy of the modifier after the last modifier in the modifier history. Repeat this step three times.

    The copy of the modifier is created exactly over the original, so you will have to move the Slice modifier's Sub-Object Slice plane to see different results. When you finish, your model should look like Figure 7.13.

    Next you will create the details on the top rear of the fire truck. The base object will be a chamfered cylinder. Some of the objects will need to be edited with face extrusions to get the shape needed.

19. First create a chamfered cylinder that will be the metal rod that is the hinge portion of the joint. Make the length a bit shorter than the length of the rear of the truck.

20. Make a copy and scale the radius to **30%** and the length to about one-tenth of the original's size. Duplicate it and slide it down the length of the truck. Place these in the middle of the rod, with an even spacing, and leave room on the ends for duplicates of them to be placed on the outer side. Duplicate them and place them on the outer side of the two cylinders.

Figure 7.13   Here all the corners have been sharpened—they're much different than the rounded holes they were.

21. The outer cylinder should be modified with an edit mesh. Select the bottom vertices and pull them down so that the object is not merely a cylinder, but more like a box with a rounded top. For the middle section, duplicate the rod cylinder and, using an Xform modifier, scale the radius and the cylinder up; scale the length to fit between the four larger cylinders.

    This resulting cylinder should be smaller in radius than the four pieces on its ends.

22. Use an edit mesh and create irregularities in the surface that match Figure 7.14. Much of this modeling is free-form and small enough for the user to create a loose model that resembles the reference image.

23. When this is done, mirror the objects.

24. Now you'll create the ladder pieces. Start with a simple box.

25. To get the ladders' split-tuning fork-like object, select the outside faces and extrude them. Figure 7.15 shows the result.

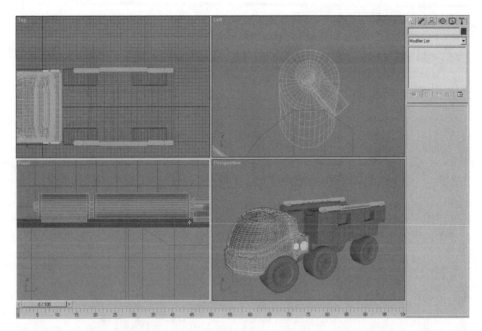

Figure 7.14   Here you can see the details on the top of the truck. Although the details are seemingly subtle, they add extra crevices for the lights and shadows to play with and increase the reality of the model.

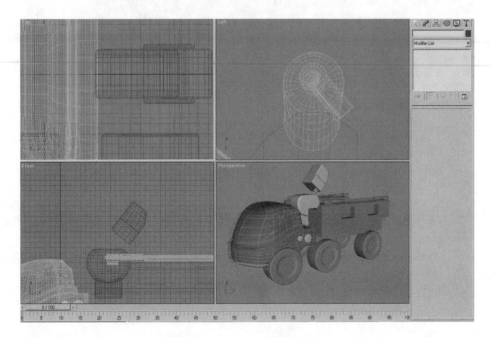

Figure 7.15   Here you have modeled some of the ladder's pieces. Again, you are just laying the groundwork and adding details later.

26. Select the pieces that will extend past the base object of the ladder. Extrude these faces and round out the shape.

27. Add two slices near the middle of the second piece of the ladder, and then use this detail to extrude the small, thin detail ridge. Your model should look like Figure 7.16.

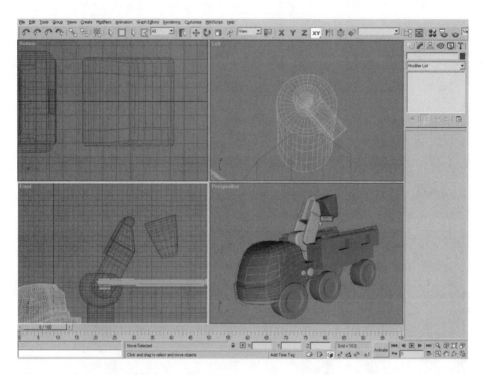

Figure 7.16   Continue to add the ladder by placing an object that will be the ladder's canopy.

28. Go on to create the hubcaps and the bottom fireman's canopy. Create the hubcaps by using a cylinder and using the same extrusion techniques used in creating the detail for the wheel. Create the fireman's canopy by taking a box and using a negative extrude for the canopy; and then select the face and extrude it for the trim of the canopy. Figure 7.17 shows the result.

29. Using some primitives, create the base of the bottom part of the fire truck. These are simple box primitives that have been shaped and rounded at some places. Other objects were duplicated. The result is mechanical detail, which adds to the intricacies of the model. Use Figure 7.18 as a reference.

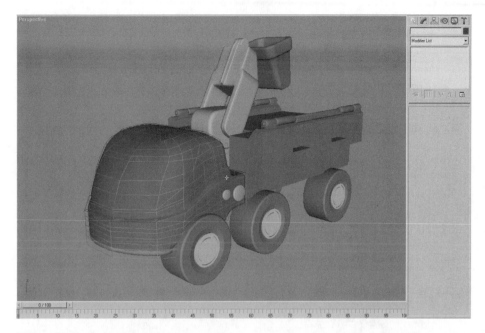

Figure 7.17 The finished detailing of the truck. All that was used were some simple
extrusions.

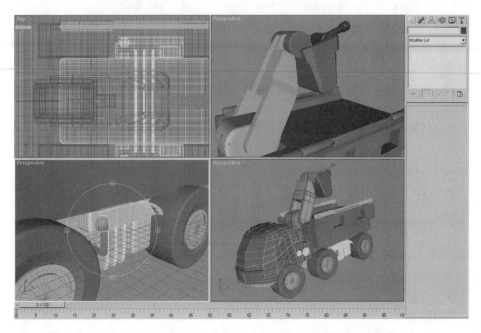

Figure 7.18 The simple shapes are clustered together. Using repeating shapes, you can
create mechanical complexity out of simple geometric objects.

30. Next, select the faces on the top of the cab and do a negative extrusion to get the fire truck's cavity for the fire truck's siren. To extrude in the negative value, make sure that you are in the Face Sub-Object mode under an edit mesh. Then drag the down spinner for the Extrusion setting.

Although this detail is not overly visible, it gives some interesting space for the light to play with, to affect the shading and rendering of the final image.

31. Model the siren from a simple box and place it into the cavity, as seen in Figure 7.19.

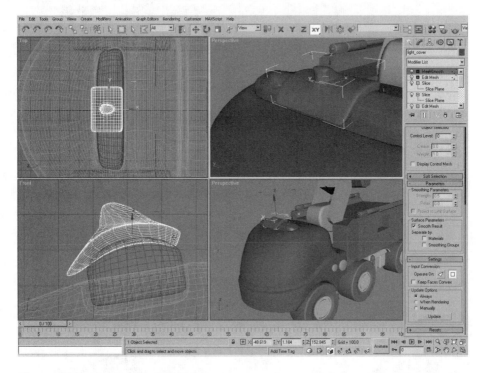

Figure 7.19   The siren is placed here.

You will use more simple box-modeling techniques to create the object on the top of the siren.

32. Create a box, and make sure that the segment settings for the box from the Top view are odd.

This generates the fin, which comes out from the top of the shape.

33. Taper the end coming toward the front end of the truck. Bend the shape of the box in the profile so that it follows the curve of the front cab. Select a few faces at the top the object, and extrude out the detail of the knob of the object.

Now that you have created most of the fire truck's volume, you will to
return to modeling the front cab of the fire truck.

34. The first thing you want to do is convert the object to an editable poly, as
seen in Figure 7.20.

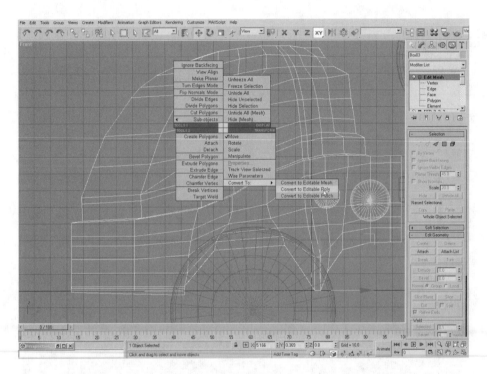

Figure 7.20   Select the object that you want to convert to an editable poly, and then
right-click and select Convert to Editable Poly.

Note

Editable poly is a new object type within 3ds max 4 that allows faces that are more than
four-sided. You might prefer to use older polygon-modeling techniques, such as editable
mesh, for more complex organic-modeling techniques, but editable poly is extremely
useful in non-organic model creation.

One of the new settings in editable poly is the new sub-object Border, which editable
mesh does not have. It selects all the edges in an open-faced area of an editable poly.
This is useful for "capping" a surface. You should cap only flat surfaces because the
results give you unpredictable shading in a curved surface. If you do cap a surface that is
not flat, use this only as a starting point to develop the manner in which the edges are
turned and what shape the faces will have. These all determine the shading of the model.
See Chapter 9, "Organic/Character Modeling Using the Patch Method for Broadcast/
Film," for more details.

The bottom part of the front of the cab has been messed up during the editing of the vertices. You will use the Border feature in editable poly to fix this.

35. Select the vertices that are to be deleted (from the Profile view), and cap this open-faced surface with the Cap option, found in the Border sub-object of the editable poly.

Note

The Border feature in editable poly calculates all the edges in an area of open faces within an editable poly. This can be capped, and the modifier does the best job to create a surface to close the hole. (See Figures 7.21, 7.22, and 7.23.)

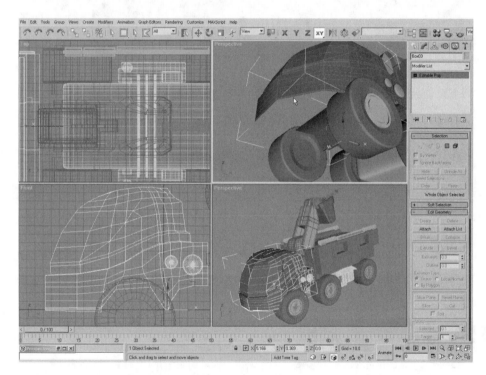

Figure 7.21   At this point, you have deleted the bottom faces and are about to perform the editable poly Border option.

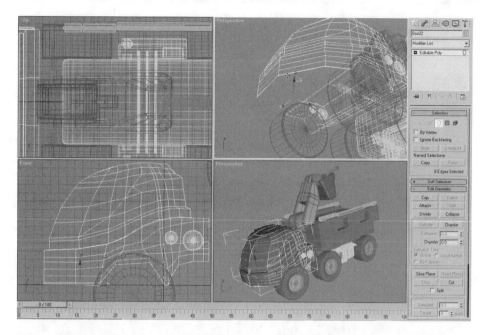

Figure 7.22   When using the Border sub-object in editable poly, select the open edge.

Figure 7.23   This is the end result of a border that has been capped with an editable poly.

36. Now you have a flat-faced object that you will detach as an object. Add an edit mesh, select Face Sub-Object mode, and click Detach. An option box pops up; select to detach as an object.

37. With the newly detached face, extrude down to create the fender of the front of the fire truck cab.

38. After you have extruded four segments, select the inside vertices of the wheel to curl to the wheel shape. Figure 7.24 shows the result.

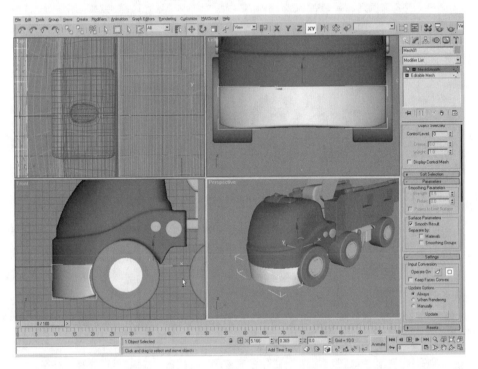

Figure 7.24   After extruding four segments, select the inside vertices of the wheel to curl to the wheel shape.

39. In the front of the view of the fender, using the Edit Mesh modifier under the Modifiers tab, shape the vertices into the border of what will be the area of the negative cavity of the front of the cab.

40. Select these faces and then do a negative extrude. Do some tweaking with some carefully placed weighted vertices to get the result in Figure 7.25.

41. Use a chamfered box and some FFDs to create the piece that represents the license plate.

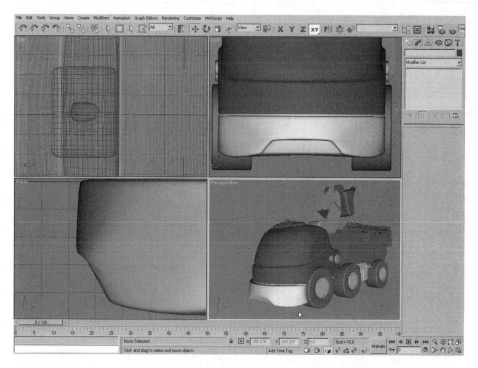

Figure 7.25   This shows the result of the negative extrude and the weighted vertices.

 Note

FFD stands for Free Form Deformation. This is a modifier that can be applied to any geometry type by going to the Modifier panel and selecting an FFD. The FFDs enable you to make global changes to an area via a lattice and control points. There are several types of FFDs, including 2×2×2, 3×3×3, 4×4×4, and an FFD box. In the FFD box, you can set the number of Free Form Deformer lattices.

42. Inspect the proportions of the model, and make any necessary adjustments.

In my initial modeling, the fender area was too small and the front cab of the fire truck was a bit too tall. Because I haven't added too much detail, adjustment to proportion can be made with out too much pain. Figure 7.26 shows how your model should look at this point.

43. Do a slight negative extrude on the face that represents the window of the front cab of the fire truck.

44. To add the front negative cavities in the fender of the truck for the lights, create two cylinders and Boolean them to cut the shapes into the fender. Figure 7.27 shows the result.

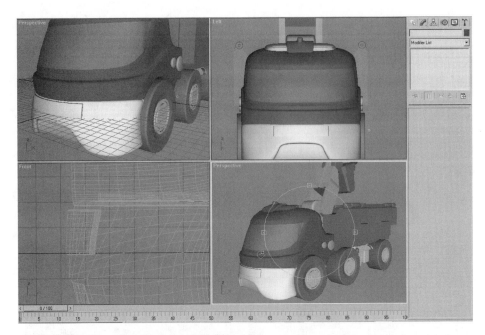

Figure 7.26   The resulting model should look like this.

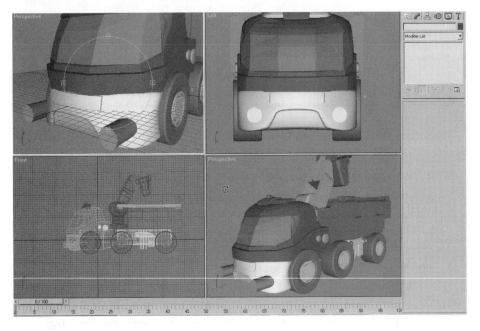

Figure 7.27   This shows the cylinders being placed before the Boolean operation.

Note

Before any Boolean operation, save and increment save so that you always have the original shapes to go back to for changes and to safeguard your design in case the Boolean operation does not perform correctly.

45. Create a cylinder and make a copy. Attach the second cylinder to the first object so that you have only one object (one cylinder must be converted to an editable mesh or poly before you can attach the other cylinder to it). Select the fender. Then select Create Panel/Compound Objects and do a subtractive Boolean.

46. The Boolean might not give you the result you want. Convert the mesh to an editable poly and select the border of the rim of the light cavities. Cap the borders and then do a negative extrusion, as seen in Figure 7.28.

47. Create the lights by creating a sphere and setting it to Hemisphere at .5. Then make a copy and place them accordingly. Figure 7.29 shows the result.

Figure 7.28 After the Boolean operation, your design should look like this.

Figure 7.29   Place the lights in all views.

48. Draw a spline in Profile view to represent the connecting hose from the truck to the tip of the hose at the top of the ladder, as seen in Figure 7.30.

49. Under the Modifier panel of the spline, check two settings, Renderable and Display Render Mesh (see Figure 7.31).

The Renderable setting enables the spline to be renderable; by default, it is unrenderable. The Display Render Mesh check box generates a mesh for any lofted geometry. These are new to 3ds max 4. Figure 7.32 shows the model at this point.

50. Add a little detail to the base of the hose by adding a small chamfered cylinder. The final result is seen in Figure 7.33.

Note

Another feature within editable poly is the Meshsmooth rollout option box. You might prefer to use a sub-object selection and then a Meshsmooth on the Sub-Object level because this retains the modifier history. The Meshsmooth option in the Sub-Object editable poly level cannot be undone within the modifier. A Modifier Stack is easy enough to collapse later on.

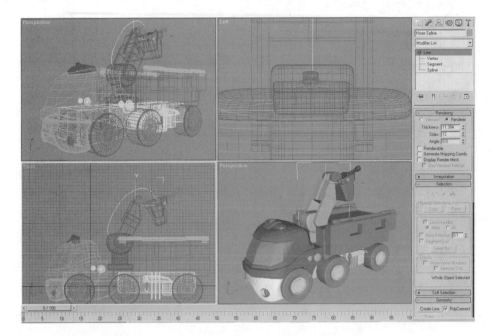

Figure 7.30   This is the spline representing the connecting hose.

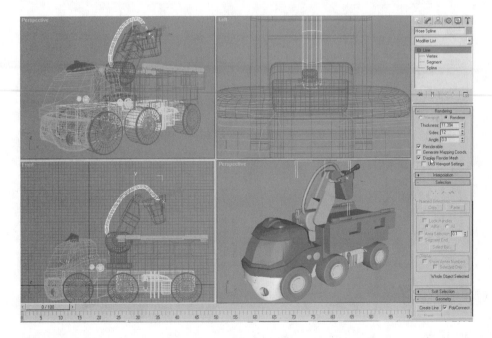

Figure 7.31   Set the spline renderable settings.

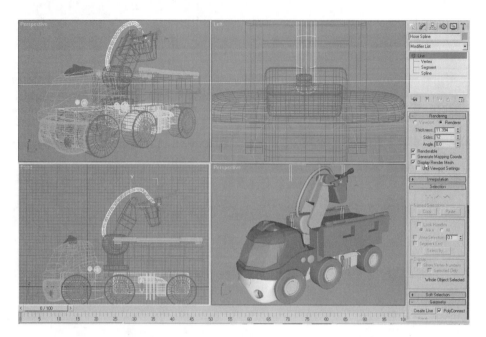

Figure 7.32   The model should look like this at this point.

Figure 7.33   The final model should look like this.

Summary

In this chapter, you learned how to use various features in 3ds max 4 to create a non-organic model: the fire truck, with all its accompanying parts. The exercise in this chapter—and the features that you used—were typical of projects and features that you would be expected to accomplish in most broadcast applications. In Chapter 8, "Nonorganic Modeling for Games/Interactive Applications," you will learn how to use the features in 3ds max 4 to create a non-organic model for games and interactive applications.

Chapter 8

Non-Organic Modeling for Games/Interactive Applications

by Mike O'Rourke

A typical game can be filled with tanks, turrets, walls, pipes, and many other items. Non-organic forms such as these are found in many places within games, so having a solid grasp on modeling these forms can be a huge asset to a game artist. To start learning how to approach non-organic modeling using 3ds max 4, you'll model the mechanical leg system for Pug (see Figure 8.1), a slimy, squid-like creature that relies on these legs as his primary mode of transportation.

This chapter covers the following:

- Modeling with primitives
- Using several modeling tools in edit poly
- Modeling with lofts, and loft deformations

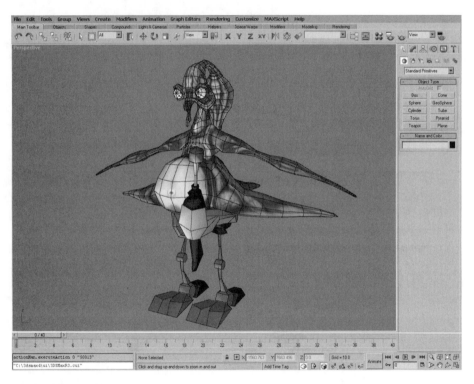

Figure 8.1   Our friend Pug relies on these legs to get around the arena. Without them he'd be reduced to a withering pile of flesh and bone—a sitting duck. You must not let him down. You need to build a powerful set of legs, with a base for Pug to sit on and a joystick unit for him to drive the whole thing with.

To start, you'll build the base for Pug to rest on (see Figure 8.2). It will be generally cylindrical in shape, with a panel on the front filled with buttons and rivets. After creating the base, you will create a joystick for Pug to control these legs. Then you will create the legs and, finally, the feet (see Figure 8.3).

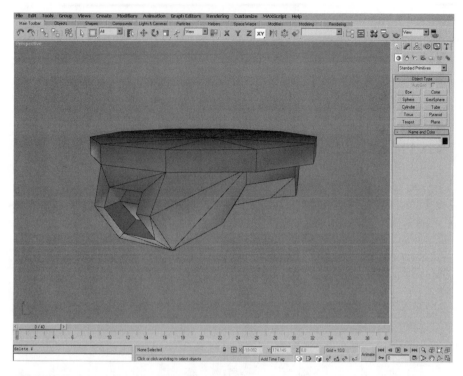

Figure 8.2 Here is the base that Pug will rest on.

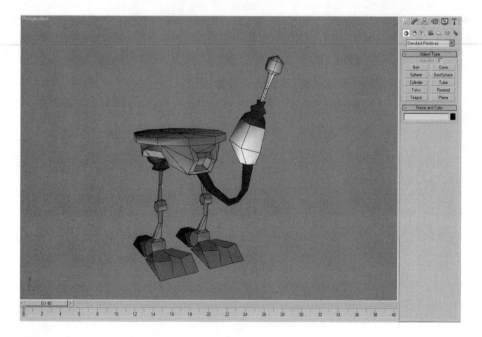

Figure 8.3 The Leg Assembly mesh looks like this.

Before you even touch max, think through what you know already: Style-wise, you want to contrast Pug's huge body with a sort of rickety, skinny pair of legs. The basic assembly will be a platform that Pug rests on, with a pair of legs and a joystick to control them.

You'll start building Pug's mechanized legs by first starting with the base.

Exercise 8.1   Building the Base

1. First create a cylinder.

   The radius should be around **30–40**, with a height at **5** or **6**, and **10** sides. Remember, this is your model, so don't worry about exact units. Feel free to make the proportions to your liking.

2. Collapse the cylinder to an editable poly by right-clicking the object and selecting Convert in the lower-right quad. Then select Convert to Editable Poly, as seen in Figure 8.4.

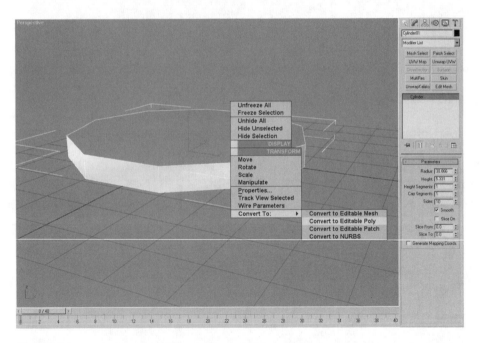

Figure 8.4   The cylinder is collapsed to an editable poly.

The cylinder is now an editable poly. This is a new geometry type for max 4. You will learn about many of the new features in editable poly later, but, for now, you'll use a couple of standard operations—bevel and extrude.

3. Rotate your view so that you are looking at the underside of the base.

4. Go into Sub-Object Polygon mode. Select the bottom polygon, and then right-click and select Bevel from the lower-left quad, as seen in Figure 8.5.

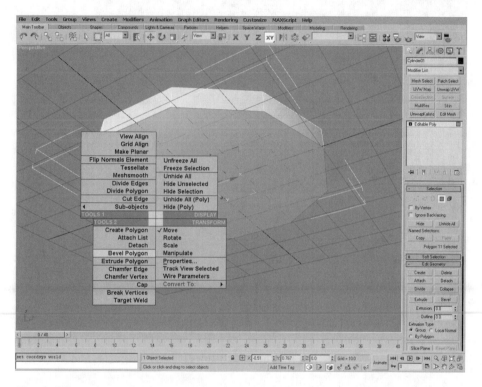

Figure 8.5 With the bottom polygon selected, right-click and select Bevel from the lower-left quad.

Your icon should now be a bit different; it should look like a white crosshair, letting you know that the next face that you click and drag will bevel.

When using the Bevel tool, first select the face and drag to extrude. Then, after letting go of the button, your mouse movement will adjust the scale or bevel of your new face.

5. For the first bevel, click the bottom face and just barely move the mouse. Keep the Extrusion counter (located in the Edit Geometry rollout on the right) at or near 0.

The new face will be created, but it will not be extruded far off of the existing plane.

6. Move the mouse down to adjust the bevel of the face so that it is pulled inside the cylinder, as seen in Figure 8.6.

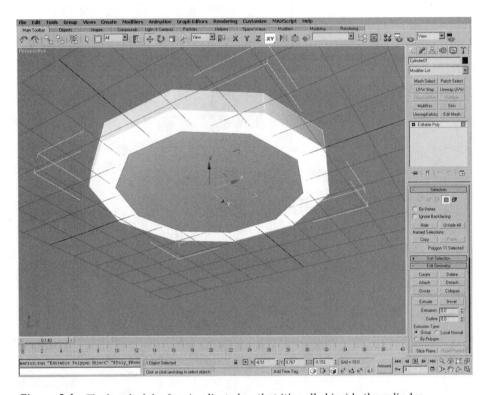

Figure 8.6   The bevel of the face is adjusted so that it's pulled inside the cylinder.

Now that you have created a new face, you'll extrude it out to further form the base.

7. Right-click to bring up the Quad menu, and select Extrude from the bottom-left quad. Click and drag the face to extrude it down, as seen in Figure 8.7.

   You have the general simple form of the base now, so you can get started adding a few details. To form the front panel, simply scale and rotate the front polygon into place.

8. Select the front polygon. Scale it non-uniformly along the Z-axis to make it a bit taller (see Figure 8.8).

9. Rotate the polygon along the X-axis, and then move it down on the Z-axis to form a front panel. Figure 8.9 shows the result.

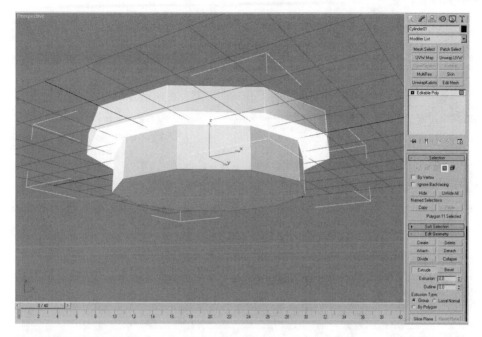

Figure 8.7   Click and drag the face to extrude it down.

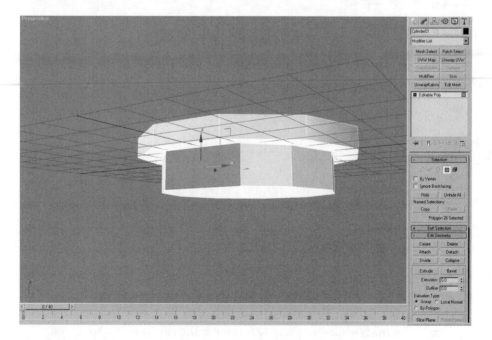

Figure 8.8   The front polygon is scaled non-uniformly along the Z-axis.

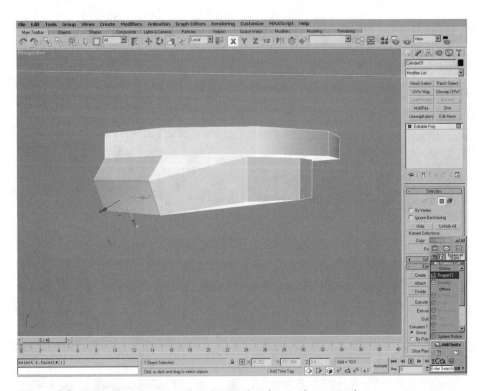

Figure 8.9   The polygon is rotated and moved to form a front panel.

The next step is to create the inset of the front panel. To do this, you'll use one of the new features in editable poly: Cut Polygons. This tool enables you to select anywhere on a polygon and cut from that point to another point on another polygon.

Note

The Cut Polygons tool is really easy to use. Just click the polygon where you want to cut it, and then pick somewhere else. The tool cuts to that point. The Cut tool works differently depending on the Sub-Object mode that you are currently in. In this exercise, you will use it in Sub-Object Polygon mode.

10. Go into the Front viewport so that you are looking head on at the model. Go into Sub-Object Polygon mode, as seen in Figure 8.10.

11. Select the Cut tool (in the Edit Geometry rollout) from the Command panel. You are now in Cut mode. To start cutting, click inside the polygons to create a box, as seen in Figure 8.11. Because you are in the Front view, you can make the box nice and symmetrical, but the cuts conform to the polygon surface.

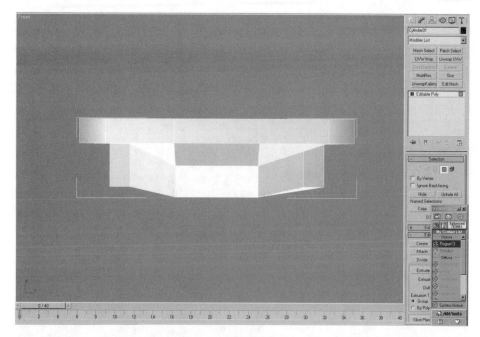

Figure 8.10   Now you're in Sub-Object Polygon mode.

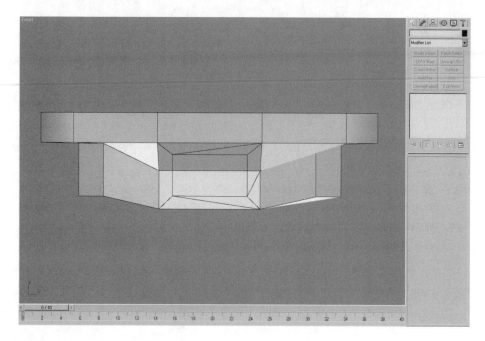

Figure 8.11   Click inside the polygons to create a box.

12. Now that you've cut the appropriate shape, you will use your trusty Bevel tool to bevel those faces, see Figure 8.12.

One more thing is left to do: chamfer some edges. You can split the edge nicely by simply selecting and dragging on an edge with the Chamfer tool. Give that a run.

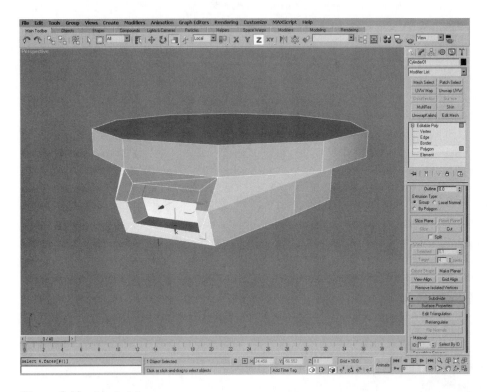

Figure 8.12   Beveled faces.

13. Go into Sub-Object Edge mode. Select the edges, as seen in Figure 8.13. You can also select the same edges on the other side, if you want to do this all in one pass.

14. When you have the edges selected, pick Chamfer Edges from the bottom-left Quad menu, and click and drag any one of those edges. Chamfer to the desired width. (See Figure 8.14.)

Now you'll move on to building the joystick.

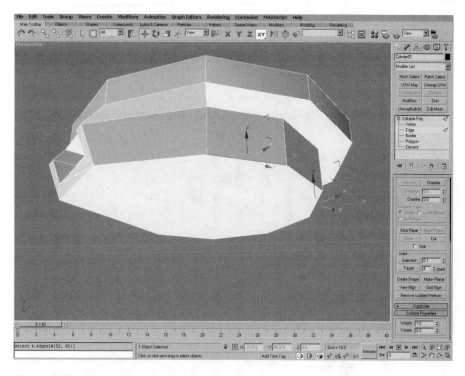

Figure 8.13   The edges are selected here.

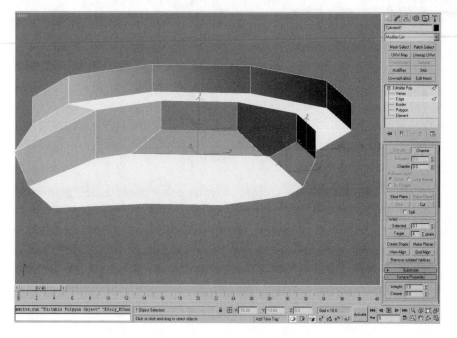

Figure 8.14   The shape is chamfered to the desired width.

Exercise 8.2   Building the Joystick Assembly

Building the joystick assembly is pretty easy because you can do it all with one loft and a sphere. You'll draw a spline to get the general shape of the assembly down, do a little work in the loft, and then add a sphere on top.

1. View the base from the Front viewport. Go to Create/Shapes/Splines/Line in the pull-down menu at the top, and draw a spline with three points, as seen in Figure 8.15.

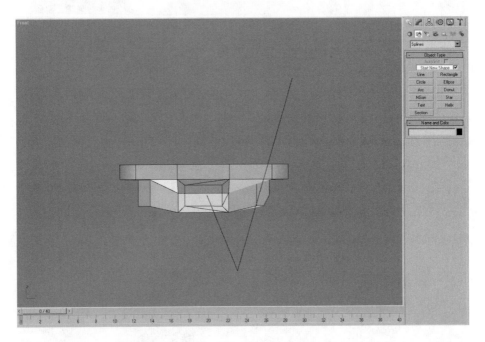

Figure 8.15   Go to Create/Shapes/Splines/Line in the pull-down menu at the top and draw a spline with three points.

2. In the Left viewport, or Perspective viewport, adjust the top and bottom vertices in the spline, as seen in Figure 8.16, by going into Sub-Object Vertices mode.

   Basically you're tucking the bottom vertex in under the base, and pulling the top one out to form the joystick handle.

3. Select the spline, and go into Sub-Object Vertex mode. Select all three vertices.

4. Right-click one of the selected vertices. In the upper-left Quad menu, find the Smooth item. Select that to make all the vertices smooth. Now you might want a little more control over them.

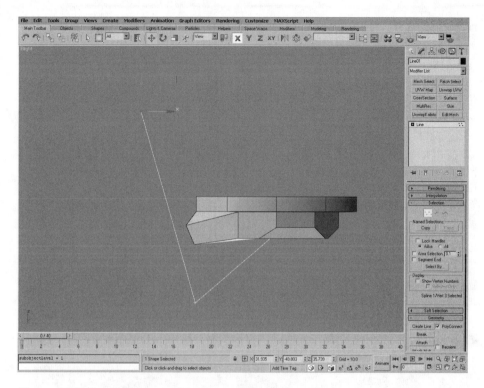

Figure 8.16   Adjust the top and bottom vertices in the spline.

5. Select the vertices that you want to control more, and follow the previous step, but this time change the vertices to Bezier. Adjust the Bezier handles to make a curve, somewhat like the one in Figure 8.17.

6. In the Perspective view, view the model from underneath. Go to Create/ Shapes/Splines, and this time press the Circle tab. Enable Autogrid by clicking its check box, found at the top of the Creation Command panel. Create a circle spline on the bottom of the base. You might need to move the spline a little bit along the Z-axis to see it. (See Figure 8.18.)

Note

The spline that you are creating will be used for the loft, so make it about as thick as you want the hosing to be. You will adjust all of this later, but it's nice to get as close as you can on the first try. Autogrid was used here so that you could see the spline on the model, making it much easier to see how big it should be.

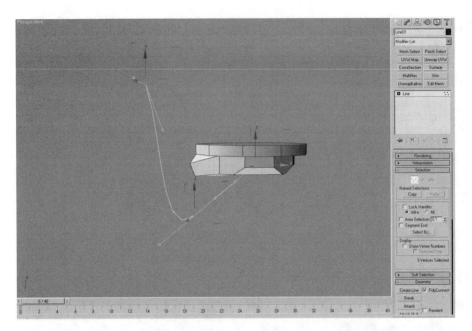

Figure 8.17   Adjust the Bezier handles to make a curve somewhat like this one.

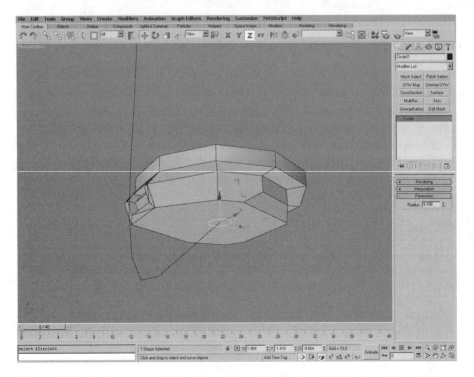

Figure 8.18   Enable Autogrid by clicking its check box, found at the top of the Creation
Command panel.

7. To make the loft, first go into the Command panel, under Create/Geometry, and select Compound Objects from the drop-down menu.

8. Select the Path spline. That is the first spline that you made, with the three points that define the length of the loft.

9. With that spline selected, press the Loft button in the Command panel.

10. Now press the Get Shape button in the Loft panel.

11. Pick the circle shape that you drew on the bottom of the base. You should now see your loft.

The loft that is created has way too much detail, so you should change that.

12. Switch to the Modify tab of the Command panel, and find the Skin Parameters rollout, which is collapsed by default. Click that to expand it.

13. Change the Shape steps to 0 and the Path steps to 1.

14. Go into the Surface Parameters rollout, and find the Apply Mapping check box. Make sure that it is clicked on.

Because you are doing this whole part of the model with the loft, you get the extra bonus of having mapping coordinates made for you. That will save time when it comes to mapping this guy. Figure 8.19 shows all these changes made.

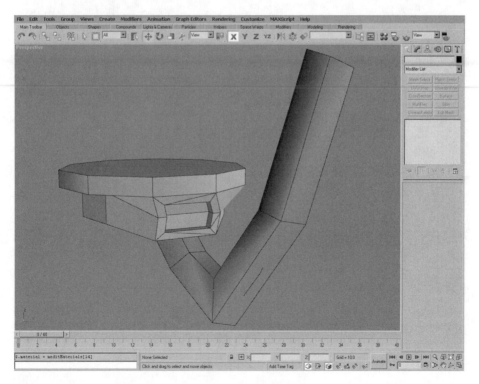

Figure 8.19   At this point, your model should look like this.

Now comes the fun part. You will shape this whole piece using the Scale Deformations tool within the Loft object. The deformations hide all the way at the bottom of the Loft Objects rollout when viewed from the Modify tab. Note that you will not see this rollout while still in the Creation tab.

15. Click the Deformations rollout to expand it.

16. Click the Scale button.

   This brings up a trackview–like editing window, as seen in Figure 8.20. Basically, this window shows you a cross-section of your loft. By adding some points and shaping them in this window, you will get the desired shape in your model.

17. To add points in the Loft window, click the icon that is a small red line with a yellow *x* on it. This is the insert corner point mode (you can also roll your mouse over the icons to check out the ToolTips).

   When this is pressed, any clicks on the line will add a point. Follow Figure 8.20 to see one way to shape the control stick. Feel free to experiment. Lots of really cool shapes can be made quickly with shape deformation in the lofter.

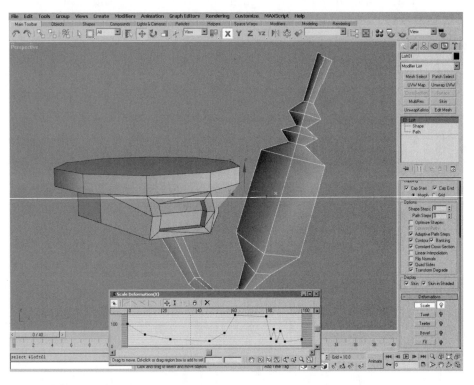

Figure 8.20   The trackview-like editing window appears.

Note

If you want to further tweak the shape of this piece, try the other deformation types. The Twist deformation does a great job of making the mesh look a little more asymmetrical.

At this point, you need to tweak the top of the pole to make it straight, and it would be good to pull and push a few vertices around. Finish everything that you can do in the Loft panel because after you collapse the model, none of that information is available to you anymore.

18. Collapse the mesh by first selecting it and then right-clicking to bring up the Quad menu. Choose Convert/Convert to Editable Poly.

19. Go into Sub-Object Polygon mode, and select the topmost polygon. To flatten this polygon, simply scale it down considerably on the Z-axis. Scaling polygons along one axis is very useful for flattening things.

    You're ready to add the ball at the top of the joystick.

20. Go into the Create/Geometry/Standard Primitives panel, and select Sphere. Turn on AutoGrid if it is not already on by checking the check box at the top of the Command panel.

21. Create a sphere on the end of the rod by clicking in the middle of the topmost face.

22. Adjust the sphere so that it has seven or eight segments.

23. Tweak vertices for a little while, if you like (see Figure 8.21). A lot of personality can be brought out of an object by just pushing and pulling on it for bit.

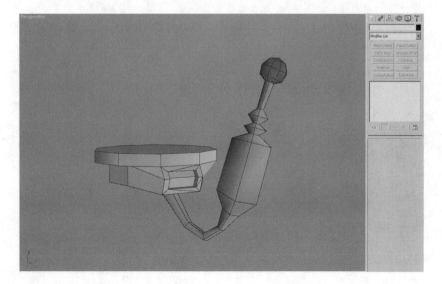

Figure 8.21   You can tweak the vertices.

Exercise 8.3   Building the Legs

The first thing you will build for the legs will be the connection point for the leg to connect to the base.

First you'll build a rubber cover for the joint that connects the leg to the base by simply adjusting a sphere.

1. Select the Top viewport and build a sphere with a radius of around 7, with 9 segments, and a hemisphere of .5. Turn on Generate Mapping Coordinates.

2. Add a Taper modifier. This can be done by going to the rollout list on the Command/Modify panel or by using the Quad menu.

Note

There is a sort of hidden Modifiers Quad menu in the Quad menu. You can access it by Ctrl+right-clicking an object and then choosing the Modifiers quad item in the upper-right quad. The menu immediately pops up a huge list of modifiers. You can get to the modifiers pretty quickly this way, and it's one more thing that's not in the Command panel, if you like working in Expert mode (Ctrl+x).

3. Adjust the taper so that the curve is at about −.9, primary axis Z, and effect XY, as seen in Figure 8.22.

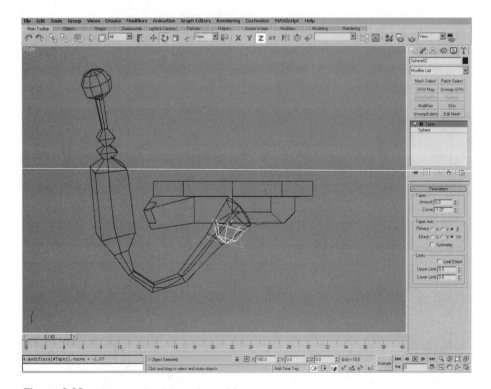

Figure 8.22   The taper has been adjusted here.

4. Convert the model to an editable poly via the Quad menu, using Convert/Convert to Editable Poly.

5. Delete all the faces on the top of the sphere, as seen in Figure 8.23. You won't see them, so they should be deleted. Before selecting these faces, be sure to have Ignore Backfacing checked, or you'll end up deleting needed faces.

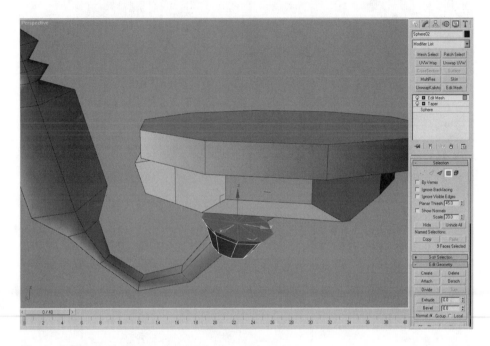

Figure 8.23   Delete all the faces at the top of the sphere.

6. Editable poly has a Border Sub-Object mode. Go into Border Sub-Object mode, and select the top border of the sphere.

7. Go into the Right viewport, and then rotate and move the border so that it is flush with the bottom of the base, as seen in Figure 8.24.

   To add more of a springy look to this connection, you'll add another row of geometry to the sphere and scale it in.

8. Select the middle row of polygons, and press the Slice Plane button in the Command panel. See Figure 8.25.

9. Move the Slice plane into place so that you are splitting the section, as seen in Figure 8.25. Then press the Slice button.

   This cuts through all your geometry according to the Slice plane angle.

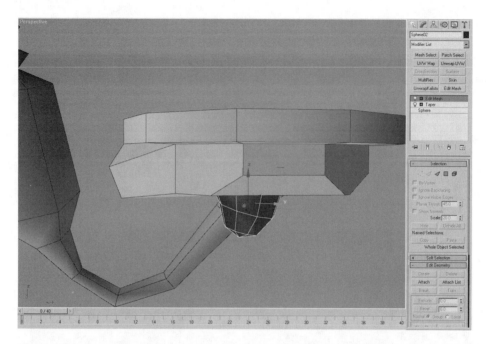

Figure 8.24   Rotate and move the border so that it is flush with the bottom of the base.

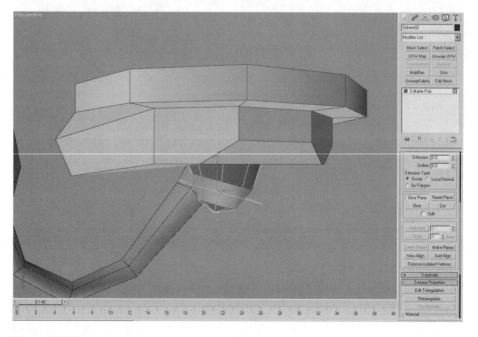

Figure 8.25   The middle row of polygons is selected.

10. Now go into Sub-Object Edge mode. Your new edges should be selected for you, but, if they are not, select the newly created edges.

11. Scale and rotate the edges as desired, as seen in Figure 8.26.

   Now, on to creating the legs. They are really easy to make as well.

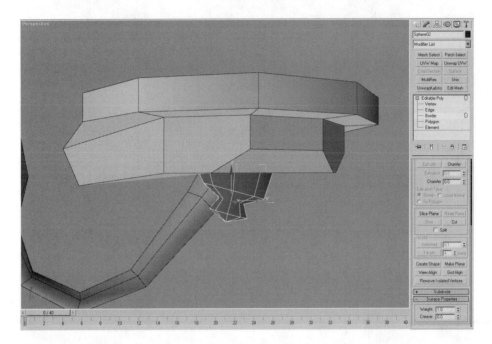

Figure 8.26   Scale and rotate the edges to your liking.

12. Create a cylinder with **4** sides and **2** height segments in the Top viewport. The height should be about **28**, with a radius of **1.7**. Turn on Generate Mapping Coordinates, as seen in Figure 8.27.

13. Move the cylinder and rotate it 15 degrees or so. Make sure that the top of the cylinder is inside the piece that you made last.

14. Convert the cylinder to an editable poly using the Quad menu.

15. Go into Sub-Object Vertex mode and select the middle row of vertices. Scale down the vertices, as seen in Figure 8.28.

16. In the Right viewport, create a cylinder with a with **4** sides, a radius of **5**, a height of **5**, and **1** height segment. Also, don't forget to turn on Generate Mapping Coordinates.

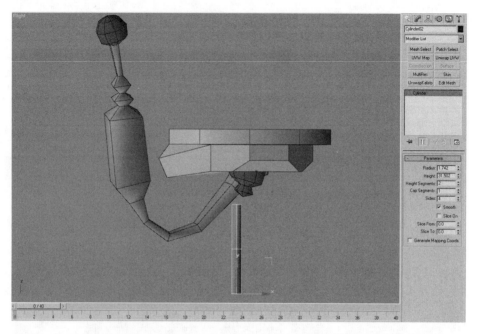

Figure 8.27 Create a cylinder with four sides and two height segments in the Top viewport. Turn on Generate Mapping Coordinates.

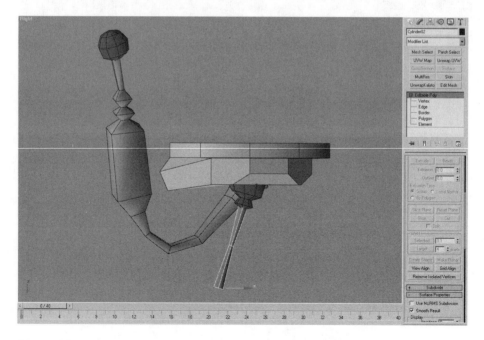

Figure 8.28 The middle row of vertices has been scaled down.

17. Select the first cylinder that you made for the leg, and right-click to bring up the Quad menu. Because you collapsed this object earlier, the Quad menu shows all the tools available to you at this time. Select the Attach List Quad menu item, as seen in Figure 8.29.

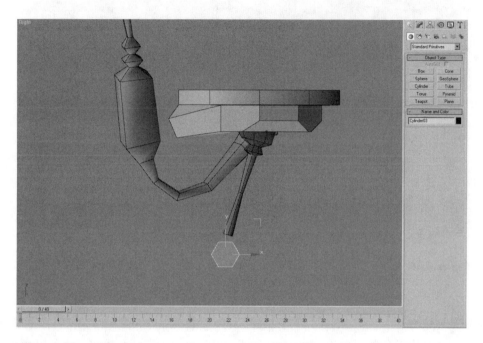

Figure 8.29   Here is the Attach List Quad menu item.

18. Attach the leg and kneecap together by selecting them in the Attach List dialog window.

19. Select the top polygon on the knee joint, and bevel it like you did earlier. Using Sub-Object Polygon/Bevel, bevel the face out until it almost touches the leg cylinder.

20. Now change your coordinate system from View to Local, and rotate the top polygon on the knee in local Z so that it matches up with the leg, as seen in Figure 8.30.

21. Delete both that top polygon (which you just rotated into place) and the bottom polygon on the leg cylinder.

22. Go into Sub-Object Vertex mode, and choose Target Weld from the Command panel, in the Edit Geometry rollout under Weld.

23. Click and drag the vertices from the open end of the kneecap to the closest ones on the open end of the leg, to bring the piece together.

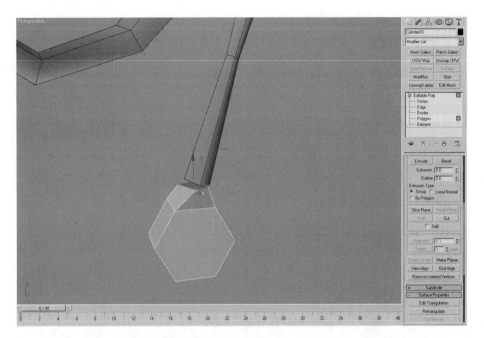

Figure 8.30   In the Local coordinate system, rotate the top polygon on the knee in local Z so that it matches up with the leg.

24. To change the way the edges lie, go into Sub-Object Polygon mode and then scroll all the way to the bottom of the Editable Poly Command panel. There you will find a Surface Properties rollout. Press the Edit Triangulation button to activate it.

25. Activate Edit Triangulation and change the direction that the edge is drawn by simply clicking one vert to start it and then clicking another to draw to it.

You can quickly go around the kneecap and retriangulate the whole thing in a few seconds. This is the editable poly equivalent to flipping edges.

Try retriangulating the polygons that were made when you beveled the kneecap. Because you rotated them, some of the edges shear a bit. Fix this by retriangulating those edges.

26. To make the bottom part of his leg, copy the leg by holding the Shift key while moving it down. Then scale it out a bit and rotate into place, moving the middle row of vertices out to give it more of a bend. Follow Figure 8.31 as a guideline.

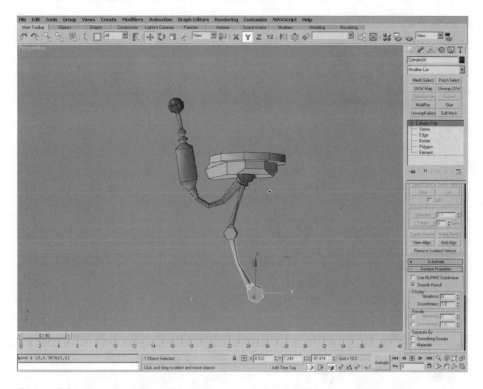

Figure 8.31   Use this image as a guide while performing Step 26.

Exercise 8.4   Building the Feet

Pug's feet are basically made up of a heel and a toe. You'll create the heel first and then the toe.

1. To make the heel, create a box right behind where the ankle would be. The box should have a length of around **20**, a width of **14**, and a height of **5**.

2. Collapse the box to an editable poly, and go into Sub-Object Vertex mode.

3. Select the vertex on the back of the heel, and scale it along the X-axis.

4. Now go into the Right viewport and pull the top-back vertex down to taper off the back of the heel. Scale and move until you like the shape. (See Figure 8.32.)

5. To make the toe, hold down the Shift key while you move the heel forward to copy it, and make the toe.

6. Scale the toe up so that it's roughly twice as big as the heel, as seen in Figure 8.33.

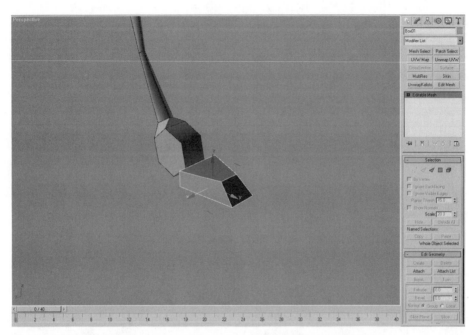

Figure 8.32   Use this figure as reference when scaling and moving the heel.

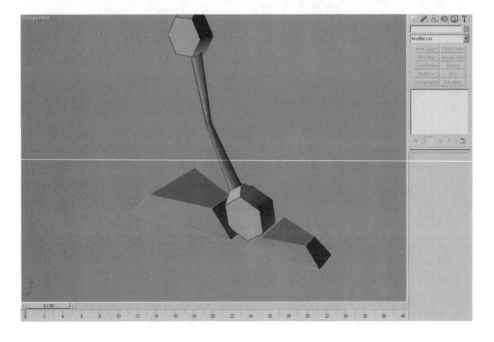

Figure 8.33   Scale the toe up so that it's roughly twice as big as the heel.

7. Select the toe and go into Sub-Object Edge mode. Find the Cut button in the Command panel, and press it.

8. Cut the edges on the front toe polygons by selecting one and then another. This will cut between those two edges right where you clicked. Cut the toe three times, as seen in Figure 8.34.

9. Select the vertex in the middle and the two outer-top vertices, as well. Move them all back along the Y-axis, as seen in Figure 8.35.

10. Select the whole leg assembly and copy it over to the other side by holding down the Shift key while you move them.

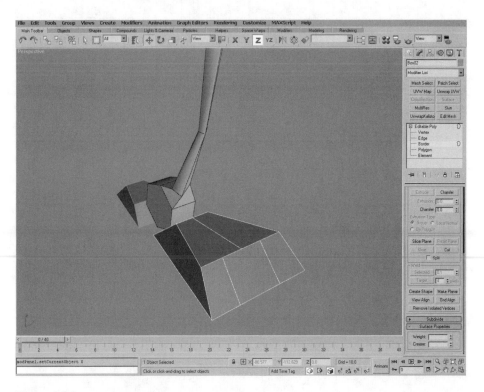

Figure 8.34   Cut the toe three times.

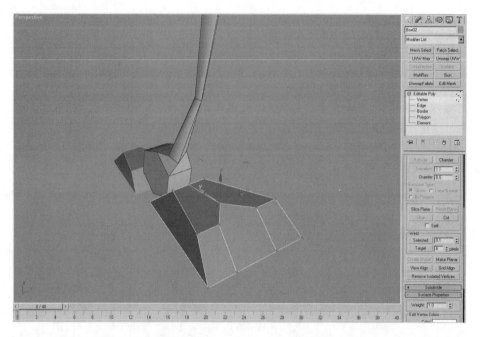

Figure 8.35   Move the vertices back along the Y-axis.

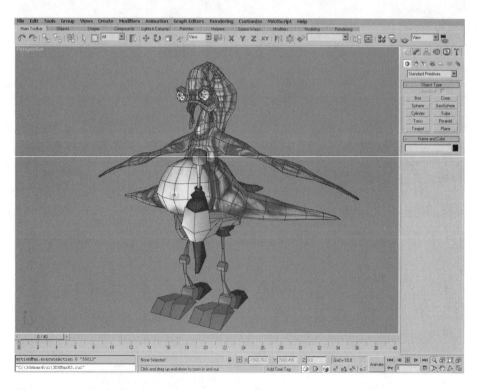

Figure 8.36   Pug has legs! He's pumped. Nice work.

Summary

This chapter used several techniques to build the various pieces comprising Pug's base, legs, and feet.

For instance, lofts are a great way to make things quickly and to use simple mapping coordinates on them automatically. When it comes time to texture-map the legs that you made earlier, the lofts can be mapped for you by enabling texture mapping in the loft object.

Edit poly, new to max 4, also offers lots of advantages, including the capability to work with borders, easy retriangulation, and cleaner cutting and slicing of polygons and edges. In Max 3, cutting across polygons caused a lot of unwanted geometry and sometimes didn't cut the way you wanted at all. Editable poly clears this up by offering greater slicing and cutting capabilities, and much more.

You'll learn how to make the fleshy part of our friend Pug in Chapter 11, "Organic/Character Modeling for Games/Interactive Applications."

Chapter 9

Organic/Character Modeling Using the Patch Method for Broadcast/Film

by Adam Holmes and Kim Lee

Of the four types of geometry and modeling categories in max—polygonal, HSDS, Bezier patch, and Non-Uniform Rational B-Spline (NURBS)—Bezier patch modeling is a great choice for characters and organic shapes. Because it enables you to up-res and down-res your topology, it's an ideal way to model for real-time games and film applications. In addition, you can work with an underlying spline cage for ultimate control, and the tools for editing the patch surface are much like the polygonal toolset. There are many little tricks to working efficiently with these tools, so pay close attention to the process.

Figure 9.1 represents the final model of the Jester character that will be used in the following chapters for skeleton rigging and animation. The same character will be modeled in the next chapter using polygonal and Meshsmooth techniques, which is a favored method by many max modelers. We wanted to explore both methods for modeling the same character for you to get the most out of this book.

Figure 9.1   Here is a finished view of the Jester model.

In this chapter you explore the basic setup for creating a CG character, from a sculpted maquette to the finishing details, including the following:

- Tracing spline contours from photographs of the real model
- Creating spline cages from these contours

- Tweaking splines
- Generating surfaces
- Editing surfaces and addressing common problems
- Attaching limbs to the torso
- Constructing faces
- Modeling clothing and accessories

We chose to create this character using patches because most film and broadcast-oriented projects have to have the highest level of resolution and detail. Patch modeling gives us this flexibility, and for many artists working on these types of projects, this modeling method more closely mimics traditional artistic techniques.

The goal is to make one seamless character, starting with each major body part and attaching the spline networks together. Planning the layout of the splines when modeling is very important to avoid unwanted pinching and creasing, as well as for animating. It's as easy as outlining the major features and muscle groups (especially for facial work) in a logical way, and "connecting the dots." There will be challenges, of course, and this chapter provides details about ways to fix or avoid common problems.

You need to have some experience in working with splines and Bezier patches to get the most out of this chapter, because you won't be spending much time on the basics or on button-to-button workflow. However, you will explore the usefulness of new features.

Your feeling of success with this chapter also depends on how much time you want to spend tweaking the model to look "right." This is completely up to you and your sense of artistry. You can learn the tools and workflow without spending a lot of time pushing and pulling points, so you can go at your own pace.

Exercise 9.1   Setting Up for Modeling

This chapter provides photographs of the character maquette, taken from the front and side views. If you're photographing your own model, be sure to use a tripod and place the character on a rotating platform so you can maintain the same image size in each picture. Don't use a wide-angle lens, because you'll distort the perspective of the features and your 3D model will not be as accurate. Use a zoom lens and have the camera as far away from the model as possible. This will flatten the perspective, resulting in greater accuracy for modeling (see Figure 9.2).

Figure 9.2   It's a good idea to use a maquette to base your model on.

To begin, start a new max scene and perform the following steps, or load the completed max scene 09_01start.max, which bypasses this exercise, and start with Exercise 9.2.

1. Create two plane primitives in the Front view at a similar proportion to the images of the model, one for the front image and one for the side (roughly 275 units length, 180 units width).

2. Rotate one plane 90 degrees on the Z-axis.

3. Move the planes so they're centered on 0,0,0.

   This is the best place to build any model, especially in a collaborative workflow with other artists.

4. Apply a UVW Mapping modifier. Select Planar mode and fit the bitmap to both plane objects.

5. Map the two images of the Jester from the CD-ROM to the diffuse channel of two new material slots in the Material Editor. Drag and drop these materials onto their respective planes. (If you don't see the textures in shaded mode, turn on the Show Map in Viewport button in the Material Editor.)

6. Select both planes, right-click to get the Quad menu and select Properties in the lower Quad. In the Properties panel, uncheck Show Frozen in Gray so you can see the textures while the planes are frozen (you'll freeze them in Step 8).

7. Align the side plane with the front plane so that the torso in the images lines up and so that the torso is split in half with the side plane.

8. Freeze both planes. Figure 9.3 shows the result.

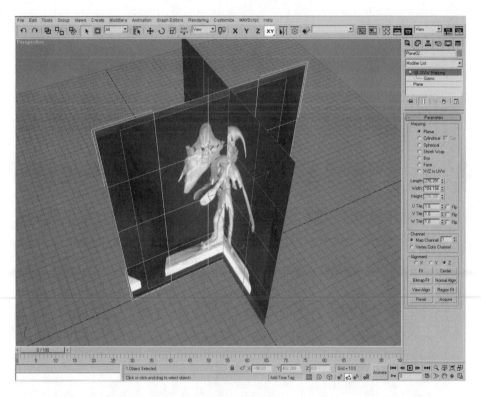

Figure 9.3   The image planes are aligned and textures are applied to them.

Now you have the references set up for placing the spline outlines and details. That wasn't so hard, was it? Again, this is just a guide, so don't feel restricted to modeling the character exactly as it appears in real life. Experiment!

Exercise 9.2   Creating Leg Circles

Next you create a series of circles to define the shape of the leg. In this exercise you define how much detail the model will have initially. By default, a circle is defined by four vertices. If you want more detail, you need more vertices. You can use the Divide tool in editable spline to add more verts, or you can start by using an Ngon shape, which has a circular option, and increase the point count. This is actually a great primitive spline object to use for modeling.

1. Draw a circle in the Top viewport. Adjust the radius to match the character's ankle.

2. Move the circle in the Front and Top viewports to match the position of the character's ankle, just below the flap on the boot.

3. Duplicate the circle up the leg five times. Position one circle between the ankle and knee, one at the knee, and one equally spaced above the knee with the one below the knee. Position one halfway up the thigh, and position the last one where the top of the leg would be, under the tunic dress.

4. Line up the circles in the Front viewport, and then adjust in the Left viewport, rotating to match the curve of the leg.

5. Right-click and convert the first circle near the ankle to an editable spline. Right-click again, choose Attach, and click the other splines sequentially up the leg.

Tip

This order of attaching is important for the Cross Section modifier to work correctly, which you'll apply later. Don't skip a spline and then go back, unless you want a surface that folds back on itself (something you'll do later for the boots).

6. You can tweak the verts to match the leg even more, pushing and pulling to get the shape you want. Figure 9.4 shows the result.

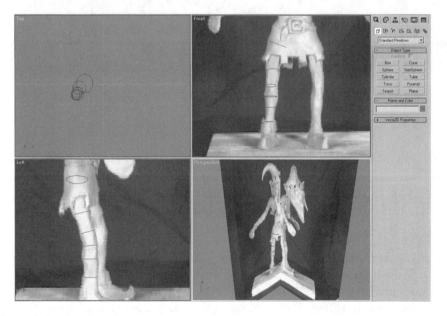

Figure 9.4   The leg circles are rotated into position.

This finished exercise can be found in the max scene 09_02leg.max.

The exercise you just completed is the foundation for creating virtually all body parts. This is just one way of doing it; as with anything in max, there is more than one way to achieve the same result.

Exercise 9.3   Creating the Torso

Now you repeat the procedure you followed in Exercise 9.2 to create the torso.

1. Create another circle in the Top viewport at 0-X and 0-Y and move it just above the belt on the Z-axis.

2. Copy the circle five times, and position and rotate each so that they match both the Front and Left views.

3. Convert the first circle to an editable spline again, and attach the others from bottom to top.

4. Because the torso isn't round, but is flatter in the front and back, a good technique for editing the verts is to select the front or back vert of one circle, and then the two side verts. Then, using the Non-Uniform Scale tool in the Use Transform Coordinate Center mode, grab the Y-axis in the Top view (make sure to be in the View coordinate system).

    Using Local Coordinate mode when performing nonuniform scaling has a different but desirable effect. Experiment with both to see each effect. Figure 9.5 shows the result.

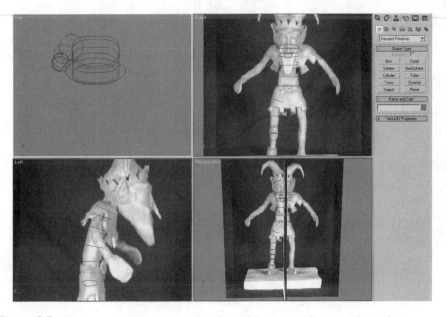

Figure 9.5   The correct positioning and scaling of the torso splines are shown here.

This finished step is the max scene 09_03torso.max. Make sure to constantly orbit around your model as you tweak the shape, which helps you determine where you need to make adjustments. Also be sure to play with editing the splines to get a feel for the tools.

Exercise 9.4   Creating Arm Splines

Next come the arm splines.

1. This time, draw the circle in the Left view and align it to the shoulder, a bit inside the shawl. Duplicate it in the Front view seven times to follow the length of the arm.

2. As in any modeling situation, you need to have more detail in the joint areas, such as the elbows. Place a concentration of four splines around this area.

3. Rotate the splines on the Z-axis (in View mode) in the Front view first, and then on the Z-axis in the Left view to align the circles down the arm. Figure 9.6 shows the result.

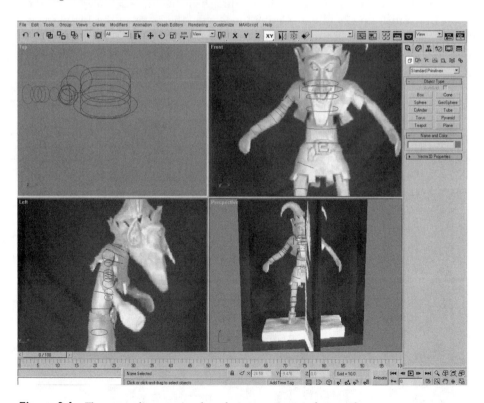

Figure 9.6   The arm splines are in place, but are not rotated correctly.

Now, you have a problem. Not a big problem, but something to be aware of. This model wasn't built in the preferred default pose for a CG character. The arms are angled down 45 degrees or so, and it's best for skinning purposes to have the arms straight out (slightly bent), palms down. You needed to align the circles to the maquette to have an accurate shape of the arm. Now you need to rotate the arm splines up to be in the best pose for skinning later.

4. In the Animation drop-down menu, select Create Point and insert a Point object in the Top view. Position it at the shoulder just to the left of the first circle that you drew.

5. While the point is still selected, select all the arm circles except the first one. In Rotate mode, choose the Pick Coordinate mode from the drop-down list and choose the Point object. Make sure you're in Use Pivot Point Center mode and rotate the circles up on the local Y-axis.

Tip

The Pick Coordinate mode is an often underused, but very useful feature for situations such as this, and for mirroring.

6. Finally, convert the first circle to an editable spline. Using the Attach button on the Editable Spline modifier, attach the other arm circles in order, down the arm. Figure 9.7 shows the result.

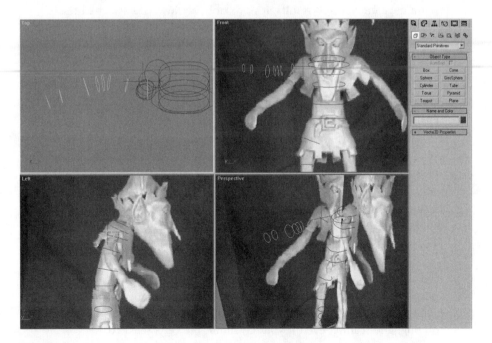

Figure 9.7   The arm splines are in position, after using the reference point for rotation.

This finished step is the max scene 09_04arm.max.

That wasn't so hard, was it? As I said earlier, this isn't about going from button to button, but more about an overall workflow, highlighting the best tools for this job.

Exercise 9.5   Attaching the Arms to the Shoulders

Ready for more? Now that you have all the splines in order for each major body part, it's time to piece them together.

1. Hide the reference planes so you can begin to work with the splines directly.

2. Add the Cross Section modifier (under the Patch/Spline Editing category) to each body part, one at a time, so each part has its own modifier.

3. Set the spline options to Bezier.

   Bezier gives you the most control over the splines, enabling you to add creases and bulges easily.

 Note

Sometimes during editing you'll change a vert from Bezier to Smooth or to Corner, but that's on a case-by-case basis. It's easier to start with every vert set to Bezier, because that's the most commonly used vert type.

If you have unexpected results, it's probably because you attached the splines (or circles, in this case) in the wrong order. Detach all the splines and reattach them in the correct order. Figure 9.8 shows the result.

This finished step is the max scene 09_05cross_section.max.

4. Next, right-click the torso's stack in the Modifier panel, collapse it to an editable spline, and attach the arm and leg objects, using the Attach button on the Editable Spline modifier.

   This absorbs the arm and leg into the editable spline, so you don't have to collapse them first. You're attaching the arm and leg to the torso so that the torso contains the appropriate pivot point for mirroring the other half of the body later.

5. In the Vertex Sub-Object mode of editable spline, tweak the shape to your liking. Two helpful tools for doing this are Area Selection and Lock Handles.

   Area Selection enables you to choose two or more *coincident verts* (verts lying on top of each other) with one click, rather than dragging a window selection around it. The threshold of .1 is usually good enough for working with spline cages where you always have two verts overlapping. Lock Handles enables you to control both Bezier handles of a spline when moving, rotating, and scaling, even if you have multiple verts selected.

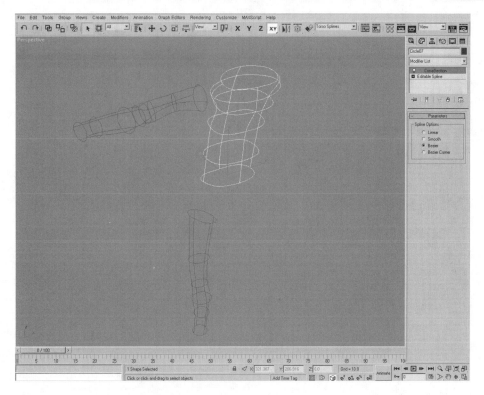

Figure 9.8   The Cross Section modifier is applied to all of the body parts.

Now you're ready for the dreaded process of attaching the arm to the shoulder. Why do I say *dreaded*? Well, in other modeling methods, attaching an arm to a torso (the shoulder is part of the torso object) is a challenging and frustrating task. Not so with splines—and the result is highly flexible.

6. In the Sub-Object Vert mode of editable spline, select the vert that's closest to the shoulder and click the Break button.

7. Move the resulting two verts apart. Select the other vert that's not broken and break that as well. Move those verts apart. Figure 9.9 shows the result.

8. Right-click any of the Snapping buttons at the bottom of the max interface. Set the snap type to Vertex Only. Then, in the Options panel, set the snap strength to **20**. Close the Snap Settings window. Move each vert you broke to its logical mate on the opening spline of the shoulder. Select each pair of verts that now lie on top of each other, and using the Weld button in editable spline, weld them together. (Make sure the Weld threshold is above 0.)

 Note

The importance of snapping cannot be overlooked. There are many options; familiarize yourself with them so you can model more efficiently and accurately.

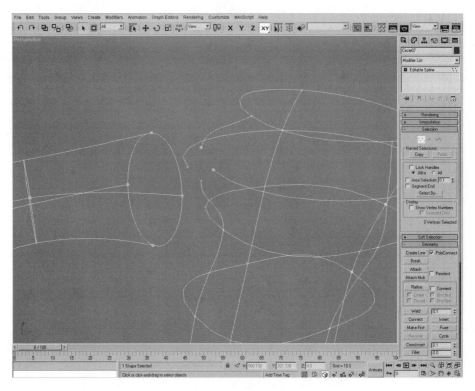

Figure 9.9   The shoulder vertices are split apart.

Welding combines the splines that run the length of the arm to the splines that you just snapped on. The circle that makes the start of the arm won't be welded, because there are no open verts that qualify to be welded. (If a vert on that circle was broken, it would weld.)

This finished step is the max scene 09_06attach_arm.max.

Tip

Here's a useful snapping tip to put into your toolbox for later:

1. Select some vertices and lock the selection.

2. Turn the snap options to Grid Only.

3. Click Rotate and set the Pivot option to Use Selection Center (the second button in the Pivot flyout.)

4. Move the mouse over any grid point to see the snapping box. Click and drag to rotate the verts about that grid point. This also works with snapping to verts of other objects or the same object, using Vertex snapping instead of Grid.

Now you have another problem that requires some attention. When you eventually apply the Surface modifier, it needs to have spline boundaries that define either a 3- or 4-sided area. Any more or less, and a surface patch won't be generated.

In the area shown, by the shoulder, there's a 5-sided boundary of splines, as seen in Figure 9.10. You need to refine that area of attachment to produce an acceptable spline boundary.

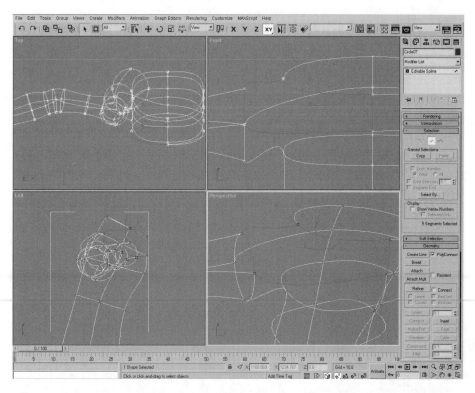

Figure 9.10 This is one of the 5-sided spline boundaries preventing a legal surface from being generated.

 Note

In the next sections I refer to objects by the terms *lines* and *splines*. These terms are used interchangeably, so I want to clarify that to avoid confusion. In the Create Line command in an editable spline, max uses these terms to mean the same thing. So do I.

9. In editable spline, Sub-Object Vert mode, choose Refine and add a vert both on the front spline that you connected to the shoulder and on the back spline.

Do this from a Front view (or User view rotated to be almost a Front view) so you can line up the vert with the other verts on the torso. It's okay if you're not 100% accurate.

10. In Segment Sub-Object mode, choose Create Line. Make sure 3D Snap is on and Poly Connect is unchecked.

    This new feature, Poly Connect (as discussed in Chapter 2, "Changes in Modeling and Materials"), won't autoweld to open or broken points as you draw them.

11. Draw the line from the front spline's vert (the one you just added) counter-clockwise to the other verts, and then back to where you started. Click Yes when asked to close the spline and No to any weld dialog. To keep this line you just drew as editable as possible, you don't want this spline's verts to weld to the others. If it's welded to the other splines, you'll lose the line's individual shape, because it becomes connected to the other splines.

12. Go to Spline Sub-Object mode and the new spline should be selected. Right-click over that spline to get the Quad menu. In Tools 1, choose Curve.

    Even though it's already checked, it's not really curved, as you can see in the viewport. Doing this actually curves the spline. Strange, I know, but it works.

    An alternative method is to select all the verts on the new ellipsoid and make them smooth and then Bezier (using the Quad menu over a vert), but the previous method saves a step.

13. Smooth out the tangencies of the verts by moving the Bezier handles. You can tweak to your heart's content or continue with the project. It's up to you. Figure 9.11 shows the result.

    This finished step is the max scene 09_07shoulder_work.max.

 Tip

To move a handle on a specific axis without choosing it from the main toolbar, click the appropriate axis on the Transform manipulator. This sets the axis constraint for movement. Then grab the Bezier handle and move. You can select the 2-axis part of the manipulator as well, to get an XY, XZ, or ZY movement.

Work in Perspective or User view, full-screen, and continuously rotate around your model to have a sense of space and dimensionality of your model. Avoid working in an orthographic view too long, or you'll lose your sense of volume and shape of the character.

It might help at this time to apply the Surface modifier, to get a better sense of how your vertex tweaking will be represented in the surface.

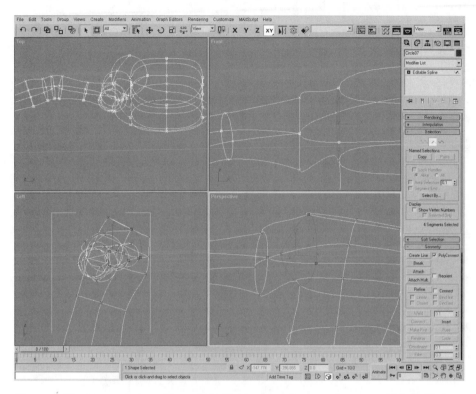

Figure 9.11   Connect a new line, which divides the spline cage into acceptable 4-sided
boundaries.

14. Add the Surface modifier from the Patch/Spline Editing section of the
Modifier List. Check Flip Normals and Remove Interior Patches to clean it
up. Set the threshold at **1.0**, which defines the distance between points that's
acceptable to make a surface. Play with the value to see different results, and
play with the Patch Topology steps to see the multiresolution capability of
the surface.

Note

Another new feature in 3ds max 4 is the capability of working with the original spline
cage and seeing the surface at the same time. Go to Sub-Object Vert mode in the
editable spline and turn on the Show End Result button in the Modifier Stack controls.
In previous versions, you had to create a reference of the spline cage and apply your
surface to it, so you had an extra reference object to deal with, making editing more
complex. Not anymore! (See Figure 9.12.)

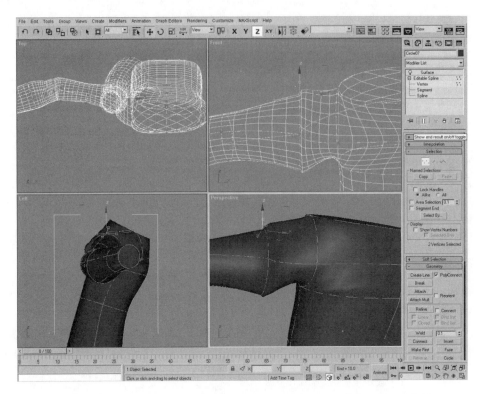

Figure 9.12 When you edit the spline cage, you can see the resulting surface at the same time.

You can see that working with splines requires few rules, and following these methods of manipulating them, you get decent results quickly. The next exercise of attaching the legs to the torso is similar to the last exercise, but it presents a few new challenges.

Exercise 9.6 Attaching the Legs to the Torso

Before you attach the legs to the torso, you need to add some detail to the base of the torso.

1. Turn off the Surface modifier by clicking the little light bulb next to it. Move the view to look up at the torso, from below, and create a line across the width of the torso (in Sub-Object Vert mode, of course). Snap it to the points on either side of it. Create another line, snapping it from front to back.

2. Choose Cross Insert and click the intersection of the two splines you just created.

   This handy tool creates a vert on each spline in the same place.

3. Window-select each group of two verts around the edge of the bottom circle (there are four groups) and weld them together.

   This connects the splines you just drew with the existing splines that go up the length of the torso.

4. Move the verts that you created with the Cross Insert tool down and round out the bottom of the torso. You can skip this step by loading 09_08torso_leg_prep.max from the CD (see Figure 9.13).

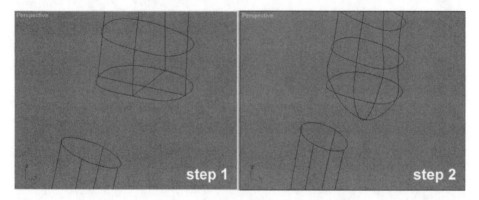

Figure 9.13   Add the lines and middle vertex, and then shape the torso to closely match the reference images.

5. Break the vert of the spline that runs the width of the torso, and move the resulting verts apart. Snap to the leg the point on the left side spline that you just broke.

6. Create a new line for the inside-thigh connection, snapping it to the crotch. Smooth out the Bezier handles to look like Figure 9.14.

   At this point, it's obvious that there needs to be more definition in the inner thigh and crotch area. This is usually a problem area after a character is skinned, so the more detail, the better. The trick is to make the detail work for the character, and not just arbitrarily add detail.

7. Draw-snap a line from the vert on the left hip to the point at the crotch.

Note

Snapping and line drawing go hand-in-hand in this process. You can turn Snapping off and on in the midst of creating a line by pressing the S hotkey. I refer to the process of creating and snapping new lines as *draw-snap*.

8. In Segment Sub-Object mode, choose that spline and divide it with a value of **1**. (I love this tool for adding verts exactly at the midpoint of a spline segment.)

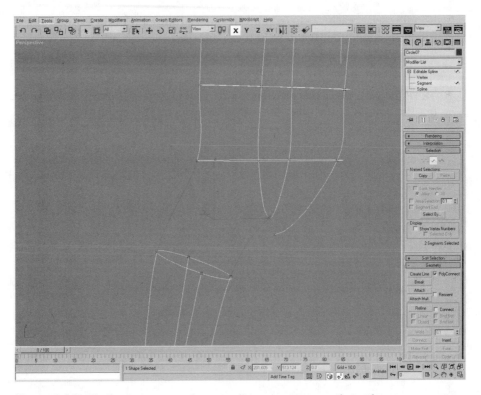

Figure 9.14   The leg-to-torso attachment splines are now correctly in place.

9. Pull this point out in the Y-axis to round it out. Notice in Figure 9.15 the middle vert is pulled outward to the front of the Jester. You can skip this step by loading 09_09torso_leg.max.

Tip

During this process you want to avoid connecting splines that make a tri-border, but sometimes you can't help it. Tri-patch surfaces tend to be not as smooth and can cause pinching. If you connect a lot of splines to a single vert, you also get a pinch that I call the "dreaded star pattern," which you now have at the hip vert. It's a better idea to add another vert below the hip and connect to that. (See Figure 9.15.)

10. Select the spline that connects from the outer side vert of the top leg circle and refine it below the hip. Then select the top end vert of the spline you drew in Step 7 and snap it to the new vert on the hip spline. Draw another spline in the back of the model, refine the segment, and pull it out in the Y-axis (that's the butt spline).

11. Create another line from the front vert of the top leg circle that isn't connected yet, and snap it to the new spline's middle vert and to the vert at the belly button. Do the same for the backside of the model. Turn on the Surface

modifier and begin to smooth out the verts and handles to get a desirable connection between the leg and torso. (See Figure 9.16.) You can skip this step by loading 09_10torso_leg_done.max.

That completes the process of attaching and refining the limbs. Now, let's move on to creating the boots.

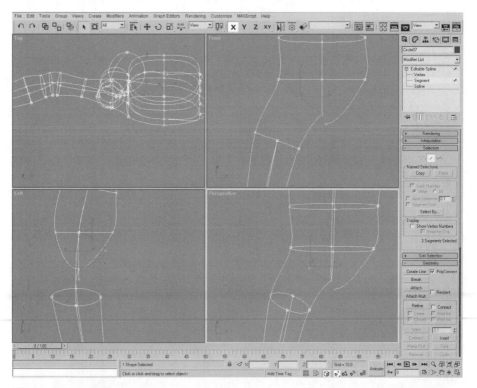

Figure 9.15   This shows too many splines connecting at the same vertex, at the hip.

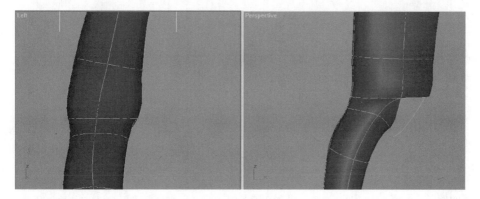

Figure 9.16   Here is the partial surface of the leg-to-torso connection.

Exercise 9.7   Creating the Boots

To create the boots, you start by unhiding the reference planes so you can create the feet splines. By now you know the drill. The splines are set up for you in the file 09_11boot_splines.max.

1. Unhide the reference planes.

2. Draw a circle in the Top viewport and move it to align with the toe, just below the tip of it.

3. Copy the circle nine times, and adjust the radii and rotations to match the reference.

4. To make the cuff of the boot, make the fourth circle from the top of the ankle bigger, the third circle smaller, the second circle a bit bigger than the third, and the top circle the same as the second.

   This boot will have an overlapping surface on the cuff. The order of attaching these circles is extremely important, or the surface won't be correct. Please follow the next step carefully.

5. Convert the toe circle to an editable spline and attach the other circles in this order: Attach the next five, skip the large cuff (fourth from the top of the ankle), and skip the next one. Grab the second from the top, the large cuff (fourth from the top), the top circle, and finally the third from the top. Figure 9.17 shows the result.

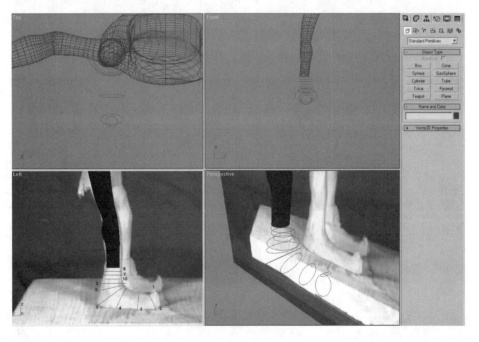

Figure 9.17   Follow the numbers displayed for the correct attachment order of the boot splines.

6. Add the Cross Section modifier and choose the Bezier option.

7. Collapse the object to an editable spline, add the Surface modifier, flip the normals, and remove the interior patches.

8. Go back to the Sub-Object Vert mode of the editable spline and start shaping the boot. Flatten the bottom by using Non-Uniform Scale on the verts, and pull the side verts down. Use your imagination editing and shaping, adding an anklebone and smoothing out the cuff.

Experiment with scaling and rotating verts while in the View and Local Coordinate modes, combined with the different Pivot Point modes. Figure 9.18 shows the result.

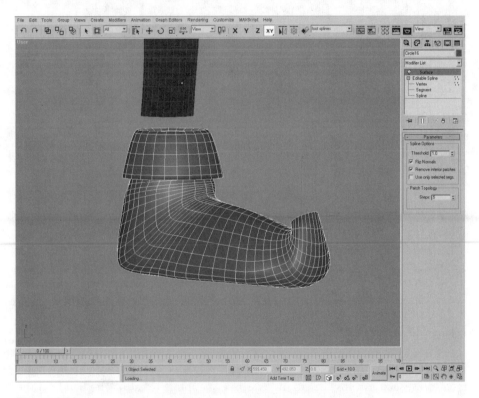

Figure 9.18   The partially finished boot model is ready for more detailing.

Cap the toe, as you did the torso in Exercise 9.6. (Load 09_12boot_toe.max.)

9. Add two lines (in Sub-Object Vert mode) and snap them to the opposite verts on the toe circle.

10. Use Cross Insert in the Editable Spline modifier to add that vert in the center crossing point. Window-select each group of two verts around the edge of the toe circle (there are four groups) and weld (or you can select all four

groups at the same time; because the weld threshold is small, it welds only those points that are on top of each other).

This connects the splines you just drew with the existing splines that go up the length of the boot.

11. Move the center points up and adjust everything to look good. (See Figure 9.19.)

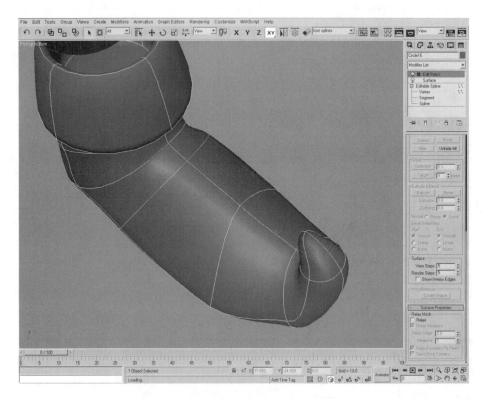

Figure 9.19   Create the toe cap splines.

That was a relatively simple procedure; by now you're getting used to a few common tools, such as Cross Insert and effective snapping. Creating the hands in the next exercise is a bit more involved and covers more useful tools, such as Binding.

Exercise 9.8   Creating the Hands

Before you get into the nitty-gritty of building the hand, you should know that you're creating the hand with these modeling techniques because you're attempting to make a seamless character (and because patch and spline tools are so cool!). You can use box modeling or Meshsmooth on a hand much faster than you can create one in spline or patch modeling. If you don't need a seamless model, go with the box-modeling method.

Note

Using the new Relax feature within edit patch enables you to box-model using patches. Relax shrinks or makes the patch surface smooth, but your edits take place on the original, unrelaxed patches. It's not exactly the same as mesh box modeling, but it has some potential use. You won't use this technique here, but it's there for you to experiment with.

1. Load the file 09_13hand_spline.max. Draw a hand shape in the Top viewport.

2. In the Left viewport, create a series of six circles down the length of the middle finger, centering two around each knuckle area, one near the fingernail, and one at the point where the finger joins the palm. Adjust them in the Top viewport.

3. Convert the circle into an editable spline and scale the top verts down to flatten the top.

4. Attach the rest of the circles, in order, to the editable spline.

5. Repeat for the other fingers.

6. The thumb needs only four splines. Rotate the thumb circles around on the local Z, and scale up the circle that connects to the palm. (See Figure 9.20.)

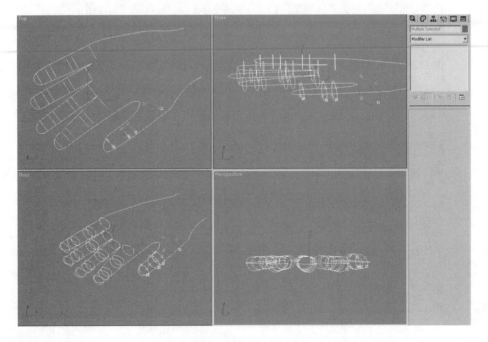

Figure 9.20 The finger and thumb circles are in place.

7. Create a circle for the wrist in the Left view and position it to match the arm. Convert it to an editable spline.

8. Copy this wrist circle and move it into the palm area a bit. Flatten the top and bottom verts.

9. Copy that flattened spline and move it into the palm area just where the thumb connects. Select all the segments and divide by 1. You'll add more detail in this area.

10. Copy that spline and move it to the area where the fingers will connect with the palm. Scale as necessary.

11. Attach all palm splines, in order, from the wrist up, and attach any finger groups together that you didn't before.

12. Apply a Cross Section modifier to the finger groups, but not to the palm. Use the Bezier parameter in Cross Section.

    The palm area requires some special attention. Add the Cross Section modifier now to see why you need to connect the verts manually. Cross Section has to guess where you want the verts connected because you have a lower vert count spline at the wrist and higher count splines connected to it. It doesn't make a pretty surface. (See Figure 9.21.) Delete the Cross Section modifier if you're continuing with this file, or you can load 09_15wrist_splines.max to see the results.

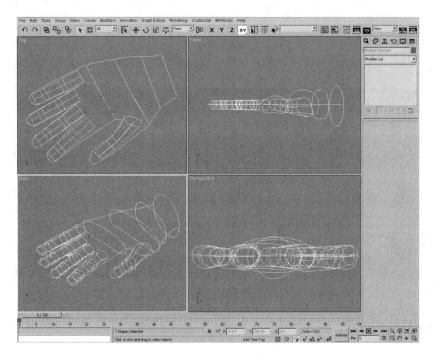

Figure 9.21   The Cross Section modifier has been applied to the fingers.

Now you begin some manual labor, but in the end it'll be worth having a well-planned surface that will deform predictably.

13. Hide the reference hand spline you started from. Attach all the finger splines together.

14. In editable spline, with Poly Connect on and Snap on, draw three splines. Draw one from the index finger to the thumb, defining the profile (like the reference hand). Draw another one from the thumb down to the wrist, and draw a third from the pinky down to the wrist.

    With Poly Connect on, the new lines will autoweld to the finger splines, saving a step later. See the max file 09_17hand_middle.max.

15. Now window-select the inner verts between the first and second fingers, the ones that would make the inner webbing between each finger when welded.

16. Click Fuse and Weld.

    Fuse brings them together at an average point, and Weld welds the open verts (that is, the verts on the splines that run the length of the finger).

17. Do the same for the other two pairs of verts, and adjust to look good. (See Figure 9.22.)

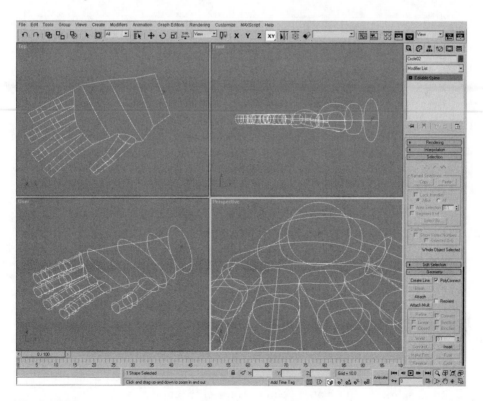

Figure 9.22   The fingers are connected to the hand outline spline.

18. Draw a line (using Create Line in Sub-Object Vert mode of the Editable Spline modifier) from the top-center vert of the wrist spline, as shown in Figure 9.23. Continue under the palm, back to the bottom vert of the wrist. Poly Connect should be off; use Vertex Snapping to be accurate!

19. Adjust the center verts to make a straighter line from the wrist to the palm.

    This ensures a more gridlike surface later, as seen in Figure 9.23. See the max file 09_18thumb_splines1.max.

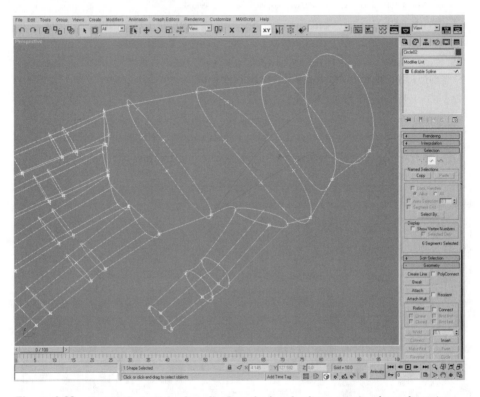

Figure 9.23   Here is the initial spline dividing the hand splines, starting from the wrist spline.

For the next thumb spline, you use the Refine tool in the Editable Spline modifier.

20. Using the Refine tool, check the two options Connect and Bind Last.

21. With 3D Vert Snap on, choose the top vert of the thumb spline that connects with the palm. When you do, you get a dialog box that asks whether you want to refine or just connect. Choose Connect Only.

22. Snap to the next spline toward the wrist and choose Connect again. The next spline doesn't have a point to connect to, but choose it anyway and right-click to create the line.

23. Repeat this procedure for a spline underneath the thumb, connecting the back two splines. See the max file 09_19thumb_splines2.max. Figure 9.24 shows the result.

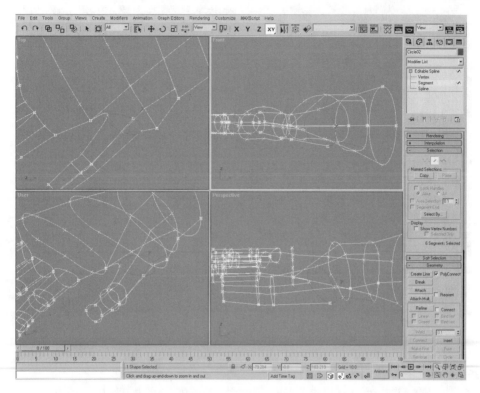

Figure 9.24   Make the thumb spline connection to the hand, which will add detail to the model.

The last point was bound to the midpoint of the spline, making Refine a very useful tool for connecting splines without creating extra verts. If you go to Sub-Object Vert mode, you'll see that the bound vert is black. You must be careful with bound verts, because they depend on vert ID numbers. When ID numbers change due to welding verts, the bound verts will be wacky. So this bind is temporary; you will unbind and rebind verts later.

24. For more detail in the thumb area, check the boxes next to Connect, Bind Last, and Bind First in the Refine menu. Draw the spline, as seen in Figure 9.25, from the palm spline to the thumb/palm connection and back to the palm spline. Make it curve using the Quad menu.

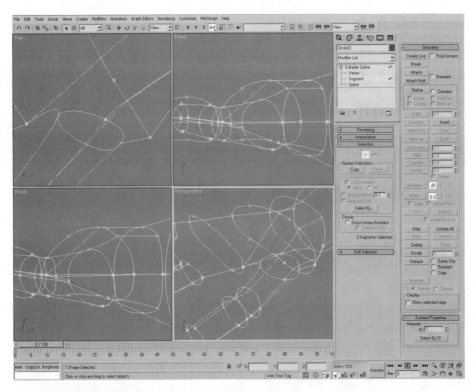

Figure 9.25   Using Refine and Connect with Binding adds detail to the thumb.

 Note

The Refine tools you just used to add splines into the model will be referred to in later sections as Refine and Connect for brevity.

25. Turn off Bind First and draw the next line from the webbing verts between the first and second fingers, connecting it to the top vert of the next palm spline and binding it to the spline after that.

26. Do the same connection on the underside of the hand.

27. On the next webbing vert, between the second and third fingers, draw backward on the top of the hand two splines and bind to the third. Don't forget to do the same binding on the fingers for the underside of the hand.

28. On the last webbing vert, between the third and fourth fingers, draw backward one spline on the top and bottom, binding to the second spline, as seen in Figure 9.26. See max file 09_20bound_hand.max.

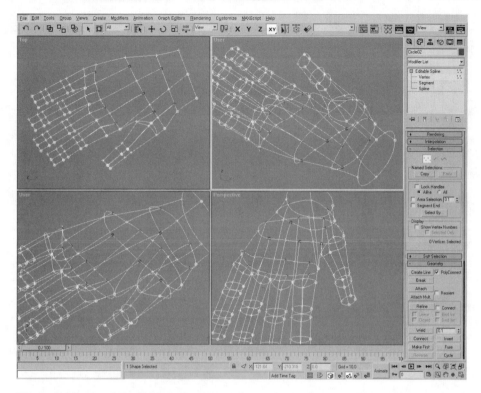

Figure 9.26   Finish by binding the lines and verts for the hand model.

29. Before you work on the tips of the fingers, window-select the entire hand in Sub-Object Vert mode and click Unbind.

In capping the fingertips, you use the same procedure you used earlier to cap the toe of the boot. After you weld the verts of the capping splines to the fingers, the vert IDs change, throwing off the binding.

30. Cap each fingertip using the boot toecap procedure.

31. Add the Surface modifier, Threshold at .1, flip the normals, and remove interior patches.

32. Click the Show End Result button. Go back to the Sub-Object Vert mode of editable spline, shape the fingers, and smooth out any creases.

It doesn't have to be perfectly smooth, because later you can add the Relax modifier, which makes the surface smooth. (See Figure 9.27.)

33. To see only the interior edges and not the tessellated patch, put an Edit Patch modifier at the top of the Modifier Stack, and uncheck the Show Interior Edges option, which is at the bottom of the Geometry rollout. See the max file 09_21finished_hand.max.

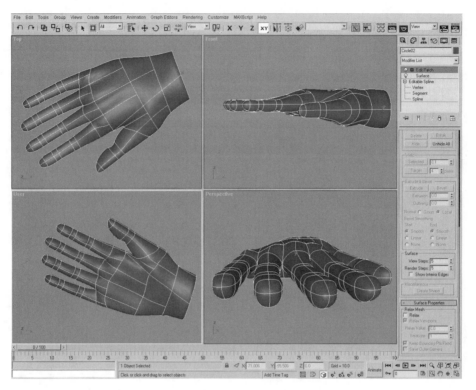

Figure 9.27   Here is the hand with the Surface modifier applied.

Now that you've completed some of the most intense spline editing, take some time to review the process, or even redo some steps to be sure you understand it fully.

Exercise 9.9   Connecting the Hand to the Body

This exercise involves connecting the hand you just made to the body.

1. Delete the Surface modifier from the hand and unhide the body.
2. Select the body and attach the hand (using Attach in the Editable Spline modifier). Now the Surface modifier that was on the body encompasses the hand. Make sure the Threshold on the Surface modifier is .1 so that the surface looks correct.

    In general, the vertices are closer together on the hand as opposed to the body, thus requiring a lower threshold to properly generate a surface.
3. Delete the last spline on the arm, near the wrist. Snap-move the logically connecting verts together and weld.

    You might have to snap-move other wrist splines together depending on your model. Keep looking for unconnected verts, using the Surface modifier as your guide (where there's no surface, there's a missed connection).

Don't worry about the surface on the hand. Patches will be missing until you can bind the verts back together. This can't be done until after the mirroring process, because the vert count will change, throwing off the whole mesh. Figure 9.28 shows the result. See max file 09_22hand_connected.max.

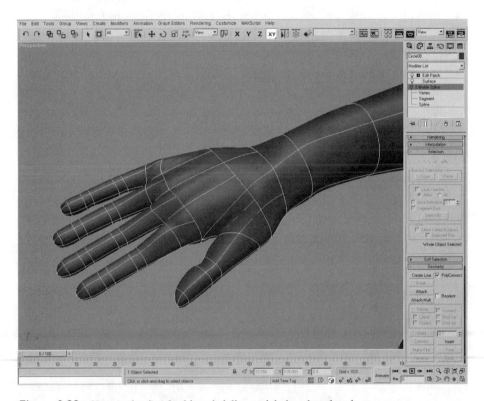

Figure 9.28   Here is the finished hand, fully modeled and surfaced.

At this point, half the body is complete. In the next exercise, you mirror what you've created to build the other half of the body.

Exercise 9.10   Mirroring the Body

For this exercise, you will start at the object level.

1. Mirror the entire model and make it an instance copy.

   Many times, it's easier to look at a completed body, rather than just half a body, to see the full dimension of the character. An instance copy was made so you can go in and tweak anything that doesn't look right and have those tweaks affect both halves of the model. (I'm sure you've done this before.)

2. When you're done tweaking, click the Make Unique button on the Stack View controls, and continue.

3. Select the original half of the body and in Sub-Object Spline mode, select the spline that runs up the middle of the body on the mirroring axis and delete it.

4. Turn off Sub-Object mode and attach the two spline cages to form one.

5. In the Front view, in Sub-Object Vert mode, select the column of verts down the middle of the body and weld them.

6. Reapply the Surface modifier if you deleted it and tweak anything that you find undesirable.

   Remember where all those bound verts were on the hand? Well, it's time to bind them back.

7. Click Bind and drag from the vert that needs to be rebound to the spline it's sitting on. This is a bit tedious, but needs to be done. Don't forget to bind the verts on the underside of the hand.

There you have it: one seamless body that is engineered for animation, with all the detail in the right places, and a logical surface. See the max file 09_23body_mirror.max. Figure 9.29 shows the result.

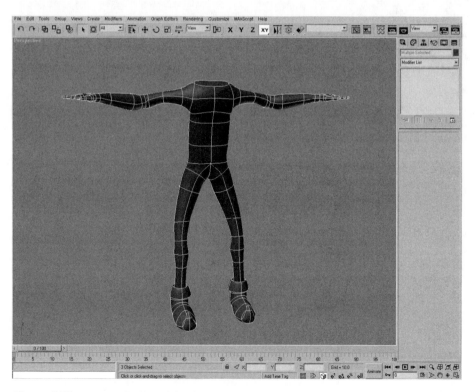

Figure 9.29   Here is the completed body model of the Jester.

Exercise 9.11   Creating the Tunic

All the Jesters these days have fashionable tunic skirts, and yours will be no exception!

1. Start by unhiding the reference planes and drawing an Ngon in the Top view.

2. Use the Circular option, in the Ngon's parameters, and enter **4** sides.

3. Center it on the waist of the character.

4. Use an edit spline and reshape it to fit the body snugly.

5. In Sub-Object Spline mode, make five copies below the first spline (hold the Shift key while translating on Z).

6. Scale each spline in the series to be gradually wider, to fit around the legs.

7. When you're done tweaking, collapse the splines into an editable spline.

8. In Sub-Object Segment mode, select all the segments and use Divide by **4**. See the max file 09_24tunic_splines.max. Figure 9.30 shows the result.

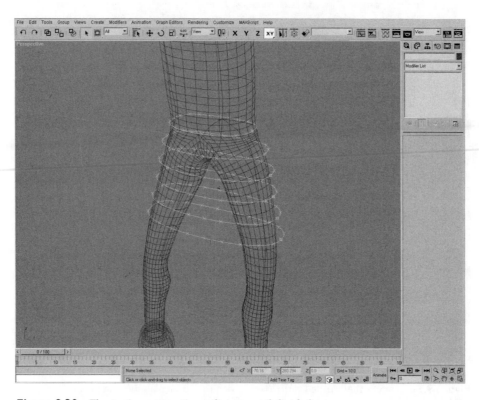

Figure 9.30   The tunic construction splines are subdivided.

9. Select the bottom-middle verts of the tunic spline cage and use Soft Selection to create a small falloff. Then pull the verts down to create a subtle droop in the skirt. Tweak as necessary.

   You've most likely used Soft Selection before on mesh editing, but now that tool is available when editing any geometry type and also splines.

10. Cross-section the skirt and collapse to an editable spline.

11. Remove every other segment at the base of the skirt to create that medieval castle look.

12. Apply the Surface modifier and tweak the underling spline as necessary. Figure 9.31 shows the result.

Without Soft Selection being available in editable spline, you would have had to use the Volume Select modifier to do something similar to Step 9, making the process more complicated. The next garment is created in a similar fashion.

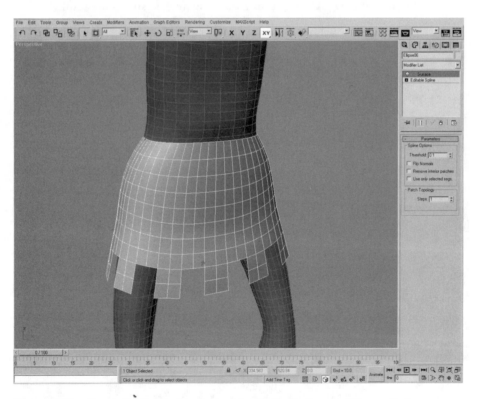

Figure 9.31   Here is the finished tunic model with the Surface modifier applied.

Exercise 9.12   Creating the Frock

Now you design the garment commonly known in Jester-land as a frock.

1. Start with an ellipse and shape it to droop over his shoulders at the base of the neck. Duplicate the ellipse four times and scale up each successive one. Duplicate one more time and scale this one down to fit around the neck area.

2. Collapse to editable spline and attach them all together in the correct order. Figure 9.32 shows the result.

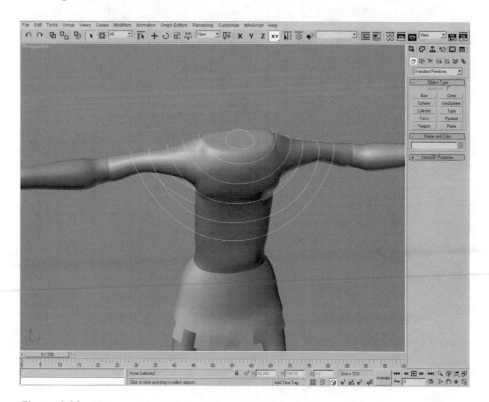

Figure 9.32   These are the initial splines needed to create the frock.

3. Select all the segments and Divide by **1**.

    This gives you the extra vert detail you need. It was easier to edit with only four verts per object than to add the detail later. See the max file 09_25frock_splines.max.

4. Cross-section and collapse the object to an editable spline. Delete every other segment on the bottom row (for that castle look) and add the Surface modifier to it.

5. Add edit patch on top of the surface. In the Surface Properties rollout, turn on Relax, Relax in Viewports, with a Relax value of **1**, and Iterations of **9**. Experiment to what you think looks best. If the body is poking through, adjust the splines on the edit patch or the body. See the max file 09_26frock_done.max. Figure 9.33 shows the result.

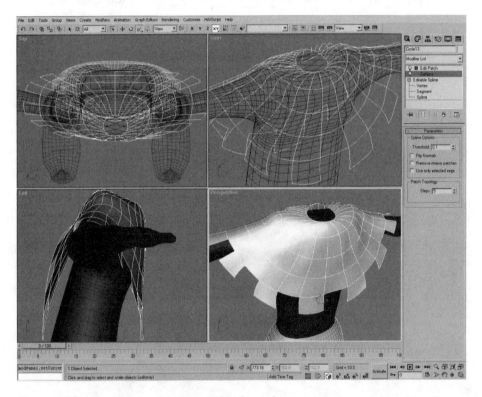

Figure 9.33   The completed frock model is shown here.

Congratulations! You're more than halfway there! Next you move on to the head.

Exercise 9.13   Creating the Head

The head is the area of the model that should get the most attention, because it is the main object used to communicate the character's feelings.

1. Unhide the reference planes and switch to the Right view.

2. Draw a spline from the base of the neck counter clockwise around to the nose. Start the next spline at the bottom lip and back to the base of the neck.

You're outlining the major curves and, as before, you'll fill in the detail where you need it. You could add a mouth cavity now, but it's simple to add it later. See the max file 09_27head_splines_begin.max. Figure 9.34 shows the result.

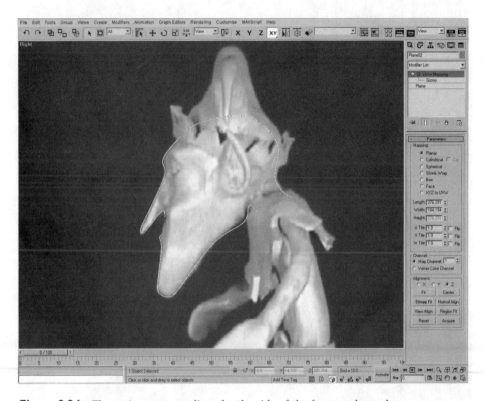

Figure 9.34   The main contour splines for the side of the face are shown here.

3. In the Front view, draw the main outline of the right side of his face, draw in the main mouth and eye outlines, an eyebrow line, and a nose hole. (See Figure 9.35.)

4. In the Right view, create a line (in Sub-Object Vert mode, using Refine as you have done in previous exercises) down the center jawline of the head, through where the ear will be. Make sure to have six verts between the two endpoints. You can choose to draw them in first, or preferably use Refine to add them later. (See Figure 9.36.)

Figure 9.35   The main contour splines for the front of the face are shown here.

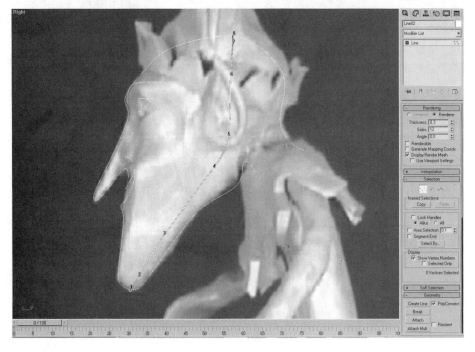

Figure 9.36   Here is the correct placement of vertices for the jaw line.

5. Turn on 3D Snapping for Vertices, and in Sub-Object Vert mode, use Create Line again to draw a line that resembles the outer edge of the lips in the Front view. Snap to the vert on the upper lip, closest to the nose, and add five verts between the start and end of the line. Finish by snapping to the third vert that's below the curve on the lower lip.

6. Compare the number and placement of your points to the one in Figure 9.37. Notice how there are more verts around high-detail areas?

7. Begin to move the verts of the eye and mouth back on the X-axis to match this view.

8. Scale down two copies of the mouth to create the lips.

9. Refine to add verts to the lip profile in the Right view so you can snap-move the lip detail from the Front view to the profile. See the max file 09_28head_splines1.max. Figure 9.37 also shows the result.

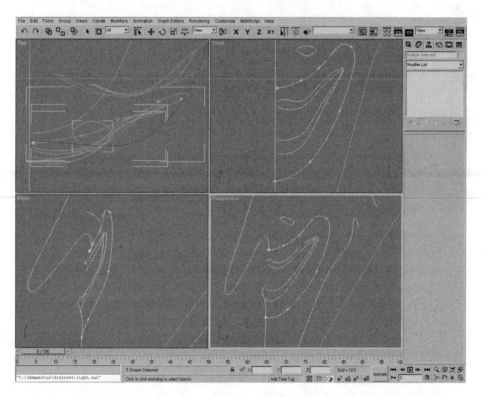

Figure 9.37   Add detail to the lips and add outlines before snapping the vertices together.

10. Make sure you have three opposing verts on the nose from the tip to the lip area.

11. Connect three lines, as seen in Figure 9.38. Divide the segments and pull the refined vert out in X.

12. For the nostril, scale down a copy of the circle you drew for the nostril hole in Step 3, and move it back in Z and Y, for a nostril cavity. Make another copy, scale it up, and move it forward slightly in Z and Y for the outer edge of the nostril. (See Figure 9.38.)

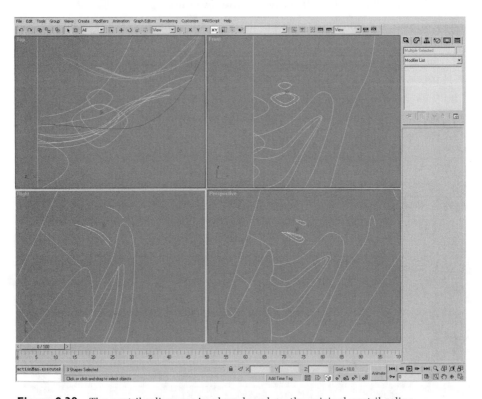

Figure 9.38   The nostril splines are in place, based on the original nostril spline.

Now that you have the rough outlines to the major parts of the head, it's time to add more detail.

Exercise 9.14   Adding Detail to the Face

Start with the eyes.

1. Scale up a copy of the eye spline and adjust its verts to match the outer portion of the eye, in the Front view.

2. Repeat, but scale down slightly to create splines for eyelids.

You're defining boundaries for geometry so skin doesn't move past that point, containing the deformations. Figure 9.39 shows the result.

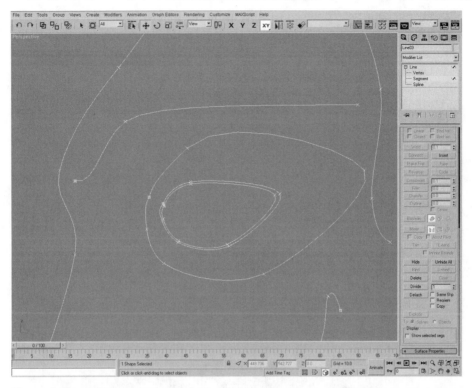

Figure 9.39   Add detail in the eye socket with copies of the original splines.

3. Attach all the splines to the main profile spline, and tweak any remaining verts to match the reference images. Keep orbiting around the head to get a sense of the volume, and tweak. See the max file 09_29head_splines2.max.

   Now move on to the interior of the face.

4. Draw-snap a line from the lower-right vert of the inner eye, connecting to the two other eye splines. Continue down the face, adding three verts in a curvature similar to the mouth, and connect to the vert between the lips and the chin.

   Now start connecting the interior face splines. It's a good idea to keep the radial area of the mouth going as the splines spread out across the face. This represents the muscle groups around the mouth and makes realistic facial animation easier.

5. Use Refine/Connect, in Sub-Object Vert mode, to add a line from the top vert of the outer mouth to the back of the head, refining the two splines between as you go. Draw-snap a new line from the outer mouth spline to the inner, at that same top vert you started with.

6. Do the same with the next three verts on the mouth, going toward the chin. See the max file 09_30head_splines3.max. Figure 9.40 also shows the result.

7. If you don't get curved lines automatically, select those splines and go to the Quad menu to select Curve.

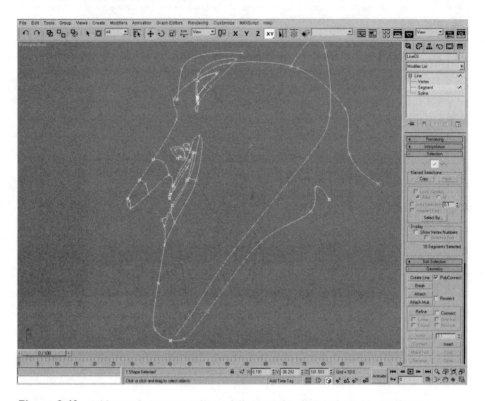

Figure 9.40   Add mouth contour splines, following the shape of major muscles in the face.

8. Connect and snap two lines from the top half of the lips to the outer, inner, and cavity of the nose splines, as seen in Figure 9.41. Make curves as necessary.

9. Refine and Connect a spline from the tip of the nose (actually, from the curve connecting the upper and lower nose splines) up to the nostril cavity.

10. Draw-snap a line from the top vert of the nose cavity, through the inner and outer nostril to the eye splines. (See Figure 9.41.)

11. Connect the brow to the front and side profile splines.

12. Refine and Connect two lines from the left verts on the eye (when looking at it in the Front view) to the nose bridge. You can connect the top line to the same vert as the eyebrow line.

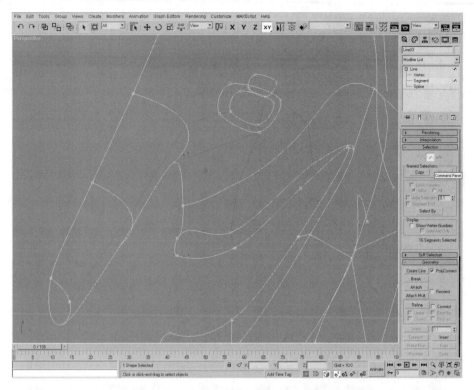

Figure 9.41   The splines connecting the lips and nose to the nostril are necessary to create a continuous surface.

13. Refine and Connect the rest of the eye to the eyebrow line, and to the front profile line.

14. Refine and Connect three lines—one from the outer nostril back to the front profile, one from the nose ridge (halfway between the eye and nose) around under the eye to the eyebrow, and a small one from the outer nostril to the nose ridge. See the max file 09_31head_splines4.max and Figure 9.42.

15. Refine and Connect two lines—one for the side of the nose and one for the smile crease—which help define the cheek area between the nose and lips. Figure 9.43 shows the result.

16. Refine and Connect a line on the side profile, from the top of the head (halfway between the eye and top of the head) to the center jawline. Then connect it to the front profile line near the base of the neck.

17. Refine and Connect from the right corner of the outer eye through the eyebrow to the line you just drew, and snap to the vert at the top of the head. See the max file 09_32head_splines5.max.

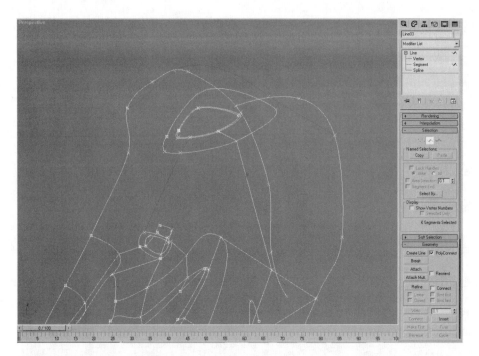

Figure 9.42   Connect splines from the nostril to the eye, and the main eyebrow spline.

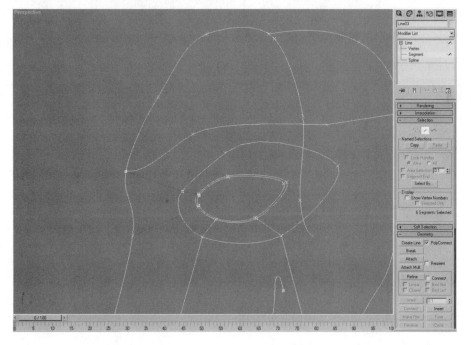

Figure 9.43   Create quad connections of splines near the eye so you'll have a legal surface later in the exercise.

18. Connect a line from the jaw area vert to the point on the side profile near the base of the neck (the bottom line as viewed from the side) and back up to the vert on the top line of the profile, just above the base of the neck.

19. Connect the neck hole with a line.

20. Refine and Connect a line from where the eyebrow meets the jawline down to the neck.

21. Refine and Connect a line parallel to the jawline so there will be a quad area to attach the ear. See the max file 09_33head_splines6.max and Figures 9.44 and 9.45.

22. Now that you've connected all the dots, go back and change the segments to be a curve (using the Quad menu) and tweak the verts.

    The vertices are set at Smooth interpolation by default. You might want to keep some that way and change some to Bezier interpolation. It's up to you.

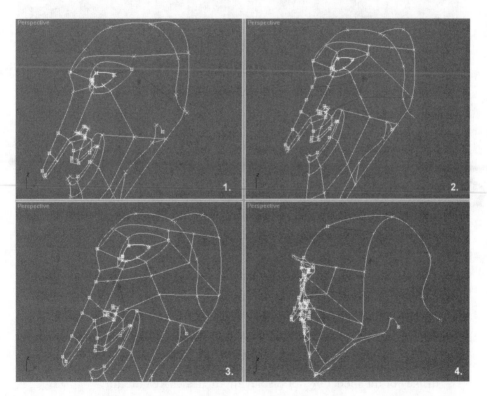

Figure 9.44   The spline connections form the top of the head and the neck, necessary for a legal surface.

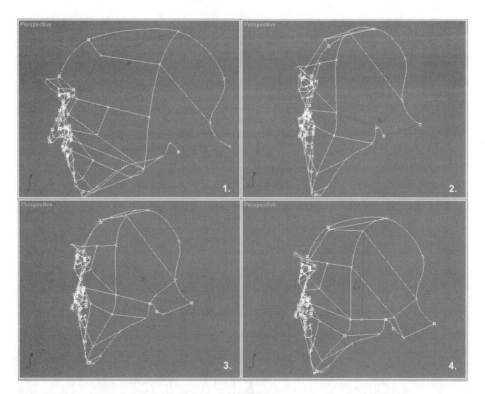

Figure 9.45   Next, create a place for the ear to connect.

 Tip

Remember to keep orbiting around to maintain your sense of space while editing verts. Use your XYZ constraints (hotkeys F6–F9) or just click an axis in the Viewport Axis gizmo and then move and rotate the vert or Bezier handle.

23. Throw a Surface modifier on the face to see your progress.

Remember, if you're snapping new lines on the spline cage, turn off the Surface modifier temporarily, because max will try to snap to verts on the surface.

You can put an edit patch on top of the Modifier Stack and turn off the Show Interior Edges option in the Geometry rollout. This simplifies the display of the model by not displaying the tessellated mesh.

You might have to create more lines if you missed some connections. If you see a quad area of splines, but no surface where you think there should be one, zoom in and make sure your verts are snapped together. If you find mis-snapped verts, select them and click the Fuse command, which moves them to the same location in space (averaging the distance between the verts). Don't worry, it doesn't weld them; you can still pull them apart.

You did most of the previous editing to minimize distortions in the surface and to define contours of the detail, while not adding any extraneous splines that would complicate the model. The next area of detail is the ears.

Exercise 9.15   Creating the Ears

Remember, you made that special quad section around where the ear would attach? You'll use that outline as a basis for the ear model.

1. Select those four segments where the ear will attach to the head, copy them (using Shift+move), and move them out from the head to start the ear.

2. Invert the selection (select pop-down menu Invert Selection) and choose Hide Selected in the Edit Spline panel. See the max file 09_34head_ear1.max.

3. Make three more copies of the segments, and begin to tweak the ear by moving and scaling the segments to form the outer edge and the inner ear. Compare your model to Figure 9.46.

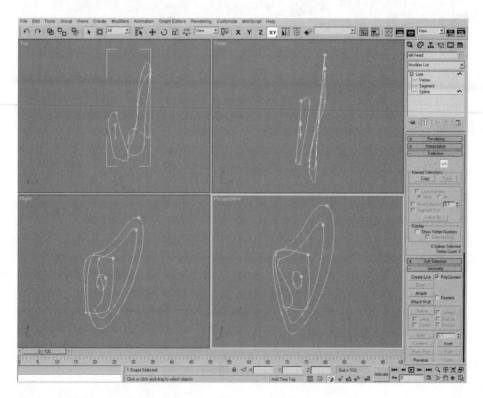

Figure 9.46   Here is the completed model of a 4-spline ear shape.

4. When you're satisfied with your edits, connect the verts from the first copied segments to the outer ear and then back to the inner ear.

5. Finalize the edits. To attach the ear to the head, click Unhide All from the Edit Spline panel, and delete the original segments that are still apart of the head.

   Now you have four open verts to connect the ear to.

6. Snap lines from the open verts to the ear and you're done! See the max file 09_35head_ear2.max and Figure 9.47.

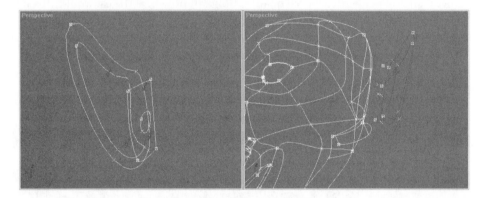

Figure 9.47   The ear is now cross-sectioned and ready for attachment.

One last addition is the inner mouth cavity.

7. From the Right view, create a spline (in edit spline) that defines the largest inside area of the mouth. Use at least five verts, but don't connect it to the lip verts yet.

8. From the Top view, center the new spline on 0,0,0 (which should line up with the edge of your head model). Copy the spline two times, in X, toward the cheeks. Scale the new splines down, and move and adjust them so they match up with the two other sets of verts on the lips, to the left of the centerline verts.

9. Move and snap the end verts to the corresponding verts on the inner lip spline, and weld the pairs of verts.

10. Connect the verts on the new splines, going from the inner corner of the smile, across the top, middle, and lower verts of the cavity splines.

11. Give the lines a natural curvature. See the max file 09_36mouth1.max and Figures 9.48 and 9.49.

   You probably still have a hole at the top of the head (visible if you've had the Surface modifier on). Let's correct that now.

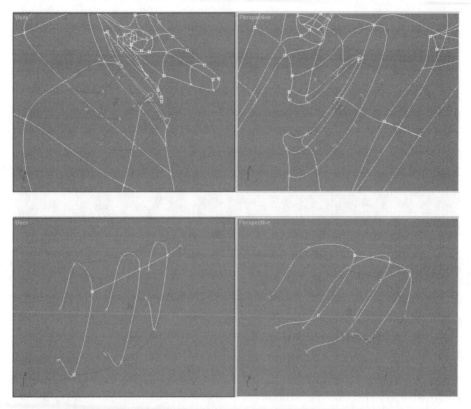

Figures 9.48 and 9.49   Create the mouth cavity splines and connect them to the lip
splines.

12. Create two lines as seen in Figure 9.50, using Connect/Bind Last in edit
spline.

 You have to unbind and re-bind it later, after you mirror the head and weld
the two halves together. (Remember the problem with binding and then
welding you had with the hands?)

13. Mirror the head (not in Sub-Object mode) and use the Instance Copy option.
Then tweak away and see the results on both sides.

 Sometimes I do this earlier in the process to make sure my proportions look
good. Because you always have the reference images available, that shouldn't
be a big deal.

Note

Sometimes working with verts in screen space is handy, as opposed to view, local, or
world, which are all locked. Screen space is essentially locked too, but orbiting enables
you to define that lock and move verts, splines, and so forth with ease.

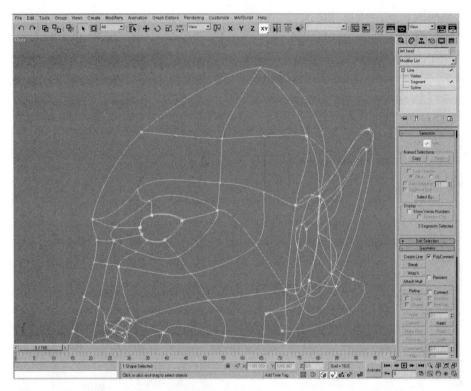

Figure 9.50   Connect missing details in the head to create quad patch areas, necessary for the Surface modifier.

14. When you've finished tweaking, make the instanced half unique by clicking the Make Unique button in the Modifier Stack controls. Attach that half to the original spline cage.

15. Delete one side profile spline that overlaps at 0,0,0.

16. Select the bound verts at the top of the head and unbind them, because you'll weld verts in the next step.

17. Window-select the center verts from the Front view and weld.

18. Now re-bind those verts you unbound just a minute ago. See Figure 9.51 and the max file 09_37final_head.max.

It takes time to make everything look just right. Don't rush that process, because it's just as important to be fast and comfortable with simple tools as it is with the complex ones.

Now that you have a head, it's time to cap it.

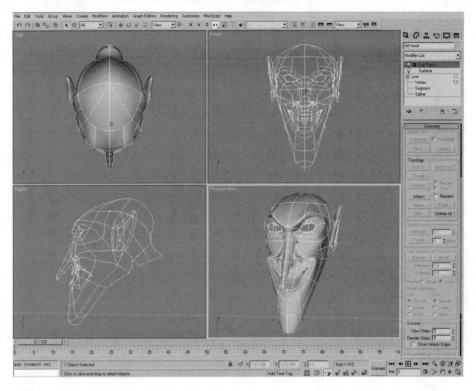

Figure 9.51   Here is the final model of the head.

Exercise 9.16   Creating the Hat

There's just a little more modeling left to do, and you'll start with the hat.

1. Unhide your reference planes and create a cone in the Top view that's close to the dimensions of the image. Give it **5** height segments, **1** cap segment, and **24** sides.

2. Convert it to a patch and select four evenly spaced edges.

3. Click Subdivide to add more detail. Select the resulting eight edges and subdivide again. See the max file 09_38hat1.max and Figure 9.52.

4. Bend the hat with either a Bend modifier, a Free Form Deformer (FFD) modifier, or simply by moving and rotating the verts. Convert to an editable patch.

5. Adjust the bottom of the hat to conform to his head, but stretching it up in the middle. See the max file 09_39hat2.max.

6. Select the underside four patches and delete them.

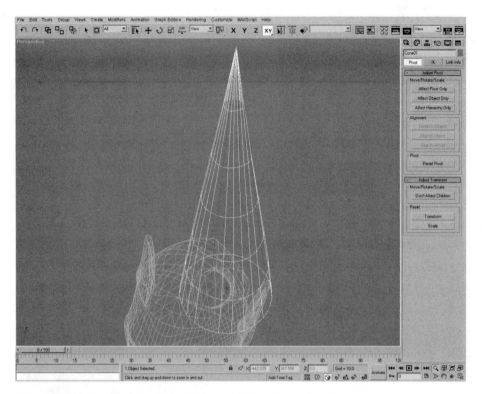

Figure 9.52   Here is the cone for the hat with the edges selected.

7. Mirror that half of the hat to the other side.

   You might have to change to coordinate systems to pick and choose the head before mirroring. That gives you a 0,0,0 reference for the Mirror tool.

8. Attach the two patches and weld the center verts.

9. In editable patch, select the edges between the two hat horns in the front and back and click Create Tri.

10. Weld the two verts of these new tri-patches, both in front and back, at the base of those tri-patches.

11. Adjust the verts to conform to the head. See the max file 09_40hat3.max and Figure 9.53.

    The hat probably doesn't appear very smooth, does it? Render it to see how bad it is. You can now assign smoothing groups to patches.

12. To fix this, select all the patches in the hat (in Sub-Object Patch mode); in the Surface Properties rollout, click Smoothing Group 1, by clicking the 1 button.

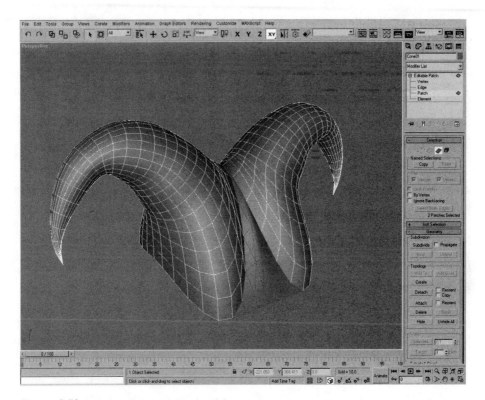

Figure 9.53 This is the rough hat model.

13. Create an Ngon spline in the Top viewport and position it where the base of the hat fringe will be. Make sure to use the Circular option and dial in **16** sides.

14. Convert to editable spline and duplicate and move up two times—one close to the first and the second a bit above the ears. (See Figure 9.54.)

15. Rotate the top copy by 11.25° in Z-axis.

    This introduces a twist in the model that you'll use soon to create the triangles for the crown. See the max file 09_41hat4.max.

16. Add a cross section and collapse it to an editable spline. Delete the top spline.

17. Hide everything else (use Ctrl+RMB and choose the Isolate tool) and manually create the lines to finish the crown effect. (See Figure 9.55.)

18. Select pairs of verts on the rim of the hat and weld.

19. Move the verts that form the tip of the crown back to shape it.

    Some randomness is good and helps enhance the realism of the model.

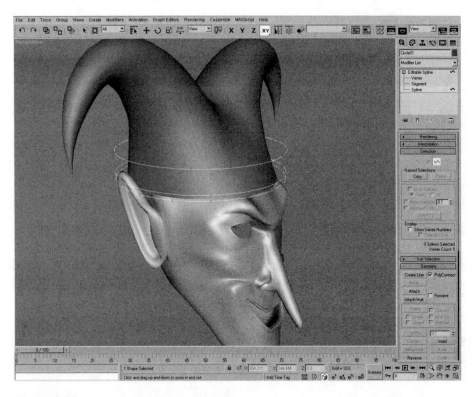

Figure 9.54   Create splines for the hat fringe.

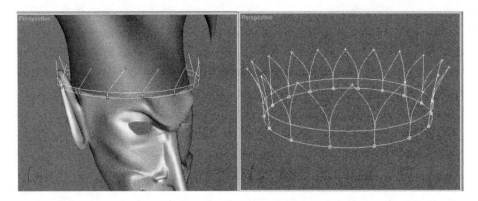

Figure 9.55   Here is the hat fringe, as created in Steps 15 and 17.

20. Apply the Surface modifier.

21. Drag a two-sided material to the hat fringe, to make seeing what you're doing easier. Adjust the verts to match the hat horns at their base. See the max files 09_42hat5.max and 09_43hat6.max and Figure 9.56.

Figure 9.56   The completed model of the hat and fringe is shown here.

Exercise 9.17   Finishing Up with the Belt, Teeth, and Eyes

With the hat done, you move ahead to the final details of the Jester's wardrobe.

1. Create a tube primitive in the Top view to fit around the waist of the Jester. Move it into position and adjust the radii to fit tightly.

2. Convert to an editable patch and adjust the verts as needed.

3. For the buckle, create a torus in the Front view. Give it **4** segments, a **45°** rotation, and **8** sides, and align it to the belt. (You won't convert this to an editable patch, because it'll reshape itself into a donut torus shape.)

4. Create a box in the Front view, with **1** length, **6** width, and **3** height segments. See max file 09_44belt1.max.

5. Convert to an editable poly and under the Surface Properties rollout, turn on NURMS Subdivision, Smooth Result, and make the Display Iterations **2** and Smoothness **1**. (It's great having this built into editable poly, eh?)

6. Tweak the two inner verts on the left side of the belt flap to taper it and bend it down, or make it look however you want.

7. Add a Capsule extended primitive with **8** sides, **6** height segments, and Smooth on. Position it to be the tongue of the buckle (the part that pokes through the belt holes). Add a Bend modifier and shape it.

Now you start on the teeth.

8. Create a box in the Front view with **11** width segments. Move it into place to be the lower teeth and adjust the size.

9. Use a Bend modifier on the X-axis, 180°, to shape the teeth.

10. Add an FFD box at 2×6×2 resolution and pull the box down in the middle to fill in the gaps and match the smile shape of the lips.

11. Repeat for the top teeth.

It helps to make the head transparent (press Alt+X) when positioning the teeth. (See Figure 9.57.)

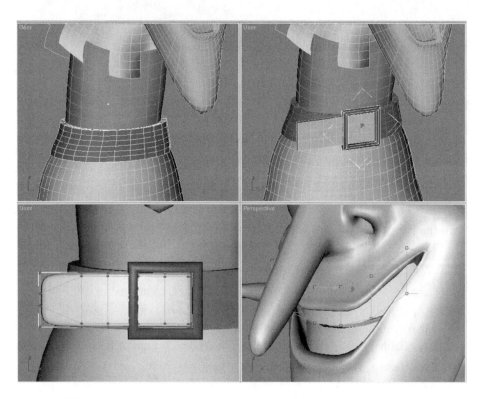

Figure 9.57   Here are the simplified belt and teeth modeling steps.

It's time to finish up with the eyes.

12. Make two spheres in the Front view, align them, and adjust their radii to fit the eye sockets. See the max file 09_45finished_model.max.

Whew! That was a lot of work! The final image is seen in Figure 9.58.

Figure 9.58   Here is the final Jester model in all its glory.

Summary

Congratulations. Building a complete character isn't for the timid 3D modeler. As you know, there are many ways to model. This chapter offers some insight into the details of Bezier patch modeling. The more you play with the tools, the more you become familiar with the workflow and idiosyncrasies that are involved.

If you want to do more tweaking, make a duplicate of the character, collapse the objects into editable patches, and tweak directly on the patch level. You lose control over the Bezier splines, but you also gain direct control of the patch surface, where you can do extrudes, bevels, and local subdivision (which most often requires binding subdivided patches to neighboring patches).

You've explored a lot of simple tools in this chapter: Editable Spline, Cross Section, and Surface. But you can see that beyond these tools, working with splines and patches is easy and flexible. In the next chapter you explore box modeling—polygonal modeling with Meshsmooth.

Chapter 10

Organic/Character Modeling Using the Box Method for Broadcast/Film

by Jerril Yoo

Chapter 9, "Organic/Character Modeling Using the Patch Method for Broadcast/ Film," focuses on modeling the Jester character using the patch modeling technique.

This chapter focuses on modeling the same character by using the box-modeling technique. In this chapter you learn the following:

- The advantages of box modeling
- Box-modeling techniques
- Using extrusion and negative extrusion techniques
- Lofting with geometry editing afterward
- Welding vertices
- Using objects other than the box for box modeling

The Advantages of Box Modeling

Box modeling is a polygonal modeling technique that uses a low-resolution model referenced to a higher-resolution model that can be interactively edited in real time. Traditionally, Non-Uniform Rational B-Spline (NURBS) was the preferred modeling method for high-resolution models because their resolution could be increased or decreased depending on what mesh resolution was needed. NURBS is a parametric surface. Box modeling enables the user to increase the resolution of a polygonal object.

The box-modeling technique, which has been available since Max 2.0, offers several advantages over other modeling techniques. Before box modeling was available, high-resolution polygonal modeling was extremely laborious and changes were neither quick nor easy to do. Making morph targets for facial animation was also very time-consuming. Box modeling enables you to make such adjustments quickly.

Box modeling also offers other advantages. For instance, with the Surface Tools modeling technique, typically a Relax modifier must be applied to know what the model's smoothing properties are. To further complicate matters, if the Surface Tools modeler is unable to achieve the final result by curves only, and the Surface Tools modeler uses the Edit Mesh modifier and Meshsmooth modifiers after the patch surface is built, the model turns into a polygonal object. As a result, the purpose of that patch modeling (Surface Tools) parametric technique is wasted.

Polygonal modeling is like sculpting clay, which for me is a much more interactive and intuitive character modeling technique than other traditional computer graphics modeling techniques using NURBS or patched surfaces. The Surface Tools method seems to be more of the paper mâché technique, where you build a framework and see the result. The deciding factors in choosing a technique are comfort and preference. As an artist, you must decide which technique is more suited for you. You will find the box modeling approach intuitive and enjoyable.

The word *box* in the term *box modeling* is a bit misleading, because you can use this process with any geometric primitive, not exclusively with a box. The advantage of starting with a box, however, is that it is easier to make an object a quadratic-faced polygonal model (a model with four edges). Making the most of a model with quadratic faces improves the smoothing values of the mesh, and it makes it easier to edit points. When you have too many triangular faces, it can be difficult to control edge curvature. The way the edges are lined up in an orthogonal view affects the smoothing of the geometry as well.

When modeling characters, typically you start with a reference of some sort. This might be a model sheet or a maquette. A model sheet typically comprises several orthogonal views of the character, as well as Perspective views. A maquette makes the modeling easier and more precise because it gives the modeler an accurate three-dimensional reference to view from multiple angles.

Tip

Trying to maintain quadratic faces does not mean that you will use quadratic faces exclusively. Use triangular faces selectively, and whenever it might be more practical. You should try to limit triangular faces to where larger areas of the geometry meet and where it would be cumbersome to get them to maintain a quadratic face structure. It is easier to go from a quadratic face to a triangular face than the other way around.

In this chapter, you model a Jester using the box-modeling method. For reference, you start with snapshots of a preliminary model, and then you refine the model until it looks the way you want.

Exercise 10.1   Box Modeling the Jester

1. Create two planes in the Front and Side views. They should intersect each other near center at a 90-degree angle. Select the planes, go to the Modifier panel, and add a UV map to each plane. Map the appropriate bitmap file onto each plane, as seen in Figure 10.1.

   3ds max 4 has a new option box, Show Frozen in Gray, that can be helpful when you want the geometry to be nonselectable, yet want the texture maps to be seen in the viewport.

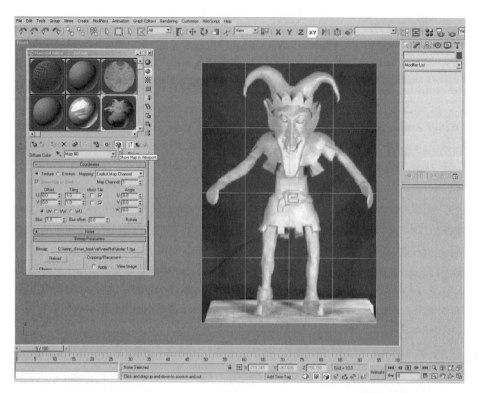

Figure 10.1   Each plane has a UV map and the appropriate bitmap file mapped onto it.

2. To access this feature, select the object—in this case the Plane—right-click it, and go into Properties. A Properties box will pop up. Uncheck the option Show Frozen in Gray, as seen in Figure 10.2. Make sure you have done this to both planes.

Now you're ready to begin modeling. You will start with generalities and then refine the mesh. Start with the body of the character and then move out to the face and hands, where there is more detail.

 Note

When box modeling, I prefer to start with rough shapes and then refine the detail. I recommend that you work in one orthogonal view (a Side view, for example) and then move to the Front orthogonal view (Left or Right) in the initial stages of geometry manipulation.

In this exercise, you start with the Jester's clothing, or frock. When creating this frock, or any item, the key is choosing the best-suited geometric object as a basis for the item being modeled. Remember, the box is only one of many primitive polygons (Standard or Extended primitives) that can be the basis of the box-modeling paradigm.

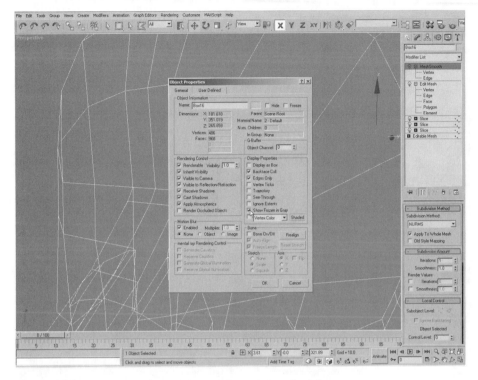

Figure 10.2   Here is the Show Frozen in Gray option check box.

3. Start with a geometric primitive. Go to the top menu bar and select Edit/Clone.

   You are prompted to choose a Clone option in the Object section of the window. You have three choices: clone as a Copy, as an Instance, or as a Reference.

4. Choose the option for cloning as a reference. This reference inherits the history of the original model's modifier. Select the new object and, in the Modifier panel, place a Meshsmooth modifier on it, as seen in Figure 10.3.

5. Reselect the original object and apply a wireframe material to its mesh through the Material Editor.

Note

Copying as a reference enables you to model a low-resolution polygonal model, on which you can see in real time the effects applied on the final-resolution geometry. You reference the model instead of applying a Meshsmooth at the end of the original model's history, because it is important to see how the final geometry is affected by the low-resolution geometry's editing, particularly when you start turning edge faces, cutting faces, and performing other tasks that affect the model's smoothness. When you are further along in the modeling process, you can delete the reference and apply Meshsmooth to the original model.

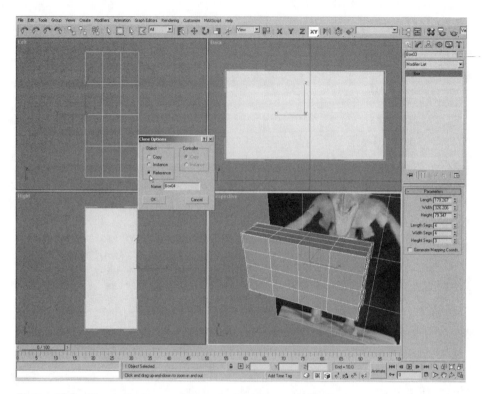

Figure 10.3   Here is the image plane and a box that you will clone as a reference.

For this exercise, you establish the frock by the front of the model.

6. Start by planning the number of pieces of the frock that extend past the main portion of the fabric, as seen in Figure 10.4.

I decided to use a box for this purpose because I felt it would be the best geometric primitive to start with. This was largely decided by the fact that I would need to establish the frock's difficult tasseled edge by working heavily in the Front and Side orthogonal views.

7. Select the faces you plan to extrude, and extrude them. You'll see that initially the extrusion amount is low. Extrude to almost the length you want, and extrude again a little bit. These small extrusion amounts act like a buffer and sharpen the edge's corners.

8. Bend the frock into shape from the orthogonal view.

Instead of just using the polygon's base levels—that is, vertex, edges, or faces—use other modifiers available at your disposal. For instance, I use Free Form Deformers (FFDs) quite a bit. FFDs enable you to make more global generalizations on the model. This is particularly powerful when in the Sub-Object level. (See Figure 10.5.)

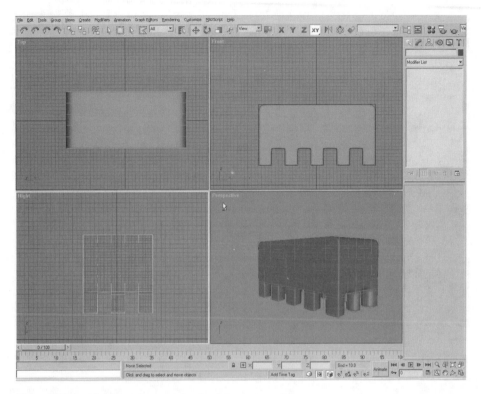

Figure 10.4   The base shape of the frock begins as a box.

Note

An *FFD* is a modifier that creates a lattice structure, which can make more global changes, and then pull in one or a few vertices at a time. It makes rapid changes to modify an existing mesh to have curves, or rounded surfaces. Remember, when working in the Modifier Stack, you can mix the modifiers and place them on the Sub-Object level and on the Object level. With this hybrid method, you can create quicker results in geometry changes than if you work in one mode at a time.

9. Round off the form. Then use the Slice modifier to slice the interior of the frock so that when the frock's extended pieces are modeled out, they will be more hard-edged and less smooth. (This helps overcome one of the disadvantages of the box-modeling technique—namely, that it can lead to overly smooth-looking corners.) Continue to round out the form and sculpt the rest of the frock, as seen in Figure 10.6. The Modifier Stack has been collapsed and more modifiers have been added.

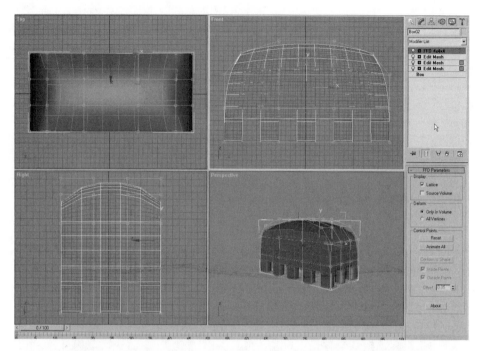

Figure 10.5   Create four FFD lattices: a 4×4×4, a 2×2×2, a 3×3×3, and a box; the box enables you to set the number of subdivisions in a lattice.

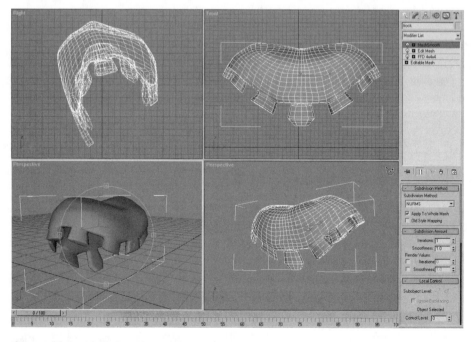

Figure 10.6   Work the shape of the frock to make a more organic-looking model.

Now you create the rest of his torso region.

10. Start by copying the frock at an earlier stage in its development. I would go back to the point where you have started to round out the corners of the frock.

11. Next, edit the model to create the torso. Extend the top of the model by collapsing the top faces and re-extruding them to create the waist and the upper part that goes under the frock. Do this by selecting the top faces and, under the Edit Mesh modifier in the Face Sub-Object level, clicking the Make Planar button under the Edit Geometry rollout.

12. Using a combination of edit mesh, FFDs, and whatever modifier you find useful, shape the torso region and add details, such as a slight indent for the spine. (See Figure 10.7.)

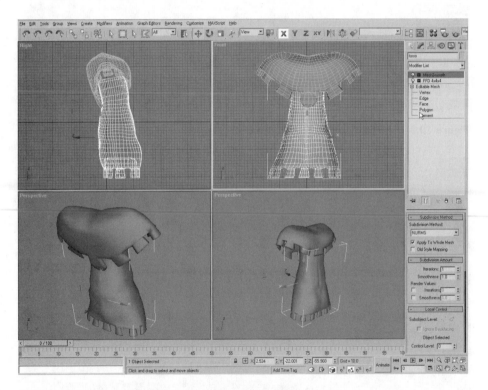

Figure 10.7   The torso region is shaped and detailed.

Now you're ready to make the buckle, and start using box modeling.

13. Begin by using a torus as your base object. Using the parametric spinners, reduce the model to a 4-sided cylinder and sharpen the corners of the buckle with carefully placed slices. (See Figures 10.8 and 10.9.)

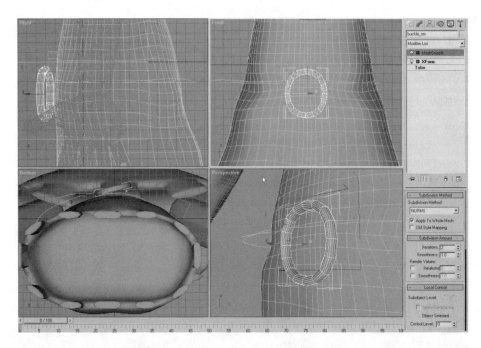

Figure 10.8   To start the initial object, use a torus object.

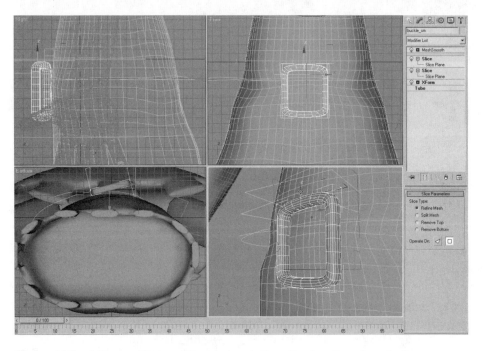

Figure 10.9   Add some Slice modifiers and push the refined vertices closer to the corners, which makes the corners a harsher angle.

14. To create the belt, create a circle with the Shape tool, found under the Create tab. This will be the cross-section of the belt. Use the Insert Vertex tool to modify the circle to a shape that more closely resembles the belt from a cross-section. Then use the Line tool to create a line that resembles the belted contour around the body. (See Figure 10.10.)

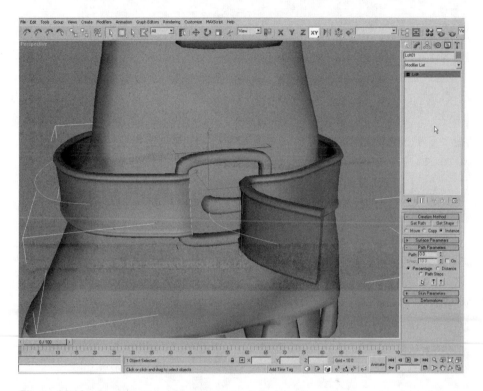

Figure 10.10 Start modifying here to get the belt shape.

15. Go to Create Compound Objects/Loft and loft the belt's cross-section shape. Then edit the points. With the Extrude tool, extrude the flat face at the end of the belt, and then scale it on a local axis so that the belt end tapers. Apply FFDs to curve the shape of the end of the belt. (See Figure 10.11.)

    You now move to modeling the shoes. The shoes will be made out of two separate objects. One piece will be the loose fabric around the ankle. The other will be the shoe around the foot.

16. Start with the loose fabric part. Create a cylinder and, with an edit mesh, push out a set of inner vertices to the edge of the mesh from the Profile view.

    This gives less of a smooth curve on the rim of the cylinder. Figure 10.12 shows the result.

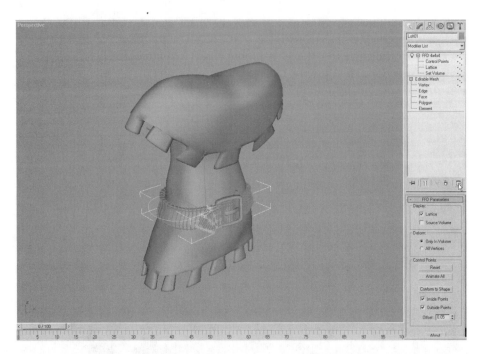

Figure 10.11   The tip of the belt is modified so that it shows the effect of gravity and feels more natural.

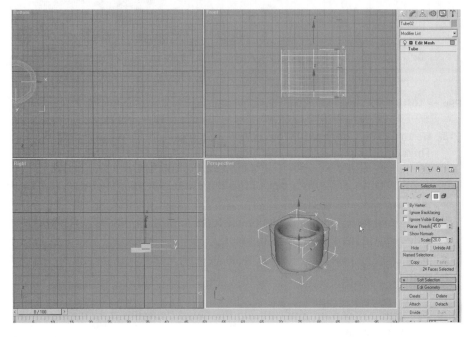

Figure 10.12   The closeness of edges affects the curve of the adjacent edge; you can use this to control the harshness of corners.

17. In the Vertex Sub-Object mode, edit the points and randomize the height of the vertices to create the feeling of cloth rather than a rigid object. Figure 10.13 shows the result.

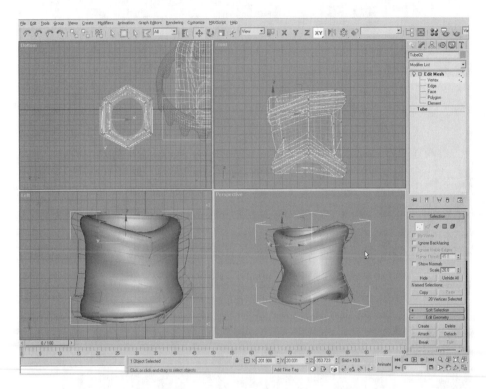

Figure 10.13   Randomize points to give a nice impression of cloth and an organic quality to the geometry.

You now move on to creating the foot.

18. Start by creating a low-resolution sphere. Use the box reference technique on it. Make sure the poles of the vertices are facing where the toes and heel would be (see Figure 10.14).

19. Apply an edit mesh, select the top pole of the vertices, and pull the vertices out to create the tips of the toes (see Figure 10.15).

20. Add a Slice modifier (found under More Modifiers in the Modify Tab panel) where the ball of the foot would be and another between the ball of the foot and the tip of the toe. Start editing the vertices with Scaling to taper the toe. (See Figure 10.16.)

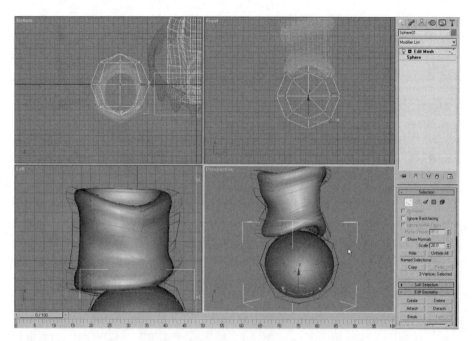

Figure 10.14   Place the sphere underneath the loose part of the shoe, and model with the object visible so you will know the object's relative scale.

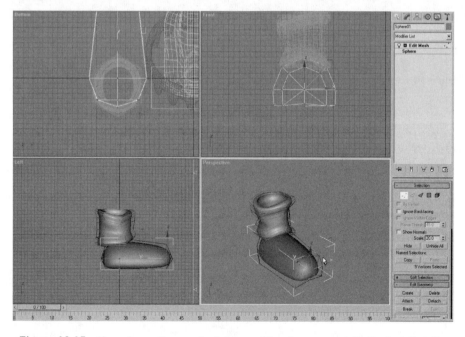

sFigure 10.15   If you know the eventual shape of the shoes, especially the fact that they will have pointy tips, you can make sure the poles are at the heel and tip of the toe.

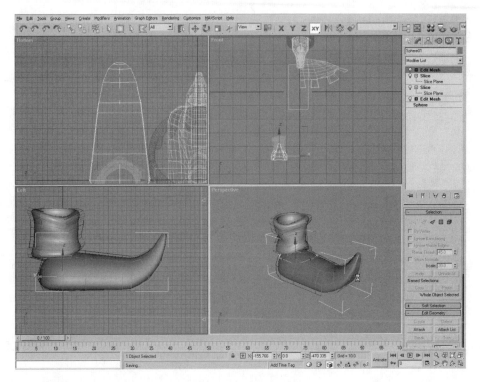

Figure 10.16   The Slice modifiers here add detail to the existing geometry and enable you to create details not possible with the original low-res reference.

 Warning

When using the Slice modifier, be careful that you slice faces and that the Slice plane does not cut too close to vertices. Otherwise, it might look as if there is only one vertex where the vertices actually have doubled up near the Slice plane. This doubling of vertices gives you rendering artifacts and makes your geometry source pinch and look weird.

21. Using the edit mesh, FFDs, and whatever modifiers you want, tweak the heel. Continue to refine the mesh and the shape of the foot by adding details, such as the curvature in the inside of the foot. (See Figure 10.17.)

Now you're ready to model the head. You start with a box and try to plan the number of divisions necessary in the head in all views. For example, you leave a vertical row of faces for eventually extruding the nose. This is important in the preliminary planning stage of the modeling. If this is done well, it saves many Slice modifiers and heavy mesh editing later.

22. Once again, start with a box, as seen in Figure 10.18.

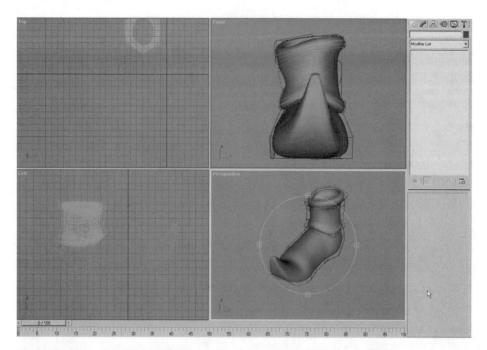

Figure 10.17   The final foot has come far from just being a sphere.

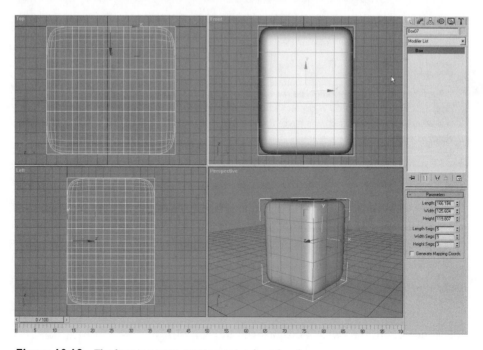

Figure 10.18   The box is a great starting point for a head.

23. Apply an edit mesh and edit the model in the Front view (see Figure 10.19). When roughly laid in, move to working in the Profile view. It is better to do the bulk of the work in one orthogonal view first and then move to the next. (See Figure 10.20.)

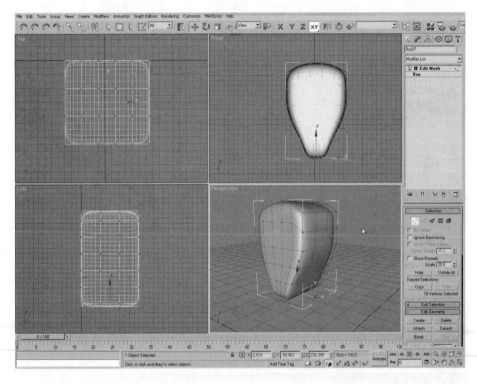

Figure 10.19   Start the model in the Front view, getting in the rough form.

24. Round out some of the head's form by working in the Perspective view and moving the corner vertices (see Figure 10.21). Then select two faces in the front-center row of faces on the side where the face of the character would be. Extrude to create the nose (see Figure 10.22). You can edit further to get closer to the shape you want.

25. Scale the faces to taper them. Repeat this step several more times and then modify the shape with an edit mesh.

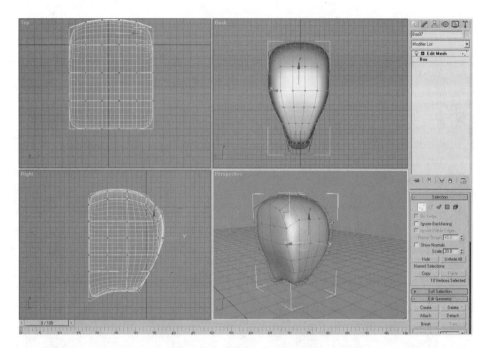

Figure 10.20   Switch to the Profile view and start to work in a different view.

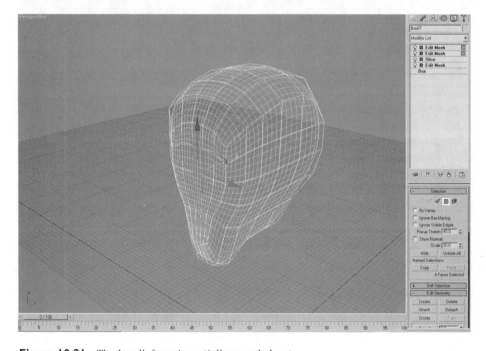

Figure 10.21   The head's form is partially rounded out.

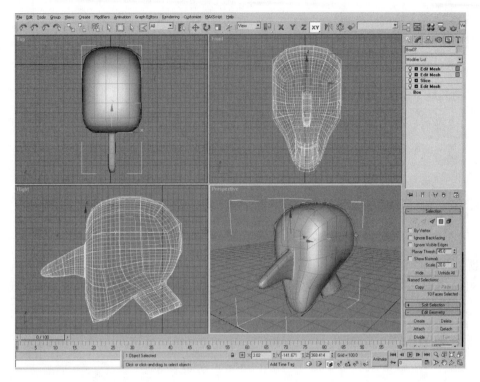

Figure 10.22   Extrude three faces to create the nose, and edit to follow a nose shape from the profile.

26. To create the nostrils, select two faces on both sides of the nose. Extrude the faces, scale them, and then modify their shape with an edit mesh so that they look like nostrils, as seen in Figure 10.23.

27. To create the chin, select the vertices around the chin area and pull them down and further away from the body. Use the Slice tool, in the Modifier panel, to refine the mesh and make it possible for more detail.

28. Follow Step 26 to create the lower and upper lips. Select some lip faces from the front and extrude them. (See Figure 10.24.)

29. Moving on to the mouth cavity, select the faces for the orifice of the mouth. This time, with an Edit Mesh modifier and in Face Sub-Object mode, use the Extrusion spinner to perform a negative extrude to make the mouth cavity. You can type the negative value into the extrusion value box, or you can hold the spinner's down arrow. Figure 10.25 shows the result.

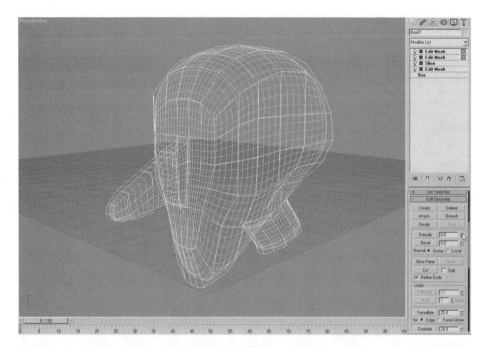

Figure 10.23   Select the faces (on both the left and right side of the character) and extrude them several times to create the nostrils of the nose.

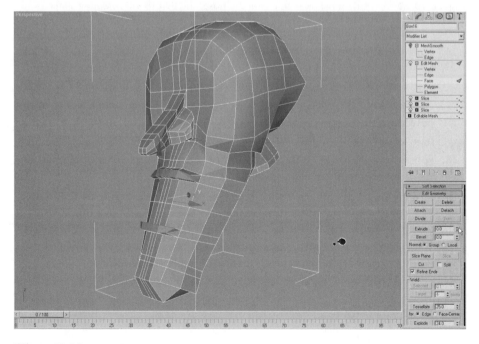

Figure 10.24   Add the lip detail.

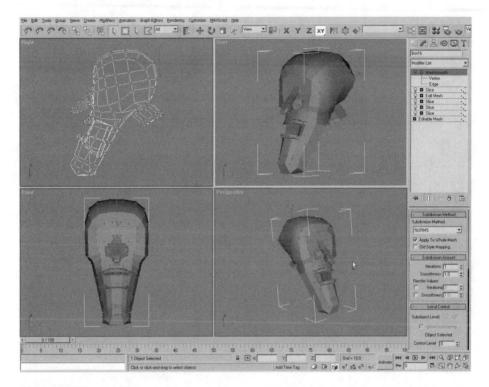

Figure 10.25   This is the head after doing a negative extrude for the mouth cavity.

30. You need to refine the level of detail with the head's geometry. To do this, change the visibility of the quadratic faces in certain areas to refine and create more areas of detail. The edges that you might make visible might reflect the curvature of a detail in the face or the curvature of the eye. Go into the Edge mode, select some of the hidden faces, and make selected edges visible. (See Figure 10.26.)

31. The Turn tool, found under the Edges Sub-Object menu, can be used to turn the edges. You use this tool by selecting the edge first and clicking the Turn button to reclick the selected edge. Do this on one side of the face.

 Note

The state of visibility of edges affects the smoothing properties of the mesh. Please note which edges are visible and invisible. You might also want to change the visibility of the mesh's edges to change the smoothing of the model. The smoothing is not only a viewport artifact, it also will appear in your final renders as a potentially funny-looking highlight.

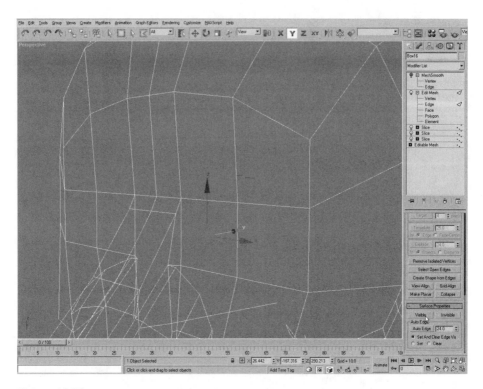

Figure 10.26   Make edges visible to define the curvature of the eyes.

32. Because you made the last changes on only one-half of the face, use the Slice Plane tool to put a slice plane straight down the middle of the face in the Front view. Select the vertices on the side of the faces you did not last modify and delete them.

You do this because later you will mirror the faces and weld the middle vertices to make the model symmetrical again.

33. On the edge level, use the Visibility tool and start to create edges that will define the curvature of the eye and other features of the face, as seen in Figure 10.27.

34. Using the Slice modifier, start adding detail in the brow region, as you did in the chin area (see Figure 10.28).

 Tip

If you have too many Slice modifiers, every so often max becomes less stable and you might crash the application. If you have more than two Slice modifiers, use the Collapse To feature. This is accessed by right-clicking the modifier that you want to collapse to and selecting the Collapse To option.

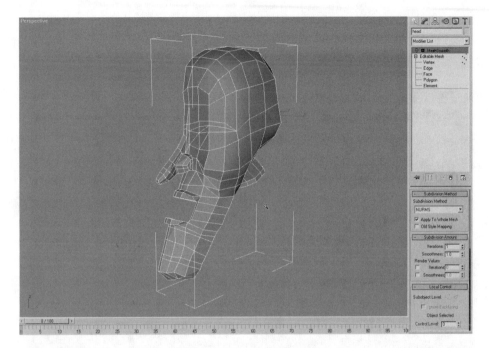

Figure 10.27 Work your way around to get the eye shape.

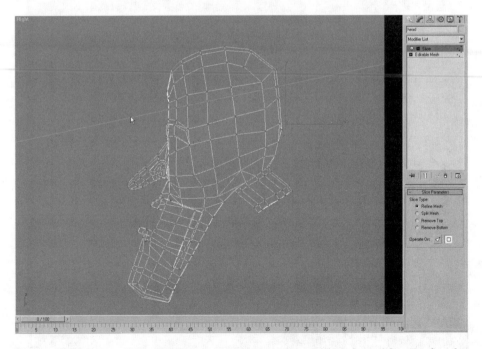

Figure 10.28 Use a Slice modifier in conjunction with an Edit Mesh modifier to refine the detail of the head and extend the height of the head.

35. When you have the detail you need, mirror the faces and, using the Weld spinner to the right of the Weld button, weld the vertices. (See Figures 10.29 and 10.30.)

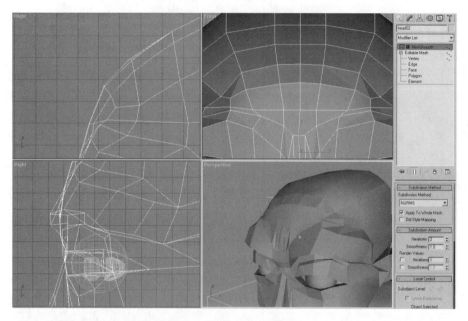

Figure 10.29   Add quite a bit of detail to the brow region.

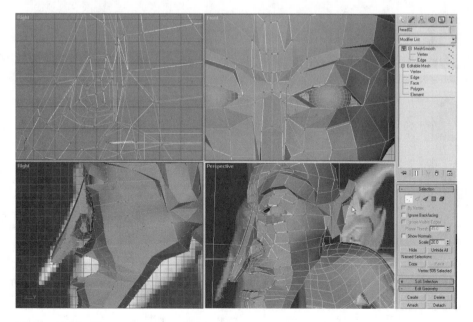

Figure 10.30   Here is some detail of the eye region.

36. Model the legs and arms in the same manner as you did the head. They are less complex because they don't have cavities where you have to apply negative extrusions. After doing the head it should be a breeze.

37. To model the Jester's hat, start with simple forms. Using the Cone primitive as a starting point, create the crown of the hat. I used a cone object with these settings (see Figure 10.31).

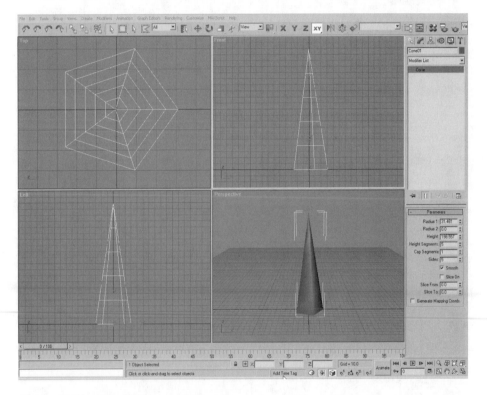

Figure 10.31   Create a low-resolution cone.

38. Use the Bend modifier, found under the Modifier tab, to apply a bend to the cone object, as seen in Figure 10.32.

39. Create a new sphere, with a step count of **10** (see Figure 10.33).

The resolution of the object is similar to the cone. You will use this object as the main cap part of the hat.

40. Adjust the size of the hat tip to the size of the sphere. Mirror the hat tip so that the hat is symmetrical (see Figure 10.34). Using the 3D Snap tool, snap the sphere's vertices to match the other part of the hat. Using the Edit Mesh tool in Vertex Sub-Object mode, adjust the bottom of the hat so that it looks less like a curve of a sphere and more like a bottom of a cap.

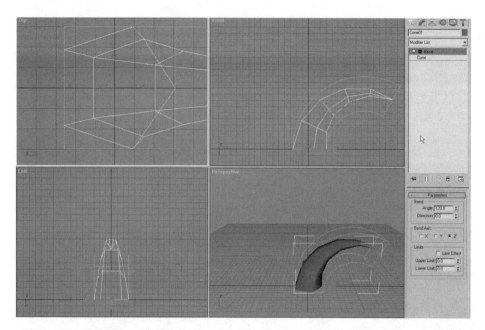

Figure 10.32   Apply a bend.

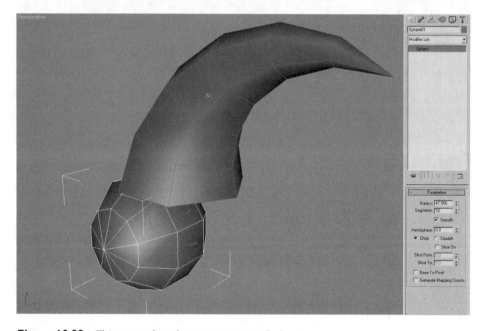

Figure 10.33   This new sphere has a step count of 10.

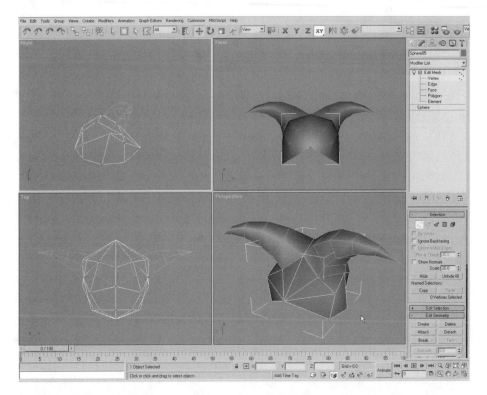

Figure 10.34   The hat tip is mirrored so that it looks symmetrical.

41. Select the faces that are now covered by the floppy parts of the hat and delete them. Attach all three objects and then weld them together (see Figure 10.35). Do this by selecting the vertices and clicking the Weld button in the Vertex Sub-Object mode of an edit mesh. Using welding techniques, attach the cone to the sphere object. Select the lower half of the sphere and delete it.

Now you create the Jester's hat trim. This will be another interesting challenge. You want a model that retains its modeling history so that you can make quick adjustments—such as trim thickness, width of tips, and so on—and update it in real time.

42. Start by creating a box with **38** segments and a circle shape the size of the head's diameter.

This number was determined because I calculated that up to 18 faces would be needed to extrude for the hat trim's tips. You will select every other face for the extrusion. The faces that are not selected become the bottom gaps between the tips of the hat's trim. The circle is the shape the box will be path-deformed to. (See Figure 10.36.)

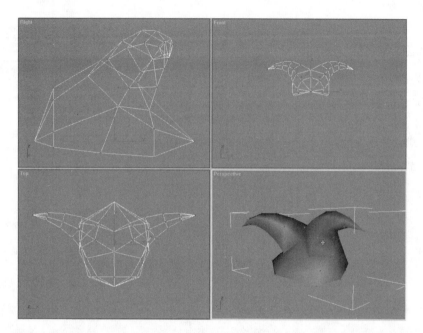

Figure 10.35   The bent cone's vertices have been snapped to the base of the hat so there is a direct connection between the base of the hat and the floppy part of the hat.

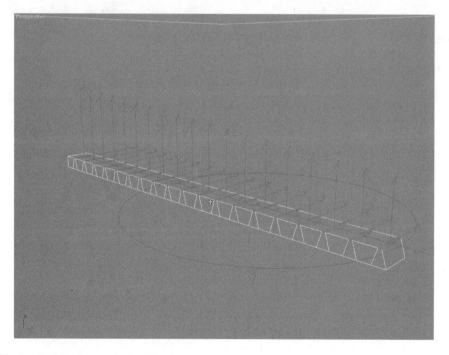

Figure 10.36   Create the length of the trim and set it up to extrude the tips.

Note

A Path Deform modifier modifies a piece of geometry to conform to a selected spline. In this case, the circle will be that spline because it is a simple shape that can be easily modified to fit the character's skull.

43. Using the Non-Uniform Scale tool, make sure the reference coordinate center is local and make sure that the transform coordinate center you are using is in Use Pivot Point Centers.

    This box is a rough estimate of the length around the head based on a Path Deform modifier. This also deforms the geometry into the base shape of the hat trim. (See Figure 10.37.)

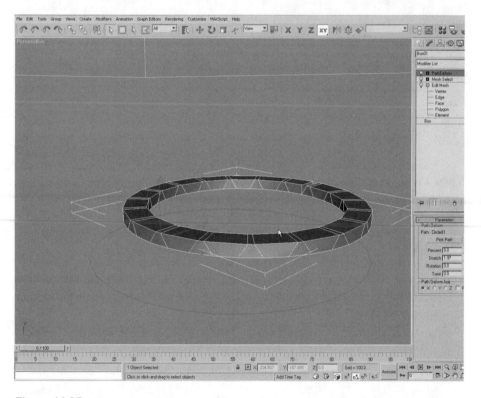

Figure 10.37   Place a Path Deform modifier on the box and use the circle as your shape.

    There still is a gap between the ends. You will connect them when you have a satisfactory shape.

44. Select every other face in the top faces of the box. These faces will be the tips of the crown. Extrude the selected faces, as seen in Figure 10.38.

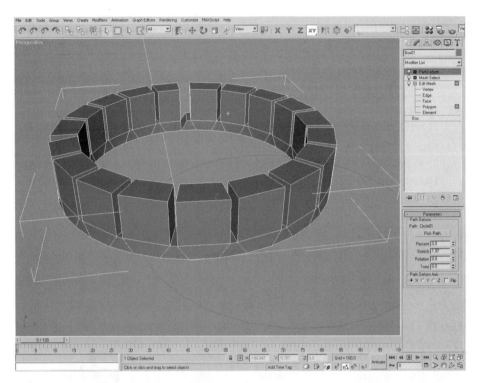

Figure 10.38   Here is the crown with the tip extrusions blocked in and not tapered.

45. Go to before the path deformer's modifier history in the Modifier Stack and add an edit mesh. Select the tips of the extruded faces and scale the local selected faces to create the sharp tips of the hat trim, as seen in Figure 10.39. You are constructing the hat's crown flat, and yet with the path deformer, you can see the object closer to the eventual form. Because you have modeling history, you can go to modifiers prior to the end result and edit and see changes interactively.

You can continue to add edit meshes, slices, and whatever modifiers before the path deformer. First you need to add a Meshsmooth.

46. Unhide the head and hat object and Xform the hat into place. Add an edit mesh and FFDs to shape the trim to the skull of the character, as seen in Figure 10.40.

A character's head typically is not a straight sphere, so you need to tailor the crown part of the hat so it fits tightly to his head.

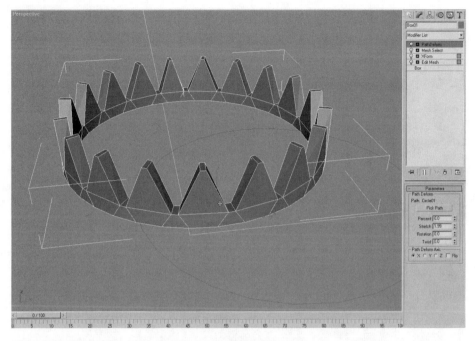

Figure 10.39   Here you see the effects of the modeling history.

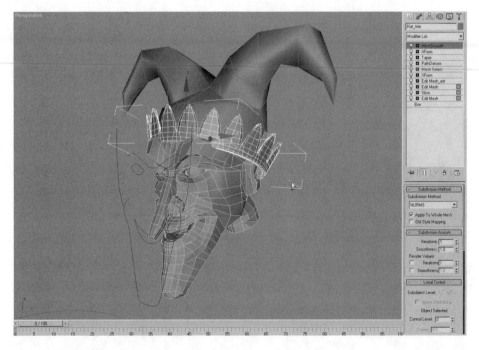

Figure 10.40   The crown portion of the hat is still a perfect circle.

47. Add an edit mesh and slices to start the curve of the cross section of the hat trim, as seen in Figures 10.41 and 10.42.

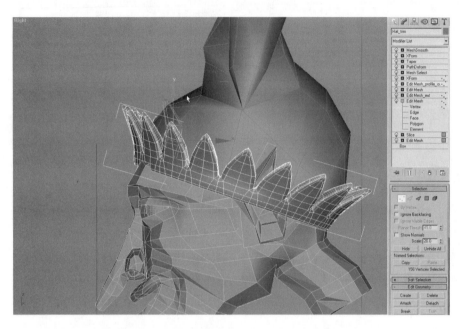

Figure 10.41   Add the Slice plane to the crown portion of the hat and tweak some of the vertices.

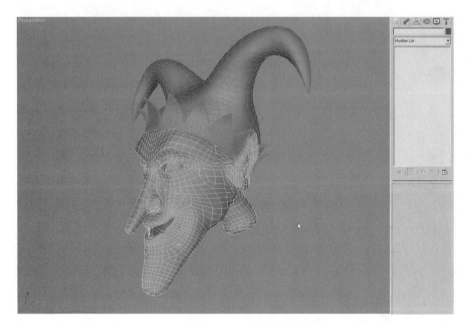

Figure 10.42   Here is the model Meshsmoothed and finished.

48. Adjust the length of the hat trim with some of the stretch settings in the Path Deform modifier or by applying an Xform modifier. If it is too long, delete the excess trim. Edit the stack until it's pleasing, and then weld the points to connect the hat trim.

Now that you have modeled the parts, the pieces might have to be adjusted to work harmoniously with the other objects. There will always be changes from the director, so these pieces were modeled in a manner to make it easier for adjustments to be made later in the production pipeline.

Summary

Planning, in box modeling and in other modeling techniques, saves you lots of time down the road. Planning the necessary subdivisions on the initial low-resolution mesh might take a bit of experimenting, depending on the model. Working separately on an individual model can decrease the time involved in the creation of the object; but do not forget about the totality of the model, and unhide or merge the rest of the model's parts to work with them in totality. You can also use a camera's clipping plane to help you model with efficiency. Whatever parts of the model extend beyond the clipping plane will not be seen or selected. This also holds true for the near clipping plane.

Chapter 11

Organic/Character Modeling for Games/Interactive Applications

by Mike O'Rourke

In this chapter you take on the task of modeling Pug, a slimy squid who rides on a set of mechanical legs, which you modeled in Chapter 8, "Non-Organic

Modeling for Games/Interactive Applications." This time, instead of using editable poly so much, you turn to spline and patch modeling.

Specifically, this chapter discusses the following:

- Creating and modifying splines
- The Cross Section modifier
- The Surface modifier
- Patch surface modeling techniques

Patch modeling has a lot of advantages, especially for games. First, you model with splines, which makes it easy to define certain shapes by simply adjusting a few points and Bezier handles. Second, the resulting surface is resolution-independent. From low resolution to high resolution, texture coordinates stay, and the mesh subdivides evenly. Finally, the tools at the Editable Patch level enable you to create and modify things quickly and easily.

You visit all these features using spline and patch modeling as you model the Pug, the final version of which is shown in Figure 11.1.

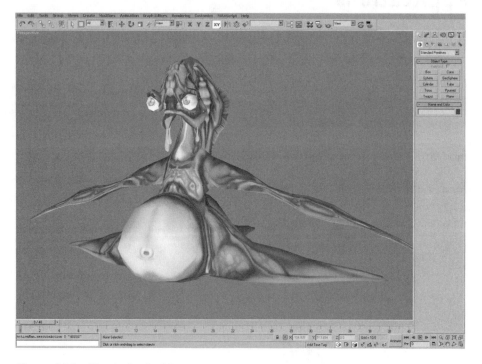

Figure 11.1   Here is the final Pug.

To start, you model his torso and back tail. Then you model all his limbs separately, including the eye sockets, tails, and arms. Finally, you attach all the limbs to the main body.

Exercise 11.1   Modeling the Torso and Back Tail

First, you model Pug's torso.

1. Create a circle in the Top viewport and make its radius about as thick as you want the neck to be. Figure 11.2 shows proportions of a previously made Pug.

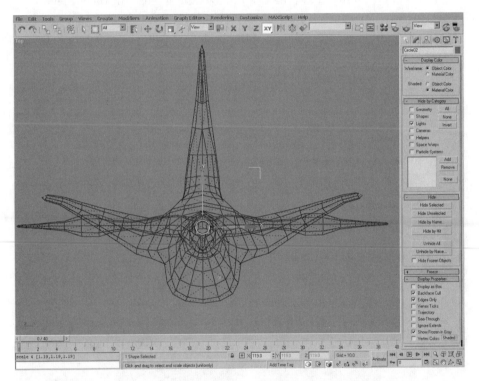

Figure 11.2   The first spline is shown here.

Next you copy this circle several times to make the main part of his body. Make sure you have your Move and Rotate hotkeys warmed up, or get nice and quick with the Quad menus.

2. Select the circle and collapse it to an editable spline by going into the Quad menu and selecting Convert/Convert to Editable Spline.

3. In Sub-Object Spline mode, select your circle (spline).

You moved to the Sub-Object Spline mode so that you can copy the spline several times and still keep it as one spline object.

This is especially handy when you use the Cross Section modifier. The Cross Section modifier looks at all the spline sub-objects within one spline object, and connects all of them, using the same numbered vertices as connection points. This means that you can copy a sub-object spline several times, and Cross Section will connect all the copies. It also means that you must be careful to copy the splines in the correct order; otherwise, the resulting splines and surface might double back on itself or give you strange results. The Cross Section modifier creates its splines based on the order the hull splines were created, or in the case of attaching splines, the order they were attached.

4. In the Right viewport, hold the Shift key down while you move the spline over a bit to make a copy. Now rotate it into place, as you want, or you can follow Figure 11.3 as a reference.

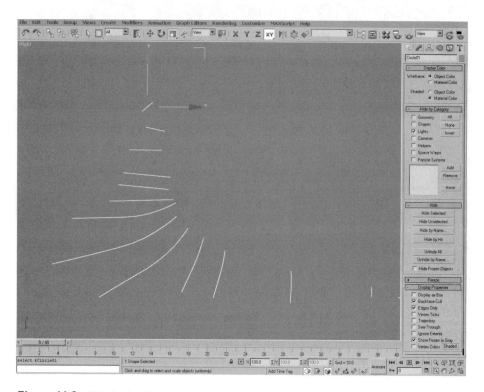

Figure 11.3   This is the Side view of the spline cage.

Note

You could have done this by just copying a regular spline over and over. If you do, however, a message box asks you to rename the spline every time you copy it, and you have to reattach them in order to get Cross Section to work. Doing it all in Sub-Object Spline mode avoids that.

5. In Sub-Object Vertex mode, move a few of the vertices that define his belly up a bit along the Z-axis.

   Follow Figure 11.1 if you like. This helps the geometry flow in a way that makes it look as if he has a huge stomach resting on something. This becomes more apparent later.

6. Apply a Cross Section modifier to the spline object.

7. Select Spline Options/Bezier in the Cross Section modifier.

8. Collapse the object by using either the Command panel, or by selecting Convert/Convert to Editable Spline in the Quad menu.

Note

Because you converted to an editable spline after changing the Cross Section type to Bezier, all your vertices in the resulting editable spline will be Bezier.

Now you have a spline cage ready to be surfaced. You can surface it now, even though you still have some spline adjustment to do.

9. Apply a Surface modifier to the spline object.

10. Check the Remove Interior Patches check box, and check Flip Normals if your surface's normals are flipped.

11. Now go back in the Modifier Stack and select the Editable Spline slot.

    This brings you back to the spline, before the Surface modifier.

    You don't see the surface anymore because you are at a place in the Modifier Stack that is before it. You can tell the Modifier Stack to show the result of all the modifier's effect, while still working on a modifier that is in the middle of the stack, by clicking the Show End Result button.

12. Click the Show End Result button. It is located at the bottom of the Stack View panel, and it looks like a little cylinder. Your model should now look something like Figure 11.4.

    You should see the surface even though you are at the Editable Spline level now.

13. In Sub-Object Vertex mode tweak the shape to your liking.

14. Select the three vertices that define the front of Pug's chest, as seen in Figure 11.5.

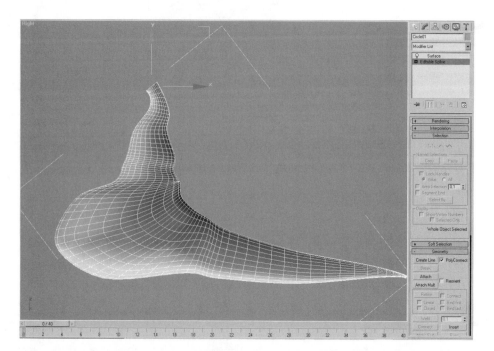

Figure 11.4   Your surfaced model should look something like this.

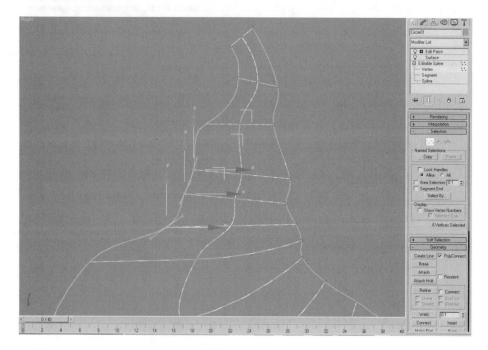

Figure 11.5   Adjust your points on the spline cage.

15. Right-click one of the selected vertices, and select Bezier Corner from the upper-left Quad menu.

This changes the vertex type from Bezier, with locked handles, to Bezier Corner, where you can move the handles independently of each other.

16. Adjust the handles to form a lumpy kind of chest. See Figure 11.6 as a reference.

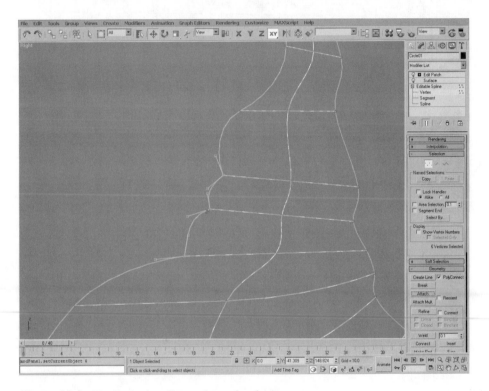

Figure 11.6   Use Bezier handles to shape the chest.

17. Move some of the middle vertices down to begin forming Pug's lumpy chest, as seen in Figure 11.7.

Now comes the part where you spend as much or as little time as you want tweaking the shape.

18. Adjust vertex types; make hard angles soft angles.

19. Rotate vertices to move Bezier handles around evenly. Scale vertices to balloon out areas, such as the stomach.

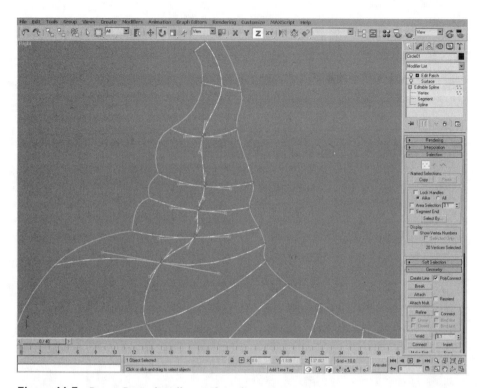

Figure 11.7   Rotate Bezier handles on the spline cage.

Figure 11.8 shows what you can do by playing around with it for a few minutes. For instance, you can put an Edit Patch modifier on the model at the top of the Modifier Stack and uncheck the Show Interior Edges check box at the bottom of the Command panel. This gives you a clean display of the surface lines, instead of showing all the faces that make it up.

 Note

At this point, you could keep the stack around so that you can go back and adjust the spline cage. When you put an edit patch on there and adjust something, however, you can't go back to earlier in the stack. This is a situation where you also might want to save the file where it is, and have that MAX file to come back to later if needed.

20. Convert the object to an editable patch by selecting Convert/Convert to Editable Patch in the Quad menu.

    It's a good idea to delete half of the model if you haven't already. There's no reason to do things twice, at least at this point.

21. In the Front viewport, in Sub-Object Patch mode, select half of the model and delete it, as seen in Figure 11.9. Figure 11.10 shows the result.

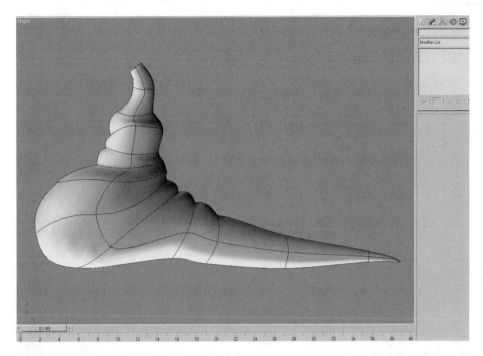

Figure 11.8   Here is the skinned model so far.

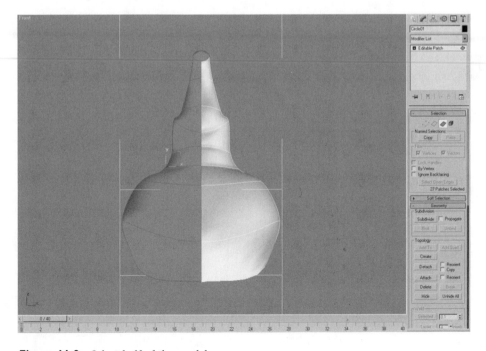

Figure 11.9   Select half of the model.

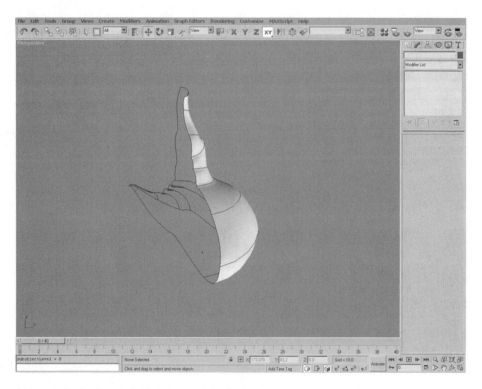

Figure 11.10   Here is half of the model selected.

Note

You will delete the patch caps at the beginning (neck) and end (tail) if you do a regular selection (refer to Figure 11.9). That is okay. You don't need these patches in the first place, and when you mirror the mesh, you end up with two of the same patch on top of each other.

Exercise 11.2   Building the Arm Tentacle

Now that you have the base of the body built, it's time to work on the arms. You first build the arm tentacle, and then you revisit the body as you attach the arm tentacle to it.

You build the arm in a similar manner to the body.

1.   Create a circle in the Right viewport. Make it as big or small as you like, but remember that you need to connect it to the body, and it helps to have the geometry line up. If you want to be sure, follow Figure 11.11.

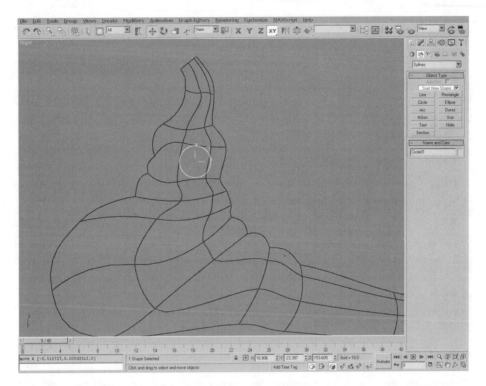

Figure 11.11   Here is the first spline for the arm.

Following the same steps you did for the body in Exercise 11.1, you copy a bunch of circles.

2. In the Perspective or Front view, collapse your circle to an editable spline.

3. In Sub-Object Spline mode, while holding down the Shift key, move and scale your copies into place. Figure 11.12 shows the copied splines.

4. Put a Cross Section modifier on the spline. Change to Bezier, under Spline options in the Command panel.

5. Collapse the spline to an editable spline.

6. In Sub-Object Vertex mode, select the two middle vertices on the underside of the tentacle. Move them up to form the underside of the tentacle, as seen in Figure 11.13.

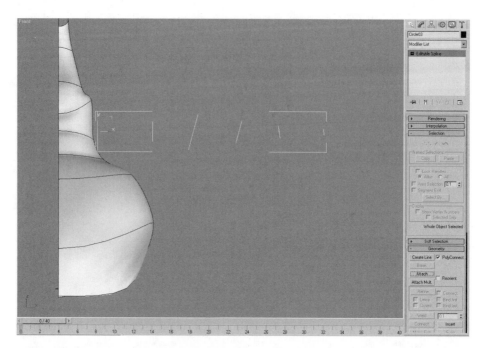

Figure 11.12   The arm splines are shown from the Front view.

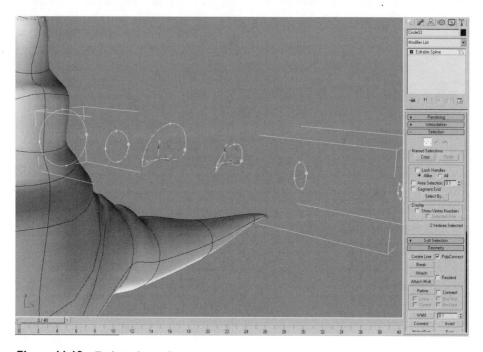

Figure 11.13   Tuck in the underarm vertices.

7. Put a Surface modifier on the spline, check Remove Interior Faces, and flip the normals if necessary, as seen in Figure 11.14.

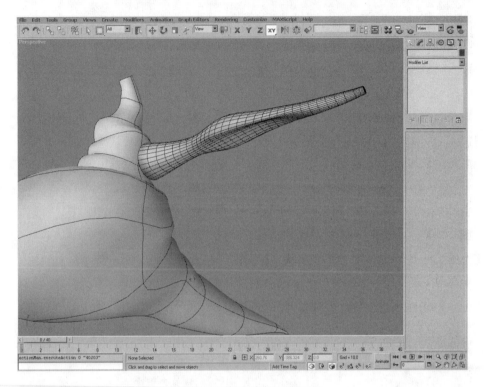

Figure 11.14   Put a Surface modifier on the spline.

8. In the Perspective viewport, look at the tentacle from the side, looking down on it. Select and rotate the four vertices that define the sides of the middle of the tentacle. See Figure 11.15 as a reference. In this case, the vertices were rotated about 30 degrees along the X-axis. This helps shape the edge of the tentacle.

   The previous image shows the flat tip at the end of the tentacle. That patch is perfectly flat because it was created with the last circle. There is no easy way to round out this end, because there are no Bezier handles right now for you to adjust that plane. But there is a way!

9. To round out the end of the tentacle, first select the patch at the end in Sub-Object Patch mode, as seen in Figure 11.16.

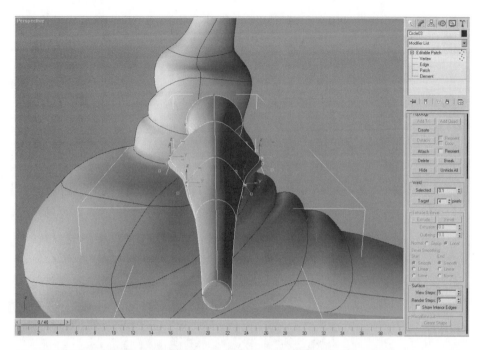

Figure 11.15   Rotate the edge vertices.

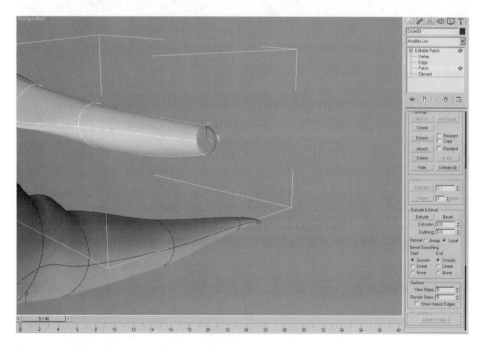

Figure 11.16   Here is the selected end patch.

10. Right-click the selected patch to bring up the Quad menu. In the upper-left Quad menu, select Manual Interior, as seen in Figure 11.17.

Although it looks as if nothing has changed at first, it actually has. The effect of Manual Interiors isn't seen until you're in Sub-Object Vertex mode.

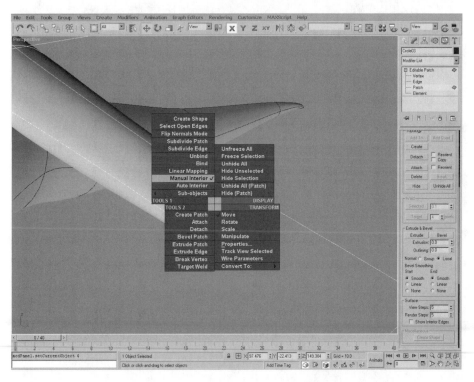

Figure 11.17   Adjust patches to Manual Interior.

11. In Sub-Object Vertex mode, observe the four vertices at the end. You now should see a tiny yellow box around each vertex. Those are the interior handles, as shown in Figure 11.18.

Note

The interior handles control how the surface is drawn between all that particular patch's vertices.

12. Move the interior handles away from the tentacle along the X-axis (away from the body) by clicking and holding them. They do not translate like normal vertices; you need to click and drag them into place. You'll see the flat patch get some curvature. Adjust to your liking. You can use Figure 11.19 as a reference.

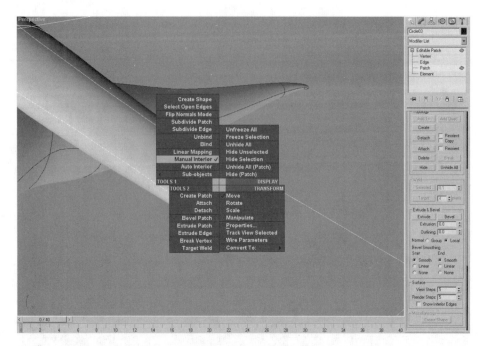

Figure 11.18   The manual interior handles (small yellow box) are shown here.

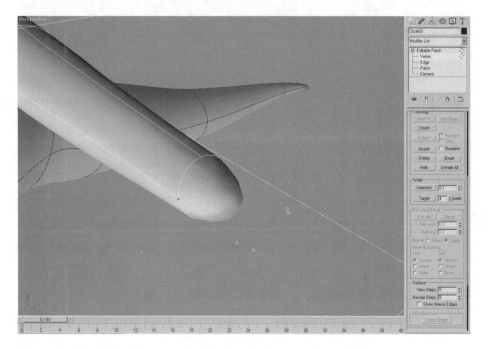

Figure 11.19   Adjust the manual interior handles.

Using Interior Handles

When you make an interior handle manual, the handles stay where they are, even when you are moving that patch's vertices. When you give a patch manual interior handles, be careful when you move it.

Because you make Pug for a real-time application, you will ultimately collapse him to a mesh, so it doesn't concern you now. The problem with manual interior handles not moving can definitely come up if you plan on animating the patch, however.

Remember this general rule of thumb (which definitely has exceptions): Don't use manual interior handles on a patch surface that you are planning to animate as a patch surface. The handles are an awesome modeling tool, but they get too squirrely when you move the surface around a lot.

Now it's time to connect the arm to the body, which is surprisingly easy with a few tricks. First you add some geometry to the body, and then you line up the geometry so that it welds nicely.

13. Select the edge, as shown in Figure 11.20.

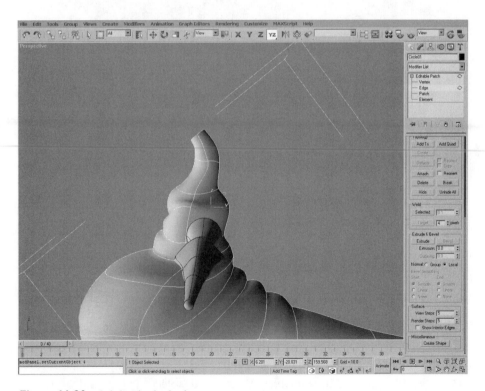

Figure 11.20   Subdivide the body.

14. Check the Propagate check box next to the Subdivide button in the Command panel, and then click the Subdivide button.

This divides those edges and all the ones that share the similar side edges. If you had clicked Subdivide with Propagate unchecked, it would have just divided that edge, leaving you with open edges.

Figure 11.21 shows the result.

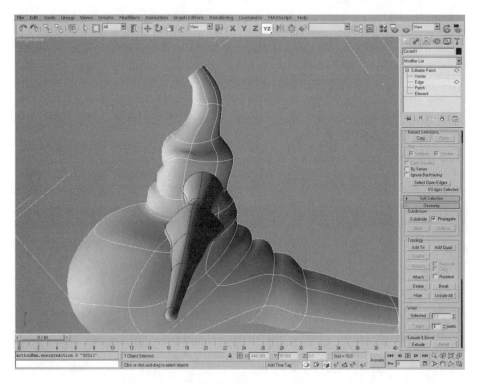

Figure 11.21   Set up the body surface to accept the welded arm.

Now you can see where to attach the tentacle to the body. Just line up the tentacle with the body and weld them.

One problem you have now is that the patch on the body that you will weld to is square, with two verts on top and two on bottom. The tentacle is round and has a vertex on the top, bottom, and both sides. (See Figure 11.22.)

It's actually not hard to deal with this. You rotate the vertices at the base of the tentacle with soft selection and then weld.

15. Select the arm, and in Sub-Object Vertex mode select the four end vertices closest to the body.

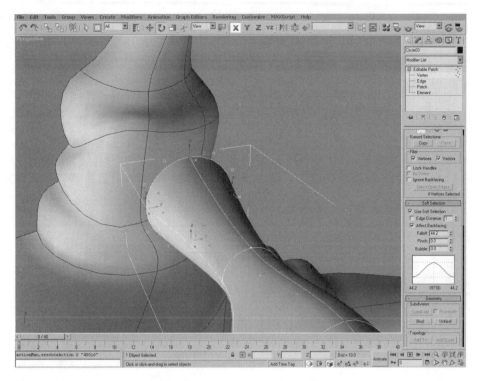

Figure 11.22   Rotate vertices to weld.

16. Turn on Soft Selection by first locating it in the Command panel and then adjusting the Amount spinner until the next row of vertices on the tentacle is yellow.

17. Change the Reference Coordinate System to Selection Center. It is the icon to the left of the X-axis icon on the toolbar. You do that so that you can rotate about the center of all the selected vertices.

18. Rotate the selection so that the vertices almost line up. Follow Figure 11.23 as a reference.

    Now that you have the vertices lined up, you need to delete the two patches that you'll weld. You don't want any patches on the inside of the model, so they need to be deleted now.

19. Select and delete the patch at the base of the tentacle closest to the body, and delete the patch on the body that is facing the tentacle.

 Note

If you just grabbed two vertices and welded them, the result would end in the middle of where each vertex was. In this case, you want the vertices on the body to conform to the arm. In other words, you want to retain the roundness of the arm and have the vertices on the body weld to the arm.

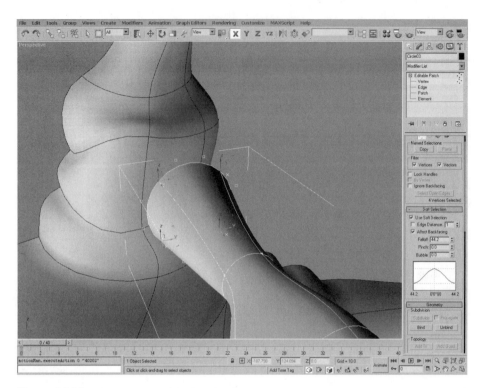

Figure 11.23   The vertices are in their final position.

To do any kind of welding with patch surfaces, you must attach them into one patch object.

20. Right-click one of the editable patches, select Attach in the Quad menu, and click the other patch to attach. Keep in mind that the order in which you attach things is important. When you attach an object to another object, the attached object gets the original object's pivot point and transformation matrix. In this case, it doesn't matter too much because you are attaching only one object, and it's easy enough to move the pivot point later.

To weld a vertex to another vertex's location, you must first select the patch that you want to weld to.

21. In Sub-Object Patch mode, select the four patches at the base of the tentacle, as seen in Figure 11.24.

22. In Sub-Object Vertex mode, select two vertices that you want to weld. Change your Weld Threshold in the Command panel to something really big, such as 200. Press Ctrl while you spin the slider to go faster. See Figure 11.25 for the result.

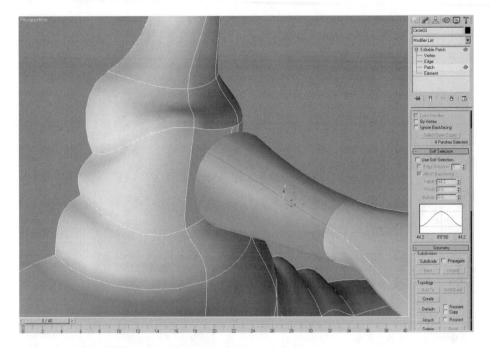

Figure 11.24   Select your patches for welding.

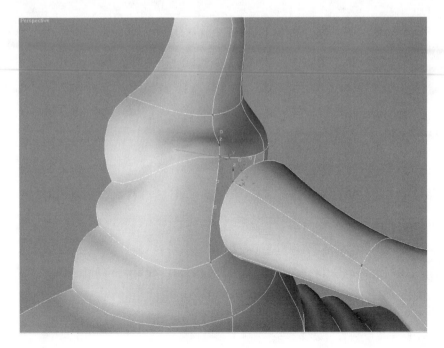

Figure 11.25   Select your vertices to weld.

23. Weld the vertices by clicking the Weld/Selected button in the Command panel, or by using the Quad menu.

Notice that the vertex from the patch you selected stayed in place, while the other vertex, from the body, welded to that vertex. See Figure 11.26 for the result.

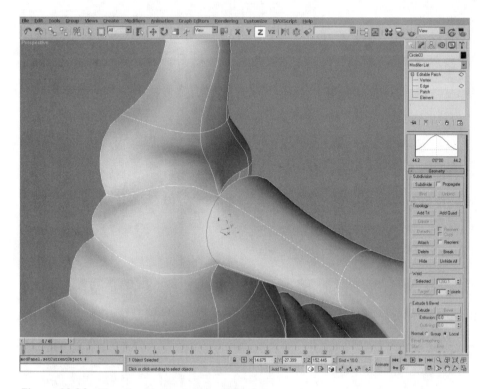

Figure 11.26   Here the two vertices are welded.

24. Weld the other three vertices to the tentacle.

25. Adjust some of the patch's Bezier handles in Sub-Object Vertex mode by moving and rotating them.

Exercise 11.3   Making the Leg Tentacle

Making the leg tentacle is exactly the same as making the arm, so let's move quickly.

1. Shape the patch that you'll attach the leg to by moving the vertices using the Move tool.

Keep in mind that by using the Move tool, the vertices will not all lie on one plane. In other words, it's not flat; but if it were, it'd be a lot easier to work on.

Figure 11.27 shows the result.

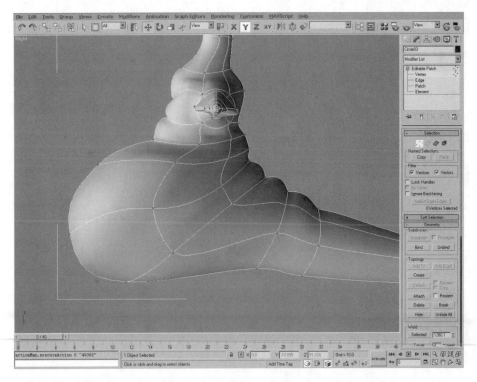

Figure 11.27   Move the vertices to shape the patch that you'll attach the leg to.

2. Make the patch flat by selecting it, and then scaling it non-uniformly along the X-axis, as seen in Figure 11.28.

   Non-Uniform Scaling along one axis is really useful for shaping patches. First you flatten it, and then you adjust the verts and handles appropriately without having to deal with all three axes at once.

3. Shape the patch so that it is round, as seen in Figure 11.29. Shaping is done by moving the vertices around a bit, and then moving the Bezier handles on those four vertices so that they create a circle. Delete the patch in the middle of those four vertices.

   You now have a nice hole in the side of your model that you can attach the leg to.

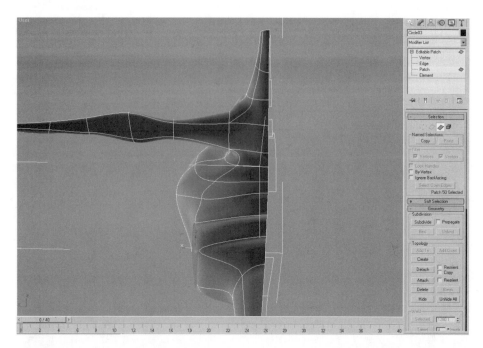

Figure 11.28   Flatten a patch for the leg.

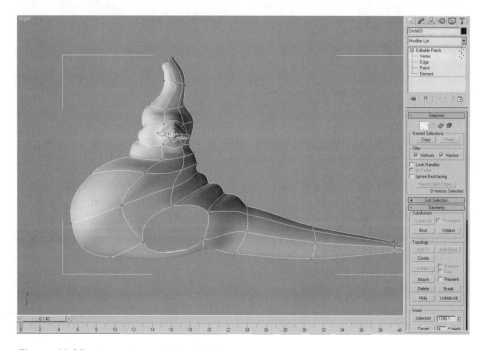

Figure 11.29   Set up the patch for the leg.

You're ready to create the leg. To do this, use the same techniques you used for the arm.

4. Create a circle spline, as seen in Figure 11.30.

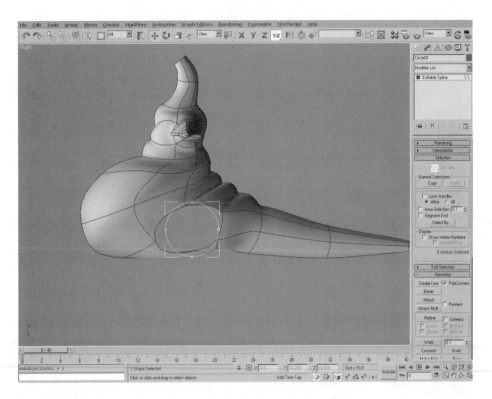

Figure 11.30   Create the first spline for the leg.

5. Collapse the spline.

6. Make copies of the spline to shape the leg, as seen in Figure 11.31.

7. Apply a Cross Section modifier to create the spline cage.

8. Apply a Surface modifier to create the surface.

9. Collapse to editable patch, and adjust Bezier handles and vertices, as seen in Figure 11.32.

Now you need to attach the leg. Again this is the same as the arm.

10. Attach the two surfaces.

11. Delete the patch on the end of the leg (closest to the body) and the patch on the body so that you don't end up with any interior patches.

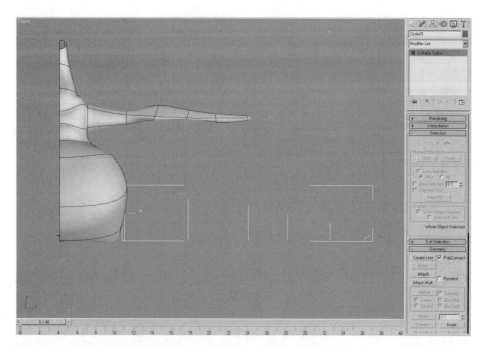

Figure 11.31   The Front view of the leg splines is shown here.

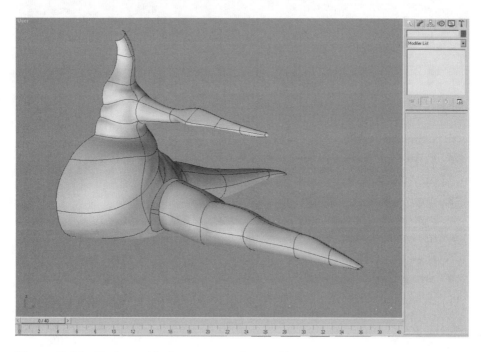

Figure 11.32   The leg and body are now ready to weld.

Note

If you can't weld two points, typically it's because these patches haven't been deleted. 3ds max won't let you weld points on a patch if it results in an interior patch.

12. Select the patches that you want to weld to in Sub-Object Patch mode, as seen in Figure 11.33.

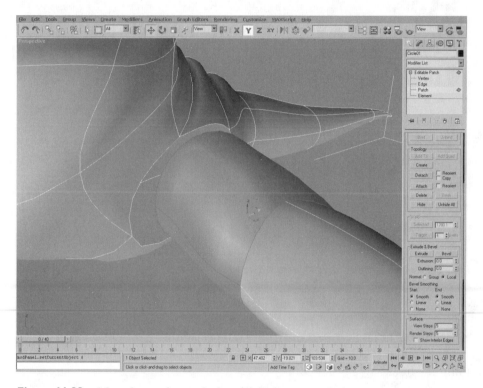

Figure 11.33   Select the patches at the base of the leg.

13. Select the vertices you want to weld, and weld them.

14. Adjust the resulting vertices and their Bezier handles to your liking. Use Figure 11.34 as a reference.

That about does it for the body. Spend as much time as you like adjusting the patch. Lots of great details, such as skin folds and lumps, can be added by rotating vertices, adjusting Bezier handles, and using many other standard techniques on the patch. When you are done with this half, mirror it, and weld all the vertices down the middle to make the other half.

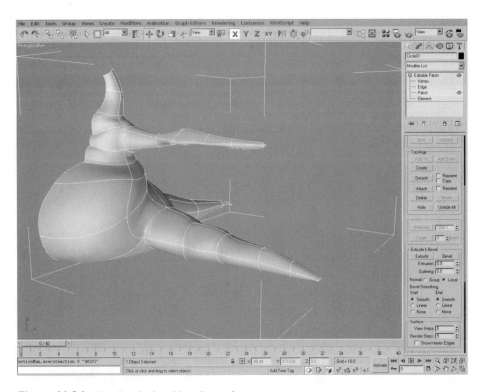

Figure 11.34   The finished weld is shown here.

Exercise 11.4   Modeling the Head

Modeling the head (as shown in Figure 11.35) is very similar to how you modeled the body and the tentacles. This time you use a loft and a few other techniques to finish the head.

1. Create a circle, collapse it, and make a bunch of copies within the spline object. Use Figure 11.36 as reference.

   Notice that the selected spline in Figure 11.36 is the first spline. When you put the Cross Section modifier on it, it gives you a tucked-in piece. Then the neck can go inside the head (see Figure 11.37).

   This is a real-time model destined to go to the Quake3Arena engine, so you must respect the factors involved in doing so. For Quake3Arena, the head needs to be a different object, so you must hide the seam somewhere. Learn more about exporting to the Quake3Arena engine in Chapter 6, "Workflow in the Games/Interactive Environment."

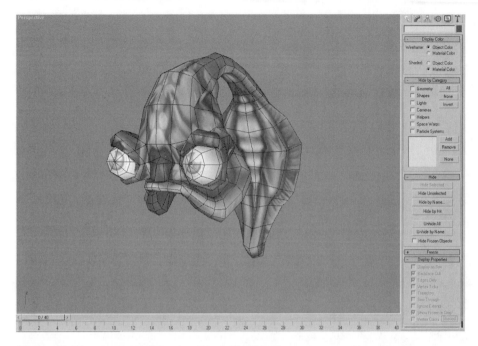

Figure 11.35 The finished head will look like this.

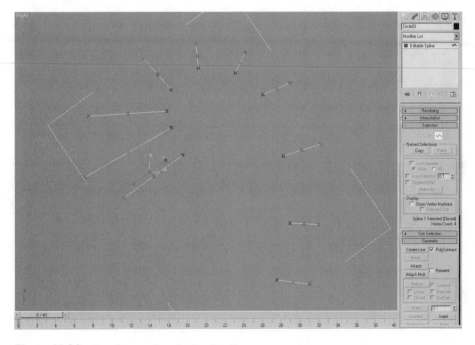

Figure 11.36 Start by creating the head splines.

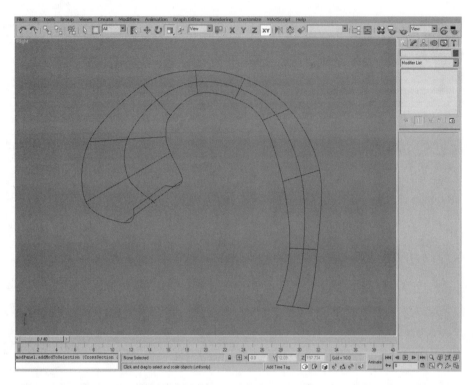

Figure 11.37   When you cross-section the head splines, the neck can go inside the head.

2. Apply a Cross Section modifier to the spline cage; adjust the spline type to Bezier.

3. Apply a Surface modifier to the spline cage. Check Remove Interior Faces and flip the normals if necessary.

4. Adjust the Bezier handles and vertices. Follow Figure 11.38 if you like.

 Tip

Convert to an editable patch. Change the last patch to Manual Interior just like the tentacle, to round out the end of the fin.

Change vertex type to Bezier Corner if you want to break the handles, or Smooth if you want an even surface. If you find that your surface is undesirably lumpy, try changing some of the vertices to Smooth.

Don't do things twice—delete half of the model. In this case, don't delete the patch that you changed to Manual Interior. It's easier to leave it there, finished. When you mirror the head, make sure you delete the extra "end cap."

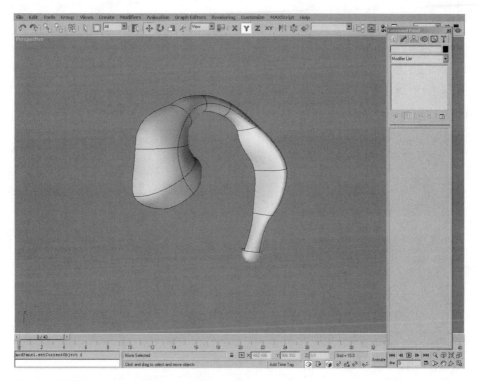

Figure 11.38   The surfaced head is shown here.

Now you will work on the lip. To do this you subdivide certain parts of the head to give the detail that you need, and then adjust the handles and vertices to get the shape you want.

5. In Sub-Object Edge mode, select the edge where the lip will be.

6. Make sure Propagate is checked, and subdivide that edge, as seen in Figure 11.39.

7. In Sub-Object Vertex mode, adjust the vertices and their Bezier handles until you have a nice lip formed, as seen in Figure 11.40.

8. Subdivide the two edges that form the upper lip, as seen in Figure 11.41. This gives you more detail to shape that section.

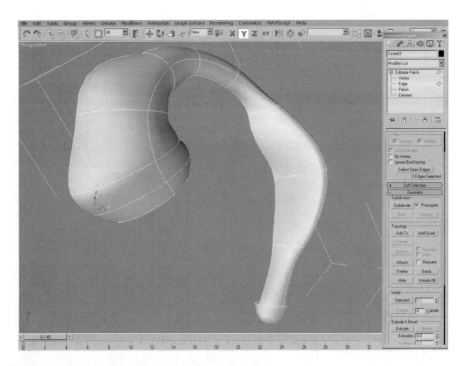

Figure 11.39   Subdivide the head.

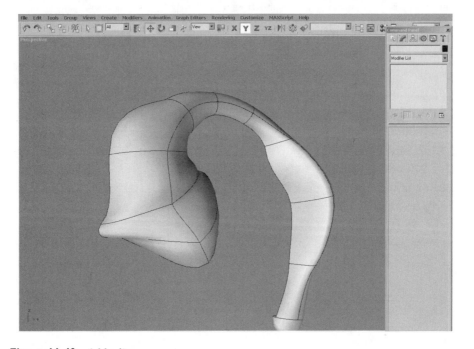

Figure 11.40   Add a lip.

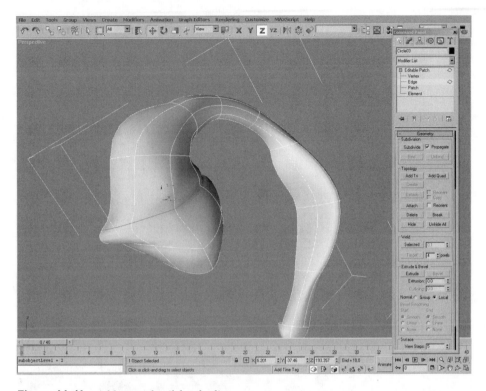

Figure 11.41   Add more detail for the lip.

9. Rotate, scale, and move the vertices to your liking. Figure 11.42 shows my result after tweaking and experimenting.

Now you have finished the base of the head, but you're missing the eye socket. Pug has an elongated eye socket. You create this in the same way that you created every other piece.

10. Create a circle. Rotate it into place.

11. Line up the first circle with the vertices on the head model and copy the circle several times, scaling and rotating each circle into place. Make the last circle small and put it inside the others. This makes the Cross Section modifier draw the eye socket the way you want it. Use Figure 11.43 as a reference.

12. Apply a Cross Section modifier to the spline. Change the Spline type to Smooth in the Command panel.

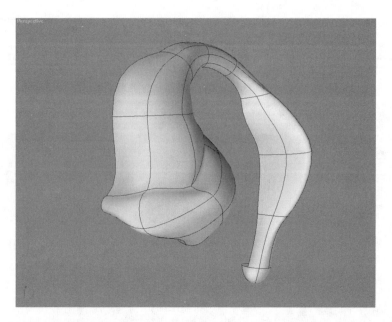

Figure 11.42   Further shape the head model.

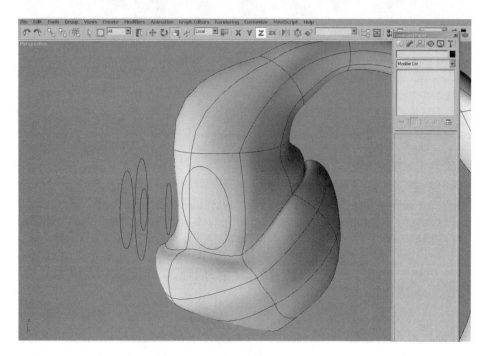

Figure 11.43   Create splines for the eye socket.

13. Apply a Surface modifier. Check Remove Interior Faces and flip the normals if necessary, as seen in Figure 11.44.

14. Convert to an editable patch. Attach the two patch objects.

15. Delete the patch at the base of the eye socket and on the head, where the eye socket will be attached.

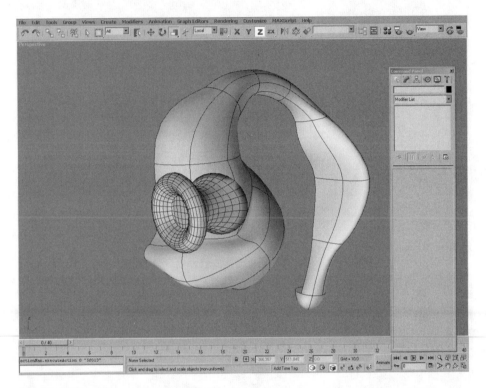

Figure 11.44   The surfaced eye socket is shown here.

16. Select the patches on the beginning of the eye socket in Sub-Object Patch mode, as seen in Figure 11.45.

17. In Sub-Object Vertex mode, select the vertices that you want to weld. Adjust the Weld value to something big, around 100 or 200. Click the Weld button to weld your vertices, as seen in Figure 11.46.

18. Create an eyeball by creating a sphere using Autogrid on the end of the eye socket.

19. Go to the Maps directory and add an eye texture to the sphere, as seen in Figure 11.47.

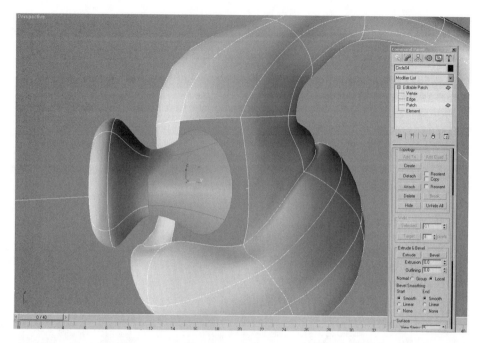

Figure 11.45   Select the base patches for welding.

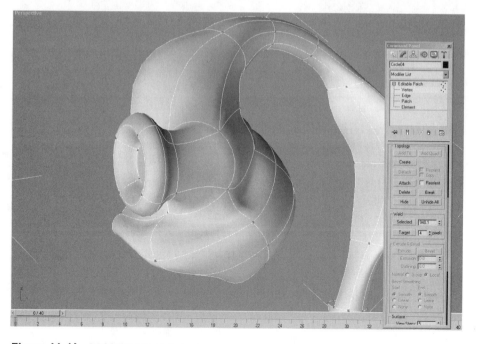

Figure 11.46   Weld the eye socket.

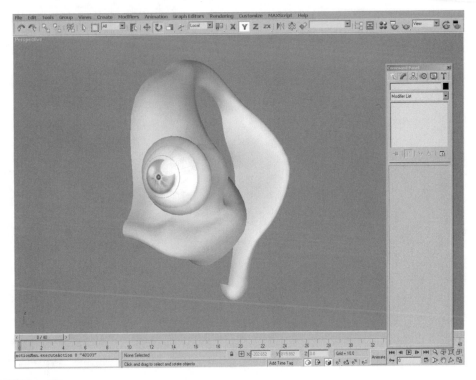

Figure 11.47   Add an eye.

Summary

Patch modeling is a great method for doing a smooth single skin mesh as was done with Pug. As you were working on him, it was pretty high resolution. That is because the Patch Tesselation Steps (otherwise known as View Steps) setting is set to 5. That means that every patch is subdivided five times. This is a little high for current games. You can lower the resolution as much as you need for your game, and as engines can handle more, raise the resolution to the detail level you want (see Figure 11.48).

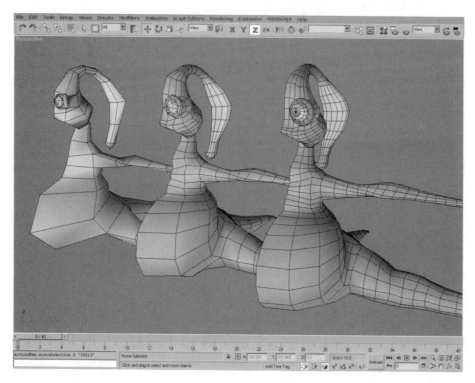

Figure 11.48   Making different resolutions is as easy as changing the Patch View steps

Part IV

Rigging

Chapter 12

Non-Organic Model Rigging for Broadcast/Film Applications

by Adam Holmes

Non-Organic model rigging sounds like a very nebulous concept doesn't it? This chapter could literally refer to any prop-type noncharacter model that needs to move a specific way. The way you approach this type of rigging is a bit different from the way you approach character rigging, though some of the tools overlap. You'll find that the nature of a mechanical model might require more precision in its movements and flexibility to extend these movements to be less mechanical.

In this chapter, you learn how to use tools that can be applied to both non-organic and organic rigging. You create controls for the fire truck model that you created in Chapter 7, "Non-Organic Modeling for Broadcast/Film." You then animate the fire truck in Chapter 20, "Animation Techniques," along with the Jester character.

Specifically, in this chapter you learn about the following:

- Effective hierarchy construction
- Position and Orientation constraints
- Path constraints and Collapse Animation
- The improved Point object
- Manipulators and Wiring Parameters
- Linked Xforms

Exercise 12.1   Setting Up the Cab Hierarchy

The key to any good model that's going to be animated is a logical hierarchy. This means that objects are linked in a parent/child relationship so that they can be easily animated in groups. In the case of the toy fire truck, there will be three main sections: the cab, the rear, and the ladder.

1. First, load up your fire truck model, or find the finished model, truck1.max, created in Chapter 7 on the accompanying CD-ROM.
   (See Figure 12.1.)

   This model is not lined up with the length of the truck pointing in positive Y on the world axis, which is usually how you want to create a model, but its orientation doesn't have any effect on the following process. The length of the truck is on the X-axis, and the truck faces negative X. I refer to specific axes that might not correspond to the model you built, so just compensate based on this information.

2. Select all the objects on the upper part of the cab above the wheel (except the cab itself) and link them to the cab using the Link tool, found in the main toolbar.

3. Link to the bumper the objects that are attached to the bumper, and link the bumper to the cab.

Figure 12.1 Use the finished fire truck model from Chapter 7.

4. Link both wheels' hubcaps to their respective wheels.

5. Select the cab and its two wheels and link them to the object beneath the cab that connects the cab to the rear of the truck.

   It makes life easier for you and the animator (assuming that's a different person and not your alternate personality) when you create groups of hierarchies like this. In max, if you double-click a parent object, you also select its hierarchy, which makes selecting any child objects easier.

   The next steps involve adjusting some Pivot points in the cab so you can get the proper rotational animation.

6. Select the cab object and go to the Hierarchy panel. Select the Pivot and Affect Pivot Only buttons.

7. Click the Center to Object button.

8. Move the Pivot on the Z-axis so it's in line with the lowest part of the bumper (best viewed from underneath the truck).

9. Move the Pivot on the X-axis so it's about where the bumper meets the main parent of the cab hierarchy.

Note

You can use three methods for linking objects. The first is the classic drag-and-drop method that you just used (selecting the Link tool and dragging the link from the child object to the parent).

The second method is selecting the child(ren) and pressing the H hotkey, which brings up the Selection dialog box and enables you to select a parent by name. This is useful if you can't physically drag the link.

The third option is using Schematic View, located in the Graph Editor's drop-down menu. This is a great way to see a graphical representation of the hierarchy. The only tool inconsistency is that the regular Link tool in max is actually select-and-link, meaning you can select objects and link with the same tool. In Schematic View, selecting and linking are two distinct tools. Fortunately, you can assign hotkeys to these tools using the Customize UI menu. Make sure you have the Keyboard Shortcut Override button on to use the Schematic View shortcuts. (This button is located at the bottom of the max interface, to the left of the Snap tools.)

10. Turn off the Affect Pivot Only button and test the cab's rotation about its Y-axis. Make adjustments to the Pivot as necessary. See Figure 12.2.

Figure 12.2   Align the cab's Pivot for proper rotation animation.

11. Double-check the centering of the wheel Pivots by repeating Steps 8 and 9 on the wheels.

12. Select the cab's parent (the big box under the cab, I'll call it cab_base) and center its Pivot.

Now you align cab_base's pivot to the base object of the ladder model.

13. Make sure Affect Pivot Only is on, and click the Align tool from the main max toolbar. Click the base ladder object (the square block under the ladder) and using X-Position, Current Object: Pivot Point and Target Object: Center, center the Pivot on the Y-center of the ladder's base object. (See Figure 12.3.)

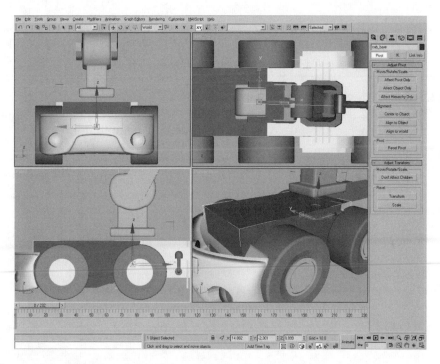

Figure 12.3   Align the cab base's Pivot under the ladder base.

14. Create a Point object (from the new Animation drop-down menu). Do this in the Top view. That way the object's axis is lined up with the world axis. Name it **Point_front_rot**.

15. Use the Align tool to center the point on the parent of the cab hierarchy (cab_base) (check X, Y, and Z and Pivot to Pivot in the Align tool). Now link the cab's parent object (the big box under the cab, truck_belly_rear) to the Point_front_rot to make the point the root of the hierarchy. Test rotating the Point_front_rot on the Z-axis to make sure the front of the truck rotates correctly.

Note

The Point object in max 4 has been revamped to include some new options, which makes it a handy tool for animation and rigging. The Cross and Box options control the look of the Point. If you need two Points on top of each other, one can look like a box and the other can be a cross, making them both easy to select. The Constant Screen Size feature makes the Point the same size, no matter how far in or out you zoom the view (otherwise, the size spinner controls the size control).

A note about the size spinner: It's locked to 10 units as its smallest integer, a current UI limitation. For small-scale scenes, 10 isn't visually small enough. You can change it with the MAXScript command

`$.size=n`

where you have a Point selected and *n* is the size you want the Point to be.

Draw on Top is also a good option if you're using a lot of Points or if they aren't scaled bigger than the geometry. Again, this makes selecting them much easier.

16. Add another point (name it **Point_cab**) and align it Pivot to Pivot on the X, Y, and Z positions to the cab. Go to the Hierarchy panel and in the Pivot section, choose Affect Object Only. Reposition the point in front of the cab.

17. Link the cab to Point_cab and link Point_cab to the Point_front_rot. Now you have an easily selectable handle to rotate the cab forward. See Figure 12.4 for a diagram of the links.

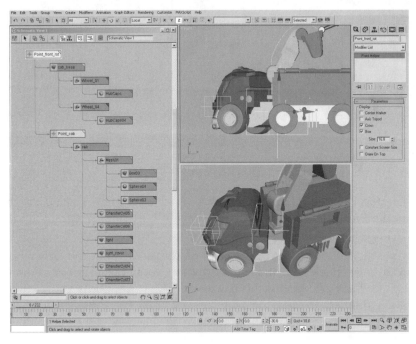

Figure 12.4 This diagram shows positions for the cab and cab_base's points for animation control.

Exercise 12.2   Setting Up the Trailer Hierarchy

Setting up the rear trailer is a similar process to what you just did with the cab. Basically, you link all the smaller parts to the larger parts.

You can start where you left off, or you can load the max file, truck2.max.

1. Link the hub cap objects to their corresponding outer wheels.

2. Link the outer wheels to the trailer base (the big box underneath the trailer, truck_belly_rear).

3. Link all the objects on the top of the trailer to the large upper trailer object, rear_trailer.

4. Link the smaller objects on the lower part of the trailer to the trailer base, truck_belly_rear.

5. Finally, link the rear_trailer to the truck_belly_rear.

   Next, you need to create a Point object to rotate the trailer.

6. Create a Point in the Top view and align it to the ladder's base using X, Y, Z and Current Object: Pivot, Target Object: Center. Adjust the size parameter of the point in the Modify panel to make it big enough so you can select it easily.

7. Name that point **Point_trailer_rot** and link the truck_belly_rearto it.

8. Test the rotation of the point on the Z-axis. The trailer should rotate from side to side. See Figure 12.5.

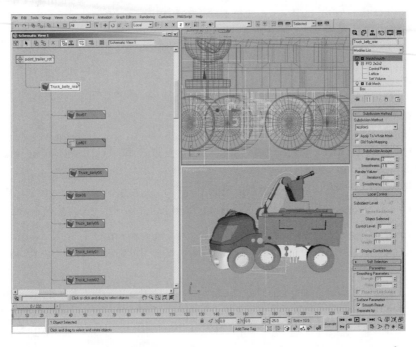

Figure 12.5   Test the rear trailer point and hierarchy to make sure it rotates correctly.

Exercise 12.3   Limiting Movement

In many rigging situations you need the controls to work on only certain axes. There is a simple way to do this in the Hierarchy panel, under Link Info. Notice there are separate locks and inherent link locks for each axis and for move, rotate, and scale. *Inherent axis* refers to the capability of a child object of transforming with its parent object (or not). *Locking an axis* refers to turning off the capability of moving, rotating, or scaling the object. See Figure 12.6.

In this exercise, you limit the transformation of the points, which makes animating these points easier and foolproof. Then an animator won't accidentally set keys of animation on axes that you don't want.

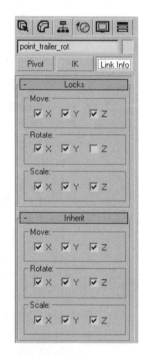

Figure 12.6
The Link Info panel locks and controls inherit transformations.

1. Select the Point_cab object and in the Lock rollout, check all the axes for Move. Lock the X and Z rotation, as well as all the scale axes. This enables you to animate the point in only the Y rotation axis.

2. Select the Point_front_rot object and lock all the movement and scale axes. A little freedom in the rotation axis is not a bad idea for the cab, so leave the rotation locks unchecked.

3. Select the Point_trailer_rot object and lock all the movement and scale axes, as well as the X and Y rotation axes.

4. Test all the rotations of the points again.

Exercise 12.4   Setting Up the Ladder Rotations

The ladder objects and hose pose the most challenge in this chapter, because you want to have control over the hose object's shape and the way it moves in relation to the rest of the ladder objects. You also dive into manipulators and Wiring Parameters to control the animation.

You can start where you left off, or you can load the max file, truck3.max.

The hose object is just a spline, and by using the new parameters in the Rendering rollout of the spline in the Modify panel, you can set the thickness of the spline and have it display in the viewport.

1. Select the hose and go to the Modify panel. In the Rendering rollout, adjust the thickness to **11** or so. Click Renderable, Generate Mapping Coords., and Display Render Mesh. Adjust the size as necessary to make it look good.

2. Link all the pieces together (except the hose spline) to build the hierarchy. Link the hose nozzle tip to the hose nozzle_mid, and the nozzle_mid to the nozzle base. Link the nozzle base to the bucket.

3. Link the bucket to the cylinder that connects it to the ladder. Link the cylinder to the ladder.

4. Link the ladder to the ladder base. See Figure 12.7.

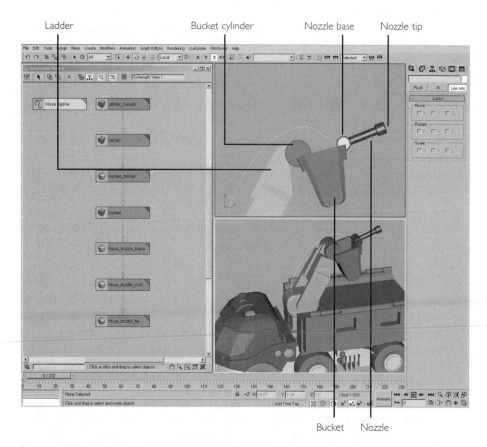

Figure 12.7   The hierarchy shows the linked ladder objects.

 Warning

Don't link the hose spline to anything, because later you're going to set up points to control the hose's shape; if you have the hose in the hierarchy, it will "double transform" when the entire truck is moved. This is a common problem in setting up hierarchies and constraints, but it's easy to avoid when you understand the order of controls. The basic rule is not to include an object in a hierarchy when it's constrained to an object within the hierarchy, or when its sub-object parts are Link Xformed to objects within the hierarchy.

You should set up the link limits for position, rotation, and scale at this point so that every object moves as expected. These controls are found in the Hierarchy panel under Link Info.

5. Select the ladder base and lock its rotation on the X-axis and Y-axis. Lock all position and scale axes.

6. Select the ladder and lock its rotation on the X-axis and Z-axis. Lock all position and scale axes.

7. Select the cylinder above the bucket and lock every axis but Y rotation, and uncheck X & Y rotation in the Inherit rollout.

   This way, the rotation of the ladder will not pass up the chain to the cylinder or the bucket, so you get a movement like the real object would have.

8. Select the bucket and check all of the axes' locking boxes. The cylinder will control the bucket's rotation.

9. Test rotation of the ladder base, the ladder, and the bucket's cylinder. If anything seems incorrect, you might have to adjust Pivot points, using the Affect Pivot Only mode in the Hierarchy/Pivot panel. The ladder's Pivot should be near the base of the geometry, but not at the extreme edge of it, as seen in Figure 12.8.

At this point you could use more Point objects to control the rotations of the ladder, but having too many control points can be confusing and clutter the viewport. Therefore, you use a new tool, called a Plane Angle Manipulator.

The Plane Angle Manipulator tool is part of the manipulator class of objects, which are custom controls that offer you more precise manipulation for your animations. They can look and act any way you can imagine, because they are a fully scriptable class of objects and you can design your own. (This chapter does not cover this, but assistance in the MAXScript help and Web resources show you how to do it.)

Imagine a 2D spline version of the truck that was an outline of the major parts. If you designed a manipulator like this, you could grab each part of the manipulator and adjust it, which would in turn move and rotate the parts on the real truck. The advantage is you have a consolidated control mechanism, and you never have to zoom in and adjust the physical pieces. There's no room for error for animators because they know only to animate the parts using the manipulator.

Excited to learn more? I bet you are, because this new technology will certainly inspire many people to create new ways of controlling animation. Be sure to read the MAXScript help file for more information on manipulators. Now back to the task at hand, which is using the Plane Angle Manipulator.

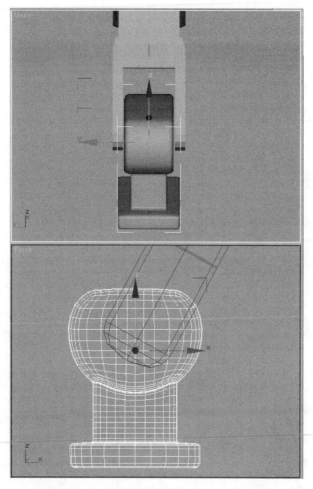

Figure 12.8   The correct Pivot placement for the ladder is at the base, but not at the extreme edge.

10. In the Create panel, choose Helpers/Manipulators/Plane Angle, and in the Front viewport, drag out a Plane Angle. Adjust the size and distance parameters so it's not too big.

11. This Plane Angle (name it **PA_bucket**) will be used to control the bucket rotation, so align the PA_bucket's position from its Pivot to the bucket_cylinder's Pivot on all axes.

12. In the Hierarchy/Link Info panel, lock all position, rotation, and scale axes.

    You might be thinking, "How am I supposed to rotate the Plane Angle if I lock all the axes?" Good question! Manipulators function in Manipulate mode, which is the button next to the Scale button on the main toolbar.

(Or you can use the right-click Quad menu to activate it.) Turn on this mode and you can adjust the Plane Angle. Because its job is only to report one axis angle, it doesn't matter what transformation tool you have active (move, rotate, scale, or nothing at all). As long as the Manipulate mode is active, you can adjust the Plane Angle.

13. Turn on Manipulate mode, and when you touch the Plane Angle, it turns red. Click and drag the mouse on it, and it rotates and pops up text that tells you how far you've rotated it, as seen in Figure 12.9.

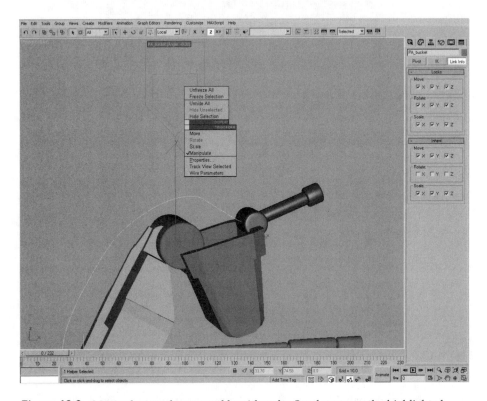

Figure 12.9   Manipulate mode, accessed by either the Quad menu or the highlighted button on the main toolbar produces an interactive readout of the angle.

 Tip

This rotation is also controlled in the Modify panel when the manipulator is selected, so you can always go there to adjust the value. Use Angle Snap so you can easily return the angle to 0 without going to the Modify panel. Using manipulators saves you from going to the Modify or Motion panels to animate.

The next step is to tie the Plane Angle's angle parameter to the Z-axis of the bucket_cylinder. The new Wire Parameters tool, found in the Animation drop-down menu or by the right-click Quad menu, does this easily. First you should set up the cylinder's rotation controller to be an Euler (pronounced oil-er) XYZ controller.

14. Turn off Manipulate mode.

15. Select the cylinder and go to the Motion panel. Open the Assign Controller rollout.

16. Select the rotation controller and press the Assign Controller button that's at the top of that rollout (it has a box and an arrow as its icon).

17. Choose Euler XYZ from the list. Now if you want subsequent objects that you create to have this controller by default (which I do because I always want direct access to the XYZ tracks), click the Default button and click OK.

Note

The default rotation controller is Quaternion TCB mathematics, which means you do not have direct F-curve control in the Track view. The controller is based on ball-joint type rotations, which is better used for a mechanical ball joint or something like a character's shoulder rotation. You won't get Gimble Lock, which is a mathematical limitation of Euler angles that causes undesired rotations. The TCB controls do take some getting used to.

In the following steps you use Wire Parameters to connect the angle of the Plane Angle to the bucket_cylinder.

Caution

Before you start working with Wire Parameters, expressions, or script controllers, *always* increase the end frame of the animation. The range of these controllers is set at their creation time, and if you expand the end time or start time into negative frames, these controllers will no longer be active. You have to manually go into the Track view and adjust the ranges (in Range mode) of each track that has these controllers assigned.

18. Zoom in to the cylinder and the PA_bucket. Right-click the PA_bucket and select Wire Parameters. A small dialog box will appear. Select Object/Angle, and then drag the dashed line to the cylinder and click it. A similar dialog box will pop up. Select Transform/Rotation/Y Rotation.

The Wire Parameters dialog box appears. The PA_bucket's parameters are on the left side and the cylinder's parameters are on the right. If you accidentally chose the wrong parameter in the previous step, now's your chance to fix it before you commit this connection.

19. The Angle and Y rotation parameters should be selected. Click the arrow pointing to the right and click Connect.

20. Leave this window open for now and test the rotation of the Plane Angle. Turn on Manipulate mode (either through the Quad menu or the button on the main toolbar) and adjust the Plane Angle.

It works! Well, almost. The rotation is most likely backward, so when you move the Plane Angle to a negative value (clockwise), the bucket rotates counterclockwise. You can easily fix that by changing the way the wire is connected using the expression window in the Wire Parameters dialog box.

21. In the Wire Parameters dialog box, in the lower-right expression window, type a minus sign in front of the word Angle so it reads –Angle. Then click Update.

22. Now manipulate the Plane Angle again and you'll get the correct rotation. Cool huh? See Figure 11.10.

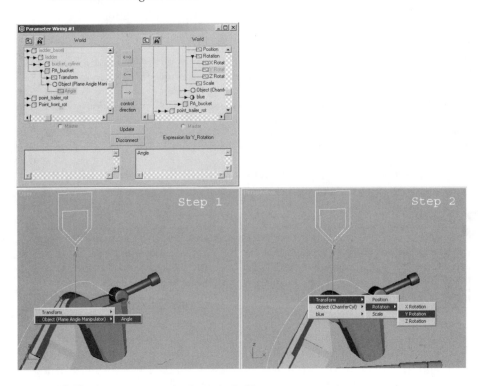

Figure 12.10   Wire the Plane Angle to the ladder.

Let's set up another Plane Angle for the ladder base and perform the same procedure as you just did for the bucket.

23. Turn off Manipulate mode and close the Wire Parameters dialog box.

24. Create another Plane Angle in the Top view. Align it to the ladder base (Pivot-to-Pivot) on all axes and make the Plane Angle big enough to select it, using its size parameters.

25. Lock the ladder base's rotations so you can't physically rotate it.

26. Change its rotation controller to Euler XYZ.

27. Right-click the Plane Angle (name it **PA_ladderbase**) and choose Wire Parameters/Object/Angle. Select the ladder base by zooming in while you're in this pick mode, or by pressing H to bring up the Select By Name dialog box.

28. Select Transform/Rotation/Z Rotation.

29. Click the right-facing arrow in the Wire Parameters dialog box, and click Connect.

30. Test the manipulator, and if it's rotating backward, add the minus sign in front of Angle in the expression window. If all is good, close the Wire Parameters dialog box.

    The only problem to solve now is a hierarchy issue.

31. Link the PA_bucket to the ladder object so they rotate together. Then uncheck Inherit Rotation for all axes.

    You won't link the PA_ladderbase to anything yet, because you haven't set up a master control point to control the truck's forward motion. That comes later.

 Warning

Don't link the controlling wired object (in this case, the Plane Angles) to anything in the hierarchy that it's wired to. This causes wired double transforms, and it should be avoided entirely.

Next, you create a Plane Angle for the ladder.

32. Make sure to turn off Manipulate mode, and then lock the rotations of the ladder.

33. In the Front view, create another Plane Angle and name it **PA_ladder**. Align it to the ladder (Pivot-to-Pivot on all axes).

34. Change the rotation controller of the ladder_base to Euler XYZ.

35. Wire the PA_ladder's angle parameter to the ladder_base's Z Rotation. Most likely you'll have to add –Angle to the expression window to get the rotation correct.

Now you're an expert at Plane Angle manipulators, Wiring Parameters, aligning, Pivot manipulation, and link locking. That's a lot of tools to use in a short period of time, so take time to experiment! See Figure 12.11, which illustrates these results.

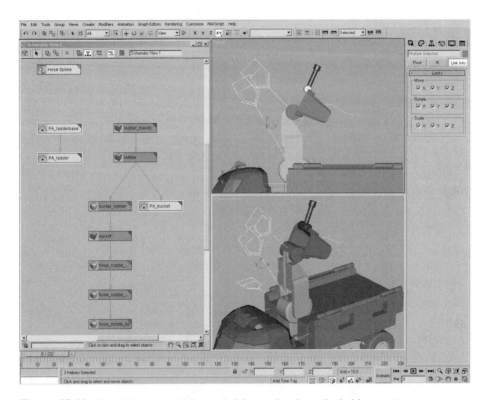

Figure 12.11   The ladder manipulators and hierarchy show the ladder rotations.

Exercise 12.5   Setting Up the Hose Controls

In this exercise, you use some new tools, called constraints, to add animation controls to the hose spline using Point objects. You can continue where you left off, or load the max file, truck4.max.

1. Select the hose spline and in the Modify panel, turn on Sub-Object Vertex mode.

2. Select the vertex near the nozzle base. Keep this vertex selected and, while remaining in Sub-Object mode, apply a Linked Xform modifier from the Modifier drop-down list.

3. Next, click the Pick Control Object button in the Linked Xform and select the hose_nozzle_base.

   Now the nozzle base object has control of that vertex. Move it around to see the effect. In the next steps, you create Point objects that control the remaining vertices. You should have four vertices on the hose spline, and you will create three Point objects.

4. Select the hose spline and turn off the Display Render Mesh in the Rendering rollout.

5. Create a Point object in the Top view and name it **Point_hose1**.

6. Keep it selected and, in the Animation drop-down menu, choose Constraints/Path Constraint and click the hose spline.

   This aligns the point with the spline and creates an animation of it following the path over the current range of frames. You need this step to align the point with the vertex on the spline, because there are no tools to directly align objects to vertices.

7. Make sure you're on frame 0. In the Motion panel in the Path Constraint rollout, change the percentage along the path spinner so the point lines up with the second vertex next to the hose nozzle. You don't have to be 100% accurate.

8. Now choose the Trajectories button at the top of the Motion panel. Change the Start Time to 0, End Time to 0, and Samples to 2 (you can't have only 1 sample).

9. In the Collapse transform, have only Position checked, and click Collapse.

   This locks the point's position in place and removes the Path constraint. This Collapse tool is very useful for "baking" procedural animation controllers, such as the Path constraint. Then you have keyframes of that motion, instead of it being controlled by another object or mathematical function.

10. With the point still selected, delete any keyframes that appear in the track bar at the bottom of the interface.

11. Rotate the point on the local Y-axis to align it with the curve.

12. Repeat the process from Step 5 to create and line up two more points to the two remaining vertices.

    Next, you add Linked Xforms to the hose spline so the points actually move the vertices.

13. Select the hose spline, and under the Vertex mode of Editable Spline, select the last vertex that lies under the hose nozzle base.

14. As in Step 2, with the first vertex, apply a Linked Xform modifier and click the Pick Control Object button, and choose the hose_nozzle_base object.

15. Add a Spline Select modifier and click the plus sign next to the modifier to expand the tool. Select Vertex to get into Sub-Object mode and select the vertex on the hose spline, under Point_hose2.

16. Add a Linked Xform modifier and click the Pick Control Object button, and choose the Point_hose1 object.

17. Repeat Step 15 for the remaining two vertices, assigning the Linked Xforms to the appropriate Point objects. You should have something that looks like Figure 12.12.

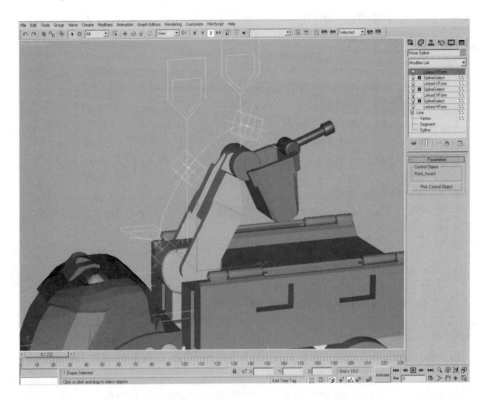

Figure 12.12   Align the points and Linked Xforms.

Note

On the accompanying CD-ROM there is a script that creates and aligns Point objects to the vertices, just as you did in the previous steps. The only thing it can't do (due to a limitation in MAXScript) is link the vertices to the Linked Xforms. It certainly saves a lot of time aligning points to vertices, however. Test it by drawing a spline and then, while the spline is selected, run pointplacer.ms.

Sure, I could have told you to do that in the beginning, but learning some new functionality is more important than running a script that does everything for you.

The next steps involve using constraints to automatically center the points between themselves and the ends of the hose. The goal is to have the hose animate its length as you move the nozzle in space, while still having manual control over each point's position and rotation. This involves a trick using list controllers.

18. Select Point_hose1, and under the Animation drop-down menu, choose Constraints/Position Constraint and drag the dashed line that appears to the hose_nozzle_base object. Point_hose1 will snap to the exact position of hose_nozzle_base until you do the next step.

19. In the Motion panel that opens, check the Keep Initial Offset box.

20. Click the Add Position Target and choose Point_hose2. Click the button again to turn off this mode.

21. Select Point_hose2 and add Position Constraint to the hose_nozzle_base object. Make sure that Keep Initial Offset is checked.

22. Click the Add Position Target and choose Point_hose3. Click the button again to turn off this mode.

23. Adjust the weight parameter of the Point_hose1 target to 75. This puts more control toward the point at the nozzle. Feel free to adjust this as necessary. See Figure 12.13 for reference.

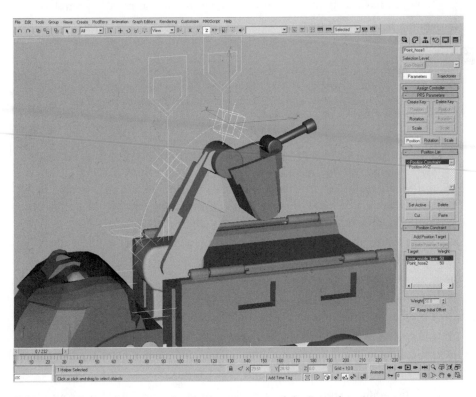

Figure 12.13   You can adjust the weight parameter of the Point_hose1 target.

24. Move hose_nozzle_base around to test the motion. Make sure to undo any movements so you can keep the alignment between the points and the vertices on the spline.

Now, you can't move Point_hose1 or Point_hose2 manually (go ahead, try it!), because of the order of the animation controllers in the position track. The controller that is active in the list takes interactive precedence and if a constraint is last, you won't be able to move the object, even if an XYZ controller is active.

25. With Point_hose2 selected, go to the Motion panel and open the Assign Controller rollout.

26. In the Position List rollout, there's an Available slot. Select Available and click the Assign Controller button. Add a position XYZ controller.

27. In the Position List rollout, click Position XYZ at the bottom of the list and click Set Active.

Now you have keyframe *and* Constraint control of that point's position. Cool!

28. Do the same procedure from Step 18 for Point_hose3.

Tip

You can edit these controllers in the Track view, which is sometimes easier than this little Assign Controller window in the Motion panel. Turn on the filter to show controllers in the Track view, and right-click over items such as a constraint or a list controller to access the editing window.

Now, do you really want to get deep into list controllers, constraints, and Wire Parameters? You need a little more control on this rig. Editing controllers are really simple after you've done it a couple of times, so dive right in. I'm going to outline the basic steps and you can conduct the edits in the Motion panel, or in the Track view (my preferred method).

29. Select Point_hose2, choose the Rotation track, and change it to a Euler XYZ controller.

30. Change the Y rotation to a float list controller.

31. Select the PA_Bucket Point and right-click and choose Wire Parameters from the Quad menu. Choose Object/Angle, and then click Point_hose2.

32. Choose Transform/Rotation/Y Rotation/Available.

33. Choose the right-facing arrow, put a minus sign in front of the Angle variable in the expression window, and click Connect.

You just added a wire between the Plane Angle manipulator (that controls the bucket's rotation) so the point will rotate automatically. See Figure 12.14 for the Track view I use for editing controllers. The highlighted tracks are the result of adding the wire and list controller to Point_hose1's Y rotation.

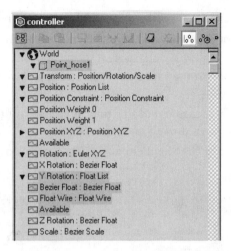

Figure 12.14   Turn off the new Hierarchy filter in the Track view to eliminate cascading tracks in the display.

34. Repeat the procedure from Step 29 for wiring the PA_ladder Plane Angle to Point_hose2.

35. Link Point_hose3 and the ladder to the ladder_base object.

After all this work, you should have a very easy-to-animate ladder using the manipulators. The hose spline should be moving along with the ladder, and you can still make manual adjustments to the hose points as needed. Make some test animations to try these new controls.

Exercise 12.6   Creating a Master Control

In this exercise, you link everything to a master control point and create an expression to make the wheels rotate as you move the truck forward.

If you need to start fresh from this point, load the max file, truck5.max.

1. Create a Point object in the Top view and align it somewhere under the cab (it really doesn't matter where). Name it **master_point**.

2. Link the ladder_base, Point_trailer_rot, Point_front_rot, and PA_ladderbase (the Plane Angle manipulator) to this new point.

3. Move the master_point around to make sure everything is moving together. If they are not, go back and link the loose objects. With so many objects, it's easy to miss a few.

   Before you create the wheel rotation expression, you need to measure the radius of the wheel.

4. Create a Tape measure from the Create/Helpers menu in the Create panel.

5. Select the root of the Tape and align its Pivot to any wheel's Pivot on all axes.

6. Use the Align tool on the Tape's target and align its Pivot to the wheel's Pivot on all axes.

7. Align the Tape target again, but this time align its Pivot to the wheel's minimum or maximum (it doesn't matter) on the Z.

   Note the readout in the Modifier panel of the Tape's length, as shown in Figure 12.15.

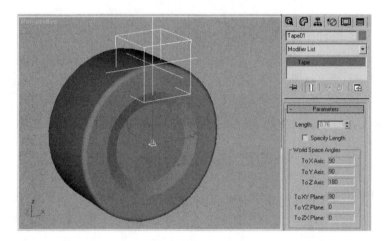

Figure 12.15   The Tape measures the wheel.

8. Make sure the master_point's position controller is an XYZ position controller. Also make sure all wheels have an Euler XYZ rotation controller.

9. Right-click the master_point and use Wire Parameter to specify its X position to the wheel's Y rotation.

10. Click the right-facing arrow and in the expression window, after the X_Position, type a slash (/) and the radius value from the Tape measure (so it reads something like this: **X_position/.76**).

11. Click the Connect button, move the master_point on the local X-axis, and watch the wheel roll (which is easier to see in wireframe display or after putting a checker texture on it).

    This is a rather simple expression, and if you turn the truck around too far, it won't work, because you won't be moving it on its local X-axis anymore.

Tip

If you closed the Wire Parameters dialog box, the best way to reopen it, displaying the connection you just made, is to open the Motion panel's Assign Controller rollout, right-click the wired controller, and select Properties. You can also do this in the Track view.

If you wired a parameter of an object and that parameter shows up in the Modify panel, you can right-click the spinner value and access the wire that way.

12. In the Parameter Wiring dialog box, type **(X_Position+ $master_point.pos.y)/.76** and click Update.

See Figure 12.16 for the Parameter Wiring dialog box.

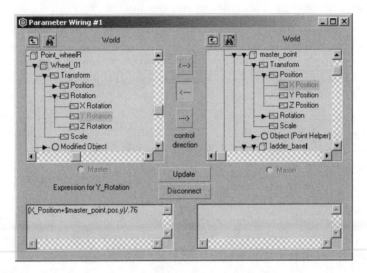

Figure 12.16   Wire the point to the wheel with this expression.

Now you're referencing both the X and Y positions of the master_point. This is necessary because transformation values in max are always calculated based on the parent object, which is the world in this case. The world axis never changes, and even if you're moving the master_point on the local X-axis, when the truck is turned, you introduce a world Y movement as well.

13. Repeat the wire connection for all the remaining wheels, starting from Step 8.

14. If you experience wheels that rotate backward, simply put a minus sign in front of the expression **–(X_Position+$master_point.pos.y)/.76**.

This wiring process works well because you can have a master wire (from the master_point) that controls any number of objects.

To finish this section, you set up a steering control for the front wheels.

15. Copy the master_point object and scale it down. Be sure to reset the scale in the Hierarchy/Pivot panel or use the MAXScript command

```
$.size= n
```

instead of scaling.

16. Name it **Point_wheel_turn**.

17. Copy the point twice and use Align to center these points on the front wheels.

18. Name them **Point_wheelR** and **Point_wheelL**.

19. Link the wheels to their respective points.

20. Link the Point_wheels (right and left) and Point_wheel_turn to Point_front_rot (the point that rotates front of the truck).

The Point_wheels aren't linked to the Point_wheel_turn because that would offset the Pivot of the wheels to the location of the Point_wheel_turn. Because you have one steering control for both wheels, they need to maintain their own Pivots. How do you get around this problem? With an Orientation constraint.

21. Select one of the Point_wheels and select Orientation Constraint in the Animation drop-down menu. Click the Point_wheel_turn, and make sure the Keep Initial Offset and World/World is checked.

22. Repeat Step 21 for the other Point_wheel. See Figure 12.17 for the Orientation constraint parameters.

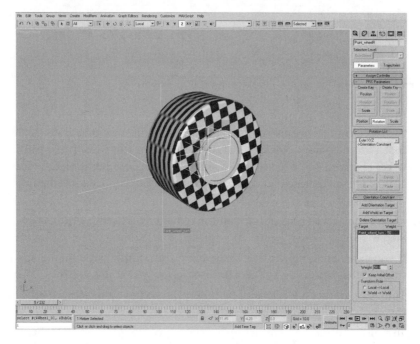

Figure 12.17   The Orientation constraint maintains separate Pivots for both wheels.

Now you have a separate control for the steering of the wheels. You might want to turn the display of the Point_wheel_turn to a cross and the master_point to a box, for easy selectability.

The finished file is named truck6.max and should look like Figure 12.18.

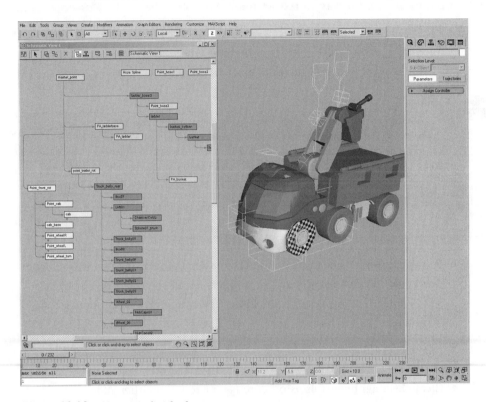

Figure 12.18   The rig is finished.

In a production studio, a technical director (TD) who creates rigs would probably freeze the geometry at this point so nothing could be accidentally moved or changed by the animator. The Point objects and the Plane Angle manipulators are all that need to be animated.

Summary

In these nonorganic rigging exercises, you explored some important aspects of rigging a prop with controls that an animator would need, keeping it as simple as possible while maintaining some flexibility. Certainly this is not the ultimate rigging you could do for this fire truck, so experiment with different control setups using the constraints and manipulators covered in this chapter.

Using Wiring Parameters is a powerful way to connect an object's parameters. Combining that tool with manipulators creates custom controls that enable an animator to focus on the motion rather than the technical details.

Constraints are a great way to restrict translations or have another object dictate that control. Animating weights presents even more options for detailed motion.

Constructing a logical hierarchy is sometimes more complicated than it first appears, and is pivotal in how pieces of a model animate.

 Warning

Watch out for reorganizing a hierarchy after constraints are in place. It's better to remove a constraint before parenting or disconnecting that object in a hierarchy. An object might fly off into space if it's trying to be constrained, and the hierarchy you make creates an invalid or cyclic loop of parents and children. Try parenting one of the hose spline points to another point along the hose spline. It'll fly off the hose—you can't undo it either!

Here are some ideas to practice and enhance this rig:

- Put all the animation controls into the master_point object by using Custom Attributes and creating sliders and spinners for all the rotations of objects. See Chapter 3, "Changes in Animation," for more information on Custom Attributes.

- Try making the truck drive along a path using the Path constraint, and having the wheels turn and steer automatically.

- Create headlight controls using Wire Parameters and either Slider Manipulators or Custom Attributes that turn on a self-illuminating texture on the headlight objects, turn on max lights, and/or turn on light-based volumetrics. Be creative!

- Use the Spring controller on various parts of the model to generate subtle secondary animation. This controller gets assigned to the Position track of an object.

Chapter 13

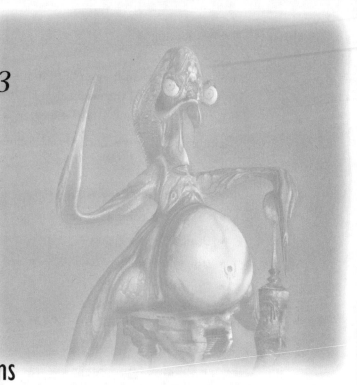

Non-Organic Model Rigging for Games/Interactive Applications

by Mike O'Rourke

3ds max 4 introduces a new set of tools

for rigging and character animation. A

new IK system, new constraints, and new

manipulators make rigging a character

faster and easier than it's ever been in max. In this chapter, you take a look at the tools necessary to rig the mechanical legs for the warrior, Pug. These legs provide a nice, simple way to understand the whole IK and constraints system inside max.

Specifically, this chapter discusses the following:

- Creating bones
- Using the new IK Solvers
- Creating IK control hierarchies
- Using IK Solver Planes
- Using manipulators
- Using the Skin modifier

Take a look at the legs in Figure 13.1 as you think through how you want to set up everything.

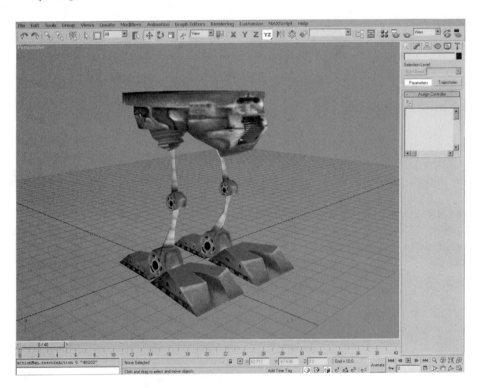

Figure 13.1   The legs are ready to be rigged.

This setup is pretty easy. You use a two-bone HI-IK chain on a leg, bending at the knee. Next you use a few one-bone HI-IK chains for the toe and heel. (For more information on HI IK, see Chapter 3, "Changes in Animation.")

You then copy the leg you build to make the second leg. Because setting up a leg isn't as easy as just setting up a few IK chains, you need to set up some constraints so that the chain works the way you want.

Exercise 13.1   Creating Bones for the Leg

Start by creating bones for the rig.

1. Open Pug_Setup_1.max on the accompanying CD-ROM and go into the Right viewport.

2. In the Create panel, under Systems, find the Bones button. Press the Bones button to go into bone-creation mode.

   Now, anywhere you click you will add a link in a bone chain.

3. Create the bones for your leg by clicking near the base, at the knee, at the ankle, at the beginning of the toe, and at the end of the toe. Right-click to end the chain. Use Figure 13.2 as a reference.

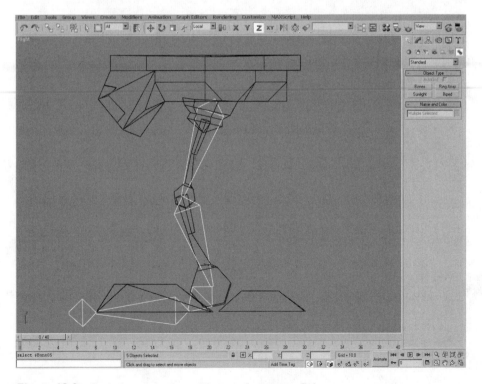

Figure 13.2   Begin bone creation with several strategic clicks.

You might notice that an extra bone was made at the end of the chain. This aids in setting up hierarchies that work well with IK. You will see why those are made as we go on.

Tip
Remember to look in the Front view to make sure the bones are lined up with the mesh. Make sure to move the bones if necessary.

4. Make one more bone off the back of the heel by using the same procedure to create bones as in Steps 2 and 3. If you followed those steps, this should be Bone06. Start the bone where you want it to rotate. See Figure 13.3.

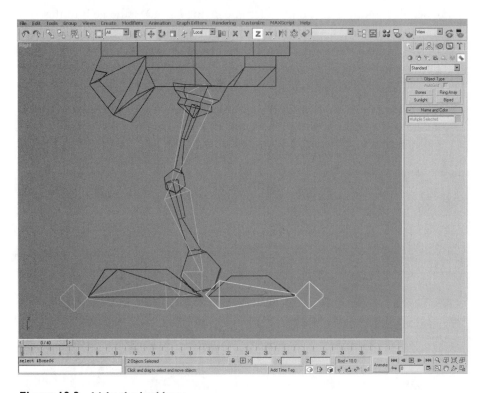

Figure 13.3   Make the heel bone.

Warning
Before you go any farther, make sure that your bones are all in the right place. If you've made everything in the Right viewport, you might need to move some bones over, laterally, so they are on the right side of the character and not down the middle. Go into a Perspective window and rotate your objects to check.

5. Link the heel bone to the small anklebone using the Link tool.

   Create the first IK chain now.

6. Select the first bone in the hierarchy; that's the one that touches the waist, Bone—Right Hip.

7. In the drop-down menus at the top of the screen, find the Animation drop-down list. Select Animation/IK Solvers/HI Solver, as shown in Figure 13.4.

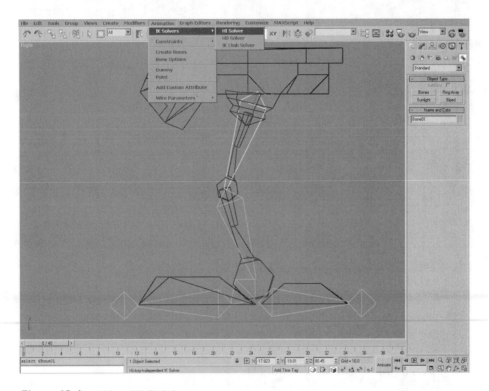

Figure 13.4   Add an HI-IK Solver.

8. Select the bone called Bone—Right Ankle, the third bone in the chain.

   Your IK chain is drawn. You can now affect the chain by moving around the little blue crosshair, known as a *goal*, at the end of the chain. Make sure to save or hold your scene before you play around with moving the goal, or do a few checks and undo them.

   While you move the goal around (see Figure 13.5), notice how the toe and heel rotate with the chain. You want those two bones to stay flat on the floor, so you need to use a constraint.

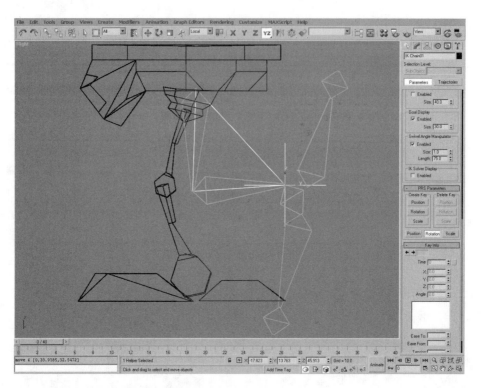

Figure 13.5   Move the IK chain goal around.

You make the constraints, along with helpers to move and rotate all of your objects. Dummy and Point helper objects make animating this assembly a little easier and are necessary to control the constraints.

9. Undo any transforms on the goal if you moved it around in the last step, or load Pug_Setup_2.max from the CD.

To fix the problem with the toe and heel rotating, make an Orientation constraint. An Orientation constraint locks an object's rotations to another object, or to the world.

In this case, instead of the toe getting its rotation from the hierarchy above it as usual, you can make a Dummy and have the toe look at that for its rotation information.

10. Create a Dummy in the Right viewport, at the ankle's pivot point. Make sure to align to the bones if they were moved in a previous step. Change the name of this Dummy to **Dummy—Right Ankle**. See Figure 13.6.

11. Select Bone—Right Ankle. Go to the Animation drop-down list at the top of the screen, and select Constraints/Orientation Constraint.

Now you should have a dotted line being drawn from the Bone—Right Ankle's pivot point to your cursor.

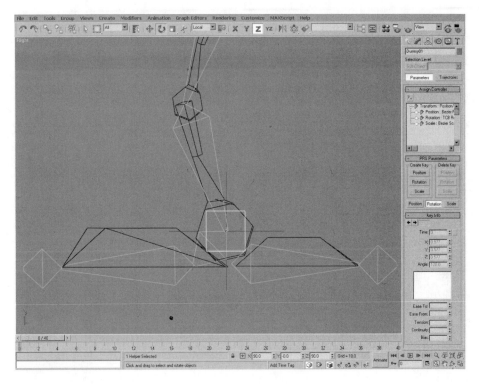

Figure 13.6   Create a Dummy for the ankle.

12. Click the Dummy—Right Ankle you just made to link the constraint to that Dummy.

13. You'll probably see your bone rotate a bit. This can occur when the Dummy is created with different local coordinates than the object being constrained. To remedy this, check the Keep Initial Offset check box in the Command panel.

Basically, you just told the anklebone to rotate only when the Dummy rotates. If you don't rotate the Dummy, the ankle won't rotate.

To see the effect, select the IK chain's goal and move it around. Notice that the toe no longer rotates. Now select the Dummy and rotate it; the toe and heel rotate. Be sure to undo any test movements you make.

Next, you make another setup so the character can go up on its toes, as if it's reaching for something high. You do this by first creating another IK chain.

14. Select Bone—Right Toe 01, go to the Animation drop-down list, and add an HI-IK Solver as in Steps 7 and 8. Click Bone—Right Toe 02 to end the chain, as shown in Figure 13.7.

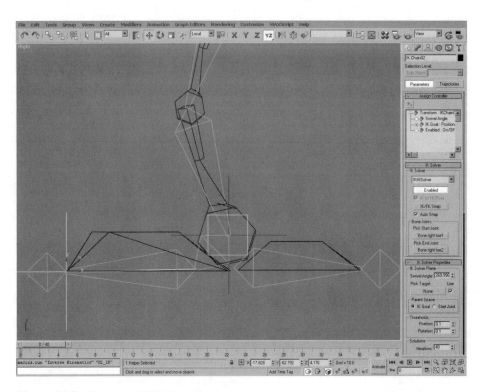

Figure 13.7   Create an HI-IK chain for the toe.

15. Link the IK Chain01 goal to the first Dummy you made, Dummy—Right Ankle. If the leg twists, don't worry about it. The next step addresses this.

Dummy—Right Ankle was previously controlling only the rotation of the ankle, but you can also use it to move the IK goal by linking it. This is useful, and all you need to do is put a Dummy where you want the whole ankle to rotate and link Dummy—Right Ankle to it.

16. To do this, create a Dummy at the toe bone's pivot. Change the name of this Dummy to **Dummy—Toe Roll**. Use Figure 13.8 as a reference.

17. Link the leg's IK chain goal to Dummy—Toe Roll.

Again, if the leg twists, don't worry about it. The next step addresses this.

18. Test to see whether the setup works by rotating Dummy—Toe Roll. It should rotate the goal and Dummy—Right Ankle, thus giving the effect of a toe roll.

In the next exercise, you take care of the knee. If the leg flipped at any time during the setup, this will fix it.

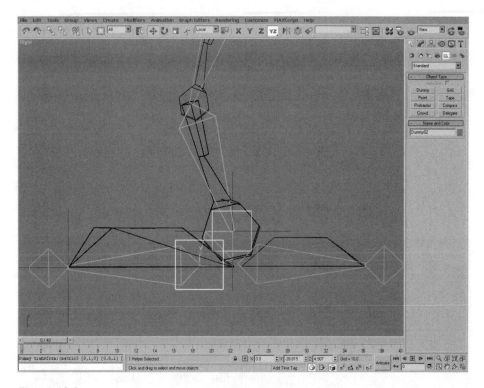

Figure 13.8   Create a Dummy to help facilitate toe roll.

Exercise 13.2   Using IK Chains and Swivel Angles

By default, IK chains have a swivel angle that determines which way the IK Solver Plane points. You can see this by going into Manipulate mode, using the Select and Manipulate button next to the Scale button in the toolbar.

In this case, you'd rather have the knee point at an object, rather than have to rotate the chain with a Swivel Angle manipulator, which is the default setup. Follow the steps in this exercise.

1. Select the leg's IK chain's goal, IK Chain01.

2. Go into the Motion panel in the Command panel. It's the tab that looks like a wheel in motion.

3. Locate the IK Solver Properties rollout in the panel. In the IK Solver Plane area, locate the Pick Target button.

   Normally the IK Solver Plane is determined by this Swivel Angle value. You will make an object for the IK Solver to point to rather than using the Swivel Angle value.

4. Create a Dummy in front of the character, about knee-high. Name it **Dummy—Right Knee**.

5. Press the Pick Target button in the Command panel. Select Dummy—Right Knee as the target.

   Now you need to address the heel. Putting a simple IK chain on the heel bones is your first step.

6. Select Bone—Right Heel 01.

7. Go to the Animation drop-down list at the top of the screen and select IK Solvers/HI Solver.

8. Select the bone at the end of the heel, Bone—Right Heel 02, to end the chain. Use Figure 13.9 as a reference.

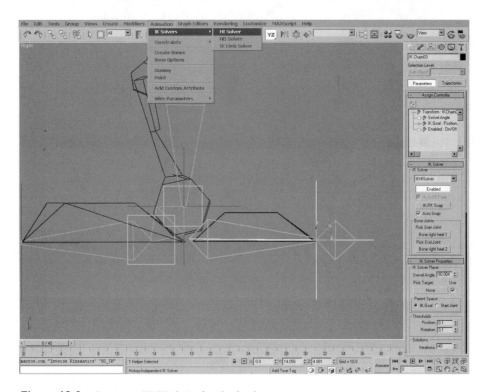

Figure 13.9   Create an HI-IK chain for the heel.

Currently you have no way to get the character up on the tip of its toe. You can roll the ankle, but you can't rotate the toe about the tip. This is actually pretty easy to fix.

9. Create a Dummy at the tip of the toe. Name it **Dummy—Right Toe Tip**. Use Figure 13.10 as a reference.

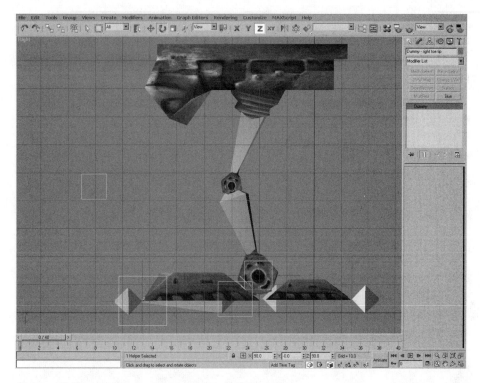

Figure 13.10   Create a Dummy for the tip of the toe.

10. Link Dummy—Right Toe Roll to the newly created Dummy—Right Toe Tip.

11. Link the toe's IK chain goal, IK Chain02, to Dummy—Right Toe Tip.

12. Test it by rotating Dummy—Right Toe Tip. The whole leg assembly should go up on its tiptoe.

 Note

The Heel bone will continue to point at its IK Solver when you rotate the tiptoe Dummy. You can either link the heel's IK chain goal to Dummy—Right Toe Tip so that it comes along for the ride, or leave it the way it is so that it keeps pointing. It's up to you.

To finish, make another Dummy that moves this whole assembly.

13. Create a Dummy somewhere around the ankle, and make it nice and big. Name it **Dummy—Right Foot Control**.

14. Link Dummy—Toe Tip and the heel's IK chain goal, IK Chain03, to the new Dummy—Right Foot Control.

15. If any bones rotate out of place, select the IK chain goal and go into the Motion panel in the Command panel. Reset the Swivel angle to **0**.

You have the basics for the leg setup now. You have constraints and IK chains to get things into place. You now need a nice interface to animate this character.

Exercise 13.3   Using Skin to Deform the Mesh

To create the interface, you use manipulators, a new feature in 3ds max 4. You also need to attach all the mesh to the bones and skin any parts of the mesh that need to deform.

First you attach the mesh to the bones. This exercise makes it easy, because there is no deformation, with the exception of the boot connection to the body.

1. Link each piece of geometry to its corresponding bone using the Link tool.

   If you've been following the previous three exercises, this should be pretty straightforward. If not, see Exercise 13.1 for details.

2. Link Bone—Right Hip to the Mesh—Base object.

   You use the Mesh—Base object as your root object. To make the boot deform when the leg is animated, you need to put a Skin modifier on it.

3. Select the Mesh—Right Boot object and apply a Skin modifier to it, as shown in Figure 13.11.

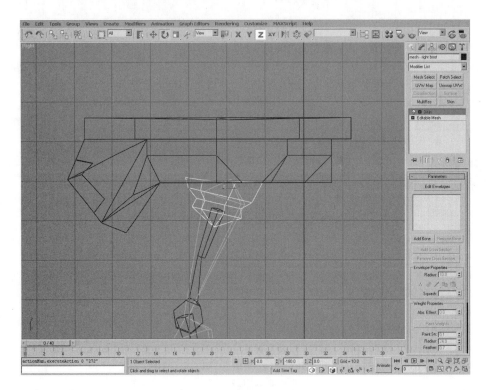

Figure 13.11   Apply the Skin modifier to the Mesh—Right Boot object.

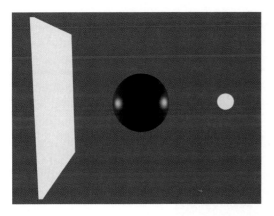 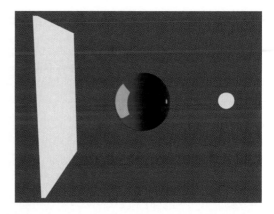

Chapter 22 - Christie
The difference between using default lights (left) and simulating light size or area (right).

Final Fire Truck toy model built in Chapter 7 (Yoo)
and textured in Chapter 19 (Austin and Diriwaechter).

Chapter 23 - Feely and Hall
Real-time game environment lighting for interiors (above) and exteriors (below).

Original clay maquette of Jester
used for modeler reference (right) .
Lee

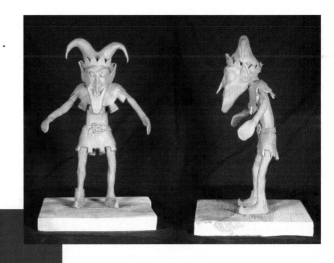

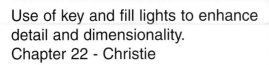

Use of key and fill lights to enhance
detail and dimensionality.
Chapter 22 - Christie

Chapter 22 - Christie

Incorrect shadow map parameters (left).

Correct shadow map parameters (below).

Chapter 22 - Christie

No ambient light simulation (above).

Simulation of ambient (bounced) light applied (right).

Diffuse Color Element

Chapter 24 - Ehrlich
The various elements (passes)
rendered for final compositing.

Specular Element

Confetti Element

Shadow Element

Particle Sparkle Element

Reflection Element

DV Video Backplate Element

VISUAL GUIDE TO 3DS MAX 4 DEFAULT ANTI-ALIASING FILTERS

The following pages are meant to serve as a quick visual guide to the various anti-aliasing filters available with the MAX Default Scanline A-Buffer renderer. For filters with user-adjustable parameters, we have included samples representing both the default settings as well as the low and high extremes of the given value range. Additionally, because the perceived affect of these filters will often vary greatly depending on the resolution of the final image, we have included samples from both NTSC D1 resolution and 2k film resolution. The master frame below illustrates the original framing of the image for print with green crop marks denoting the NTSC (D1 720x486) framing used and red crop marks denoting the 2k film (35mm 1.85:1 (cine) 2048x1107) framing used. The blue crop marks represent the area that has been magnified for our sample swatches. Readers should note that perceived results may vary depending on the nature of your image.

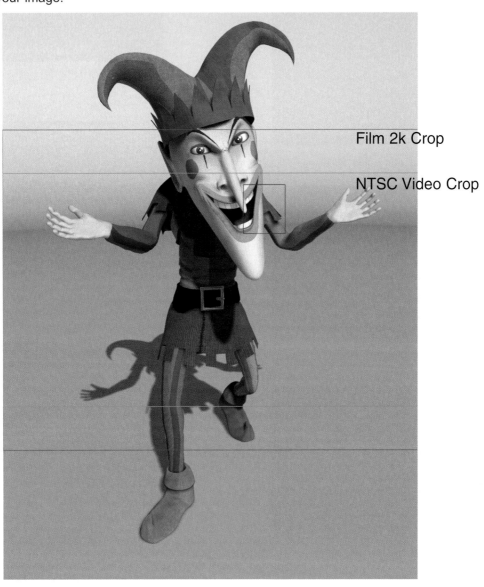

Film 2k Crop

NTSC Video Crop

Anti-Aliasing at
NTSC Resolutions

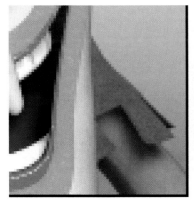

Area (Filter 1.0)

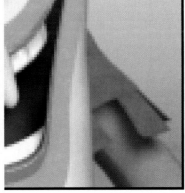

Area (default 1.5)

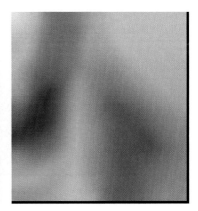

Area (Filter 20.0)

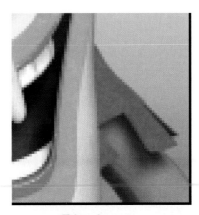

Blackman

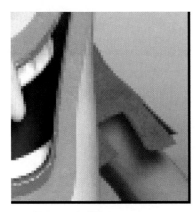

Blend (Filter 1.0,
Blend 0.0)

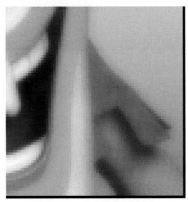

Blend (Filter 8.0,
Blend 0.3) default

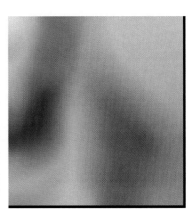

Blend (Filter 20,
Blend 1.0)

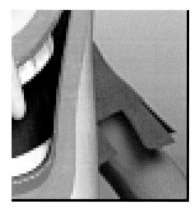

Catmull-Rom

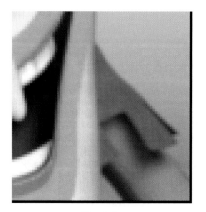

Cubic

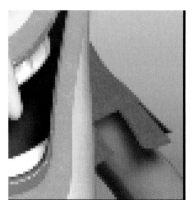

Cook Variable
(Filter 0.1)

Cook Variable
(Filter 2.5) default

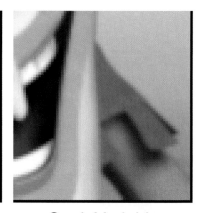

Cook Variable
(Filter 20.0)

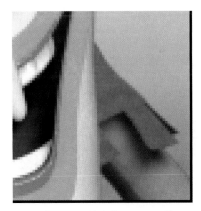

Mitchell-Netravali
(Blur 0.0, Ringing 0.0)

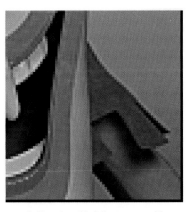

Mitchell-Netravali
(Blur 0.0, Ringing 1.0)

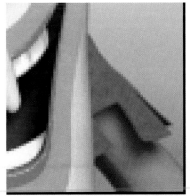

Mitchell-Netravali (default)
(Blur 0.333, Ringing 0.333)

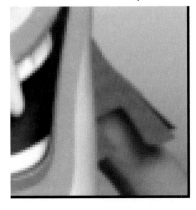

Mitchell-Netravali
(Blur 1.0, Ringing 0.0)

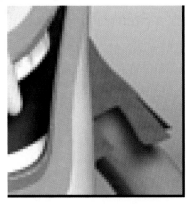

Mitchell-Netravali
(Blur 1.0, Ringing 1.0)

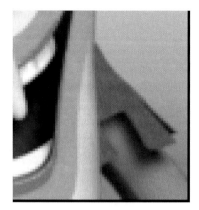

Quadratic

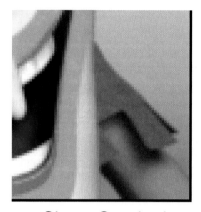

Sharp Quadratic

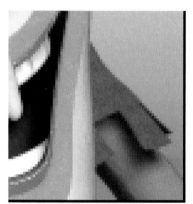

Plate Match/MAX R2
(Filter Size 1.0)

Plate Match/MAX R2
(Filter Size 1.5)
default

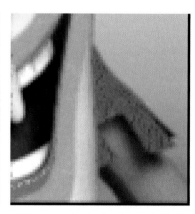

Plate Match/MAX R2
(Filter Size 2.0)

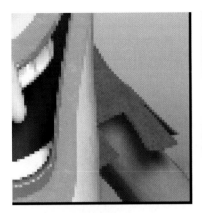 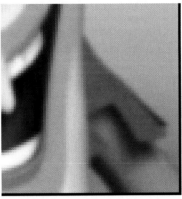 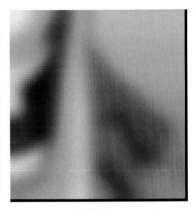

Soften	Soften (default)	Soften
(Filter Size 1.0)	(Filter Size 6.0)	(Filter Size 20.0)

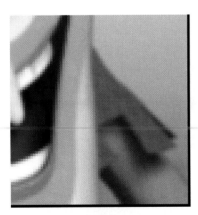

Video

Anti-Aliasing at Film Resolutions (2k)

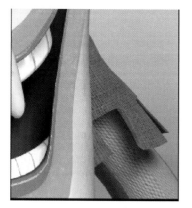

Area (Filter 1.0)

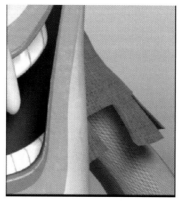

Area (default 1.5)

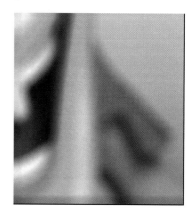

Area (Filter 20.0)

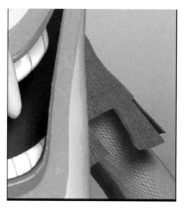

Blackman

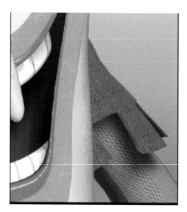

Blend (Filter 1.0,
Blend 0.0)

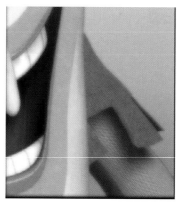

Blend (Filter 8.0,
Blend 0.3) default

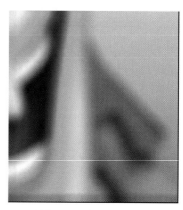

Blend (Filter 20,
Blend 1.0)

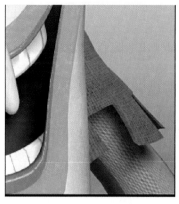

Catmull-Rom

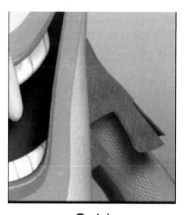

Cubic

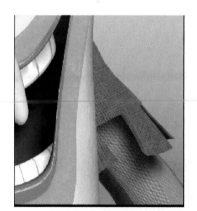

Cook Variable
(Filter 0.1)

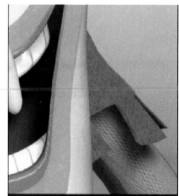

Cook Variable
(Filter 2.5) default

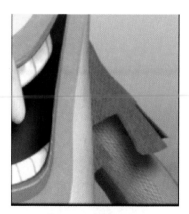

Cook Variable
(Filter 20.0)

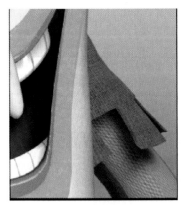

Mitchell-Netravali
(Blur 0.0, Ringing 0.0)

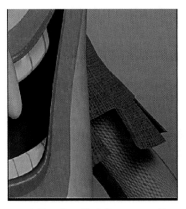

Mitchell-Netravali
(Blur 0.0, Ringing 1.0)

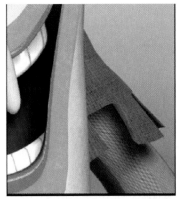

Mitchell-Netravali (default)
(Blur 0.333, Ringing 0.333)

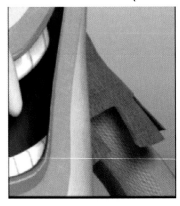

Mitchell-Netravali
(Blur 1.0, Ringing 0.0)

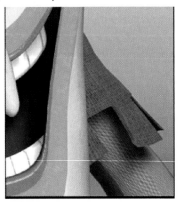

Mitchell-Netravali
(Blur 1.0, Ringing 1.0)

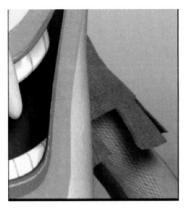

Quadratic

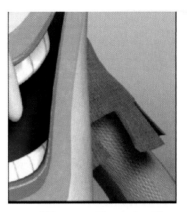

Sharp Quadratic

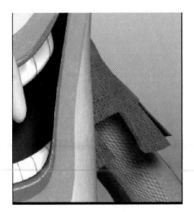

Plate Match/MAX R2
(Filter Size 1.0)

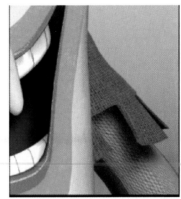

Plate Match/MAX R2
(Filter Size 1.5)
default

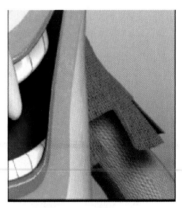

Plate Match/MAX R2
(Filter Size 2.0)

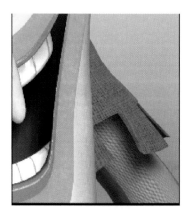

Soften
(Filter Size 1.0)

Soften (default)
(Filter Size 6.0)

Soften
(Filter Size 20.0)

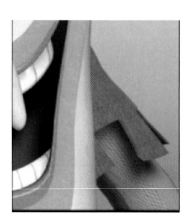

Video

4. Inside the Skin modifier, press the Add Bones button. Add the Mesh—Base object and the Bone—Right Hip object as bones.

   The Skin modifier makes an envelope for each bone that you add to it. All vertices that are inside an envelope follow that envelope. If a vertex is in two envelopes at one time, a weight value determines which envelope that vertex should be in. This is easily visualized, because skin turns the mesh different colors to show weighting.

5. In the Skin modifier, press the Edit Envelopes button.

   The Bbot turns red where there is an envelope affecting it. It turns blue where it is not being affected.

   The Skin modifier looks at the bone-bounding box to determine the envelope size. Because the Mesh—Base object is a big object, the envelope made for that bone is too big.

6. Adjust the size by either selecting the handles on the outside of the envelopes in the viewport, or by adjusting the Radius property in the Skin Modifier panel. See Figure 13.12.

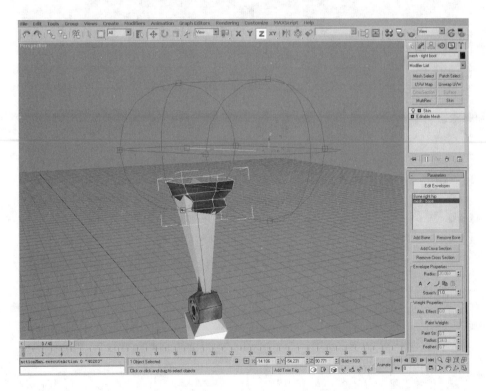

Figure 13.12   Adjust a Skin envelope.

7. Adjust the other bone's envelope, Bone—Right Hip, to cover the bottom half of the boot. You want each envelope to have about half of the boot object inside it.

8. Check the deformation by moving the Mesh—Base object up and down.

This leg is now set up, and you should copy it to make the left side.

9. Select all the pieces of the leg and, while holding down the Shift key, move the selection over to the left to copy all the pieces.

You need to adjust the Skin modifier on your new boot object.

10. Remove Bone—Right Hip Bone, and add Bone—Left Hip Bone, as shown in Figure 13.13.

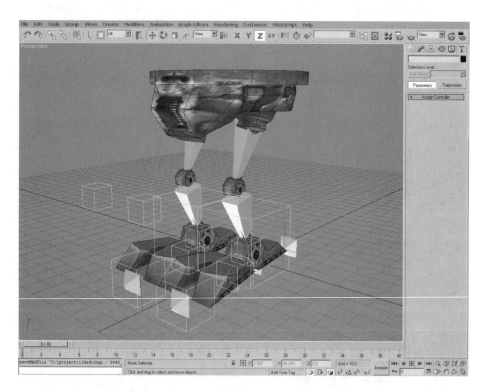

Figure 13.13 The leg is set up with all the IK and constraints completed.

If you plan on using this setup for a while, rename all the objects to reflect that they are now on the left side. For now open a previously set-up file that has all the naming correct.

11. Open Pug_Setup_3.max from the CD.

You will create some UI elements to make animating this cleaner and easier. First you make some manipulators, and then you make them work using Wire Parameters.

12. In the Command panel, under Create/Helpers/Manipulators, press the Slider button. Click in the viewport to create a Slider manipulator in the viewport.

This manipulator is a simple slider that you can attach to any attribute in max. See Figure 13.14.

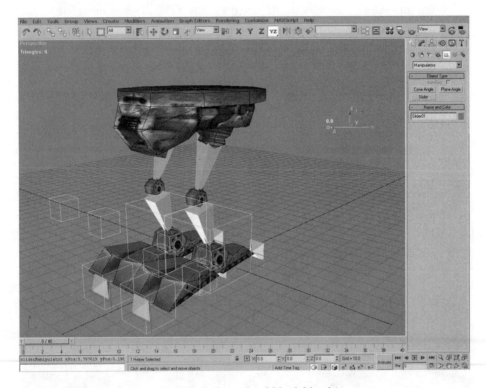

Figure 13.14   Your first Slider manipulator should look like this.

13. Customize this Slider manipulator by selecting it, going into the Modifier panel, and putting Right Toe Roll in the Name box. This names the manipulator in the viewport.

You are going to take the value from the Slider and pass it into another object's controller. In order to do this easily for rotation, you need to change the target object's rotation controller to Euler XYZ.

14. To change the target object's rotation controller to Euler XYZ, right-click the object's rotation controller in the Motion tab of the Command panel, and change it from TCB Rotation to Euler XYZ. This is already done for the dummies you will use in this file.

15. Make sure the Slider is still selected and right-click it. Select Wire Parameters from the bottom right Quad menu. A small dialog box opens up with two choices: Transform and Object(Slider).

16. Because you want the Slider to adjust the rotation of another object, choose Object(Slider)/Value.

max then draws a dotted line from that object to your cursor.

17. Pick the object that you want to wire the slider to. In this case, it's the Dummy—Right Toe Roll object. When the dialog box comes up again, choose Transform/Rotation/Z.

The Wire Parameters window opens, in which you determine where the value comes from and where it is wired. In this case you wire from the Slider's value to the Dummy's rotation.

18. Press the arrow in the direction that points right (Object Slider/value to Dummy—Right Toe Roll/Z rotation). See Figure 13.15.

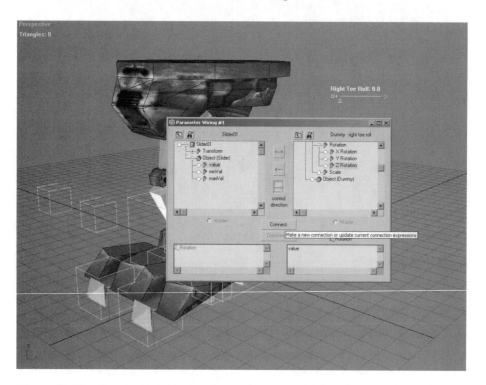

Figure 13.15   Wire the Slider's value to the Dummy's rotation in the Wire Parameters window.

Now that the connection is made, you can try your manipulator by going into Manipulate mode.

19. In Manipulate mode, try sliding the slider.

The leg should go kind of crazy, because the value that is being sent from the slider is too high.

20. Select the manipulator and go into the Modifier panel.

21. Change the Max Value to 1. Now try it. Much better.

22. Create another manipulator for the tiptoe roll using the same steps.

Note

Pug_Setup 4.max has all the manipulators set up. Take a look at it if you have any problems.

There you go. It's a nice easy-to-use leg setup.

Summary

Keep a couple of things about rigging in mind. First, you can approach rigging many ways. You might have 2 legs, 4 legs, or 40 legs. It's important to be comfortable with the components that make up the rig. Second, try to think about where to use IK, and how combinations of constraints can give you different results. Sometimes you might want things to be automated, using constraints and expressions, but there are also times where a simple manual setup is the best bet. This all depends on the artist and the situation. Happy rigging!

Chapter 14

Organic/Character Model Rigging for Broadcast/Film Applications

by Adam Holmes

Many 3D artists have a desire to be a character animator. They might feel that it's the only way to break into a large studio, or they are influenced into focusing all their efforts to character work by the incredible 3D films that have come out in recent years. The reality is, without an experienced technical director/character engineer you have no control over your character, and nothing to animate.

Character rigging involves more of a technical mind and thus turns a lot of 3D artists off. This job is as important as the animator, but tends not to be as high profile. This chapter explains character rigging in 3ds max 4 so you can understand the concepts and commands, expand your mind, and try new ways of working.

As 3D packages get more powerful, they offer more options for setting up controls for a character. This also means you need to be more selective about the tools you use, so you don't engineer yourself into a corner.

There are tools, such as Discreet's character studio, that provide a procedural IK skeleton system (Biped). This enables you to basically start animating out of the box for bipedal and quadripedal characters. Depending on your situation, this might be a very effective solution for you. In other situations, such as creating a spider character, you'll want to engineer your own controls. In that case, you need to know about the many new tools max 4 has to offer and how they all interact in a very technical way.

There are about as many character rigs as there are characters in your imagination, because each character you design presents unique challenges in its animation controls. Fortunately, there are guidelines that allow consistency in professional rigs. The process of rigging involves many new tools within 3ds max 4. Each topic is discussed in depth in this chapter, so be sure to pay extra attention to the details and you'll build a successful character rig.

IK Rigging

I asked a valued Discreet customer, Paul Neale, CEO of PEN Productions in Toronto, Canada, to comment on his approach to IK rigs. His current experience is in production of 3D animated TV series with 3ds max 4, which inherently has specific challenges and workflow, as opposed to creating a short animated film by yourself. Here is what he had to say:

"I find character setups to be sort of an art form in themselves. Speaking from the experience I've had on the production of an animated TV series, the way that I approach a character is to first find out what the character's personality is in relation to the story. This has an affect on how the character is to be animated and therefore might change the way I create controls. For example, if a supporting character doesn't have many spoken lines, I'd spend more time on other facial controls like eyes and eyebrows, so the character still has a wide range of expression and doesn't appear 'dead' next to the main character."

"The next step is to determine just how big a part the character plays in the production and if there are any special needs the animators are going to run into—for example, a scalable IK rig or removing an item from the character like a hat or piece of clothing. If the character is only going to have a small part in the show, I might be able to reduce the amount of work by not creating a full set of controls for it. In general, I try to give animators the most amount of control over a character with the least amount of physical control over objects and parameters that I can. The more control over the character you have, the potential for superior animation is much higher. You don't want an animator to feel restricted in how a character can 'act,' but also you want them to be efficient in bringing the character to life. With 30 animators creating an 11-minute show in two weeks, balancing quality with quantity is a science."

"The way I approached controlling IK rigs, I used the concept of control handles that have been created with spline objects. The animators can filter out the spline controls from the rest of the character by using the Shapes filter. This way, they don't have to worry about selecting the wrong object. I'll give credit here to my friend Sergio Mucino for coming up with the idea for the spherical controls that I now use (Sergio is a Discreet Certified Instructor)."

"I also use List Controllers on all parts of the IK rig (bones, IK goals, control objects, and so on) in the Position and Rotation tracks of those objects. It may sound like List Controllers complicate the rig, but they're actually easy to set up and reuse. For example, the first controller in a Rotation List holds the current offset from its parent object, and if there is no parent the world is the considered to be the parent. The second controller in the List is the one that is used for animating and is an offset from the first controller. So you have two Euler Rotation controllers in the List, but only the second controller holds the keyframes."

"Because of this, the second controller has a starting value of zero, and this makes it very easy to reset the character to the default position and rotation by just returning the second controller to a value of zero. Using expressions and Wire Parameters becomes easier with this setup as well. For example, you can wire the Position or Rotation of a bone to a control object (like a dummy or point) using the second controller, and the bone will have a relative offset from that control object and not an absolute value. Again, this is because the second controller has a starting value of zero, no matter what its world position or rotation is."

"I have created two MAXScripts that aid in creating List Controllers for this purpose, as well as for animating the second controller and resetting it. The scripts are PEN_Character_setup.mcr and PEN_Animation_controls.mcr. These can be found on the accompanying CD in the Pentools.zip file, as well as an IK rig (pen IK system35.max) that uses the principles I spoke about."

Both Paul and Sergio are frequent contributors to Discreet's free Web board, http://support.discreet.com.

This book is designed for the intermediate-to-advanced user, so this chapter doesn't explain the basic concepts of each tool. Instead, you learn how 3ds max 4 implements these industry-standard tools and how you can leverage the features to your benefit.

In this chapter you learn the following

- Creating bone objects
- Inverse kinematics (IK)
- Using Script controllers
- Setting up constraints
- Using Link constraints
- Setting up LookAt constraints
- Wiring Parameters
- Assigning the Reactor controller
- Creating Custom Attributes
- Using manipulators
- Skinning

Defining Bones

Let's start by talking about bones, which is a common term in all of 3D animation. Just like human bones, the bones in 3ds max define the linkages between joints (a hierarchy) and the rotations of your character's joints. In reality, a bone system is nothing more than a set of parented Pivot points, with some kind of visual connection between the Pivot points. In 3ds max 4, that visual representation can be anything: standard bone objects, teapots, lights, spheres, dodeca-whatevers. You get the idea. In fact, every object in max 4 carries a bone property that can be toggled on or off, and that has special squash and stretch capabilities.

A bone object in max has parameters, which are width, height, taper, and fin properties. These help you define the shape of the bone to fit the volume of each limb accurately, filling out the volume of the character. This is important because displaying the skin of a character while animating usually slows your computer down to the point where you're not interacting with the character in real time. Working with just the bones is very fast, but without a volumetric display of the bones (that is, without the bones being a 3D object), you have no reference of the character's size and shape. The fins also help you visualize and troubleshoot rotations of the bones.

Exercise 14.1   Creating a Bone System

In this exercise, you build a simple leg and apply an IK Solver to it to test some of the features on a small scale before you start to rig the Jester character from Chapter 9, "Organic/Character Modeling Using the Patch Method for Broadcast/Film."

1. Make the Front viewport full-screen and zoom in a little.
2. Turn on Grid Snapping.
3. Under the Animation drop-down menu, choose Create Bones.
4. Click once at the location of the top thighbone at about 100 units on the Z-axis and 0 on the X-axis.
5. Click again where the angle would be, straight down at coordinate 0,0,20.
6. Click where the ball of the foot would be, about 20 units on the X-axis, and 0 on the Z-axis.
7. Click where the toe would be, about another 20 units more on the X-axis, and 0 on the Z-axis.
8. Right-click to finish. Right-click again to cancel the Bone command.

   You should see a little bone nub at the end of your toe. This is a bone that gets automatically inserted after the last one you created. It's not needed all the time, but it is if you intend to assign an IK Solver to the previous bone. You can always delete it and substitute a Point object or a dummy if that's what you prefer.

   Your result should look something like Figure 14.1.

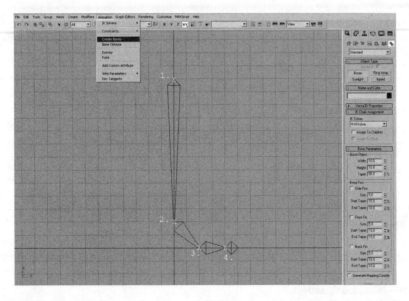

Figure 14.1   The little bone nub at the end of the toe gets automatically inserted after the last one you created.

I didn't instruct you to draw in a lower-leg bone so that you can learn to use the new Refine feature in the Modify panel. (Sneaky, aren't I? I warned you to pay attention, so if you drew it in, delete everything and start over!) It's not really a better method than drawing a lower-leg bone to begin with; this workflow just shows how to use some new tools.

9. Select the thighbone and open the Modify panel. Play with the different spinners and values for sizing and fins. Turn on Shaded Mode and orbit around the bones to see how they look in 3D.

10. Go back to the Front viewport and, with the thighbone still selected, choose the Refine button in the Modify panel.

11. Click the thighbone and it will split where you selected it. This might not be exactly where you want to have the knee, so you adjust it in the next step.

12. Go to the Hierarchy panel and click the Don't Affect Children button in the Adjust Transform rollout.

13. Select the calf bone and move it out on X to define the knee bend.

Note

Defining the Preferred Angle is important in an IK system, and you just did it by creating a knee bend. You can always adjust this later in the process, but it's generally better to have it as close as possible up front to give you a better starting point if you need to tweak it.

Tip

If you want to create a new bone and have it look like a previous bone in your scene, there's a little trick to do that. Select the bone you want to mimic and open the Modify panel. Then create a new bone like usual, and it will have the same parameters as the one you just selected!

Drawing bones is very easy, and you can see that there's some new ways to work with them. Now, on to assigning an IK Solver to those leg bones.

Exercise 14.2   Assigning HI IK

3ds max 4's solvers are a plug-in class, which makes adding new solvers very easy. There are currently three solvers, the HI IK (history-independent), the HD IK (history-dependent, the max 3.1 IK Solver), and the IK Limb (a subset of the HI IK for two-bone chains). This means that it's easy for new solvers to be added to the system. In fact, the IK Limb is open source code that can be modified for further development, and is mainly geared toward video game developers, but it's useful in any two-bone IK situation.

The main differences between the solvers was explained in Chapter 3, "Changes in Animation," so I won't go over them again here.

In this exercise, you assign the HI-IK Solvers.

1. Select the thighbone and, in the Animation drop-down menu, select IK Solvers/HI Solver.

2. Click the third bone (the anklebone).

3. Select the IK goal that appears (the little blue cross) and move the IK chain around.

4. With the IK goal still selected, turn on Manipulate mode (use the Quad menu) and you'll see a Swivel Angle manipulator appear.

5. Move it around to twist the knee joint.

   In a slightly orbited view, you see the effect better. If you open the Motion panel, you see the Swivel Angle parameter's value change as you move the manipulator, as seen in Figure 14.2.

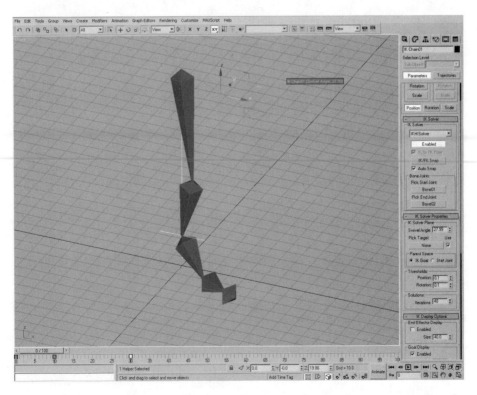

Figure 14.2   In this example, the Swivel Angle parameter's value changes as you adjust the manipulator.

Now try some animation and test the new IK/FK switch. This enables you to seamlessly transfer animation control from the IK goal to the bone's rotation (forward kinematics) and back. This feature is necessary because not all limb movements are IK or forward kinematics (FK) all the time.

6. Reposition the IK goal to its original position.

7. Turn on Animate and move to frame 10.

8. Move the IK goal straight up on the Z-axis for an IK movement.

9. Stay on frame 10 and, in the Motion Panel/IK Solver rollout, turn the Enabled button off.

10. Move to frame 30. (See Figure 14.3.)

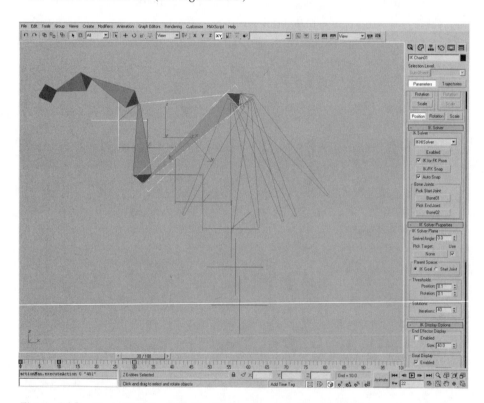

Figure 14.3   Max's Ghosting effect is displayed to visualize the rotations and movements.

11. Select and rotate the thighbone back on its Local Z.

12. Scrub the timeline to see the animation transition from IK to FK at frame 10.

13. Move the time slider to frame 30 and turn the Enabled button back on.

The IK goal snaps back to the ankle. If you're in a situation where you need it to snap back, click the IK/FK Snap button in that same rollout.

14. Move the time slider to frame 40 and animate another IK move of the IK goal.

Let's see what's going on "under the hood."

15. Select the IK goal and go to Track View Selected in the Quad menu.

16. Expand the tracks and you see that there's an Enabled track that enables the IK Solver to be turned on or off over time, as seen in Figure 14.4.

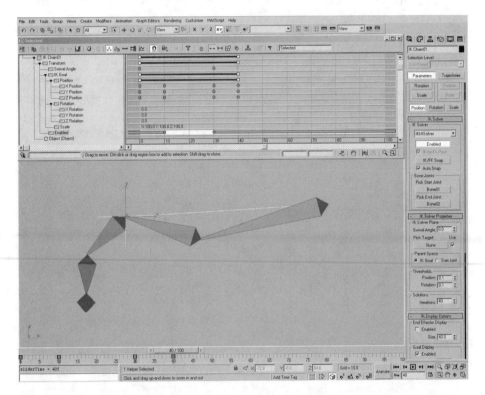

Figure 14.4   When editing keyframes, remember that the Swivel Angle parameter has keyframes added automatically to prevent joints from flipping unnaturally.

17. Click bone01.

In the Track view, the bone has an FK subcontrol on its transform track. This enables the bones to have rotational FK control when IK is off. Pretty cool, huh?

Tip

In editing IK/FK animations, be aware of all the keys that are taking place to make the movement transition natural. Because of this, always select both the IK goal and the bones in that IK chain (in this case, the thigh and calf bones) to do timing changes in the track bar or Track view. This way, you keep the groups of keys that need to be together intact. Having the Modify Sub-Tree button on in the Track view also makes this process easier.

It's also advisable not to add keys manually in Track view to the IK Enabled track, because it can mess up your animation and might lead to a crash.

18. Move the time slider to frame 20 and turn Animate on.

19. Select the IK chain and click the IK/FK Snap button to reset the IK goal's position.

20. Move the IK goal around to pose the bones.

In this mode, IK is temporarily turned on so you can pose the bones, but it's the *rotations* of the bones that are still being animated. I'll say it again—pretty cool, huh?

If you want to alter the Preferred Angle of a bone after the IK Solver has been applied, you do it in the Hierarchy Panel/IK section, as seen in Figure 14.5.

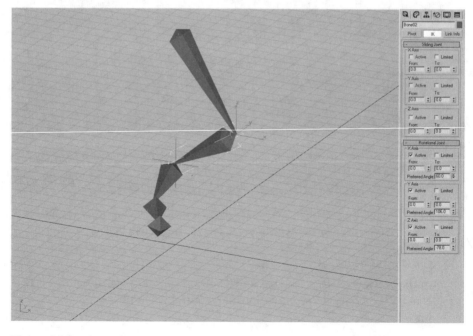

Figure 14.5   The Preferred Angle parameters of the bones are shown here.

21. Select the calf bone, and adjust the X-axis Preferred Angle spinner.

    If you move the thighbone down on the Z-axis, the foot follows the rotation and goes through the floor. You're going to use another IK chain to lock down the foot.

22. Select the anklebone (bone03) and choose the HI Solver in the Animation/IK Solvers drop-down menu.

23. Select the ball bone (bone04) to apply the IK.

24. Move the ankle IK goal and see how it behaves.

25. Move the thighbone down and notice that the foot now sticks to the ground.

26. Adjust the Swivel Angle; you'll probably see both the knee and the ankle rotate.

27. To fix that, select the second IK goal and, in the Motion panel, make sure the Parent Space option is set to IK Goal and the Swivel Angle is 0. This prevents the two Swivel Angles from interacting.

28. Create one more IK chain from the ball bone to the bone nub (bone05). This sticks that bone down and sets up rotational control of the toe for a step later in this section.

29. Make sure that this IK goal is in IK goal space as well. (See Figure 14.6.)

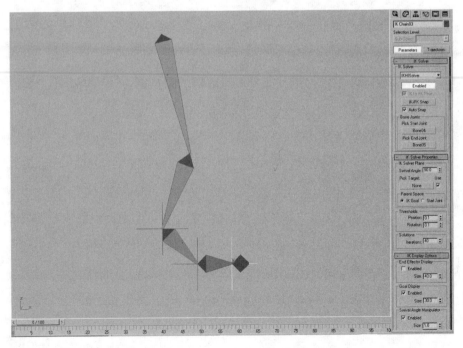

Figure 14.6   Make sure that the IK goal for the ball bone to the bone nub is in IK goal space.

Move the different parts of the bones and IK around to get a feel for how it moves. If you pull the thighbone forward on the X-axis, the foot bones don't quite "peel off" correctly. There is no Precedence setting in HI IK, as there is in HD IK. HD IK is designed more for mechanical IK systems, and it has this parameter. It essentially enables you to weigh the IK chains so one chain has to reach its limit before the next one can take effect (which is great for a retracting telescope effect).

There is a small IK trick to overcome this HI-IK limitation.

30. First, hold the scene.

31. Select bone02 and add a HI-IK chain from that bone to bone04. Make sure the Parent Space is set to IK Goal and the Swivel Angle is **0**.

32. Select bone03 and add an HI-IK chain from that bone to bone05. Make sure the Parent Space is set to IK goal and the Swivel Angle is **0**.

You've just made some overlapping IK chains, which is another nice feature of HI IK.

33. Move the thighbone forward on the X-axis and you'll see the peel-off effect, as seen in Figure 14.7.

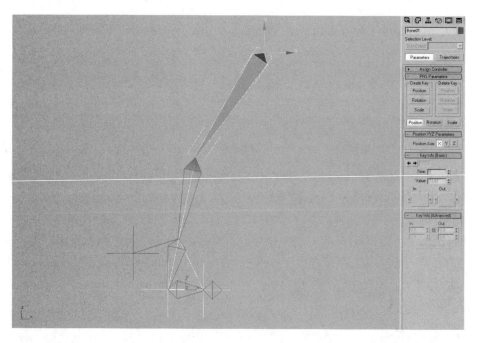

Figure 14.7   As you move the thighbone forward on the X-axis, the foot bones peel off from the IK Solvers correctly.

Because there's never a perfect rig that works best in all situations, use this method only if you really need that kind of movement. It's better to keep the IK system as simple as possible for speed and editing animation. Many times in a large animation house, they'll engineer characters with different rigs for special shots and animation needs. That way they're not trying to make a rig animate in a way it wasn't designed to.

Exercise 14.3   Creating a Stretchy Leg

Now you start to have fun with the IK system. You're going to look at a way to make the leg stretchy automatically when the IK goal is moved past the IK limits. This is great for those cartoony character setups, and though you can do it manually, as explained in Chapter 3, this is a good exercise for learning more advanced max tools (which is why you're reading this book in the first place, right?).

In this exercise, you write some MAXScript that enables you to extend the capabilities of the IK system to automatically stretch the bones as you move the IK around.

1. Fetch the scene to get back to your original IK setup.

   You need three numbers: the X Position that the Track view reports for bone02 and bone03, and the distance at which the IK chain reaches its limit.

2. Select bone02 and look in the Track view to find the X position value.

   If your controller is not a Position XYZ, you have to change the controller.

3. Select the Position controller and click the Assign Controller button, just above the Position track.

4. Select the Position XYZ and click Make Default, Yes, and OK. (See Figure 14.8.)

5. Select bone03 and find its X value, for use in line 4 of the script you'll enter shortly.

6. Move the IK goal down until the leg is completely straight, but the goal isn't off the ankle. Move slowly to get it right.

7. In the MAXScript Listener window, type the following: **distance $IKChain01.pos $Bone01.pos**. Then press Enter. Write down the number that MAXScript gives you; you'll use it in line 3 of the script. This is the distance from the IK Goal and the position of bone01.

8. Move the IK goal back to its original position.

9. Change the X Position controller to a Float Script controller. The Script Controller Editor pops up. Note the X Position Value in the window.

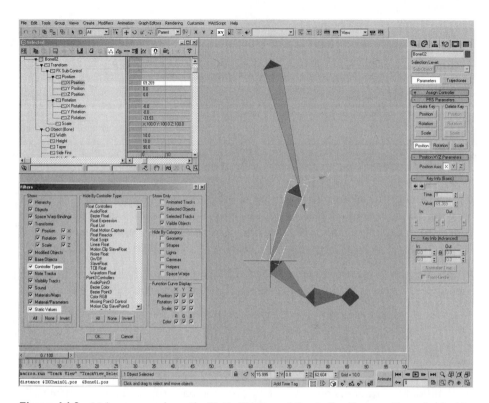

Figure 14.8   Make sure you have the Static Values and Controller Types options checked in the Track view filters.

10. Type the following script (pressing Return after each line), substituting the values presented for your own:

```
dependsOn $IKChain01.pos.controller $Bone01.pos.controller
d = distance $IKChain01.pos  $Bone01.pos
ex = (d - 114.75)
orig = 69.269
if (ex < 0) then
    ex = 0
p = orig + (ex/2)
```

 Note

The dependsON command in line 1 is new to MAXScript. It enables you to tell max when to interactively evaluate the script based on any number of object parameters changing. Previously you'd have to move the time slider to see a Script controller update. Now it updates interactively.

Line 1 in the script sets Interactive Update to occur when the IK goal's and bone02's position changes.

Line 2 measures the distance between the IK goal and bone01, just as you did before, and sets it to a variable.

Line 3 subtracts the extended leg distance from the current distance, and sets it to a variable.

Line 4 sets the original X position of bone01 to a variable.

Line 5 determines whether the leg is not extended and sets the extended distance to 0 if that's true.

Line 6 is the last line in the script, and the output of this line actually sets the value of X position, which controls the stretch of the leg. Take the original X Position value, add the extend value, and divide by 2 to get an even stretch over both bones (you'll repeat this script on bone03).

11. Click Evaluate and Close.

12. Select bone03 and repeat the procedure beginning at Step 1, substituting the original X Position value for bone03.

You should have a stretchy leg now when you move the IK goal.

13. Load the max file 01stretchyLeg.max to see the final result, as seen in Figure 14.9.

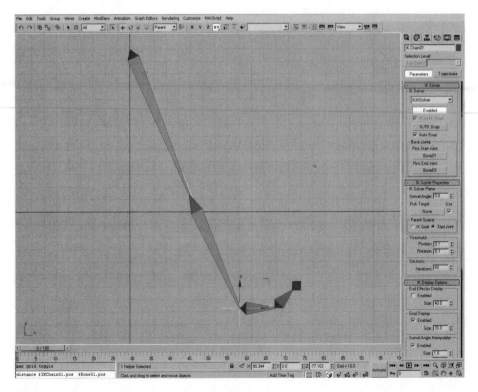

Figure 14.9   This figure shows the final stretchy leg.

Note

This procedure was based on the work of my talented friend, Michael Comet. He has a great Web site with max tutorials. Visit www.comet-cartoons.com.

Now that you've gotten some experience in the new IK and bone tools, it's time to move on to designing the Jester character's bones.

Exercise 14.4   Creating Jester's Leg Bones

If you felt lost in the previous exercises, go back and do them again to be sure you're comfortable with the terminology, the rollouts, and the procedures. Experiment a bit and then continue here.

You're going to start with leg bones and IK for the Jester character that you modeled in Chapter 9. Let's look at some more tools to add to your bag of tricks and get this guy moving!

You can load the Jester you created previously, or load the max file right_leg_start.max from the CD-ROM.

1. Choose Create Bones in the Animation drop-down menu and before you start drawing, change the height and width to .5.

   The Jester model is small and the default bone size of 10 is too big.

2. In the Left viewport, draw two bones starting at the hip and continuing to the knee, and then to the ankle.

3. Right-click two times to end bone creation.

4. In the Front viewport, move the bones over so the ankle joint lines up to the center of the leg.

5. Use the Don't Affect Children mode in the Hierarchy/Pivot panel to move the hipbone back toward the pelvis. This model is rather bowlegged, which will present some challenges later in skinning and animation.

6. Do some adjustments on the width, height, taper, and fins to make the bones fill the model space, as seen in Figure 14.10.

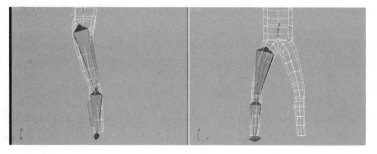

Figure 14.10   Adjust the width, height, taper, and fins to make the bones fill the model's volume.

7. Select all the bones, make sure you're in world-coordinate space, and Use Pivot Point Center in the Active Pivot option (the button next to the coordinate space dropdown in the main toolbar).

8. Select the Mirror button on the main toolbar and choose X, Copy, and Mirror Bones.

9. Use the Offset spinner to adjust the mirrored bone's position.

10. Click OK.

11. Hide the mirrored bones, because you work with that leg later.

Note

The Mirror Bones option counteracts the effects of a negative scale when mirroring. As you know, mirroring is actually a negative scale effect. Having mirrored axes and a negative scale on an object can lead to problems later as you work with more advanced tools, such as constraints. Face all axes the same way on similar body parts and scale at positive 100%.

Mirroring IK chains and bones is not really the best idea, because that might lead to a crash or unpredictable behavior of the mirrored IK chain. It's safer to mirror just the bones and assign each IK chain individually.

Next you draw the foot bones. The hierarchies of the leg and foot remain separate for maximum flexibility. You'll connect them later using a Position constraint.

12. Unhide the Shoe Right object.

13. In the Left view, draw the anklebone starting from the shinbone. Click on the shin to draw off its pivot.

14. Add the ball and right-click to add the toe nub.

15. Make sure the foot bone's Z-positions are set to 0, so they will be on the "floor" of the world.

16. Play with the width, height, fins, and tapering to get the bones to fill the shoe.

17. Adjust the bones with the Don't Affect Children tool in the Hierarchy/Pivot panel.

18. You might need to set Non-Uniform Scale for the toe nub. That's fine; just reset the scale in the Hierarchy panel.

19. Make sure everything lines up in the Front view as well. (See Figure 14.11.)

After setting up the leg bones, you're ready for the next exercise, setting up the IK and constraints.

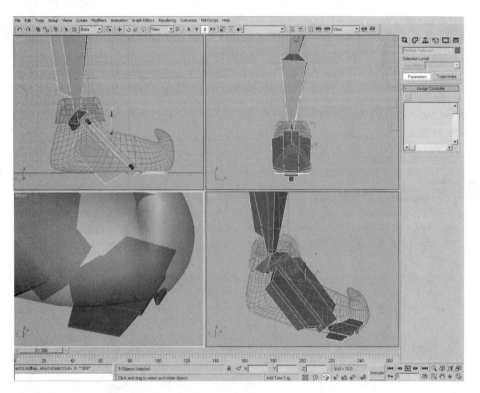

Figure 14.11   Use Non-Uniform Scale to adjust the toe bone nub, and make sure all the bones line up in the Front view.

Exercise 14.5   Setting Up Leg IK and Constraints

These steps are similar to Exercise 14.1, so you should be able to breeze through it!

1. Add a HI-IK Solver to the leg from bone01 to bone03.

   You'll notice immediately that two things are wrong. The IK goal is huge, and when you move the goal, the foot moves. (Remember I said it shouldn't be part of the hierarchy?)

2. Unlink bone04 (the anklebone).

3. Select the IK goal and go to the Motion panel.

4. Adjust the IK goal size in the IK Display Options rollout to be more reasonable.

5. If you turn on Manipulate mode, you'll see that the Swivel Angle is huge. Use the Display options in the same rollout to fix this.

6. Set the Parent Space to IK Goal.

Later, you'll parent this leg to another control object. Setting the Parent Space to IK Goal stops unwanted rotations from being passed to the leg.

7. Turn off Manipulate mode and animate the IK goal moving up in the Z-axis over a few frames.

Notice that the knee swings out a little too far? You can fix that by adjusting the IK limits.

8. Select bone04 and go to the Hierarchy/IK panel.

9. In the Rotational Joint rollout, make the Preferred Angle on the Y-axis about 8.

10. Turn on the Limited check box and type **8** in the To field. Leave the From field at 0. (See Figure 14.12.)

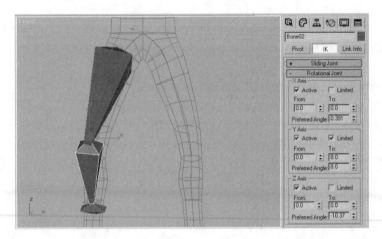

Figure 14.12   When you limit rotations, this constrains the joints to behave more predictably during animation.

11. Select bone04 and add a Position constraint from the Animation/ Constraints drop-down menu.

12. Select bone03, the nub at the base of the ankle, as the target.

The reason you didn't constrain the bone to the IK goal is that the goal can be pulled off the bones, and you want the anklebone to stay locked in position with the leg.

13. Test the movement of the IK goals. Notice that the bones are jiggling a little bit? This is because the IK threshold values are too large.

14. Select the leg IK goal and go to the Motion Panel/IK Solver Properties rollout. Change the position and rotation thresholds to **.01**. You need this step because your model is at such a small scale.

15. Test the movement again. It should be much smoother.

16. Now unhide the left leg, and before you copy the foot hierarchy over, delete the target from the Position constraint. Do this in the Motion panel.

17. Now copy the foot over and align it to the left leg.

18. Add the correct targets to each anklebone for the Position constraint.

19. Next, add an HI-IK Solver from each anklebone to its corresponding foot bone.

20. Add another one from the foot bone to the toe nub, on each foot.

21. Again, adjust the IK goal display, and turn off the Swivel Angle manipulator's Enabled switch for each IK chain.

22. Set the Parent Space of each IK chain to IK Goal and set the thresholds to .01.

Now that you have one leg working with IK on a basic level, it's time to add some sophisticated controls to make the typical heel-ball-toe foot animation easy.

Exercise 14.6   Designing Spline Controls and Linking

Now that the leg is set up, your challenge is to design some custom controls to rotate the feet on the ankle, heel, ball, and toe. There are several ways to do this with Point objects or dummies, but you're going to use splines. Why splines? Because they can look like anything, not just a box.

I've provided a file with some spline controls that I created that should work for you, but feel free to design your own.

1. Choose File/Merge command and load spline_controls_foot.max.

2. Using the Align tool, move these splines around to fit your exact IK rig. Align from the pivot of each spline to the pivot of each corresponding bone. The footpad has its pivot above the spline, where the ankle's pivot is. Use Affect Pivot Only mode in the Hierarchy panel to align.

The front two splines with the balls on the ends should line up with the toe IK and the ball joint IK.

Keep the spline/ball at the heel lined up with the back of the footpad. Unhiding the geometry might help you as well. (See Figure 14.13.)

Now for some hierarchy magic! How you link the spline controls to the IK goals is very important. You want all the rotations to work correctly to make a foot roll from heel to ball to toe, and to have ankle rotation.

Refer to Figure 14.14 while you make the following connections.

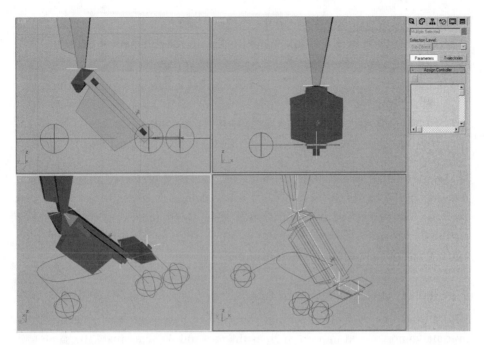

Figure 14.13   Align the spline controls to the foot bones.

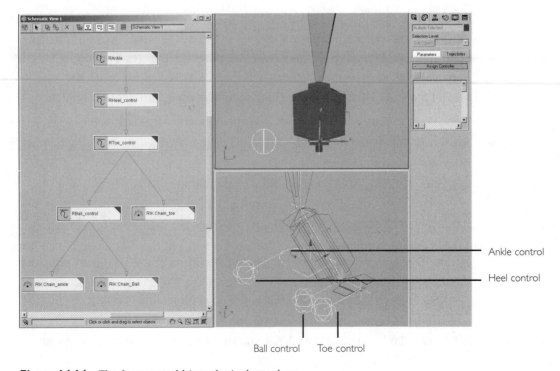

Figure 14.14   The foot control hierarchy is shown here.

3. Link the IK goal on the toe to the toe control spline.

4. Link the IK goals on the ankle and the ball to the ball control spline.

5. Link the ball control spline to the toe control spline.

6. Link the toe control spline to the heel control spline (the spline with the ball at the end).

7. Finally, link that spline to the footpad or ankle control.

8. Now test the control splines by rotating them on their local Y-axis.

That wasn't so bad, was it? You have some very fine control now of all the pertinent rotations of the foot. Bear in mind that this system isn't 100% perfect, but it gets the desired movement with minimal work. The only thing lacking is the capability for the heel rotation control (footpad) to follow the foot's ball rotation, but it's a minor thing to deal with during animation.

Exercise 14.7   Adding an Automatic Foot Roll

With all this fine control, sometimes you want to have some fast general control over a commonly used motion, such as the foot roll. Why animate the same four objects over and over to get the foot to "walk" when you can consolidate that movement to one spinner or slider?

This is a good test of combining some new and updated tools: Custom Attributes (CAs) and the Reactor controller. Max 3.1 provided the Reactor controller, but improvements have been made to it in 3ds max 4. (The Reactor controller is not to be confused with Discreet's reactor plug-in for dynamics and physics simulations.)

If you want to start from this point, load the file right_leg_linked.max.

Before you get started, you need to run a scripted plug-in that creates a modifier necessary for the next steps.

1. Select the drop-down MAXScript/Run Script and find your max 4 folder. In there, open the scripts/PluginScripts folder.

2. Open the Modifier-Attribute Holder.ms script.

3. Select the footpad (RAnkle control) object and add the new modifier you just installed. Look for Attribute Holder at the bottom of the Modifier List, under Unassigned Modifiers.

   This is just a blank modifier that is designed for adding CAs to it.

4. Under the Animation drop-down, choose Add Custom Attribute.

5. Make the Parameter type a Float, the UI type a Spinner, and the width **80**.

6. Set the Range so that it's from –20 to 50, default: 0.

7. Under the Finish rollout, choose Object's Current Modifier in the drop-down list.

8. Click Add.

   This spinner now can be used to control anything within the scene, much like a Slider manipulator or Plane Angle manipulator that you used in the setup of the fire truck. See Figure 14.15 for the Custom Attribute dialog box.

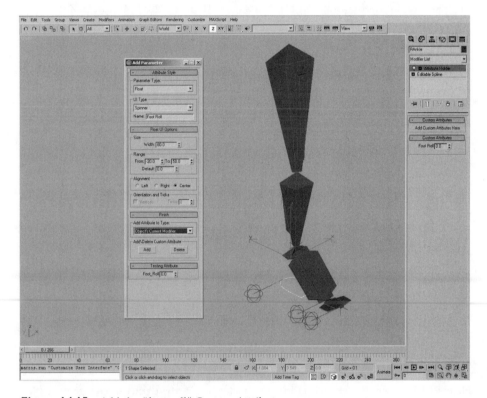

Figure 14.15   Add the "foot roll" Custom Attribute.

There's one more setup procedure you need to do before getting into the Reactor controller: Freezing Rotations. This is not a critical step, but more of a slightly hidden feature that can come in handy later.

9. Choose Customize/Customize User Interface and go to the Quad menu.

10. Choose Animation 1 Quad [Alt+RMB] from the drop-down list and in the Category on the left side, find Animation Tools. These are little scripts you can add to your Quad menu.

11. Drag the Freeze Position and Position to Zero commands to the Position Quad listing (lower-right quad). Add a separator to keep things neat.

12. Drag the Freeze Rotation and Rotation to Zero commands to the Rotation Quad (upper-right quad).

13. Close the dialog box and save your UI scheme. Choose whatever name you like.

14. Select the heel spline control and press Alt+right-click to call up the Animation Quad.

15. Select the Freeze Rotation command.

16. Rotate the heel control on the X-axis and then try the Rotation to Zero command.

See Figure 14.16 for the Customize User Interface dialog box.

Figure 14.16   The Customize User Interface dialog box is where you can change the look and feel of the interface.

The List controller has two layers of rotation. One layer always remains constant, at the rotation where you froze it. The second Rotation controller is the one you animate. Setting that one back to 0 resets the rotation, and the first controller's value is then visible. Think of the second controller that you animate as an offset of the first one.

Look in the Track view to see these controllers. If you used the scene files on the CD-ROM, they include a custom Track view found in the drop-down menu of the Graph Editors/Track view menu called Controller Edit. Click it in the Graph Editors drop-down menu to see the List controllers.

17. Repeat Steps 14 and 15 on the other spline controls. (You can select them all at once and freeze the rotations.)

Finally, you're ready to add the Reactor controller.

18. Select the heel spline control and open that custom Controller Edit Track view, or just open the Track view and make sure Selected Objects Only and the Controller Types filters are on.

If you want, you can turn on the Show Hierarchy filter to see a cascading list of your objects, modifiers, and controllers, but I find this too cluttered in the display.

19. Expand all the tracks (you remember, right-click, and so forth).

20. Click on the X Position track of the Keyframe XYZ: Euler XYZ track.

21. Click the Assign Controller button and add a Float Reactor.

A little dialog box pops up and you're ready for action!

22. Click the React To button and then click the footpad (RAnkle control).

A Wire Parameter style pop-up menu appears.

23. Choose Modified Object/Attribute Holder/Custom_Attributes/Foot_Roll.

You assigned the Reactor controller to the X Rotation track and linked it to the Foot_Roll Custom Attribute. Reaction01 is 0 rotation of the heel spline and 0 value of the Foot_Roll spinner. See Figure 14.17 for the menus.

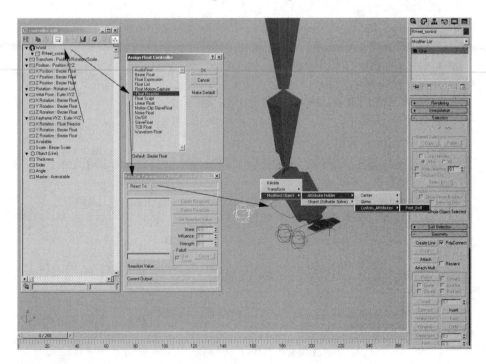

Figure 14.17   Assign the Reactor controller to create the automatic foot roll effect.

Now you need to set up a second reaction for the motion of rocking back on the heel.

24. Select the footpad and make the value of the Foot_Roll –20.

25. In the Reactor Parameters dialog box, click Create Reaction. Now you have Reaction02.

26. Next, adjust the value of the State spinner (which is controlling the X Rotation of the heel control) to –.9, or just before the knee of the leg becomes straight.

27. Test the reaction by adjusting the Foot_Roll spinner from 0 to –20 and back. Pretty cool, huh?

28. Click the Curve button to see the linear interpolation of the reactions. You can edit the reactions here as well, adding more, or ease in and out points, to the curve.

29. Close the Reactor dialog box.

Now you can do a similar procedure for the rotation of the ball of the foot.

30. Set the Foot_Roll spinner back to 0.

31. Select the ball rotation spline and replace its X Position track with a Float Reactor, as you did in Step 21.

32. Click on the React To button and click the footpad. Connect to the same Custom Attribute as in Step 23.

33. Select the footpad (RAnkle), change the Foot_Roll spinner to 25, and click Create Reaction.

34. On Reaction02, set the state value to about .66, or just before the ball of the foot is vertical.

35. Close the Reactor dialog box and test the Foot_Roll.

Finally, place a reaction on the rotation of the toe spline control.

36. Set the Foot_Roll spinner to 25.

37. Select the toe rotation spline and replace its X Position track with a Float Reactor, as you did in Step 21.

38. Click on the React To button and click the footpad. Connect to the Foot_Roll Custom Attribute.

39. Select the footpad, change the Foot_Roll spinner to 50, and click Create Reaction.

40. On Reaction02, set the state value to about 1.7, or when the toe of the foot is vertical.

41. Close the Reactor dialog box and test the Foot_Roll.

That's working very nicely—and the beauty is that nothing is time-based. Everything is parameter-based, which means you can change the reactions and affect all the animation in the entire scene. Just don't delete the Attribute modifier, or you'll lose the connection to the Reactor controller and have to do this exercise again!

The only problem with this setup is that you lost manual control of the splines. Get it back by using a List controller on those Reactors.

42. Select the heel spline control and in the Track view, select X Rotation: Float Reactor.

43. Click the Assign Controller button and add a Float List.

44. Expand the list and click the Available slot.

45. Click the Assign Controller button again and add a Bezier Float.

46. Select X Rotation: Float List and right-click to open its properties.

47. Click the Bezier Float and click Set Active.

48. Close that window and test-rotate the control manually, and then with the Foot_Roll spinner.

49. Repeat from Step 42 for the other ball and toe spline controls. See Figure 14.18 for the menus.

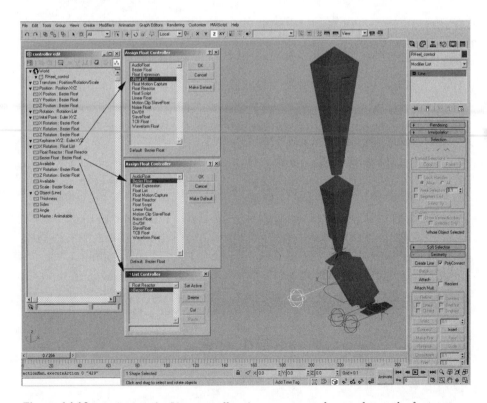

Figure 14.18   Assigning the List controller gives you manual control over the foot movement while maintaining automatic control through the Custom Attribute.

This might seem like a complicated procedure, and writing some MAXScripts could automate this process, if you want this to be a default setup when rigging another character. It's important to know the nuts and bolts of a procedure such as this so you can take that knowledge and apply it to creating scripts. Try this on your own if you're interested in scripting. For now, continue with creating this rig the old-fashioned way.

50. Unhide the other leg and foot you copied/mirrored. You get to do the whole process again! It's good practice, though. Start with Exercise 14.5.

You might also want to use the Freeze Position command that you put into the Animation Quad on the footpads in case you move them accidentally. The next exercise covers the design of the hip control.

Exercise 14.8   Designing the Hip Controls

In this exercise you create the hip controls that will be the master parent of the hierarchy (except the feet, which always remain separate). This is also commonly referred to as the *Center of Mass*.

If you need to start from this point, load the max file leg_torso_start.max.

To begin, create four objects: an ellipse, two control splines like the ones you used for the feet, and a Point helper.

1. Create an ellipse in the Top viewport and center it on the Jester's waist, just above the thighbones (bone01 and bone07). Name it **COM**.

2. Merge in two spline controls from the file hip_controls.max and align their pivots with the center of the ellipse.

3. Unlock the spline's Z Rotation in the Hierarchy/Link Info panel.

4. Face the spline controls to each other, one sticking out of the front and one sticking out the back.

5. Be sure to have the pivots of all objects aligned to the world. In the Hierarchy/Pivot panel, choose Affect Pivot Only/Align to World.

6. Name the spline that's pointing out the front **Pelvis_control** and the one sticking out the back **Spine_control01**.

7. Create a Point object in the Top viewport and align it to the center of the ellipse named COM. Scale it down and reset the scale. Name it **Master Point**.

Now you're good to go. See Figure 14.19 if there's any confusion.

It's time to link it all.

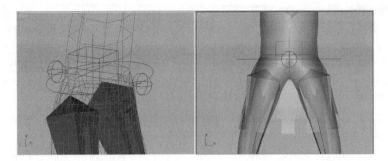

Figure 14.19   In this figure, the Point object is aligned to the center of the ellipse.

8. Link bone01, bone07, bone04, and bone10 (thighbones and anklebones) to the Pelvis_control spline.
9. Link the Pelvis_control and the Spine_control to the COM, as seen in Figure 14.20.

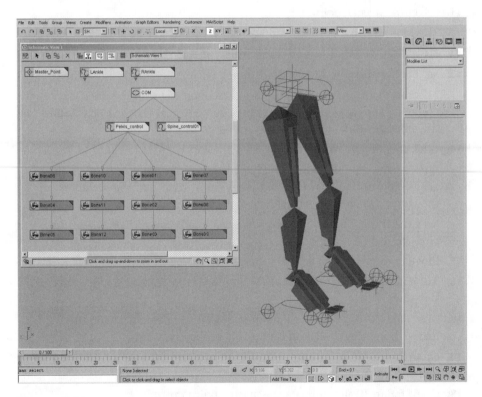

Figure 14.20   In this figure, the Pelvis_control and the Spine_control are linked to the COM.

Test the movement of the character now. Move and rotate the COM ellipse and the spline controls. The Spine control isn't supposed to do anything at this point, because you haven't built the spine bones. Make sure that the feet are behaving and that when you move the ellipse down, the feet don't rotate. If they do, you probably don't have the IK Parent Space set to IK Goal on the ankle and ball IK chains.

Optionally, you might want to use Freeze Rotation and Position on the COM and Freeze Rotation on the spline controls.

Now you're probably asking yourself, "Why is that Point object in the scene when it's not doing anything?"

That master_point is going to be a temporary parent/COM when you want the Jester to fly through the air and do flips. You can do this with the fancy new Link constraint, which is essentially an animated hierarchy tool.

10. Select the COM ellipse and under the Animation drop-down, select Constraints/Link Constraint.

11. Select the master_point.

    The Motion panel pops up and you can do some editing.

12. First, delete the master_point link. You don't need it now.

13. Set the Key mode to Key Nodes/Parents.

    This sets PRS keys (position, rotation, scale) on the ellipse to lock it between hierarchy switches. If it didn't do this, you'd get unwanted interpolation of the animated link as you edit the animation.

14. Click the Link to World button.

    This is handy because you don't have to have a dummy or another object act as the world link. The COM behaves as if it has no other parent except the world, which every object has by default.

    Let's test this animated link. You can use as many frames as you want to animate.

15. Move to frame 10 and animate the COM moving forward.

16. Animate the master_point so it's centered on the COM at frame 10 (using the Align tool).

17. Select the COM. Click Add Link in the Link parameters and add the master_point. Right-click to cancel that mode.

18. Go to frame 20 and animate the master_point up into the air. Does the COM follow?

19. Go to frame 30 and animate the master_point down.

20. Select the COM and click Link to World at frame 30. Right-click to cancel that mode.

21. Go to frame 40 and animate the COM again. Now it's free again. (See Figure 14.21.)

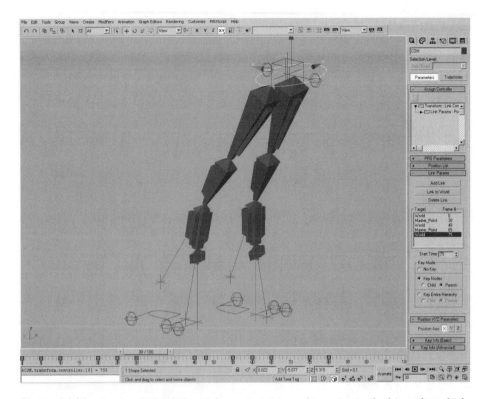

Figure 14.21 Leaping Jesters! The Link constraint is used to animate the hierarchy, which allows the character to flip and fly.

The finished torso file, leg_torso_done.max, is located on the CD-ROM.

You've just built some precise animation controls into the IK system in a short amount of time. Be sure to review anything that didn't make complete sense, because this is the foundation for the character's movement. Ideally, to be an effective character engineer, you should be able to re-create this in your sleep.

In the next exercise, you set up the controls for the spine to do both automated and manual rotations.

Exercise 14.9 Setting Up Back Controls

For this exercise, load the file back_neck_head_start.max from the CD-ROM. It contains all the previous steps plus the bone structure for the back, neck, and head (which are not complicated to create and don't need any special instruction) .

This exercise covers setting up the Wire Parameters to control the automatic/manual bone rotations for the back, neck, and head, instead of creating the basic structure, which you should already have a good grasp of by now.

The only difference in the way the bones are linked, compared to what you've been doing, is that they are directly linked to the controlling splines. The splines are in a hierarchy that will be animated. This is done because you're using the splines to animate the bones. See Figure 14.22 for the Schematic View of this hierarchy.

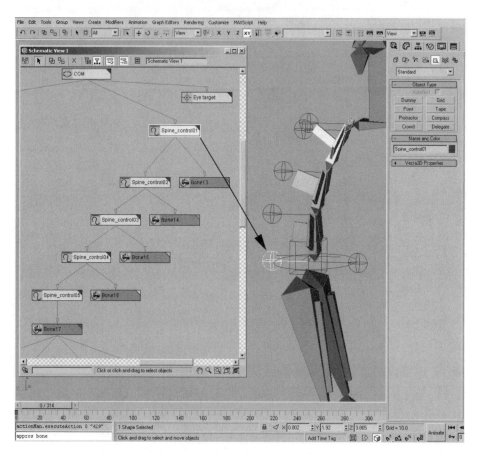

Figure 14.22   Examine the Schematic View shown and compare to your scene to create the correct hierarchy.

Bone13 is the child of Spline_control01, and this spline is also the parent of Spline_control02.

Now you're going to use Wire Parameters to add a gradual rotation to the hierarchy.

1. Select Spine_control01, right-click, and select Wire Parameters from the Quad menu.

2. Select Transform/Rotation/Keyframe XYZ/X Rotation. (A Freeze Rotation was done on the spine controls, which is why you see two rotation controllers.)

3. Select the Spine_control02 and wire to the same X Rotation.

4. In the Wire Parameters dialog box, click the right-facing arrow and in the expression window add **/1.2"** after X_Rotation so it reads X_Rotation/1.2.

5. Click Connect and rotate Spine_control01 on the X-axis to see the effect on Spine_control02.

   If you want to see a greater rotation effect, make the dividing number smaller, and click Update.

6. Close the Wire Parameters dialog box.

7. Use the same procedure, starting with Step 1, to wire Spine_control02's X Rotation to Spine_control03's X Rotation, and type **X_Rotation/1.2** into the expression window, as well.

8. Do the same procedure starting with Step 1 for the next two spine controls, wiring each spine control to the previous one, and typing the **X_Rotation/ 1.2** expression, as before.

9. Test the rotation of Spine_control01. Spine_control02 through Spine_control05 rotate as they follow the rotation of Spine_control01. You can rotate only Spine_control01 and not the others because each rotation is now controlled solely by the spine control it has been wired to. You remedy this in the next exercise.

   Figure 14.23 shows the first step in wiring the spine control.

   Follow this exercise, beginning with Step 1, to wire the rotations of the Y-axis and Z-axis. You can experiment with different values for the expression depending on how you want the automatic rotations to happen.

   The next order of business is creating manual rotational controls for each Spine_control object. You use the List controller to accomplish this. In fact, the List controller is used frequently on this character rig, so it's a good idea to get familiar with the process quickly because it can get repetitive.

   If you want to speed up the next few steps, make sure the MacroRecorder is on for the MAXScript Listener, and that the relative options are all turned on.

10. Select Spine_control02, and select Graph Editors/Track View/Controller Edit. (This is the custom Track view I saved with the scene.)

11. Expand the Rotation tracks and select X Rotation: Float Wire under the Keyframe XYZ listing.

12. Click the Assign Controller button and choose Float List from the menu that pops up.

13. Expand the Float List and choose the available track.

14. Click Assign Controller again and choose Bezier Float.

15. Click X Rotation: Float List, and then right-click and select Properties.

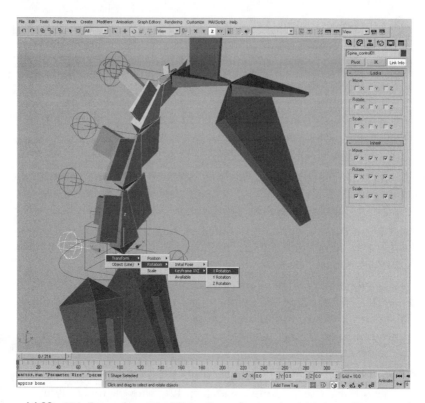

Figure 14.23   This figure shows the Wiring Parameters tool, which is used to create the back controls.

16. Double-click Bezier Float to make it active.

17. Test rotate Spine_control02 on the X-axis.

Using MAXScript to do repetitive tasks is a real time-saver, and will save you many clicks in this process.

18. Open the MAXScript Listener and find the following two commands:

```
$.rotation.controller.Keyframe_XYZ.controller.X_Rotation.controller
= float_list ()

$.rotation.controller.Keyframe_XYZ.controller.X_Rotation.
controller.
Available.controller = bezier_float ()
```

19. Copy and paste these commands from the gray Listener area to the white output pane (press Ctrl+C to copy and Ctrl+V to paste).

20. Type a third command based on these commands:

```
$.rotation.controller.Keyframe_XYZ.controller.X_Rotation.
controller.
active=2
```

(MAXScript didn't record the step of making the Bezier controller, number 2 in the list of controllers, active.)

21. With the max Tab panel visible (Customize UI/Show UI/Show Tab Panel), select all three lines of text and drag them into a toolbar, which creates a button.

22. Select the next spine control and click the button you just made. All the controllers will be set correctly for the X-axis. Repeat for the remaining spine controls.

23. Duplicate these commands, changing the X_Rotation for Y and X_Rotation to make two new buttons to do the controller editing for you.

It does take manual labor to fully rig these back controls, but it's worth it when you can have an automated rotation and manual rotation at the same time. With more MAXScripting, as you did in this exercise, you could automate this process even more. Feel free to experiment.

The next section introduces the LookAt controller, which you'll use to target the eyeballs to control objects.

Exercise 14.10   Targeting the Eye

Eye targeting is an important control to have, because animating the rotation of the eyes would be a very tedious process if you were dealing with rotation data versus simpler position data of a control object. Using the new LookAt controller also enables you to animate the targets, which the eyes will follow. For instance, you want the character's eyes looking at the camera for a comedic effect. Animating the weight of the LookAt target from the main control object to the camera is a snap.

Notice the small Point object in front of the head and the letters *R* and *L*. Those are eye target controls. The letters are parented to the point and the point is parented to the COM ellipse. You'll use these objects as the LookAt targets.

1. Turn off the Hide Geometry filter in the Display panel.

2. Select the left eyeball (Sphere01) and choose the LookAt constraint from the Animation/Constraints drop-down menu.

3. Select the *L* text to be the LookAt object.

4. In the LookAt constraint parameters, make sure the LookAt Axis is set to Y, and the Viewline Length Absolute is checked off.

5. Repeat these steps for the right eyeball (Sphere02). (See Figure 14.24.)

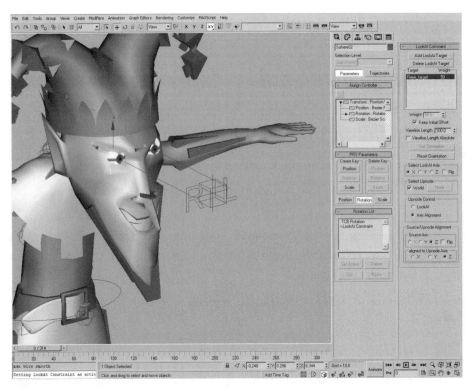

Figure 14.24 This figure shows the Look-At constraint to create the eye targeting effect.

 Note

This step was initially skipped during the production cycle of the book, so you'll see only a single eye target in the final animated max scene that comes on the CD-ROM.

With the eye controls set up, you can create a lot of personality quickly during animation. After that easy section, let's move on to something more difficult, the arms and hands. Please pay close attention to the steps to get the correct results.

Exercise 14.11   Setting Up the Arms and Hands

In this exercise you set up the arms and hands. Another file is located on the CD for you to start from, so you don't have to go through some tedious steps of bone creation. Take time to examine the scene closely, so you can see how the bones are laid out.

Load the file arms_hands_start.max. The clavicle and arm bones are already created. Zoom into the end of the arm where you see a controlling sphere (Rwrist_control) and a very small Point object, which is part of the arm hierarchy. When I created the arm, I substituted the bone nub that appears automatically with a Point object. This was a visual decision, but not absolutely necessary.

This Point object is the end of the IK chain that you're going to create.

1. Select the upper-arm bone and select the HI-IK command in the Animation menu.

2. Select the Point object at the end of the arm to add the IK to.

3. Adjust the large goal size to something more reasonable, but not bigger than the controlling sphere, and set the position/rotation thresholds to **.01**.

4. Link the IK goal to the controlling sphere (Rwrist_control).

   The goal of this process is to make the controlling sphere the animated object (you rarely want to animate just the IK goal). As you've already experienced with the foot setup, linking the IK goal to helper objects gives you pivot control.

   The elbow rotation is left up to the automatic Swivel Angle, which you can access through the Motion panel or as a manipulator in the viewport. You could link the Swivel Angle to a Point object and then link the point to the COM ellipse, but it's not really necessary and just creates more nodes to deal with.

   Now, it's time to set up the hand hierarchy.

5. Duplicate the Point object, scale it up a bit, and reset the scale. Name it something like **R_handParent**.

6. Link that duplicate Point to the lower-arm bone.

   The R_handParent point is going to be the parent of the hand bones and can't be linked to the controlling sphere, because you don't want it to move with the sphere.

7. Select R_handParent, and assign an Orientation constraint from it to the controlling sphere.

8. Make sure the Orientation properties are set to Keep Initial Offset on, and that World/World is selected. (See Figure 14.25.)

   To save some time in modeling the hand bones, I've provided the bone structure I created; it's just hidden. There was nothing special done with respect to the creation of these bones, other than that they fit within the mesh, the thumb bones are rotated to match, and they were drawn in the Top viewport.

9. In the Selection Sets drop-down menu there's a selection called Rhand. Select it and click Yes to the dialog box that pops up to unhide the hand bones.

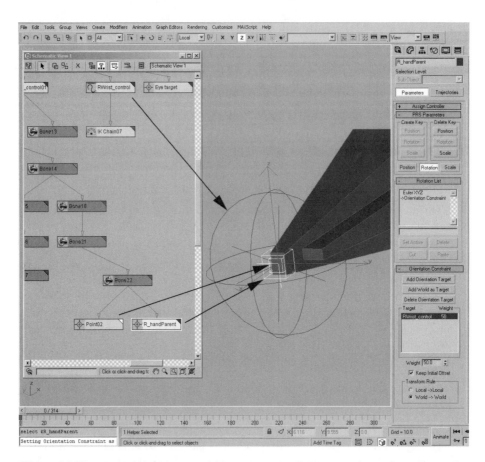

Figure 14.25   The Orientation constraint properties and the proper hierarchy to begin the hand setup are shown here.

The bone hierarchy might be a bit different from what you'd expect. There are three parent bones: one for the thumb bones, one for the center three fingers, and one for the pinky bones. Between the first and second pair of bones on each finger is a Point object (the little plus signs in the viewport and the green boxes in the Schematic View in Figure 14.26). You'll use these Point objects later to assist in the finger curling.

The next step links the hand bones to the hand controls you just set up.

10. Select bone32 and bone28 (the parents of the pinky bones and the thumb bones). Link them to bone23, the parent of the middle fingers.

11. Link bone23 to the R_HandParent Point object (the larger of the two points at the wrist).

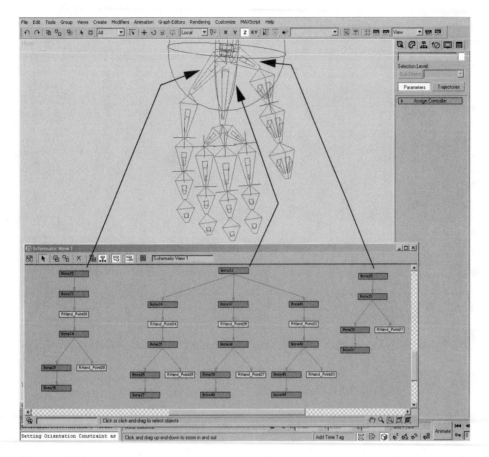

Figure 14.26   A Point object is located between the first and second pair of bones on each finger in order to create more intricate controls for animating.

12. Test the movement (position and rotation in local coordinates) of the hand by working with the Rwrist_Control sphere.

   See Figure 14.27 for the hierarchy you just set up.

   You can move the wrist control off the arm, but the hand does not pop off. This is because the hand is not linked directly to the wrist control, but to the point that is only Orientation-constrained to the wrist control (R_HandParent).

Tip

If you move R_HandParent around, the hand will pop off the wrist. To make sure you don't accidentally do that during animation, lock the position in the Hierarchy/Link panel.

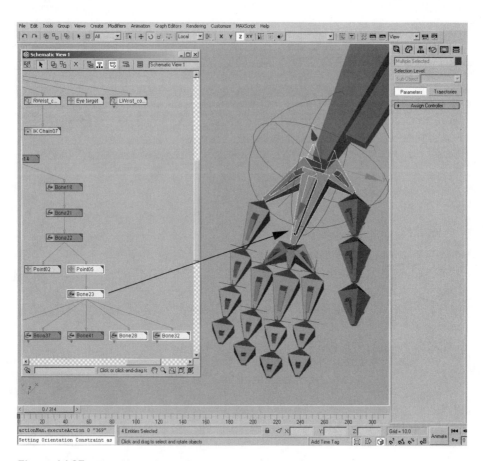

Figure 14.27   This figure shows the wrist control hierarchy.

13. Select R_HandParent, open the Hierarchy/Link panel and check all Move and Scale locks.

    Repeat this entire exercise for the left arm and hand to duplicate this setup and to practice working with these tools.

Proper constraints are important for predictable movement, especially if you're handing off this work to an animator. For the hand that you just rigged and now the upcoming Link constraints, the goal is to make the animation system as flexible as possible while adding acceptable limits so the character won't fall apart.

Note

There's a technique for rigging a forearm twist that I wasn't able to include in the actual rig used in the final animation.

A max file called arm_twist.max shows this example. It's simply two two-bone IK chains with HI IK on either side of the forearm, linked to the parent of the hand. (See Figure 14.28.)

The bone and IK direction are actually facing the opposite direction of the arm bones, so as the wrist twists, the twist bones rotate about the pivot point on the wrist and the IK keeps the ends of the bones locked in place.

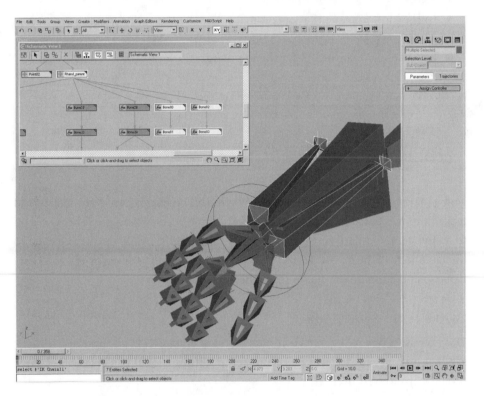

Figure 14.28   This figure shows the two two-bone IK chains with HI IK on either side of the forearm, linked to the parent of the hand to create a forearm twist.

Exercise 14.12   Using Link Constraints

This short exercise locks the IK space of the hands. Sometimes you want the hands to move with the body, putting the IK into body space; other times you want it locked to world space, where the hands don't follow the body and stay locked in position (like when the character's doing a push-up or hanging from the rim of a basketball hoop).

To do this, use a Link constraint, which you used in Exercise 14.8, to make the character fly through the air.

1. Make sure you're on frame 0.

2. Select the right control sphere (Rwrist_control) and select Constraints/Link Constraint in the Animation menu.

3. Select the COM ellipse to link it to.

4. In the Motion panel that opens, make sure the Key mode is set to Key Nodes/Parents.

5. Repeat Steps 1 through 4 for the left hand.

 Tip

This isn't the only way to do it. You could have another hand control that's used only to animate the hand in world space. This additional control would never be parented to anything. The original hand control would then be Position-constrained to both the COM and the second hand control. Then the weight would be animated over time.

Now you can easily create animations where the character can grab objects and make IK moves based on these objects. An example occurs when the Jester grabs on to a table and you Link-constrain the hand to the table. The hand stays locked to the table for as long as you keep it linked. You also could Link-constrain the hand to a cup and animate the cup to drive the arm motion.

Exercise 14.13   Rotating Fingers

This exercise is one of the most complex in this chapter, so I'm giving you fair warning that any missed step can make this setup nonfunctional or make you go back several steps to start over.

Why is it so complex? I wanted to make a versatile finger-curling rig that allows as much manual control as there is automatic control. If I know animators, they always want some way to tweak every movement of the character, despite the attempts of the people rigging the character to make repetitious animation easier with consolidated controls. This is not to say animating everything by hand slows down a production, because you need to do this to add more life into the character. Do you really want every foot rotation or finger curl to be exactly the same? No, because your character would become very robotic, very quickly. Why not start with some automated controls to get you 90% of the way for rough animation, and then tweak and add "specific randomness" by hand?

To do this, you incorporate—rather judiciously—Wire Parameters, Link controllers, and Custom Attributes.

This complexity might also lead to some unexpected software crashes—I encountered a few. Most likely, many of those will be fixed in a maintenance release that should be out on the Discreet Web site (http://support.discreet.com) at the time of this publication. To make sure you don't lose any work, as always, turn on the Autoback feature in the Customize/Preferences/Files, and be sure to save multiple versions of your work as you go so you have a complete track record of your steps. I recommend entering comments into the File/File Properties area to help you remember what a file's state is at the time of a save.

Warning

It seems like more stable workflow to not use Undo if there is the option of deleting a step you did in this section. You might run across an Undo bug at the wrong time. I don't want to imply that there are rabid Undo bugs—just be careful.

Remember that early in the chapter, you were instructed to run the MAXScript modifier_custom attributes.ms, which resides in your max4 folder/scripts/PluginScripts. This creates a new modifier, Attribute Holder, which is listed at the bottom of the Modifier List in the Unassigned Modifiers section. It is a blank modifier that is useful for adding Custom Attributes for animation control.

You're doing this to consolidate animation control onto one object that you'll work with a lot: the wrist control sphere. If you are always using that object to control the hand, it should contain all the finger rotation controls.

Tip

I usually use a Slider manipulator (in Create Panel/Helpers/Manipulators) to test controls before I create a Custom Attribute to perform the same function. The sliders are more versatile than CAs. You can change their value ranges and default values, which makes testing interaction between two objects' values much easier. You can also add and delete sliders easier than CAs, and as of now, there is not an editing tool for CAs.

1. Select the wrist control sphere and add the Attribute Holder modifier.

2. In the Animation drop-down menu, select Add Custom Attribute. A dialog box pops up with many options.

3. Use the default options, Float parameter and Spinner. Name the first attribute **Finger1_curl**.

4. In the Float UI Options, make the width about **70**, range **0–100**, and default **0**. Alignment doesn't matter—use whatever you want.

5. In the Finish rollout, choose to add the Attribute to the Object's Current Modifier (in the drop-down menu).

6. Click Add.

7. Repeat Steps 3 through 6 for the other finger controls, as seen in Figure 14.29 (Finger2 through 4 curls, Thumb_curl, Finger_curl_All, Fist).

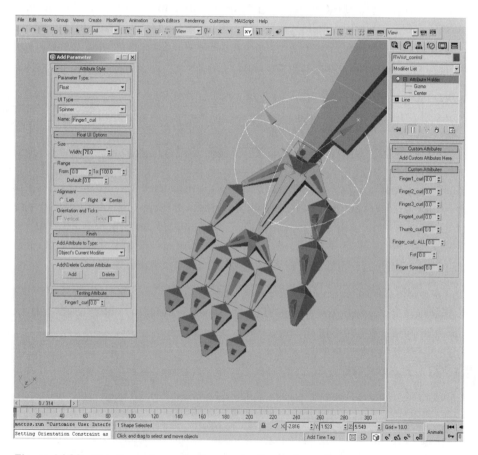

Figure 14.29   This figure shows the Custom Attributes that will drive the finger rotation.

8. Add a Finger Spread attribute, but make the values **–30** to **30** and default **0**.

Note

If you misspell a name, make sure the wrist control sphere is selected, and delete the CA through the same dialog box. Optionally, you can delete the Attribute Holder modifier and start over.

Tip

If the Add Attribute dialog box starts to act strange, close it down and restart it. At times I have seen some additional "testing attribute" rollouts pop up in the dialog box, which made it clear I needed to restart the process.

In the next section, you apply the wires to link up the Custom Attributes to the rotations of the fingers.

9. Select the Rwrist_Control sphere and right-click to select Wire Parameters.

10. Select Modified Object/Attribute Holder/Custom Attibutes/Finger1_curl.

11. Select the index finger's first joint (bone42) and choose the Y Rotation axis as the wired parameter.

12. In the Wire Parameters dialog box, select the bidirectional arrow and type the following into the expression windows:

    Left side: **radtodeg Y_Rotation**

    Right side: **degtorad Finger_curl1**

Note

The expression you just entered converts the values from radians to degrees and vice versa. The value coming out of the Custom Attribute is considered a degree, and because the max rotation units of Euler angles are computed as radians, you must convert the values. In the expression for the CA, you convert the incoming radians into degrees. There are 5729.598 degrees in 100 radians. Look up Euler XYZ controller in the max online help file for more information.

13. The next wire goes from the same Finger1_curl Attribute to the Y-axis in the point that's named Rhand_Point03. It's in the index finger's hierarchy between the bone42 and bone43.

14. In the Wire Parameters dialog box, click the right-facing arrow and type **degtorad** in the expression window before the Finger_curl1 variable.

15. Click Connect to complete the process.

16. Wire the Rhand_Point03's Y-axis to bone43's Y-axis.

17. Click the right-facing arrow. You don't need to do any unit conversion in the expression window.

18. The last wire is from bone43's Y-axis to bone44's Y-axis. Again, use the right-facing arrow, and in the expression window type **Y_Rotation/.8**. This speeds up the rotation of the tip of the finger.

19. Close the dialog box.

Test the Y Rotation of the finger by rotating bone42 and adjusting the spinner. Because you set a bidirectional wire from the Custom Attribute and bone42, you can use either to animate.

Now the rotation looks okay, but let's do some expression editing to make it more realistic. Normally, the first joint of a finger doesn't rotate that much before the other two joints begin to curl.

20. Open the custom Track view named Controller Edit.

21. Select Rhand_Point03 (the point between the first and second joint on the index finger).

22. In the Track view, expand the Rotation track, and select Y Rotation: Float Wire. Then right-click it and select Properties.

The Wire Parameter dialog box pops up with the Rhand_Point03 on the left side. If it doesn't show the wrist control's Finger1_curl attribute on the right side, click the little binocular icon on the right side of the dialog box. This searches for the matching wire to the left side.

You should see the left-facing arrow highlighted, showing that the attribute controls the point's Y Rotation.

23. In the left side expression window, type **(degtorad Finger_curl1)/.5**.

24. Click Update and test the rotation of bone42.

25. Close the dialog box. (See Figure 14.30.)

Another tweak to the rotations of the bones involves limiting the second and third joints so they don't bend back unnaturally when you rotate bone42 into negative values (rotating the finger up).

26. Select bone43, and using the Controller Edit Track view, open the Wire Parameters dialog box as you did in Step 22.

27. In the expression window of the dialog box, type **if Y_Rotation<0 then Y_Rotation = 0 else Y_Rotation**.

28. Click Update and test the rotation of bone42.

This expression limits rotations based on the incoming values. If the values are less than 0, it locks the rotation to 0; otherwise, accept the incoming value.

All of this is great for automatic controls, but what if you want to manually tweak the rotations of each joint? That's where our friend the List controller comes in.

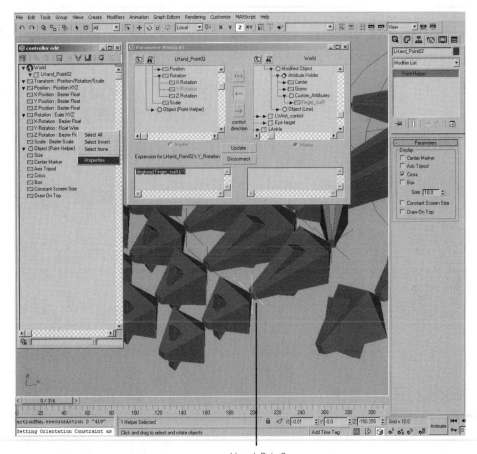

Lhand_Point2

Figure 14.30 Wire the Point object to the finger bone.

29. Select bone43, and in the Controller Edit window, change the Y Rotation controller from a Float Wire to a Float List.

30. Add a Bezier Float to the active slot and make it active.

31. Test the rotation of bone43, both manually and with the attribute spinner on the wrist control.

32. Repeat Steps 29 and 30 for bone44 and test its rotation.

The next addition to these controls is the ability to control the fingertip curling manually. This is done by wiring the Rhand_Point03 to bone43.

33. Make sure all rotations are set back to 0, and the Custom Attribute is 0.

34. Select Rhand_Point03 and change its Y Rotation track to a Float List.

35. Add a Bezier Float to the Available track and make it active.

36. Wire from the Rhand_Point03's Y Rotation/Bezier Float to bone43's Y
Rotation/Bezier Float. (See Figure 14.31).

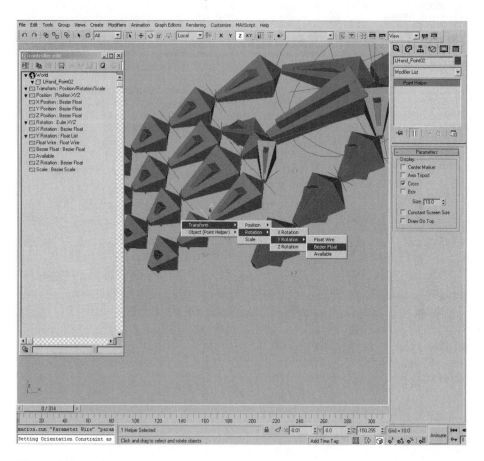

Figure 14.31   The Wiring Parameters tool is used for manual control over the fingers.

37. Continue by wiring bone43's second Y Rotation float wire to bone44's Y
Rotation/Bezier Float.

You're layering wires in the List controller, which enables you to have multiple controls going on at once (the Custom Attribute wire and the Rhand_
Point03 wire).

Next, you need to add the manual rotation control back into bone43
and bone44.

38. Select bone43, and in the Available slot of the Y Rotation Float List, add a
Bezier Float and make it active.

39. Do the same for bone44.

40. Test all the rotations of each object and the Finger1_curl Custom Attribute, and you should be able to contort the finger like the one in Figure 14.32.

The manual rotations act like an offset to the finger-curling spinner, which is very useful, especially when you add the attribute to curl all the fingers simultaneously.

If you can't undo all the Y Rotations back to the 0 reference, the order of objects you zero out matters; otherwise, the bones might flip 180.

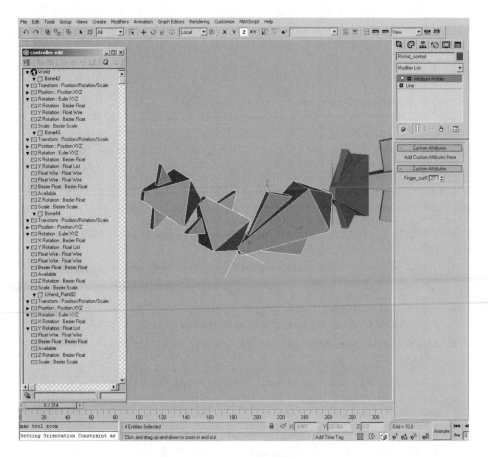

Figure 14.32   The objects and their List controllers are highlighted in the final wiring of the fingers.

41. Zero the Y Rotation of bone42 (the Finger1_curl Custom Attribute will also zero out because of the bidirectional wire).

42. Zero Rhand_Point03's Y Rotation.

43. Zero bone44, bone43, and finally bone44 again.

Note

This process is pretty easy to script. In the Chapter 14 folder on the CD-ROM you'll find a scripts folder with the file zero finger.ms. It's a basic script that installs in the MAXScript Tools section of the Customize UI menu, so you can hotkey it or put it into a menu, toolbar, or Quad menu.

To use it, select the first finger joint (in this case, it's bone42) and activate the script.

Now that you have one finger down, you can practice this process three more times! Repeat these steps for each finger except the thumb; you set up the thumb rotation in the next exercise. Think about where you might use the MacroRecorder to save steps in assigning controllers. This speeds up this task and reduces the number of mouse clicks.

Exercise 14.14   Rotating the Thumb

The thumb is slightly different from the rest of the fingers; the Z-axis and Y-axis rotate together. The rest of the rigging method is the same as in the last exercise, so you should be a pro by now! Therefore, I don't lay it out click-by-click here; I just describe the connections, the expressions, and the List controllers.

1. Wire the Thumb_curl Custom Attribute to the Z-axis on the first joint of the thumb (bone29) as a bidirectional connection.

2. Make sure to add the expressions **radtodeg Z_Rotation** and **degtorad -Thumb_curl**. (Notice the negative sign before Thumb_curl.)

3. Wire the Thumb_curl Custom Attribute again, but to the Y-axis on bone29, and make it a one-way connection to the bone.

4. Add the expression **degtorad Thumb_curl/4**. This rotates the thumb only slightly on the Y-axis.

5. Wire the Thumb_curl Custom Attribute again, to Rhand_Point01 (the Point object in the thumb hierarchy). Make it a one-way connection to the point and add the expression **degtorad Thumb_curl**.

6. Wire a one-way connection from Rhand_Point01's Z Rotation to bone30's Z Rotation and add the expression **-Z_Rotation**.

7. Wire a one-way connection from bone30's Z Rotation to bone31's Z Rotation and add the expression **Z_Rotation/.8**.

   Next, you add some List controllers for manual rotation control.

8. Change Rhand_Point01's Z Rotation:Float Wire to a Float List controller.

9. In the Available slot, add a Bezier Float.

10. Do the same with bone30 and bone31.

    Now add the wires from the manual rotation controls.

11. Wire a one-way connection from the Rhand_Point01's Z Rotation/Bezier Float to bone30's Z Rotation/Bezier Float.

12. Wire a one-way connection from the bone30's Z Rotation/Float Wire #2 to bone31's Z Rotation/Bezier Float.

13. Add the expression **Float_Wire/.8**.

The last step finalizes the manual controls.

14. Add a Bezier Float to the Available slot of bone30 and bone31's Z Rotation Float List controller.

Figure 14.33 shows the final thumb controller setup.

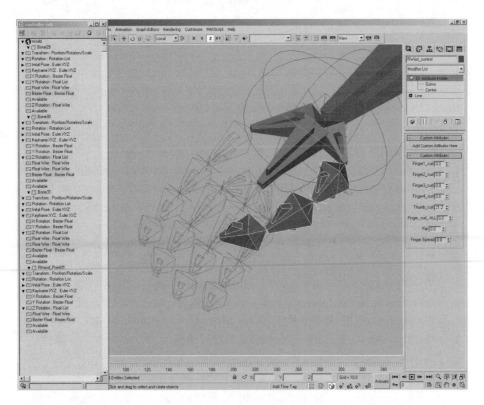

Figure 14.33 The controllers for the thumb rotation setup are shown here.

I hope you're excited at your progress! By now you should have all fingers able to be animated by the Finger_curl spinners and by manually animating the rotations of the Bones and Points. In the next exercise, you combine even more controls into one spinner.

Tip

To make your work more decipherable by others on your team, I suggest renaming the controllers to be more specific than the general *Float Wire*. Use something that makes sense to you, maybe **wire_from Attribute** or **wire_from Point01**.

Select the object and open the List Controller Properties window to change the names of the subcontrollers in the list. This is the same dialog box you pull up to set the active controller (right-clicking the List controller in the Track view, or in the Motion panel, clicking the Rotation button). There's a small box at the bottom of the dialog box where you can enter text to change the name.

Because the current Schematic View does not show this information, doing this eliminates the need for opening the Wire Parameters dialog box to find out what's wired to what.

Exercise 14.15   Curling All Fingers

This exercise adds even more List controllers to the mix to control all the fingers (without the thumb) in one big curling motion.

1. Select the wrist control sphere (Rwrist_control) and right-click in the Finger1_curl spinner. A pop-up menu appears. Select Show In Track View.

2. Make sure the Modified Objects filter is on and expand the Custom Attributes track and all the Finger1_curl tracks.

3. You'll notice an Animation: Bezier Float track under the Finger1_curl track. Select this track and change it to a Float List controller.

4. Repeat Steps 1 through 3 for each finger and thumb curl Custom Attribute.

5. Wire the Rwrist_control/Modified Object/Attribute Holder/Custom Attributes/Finger_curl_all to itself, selecting the Finger1_curl attribute.

6. When the Wire Parameters dialog box appears, expand the Finger1_curl tracks to reveal the Animation track and select the Available track.

7. Click the right-facing arrow and click Connect.

8. Keep the Wire Parameters dialog box open and test the Finger_curl_all attribute spinner.

   It should curl finger1 and you should be able to curl or uncurl finger1 with its own spinner or by rotating bone42.

9. Because the Wire dialog box is still open, you can expand each finger curl track and wire the curl_all parameter to each available animation track, as you did with finger1.

   See Figure 14.34 for the controllers and Wire Parameters dialog box.

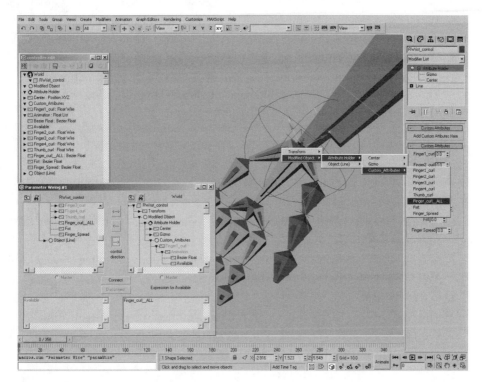

Figure 14.34   This figure shows the controllers and Wire Parameters dialog box for the Finger_curl_all attribute.

Is this getting easier? The tools should be making sense by now, and these exercises are good practice because they're all similar setups. Another global control for the hand is the fist, which you create in the next exercise.

Exercise 14.16   Making a Fist

This exercise is like the last, because you add more List controllers and wires to make the fist spinner work. You've already added the Float List controller to the Thumb_curl Attribute, so the next step is to wire the Fist Attribute to each Finger_curl and the Thumb_curl.

1. Wire the Fist Attribute to Finger1_curl.
2. Expand the tracks in the Wire dialog box, and select the Available slot to wire, using the right-facing arrow.
3. Add the expression **Fist/2** in the Wire Parameter dialog box to slow down the finger rotations.
4. Click Connect.

5. While the dialog box is still open, wire the rest of the fingers using Steps 1 through 4.

6. When wiring the Thumb_curl, add the expression **Fist/10**.

This slows down the rotation of the thumb so it doesn't intersect the fingers. This expression value can vary, depending on how fast you want the thumb to curl in relation to the rest of the fingers.

Exercise 14.17   Spreading the Fingers

In this final Custom Attribute wiring, you connect the Finger_Spread spinner to the Y Rotations of the Point objects that are parents of each finger hierarchy.

1. Wire the Finger_Spread attribute to Rhand_Point02's Z-axis. It's the point just before bone42.

2. Use a bidirectional connection the standard expressions **radtodeg Finger_Spread** and **degtorad Z Rotation**.

3. Click Connect.

The finger's rotation jumps, which is a problem because the default value of the spinner is 0 and the finger's initial rotation is not 0. You need a way to keep the initial offset and then apply the wire. Again, the List controller comes to the rescue.

4. Undo the wire operation.

5. Select Rhand_Point02, and in the Controller Edit Track view, select its Z Rotation track in the Keyframe XYZ track.

6. Change the controller to a Float List.

Now you have the Bezier Float as the first item in the List controller for the Z-axis. This keeps the initial rotation offset of the bone and enables you to layer in the wire.

7. Wire the Finger_Spread attribute to Rhand_Point02's X-axis/Available track. Use a one-way connection (right-facing arrow) and type the same degtorad conversion you used before. (See Figure 14.35.)

8. Use the wiring procedure in Steps 1 through 7 for Rhand_Point06 and Rhand_Point08 (skipping the middle finger, which doesn't need to spread). Input the following expressions as you perform the wiring:

Rhand_Point06 needs an expression like **degtorad finger_spread/2** to slow it down.

Rhand_Point08 needs an expression like **degtorad finger_spread/.9**.

The original Bezier Floats are still the active controller, so you can manually rotate the Points to control the finger spread.

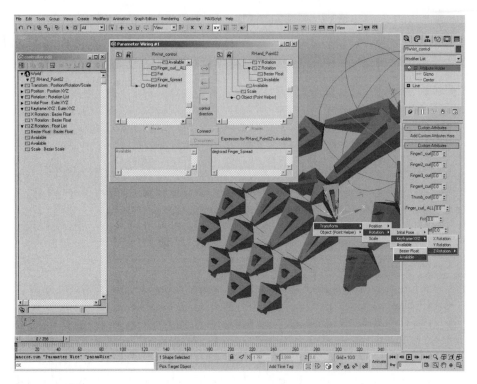

Figure 14.35   Wire the finger spread attribute to the correct axis tracks.

That's it! You should have a fully functional hand with some in-depth finger controls.

Exercise 14.18   Setting Up the Left Hand

Practice all these steps. You have to do it all over again for the left hand. Remember that because you are mirroring the bones from the right hand, all the rotation values in the wired expressions have to be reversed by putting a negative sign (-) in front of the values.

For instance, when you wire the first bone of the first finger, you add the expressions **degtorad -Finger1_curl** and **radtodeg -Y_Rotation** (because it's a bidirectional wire). It is obvious if you need to reverse the rotation, because your joints will rotate backward.

Remember also that on the expressions that limited rotation, you have to switch the less-than sign (<) to greater-than sign (>). This was done on the second finger joint in Step 27 of Exercise 14.13. The new expression should read if **Y_Rotation > 0 then Y_Rotation = 0 else Y_Rotation.**

It's possible to clone the right hand and modify the resulting wires to these negative expressions. I haven't fully tested it to see whether there are problems later, but initially it appeared to work.

1. Unlink the Rwrist_control object and the Point object that's the parent of the hand bones.

2. Select the Rwrist_control, that point, and all the hand bones and points.

3. Press Shift+move to clone the objects.

4. Test the Custom Attributes on the cloned Rwrist_control01.

   Now you need to mirror the objects, and to do that you have to remove the Orientation constraint from the hand's parent point.

5. Select the Point in question and in the Motion panel, select Trajectories.

6. Be sure you're on frame 0, and set the Sample Range to 0 start, 0 end, and 2 samples.

7. In the Collapse Transform, check Rotation only and click Collapse.

   This effectively deleted the Orientation constraint and kept the Point object in the same position it was before the deletion. If you were to just delete the Orientation constraint, the point and the hand would flip around and you'd waste time reorienting it. Next you mirror everything.

8. Select all the cloned objects and in the coordinate space pull-down menu, select Pick and choose the COM ellipse.

9. Select the third button option in the Pivot drop-down menu (next to the coordinate pull-down).

10. Click the Mirror button, mirror on X, no clone, and Mirror Bones should be checked.

    The hand should pop in roughly where you want to have it, and you have to align it.

11. Add negative signs in front of any expression in the wire that's a value conversion, such as **radtodeg -Y_Rotation** or **-(degtorad Float_Wire)/.5.**

12. For the second joint of the fingers that have two Y Rotation wires and an expression on the first wire that reads "if Y_Rotation < 0 then Y_Rotation = 0 else Y_Rotation," change it so that it reads **if Float_Wire > 0 then Float_Wire = 0 else Float_Wire.**

Note

The less-than sign (**<**) changes to a greater-than sign (**>**), and because you're redoing the expression, you have to rereference the current incoming value name, which is **Float_Wire**. (It used to be Y_Rotation, but you added a wire to that track after the initial expression was made.) For some reason, this value name doesn't update automatically, and you need to change it only if you touch the expression and click Update. You'll see an error if you don't change the value name prompting you to do something to fix it.

13. As a last step, re-add the Orientation constraint and make sure the hierarchy is correct to attach everything as it is on the right hand.

Note

If you have a firm grasp on these technical details and are comfortable with all the finger setup, this cloning option might be for you. It can save a lot of time. If not, I recommend going through the process again from scratch on the left hand.

Here are some tips to remember:

- If you make a mistake with a List controller and need to reset it, change the List controller to a Bezier controller. It wipes out the entire List controller and you can start over. This isn't the greatest workflow—destroying work and starting over— but it's necessary because there's no interface to cut/paste/delete subcontrollers within a List controller that resides in a subtrack, such as the X-axis.

- There is MAXScript exposure, though, which does enable you to do this, so I suggest reading the online help to get the most out of this functionality. Maybe one of you clever users will write an interface and post it as a free script at http://support.discreet.com (if we don't beat you to it)!

- Rename your List controllers to more easily understand what the different tracks refer to.

- You can right-click any parameter spinner in the Modify panel to access the Track view or the Wire Parameters dialog box (if there's a wire to edit and it's wired to only one object).

Exercise 14.19   Skinning the Legs

The Skin modifier in max 4 has some major new features, as described in Chapter 3. You use some of these features as you skin the Jester.

There is a lot of tweaking involved in this process, so I cover the new tools only as they apply to this character and leave the fine-tuning to you.

Even though you can skin a patch model, it's not an easy task; unless you have a lot of vertex detail it's not worth trying. The time you spend manually weighting individual vertices and Bezier handles is substantial, because the enveloping system works best with a regular distribution of vertices that a mesh gives you.

Caution

In our production pipeline, we ran into problems merging the animated Jester skeleton onto the skinned model, and we didn't have a lot of time to troubleshoot the problem. So we ended up skinning the animated skeleton to the textured model. This doesn't mean it can't be done, because there are tools for merging and replacing objects and animation. We realized that when you merge in an object, it comes with its parent, if it has one. This is true on a Link constraint too, where there is not a real hierarchy, but an animated link. Be careful when merging so that you don't end up with duplicate or extraneous nodes that can wreak havoc on your scene like gremlins. This is especially true when you have Custom Attributes and wires that could easily refer to duplicate objects (with the same name) and confuse the system.

The goal is to keep the character as a patch-based model so you can go back and make changes without losing any of the patch detail. There are three new modifiers that enable you to translate geometry in midstack: Turn to Mesh, Turn to Patch, and Turn to Poly. You use poly because it's the newest modeling geometry (true quad polys), which matches elegantly with the quad output that patches have. Of course, if your patch model has a tri-patch, Turn to Poly handles that as well.

Note

One new tool that I use all the time is the Display Filter box in the Display panel. This enables you to add specific object classes to be hidden. In this case, I add Bone to the list and another object that I'm not using right now, such as CamPoint. Click the name in the box to hide it, and click the None button to show it.

I use the Display Floater more than the Display panel, because I can pop it up anytime and not have to change panels (it's in the Tools drop-down menu). In this floater, there is no None button like the one in the Display panel, so I click the name of that other unused object (CamPoint) to show the bones, and click Bones again to hide them.

For this exercise, either load the final rigged character you made or load rig_ FINAL.max from the CD-ROM.

1. Unhide just the body geometry, because you start with the legs.

2. Select the body and collapse it to an editable patch. Make sure the Patch view and Render steps are set to **1**.

Tip

Before you skin the model, decide what resolution you want the character, because any per-vertex weighting you might do is lost if you change the patch resolution. The best idea is to skin it at a patch tessellation of 1 and then add Meshsmooth after the skin. The body will look slightly different, as you'd expect from the differences in tessellation of Meshsmooth and patches. So decide which looks better to you, a higher patch tessellation and no Meshsmooth or a low tessellation and Meshsmooth later. Remember that having Meshsmooth on in the viewport slows down interactivity, so keep it off until you're ready for test renders.

Either start from the file you finished with from the last exercise, or load the file rig_FINAL.max.

3. Add the Turn to Poly modifier, which is under the modifier heading of Conversion Modifiers near the bottom of the list. Use the default parameters.

4. Add the Skin modifier.

5. Add bone01 and bone02 (the right leg bones).

6. Click the Edit Envelopes and adjust the outer envelope's radii so there's a little overlap in the knee area. Because the model is so small, adjusting the radii in the viewport doesn't work very well. Just select one of the four control points of an envelope and adjust the Radius spinner in the Envelope Properties area of the Skin modifier.

   Now you should create a keyframe of the foot moving up, so you can test the knee and make adjustments based on the limits of the animation.

7. Animate the foot moving up in the Z-axis, over 10 frames, using the foot control spline named RAnkle.

8. Select the body and edit the envelopes again to make the knee and rear end of the Jester look as good as possible.

Tip

Play with both inner and outer radii while the limb is at maximum bend. Don't forget you can move either end of the envelope (by turning on the Envelope filter) and select the small box at the center of the envelope. Sometimes an envelope appears 90 degrees off axis by default, and you have to move the ends of the envelope to line it up to the skin.

In the case of the Jester's rear end, I moved that end of the envelope toward the front of the model (in World Y).

See Figure 14.36 for an example of the leg envelopes.

The next step is to assign a Joint Angle Deformer (JAD) to the knee joint, because adjusting the envelopes themselves is not enough to make a good crease and bulge in the knee.

9. In Edit Envelope mode, select bone02's envelope.

10. Turn on the Vertices filter and select several rows of verts surrounding the knee.

11. Use the Ctrl and Alt keys to add or subtract from the selection. Orbit the model to make sure all verts that you want are selected.

12. In the Gizmos rollout, add a Joint Angle Deformer.

13. Go to frame 10 of the animation and look at how the JAD lattice affects the joint. To compare the joint with and without the JAD, you can uncheck the Enabled Gizmo box in the Gizmos rollout.

    See Figure 14.37 for the Joint Angle Deformer assignment.

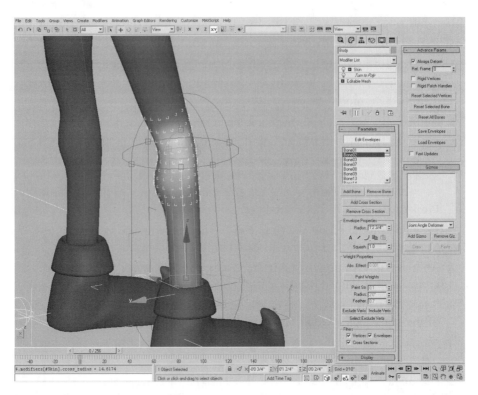

Figure 14.36   Test the leg envelopes.

14. Go back to frame 0 and turn on the Edit Lattice mode from the Gizmo Parameters rollout of Skin.

15. Select the second row of lattice verts, on the calf side of the leg.

16. Scrub to frame 6 and move the points down to shape the calf. Go to frame 10 and continue to shape the calf.

17. The lattice gets rotated because the leg bones give the Jester a slightly bow-legged look. To counteract that, set the Twist parameter in the Gizmo Parameters rollout to something like **–40**.

18. Continue to select rows of two lattice verts at frame 0 and then adjust them at frames 6 and 10. Some verts will have a desirable effect, and others won't.

19. Grab the inner row of two verts that define the crease of the joint. Pull those back on the Y at frame 10, to smooth out the crease.

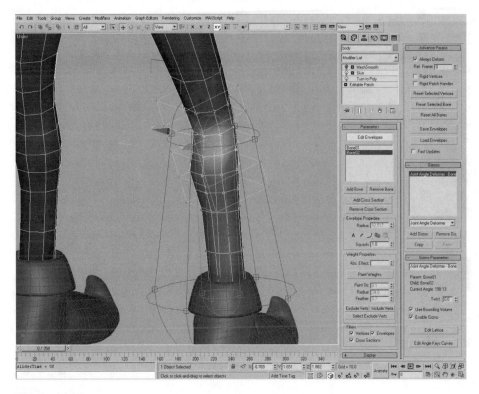

Figure 14.37   The Joint Angle Deformer assignment is shown here.

 Tip

Undoing a lattice vert move is kind of weird. You'll see the point slowly move itself back into place. I avoid undoing lattice vert moves. Instead I use the right-click to cancel feature. It's the best instant undo function anywhere. While you're holding down the left mouse button to do something (draw a line, move a lattice vert, and so forth), click the right mouse button without letting up the left button, and that command is canceled.

Be sure to turn off Meshsmooth once in a while to see how it looks with it on, unless you opted to skin a higher-resolution patch.

Every vert move you make is recorded as a keyframe at that joint angle, so in this case you can have up to 10 specific lattice tweaks on each vert. That translates into a lot of data, so try to limit the number of angles you apply edits to. Because this is all angle-based, nothing is tied to the timeline; it's just convenient to scrub the timeline to see your changes.

See Figure 14.38 to see the lattice editing.

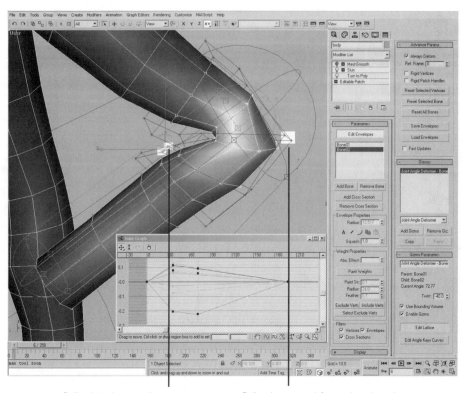

Pull points down to shape crease   Pull points up and forward to shape knee

Figure 14.38   The Joint Graph displays the lattice edits and the selected verts' X, Y, and Z
curves.

The rig_skin_knee.max file on the CD-ROM shows how the Joint Angle
Deformer should work on the knee.

Now that you have one leg done, you copy and paste the information to the
other leg.

20. In the Skin modifier, click Add Bones and add the other left leg bones in
    (bone07 and bone08).

21. Click Edit Envelopes and select bone01. Click the Copy icon in the Envelope
    Properties rollout; it looks like two overlapping pieces of paper.

22. Click bone07 and click the Paste icon (which is next to the Copy icon).

23. Copy bone02 to bone08.

    To copy the Joint Angle Deformer parameters, you have to make another
    one on the left leg.

24. Select the same rows of verts on the left leg as you did on the right.

25. Add a Joint Angle Deformer.

26. Click the JAD for the right leg and click the Copy button in the Gizmos rollout.

27. Click the new JAD you just made and click Paste.

28. Adjust the Twist value to –80, or whatever looks good and matches the right leg.

29. Create a similar animation for the right leg and test the JAD.

    You still need to move the Envelope control by the waist forward to correct the rear end copy-and-paste copies only the envelope sizes and not the positions.

Tip

Start naming your Angle Deformers so that you know which one controls which joint. Rename them in the Gizmo Parameters rollout.

See Figure 14.39 for a reference of the two JADs.

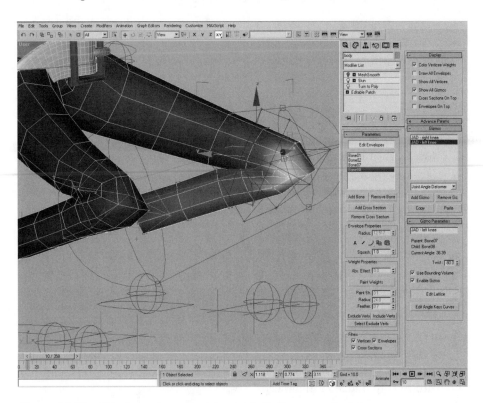

Figure 14.39   This figure shows the Joint Angle Deformers on both knees.

Tip

To quickly jump between two keyframes, use either the Key Mode Toggle on the frame control bar by the Animate button, or Time Tags. Time Tags are useful for marking animation points, audio cues, or—in this case—simple beginning and ending keys for skin tests.

Click the bar at the bottom of the max window that says Add Time Tag (yes, this feature was in max all along). Then you can set up a 0 tag and a 10 tag to quickly jump between frames without anything selected (if you use the Key Mode Toggle, you have to have an object selected).

Exercise 14.20   Skinning the Feet

In creating the leg skin, we purposely left out skinning the feet with the same modifier as the body—not only because it's a separate object, but to allow more control over the final result. You can use the same leg bones to drive the deformations, but because you're using a unique Skin modifier, you can control those bone's' envelopes independent of the body skin's envelopes.

1. Select the right foot, collapse it to an editable patch and leave the View and Render steps at 4.

    Meshsmooth in this case flattens out a lot of the work done in editing the foot, so you skin it at a higher resolution.

2. Add a Turn to Poly modifier to it and a Skin modifier.

3. Next, add in bones 02, 04, 05, and 06.

    Remember that handy Foot_Roll Attribute that you set up a long time ago? Now's a great time to use it!

4. Select the footpad (RAnkle) and use the Foot_Roll spinner in the Modifier panel to animate the movement.

5. Select the foot again and edit the envelopes.

    Bone04 probably doesn't line up down the length of the foot.

6. Adjust the envelope ends to realign it, as seen in Figure 14.40.

7. Adjust the toe envelope's outer radius to include the toe vertices of the foot.

8. When it's looking good, go to the Advance Params rollout (you're an advanced user right? OK then, you can proceed).

9. Click Save Envelopes and put them in a place where you can find them in a minute.

10. Get out of Sub-Object mode and prepare the left foot (collapse to patch, Turn to Poly, and Skin modifier).

11. Add bones 08, 10, 11, and 12.

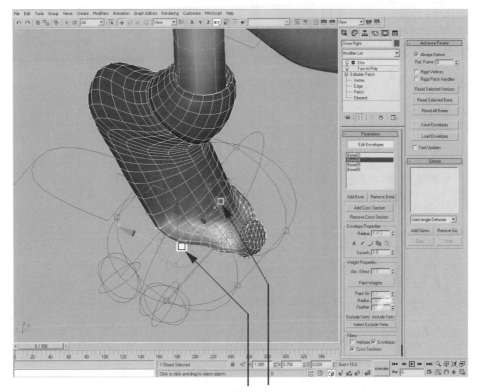

Move Envelope points to align down the length of the foot

Figure 14.40   Adjust the envelope ends for the feet.

12. Open the Advance Params and load the envelopes from the right foot.

    Because you can't cut and paste between Skin modifiers, you copy envelope data between similar models.

13. A dialog box comes up that enables you to remap the incoming envelopes to the current set of envelopes. You don't have to remap anything here, so just click OK.

14. Test the Foot_Roll parameter on the left foot. If anything looks bad, go back and tweak the envelopes.

    See Figure 14.41 for reference.

This was a good introduction to the new features in Skin. You can see how Angle Deformers help you achieve precision skinning with minimal effort. They can get messy if you're not carefully selecting and moving the vertices. The next exercise reiterates these basic skinning steps for the back, but the arms are more difficult.

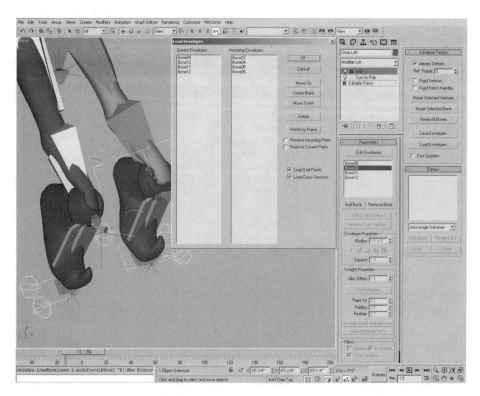

Figure 14.41   The envelope data is loaded onto the opposite foot, which saves a little work.

Exercise 14.21   Skinning the Back and Arms

There's nothing really special about the back.

1. Add all the back bones (bone13 through bone16) to the Skin modifier and work the envelopes to make a natural-looking bend in the skin, as seen in Figure 14.42.

 Tip

It's usually easier to skin a character by adding bones to the Skin system as you go, rather than adding all of them at once. Then you can see the effect of the major influencing bone and add the other bones—the ones that will have less influence—later.

The arms take more work.

2. Animate the wrist control splines on both hands to cause the arms to bend naturally. Then add all the arm bones (bone21 and bone22: right arm, bone46 and bone47: left arm) to the Skin modifier and work the envelopes to make a natural-looking bend in the skin.

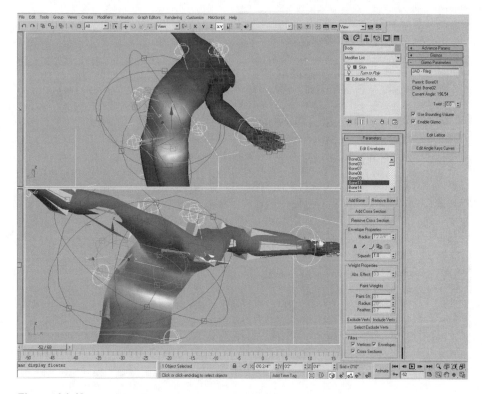

Figure 14.42 Test the skin envelopes for the back.

3. Use the Joint Angle Deformers again to fix the creasing in the elbow.

   In Figure 14.43, the left side is the before image and the right side is the result of adding and editing the Joint Angle Deformer to the elbow.

Tip

When assigning any Angle Deformer, remember to always select the bone that's driving the rotation. In this case, it's the forearm bone. Then select the vertices surrounding the joint and add the Angle Deformer.

4. Tweak the lattice verts as you did for the knees, pulling the crease in and bulging the elbow out a little.

   You can load the max file rig_skin_elbows.max from the CD-ROM. This file has the right elbow completed, and you can practice on the left elbow.

   The movement you see here is done to test the elbows, but you need to raise the Jester's hands above his head to test the sides of the torso. Don't worry about the shoulder or armpit too much because the clothing will cover that up.

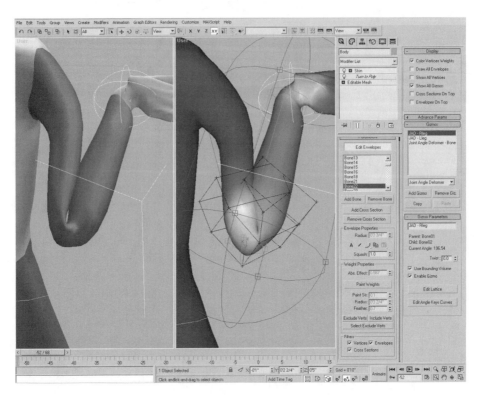

Figure 14.43   This figure shows the correcting effect that the Joint Angle Deformer has on the elbow.

Exercise 14.22   Skinning the Wrists and Fingers

The wrists and fingers take time to tweak the envelopes. The following steps make the process go faster.

1. The best approach is to animate a simple rotation of the wrist on a single axis and work the envelopes to make good bends, as seen in Figure 14.44.

    The fingers often need larger envelopes than the gap between the fingers allows before there's unwanted overlap in the weighting. You need to exclude vertices from the surrounding fingers. Sound hard? Not at all! Fortunately, there's a couple of new buttons in Skin to help you deal with that.

2. Animate the finger curl 1 parameter over 10 frames to the maximum curl that looks natural.

3. In the Envelope mode of Skin, select the first index finger envelope to work on (bone58), and then select the vertices on the other fingers that shouldn't be affected, and click Exclude Verts. (See Figure 14.45.)

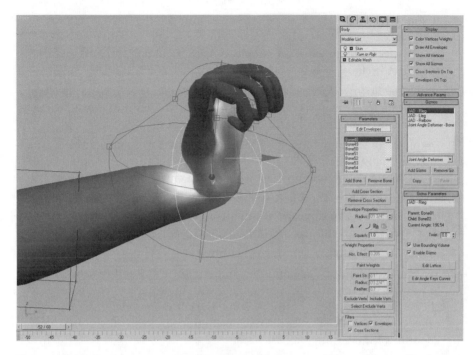

Figure 14.44   Animate all the possible rotations, one axis at a time, to find skinning errors.

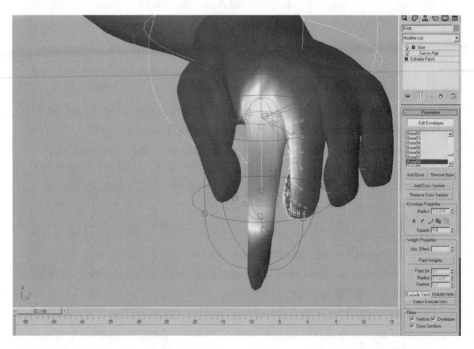

Figure 14.45   As you can see, vertices on the fingers need to be excluded from the index finger's envelope.

If you want to exclude those same vertices from another envelope, turn off the Vertex filter and press the Ctrl key while you select another envelope. If you deselected them, click the envelope that's excluding the verts and click the Select Exclude Verts button.

4. When the first two joints on the index finger are done, select the envelope or bone60. Its envelope is oriented vertically, so you have to move the envelope ends to make them align along the length of the fingers.

5. Do plenty of experimenting with moving the envelopes and adjusting radii, looking at all the frames of animation for the finger curl. You should be able to get decent deformation by just working the envelopes.

6. There are extra bones in the hand, just above the fingers in the hierarchy. Select them one at a time and shrink their envelope's radii to 0, because they don't need to influence any vertices.

7. Repeat Steps 2 through 6 for the other fingers.

8. To get a head start on the opposite hand, use the Copy and Paste Envelope buttons. Select an envelope on the hand with the complete envelopes and click the Copy Envelope button. Choose the corresponding envelope on the other hand and click the Paste Envelope button. There's really nothing new about this feature from Max 3.1.

   You'll still have to reorient any vertically aligned envelopes (which occur mainly on the tips of the fingers) and do all the vertex exclusions again.

Exercise 14.23   Skinning the Hat, Head, Eyes, and Teeth

The hat is easy to skin, because you're just adjusting envelopes and radii to make a decent deformation.

1. The only specific step for the hat is to exclude the bottom two rows of vertices from the two closest hat bones, as seen in Figure 14.46.

2. For the crown object surrounding the hat, link it to the head bone so it rotates with that bone. You might have to scale the crown object slightly to prevent interpenetration with the hat.

   The head has a couple of specific areas that need some work, to make sure the neck stays put, and to add the jawbone. Because the head is a patch and Morph targets were already created from this head, leave it a patch. If you want to start from here, load the max file skin_head_start.max.

3. Assign the Skin modifier to the head and add bone17 and bone20, the main head bone and the jawbone.

4. Dial up the Morph target for opening the mouth to 100%.

5. Go back to Skin and edit the jawbone envelope to encompass the jaw but not the upper teeth.

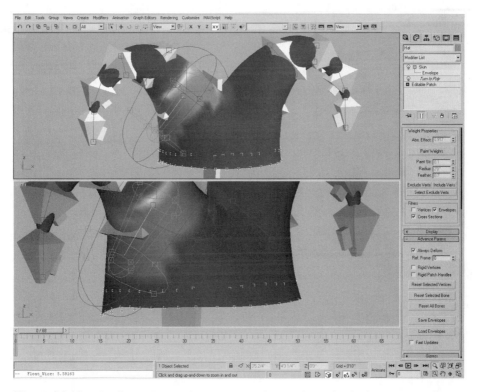

Figure 14.46 This figure shows adjustments on the envelopes for the hat.

6. Select all the vertices other than the ones being affected by the jawbone and click the Exclude Verts button, as seen in Figure 14.47.

7. Go to the Edit drop-down menu, choose Select Invert, and select the jaw-bone vertices.

8. Press Ctrl, select the head bone, and click Exclude Verts.

9. Select the bottom row of verts at the base of the neck and click Exclude Verts.

10. Adjust the head bone envelopes to include all the remaining verts.

11. Test the rotation and shape of the head using the spine controls and the Morph targets, and make adjustments as necessary.

If you see a light-gray line shooting out from the head, that's a patch handle that hasn't been weighted. Just window-select around the end of that line to select the handle. Then, press Ctrl and select an envelope in the viewport or select the name in the envelope list, and turn up the Abs. Effect spinner under Weight Properties to give it some weight.

12. For the eyes and teeth, simply them directly to the head bone (bone17).

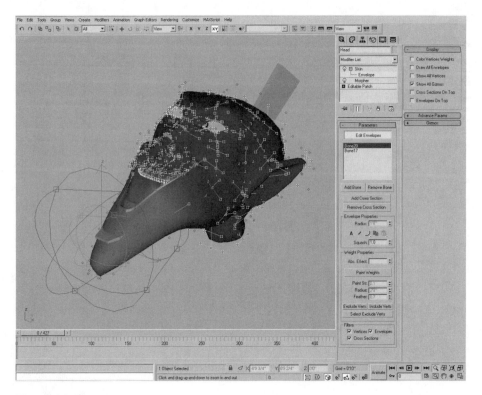

Figure 14.47   Adjust the envelopes on the jaw, with the mouth wide open.

Exercise 14.24   Skinning the Tunic

That title sounds like a really bad punk band. Before you skin the Jester's dress (tunic), let's deal with the belt objects.

1. Parent all the loose objects to the main belt that encircles the Jester.

2. Parent the belt to bone13, the base of the spine.

   Refer to Figure 14.48.

   Next you need to add two bone/IK chains that will be used later in the animation for secondary clothlike animation, and they assist in skinning as well.

3. Draw two bones vertically in the Front view, at the center of the tunic, and right-click to add the bone nub.

4. Adjust the bone widths to fill out the center of the tunic.

5. Align the bones to be just below the belt and in the front of the tunic.

6. Copy this bone chain and move it to the back.

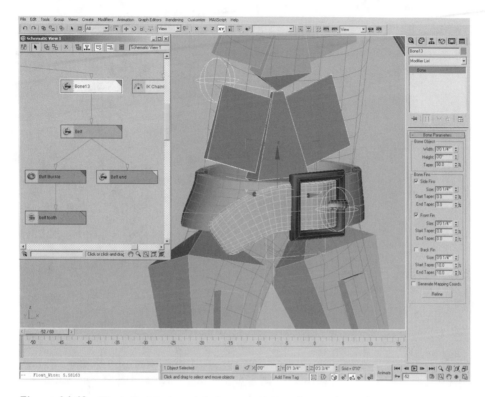

Figure 14.48   The belt objects and their correct hierarchy are shown here.

7. Link the parent bones to the COM ellipse. If you don't want them to rotate with the COM, turn off the Inherit Rotate in the Hierarchy/Link Info panel.

8. Add HI IK to each bone chain, as seen in Figure 14.49.

9. Add the Skin modifier to the tunic, and add the bones you just drew (without the bone nubs), the two upper-leg bones, and the base spine bone.

10. Click Edit Envelopes and select bone13 (spine bone) and shrink the radii to 0.

11. Select the top row of vertices on the tunic and set the Abs. Effect to 1.0. This locks the verts to the spine bone.

12. Use the envelopes to evenly divide the weight distribution between the leg bones and the secondary animation bones, as seen in Figure 14.50.

13. Animate the IK feet doing some front and back movements to "exercise" the Jester. Doing so enables you to view problems in the skin.

    This might be a good time to experiment with the Paint Weights feature. Although nothing new has been added in max 4, it's much easier to see what you're doing because of the new shaded display.

14. If you see a lot of penetration with the body, you could pull out some verts in the Editable Patch modifier to separate it.

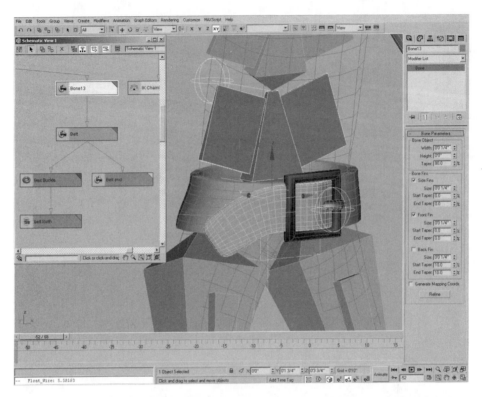

Figure 14.49   These are the bones for skinning and secondary clothlike animation on the tunic.

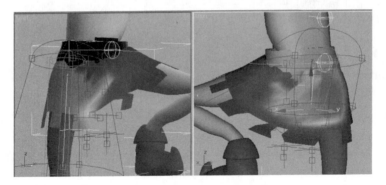

Figure 14.50   This figure shows the envelopes adjusted on the tunic.

The tweaking process was somewhat time-consuming, so be patient and always double-check the effect one tweak to the skin has on other movements. It might look good when the leg moves forward, but how about when it moves backward?

Exercise 14.25   Skinning the Frock

You're almost finished! Of course I've saved the most difficult task for last. There were some strange things Skin did when I applied it to the frock and added the arm bones. The envelopes did not appear in a nice predictable shape, and they were extremely difficult to edit. I attributed this problem to the way the frock is modeled and to the fact that Skin likes nice regular rows of vertices over a folded-over piece of cloth.

To solve this problem, add an FFD space warp to the scene.

1. Create an FFD space warp. Move it to encompass the frock and bind the frock to it. Make the FFD a resolution of 2×7×5.

2. Apply a Skin modifier to the FFD and add the upper-arm bones and the spine bone15 to the Skin modifier. (Bones 46, 21, 15, and 14).

3. The envelopes don't help you very much here, so shrink all of them to 0; you'll do a lot of vert weighting by hand.

4. You need to add another bone into the neck area to lock down verts. Create a small box, position it around the neck area, and link it to the spine hierarchy.

5. Add the box bone into the Skin modifier, and shrink its envelope radii to 0 as well.

   You add Step 4 to get a bone in that part of the skin that won't rotate directly like the spine bones, one that will follow the rotation of the spine. That seems to clean up the neck area from being bent down by rotating bones to being locked down and moving with the skin in a more rigid manner.

6. Animate the back bending forward and backward (using the Spine_control01 object). If you do see extra stretching in the neck area, assign those verts that aren't deforming realistically to that box bone at **100%** Abs. Effect.

   Editing FFD weights can be tricky, but if you stick to selecting groups (rows or columns) it makes the process easier.

7. Animate a raising hand movement, an arm forward movement, and a straight-down movement over a short range of frames, as seen in Figure 14.51.

8. In the Envelope Sub-Object mode of the Skin modifiers, select bone21's envelope.

9. Turn on the Vertex filter and select the first three columns of vertices of the FFD that surround the upper-arm area. Dial the Abs. Effect spinner up and down in Skin to see how the weighting adjustments affect the frock.

10. Continue to select groups of verts and make adjustments in problem areas in your animation.

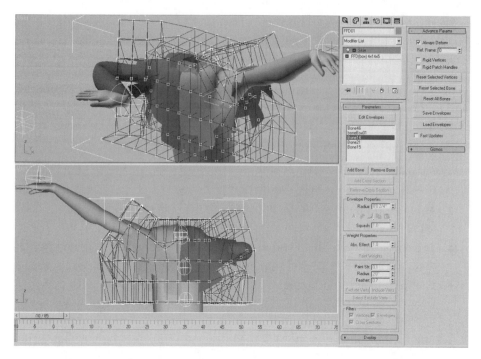

Figure 14.51   The weighting on the skinned FFD for the frock is adjusted.

11. Select the other bone's envelopes, one at a time, and make similar adjust-
    ments, always scrubbing the time slider to see how your weighting adjust-
    ments are affected by the different movements.

    It takes some experimenting to get this to look right. After you get the basic
    blocks of verts assigned in a logical way to the arm and spline bones, tweak
    individual rows of verts and finally individual verts.

12. Add weighting to the verts from different bones in the Skin modifier. This is
    where the most experimenting takes place. What happens when you assign
    the weighting of a particular vert to a particular bone?

Depending on the deformation you're getting, assigning the inner verts of the FFD
to that little box bone you created around the neck tends to lock them in place,
avoiding penetration of the clothes and skin. Again, it depends entirely on your particular weighting.

In the final example on the CD-ROM, I used an FFD that had more vertices (4×15×5),
which gave me some good results. In writing this chapter and experimenting more,
I found that a less-dense FFD is easier to deal with (less points, less data to organize),
and I got equally acceptable results. Unfortunately, this discovery was too late, and
the final skinned character had already been passed on to the animator.

If you're finding a lot of penetration between the clothes and the skin, consider scaling up the frock geometry a bit.

Summary

If you wanted more in-depth information about character engineering in max 4, this chapter definitely gives you a good head start—even if you didn't have time to tweak all the controls and skinning to make it perfect. It took me about a week to get this going from scratch, but that included a lot of experimenting, pushing the system, finding some bugs and being picky about the outcome.

If you can learn the basic concepts of engineering and what an animator needs and wants, you make the entire pipeline go faster. I asked the animator if he wanted the character to have an auto-centering pelvis or to be able to flip and fly the character through space. I explained why I couldn't rig both controls because they conflicted in engineering methods, so he chose flipping/flying ability. This set me along a path that had a well-defined goal.

A major topic in this chapter is automation versus manual control. When you want the best of both worlds, it can create some complexities that don't necessarily have to be there if that's not what the animator wants. Remember, it's more efficient to have multiple characters that are engineered to move and behave in specific ways. For long shots, the character can have simple controls for the fingers, because an animator might not spend time doing very detailed animation. For close-ups, a version is needed to allow the animator to adjust every little joint.

Some issues didn't make it into this chapter for space and time reasons, such as file merging and Xrefing, which are part of the studio workflow. In a basic sense, you can Xref this entire character into a scene for animating, but you can't access any modifiers when you Xref an object. This means you can't animate any Morph targets or the Custom Attributes. It's a current limitation, so for now, merging a complicated character like the Jester into a scene is the best method.

With tools such as the Reactor controller, Wire Parameters, constraints, and your new best friend the List controller at your disposal, you can create amazing character rigs. Learning a bit of MAXScript will go a long way toward solving problems that you can't solve using the interface alone. Step out of the UI as much as possible, because when you get a grasp for what's going on under the hood and how to manipulate it, you'll feel empowered rather then restricted.

C h a p t e r 15

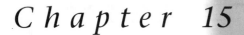

Organic/Character Model Rigging for Games/Interactive Applications

by Mike O'Rourke

The new IK and skinning improvements

in 3ds max 4 add much-needed func-

tionality for the character animator and

rigger. In this chapter, you use the new

bone system, IK, skinning, and a few other new tools necessary for rigging Pug, shown in Figure 15.1.

This chapter discusses how to do the following:

- Create a skeletal system using the new max 4 bones
- Use Wire Parameters
- Use Manipulator helpers
- Use the Skin modifier
- Use deformers

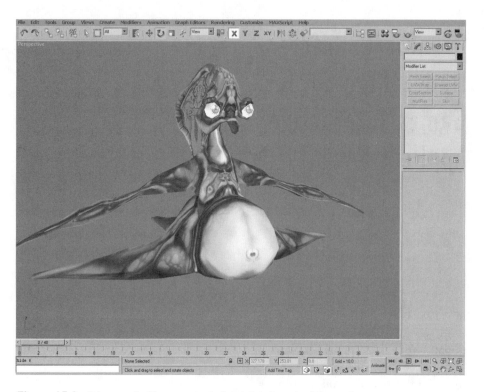

Figure 15.1   3ds max 4 offers new tools for animating the Pug mesh.

Pug has two arm tentacles, three leg tentacles, a head with a huge backflap, and a pair of bulged-out eyes. In addition to a basic setup for the bones and skinning, you also work on making a UI to facilitate easier animation later.

Exercise 15.1   Creating Bones

For this exercise, you create bones for all the tentacles.

1. Open the pug_chapter15_start.max file.

2. In the Command panel, choose Create/Systems. Press the Bones button to start creating bones.

3. In the Front viewport, create six bones for the arm. Figure 15.2 illustrates the bone placement. The last bone is created automatically for you, which is technically the seventh bone.

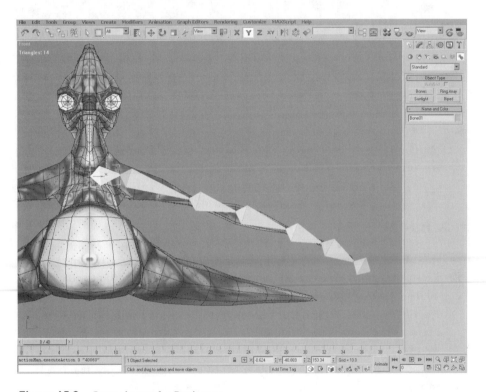

Figure 15.2   Create bones for Pug's arm.

4. In the Top viewport, position the bones so that they are inside the mesh, as shown in Figure 15.3.

5. In the Perspective viewport, select the bones and resize them to your liking using the bone's parameters in the Modifier panel.

Tip

To help resize the bones, select the mesh and press Alt+X to put that mesh in See-Thru mode. Now you can see the bones more clearly.

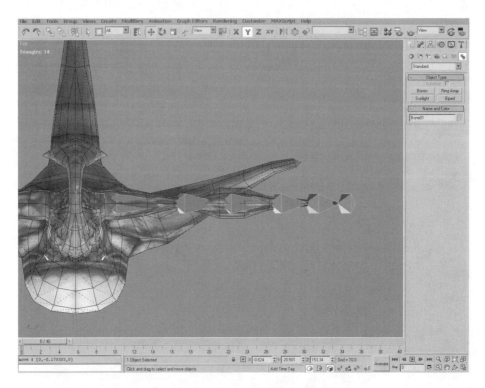

Figure 15.3   Position the bones in the Top view of bone placement.

6. Add fins to the bones by checking the appropriate Fin check box in the Command panel. You can add fins to the sides, top, or bottom; you can also adjust a fin's length and taper.

7. Change the bones' colors by changing the object color of the bone, to make them a little easier to differentiate.

   Figure 15.4 shows the bones after the sizes were adjusted, fins added, and colors changed from dark to light. The last bone on the tip of the tentacle was resized to fit the end.

8. Name the bones so that they make sense to you when you need to pick them in a dialog box, such as in the Skin modifier. The following names were used in the pug_chapter15_ArmBones.max file:

   Bone L-collar, Bone L-Bicep, Bone L-Elbow, Bone L-Flipper, Bone L-Flipper2, Bone L-Flipper3, Bone L-Flipper4.

   Now you create an IK chain for the arm. You want the chain to bend at the proper angle, and currently the arm bones form a perfectly straight line when viewed from above. If you bend the bones slightly, the IK chain will be made properly. This sets a Preferred Angle.

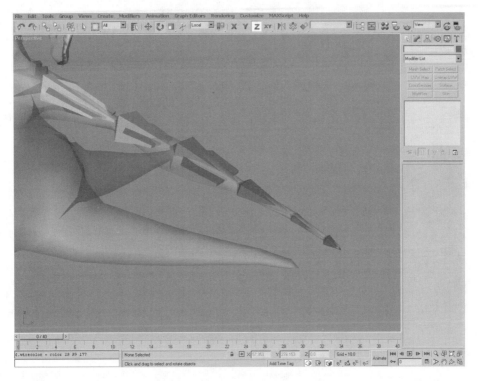

Figure 15.4   Adjust the appearance of the arm bones.

In this situation, you want the Preferred Angle to point toward the elbow. If the bones were perfectly straight, the IK solver that you apply later in the process would not know which way to bend at the joints.

9. Bend the Bone L-Elbow and Bone L-Flipper along their Local Z-axis about 10 degrees, as shown in Figure 15.5.

10. To create an IK chain for the arm, select Bone L-Bicep. Then, in the Animation drop-down list, select IK Solvers/HI Solver. Select Bone L-Flipper2 to end the chain, as shown in Figure 15.6.

    You need to control the IK chain by adding an object—in this case, a Point helper—and using it for the IK chain's Solver Plane, otherwise known as a Swivel Angle.

11. In the Command panel, choose Create/Helpers/Point. Create a Point helper in the Top viewport, behind the arm.

12. Move the Point helper along the Z-axis so that it is at the same height as the elbow in the Front viewport.

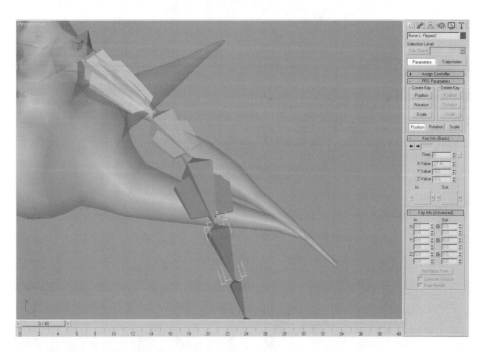

Figure 15.5   Bend the Elbow bones.

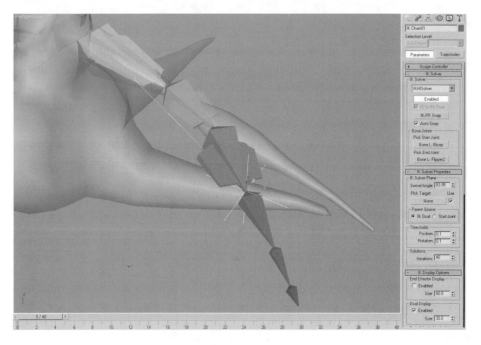

Figure 15.6   Create the HI-IK chain.

13. Select IK Chain01, and in the Command panel, go to the Motion tab to access the IK Chain parameters. Find the IK Solver Plane rollout (in the IK Solver Properties section).

14. Press the Pick Target button, which currently reads None.

When pressed, the button turns yellow, indicating that you are in Pick mode. The next object you pick will be the target.

15. Select the Point helper. Rename the Point helper **L Elbow Point**.

16. Move the IK chain's goal along the Y- and Z-axis to bring the bones back to their original position, as shown in Figure 15.7.

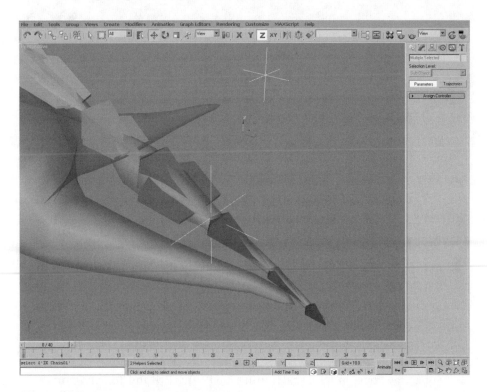

Figure 15.7   Move the Elbow Point helper.

17. Select the bones, IK chain, and Point helper.

18. Mirror the setup by pressing the Mirror button on the top toolbar, as shown in Figure 15.8.

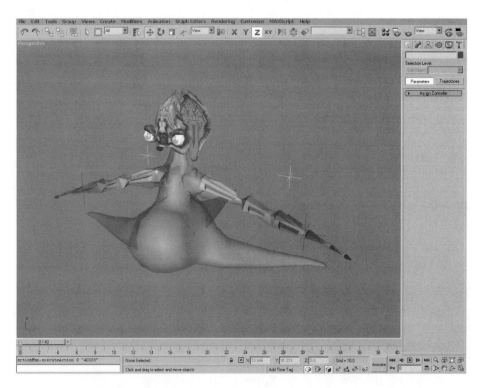

Figure 15.8   Press the Mirror button for a mirrored bones setup.

Now you make bones for the leg tentacle, using a similar technique.

19. In the Command panel, choose Create/Systems. Press the Bones button to start creating bones.

20. In the Front viewport, create eight bones for the leg. Figure 15.9 illustrates the bone placement.

Unlike the previous limb you worked on, this leg is bent in the Z-axis. To account for this, you must rotate the bones into place.

21. Rotate the bones in local space, using the Perspective and Top viewports.

22. Resize the bones, add fins, and change their colors to make them easier to work with.

Figure 15.10 shows the final adjustments. The bones are set up thus far in the pug_chapter15_bones.max file.

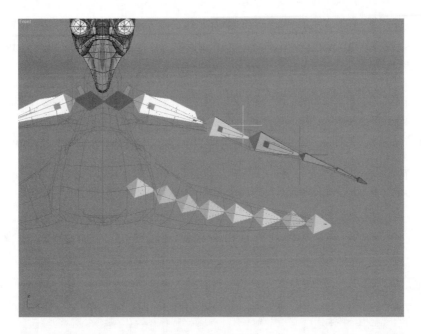

Figure 15.9   Create the bones for the leg.

Figure 15.10   Make the final adjustments for the leg bones.

Exercise 15.2   Using Manipulators to Create a Leg Rig

The bones are in place. Now you need to make a few manipulators to animate the leg tentacles.

1. In the viewport, create three Slider manipulators by choosing Create/ Helpers/Manipulators in the Command panel. Sliders are created in screen space, so it doesn't matter what viewport you are in.

2. Create the Sliders somewhere around the outer edge, as shown in Figure 15.11. I named the Sliders Bend Left Leg Base, Bend Left Leg Mid, and Bend Left Leg Tip. You can name them whatever you like. It doesn't matter, as long as you can easily remember what each is.

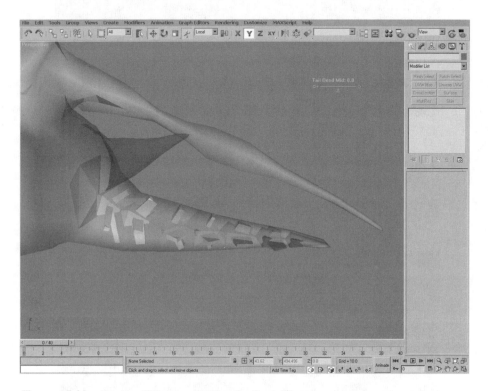

Figure 15.11   Create a Slider manipulator for the tail bend.

Now you wire the bone's Z-axis rotation to the appropriate manipulator. Unfortunately, in this situation the default controller for rotation on the bones is a TCB controller (unless you changed the default controller type, which is easy to do). You need to use the Euler XYZ controller in this case, giving you access to wire just the Z-axis to the manipulator.

3. To change the last six bones' Rotation controllers to the Euler XYZ Rotation controller, select the object, and then go to the Motion tab in the Command panel.

    You'll see a white dialog box in the panel named Assign Controller.

4. Select the Rotation item, and then press the Assign Controllers button (the green arrow at the top of the box). Another window will pop up. Select Euler XYZ in that window.

    To check your work, load the pug_chapter15_Euler.max file, which has all the proper bones assigned.

    Now you wire the bone's parameters to the manipulators you made earlier.

5. Select the last bone on the leg, Bone L-Flipper4. Right-click to bring up the Quad menu.

6. Select Wire Parameters in the lower-right quad.

    A small dialog box appears. This box enables you to choose what is wired.

7. Select Transform/Rotation/Z Rotation.

    Your cursor now has a line being drawn from it to the bone you have just selected to wire. See Figure 15.12.

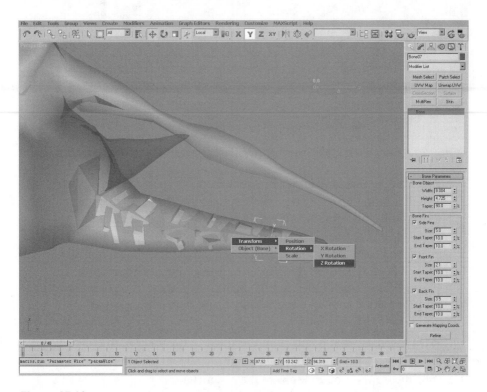

Figure 15.12   Select Wire Parameters to choose what to wire.

8. Left-click the Slider manipulator you made earlier. A menu of available parameters will pop up.

9. Choose Object(Slider)/value.

A new dialog box appears, as shown in Figure 15.13.

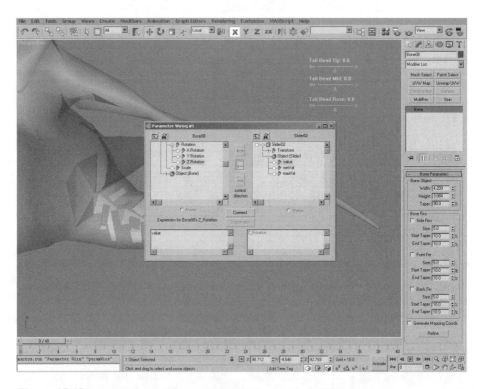

Figure 15.13   You will wire the two objects in the Parameter Wiring window.

This window enables you to wire the two objects that you have selected. By default it brings up the two properties that you selected, but anything that shows up in this window can be wired.

In the middle of the window, there are three arrows. These arrows determine in which direction the information is being passed. It can go one way, thus only one object controls the other, or it can go both ways, enabling the objects to drive each other. In this situation you want it to go one way with the information coming from the Slider, and then getting passed on to control the bone's Z rotation.

10. Select the arrow that points from the Slider to the rotation. If objects were selected in the order described previously, it should be the left arrow.

11. Press the Connect button to wire the parameters.

12. Go into Manipulate mode and slide the Slider back and forth to check it out.
The flipper rotates wildly! Undo your moves, or just set the Slider back to 0.

The bone went crazy because the value the manipulator is sending to the
bone is too high. You can easily adjust this by going into the Modifier panel.

13. Select the Slider manipulator. Double-click it if it doesn't select.

14. Adjust the Minimum value to **–1**, and the Maximum to **1**.

Try the manipulator now. It works just the way you want. You can adjust the
limits by adjusting the Maximum and Minimum values for the Slider.

Now that the manipulators have been created, you need to wire the leg bones in
groups of two to the three manipulators. This is done by repeating the previous
couple of steps. All the bones need to be mirrored to account for the right-side leg
tentacle. They then need to be parameter-wired to a new set of manipulators. The
file pug_chapter15_Manipulators.max has all the manipulators wired.

Exercise 15.3   Creating Bones for the Spine, Head, Stomach, and Tail

1. Open pug_chapter15_Manipulators.max. Figure 15.14 shows what the
character should look like.

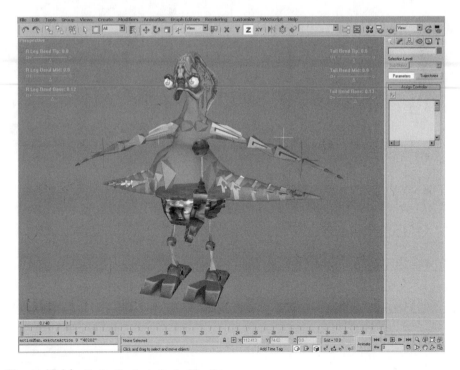

Figure 15.14   So far Pug's rig looks like this.

2. Hide everything except the body, head, and eyes.

3. In the Right viewport, draw bones for the tail. Seven bones should do fine. Use Figure 15.15 as a reference for drawing the bones. Taper them and add fins as you did with the legs earlier in this chapter.

4. Draw bones from the pelvis to the end of the neck. Figure 15.15 shows the setup.

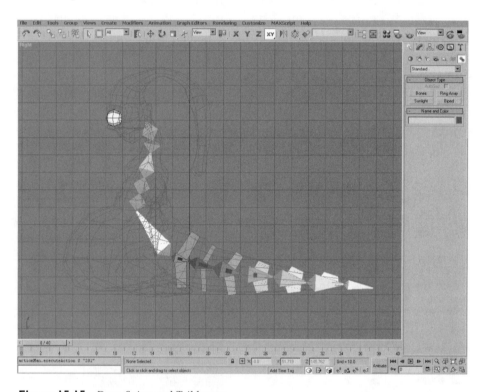

Figure 15.15   Draw Spine and Tail bones.

5. Now create one big bone for the head, starting from the back of the neck.

   Make sure the Pivot point is in the proper place. It should be right where the neck attaches to the head. See Figure 15.16 for reference.

6. Create more bones for the flipper on the back of the head.

7. Create three bones for the eye sockets, starting from the base, out toward the eyeball. Mirror those three bones for the other side. Figure 15.17 shows how these should be arranged.

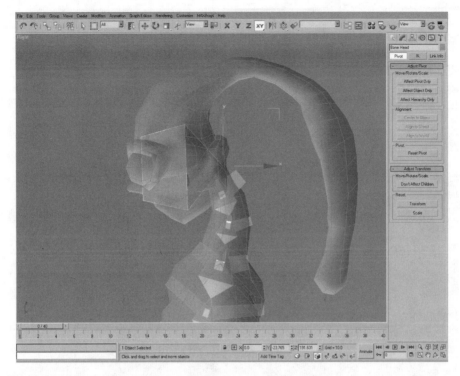

Figure 15.16   Create a bone for the head.

Figure 15.17   Create additional bones for the head.

8. Create three more bones, separately, for the stomach. See Figure 15.18.

Next, you need to link a few objects to get the hierarchy set up properly.

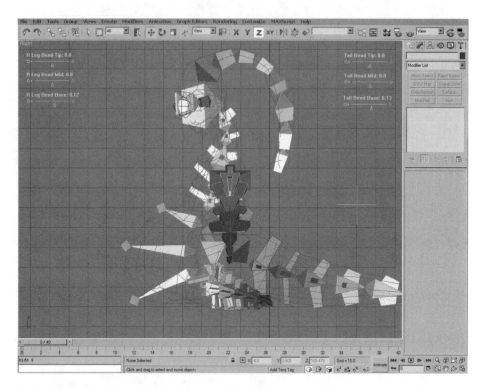

Figure 15.18   Create bones for the stomach.

   9. Link the Pony Tail parent bone to the Head bone.

10. Link the first Eye Socket bone to the Head bone.

11. Link the Head bone to the first Neck bone.

12. Link the first bone of each tail to Bone Pelvis.

13. Link the first bone on each arm to Bone L-Collar.

One of the best ways to get this right is to look at a file that is set up and compare it to what you have so far. The pug_chapter15_AllBones.max file on the accompanying CD-ROM shows you how it should look. You also can use Figure 15.19 as a reference.

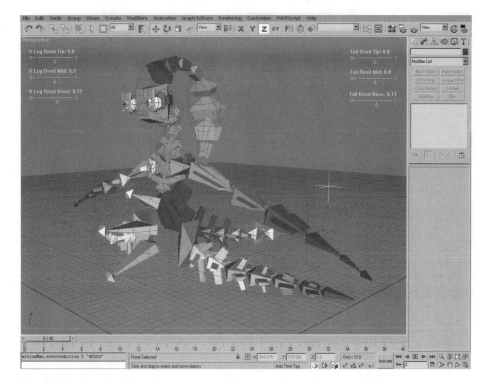

Figure 15.19   Check the Pug bones setup.

This file has all the bones and manipulators that you made previously. The red Pelvis bone is the parent of all the other bones. You will link the Pelvis bone to the base later so that Pug rides the mechanical legs. At this point you have all the bones you need for now. Let's move on to skinning the model.

Exercise 15.4   Skinning the Model

You use the Skin modifier to apply the mesh deformation using the bones you've created. There are a lot of new features in the Skin modifier in max 4, such as deformers, which you explore in this exercise.

1. Unhide your mesh and get it out of See-Thru mode if it is active by using Alt+X.
2. Hide everything in the scene except the Pug meshes and the bones. This makes everything a lot easier to see while you're skinning. See Figure 15.20.
3. Select Pug–Body. Apply a Skin modifier to it.

    Next you add bones to the Skin modifier so that the model knows which bones it should eventually be deforming to.

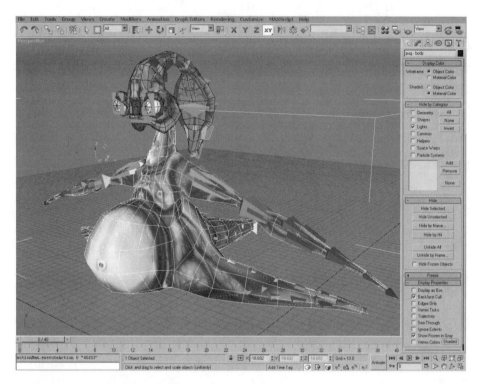

Figure 15.20   Hide everything but the Pug mesh and bones.

4. Press the Add Bone button in the Skin Modifier panel.

   A window pops up, enabling you to add bones to the skin.

5. Select everything that starts with bone, except Bone Head, Bone Necks, Bone Eyes, and Bone HeadTail.

6. Press the Edit Envelopes button to start editing envelopes. Select the part of the envelope you want to edit: the inner envelope, outer envelope, or envelope handles. After the item is selected, you can adjust it using the move tool in the viewport, or you can adjust its Radius spinner in the Modifier panel.

 Note

A mesh turns color to show weighting (see Figure 15.21). When a bone's weighting is heavier on that particular area of the mesh, the mesh's color turns toward red. Blue means it's not weighted to the current bone.

7. Select Bone Pelvis and move it around. Look for any parts of the mesh being left behind, or other weirdness.

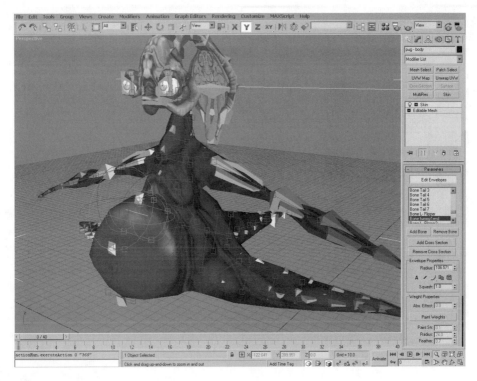

Figure 15.21   Mesh color shows skin weighting.

 Tip

> If a part of the mesh does not move, there is no envelope encapsulating those vertices.
> Try making a nearby envelope bigger by adjusting its radius in the Modifier panel.

Try to get a basic skin working, but don't spend a whole lot of time tweaking it. You'll want to put Pug in a few poses later on and tweak the skin then.

8. Apply a Skin modifier to the Pug–Head object, as you did in Step 3 for the body.

9. Add all the bones that you want to use to control the model.

10. Edit the envelopes until you have a basic skin setup where all vertices fall within the envelope of at least one bone.

11. Link the eyes to the last bone in each eye bone chain.

12. Rotate Bone Head to check the skinning. Make sure none of the mesh is getting left behind.

Refer to the pug_chapter15_Skinned.max file on the accompanying CD-ROM, or Figure 15.22, to see the Pug model with all the previous steps completed.

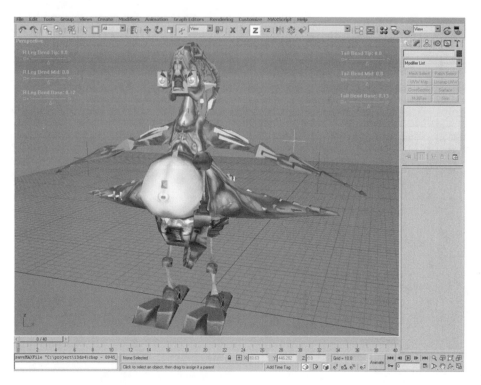

Figure 15.22   The Pug model with rig looks like this.

Exercise 15.5   Using Skin Deformers

Now you use Skin's new deformers to help shape the top of the belly when Pug bends forward. Currently if you rotate Bone Spine 1, a cavity forms in his chest, as seen in Figure 15.23. You want the skin to bunch up there. This is pretty easy to do with a Skin deformer.

1. Go to Frame 5 or 6 by sliding the time slider at the bottom of the screen. Turn on the Animate button.

   You give Pug an extra keyframe of animation so that you can set limits for the Skin deformer. You want a standard frame (Frame 0) and then the upper limit of rotation, where you adjust the Skin deformer (Frame 5).

2. Rotate Bone Spine 1 as far forward as you want Pug to be able to lean forward.

3. Select Pug–Body. In the Skin Modifier panel, select Edit Envelopes. Select the Bone Spine 1 envelope in the small dialog box, as shown in Figure 15.24.

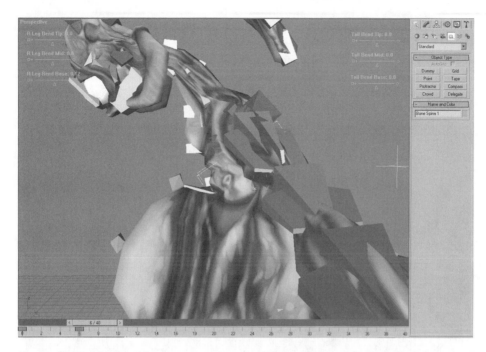

Figure 15.23   A Skin deformer will fix the crease in Pug's chest.

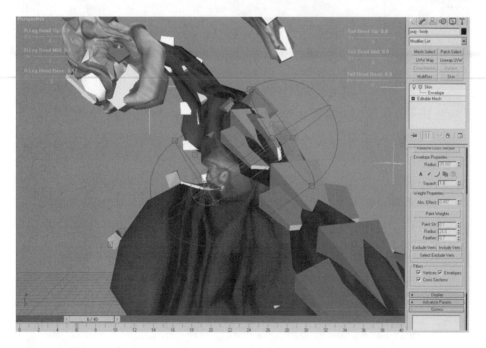

Figure 15.24   Select the Skin envelope.

4. Check the Vertices check box in the Filter section of the Skin Modifier panel. This enables you to select vertices.

5. With the Bone Spine 1 envelope selected, select the front six vertices, as seen in Figure 15.25.

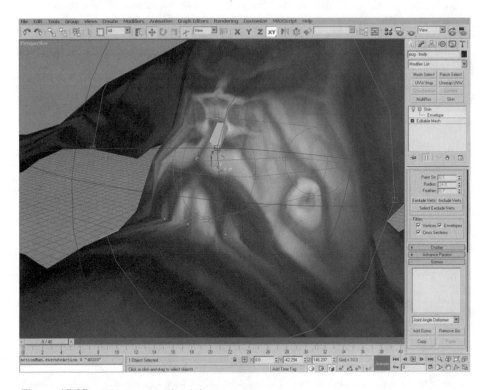

Figure 15.25   Select vertices for deformer.

6. Make sure you are currently at Frame 0, and slide the Skin command all the way to the bottom. Expand the Gizmos rollout.

7. Add a Joint Angle deformer by pressing the Add Gizmo button.

   You should see a lattice around your vertices. This is the Angle Deformer Lattice. If you don't see the lattice, try going into Wireframe mode.

8. Press the Edit Lattice button in the Gizmo Parameters rollout, located right below the Gizmos rollout. This enables you to select Lattice points.

9. Go to Frame 5 and adjust the Lattice points by moving them into place, as shown in Figure 15.26.

10. Move the points around until you are satisfied with the result.

    Try not to worry about how the lattice cage ends up, but look more at the effect on the mesh. Figure 15.27 shows the mesh after the gizmo was adjusted.

11. Slide the Time Slider to see the effect of the gizmo.

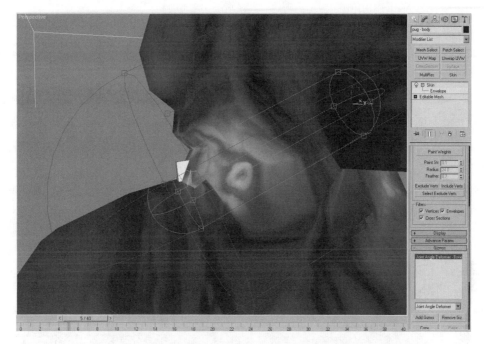

Figure 15.26   Adjust the Deformer lattice points.

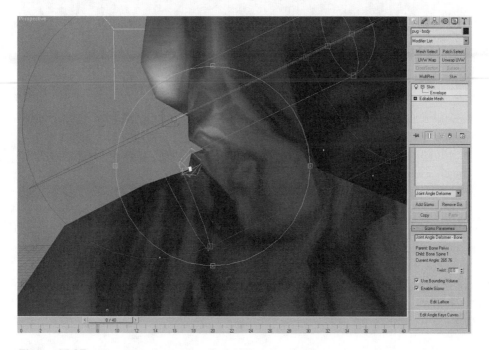

Figure 15.27   The mesh shows the effect of the gizmo adjustment.

This is great for fixing problem spots, such as armpits and crotches. It's also great for adding details, such as muscle bulging. Figure 15.28 shows the result.

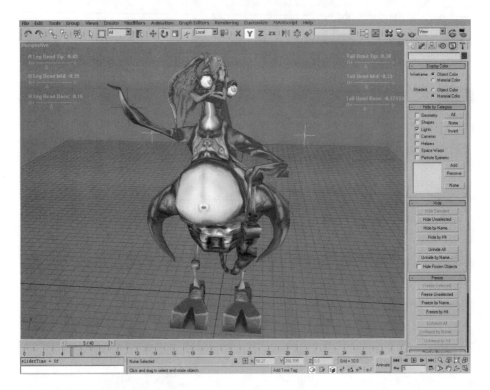

Figure 15.28   Slide the Time Slider to see the gizmo's effect.

Pug is rigged up and ready to go. Sometimes rigs can take a long time to set up, but setting them up right can save you a lot of time when it comes to animating. The new manipulators and Skin deformers in max 4 give you more control in rigging the character.

Summary

Try to come up with new ways to use manipulators, constraints, and all the other features covered in this chapter. There is no one way to rig a character, so the more you understand the tools, the better suited you are for whatever situation might arise. The final rigged file is called pug_chapter15_Posing.max, and is on the CD-ROM.

Part V

Materials and Mapping

Materials/Shaders/ Mapping for the Fire Truck

by Brian Austin and Diana Diriwaechter

In this chapter, you give the little fire

truck you made in Chapter 7, "Non-

Organic Modeling for Broadcast/Film," a

life by adding materials and textures.

The model looks rather lifeless now and, well, just gray (see Figure 16.1). It is impossible to tell what the fire truck is made of. We need to change that.

Figure 16.1   The fire truck from Chapter 7 has no materials or texture.

In this chapter you learn how to

- Set up custom mapping and Material IDs
- Use various sub-object selection tools
- Work with multiple shaders
- Work with Alpha Channels
- Work with displacements

The best way to approach this task is to take a moment to analyze the model. It is supposed to be a toy—a toy for a 2- to 3-year-old. In this chapter you make it look so plastic that someone wants to pick it up.

You need to work on the model in separate parts and yet maintain the same materiality throughout. Start with the rear trailer.

Exercise 16.1   Texturing the Rear Trailer

A good plan for a model like this, in which all the individual pieces are made of the same material, is to create a base texture and then slowly add more detail.

First, open the Max file of the truck you created in Chapter 7, or use the firetruck.max file from the accompanying CD-ROM.

1. Open the Material Editor and select the first sample slot, or Material #1. Change the name to **rear trailer**.

Let's choose a standard Blinn material and set the base color. It's a fire truck, so give it a reddish tone.

2. In the Diffuse channel, set the color channels to R: **187**, G: **38**, B: **63**. Because the material is supposed to be plastic, you want to give it some specularity. In the Specular Highlight parameters, set the Specular Level to **77** and the Glossiness to **56**.

Now that you have a basic material, add some detail with a bump.

3. Open the Maps Parameters rollout and select the empty Bump slot. To avoid a very uniform, tiled look, you use a Mix material. In Color #1, put a Smoke material. The only thing to change within the Smoke Parameters rollout is the size. By default it is set to 40, which would generate a huge pattern, so set that number to **5**.

4. Back in the Mix Level, add a Noise material to Color #2. Within the Noise Parameters rollout, change the size to **3.00**, and instead of going with the default Regular Noise Type, choose a Fractal Noise Type.

5. To soften the noise, change the Blur to **0.01** and the Blur Offset to **5.0**. To have the two materials actually mix, you need to change the Mix Amount from 0 to a higher number. We chose 80.0. (See Figure 16.2.)

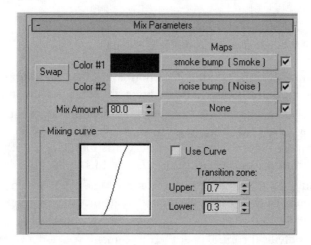

Figure 16.2   Change the Mix Amount in the Mix Parameters rollout.

6. Change the Bump Amount to **5** so the bump won't be too strong.

Still missing is some kind of a reflection. A plastic object almost always reflects its environment at least a little. If you were on a live-action set, most likely white cards would be used to give the artists control of the reflections seen in the objects they were shooting. We had white cards in mind when we created our map in Photoshop to use as a reflection (see Figure 16.3).

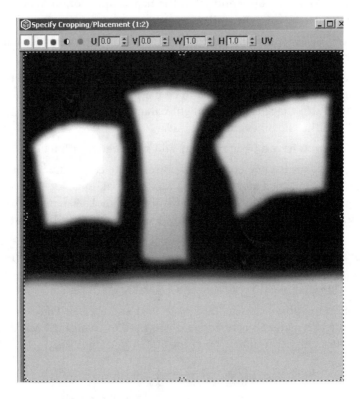

Figure 16.3   Our reflection map was created in Photoshop.

7. Place bounce_card.jpg into the Reflection slot. Soften the reflection a little by changing the Blur Offset to **.001** and bring the Reflection Amount down to **15**.

Now that you have a pretty good plastic foundation, add some fun details. Plastic toys often have stickers on them, so we added a ladder and a logo. In Photoshop we drew a ladder and made a little round logo. Both need to be saved with their Alpha Channels (see Figure 16.4).

To see both decals at the same time, on the same surface, each successive texture must have an Alpha Channel that enables the other texture to be seen underneath it.

To have individual control over their placement, you add a UVW Map for each decal in the Modifier Stack (see Figure 16.5).

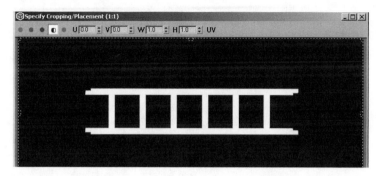

Figure 16.4   Draw a ladder and save it with its Alpha Channel.

8. The first UVW Map will be for the ladder, so make it Planar with a Z alignment. Set the Map Channel to **1**.

9. Now add another UVW Map modifier for the logo. Make this one Planar, also with a Z alignment, but change the Map Channel to **2**.

 Note

By adding these different Map Channels, you can control which bitmap gets applied to which UVW Mapping Coordinates. Should you need extra control over the scale and placement of these bitmaps, the UVW Gizmo can be adjusted.

You are ready to add these two decals to your material. In the Material Editor, you use a Composite material in the Diffuse slot (see Figure 16.6).

10. While in the Composite Parameters rollout, add ladder.tga in Map 1.

11. In the Bitmap Parameters rollout, you want to make sure that Image Alpha is checked and that Premultiplied Alpha is unchecked. In the Coordinates rollout, use Offset to move the map around on the object and place it correctly. We changed the V Offset to –0.14. To make certain the texture is looking at the correct UVW Map, set the Map Channel to **1**.

Now that the ladder decal is on, you are ready for the logo.

12. In the Composite Parameters rollout, select Map 2 and add logo.tga. Again, make sure the Alpha Channel is being used and that Premultiplied Alpha is unchecked. Set the Map Channel to **2**. The bitmap won't automatically be in the right place, so move and scale the UVW Gizmo until the placement looks correct to you.

Your Material Editor should ultimately look like Figure 16.7.

Figure 16.5
Add a UVW Map for each decal in the Modifier Stack.

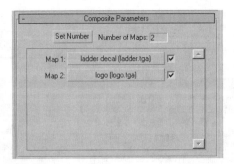

Figure 16.6   Add the decals to your material.

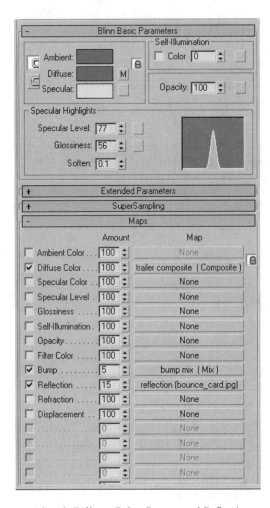

Figure 16.7   The material with Diffuse, Color, Bump, and Reflection applied.

You're finished with the first part of the fire truck. Render a preview and check it out. Let's move on to the little ladder.

Exercise 16.2   Texturing the Yellow Ladder

The base material is exactly the same as for the rear fire truck. You use a Displacement map, adding detail via materials, rather than modeling.

1. Open the Material Editor and select a new sample slot. Change the name to **yellow ladder**.

2. Start with a standard Blinn material, and to adjust the base color set the Diffuse channel color to R: **243**, G: **197**, B: **73**. In the Specular Highlight parameters, set the Specular Level to **77** and the Glossiness to **56**.

3. To keep a consistent look on the plastic, you use the same reflection map all over. So in the Reflection Map slot, add bounce_card.jpg and set the Reflection Amount to **15**. To soften the reflection map, change the Blur offset to **.011**.

   Now let's add some detail with a bump. Instead of a Mix map, use a Composite material so you can use two maps equally.

4. For Map 1, use the same Noise map that you used on the rear fire truck. Change the Noise Type to Fractal and adjust the Size to **3.0**.

5. In Map 2, add yellow_ladder_bump.tga from the CD. This map, created in Photoshop and saved with our trusty friend, an Alpha Channel, adds some detail to the ladder. In the Bitmap Coordinates rollout, make sure the Map Channel is set to **1**.

   What's missing? Correct! You need to add a UVW Map.

6. Go to the Modifier Stack and add a UVW Map modifier to the object. Make it Planar and align it to the Y-axis. Make sure the Map Channel is set to **1**.

   If you now render this object, you will definitely notice a difference with the added bump. (See Figure 16.8.)

   However, a texture artist is usually given a "final" model to work on. Often, having gotten approval for a final model by the director and/or client, the modeler has collapsed the Modifier Stack and sometimes, as is the case here, rigged the model for animation.

   Then, because we live in an ever-changing world, the director tells you to add some new detail to the model.

   For example, the client wants to see the ladder as if it were really there! Do you call the modeler back in? Do you panic? No, you add a Displacement map!

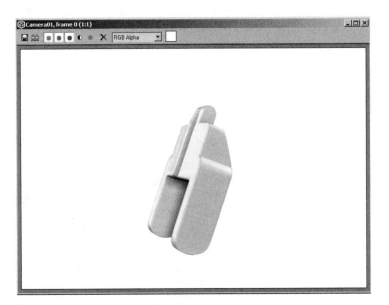

Figure 16.8   Render the object to get this ladder.

7. Drag and drop a copy of the same bitmap you used for the bump into the yellow ladder's Displacement slot in the Maps rollout. You don't have to change any settings on the bitmap level. Make sure, however, to set the Amount no higher than 3 or you'll get a very deformed object.

8. Before you can see the results, you have to add one more modifier. Add a Displacement Approx. modifier to the model's Modifier Stack.

9. Click Render Last.

Now *that* should satisfy your client. The ladder is very apparent in the render.

As a last detail, add the same logo from the rear ladder to the bottom of the ladder.

10. Add another UVW Map modifier, and set the Map Channel to 2.

11. In the Diffuse Color Map slot, add logo.tga from the CD. You don't have to adjust anything—just make sure that you're using the Alpha and that Premultiplied Alpha is turned off (see Figure 16.9).

We often hear it said that computers free us of repetitive tasks. Although that statement is sometimes exaggerated, you are about to save some time copying parameters for the next few materials.

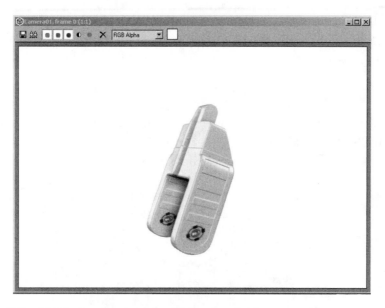

Figure 16.9   Add displacement and the decal to your ladder.

Exercise 16.3   Texturing the Back of the Fire Truck

In this exercise, you texture the details on the back of the fire truck. Start with the ladder.

1. Instead of starting from scratch, make a copy of the yellow ladder material by dragging its sample slot to an empty slot. Be sure to rename it.

2. Now delete the Diffuse map and the Displacement map. Instead of using both the bitmap and the noise in the bump, use only the noise.

   Next you texture the bucket cylinder and bucket

3. For the bucket, make a copy of ladder base and rename it **bucket**.

4. Change the color from yellow to blue. Then select the Ambient color and set the RGB values to R: **14**, G: **41**, B: **84**. Select the Diffuse color and change the RGB to R: **44**, G: **121**, B: **255**. Be sure to turn off the Ambient/Diffuse Lock.

   Now it's time to texture the hose.

5. Again, copy ladder base, and rename it **hose**.

6. In the Basic Parameters rollout, change the Ambient and the Diffuse color to almost black.

7. To soften the black, and to make the hose feel a little more detailed, add a Falloff map to the Diffuse slot. In the Falloff parameters, change the first color channel to a dark gray and the second one to black.

The back of the fire truck is now done! Take a break—or move on to the front of the fire truck. The front is easier because you can use many of the same techniques you used on the back.

Exercise 16.4   Texturing the Cab

Texturing the cab will be fun because this is a great area to add some decals. You use a Multi/Sub-Object material (see Figure 16.10). You texture both the window and the outside of the cab with one shader, combining two materials into one.

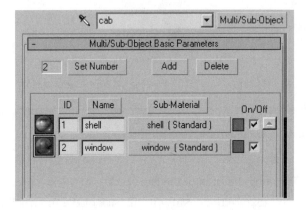

Figure 16.10   At this point your Multi/Sub-Object Basic Parameters rollout should look like this.

1. In the Modifier Stack, open the Modifier List and select an Edit Mesh modifier. In Sub-Object mode select all the faces except the window (see Figure 16.11).

2. In the Modifier Stack, open the Modifier List, select a Material modifier, and set the Material ID to 1.

3. Repeat Step 1, this time selecting just the window.

4. Apply a second Material modifier and set the Material ID to 2.

5. Return to the Material Editor and click the Standard button to open the Material/Map Browser. Select Multi/Sub-Object as your material.

   Having assigned two Material IDs, you know you'll need two materials.

6. Drag and drop the material named rear trailer into ID 1 and rename it **shell**.

   To control the placement of the stickers, you have to apply four UVW Map modifiers—one for each sticker (see Figure 16.12).

Figure 16.11 Select the faces in Sub-Object mode.

7. In the Modifier Stack, open the Modifier List and select a UVW Map modifier. In the Mapping parameters, select Planar and align it to the Y-axis. Set the Map Channel to **1**.

8. On top of that, add another UVW Map modifier. Make this one Planar and also align it to the Y-axis. Set the Map Channel to **2**.

9. Add a third UVW Map modifier. Make it Planar and also align it to the Y-axis. Set the Map Channel to **3**.

10. Add one more UVW Map modifier on the very top of the stack. Make this one Planar, align it to the X-axis, and set its Map Channel to **4**.

    Now you're ready to go back to the Material Editor. To show all decals at the same time, you have to add a Composite map to the Diffuse channel of Multi/Sub-Object 1.

11. Go to the Composite Parameters rollout, and set the number of maps to **4** (see Figure 16.13).

12. In Map 1, open light_icon.tga on the CD, a map created in Photoshop with an Alpha Channel. In the Coordinates rollout, make sure Premultiplied Alpha is

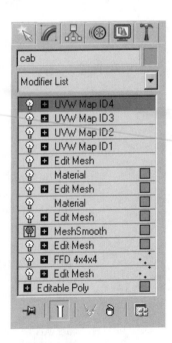

Figure 16.12
Apply a UVW Map modifier for each sticker.

unchecked and set the Map Channel to **1** so that it looks at the correct UVW Map. You might also (in the viewport) scale the UVW Map Gizmo so the bitmap is placed correctly.

Next you add a no1 decal. Because you're using planar UVW mapping, you can't use one Map Channel for both the left and right side of the cab. By default the no1 would show up reversed on one of the sides. To solve this problem, you create two UVW Map modifiers—one for each side—and two separate composite maps.

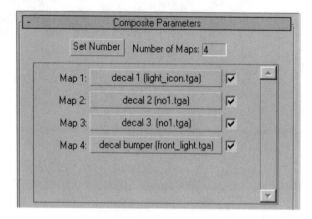

Figure 16.13   Your Compositor Parameters rollout should look something like this.

13. Go back to the Composite Parameters rollout and add no1.tga from the CD to Map 2. When you're in the Coordinates rollout, make sure Premultiplied Alpha is unchecked and set the Map Channel to **2**. Again, you can scale and move the UVW Map to get the desired size and placement.

14. In the Composite Parameters rollout, drag and drop Map Channel 2 into Map Channel 3, creating a copy. In the Bitmap Coordinates rollout, change the Map Channel to **3**. Because the whole point of this second map is to avoid the map being reversed, you now need to rotate the V Angle to 180.

15. One last time, go back to the Composite Parameters rollout, and put front_light.tga from the CD in Map 4. Make sure Premultiplied Alpha is unchecked. Change the Map Channel to **4**. Use the UVW Map Gizmo to adjust the placement.

The cab was the most difficult material yet. The fire truck's belly will be a breeze. Let's get started!

Exercise 16.5   Texturing the Fire Truck Belly

For the belly of the fire truck, you create a matte plastic.

1. Start with a new material and name it **belly**. In the Basic Parameters rollout, lock the Ambient, Diffuse, and Specular color. Then change the RGB values to R: **222**, G: **212**, B: **212**.

2. Because this material is supposed to be matte, set both the Specular Highlight and Glossiness to **0**.

3. All you need now is a little bit of a bump. Select the Bump Map slot and apply a Smoke map. While you're in the Smoke Parameters rollout, change the Size to **2**. Bump Amount should be set to **3**.

Now that you've finished the belly of the truck, move on to the wheels.

Exercise 16.6   Texturing the Wheels

The wheels, like everything else, will be plastic. You use a Multi/Sub-Object material again so you can give the top of the tires a tread bump without affecting the sides.

1. In the Modifier Stack, open the Modifier List and select a Poly Select modifier. In Sub-Object mode, select all the outside polygons. Open the Modifier List again and apply a Material modifier to the top of the stack. Set the Material ID to **1**.

2. Repeat Step 1, this time selecting the inside of the wheels and setting the Material ID to **2**.

3. Open the Material Editor and create a Multi/Sub-Object material. Name the material **wheels** and set up two Material IDs. Name the first Sub-Object material 1 **treads**. The other one you will name in a few steps.

   Thus far you have relied on Blinn shaders. This time you open a Multi-Layer shader (see Figure 16.14).

   The Multi-Layer shader is really nice because you can play around with an extra Specular Level.

4. In ID 1, select Multi-Layer from the Shader Basic Parameters pull-down menu. Change the Ambient and Diffuse color to a dark gray.

5. Adjust the First Specular Layer, changing the color to a dark gray. Set the Level to **55**. Leave all the other parameters on 0. This gives a nice falloff to this highlight.

6. In the Second Specular Layer, change the color to a whitish gray and set the Level to **110**. Leave the Glossiness and Orientation on 0, but change the Anisotropy to **80**. These settings increase your highlight's strength and give it a sharp falloff.

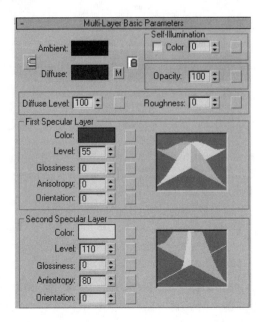

Figure 16.14 Use these settings in your Multi-Layer Basic Parameters rollout.

Play around with these levels for a few minutes. They are very powerful, flexible controls.

7. Now open the Maps rollout. In the Diffuse slot, place a Falloff map. In the Falloff Parameters rollout, change the first falloff color to a dark blue. We set the RGB parameters to R: **0**, G: **11**, B: **58**. Set the second falloff color to a dark gray (see Figure 16.15).

   By giving it a slightly dark blue falloff, you break up the overwhelming blackness and give it some detail.

   Next you create a Mix map. Instead of mixing two procedural maps, you mix a noise and a bitmap, which will be used as the treads.

8. Go to the bump map, and in Color #1, place a Smoke map and change the size to **5**.

9. In Color #2, place the bitmap wheel_tread.tga from the CD. In the Bitmap Coordinates rollout, you need to tile the image. Set the U offset to **0** and the V offset to **0.35**. The U tiling should be on 8.0 and the V tiling 0.8.

10. In the Mix Parameters rollout, set the Mix Amount to **95** so that the tread texture is dominant over the Smoke texture.

11. Back in the Maps rollout, set the Bump Amount to **35**.

12. Still in the Maps rollout, apply your much-used—but not tired— bounce_card.jpg in the Reflection slot. Set the Amount to **15**.

    You still need to give the inside of the wheel a texture.

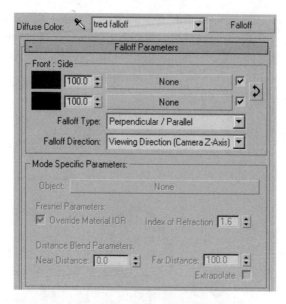

Figure 16.15   Set the RGB colors in your Falloff Parameters window.

13. Copy the first material, treads, into Sub-Object slot 2 and name it **sides**. Leave all the basic parameters the way they are.

14. Because there should not be any treads on the sides, we can use the same Mix map used in the rear fire truck. Drag and drop a copy of it over to this material's Bump slot and set the Bump Amount to 1.

The wheels wouldn't be complete without the hubcaps. Move on to the hubcaps.

Exercise 16.7   Texturing the Hubcaps

For the hubcaps, you can start with the standard plastic material you've been using all along. However, to add more detail, use hub_cap.tga from the CD as both a decal and a Displacement map.

1. Because you are dealing with bitmap placement, you, as always, have to apply a UVW Map modifier. This should be easy for you by now.

2. Drag and drop a copy of the basic Plastic material you have been using, and rename it **hubcaps**.

3. Change the Ambient, Diffuse, and Specular color to white.

4. Make sure the Reflection Map parameters are the same as on all the other materials.

5. Load hub_cap.tga into the Diffuse slot. You can leave all the parameters in the bitmap channel the way they are by default.

6. Load hub_cap.tga into the Bump slot. Set the Bump Amount to **2**.

7. Open hub_cap.tga one more time and load it into the Displacement slot. Set the Displacement Amount to **4**.

   Remember that in order for the displacement to show up, you have to add a Displacement Approx. modifier in the Modifier Stack.

8. Click Render (see Figure 16.16).

Figure 16.16   You are done!

Summary

We quickened the pace a little toward the end, because many of the steps in the second part of this chapter were repetitions of previous tasks.

Keep in mind that there is beauty in repetition, and we begin to remember what we repeat. With each repeated step, you gain a little more confidence.

Never be afraid to make mistakes. Every material you create is only the result of your limited experience and finite knowledge meeting the demands of the client and the job. Each production situation is different.

You can never go over the steps of creating materials enough. If you need to review, do so now, because you are about to enter the Jester's realm.

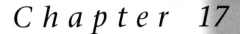

Chapter 17

Materials/Shaders/ Mapping for the Jester

by Brian Austin and Diana Diriwaechter

In this chapter, you give the Jester model,

which you created in Chapters 9,

"Organic/Character Modeling Using the

Patch Method for Broadcast/Film," and

10, "Organic/Character Modeling Using the Box Method for Broadcast/Film," a bit of character—a slightly menacing character, to be precise (see Figure 17.1).

Figure 17.1   Here's the direction you're headed.

Specifically, you will learn how to do the following:

- Set up multiple levels of UVW mapping and Material IDs
- Work with the Material modifier
- Use the UVW Unwrap modifier
- Create Composite materials
- Work with displacement mapping
- Use the Oren-Nayar-Blinn shader

The production pipeline for a project like this, done over an ftp site and working remotely, sharing files with artists all over the country (many of whom will never meet), taking direction over a DSL line, and using Windows Netmeeting, limits what you can know about each artist's decisions. You need to turn these constraints into opportunities.

One of the technical challenges here, which mirrors many real-life production situations, is that you have to texture the Jester with only a rough notion of what the final animation will be. That is, your Jester might come very close to the camera, or he might not. His face might be full frame, or he might remain in the background, far away from the camera.

What you need to do as a texture artist is make sure that you build a level of detail into the shaders and textures that will hold up, in case the character animator or director decides to push his nose in your face.

Speaking of noses and faces, you begin by mapping and texturing the Jester's face.

Exercise 17.1   Selecting Material IDs for the Jester's Head

If you isolate the patch model of the head—which you can do using a new feature of max 4 by simply right-clicking over the selected patch model and hiding all uns-elected models—the first thing you should notice is that the modeler has attached the Jester's teeth to his head. So, right off the bat you know that you will probably need to use a Multi/Sub-Object material with at least one extra ID.

Open Jester_no_materials.max from the CD. You'll add your first Patch Select.

1. With the patch model selected, open the Modifier List and select Patch Select. This is near the top under the heading Selection Modifiers. These Modifier Stacks can get pretty long, so right-click over this Patch Select and rename it as **Patch Select Teeth**.

Note

In a production environment, it is essential to name things clearly at every step of the way because you will eventually pass on the file to another artist. Likewise, if you ever get hired on to a project midstream, you will be grateful that a particular texture map is named Jester left_eye_brow.tga instead of Untitled03_copy.tga.

2. Click the + sign (to the immediate left of the Patch Select in the Modifier Stack), and select the Patch option to activate the Patch Sub-Selection tool.

3. Now move your cursor back into the viewport, and select the teeth (see Figure 17.2).

    You might find it easier to select everything but the teeth and then invert that selection.

    This selection will eventually correspond to a Material ID number in your Multi/Sub-Object material, so we need to add a Material modifier so that your material knows where to go.

4. With the teeth selected, open the Modifier List and add a Material modifier, located near the bottom under the heading Surface Modifiers. Rename this as **Sub-Object Modifier to Material Teeth**, and change the Material ID number to **5**.

5. With the patch model still selected, open the Modifier List and add a second Patch Select to the Jester's head. Right-click over this Patch Select, and rename it as **Patch Select Mouth Inside**.

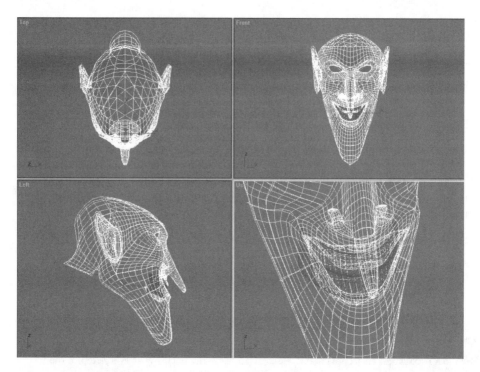

Figure 17.2 Your selection of the teeth should look like this.

 Tip

As these names get longer, the only way to see the whole name is to simply place your cursor over the modifier, and its full name will show up.

6. Click the + sign (to the immediate left of the Patch Select in the Modifier Stack) and select the Patch option to activate the Patch Sub-Selection tool.

7. Now move your cursor back into the viewport and select the area inside the mouth.

8. Repeat Step 4, and add another Material modifier. With the inside of the mouth selected, open the Modifier List and add a Material modifier. Rename this as **Sub-Object Modifier, Material Mouth Inside**, and change the Material ID number to **4**.

9. Repeat Steps 5, 6, 7, and 8 for each head area that you want material control over. These are the back of the head (Material ID 6); the lips (Material ID 3); the outer lips (Material ID 2); and the face, including the skin and makeup (Material ID 1). Your Modifier Stack should now look like Figure 17.3.

   Having established which surfaces of your model will receive which materials, you are ready to add UVW mapping so that you can control how your textures are projected onto your model.

10. Open the Modifier List, and add a UVW Map.

11. Make this UVW Map planar, select Fit, align it to the Z direction, and make sure that the Map Channel is set to 1. This map gives you control over your various bump maps.

    Use procedurals for as many of your bump maps as you can; these are easily mapped and very easy to adjust.

12. Now rename the UVW Map in the Modifier List as **UVW Map ID 1**.

13. Open the Modifier List and add another UVW Map.

14. Make this UVW Map cylindrical (that is the way it is spelled in max), select Fit, align it to the X direction, and make sure that the Map Channel is set to **2**. This map gives you control over your Jester's painted clown decal.

15. Rename the UVW Map as **UVW Map ID 2**.

16. Open the Modifier List and add another UVW Map. Set this UVW Map to cylindrical, and scale its gizmo to fit around the area of the teeth (see Figure 17.4).

    This UVW Map gives you control over your Jester's teeth texture.

17. Align it to the X direction and set the Map Channel to **3**.

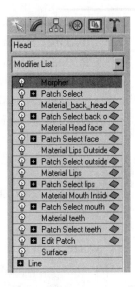

Figure 17.3
Here's an image of how your Modifier Stack should look at this point.

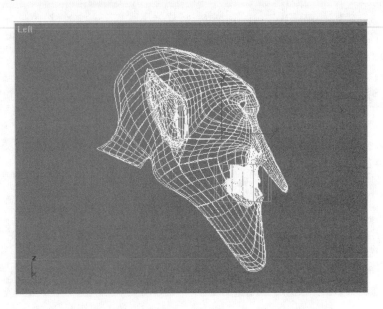

Figure 17.4 Your UVW Map should fit around the teeth, like in this image.

18. Now rename the UVW Map in the Modifier List as **UVW Map ID 3**.

19. Open the Modifier List and add another UVW Map.

20. Make this UVW Map planar, select Fit, align it to the Z direction, and set the Map Channel to **4**.

This UVW Map gives you control over your Jester's wrinkles.

21. Now rename the UVW Map in the Modifier List as **UVW Map ID 4**.

Congratulations! That's it for assigning Material IDs and mapping coordinates. You can now move on to the fun stuff!

Exercise 17.2   Color and Texture

In this exercise, you will be playing more with the artistic side. For now, you are done with the Modifier Stack and will be moving on to the Material Editor. This is where you'll have the chance to create the actual texture.

1. Open the Material Editor, and create a Multi/Sub-Object shader. Name this material **Head**, and set the slot number to **6** in the Basic Parameters rollout. If you remember, you created six Material IDs in your Modifier List for the head.

2. Now quickly adjust the Diffuse Color setting in each material slot; something extreme is preferable. Assign this material to your model so that you can quickly check to make sure that all your Material IDs are correct (see Figure 17.5).

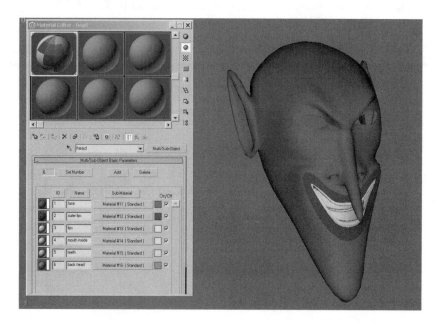

Figure 17.5   In this image, you can see that the subselections are in the right place on the geometry.

3. Rotate the head, and make any adjustments to your patch selections that you need to.

4. Name the material in the first slot **Face**. Use a Blinn shader type, and leave both the Specular Level and Glossiness at 0 because you want to give the face a matte look.

5. To have control over two materials (a skin texture and "clown paint") on the face, place a Composite material in the Diffuse slot.

   The first material that you will create is the skin texture for the Jester's face.

6. Load face_skin.jpg from the CD into Map 1. Make sure that Map Channel 4 is selected.

   This will correspond to UVW Map ID 4 in your Modifier List for the head.

Note

At this point, it's a good idea to make sure that you understand the distinction between the Map Channel and the Material ID. The Material ID, which you set earlier with Patch Select modifiers, corresponds to your Material ID number in your Multi/Sub-Object Basic Parameters rollout (in the Material Editor). The Map Channel number refers to the UVW Maps that you set and named in the Modifier Stack.

7. Next, fill the Map 2 slot with jester_mask.tga from the CD.

   This Targa image goes into slot Map 2 because you saved this image with an Alpha Channel, which allows the texture in Map 1 to show through (see Figure 17.6).

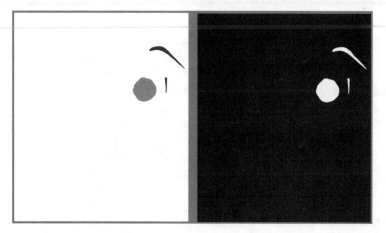

Figure 17.6   Here you have the actual color map on the left and the Alpha Channel of the same map on the right.

Figure 17.6 shows jester_mask.tga on the left, with its alpha channel on the right. You can add many layers of texture, as long as each one has an Alpha Channel, to let the previous map come through.

8. You now need to ensure that your Alpha Channel is actually being used. In the Bitmap Parameters rollout, make sure that in the Alpha Source panel, Image Alpha is checked and Premultiplied Alpha is unchecked (see Figure 17.7).

9. Switch the Map Channel to 2 in the Coordinates rollout in the Material Editor, and adjust the Offset and Tiling (see Figure 17.8).

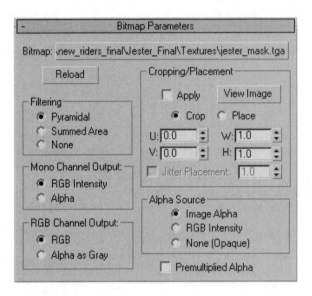

Figure 17.7   All your settings should be set to the same parameters, like in this image of the Bitmap Parameters rollout.

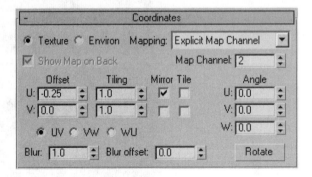

Figure 17.8   Here's an image of the Coordinates rollout with all the new adjustments.

10. Make sure that the U Offset is –0.25, leave the V Offset at 0.0, turn off Tile, and check Mirror in the U direction.

11. Check the Show Map in Viewport option, and adjust the map visually in a Shaded viewport (see Figure 17.9).

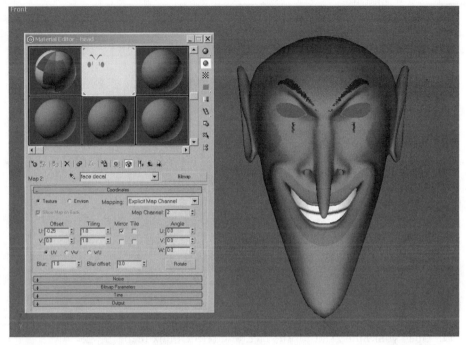

Figure 17.9   In this image, you can see the Material Editor with the Show Map button selected, which enables you to adjust the offset and interactively see the changes on the head.

 Note

Here's a classic production situation, where you can see flexibility and ingenuity. Chapters 16 and 17 were not only co-written, but the models were passed back and forth between two artists: They were mapped and textured by one person and then were altered and tweaked by the other. Because jester_mask.tga was being used as a decal, the artists did not need to worry about any seams. They saved time by painting only one side of the image, saving it with an Alpha Channel, and then mirroring it, as seen in Step 8. Looking at the textured model, they decided to add another level of detail (in the form of a diffuse color texture map that needed to cover the whole face) (see Figure 17.10).

At this point, Diana had the model. She simply turned the original Diffuse material into a Composite material, added face_skin.jpg (using different mapping coordinates), and, as explained previously, used the alpha from jester_mask.tga to allow the Skin map to show through.

Now that your textures are established, you are ready to move on to a bump map. You will often find a Procedural (noise, smoke, and so on) being used as one of your bump maps. In production, the most flexible solution should *always* be your first choice. Because Procedurals can easily be manipulated without leaving the program, and because no maps need to be saved out, they make ideal textures. No confusion can result from missing map files, especially when you are sharing files over a network with other artists.

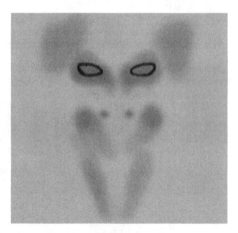

Figure 17.10   This is what the file face_skin.jpg looks like.

12. Open your Bump slot for the face, and select a mix map.

A mix map gives the bump a more varied look than a single map would.

13. In the top slot, labeled Color 1, place the bitmap face_wrinkles.jpg. Make sure that it is using Map Channel 4, and change the Blur value to **3**. Then add a noise map to the Color 2 slot. Remember to check that the Map Channel is set to **1**, and then adjust the Noise parameters to Fractal and set the size to **1.6**.

14. Move back up by pressing the Go to Parent icon, and experiment with the Mix Amount slider. In this case, a value of 15 gave the right mix of noise bump and wrinkle.

Here's an opportunity to use your ActiveShade Floater, checking the effect of altering the Mix amount.

15. Set the Bump amount in the Maps rollout to **30**.

That's it for the material in ID 1. Feel free to open the individual texture maps and alter the wrinkles and face paint to get varied results.

Note

What if the client wanted the clown face material to be shiny? How would you achieve that? Simply make the Reflection slot a Mask material, and, in the Mask slot, place your jester_mask.tga (making sure that the Map Channel is set on **2**), to add any Reflection map or even a Raytraced material. You begin to see here how robust 3ds max 4's Material Editor is when you begin to layer and mask materials.

16. Before you leave the face material, drag the mix map in the Bump slot up to an unused Sample window. Select Instance because you might want the same bump on other features of the face.

Now you'll move on to the other shaders in the remaining IDs.

17. Name the material in ID 2 **Outer Lips**.

Remember all the extra time you took in naming conventions in your Modifier Stack? Here is where it really pays off. You could hand off this model to another artist, and he would be able to "read" the Modifier Stack and know which materials get which Map Channel and Material ID.

18. Drag and drop that Mix material into your Bump slot as an instance. Set the Bump amount to **30**.

That's it for the bump! It should match the face bump map. Now you should notice that your wrinkle texture is also seen on our outer lips.

Now you'll try something new with your Reflection map.

19. Click on the Reflection slot, and choose Mask from the Material/Map browser.

20. As a Reflection, choose house.jpg, which is one of 3ds max's default maps. This image is located in the 3D Studio Max4/Maps/Background folder.

21. In the Mask slot, choose Mix from the Material/Map browser (see Figure 17.11).

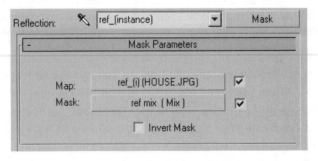

Figure 17.11   At this point, your Mask Parameters rollout should look like this.

22. In Color 1, place a cellular map. Set the size to **0.6**, and check Fractal. Make an instance of the noise map, from the face material, and place it in Color 2. Set the Mix amount to **50** and the Reflection amount, in the Maps rollout, to **50**.

Note

Here you created a reflection, using house.jpg, and then used your noise bump, mixed with a little cellular for variety, to mask the reflection in the outer lips. Overkill? Maybe. But you will find that the more subtle layers you can add to your materials without losing control of them, the richer they will look.

On to the shiny lips!

23. In ID 3, you need to set the Specular Level to **84** and the Glossiness to **48**. Your Diffuse Color setting should use a hot red. Set the RGB to **214, 0, 0**. All you need for bump here is your trusty mix map, with the instanced noise map in the Color 1 slot. Add Smoke to the Color 2 slot, sized at **0.3**, to give those lips a little shimmer. Set the Mix amount to **50**, and set the Bump Map amount to **10**.

    Again, you can use the ActiveShade Floater to adjust your bump parameters.

24. You can reuse house.jpg as a simple Reflection map. Keep the Map amount low for a subtler look.

25. All you need for Material ID 4, the inside of the mouth, is a copy of the Lips shader with some slight adjustments. Because this is in the inside of the mouth, set the RGB values a little darker. Set the Specular Highlight levels back to their default settings (Specular Level **0** and Glossiness **10**), and get rid of the Reflection map.

    If your client wanted a wetter look in the mouth, you could turn the Reflection back on, and maybe even add a Raytraced reflection.

    Now you'll focus on the smile.

26. The material in ID 5 is for the teeth. Because you want something shiny here, you need to set the Specular Level to **100** and the Glossiness to **91**. Both your Diffuse Color and Specular Color settings should use 100% white.

27. In the Diffuse Color slot, open teeth.jpg. This image needs to be tiled **16.0** in the U direction and cropped, leaving all the white and just enough gray to create a line between each tooth.

28. Drag and drop this material into the Bump slot. When you replace the image with teeth_bump.jpg from the CD, you already have your tiling and cropping set up. Set the Bump amount to **50**.

    Did you forget anything? You bet. Remember that cylindrical UVW Map that you scaled to fit around the teeth selection? You named that one UVW Map ID 4. Well, you have to make sure that your teeth textures are being projected using that UVW Map.

29. Set your Map Channel to Diffuse and the Bump slot to **3**.

All that's left to do is texture the back of the head. This is very simple. Because your Jester is wearing a hat and has big ears, you do not have to worry about seeing a seam: It will be covered.

30. Open the slot for Material ID 6, and name it **Back Head**. Leave it a Blinn, with the Specular Level and the Glossiness set at 0. You need it to match the face.

31. Go to the Maps rollout and open the image face_skin.jpg from the CD in the Diffuse Color slot. When you're in the Bitmap Parameters rollout, go into the View Image panel and crop the Image Map in the lower-right corner so that you do not pick up any of the airbrushed part of the image. The actual coordinates for the cropping are U: **0.664**, V: **0.657**, W: **0.336**, and H: **0.343**, in case you prefer typing in the values. Do not forget to check the Apply box, immediately to the left of the View Image button.

32. Now add your instanced noise map in the Bump Map slot, and set the amount to **10**.

   You have to love the idea of an instanced material map! Any adjustment that you now make to the noise bump on the face will be updated automatically on the back of the head. That's what you call control.

   While you're here, you can do the eyes.

   Your mapping for the eyes could not be any easier: Planar and Fit in the Z direction.

33. Use a Blinn so that you get a nice round highlight. Make that highlight white by making the Specular color white, the Specular Level **174**, and the Glossiness **61**.

34. For a diffuse map, load eyecolor.jpg from the CD. Notice that a little character has been added to the eyes by making them slightly bloodshot. Blur the image—try **5.0**—and increase the Output (in the Output rollout) to **1.2**. This will make your Jester's eyes pop yet still feel soft.

35. A bump, eyecolor_bump.jpg (on the CD), also has been added to give a little more definition.

36. Last but not least, in the Reflection slot, add a Raytrace. In the Raytrace Parameters rollout, click the Global Parameters button. Make sure that the Ray Depth Control is set to a Maximum Depth of **2**. This limits the amount of times that your reflections bounce. You also might as well exclude everything but the head from your reflections. You will find this option in the Raytracer Parameters rollout, under Local Exclude.

   You have just completed the head successfully, so you can move on to the body.

Exercise 17.3   The Body

Your biggest challenge, and the thing that will take the longest to set up, is the Jester's body suit. You will have to pull just about every trick, and then some, to set this up. But, after you succeed, you'll be able to master almost any texture challenge.

Because this body is a single patch model, you'll need to isolate different faces. You'll split up the body using a series of Patch Selects, Material IDs, and multiple mapping coordinates. Finally, you'll texture the individual parts.

The legs are one of your most difficult tasks. You will begin with one of them, learning everything in great detail as you proceed. After you master the one leg, you will find the other parts of the body easier to understand because there is a lot of repetition in the different steps.

Beginning slowly with the right leg, you'll pick up speed as you work up the rest of the body. Enough talk—it's time to get to work.

1. Start with the right leg. Apply a Patch Select modifier. Now select the patches for the right leg (see Figure 17.12).

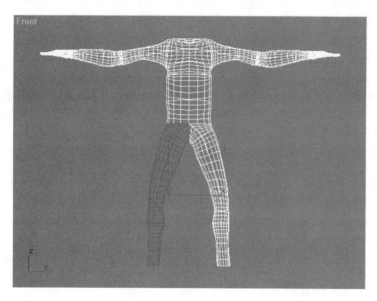

Figure 17.12   In this image, you see the patch selection for the right leg.

Note

You use the Jester's point of view when deciding which is the right side and the left side.

2. Apply a Material modifier so that you can texture it individually. Set this Material ID to **1**, and rename it as **Mat 1 Rght Leg**. (This naming will be invaluable for subsequent artists, including you, who might need to navigate this Modifier Stack.)

Now that you've defined the leg, you can set up UVW Map coordinates for the different maps that you'll apply in the Material Editor. You'll need three UVW Map modifiers: two for the stripes (one on the sides and one on the front) and one for the base texture.

3. Go ahead and add three UVW Map modifiers. Rename the first UVW Map as **UVW Map ID1**, and set the Map to Channel **1**. Rename the second one as **UVW Map ID2**, and set the Map Channel to **2**. Rename the third as **UVW Map ID3**, and set the Map Channel to **3** (see Figure 17.13).

Don't worry about the mapping coordinates; you'll change that later after the bitmaps are set up.

You already know that you're going to be dealing with several materials on one surface. You even know the number of Material IDs you're going to need—six: right leg, left leg, main body, right arm, left arm, and hands.

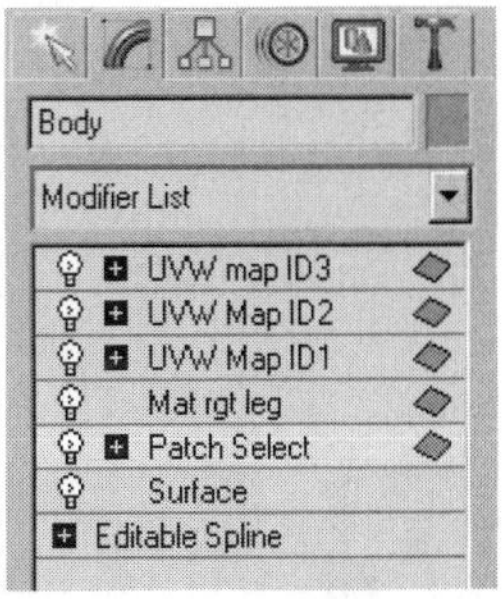

Figure 17.13
After you've applied all the UVW Maps, your Modifier Stack should look like this.

4. Open the Material Editor, create a Multi/Sub-Object material, and name it **Body**.

5. Select Sub Material ID 1 and name it **Right Leg**.

6. Because this material is supposed to be fabric, it should be rather matte. A shader that works wonderfully for matte materials is the Oren-Nayar-Blinn shader. Select this shader from the Shader Basic Parameters rollout. You should notice an immediate change in the Material Sample window.

7. Next, adjust the Basic parameters. Lock the Ambient Color and Diffuse Color settings, to make both the same. Select Diffuse Color, and set the RGB values to **106**, **2**, **121**. This combination should give you a nice purple.

8. To keep the material from looking completely matte, give it just a little bit of specular highlight. Set the Specular Level to **15** and the Glossiness to **0**.

You're ready to move on to the Maps rollout.

9. Put a composite map in the Diffuse slot. The composite map enables you to place two stripes on the base material. In the Composite Parameters rollout, set the Number of Maps to **3**.

Note

As you work on these Composite materials, take advantage of the fact that you now can display multiple maps in Shaded viewports.

10. Start by choosing a mix map for Map 1 (see Figure 17.14) .

To give the base material a little variety and more detail, you'll be mixing the base fabric with a procedural checker map.

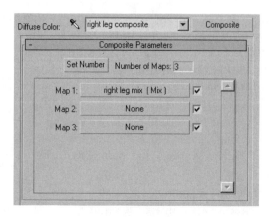

Figure 17.14   At this point, your Composite Parameters rollout should look like this image.

11. In Color slot 1, add base_fabric_purple.tga from the CD.

12. Set the Alpha Source to None (Opaque) because it should use the entire map with no mask (the Alpha will be used when you're working on the stripes).

Select the Show Map in Viewport button so that you can see the way the map will look on the object. The bitmap looks a little too large over the leg. You can tile it some.

13. Set both the U and V Tiling to **3.5**. Also make sure that the Map Channel is set to **1** so that you get the placement from UVW Map 1.

14. Select Go to Parent. In the Mix Parameters rollout, add a checker map to Color 2. Tile the checker map so that it starts looking like a texture on fabric. Set both the U and V Tiling to **60**.

15. Adjust the Mix amount in the Mix Parameters rollout. You'll want the bitmap to be the more dominant map, so set Mix Amount to **30** (see Figure 17.15).

16. Also adjust the UVW Map modifier.

17. In the Modifier Stack, select UVW Map ID1. By default, it's set to Planar.

If you preview this in your render, you'll notice that the mapping doesn't look correct. It's all stretched.

18. First, scale the gizmo to roughly the size of the right leg, and move the gizmo over so that it's placed around the right leg. Select Box as your mapping parameter.

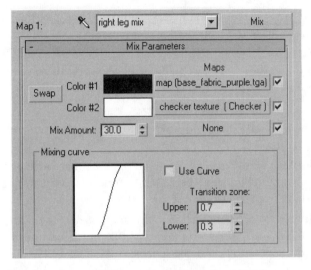

Figure 17.15   This is how your Mix Parameters rollout should look.

19. Go ahead and play around with the different mapping parameters, but you'll find similar stretching or artifact results. You'll likely find that a box map with a 45° rotation on the Z-axis works best. The alignment in the UVW Map is set to the Y-axis (see Figure 17.16).

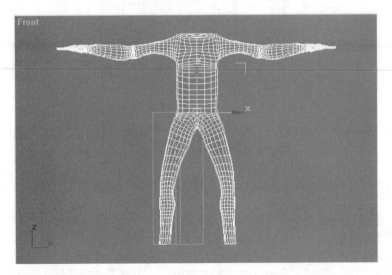

Figure 17.16   Your screen should look like this with the correct mapping.

Now you are ready to move back to the Material Editor. The next map will be for one of the stripes.

20. Return to the Composite Parameters rollout and add base_fabric_purple.tga to Map 2. To make the stripe look like a separate piece of fabric, change the U and V Tiling to **1.5**. It's very important to set the Map Channel to **2**.

21. Make sure that the Alpha is actually being used and that Premulitiplied Alpha is unchecked.

The Alpha is what's making it a stripe.

22. Still in the Material Editor, move down to the very bottom and open the Output rollout.

The Color Map graph enables you to adjust the tonal range of an image. Here, you want the image to be darker to further accentuate the stripe's separate look from the base material.

23. Check Enable Color Map to activate the graph. Select the point on the right, and move it down 0.7. You can also type **0.7** on the bottom. The image should now appear to be a darker purple (see Figure 17.17).

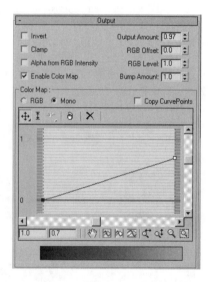

Figure 17.17   This shows your settings for the Color Map rollout.

Because this stripe is going to be on the side of the Jester's leg, you now have to adjust UVW Map ID2.

24. Select the UVW Map ID2 modifier in the Modifier Stack. Double-check to make sure that the Map Channel is set to **2**. Make it planar and align it to the X-axis.

You are going to adjust the gizmo so that it follows the contours of the leg from the side. The short yellow line should be on the top, indicating the top of the map.

25. Rotate the gizmo slightly and scale it to the length of the leg, as seen in Figure 17.18.

Note

Notice that, even with an adjusted UVW Map, the stripe still is not following the leg correctly. You will use a powerful modifier to control the placement of the stripe.

An Unwrap UVW modifier is used to assign planar maps to sub-object selections and to edit the UVW coordinates of those selections. Unwrap UVW supports polygonal faces, both Bezier quad and tri-patch faces, in addition to triangles and quads.

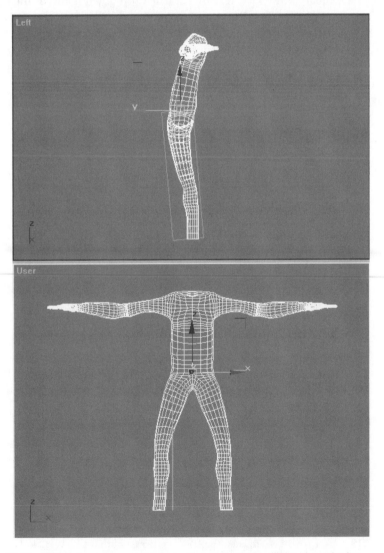

Figure 17.18   This image shows how your gizmo should be adjusted on the leg.

26. In the Modifier List, add an Unwrap UVW modifier above UVW Map ID2. First change the Map Channel to **2**.

Now you are ready to edit the UVW coordinates.

27. In the Unwrap UVW Parameters rollout, select Edit.

Edit displays the Edit UVW dialog box. The Edit UVW dialog box is a window that displays a lattice made up of UVW faces and vertices. Within this window you manipulate the UVW coordinates relative to the map by selecting the lattice vertices and moving, rotating, or scaling them.

28. On the toolbar, in the Pick Texture list (the drop-down menu in the upper-right corner of the Edit UVWs window), you can select your composite map with the stripe as a background image. Go ahead and move around those texture vertices, centering the stripe to the leg. Keep an eye on a Shaded viewport, where you can interactively see the stripe being adjusted on the geometry, as long as the Show Map in Viewport button is selected (see Figure 17.19).

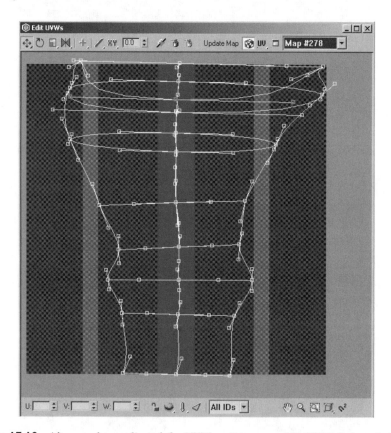

Figure 17.19   After you have adjusted the UVW vertices, your Edit UVW dialog window should look similar to this.

After successfully placing the stripe on the leg, it's time to move on to the next stripe. This one, of course, will be a lot easier, because you've already done it.

29. In the Material Editor, go to the Composite Parameters rollout and add base_fabric_purple.tga to slot Map 3.

30. The Bitmap Parameters rollout should be the same as for the first stripe, except that you'll want to set the Map Channel to 3.

31. You already have a UVW Map modifier for this material's ID in your Modifier Stack. Just double-check that the Map Channel for UVW Map ID3 is set to 3.

    This stripe will be on the front of the leg, so you have to adjust the mapping.

32. Select UVW Map ID3, make it planar, and align it to the Y-axis.

33. Scale the gizmo and rotate it a little so that it follows the contour of the leg more (see Figure 17.20).

    The next step is much the same as Step 26.

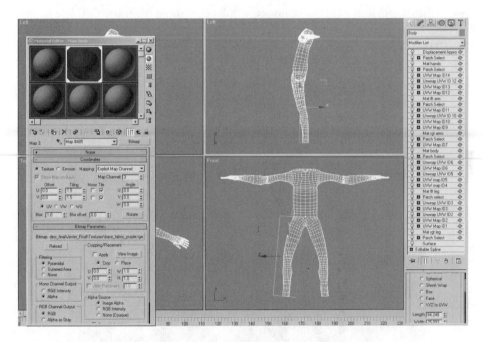

Figure 17.20   Here's the UVW mapping for the stripe on the right leg.

34. Apply an Unwrap UVW modifier, this time setting the Map Channel to 3. Again, open the Edit dialog window. Make sure that the stripe map is visible as a background, and align the texture vertices to the stripe.

You're almost finished with the right leg. Although the texture has a nice feel, it has too smooth a surface and therefore is not very realistic. You need some bumpiness.

35. Go back to the Maps rollout. In the Bump slot, add a Mix material.

As mentioned earlier, it's handy to use a Mix material, especially for a bump map, to make the texture feel less uniform and tiled.

36. In the Mix Parameters rollout, put base_fabric_
bump.jpg from the CD in Color 1. All the settings should be the same as those for the base_fabric_purple.tga bitmap in the Diffuse slot.

37. In Color 2, add an instance of the checker map that you made for the Diffuse slot. Simply drag and drop the checker into the slot labeled Color 2.

38. Set the Mix amount to **20**. Again, the base_fabric_bump.jpg should be predominant.

39. Set the Bump amount to **30**.

To give the fabric an even truer feel, you can add some little wrinkles.

40. In the Displacement slot, open leg_displacement.jpg from the CD. Tile it, in both the U and V, as **3.5**. Try softening the displacement a little by adding a **0.003** Blur offset.

41. Set the Displacement amount to **1**. You could add a Displacement Approx. Modifier to your Modifier Stack now, but wait until later to do this.

That's it for the right leg! (See Figure 17.21.)

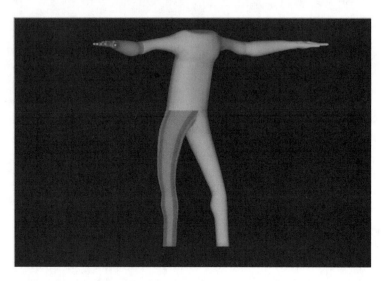

Figure 17.21   In this image, you can actually see what your finished material for the right leg should look like.

Exercise 17.4   The Left Leg

Of course, the left leg will be easier. Because you are repeating exactly what you did on the right leg, this exercise will explain less and move a little quicker.

1. Using a Patch Select modifier, select the left leg.

2. Open a Material modifier. Set the Material ID to 2. Rename it as **Mat 2 Lft Leg**.

3. Add three UVW Map modifiers: one for the base material and two for the stripes.

   Now you'll set up the UVW Maps for your bitmaps.

4. The first UVW Map should again be a box, scaled to fit the leg. Rotate the gizmo 45° on the Z-axis. The actual alignment in the UVW Map should be set to Z (see Figure 17.22).

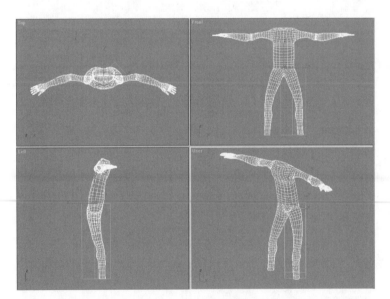

Figure 17.22   The gizmo for the left leg should be placed with its 45° angle, as this image demonstrates.

5. Rename this UVW Map modifier as **UVW Map ID4**. Set the Map Channel to 4 because you will use a different texture for this leg.

6. Rename the next UVW Map modifier as **UVW Map ID5**; you will use this for one of the stripes. Make sure that the Map Channel is set to **5**.

7. Make it planar, with an X-axis alignment. Scale and rotate it to the contour of the leg. The little line should be on the top of the map (see Figure 17.23).

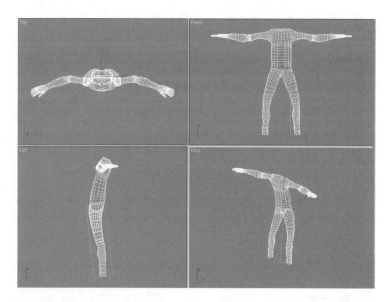

Figure 17.23   This is what the placement of the UVW Map, this time a planar map, should look like on the leg.

8. Add an Unwrap UVW modifier. Set the Map Channel to 5. Rename it as **Unwrap UVW ID5**.

9. Rename the third UVW Map modifier as **UVW map ID6**. Set the Map Channel to 6, and make it planar, with a Y-axis alignment (see Figure 17.24).

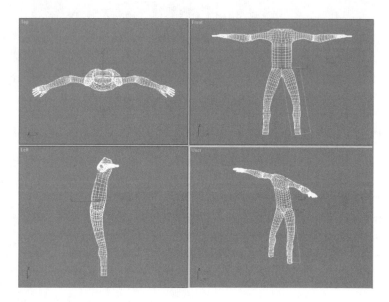

Figure 17.24   Here's how the planar UVW map for the front stripe should look on the leg.

10. Add another Unwrap UVW modifier. Set the Map Channel to **6**. Rename it as **Unwrap UVW ID6**.

11. Open the Material Editor. In the Multi/Sub-Object Basic Parameters rollout, drag and drop the material for the right leg into Sub-Object ID 2. It will ask you if you want to make this an instance or a copy. Because you are going to want to make some changes to this material, make it a copy.

12. Rename this material as **Left Leg**.

13. Adjust the Ambient Color and Diffuse Color RGB settings to **165, 125, 3**. Everything else in the Basic Parameters should already be set.

14. In the Composite material's Mix Parameters rollout, replace what's in Color 1 with base_fabric_yellow.tga from the CD. Set the Map Channel to **6**.

15. Set the Map Channel for checker to **4**.

16. Back in the Composite Parameters rollout, load base_fabric_yellow.tga in Map 2. The only thing you need to do within the Bitmap Parameters is set the Map Channel to **5**.

17. Open the Edit dialog window of Unwrap UVW ID5, and adjust the lattice vertices until the placement of the stripe looks correct on the side of the left leg. Select the stripe map as a background, centering the stripe to the leg texture vertices.

18. In the Composite Parameters rollout, open Map 3. Replace the existing bitmap with base_fabric_yellow.tga. Set the Map Channel to **6**.

19. Open the Edit dialog of Unwrap UVW ID6, and move around the lattice vertices until the placement of the stripe looks correct on the front of the left leg.

20. In the Bump slot, all you have to do is change both Map Channels to **4**.

21. Finally, change the displacement's Map Channel to **4**.

You've now successfully completed both legs! Your Modifier Stack is getting pretty long (see Figure 17.25).

You are just getting started, though, so take a break. Have an espresso or a latte. You deserve it.

Figure 17.25
At this point, your Modifier Stack should look like this.

Exercise 17.5   The Upper Body

The upper body is next. Don't sweat—you have no stripes to worry about, so it will be a simpler setup. For starters, there will be only one UVW Map modifier.

1. Open a Patch Select modifier from the Modifier List. Select the patches for the upper body, without the arms, legs, and hands (see Figure 17.26).

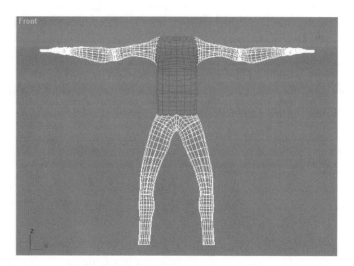

Figure 17.26   This image highlights the patch selection for the upper body.

2. Add a Material modifier and set the Map Channel to 3. Rename it as **Mat 3 Body**.

3. Also add a UVW Map modifier. Rename it as **UVW Map ID7**. Set the Map Channel to **7**. Make it cylindrical with a Z alignment (see Figure 17.27).

   You can also scale the UVW Map gizmo to the size of the upper body.

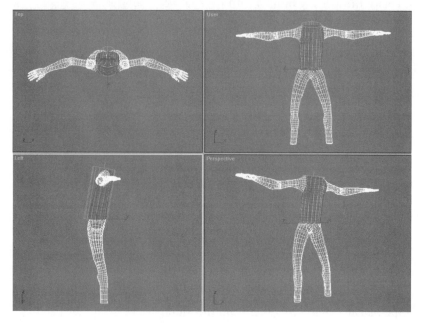

Figure 17.27   With this image, you can see how the placement of the cylindrical mapping should look.

4. In the Material Editor, select Sub-Material 3 and rename it as **Upper Body**.

5. Get the settings from the Oren-Nayar-Blinn Basic Parameters rollout from one of the other materials.

6. Add a Mix material in the Diffuse slot. In Color 1, open base_fabric_y_p.jpg from the CD. Set the Map Channel to **7**.

7. In the Bitmap Parameters rollout, select the View Image button. Notice that you have both the purple and the yellow material in one image. Move the crop marks down toward the center. If you prefer to use the exact parameters used here, you can also just type in the values for the cropping. On the top of the Specify Cropping/Placement window, you can type in the following numbers: U: **0.165**, V: **0.213**, W: **0.673**, H: **0.581** (see Figure 17.28).

   Instead of using the whole image, you will use only this smaller section, so the texture will appear larger on the upper body.

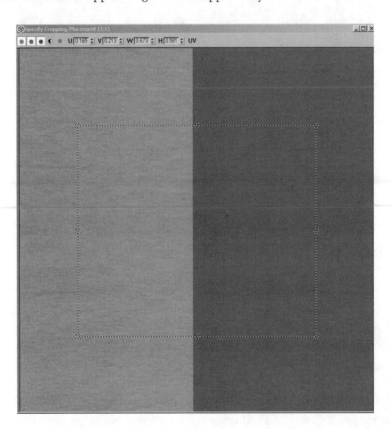

Figure 17.28   In this image, you can see the Specify Cropping/Placement window parameters.

8. You can alternatively type in the crop values U: **0.165**, V: **0.213**, W: **0.673**, and H: **0.581**.

9. Check the Apply box for the cropping to actually take effect.

10. Apply a checker map in the Mix Parameters rollout for Color 2. Set the Map Channel to **7**, and adjust the Tiling to U: **120** and V: **105**.

11. Set the Mix amount to **10**.

12. In the Maps rollout, drag and drop the Mix material from the Diffuse slot as a copy into the Bump slot. Change the map in Color 1 to base_fabric_bump.jpg.

13. Set the Bump amount to **15**.

14. Now do a render to see where you are. It should look like Figure 17.29.

Figure 17.29   This image shows you a final render of the upper body.

Not bad, but what if you add some extra detail to give the image some folds?

15. Select the Displacement slot and add a mask map.

A mask map lets you view one material through another, controlling where the map appears on the surface.

This will be very useful with your displacement. You'll use a gradient as your mask; that way, the folds will appear only toward the bottom of the shirt, fading toward the top.

16. In the Mask Parameters rollout, add shirt_displacement.jpg from the CD to the Map slot. In the Bitmap Parameters rollout, set the Map Channel to **7** (see Figure 17.30).

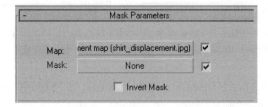

Figure 17.30   Here's an image of how your Mask Parameters rollout should look at this point.

17. Using the Show Map in Viewport button, adjust the placement of the image on the object.

Your final placement is Offset U: **0.0**, Offset V: **0.34**, Tiling U: **1.0**, Tiling V: **0.5** (see Figure 17.31).

18. In the Mask Parameters rollout, add a gradient map in the Mask slot (see Figure 17.32).

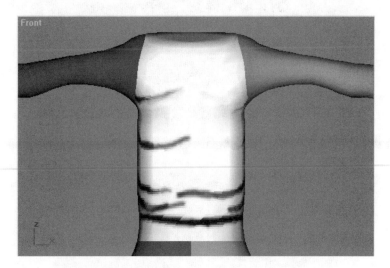

Figure 17.31   This image demonstrates how your bitmap should look on the upper body, with the correct placement.

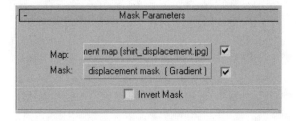

Figure 17.32   The final settings in the Mask Parameters rollout should look like this.

19. In the Gradient Parameters rollout, set the Map Channel to **7**.

To control where the folds are, you'll change the colors a little, adjusting the mask area. Where it is black, the displacement will not be visible (see Figure 17.33).

20. Also in the Gradient Parameters rollout, Color 1 should be just solid black, and Color 3 should be a solid white. Color 2 can be a dark gray. RGB values of **23**, **23**, **23** were used here. Set the Color 2 position to **0.65**, to make sure that it uses more of the white color (see Figure 17.34).

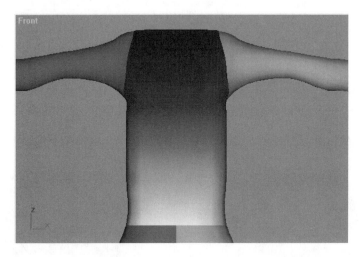

Figure 17.33   Here you can see what will be masked out by the gradient.

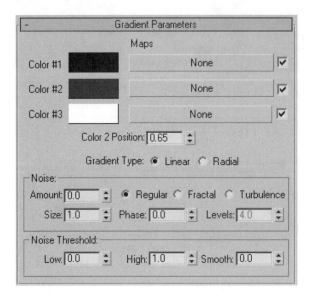

Figure 17.34   This image shows you the settings for the Gradient Parameters rollout.

21. Set the Displacement amount to 5.

22. Add a Displacement Approx. modifier to your Modifier Stack (see Figure 17.35).

The Displacement Approx. modifier basically converts its input object to an editable mesh, so you can use this modifier to add displacement mapping to geometry primitives and any other kind of object that can convert to an editable mesh. Without this modifier, your displacement would not show up on the object. You don't need to adjust any of the parameters for this modifier.

23. Hit the Render button. Figure 17.36 shows the result.

Note

The Displacement Approx. modifier takes a lot of processing power to calculate, so if you do not have a suitably fast machine, you might want to leave this modifier inactive when rendering.

Now, those are folds! That's it for the upper body; you'll now move on the arms. You will find that the arms will be similar to the legs.

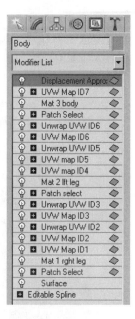

Figure 17.35
Your Modifier Stack should now look like this.

Figure 17.36   This image almost looks like Figure 17.29, except that now you have added folds.

Exercise 17.6   The Arms and Hands

Our next big task will be the arms. You'll notice that most of these steps are the same as for the leg materials. The main difference is that here you have only one stripe.

As with every material so far, you first want to assign Material IDs.

1. Open the Modifier List and add a Patch Select modifier. Select all the patches on the right arm (see Figure 17.37). Make sure that you don't select the hands.

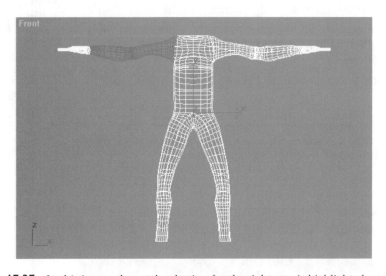

Figure 17.37   In this image, the patch selection for the right arm is highlighted.

2. Add a Material modifier and set the Material ID to **4**.

   You'll need three UVW Map modifiers: one for the base material, one for the stripe, and, because you'll add folds by the elbow, one for a displacement map.

3. Name the first **UVW Map ID9**. Set it to box mapping and align it to the X-axis. In the left viewport, rotate the gizmo 45° on the Z-axis (see Figure 17.38). Set the Map Channel to 9.

4. Name the second map **UVW Map ID10**. Select Planar and align it with the Z-axis. Set the Map Channel to 10.

5. Rotate the gizmo so that the short yellow line, indicating the top of the image, is pointing to the neck area (see Figure 17.39).

   The stripe will run along the top of the arm.

6. Name the third map **UVW Map ID11**. Select Planar and align it with the Y-axis. Set the Map Channel to **11**.

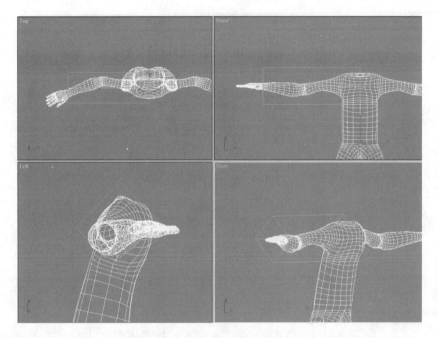

Figure 17.38   Again, here you can see what the placement of the box mapping should look like on the right arm.

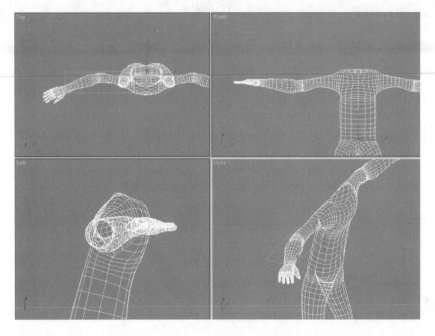

Figure 17.39   This image shows the placement of the planar map, which is for the stripe on the right arm.

7. Scale down the gizmo and move it to the elbow area. Don't worry too much right now about the correct placement. You can always further adjust it when you're actually assigning the displacement image (see Figure 17.40).

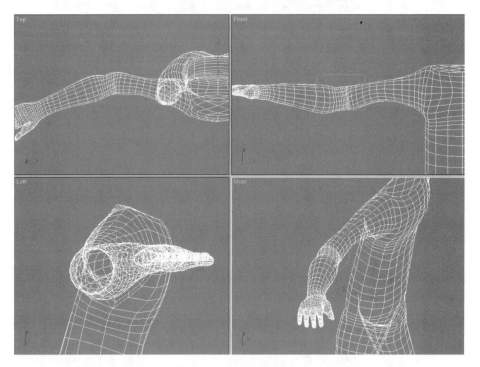

Figure 17.40   Here you see the placement of the planar mapping for the displacement folds.

This mapping is for the fabric folds on the elbow.

8. In the Material Editor, select the material in ID 4 and rename it as **Right Arm**. Because your settings in this material's Basic Parameters rollout will be identical to the settings in the material that you created earlier for the right leg, you can copy those settings. Do that now.

9. In the Maps rollout, add a Composite material in the Diffuse slot (see Figure 17.41).

First, you'll create the base material.

10. In Map 1, add a mix map. Open base_fabric_purple.tga in Color 1 (see Figure 17.42). Set the Map Channel to **9**.

11. Add a checker map in Color 2 of the mix map. Set the Tiling to **65**, in both U and in V. Set the Map Channel to **9**.

Figure 17.41   This image shows your Composite Parameters rollout.

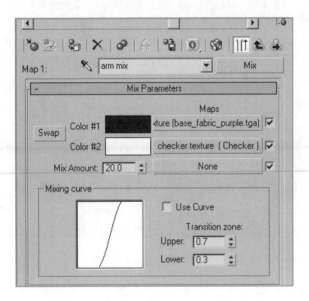

Figure 17.42   This image shows the Mix Parameters rollout for this material's bump.

12. Because base_fabric_purple.tga should be dominant over the checker, set the Mix amount to **20**.

Now you'll move on to the stripe.

13. In the Composite Parameters rollout, open base_fabric_purple.tga. In the Bitmap parameters, set the Map Channel to **10**. Make sure that Image Alpha is checked that and Premultiplied Alpha is unchecked.

It's time to unwrap.

14. Add an Unwrap UVW modifier above UVW Map ID10 in the Modifier Stack. Set the Map Channel to **10**.

15. Open the Edit dialog box, and, just like with the stripes on the legs, select the stripe map as a background and continue to center the stripe. Adjust the lattice vertices until the placement of the stripe looks correct on the top of the right arm (see Figure 17.43).

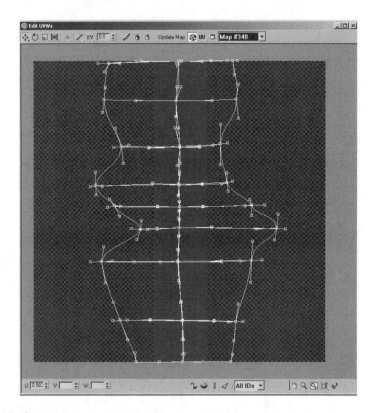

Figure 17.43   Here's your edited UVW Unwrap dialog box.

Now you need a bump.

16. In the Material Editor, create a Mix material in the Bump slot. Open base_fabric_bump.jpg, in Color Map 1. Set the Map Channel to **9**.

17. Open a checker map in Color Map 2. Set the Map Channel to **9**. Adjust the Tiling to U: **65**, V: **65**.

18. Set the Mix amount to **20**.

Just like with the upper body, you'll apply a mask map in the Displacement slot, controlling the creasing around the elbow.

In Adobe Photoshop, a simple map was created here to simulate some folds (see Figure 17.44).

Figure 17.44   Here is the image created in Adobe Photoshop.

19. Add a mask map in the Displacement slot.

20. In the Mask Parameters rollout, open arm_displacement.jpg from the CD in the Map slot. Set the Map Channel to 11.

21. To interactively see where the image will be placed on the arm, turn on the Show Map in Viewport button (see Figure 17.45).

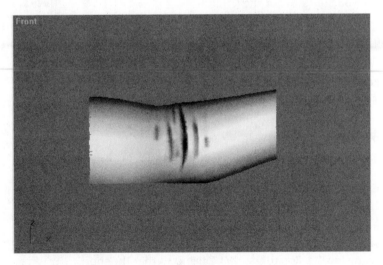

Figure 17.45   Here is the map, as seen in the viewport.

Now you can adjust the mapping gizmo if the placement or scale doesn't look right.

22. The creasing should show up just on the inside of the elbows, so uncheck both the U and V Tiling options.

23. Move back up to the Mask Parameters rollout. Drag and drop from the Map slot (an instance or a copy) of the arm_displacement.jpg into the Mask slot.

24. Where the image mask is lighter (whiter), the map will be visible; where the image is darker, it will be transparent. You need to check the Invert Mask box (see Figure 17.46).

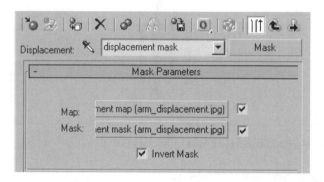

Figure 17.46   Here is your Mask Parameters rollout.

25. Set the Displacement amount to **3**.

Your Modifier Stack should now look like Figure 17.47.

Now you are ready for the left arm.

26. Add a Patch Select and select all the patches for the left arm. Again, be careful to exclude the hand.

27. Add a Material modifier, setting the Material ID to **5**.

28. Rename the modifier to **Mat 5 Lft Arm**.

29. Because you are basically repeating all the steps from the right arm, go ahead and open three UVW Map modifiers and one Unwrap UVW.

30. Name the first UVW Map as **UVW Map ID12**. Set it to box mapping, aligned to the Z-axis. In the left viewport, rotate the gizmo 45° on the Z-axis. Set the Map Channel to **12** (see Figure 17.48).

31. Name the second UVW Map modifier **UVW Map ID13**. Use a planar map, aligned to the Z axis. Set the Map Channel to **13**. Rotate the UVW gizmo so that the short yellow line, indicating the top of the image, is pointing to the neck area (see Figure 17.49).

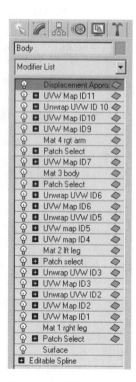

Figure 17.47
As you can see, your Modifier Stack is pretty long.

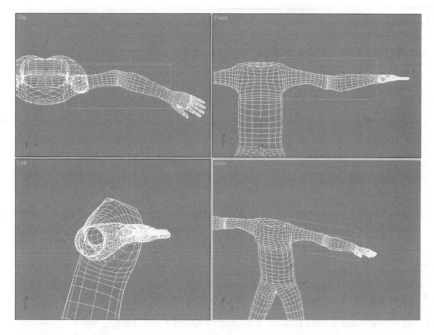

Figure 17.48   Your first UVW gizmo should be adjusted as in this image.

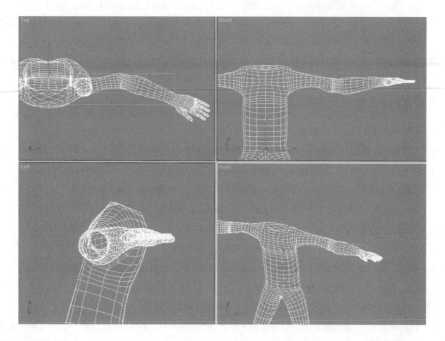

Figure 17.49   Your second UVW gizmo should now be adjusted as shown in this image.

32. For the third UVW Map modifier, instead of having to align it and scale it, simply copy and paste UVW Map ID11 from the Modifier Stack and rename it as **UVW Map ID14**. Now you have all the same settings, but it's not in the right place yet. Move it over to the left arm elbow. Then set the Map Channel to **14**.

33. Open the Material Editor. As with the legs, instead of having to create a whole new material, just drag and drop (an instance or a copy) the material from the right arm, down to the Sub-Material slot ID5. This way, you'll have most of the settings.

All that remains is to adjust the Map Channels and change some of the bitmaps.

34. Rename the new material **Left Arm**. The only things you want to change in the Basic Parameters rollout are the Ambient Color and Diffuse Color settings. Just copy the parameters from the left leg.

35. Start with the Composite slot. Open the mix map in Map 1. Select Color Map 1. Simply exchange the bitmap for base_fabric_yellow.tga, and check the Alpha Source to None. Set the Map Channel to **12**.

36. In Color Map 2 you should find the checker map. Simply set the Map Channel to **12**.

37. In the Composite Parameters rollout, replace the bitmap in the Map 2 slot with base_fabric_yellow.tga. Make sure that Image Alpha is checked and that Premultiplied Alpha is unchecked. Set the Map Channel to **13**.

38. Open the Unwrap UVW modifier in the Modifier Stack, and make sure that it is directly above UVW Map ID13. Set the Map Channel to **13**.

39. Open the Edit dialog box and, just like you did with the right arm, move around the lattice vertices until the placement of the stripe looks correct on the top of the left arm.

40. Set both Map Channels in the Bump slot to **12**.

41. The last step here is to set both the map and the mask within the Mask Parameters, within your displacement map, to Map Channel **14**.

Now you'll move on to the hands, which will be really simple.

42. First, add a Patch Select. Select the patches for just the hands. Apply a Material modifier, rename it as **Mat 6 Hands**, and set the Material ID to **6**.

43. Back in the Material Editor, open Material ID 6 and name it **Hands**.

44. Change the Ambient Color and Diffuse Color RGB settings to **223, 174, 150**. Set the Specular Level and Glossiness settings to **0**.

45. Put a noise in the Bump slot. Set the size to **2.0**, and keep the Noise Type set to Regular.

That's it for the Material Editor. It should look like Figure 17.50.

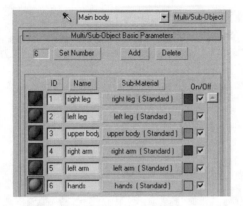

Figure 17.50   Your Multi/Sub-Object Parameters rollout should look like this.

46. Just for safe keeping, add a final Patch Select to the top of the Modifier Stack, to close the stack. Make sure that you still have a Displacement Aprox. modifier on the very top of the stack. Without the displacement modifier, all those nice displacement maps that you set up won't work correctly.

That's it for the Modifier Stack, which should now look like Figure 17.51.

Not bad for a day's work. You are done! You have successfully completed one of the most difficult, not to mention time-consuming, parts of the Jester.

You also learned a lot by setting up some pretty detailed materials. Plus, you managed a fairly elaborate set of UVW mapping problems. And who can forget the Unwarp UVW modifier?

47. Hit the Render button. You deserve it! (See Figure 17.52.)

Ready for some more? Most, but not all, of your big challenges are out of the way. It's time to move on.

Figure 17.51
This is what your final Modifier Stack should look like.

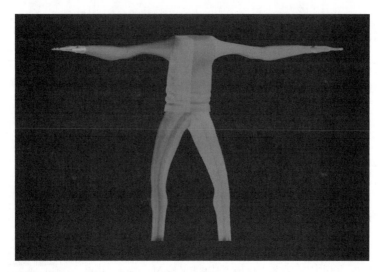

Figure 17.52   Here's where you are at this point.

Exercise 17.7   Texturing the Hat

Our Jester will wear a hat made out of rough linen. To have some fun with it, you'll break the hat into different colors. At first glance, the task of texturing the hat looks quite simple.

Well, it's not as difficult as rendering the body, but it is a little tricky. The ends are bent, so the mapping won't be totally straightforward. The good news is that you're going to reuse some of the techniques that you learned for the body.

Like everything else so far, start with breaking up the hat into different Material IDs.

   1. Open up a Patch Select, and select the patches for just the center part of the hat (see Figure 17.53).

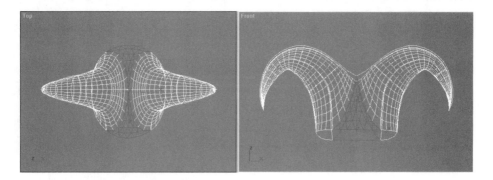

Figure 17.53   Here you can see the selected faces.

2. Above the Patch Select, open a Material modifier, rename this **Mat Center ID1**, and set the Map Channel to **1**.

3. Place a Planar UVW Map modifier and rename it as **UVW Map ID1**. Set the alignment to the Y-axis. Set the Map Channel to **1** (see Figure 17.54).

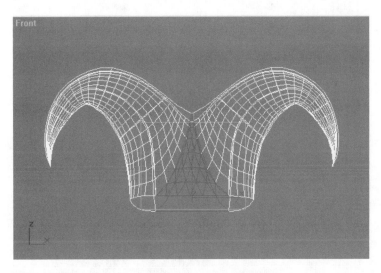

Figure 17.54   The UVW Map is applied to your selected faces.

4. Adjust the map to the center of the hat by scaling and moving the gizmo.

5. Open the Material Editor and create a Multi/Sub-Object material with a total of five IDs.

6. Name ID 1 **Hat Center**. Choose an Oren-Nayar-Blinn shader.

   You will use one handy utility while working with this material to help your workflow. You're going to have all these different parts on the hat, so instead of having to always adjust the Ambient Color and Diffuse Color settings each time, you will work with the Color Clipboard. This utility stores color swatches for copying and pasting from one map or material to another.

7. Open the Utilities panel. Select the Color Clipboard channel. Hit the New Floater button (see Figure 17.55).

8. Select the first slot and set the RGB values to **221, 166, 0**. Select the second slot and set the RGB values to **91, 0, 84**. You just created colors of yellow and purple.

9. Now drag and drop a copy of the yellow color slot into the Diffuse Color and Ambient Color slots in the Oren-Nayar-Blinn Basic Parameters rollout.

Figure 17.55
This is the Color Clipboard.

10. Minimize the Color Clipboard. You'll be using it again.

11. Set the Specular Level and Glossiness settings to **0**.

12. Add linen_color.jpg from the CD to the Diffuse Color slot.

13. In the Bump slot, open linen_bump.jpg from the CD. Leave the map settings alone for now.

    The left side of the hat will be split into four sections, two purple and two yellow.

14. Add a Patch Select in the Modifier Stack.

15. On the left side of the hat (the Jester's left), select the top patches, all the way to the tip; in the back, select all the bottom patches (see Figure 17.56).

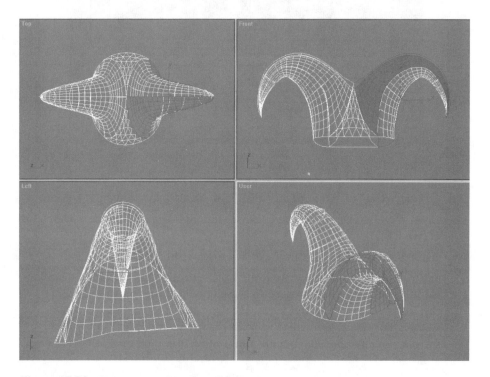

Figure 17.56   Here you see the selected faces.

16. Add a Material modifier, set the Material ID to **2**, and rename it as **Mat ID2 Lft Top**.

    Next, you're going to set up proper mapping. This is a little tricky. The hat is so bent that, at the ends, the texture usually wants to stretch a little.

17. Add a UVW Map modifier, rename it as **UVW Map ID2**, choose box mapping. Set the Map Channel to **2**. Align it to the X-axis.

18. In the left viewport, rotate the gizmo on the Z-axis 45° (see Figure 17.57).

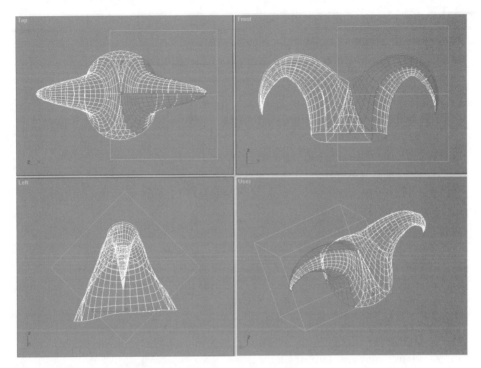

Figure 17.57   The UVW Map is applied to your selection.

The nice thing about using the rotated box is that the seam of the box will be where the end of the patch is, so it's almost being used like a planar map.

19. In the Material Editor, select ID 2 and name the material **Left Purple Stripe**.

20. Maximize the Color Clipboard, drag and drop a copy of the purple color into the Ambient Color and Diffuse Color channels, and set the Specular Level and Glossiness settings to **0**.

21. Add linen_color.jpg in the Diffuse Map slot. Set the Map Channel to **2**. Adjust the UV Tiling to U: **1.5**.

    If you look at the actual image file, you'll notice that it has both a purple and a yellow side. Because this section of the hat is supposed to be only purple, you'll have to crop the image to use only the purple part.

22. Select the View Image button in the Bitmap Parameters rollout. Drag the handle in the center on the right side toward the center, isolating only the purple area. Close this window, and check the Apply box in the Cropping/Placement parameters.

23. Add a mix map in the Bump Map slot.

    You will mix a linen bump map with a noise map. The linen bump map will give you a little bit of roughness, and the noise map will make the hat feel a bit dented.

24. In Color 1, open linen_bump.jpg.

25. Set the U Tiling to **1.5** and the Map Channel to **2**.

26. In Color 2, add a noise map. Change the size of the noise to **8**.

27. Set the Mix amount to **75**, giving the noise map dominance over the bitmap.

The first hat section is done. It's time to move on to the other sections, on the same side of the hat.

28. Add another Patch Select modifier. This time select the patches for the remaining two stripes.

29. Add a Material modifier, rename it as **Mat ID3 Lft Bottom**, and set the Material ID to **3**.

30. Copy and paste the UVW Map ID2 modifier. Change the name to **UVW Map ID3**, and set the Map Channel to **3**.

31. Instead of creating the next material from scratch, drag and drop (an instance or a copy) the material in ID 2 into the Material ID 3's slot. Rename the new material as **Left Yellow Stripe**.

All you have to do is adjust some of the parameters.

32. Maximize the Color Clipboard, and drag and drop the yellow color into the Ambient Color and Diffuse Color slot.

33. Open the Bitmap Parameters for linen_color.jpg. Because you cropped the image to use the purple part, you must now change the cropping to use only the yellow part of the image.

34. Set the Map Channel to **3**.

35. Now set the Map Channels in the bump map to **3**.

You're done with the left side of the hat. The right side will work exactly the same, so you can move a little more quickly.

36. Add a Patch Select. On the right side of the hat, select the top patches all the way to the tip. In the back, select all the bottom patches.

37. Add a Material modifier, rename it, and set the Material ID to **4**.

38. Copy and paste the last UVW Map modifier to the top of the stack. Rename it, and set the Map Channel to **4** (see Figure 17.58) .

Next you'll adjust gizmo to the right side of the hat that you are about to texture.

39. In the Material Editor, you want to drag and drop a copy of the Sub-Material ID 3 into the Sub-Material ID 4. Rename this material as **Right Yellow Stripe**.

Now you'll move on to the Map Channels.

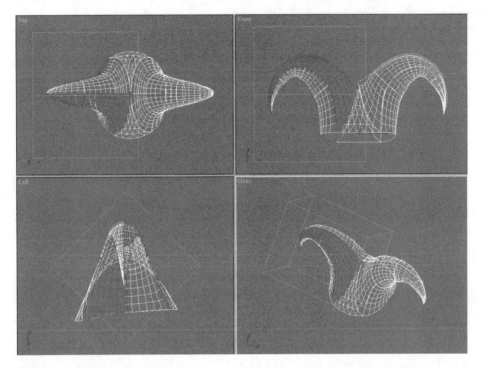

Figure 17.58   Here you see the UVW Map applied to your selected faces.

40. Set the diffuse color map and the bump maps to Map Channel **4**.

    Next you'll tackle the two remaining stripes on the right side of the hat.

41. Add another Patch Select. On the right side of the hat, select the bottom patches all the way to the tip. In the back, select all the top patches.

42. Add a Material modifier, rename it, and set the Material ID to **5**.

43. Copy and paste the last UVW Map modifier. Rename it, and set the Map Channel to **5**.

44. In the Material Editor, drag and drop a copy of the Sub-Material ID 2 into the Sub-Material ID 5. Rename this material as **Right Purple Stripe**.

    Again, you'll adjust the Map Channels.

45. Set all the Map Channel IDs to **5**.

46. To close off the Modifier Stack, add a Patch Select to the very top. You have just completed the hat!

47. For the hat rim, simply add a cylindrical UVW Map, and drag and drop your purple material from the hat Sub-Object Material. Then rename it. Make sure that the Map Channel is set to **1**.

Exercise 17.8   Texturing the Shoes

Maybe you should change your perspective for a while. It's time to turn from the head to the toes—to the shoes, to be precise.

Unlike the Jester's head, which he might stick in your face, so to speak, it's probably safe to reason that, despite his menacing character, the Jester is not going to kick us. But we'll give the shoes a little detail anyway.

1. Your Modifier Stack will be very simple here. Just add a UVW Map and select Face from the Parameters rollout. That's it!

2. You are after the feel of a matte fabric here, so create a new Standard Material and select Oren-Nayar-Blinn from the Shader Basic Parameters.

3. Name this material **Left Foot**, and apply it to the left foot.

4. Set the Specular Level to **10** and the Glossiness to **30**. This gives the shoes a soft highlight.

5. While in the Orin-Nayar-Blinn Basic Parameters rollout, set the Roughness value to **100**. This will increase the material's matte appearance.

6. Now load linen_color.jpg into your Diffuse Color slot. Adjust the Tiling, in both U and V, to **0.5**.

7. This image contains your color palette, side by side, so go into the Bitmap Parameters rollout and crop it. You need a square pattern that your face mapping can read, but you also need to isolate the color purple (see Figure 17.59).

8. Create the mix map in the Bump Map slot. Set the Bump amount to **30**, and now drag and drop a copy of linen_color.jpg into Color 1. You are doing this only to get the Tiling and Cropping parameters in one move.

9. When linen_color.jpg is in your slot, go ahead and replace it with linen_bump.jpg. You now have a grayscale version of linen_color.jpg, and you do not have to make any adjustments to it.

10. Add a noise map into the Color 2 slot in the Mix Parameters rollout. Experiment, using the ActiveShade Floater, with Mix amount and Noise parameters.

    For the other material, you can repeat Steps 1 through 9, change your cropping area, select the yellow/gold color, and apply this new material to the right foot.

    Congratulations again! The feet are done.

Figure 17.59 This is your cropping placement.

Exercise 17.9   Cheap Shiny Vinyl and Tacky Chrome

What else would you expect our Jester's belt to be? Now you get to play around with another shader: Anisotropic. You are actually going to use the Multi-Layer shader, which is *two* Anisotropic shaders together.

1. The UVW mapping for the belt is very simple. As you might expect, you'll place a cylindrical UVW Map on the belt patch itself. Select Z Alignment and Fit.

2. In the Material Editor, select Multi-Layer from the Basic Parameters rollout.

   As indicated previously, you now have two levels of Anisotropic parameters to adjust.

3. Because your belt is jet black, lock the Ambient Color and Diffuse Color parameters, and set them to black. Also bring the Roughness down to **0** because you want the highest contrast possible.

4. You need your first specular layer for control over a tight specularity. Set the Color to pure white, the Level to **64**, and the Glossiness to **0**. Now set the Anisotropy to **100**. As you make these adjustments, watch the material in the sample window change. You can see the effect that changing the Anisotropy has on the highlight.

    For the second specular level, you'll want a softer specularity, with a falloff.

5. Set the Color to a light gray of R: **0**, G: **0**, B: **178**. Bring the Level to **42**, the Glossiness to **55**, and the Anisotropy to **0**.

    You should see a soft, light-gray highlight now in the Sample window. Move down to the Maps rollout and add some more details to your new shader.

6. In the Bump slot, select a mix from the Material/Map browser. Place a Noise in Color 1, change the Noise Type to Fractal, and set the Size to **5**. Also, to make a high-contrast map, in the Noise Threshold, set the High slider to **0.74** and the Low slider to **0.455**.

7. Copy this noise into Color 2, keeping all the parameters the same, but set the Noise Size to **1.0**.

8. A Mix amount of **50** and a Bump amount of **3** should give you almost what you need.

    The second specular color looks too bright. A quick way to fix that is to add a map to the Specular Color 2 in your Maps rollout.

9. Simply drag and drop a copy of the map in the Bump slot up to the Specular Color 2 slot.

    This will mask out some of the color.

10. The last step on the belt strap is to apply the belt material to your patch models, the belt, and the belt end.

    For the buckle, you will choose Spherical Environment for your Reflection, so you do not need a UVW Map. Go directly to the Material Editor.

11. Choose Anisotropic as the base shader type. Because you will get your color from a reflection map, go ahead and lock the Ambient Color and Diffuse Color, and set them to black. Now set the Specular Color to pure white. Set the Specular Level to **119**, the Glossiness to **18**, and the Anisotropy to **54**.

12. To save a little time, drag and drop the Bump Mix channel from your belt material into your Bump Map slot. Make it a copy because you modify it slightly.

13. Select one of the noise maps, and change its Size to **0.125**. This smaller bump size will give the buckle a slightly brushed look. Now turn up the Bump amount to **7**.

14. In the Reflection slot, go ahead and load house.jpg. Notice that your chrome has too much color in it. Well, that's an easy fix.

15. With your house.jpg parameters rollout still open, click the Bitmap button, as if you were going to load a new bitmap. From the Material/Map browser, select RGB Tint. Make sure that the Keep Old Map as Sub-Map button is selected, and hit OK.

16. Set the red value to a light gray of **205**, and set both the green and the blue values to jet-black (see Figure 17.60).

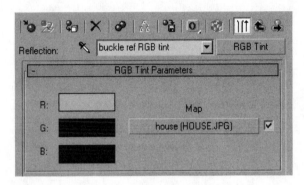

Figure 17.60   Here is your RGB Tint Parameters rollout.

Notice how this gives you control over the reflection color.

17. As a final step, put a heavy blur on the house.jpg map.

18. Apply this shader to Belt Buckle and Belt Tooth.

That was easy, compared to some of the other challenges you have faced. Now you will move on to the tunic and frock.

Exercise 17.10   Tunic and Frock

In this exercise, you will again go back to a matte material (see Figure 17.61).

You are going for a matte, linen material here, so, you guessed it, the Oren-Nayar-Blinn shader is your best bet.

You'll do the frock first. Your first order of business is the Modifier Stack. You should already be familiar with these steps from previous exercises.

1. Add a Patch Select modifier, and select the right half of the model (see Figure 17.62).

2. Add a Material modifier, keep the Material ID on 1, and name it **Material Yellow ID 1**.

3. Add a second Patch Select modifier, and select the left half of the model.

Figure 17.61   This is your texture map.

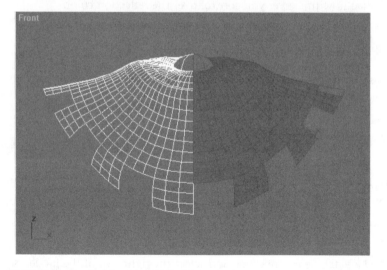

Figure 17.62   Your Patch Select should look like this image.

4. Add a second Material modifier, change the Material ID to **2**, and name it **Material Purple ID 2**.

   You no doubt have the hang of this by now.

5. Add a UVW Map modifier and select Face as the mapping type.

While you're in this mode, edit your Modifier Stack for the tunic as well.

6. Select the tunic, add a UVW Map modifier, and select Cylindrical as your mapping type. That's it, for now.

On to the material.

7. Create a Multi/Sub-Object material, and name it **Frock**. After a quick look at your Modifier Stack, you know to set the number of sub-materials to **2**.

8. Click Sub-Material 1, and choose Oren-Nayer-Blinn. Bring the Specular color to a light gray, with a value of **200**. Keep the Roughness at **50**, and set the Specular Level and Glossiness settings to **0**.

9. Load yellow_frock_tile.jpg from the CD, and tile it to **15** in both U and V. This will tighten the look of your texture a little.

10. Go into View Image, in the Bitmap Parameters rollout, and crop the texture to U: **0.221**, V: **0.248**, W **0.494**, H **0.653**.

11. Remember how you made a copy of the shoe texture to get your coordinates and then replaced it with the linen_bump.jpg? Just repeat that here. But first, make your bump map a mix map. Into Color 1, drag a copy of yellow_frock_tile.jpg, and then replace it with bump_frock_tile.jpg from the CD.

12. Into Color 2, place a noise. Adjust the noise Size and the Mix amount, to give a little variety to your bump.

13. Bring the Bump amount up to about **70**.

14. As one last detail, make sure that you check 2-Sided in the Shader Basic Parameters rollout. You will then be able to see the inside faces of the model.

That's it for your yellow linen.

All you do now is move back to the Multi/Sub-Object Basic Parameters rollout, copy this material into ID 2, rename it, and then replace the yellow_frock_tile.jpg with the purple_frock_tile.jpg. Then repeat Step 5 in this material to make sure that your new cropping placement for the texture matches the cropping on the bump texture.

For the tunic, most of the shader parameters will be the same as those for the frock, so you will not spend much time on them. Your main focus will be the stitching that you added (see Figure 17.63).

You will also need to revisit the handy UVW Unwrap modifier to control how your linen material conforms to the tunic.

15. From the frock material, make a copy of the Sub-Material ID 2 (purple side) as a starting point. Rename it as **Tunic**. By doing this, you already have all the settings for the Oren-Nayar-Blinn basic parameters. All you have to adjust now are the Diffuse and the Bump Map slots.

16. A quick render tells you that you have to adjust the Tiling in V. Bring it back down to **1**. Make sure to do the same for the texture in the Bump slot.

Figure 17.63   This is the map used for the stitching.

17. Because you need to get your stitch onto this model, change the diffuse color map to a Composite material. Make sure that Keep Old Map as Sub-Map is selected.

18. In Map 2, load stitches.tga from the CD.

19. Adjust the UV Offset and Tiling so that the stitches line up where you want them. Be sure that Image Alpha is selected in the Alpha Source panel. Make sure that Premultiplied Alpha is unchecked.

20. Now for the bump map. Replace Color 1 in the Mix Parameters rollout with linen_bump.jpg. Tile the map in U: **1.5**, and also crop the image to U: **0.0**, V: **0.085**, W: **0.472**, H: **0.653**. This cropping should match what you already have in the diffuse map. Back in the Mix Parameters rollout, replace the noise map in Color 2 with an instance of stitches.tga from the Diffuse Map slot.

If you render this material on the tunic, you can see that some adjustments are in order. Add your trusted Unwrap UVW to the tunic's stack.

21. Make adjustments to the stitches by adjusting the control vertices in the Edit UVW's window. You want to make it feel like it is conforming to the tunic.

Summary

This chapter demonstrated one of many possible approaches to mapping and texturing. This is not the last word, by any means. Some of the techniques used here are the result of the collaboration between two artists. Each artist, or group of artists, will always find their own way through a project like this.

You should now take the Jester model and create something of your own with it. Give yourself some art direction; and then stick to your objectives. Test yourself as if it were a real production situation. The key is to always do the best you can in every situation.

Chapter 18

Materials/Shaders and Mapping for Games/Interactive Applications

by Doug Barnard

As you look about, most of the non-organic objects that you see around you are fairly simple. If you were tasked to model them for a real-time application, you could probably accomplish the job without much effort. But your scene would be almost indistinguishable from dozens of other studios—that is, until you applied *texture* to your scene. The various colors, the way that light reflects off the objects, and small surface detail make your work area stand apart from others similar to it.

In this chapter, you explore the construction and precision application of textures in a real-time setting. After completing the exercises in this chapter, you should be familiar with the following:

- Building sub-object materials
- Defining sub-object selections to apply the materials to
- Applying UVW mapping coordinates to the geometry to place the materials precisely

Material IDs Versus Sub-Object Materials

Using textures for low polygon-count applications is both simpler *and* more difficult than using textures for traditionally modeled high polygon-count scenes. It's simpler because the scenes are far less complex, so the materials or textures are far simpler. It is more complex, because materials also have to compensate for the more simplistic geometry, and any bungling in this area will most likely wreck the scene.

All your artistic prowess will be called into play as you manipulate the geometry, adjust the colors, and play with the mapping to get an optimized scene that uses the fewest resources possible to give the maximum visual punch. Optimization is the final goal; your scene can be incredibly beautiful, but if it brings the target platform/application to its knees, you have failed.

To avoid catastrophes it is imperative that the artists maintain a close communication with the programmers. This cannot be stressed enough, because some of the most tedious work will have to be completely redone if the textures won't work on the target platform.

Most texts on this subject make light of these potentially horrendous calamities by covering the necessary material in noncontiguous sections. Creating textures, defining the places that they reside on the models, and their interactive positioning is an iterative process that needs to be viewed as a whole for easy comprehension.

If you are working on a large project, someone else might have built the model, and it's your job to texture it. It is still necessary to check over the model before you begin your work, and make sure that it is fully optimized, that it is "airtight" (no open edges or stray vertices), and that the Material IDs and smoothing groups are properly set. To avoid a precheck is to compound someone else's poor workmanship and perpetuate an even more costly mistake.

Tip

An easy way to check models for errors is to use the STL Check modifier in the Mesh Editing area of the Modifier List. Even though you probably aren't preparing your file for stereolithography, STL Check informs you of your model's foibles. It checks for all the errors that keep your model from being airtight, such as extra vertices, T-junctions, unconnected edges, and open edges. When you have a clean bill of health from STL Check, you can delete the modifier or collapse the Stack.

The complex texturing of objects necessary for gaming and interactive applications takes three steps:

1. Define Sub-Material IDs. This tells 3ds max 4 where the different materials are supposed to go.

2. Build sub-object materials. This specifies the various materials that go in those locations.

3. Apply the UVW mapping coordinates to the objects. This ensures that the bitmaps lie in the correct orientation.

Even though in production, these three procedures are intermixed, in this chapter they are covered systematically for clarity.

Assigning Material IDs

You might be familiar with the standard method of assigning materials to objects: select the object in the viewports, select your material in the Material Editor, and click Assign Material to Selection. Missing in this method is the way to assign multiple materials to the same object.

Navigating the Sub-Object Panels

Open the file cube.max from the CD-ROM. You will see a simple cube, colored red, green, and blue (see Figure 18.1). The cube is an editable mesh, with various polygons selected and assigned the different colors as sub-object materials.

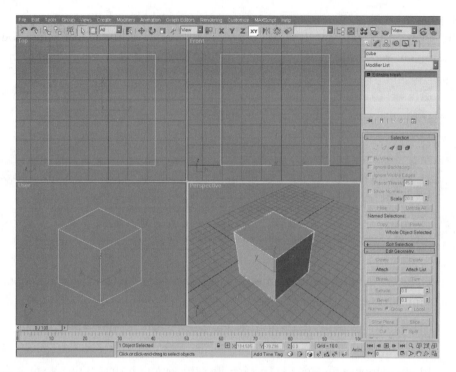

Figure 18.1   This simple cube, with sub-object textures applied, is an Editable Mesh.

Under the Selection panel of the Modify tab, you can see icons of the five different sub-object types: Vertex, Edge, Face, Polygon, and Element (see Figure 18.2).

Figure 18.2
Polygon is selected among the sub-object icons.

 Note

For a more complete discussion of sub-objects, please see Chapter 8, "Non-Organic Modeling for Games/Interactive Applications."

If you select the Polygon icon and scroll down to the Surface Properties menu of the rollout, you can see the Material box. Clicking the red polygon shows that it is Material ID 1 and Smoothing Group 3 (see Figure 18.3).

If you click Face or Element, nothing in the Surface Properties menu changes. You now have seen half of the equation: Material IDs can be specified on the Face, Polygon, or Element level.

The other half of the equation lies in the Material Editor. If you open the Material Editor, you can see that four materials have been specified (see Figure 18.4).

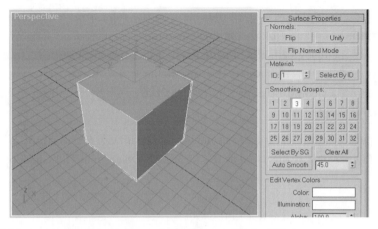

Figure 18.3   Select the red polygon to learn that it is Material ID 1.

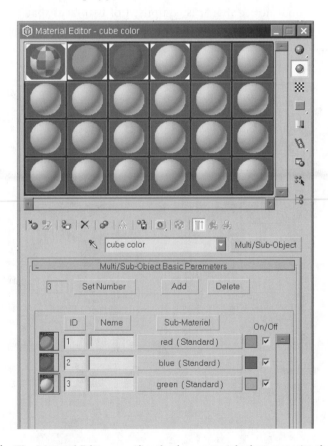

Figure 18.4   The Material Editor specifies the four materials that comprise the cube.

The three on the right are each of the colors on the cube, and the first material on the left is the Multi/Sub-Object combined material. This material is actually assigned to the cube; the red, green, and blue materials are all instances of their counterparts in the Multi/Sub-Object material. This instancing is not strictly necessary, because the sub-materials could be edited by clicking the appropriate button in the Basic Parameters rollout.

Notice that the red sphere is listed as having an ID value of 1; this confirms that the cube's Material ID 1 is the same as the Multi/Sub-Object material cube color value of ID 1.

Assembling Faces into Logical Groupings

Returning to the Multi/Sub-Object rollout, if you select the Face icon and click the green polygon, you'll notice that it is comprised of two faces that both share the ID 3. The edge that both of these faces share is invisible, as shown in Figure 18.5 by the dotted line.

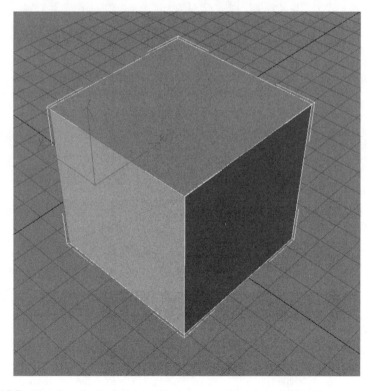

Figure 18.5   The shared edge between the two green faces is invisible.

For the most part, deciding which edges are visible and which aren't is strictly a convenience measure to make models more easy to read and to divide them into easily understood groupings. An exception to this is a game or dynamics engine that uses quadrilaterals to perform its calculations, instead of the three-sided polygons that 3ds max 4 produces. To avoid later confusion, be sure to discuss this subject with your programmers before modifying any edges.

Because producing artwork for games and interactive applications is an iterative process, it's prudent to make your models as neat and concise as possible because either you or someone else will probably make modifications later. Clicking a single polygon is far easier than selecting many faces. These polygons can then be assembled into a single Material ID, which can be selected using the Select By ID dialog box from the Surface Properties rollout.

Using Smoothing Groups

Another tool in the texturing arsenal is smoothing groups. Smoothing groups help define the contiguous areas of a mesh and add visual seams to separate elements that might be attached. Smoothing groups can add the appearance of additional geometry and make the texture artist's job easier.

As you can see in Figure 18.6, judicious use of smoothing groups can help delineate the different sections of this antishipping mine. When every polygon counts, smoothing can make the difference between a tight model and an amorphous blob. Smoothing groups can also add shading to sections of textures that have a much larger repeating pattern. Remember, you have to be as aware of the texture load to the target platform as the modeler has to be aware of the polygon load!

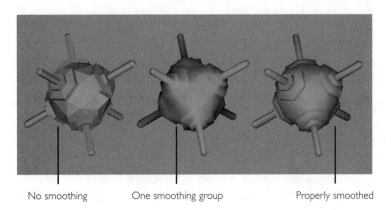

No smoothing   One smoothing group   Properly smoothed

Figure 18.6   This illustration of antishipping mines shows the differences that smoothing groups can make.

Smoothing groups are assigned in either the Face, Polygon, or Element level by first selecting the appropriate geometry and then clicking one of the numbered buttons. Figure 18.7 shows the main body of the mine being given Smoothing Group 1. Faces can be assigned multiple smoothing groups; this practice enables selective creasing across designated portions of a mesh.

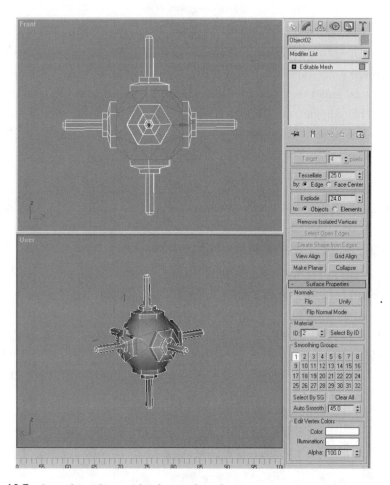

Figure 18.7   Smoothing Group 1 has been selected.

A character's nose is an example of where multiple groups might be used. You want the nostrils to smooth with the nose, and you want the nose to smooth with the rest of the face. You want a crease where the nostrils intersect the face, however. If the face is Smoothing Group 1, and the nostrils are Smoothing Group 2, the nose should be a member of both groups.

Exercise 18.1   Assigning Material IDs and Smoothing Groups in a Simple Room

In this exercise, you assign Material IDs and smoothing groups in a simple room.

1. Open room01.max on the CD-ROM. (See Figure 18.8.)

Figure 18.8   The room at the beginning of the exercise has smoothing problems on the wall with the door.

The part of the room that you will be dealing with is the front boxlike section. You can see that the normals have already been flipped by the modeler, but there are some smoothing problems on the wall with the door that need to be fixed.

2. Right-click the title of the User viewport, and select Edged Faces, as shown in Figure 18.9.

   Edged Faces is a real asset when it comes to editing faces. Be selective in its use—not checking your work with Edged Faces off can mask smoothing problems.

3. Select the room and go into Polygon mode.

4. Turn on Ignore Backfacing; this keeps the polygons facing away from you from being selected.

5. Click the polygons in the door wall one by one. If you look in the Smoothing Groups section of the Surface Properties rollout, notice that they are all in Smoothing Group 3.

Figure 18.9
Select Edged Faces in the viewport right-click menu.

Why does that door wall look so bad if the whole wall shares the same smoothing group? The wall in the passage is also a member of the same group.

6. Control-click all the polygons in the door wall and click Smoothing Group 9 from the Surface Properties rollout.

7. Click Smoothing Group 3 to turn it off. The wall looks smooth, as shown in Figure 18.10.

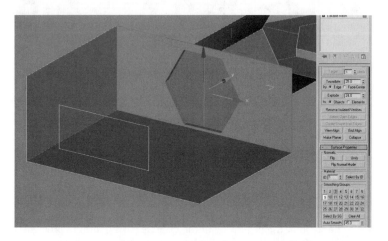

Figure 18.10   The door wall is properly smoothed.

8. Change the door wall polygon's Material ID setting to **4**.

9. Select the side wall and change its Material ID setting to **2**.

10. Using Arc Rotate Sub-Object and Pan, adjust the view so that you can see the other side wall and the front (window) wall.

11. Assign the side wall Material ID 2, and the front wall ID 3, by first selecting the proper polygons and then setting the Material ID number.

12. Get out of Sub-Object mode by clicking the Editable Mesh title or pressing Ctrl+B.

13. Open the Material Editor. Assign the material controlRoom, which is in the first slot.

    Your room should look like Figure 18.11, with each of the surfaces showing a different texture. If it doesn't look like this, open room02.max from the CD-ROM to see the Material ID assignments. It's easy to get confused when specifying your Material IDs, so be sure that you're selecting the right polygons before you give them their number.

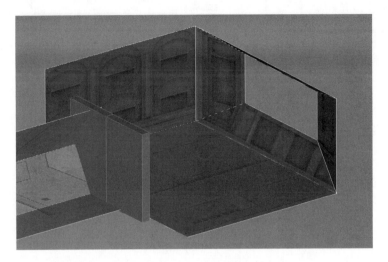

Figure 18.11   The room has all its Material IDs assigned.

Building Sub-Object Materials

The material that you assigned in the previous exercise was a custom-built Multi/Sub-Object material. You access it by selecting a free slot, and clicking the New button, as shown in Figure 18.12.

Most of the power of the 3ds max 4 Material Editor is wasted when setting up materials for real-time applications. As mentioned before, discussing all the parameters in the target application or platform with your programming crew *before* starting to texture your models is crucially important. Computers are notoriously unforgiving when it comes to input that they can't digest.

Checking Constraints on the Target Platform

Many game engines require that bitmaps be of a certain type (usually Targa files), and that they be sized in powers of 2. In this scenario, bitmaps could be 256×256, 128×128, and so forth. Some older engines also require the maps to be square.

The old 3D Studio DOS (3DS) is a popular format for 3ds max 4 artists to export to. One of the problems with this is that 3ds max 4 lops off the last letters of long filenames to make them "legal" for DOS 8.3. If you're a Windows 2000 user, all your bitmap filenames should be no more than eight characters long, excluding the extension. Otherwise, if you reimport the 3DS file, you have to go through and reassign the textures. The programmers also have to manually assign texture names, which will not cause great happiness among them, either.

Figure 18.12   Click the New button in the Material/Map Browser.

 Tip

Whenever you're scanning in material to make into textures, it's almost impossible to get the source perfectly straight on the scanner bed. After it's scanned in, there is usually a back-and-forth seesawing in Photoshop as you try to rotate the picture to square up the edges.

A little-known use of the Measure tool in Photoshop makes this odious task a breeze. Scan in your image any way you want. Use the Measure tool (it's underneath the EyeDropper) to draw a line that *should* be vertical. This can be along an image element or even the edge of the picture. Select Image/Rotate Canvas/Arbitrary. There should be some number in the Angle box; click OK. The picture is rotated perfectly! (See Figure 18.13.) You should check your work using the Marquee tool to make sure that the alignment is the way that you want it.

There are two methods for building Multi/Sub-Object materials. You can manually construct the Multi/Sub-Object material from the Get Material tool. You then need to use the Select By ID button in the Surface Properties rollout to figure out where your materials are supposed to go, and refer to the Material Editor to edit the numbers. Not much fun!

Figure 18.13   Use the Measure tool and Rotate Arbitrary in Photoshop to straighten a scan.

The easiest method is to select faces and assign standard materials by dragging and dropping. Exercise 18.2 explains how to do this. 3ds max 4 takes care of all the sub-object business; this includes Material ID selections, constructing a Multi/Sub-Object material, and assigning it to the object.

Exercise 18.2   Sub-Object Materials—The Easy Way

  1. Open cube01.max on the CD-ROM.
  2. Select the cube and go into Polygon mode.
  3. Open the Material Editor and position it so that you can see the cube and the tool rollouts.
  4. Select the top surface of the cube and drag the red material on to it. The top of the cube turns red.
  5. Assign the green material to the left face by first selecting the face and then dragging the green material on to it.
  6. Repeat Step 5 with the blue material and the right face. (See Figure 18.14.)
  7. Select a free slot in the Material Editor and click the Get Material button on the left side of the Material Editor toolbar.
  8. Select the Scene radio button in the Browse From area. Select the material in the browser window.

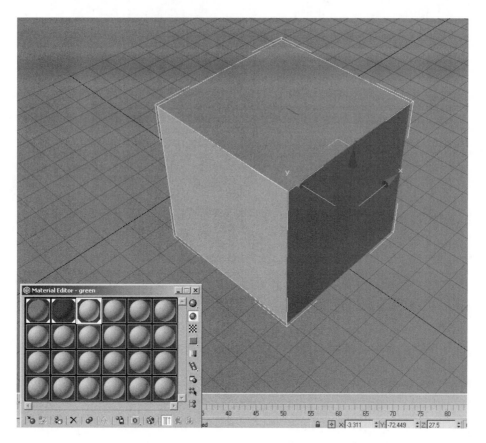

Figure 18.14   Assign materials to the cube by selecting the face and dragging the material on top of it.

A Multi/Sub-Object material with four sub-materials has been built and assigned to the cube. The faces on the far cube are still Material ID 1, so they are still gray. The file cube02.max on the CD-ROM has the completed exercise with the new Multi/Sub-Object material.

Although this is a perfectly acceptable way to apply materials, you still need to be able to further edit them. This dragging method is a good way to begin when approaching a complicated model involving many Multi/Sub-Object materials. You don't want to make up new materials if you don't have to, however. This can lead to confusion when they need to be edited; global changes cannot be made if dozens of copies of the same material are used throughout the scene. You want to maintain consistency in your materials.

Always remember that after a bitmap has been loaded into the game engine, reusing it (or even just a piece of it) is "free"; there will be no additional machine resources allocated for its use.

Assigning Mapping Coordinates

The last procedure is assigning the UVW mapping coordinates to the mesh to line up the bitmap in its proper location.

Mesh Select/UV Map Pairs

Mapping coordinates are applied by adding the UVW Map modifier. You have probably done this many times on an object-level basis, and sub-object mapping is fairly similar. A Mesh Select modifier is added to the stack, an area is selected, and a UVW Map modifier is placed directly after (without clearing the relevant sub-object selection). The next area is mesh selected, and so on. In the next exercise, you practice setting the UV coordinates in the room from the last exercise.

Exercise 18.3   Applying Mapping to the Simple Room

   1. Open room03.max on the CD-ROM. The room's textures aren't showing because of the lack of mapping coordinates (see Figure 18.15).

Figure 18.15   The room's textures aren't visible because of the lack of UVW mapping.

2. Using the Min/Max toggle, or the W hotkey, go to a 4-viewport layout.

3. Select room01. Then, from the top of the Modifier List drop-down list, under Selection Modifiers, choose Mesh Select.

4. Click the Polygon tool and check Ignore Backfaces.

5. Select the floor, use Arc Rotate to adjust the view, and select the ceiling.

6. From the Modifier List drop-down list, under UV Coordinate Modifiers, select UVW Map.

   The floor and ceiling look fine, but there are some stray UVs in the rest of the room (see Figure 18.16). Not to worry—you'll be fixing them straight-away.

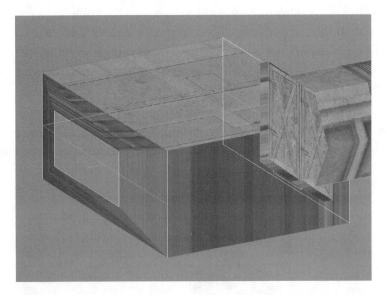

Figure 18.16   False UV coordinates can appear when you're sub-object mapping; they are taken care of by applying more UV coordinates.

7. Add another Mesh Select modifier and select the two side walls.

8. Add another UV modifier.

   This time, the modifier's initial position is incorrect. It is in the same orientation as the floor/ceiling UV modifier.

9. In the Alignment section of the UVW Mapping modifier, activate the Normal Align function.

10. Click and drag on one of the side walls, as if you were rubbing the wall with the cursor. The UV mapping gizmo snaps to the wall.

11. Click Fit from the same area of the UV Mapping Parameters rollout. The UVs are now aligned and sized properly, as shown in Figure 18.17.

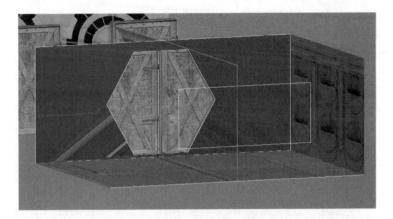

Figure 18.17   The UV mapping gizmo is aligned and sized to the side walls.

12. Use Arc Rotate to adjust the view so that you can see the front window wall.

13. Add another Mesh Select/UVW mapping pair on the front wall. Try to align and fit the gizmo the way that you did in Steps 9 through 11.

Because the walls are sloping, Normal Align is inappropriate. Normal Align is typically the first choice because you can continue work in the User view.

14. Right-click the Front viewport.

15. Choose View Align/Fit from the Alignment section of the Parameters rollout.

The front wall's gizmo is aligned and sized properly (see Figure 18.18), but the wall could look better.

Figure 18.18   The UV mapping gizmo is aligned and sized, but still needs to be repositioned.

16. In the stack, click the plus symbol next to the top UVW Mapping modifier. The Gizmo subheading appears.

17. Click the Gizmo subheading and select the Move tool from the main toolbar.

18. Move the gizmo in the Z-axis and X-axis until the design is centered in the wall area and the frames around the edges of the bitmap line up with the outer edges of the wall. See Figure 18.19.

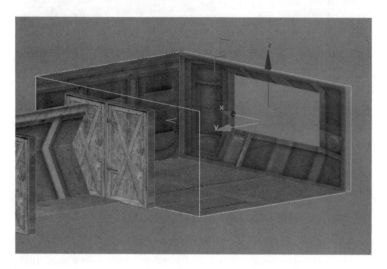

Figure 18.19   The UV mapping gizmo is now positioned properly.

Use Arc Rotate to adjust the view so that you can see the back wall.

19. Add another Mesh Select/UVW mapping pair on the back wall. Try to align and fit the gizmo the way that you did in Steps 9 through 11.

    This time, it works fine. However, the bitmap looks strange, because the design elements intersect the doorway (see Figure 18.20).

20. Go to the Gizmo Sub-Object for the current UVW Mapping modifier and select the Non-Uniform Scale tool.

21. Scale the map in to about 35% on the X-axis so that there are two sets of canisters on the wall and the third set is entirely inside the doorway. See Figure 18.21.

You have now completed the final element of real-time texturing, applying the mapping coordinates. If you had any problems, you can open room04.max from the CD-ROM to compare your work.

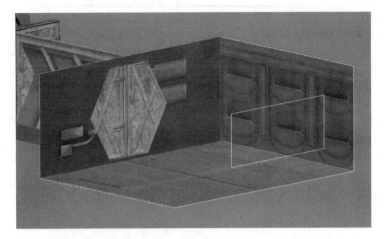

Figure 18.20   The UV coordinates need scaling.

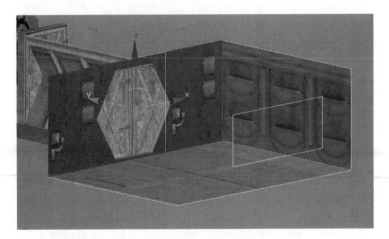

Figure 18.21   The texture is properly set on the back wall.

This system enables the texture artist to go back in the stack and change mapping coordinates at any time. Different areas on the mesh can have their Sub-Object Material IDs changed in the original editable mesh, to assign different materials as the artist sees fit. The materials themselves can be added to as the design develops, keeping the entire process fluid and flexible.

Using Unwrap UVW

There are times when merely transforming the gizmo isn't enough, and a finer level of control is needed. The Unwrap UVW modifier can give you a graphic representation of where the mapping coordinates fall on a given mesh.

It's helpful to think of the UV coordinates as "stuck" exactly on top of the vertices of the underlying mesh. That is the situation after you have applied the UVW Mapping modifier. As you have seen in the preceding exercises, however, the mapping coordinates can be transformed and manipulated in the same way that geometry can be altered.

Unwrap UVW enables UV editing on a vertex-level basis. This gives the finest level of control possible and is perfectly suited for low polygon-count applications. The next exercise shows Unwrap UVW's ease of use when fine-tuning mapping coordinates.

Exercise 18.4   Unwrap UVW Hits the Road

1. Open the file road.max from the CD-ROM.

   You have a model of a curvy road with bad mapping coordinates, as shown in Figure 18.22.

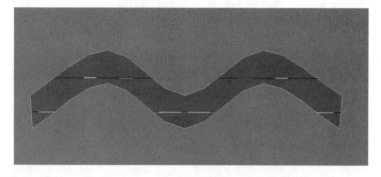

Figure 18.22   The road texture has to be curved to fit the road model.

2. Select the road. You can see the UVW Gizmo; it has been sized to fit the ends and the center curve.

3. From the Modifier List, under UV Coordinate modifiers, select Unwrap UVW.

4. Click the Edit button in the Parameters section of the modifier.

5. Click the Zoom Extents icon in the lower-right corner of the Edit UVWs window, as shown in Figure 18.23. The lower UVW coordinates have been selected.

6. Carefully region-select all the texture coordinates on the bottom half of the road. There are a couple of coordinates at each location, so you can't just click them individually. Figure 18.23 shows the coordinates that should be selected.

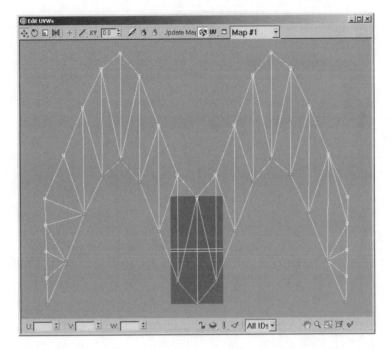

Figure 18.23   The Edit UVWs window shows how the asphalt texture fits on the road mesh.

7. Click and hold on the Scale flyout, so that you choose the Vertical Scaling tool.

8. Scale down all these points until you have a flat, horizontal line. Use the Move tool in the Edit UVW window's toolbar to move these coordinates down so that they align with the bottom of the road texture. (See Figure 18.24.)

9. Region-select the coordinates on the top curve of the road, and scale them as you did the bottom ones.

10. Move the coordinates so that they line up with the top edge of the road texture.

11. Close the Edit UVWs window. Figure 18.25 shows the road with the correct UV mapping coordinates.

Now your road's textures should look aligned properly with the road geometry. If your road isn't similar to Figure 18.25, you should open road01.max from the CD-ROM and check your work.

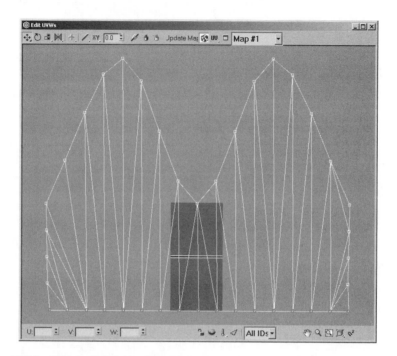

Figure 18.24   Half the UVW coordinates have been moved; the texture updates automatically in the viewport as the UVWs are moved.

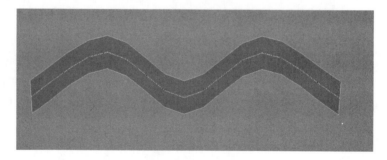

Figure 18.25   The road textures are aligned with the road geometry.

Finishing Off

There's still a few tricks up the sleeve of 3ds max 4 that the texture artist can take advantage of to make the scene as realistic as possible. Using opacity maps and vertex shading should be part of every texture artist's repertoire.

Adding Maps

Depending on your target application, you might be able to add bitmaps that make your textures richer and provide additional functionality.

Some game engines support bump mapping, which distorts the surface normals so that the appearance of lumpiness is given. Although bump mapping plays a large role in dense polygon meshes, it is of little importance on a low polygon mesh. Of primary importance is opacity mapping, which enables portions of the mesh to be transparent. In 3ds max, pure black is clear, and pure white is opaque.

 Tip

A good way to get a handle on the black/white opacity convention is to imagine that you are in a brightly lit room looking out to a nighttime sky. This scenario makes some sense, but the reverse could never be true; a blinding bright exterior could never produce a completely dark interior.

These maps need to be in grayscale (shades of black and white), but this information might be contained in a standard 24-bit Targa file. Typically, the extra information is contained in an Alpha Channel. Many game engines will accept only Alpha Channel opacity *or* bumping, so you have to decide which you want. Real-time opacity mapping (aside from setting the mapping coordinates) takes place in the Material Editor. The following exercise uses an opacity map to simulate the transparency of a cabin's window.

Exercise 18.5   Making a Window See-Through

1. Open the file window.max from the CD-ROM.
2. Open the Material Editor and select the first material, window.
3. Assign this to the purple rectangle named window, as shown in Figure 18.26. The sky in the window doesn't look at all like the sky in the background.
4. Scroll down in the Material Editor to the Maps rollout. Click the Map button for Diffuse Color.
5. Scroll down so that you can see all of the Bitmap Parameters rollout.
6. Under Cropping/Placement, click View Image.
7. Click the Display Alpha Channel button, which is next to the Blue button. The picture shifts to show a black-and-white window (see Figure 18.27).

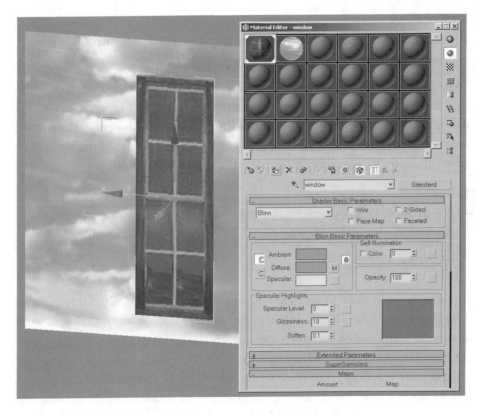

Figure 18.26   Assign the basic material to the window.

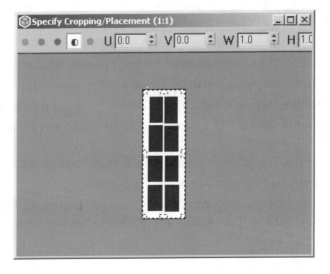

Figure 18.27   The window's Alpha Channel shows as a black-and-white window.

8. Close the Cropping/Placement window.

   If Image Alpha is selected as the alpha source, why isn't the window clear? If you look at the representation of the texture on the sphere in the Material Editor window, you can see that it looks much brighter and more washed out than the window in the scene. This is because the Alpha Channel is adjusting the transparency to reveal the underlying gray texture. To adjust the actual opacity, you must add another map.

9. Click the None (Opaque) button in the Alpha Source area. The image in the Material Editor now more closely resembles the image in the viewport.

10. Click the Go to Parent button in the Material Editor. This returns you to the top level in the material.

11. Drag the Map #2 (window.tga) button down and drop it on the Opacity Channel's None button. When the dialog appears, be sure that the Copy radio button is selected. Click OK.

12. The entire window should now be mostly transparent. Open the Opacity Channel's map by clicking the button that you just dropped the texture onto.

13. In the Mono Channel Output area, click the Alpha button. The glass area is completely transparent.

   Even though the window is totally see-through, now it looks as if there's no glass there. This is supposed to be a funky, log-cabin window; more work is needed to get the right effect.

 Tip

Some video cards have problems making the window transparent after the drag-and-drop. Try reloading the texture by clicking the Bitmap button in the Bitmap parameters area. Right-click the title in the User window and select Configure. Make sure that Transparency is set to Stipple or Blend. Make sure that the Show Map in Viewport button is off in both the Opacity and the Diffuse mapping channels and on in the top level of the material.

14. Load the window2.tga texture by clicking the Bitmap button in the Bitmap parameters area. You can find it in the Chapter 18 Textures folder on the CD-ROM.

   The window becomes semi-transparent, and it looks like it is reflecting something. If you look at the bitmap's Alpha Channel (by clicking View Image/ Show Alpha Channel), you can see that instead of solid black window panes, they are now light gray.

   If this doesn't ring a bell, load window01.max from the CD-ROM to troubleshoot your material.

Using Vertex Shading

Adding additional maps can be quite useful when it comes to opacity, but somewhat weak when considering bump mapping. Aside from playing with the smoothing groups, there is another way to give your scene more depth and realism: by using the Vertex Shading modifier.

Warning

Not all rendering engines support vertex shading, and that includes 3ds max 4. If you use vertex shading, you will see it only in the viewports and not in a sample rendering.

Use vertex shading when you want to permanently shade an area, such as the corners of a room or the top of a character's neck. In this next exercise, you use the VertexPaint feature in 3ds max 4 to interactively add vertex shading. This adds more depth and realism to the room.

Exercise 18.6   Adding Drama to the Room

1. Open the file room05.max from the CD-ROM.

2. Select the front room, room01.

3. From the Modifier List drop-down list, in the Mesh Editing area, select VertexPaint (see Figure 18.28).

4. Change the default Opacity value of 100% to 5%.

5. Make sure that Affect Channels/Colors is checked, and that black is selected as the paint color.

6. Click the Vertex Color Paint icon.

7. Click the VertCol button to turn on the vertex colors display.

8. Carefully click a few times in the corner where the walls meet the floor. You should see the area start to darken.

9. Use Arc Rotate to adjust the view so that you can see the front window wall.

10. Click and drag in the hollow-looking area to the left of the window. Vertex painting can make this look a lot more three-dimensional.

11. Paint along the top of the window, so that the area that slants out is in shade. (See Figure 18.29.)

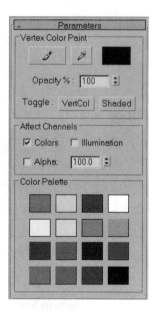

Figure 18.28
Select the VertexPaint parameters palette.

Figure 18.29   Use vertex painting to prelight the scene and make it more dimensional.

You can continue to use Arc Rotate and paint in the corners to get a feel for how vertex painting works. Be sparing in its use, or your scene will get so dark that the lighting guys will never get it lit right!

A completed vertex painting of the room can be seen by loading room06.max from the CD-ROM.

Using Texporter

A plug-in that no 3ds max 4 texture artist should be without is Texporter, created by Turkish programmer Cuneyt Ozdas. It can be downloaded free from the following URL: http://www.cuneytozdas.com/software/max/texporter/index.htm.

This utility constructs a bitmap representation of the mapping coordinates that can be loaded into your favorite painting program (Photoshop, Fractal Painter, PaintShop Pro, and so on.). There are other free plug-ins that are versions of Texporter, and they can be used in a similar fashion.

You might wonder why it is necessary to go back into a paint program when you have tools such as UVW Unwrap available. It is easy to make a texture unusable by stretching it too far to get the proper image elements to line up with the geometry. When stretching happens the texture should probably be repainted.

As you can see in Figure 18.30, a simplified map of where the texture will fall on the model can greatly assist in the painting process. A good way to do this in Photoshop is to make another layer above the Texporter output. The opacity of the new layer can be adjusted so artists know exactly where they are painting in relationship to the model.

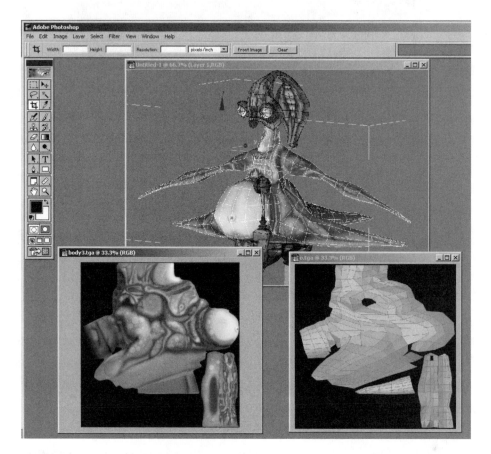

Figure 18.30   Texporter output from 3ds max 4 has been brought into Photoshop with the original painting of the skin.

Using Other Texturing Tools

There are other commercial tools available for the texture artist that can greatly enhance the look of your scenes; you should consider them if there is room in the budget and if the results must be first-class.

3D paint programs such as BodyPaint 3D (http://www.maxon.net/usa/index.html), DeepPaint 3D (with Texture Weapons, http://www.us.deeppaint.com/dpaint/deep_paint_home.htm), and Zbrush (http://pixologic.com/) can make the complicated task of painting on 3D surfaces somewhat easier.

Remember that these tools can make a great artist's job easier, but they are just another layer of complexity for a beginning artist. Additional tools aren't replacements for lack of facility in basic real-time texturing, and should be considered only after complete comprehension of the tools that are available with 3ds max 4.

Preparing for Export

After your models are completely textured, you still need to do a little work before exporting to the target application.

First, you should save a copy of the scene as a reference. This leaves all your models in a state that can be easily edited. Using the copy, you reset the transforms for all the objects in the scene. This "burns in" any transforms that you (or the modeler) have made in the scene.

3ds max 4 figures out where objects are by first determining where the object was created and then figuring out how much it was moved, rotated, or scaled. Although this is an invisible activity in 3ds max 4, a game engine can easily become hopelessly confused. Most engines ignore the transforms, placing objects in strange positions all over the scene.

The easy way to reset the transforms is to use the Reset XForm utility (found in the Utilities section of the Command Panel). It consists of a single button that should be pushed when all the objects in the scene have been selected. A way to make sure that the reset has taken is to look in the Track View of the object in question. If you go to the Transform heading, you can see the Position, Rotation, and Scale headings. Of these, Rotation should be zero, and Scale should equal 100%.

Next, collapse all the Stacks for each object (by right-clicking the stack in the Modifier panel and selecting Collapse All). The Collapse utility enables collapses to Multiple Objects as a mesh. Make sure that you don't have any spare splines left in the scene, or they also will become meshes.

Using the exporter of your choice, and write the file. Consult with the programming team to get the settings for your application.

Finally, archive the scene by choosing File/Archive. This process automatically collects every texture map used and places it neatly into the archive, along with a convenient file listing and a copy of the current scene. Using Windows Explorer and your favorite archive utility (such as WinZip), add the exported file to the archive that was built by 3ds max 4.

This produces a handy package with all the necessary information, even if you have to go back and edit your textures.

Summary

If the proper procedures are followed, real-time texture mapping can be a straight-forward exercise. Proper communications with the programming team and the art director can keep the redos to a minimum. Because you, as the texture artist, have maintained proper fallback positions, any aesthetic changes that need to happen as the game comes together can be made as painless as possible.

Many prerendered 3D artists love to brag about how many polygons their scene has. The real-time artist looks with pride on work that uses the fewest machine resources, and makes the programmers look as if they know what they're doing!

Here are some tips to remember when working with textures for real-time applications:

- Resist the urge to zoom ahead by slapping on textures. Take the time to plan your directory structure, naming conventions, and archive files.
- Be creative in the way that you use bitmaps. If a model in the scene is seen from only far away, a mottled gray can serve as old metal, concrete, or calcified slime. Avoid adding extra bitmaps when a currently loaded bitmap will serve the purpose.
- Don't be overly sensitive when programmers harp at you about seemingly inconsequential details. Sloppy models and textures can bring a game engine to its knees; it's always best to do it right the first time, even if it takes a bit longer!
- Be careful about leaving unassigned (default) materials and sub-materials. Some game engines expect to see a true material assignment, and aren't happy when they don't get the proper material.

- Bump mapping can look great, but can cause excessive shimmering because of the way that the surface normals are facing—and the shimmering can be difficult to track down. If your bump-mapped textures are sparkling, try turning down the intensity or removing the bump map.

- Try to create a basic material that has all the right attributes, and copy it to all of the Material Editor slots. This helps keep you from accidentally adding a material that will cause the game engine to choke.

Part VI

Animation

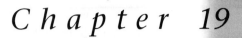

Chapter 19

Camera Matching

by Adam Holmes

Camera Tracker is a tool within 3ds max

4 that enables you to extract 3D camera

data from film or video footage. You can

add CG elements into your footage, and

they appear to be a real part of your scene. With camera tracking, you can add your new skyscraper design to an empty parking lot scene, add digital props to a set that lacked detail in the original footage, or—as in this chapter—place an animated character into a live action scene.

Camera Tracker and the associated Camera Matcher tool were part of 3ds Max 3, and no new features were added to it in max 4. We created this project to use a wide variety of max tools, which will give you broad exposure to max as a whole.

In this chapter, you learn how to

- Import background video footage and create matching geometry to represent real-world objects.
- Create tracking points to match objects in the live action footage.
- Batch-track and match-move to assign the tracking data to the camera.
- Edit tracking data and manage errors to clean up the animation.

With any complex tool, there is a lot of room for user error. You can achieve different results from subtle variations in the way you set up the scene. Because this tool reads motion off the moving pixels in the video footage and the video is not perfect quality, the adjustments you make to the tracking objects that read the pixels are what affect the final camera motion. Some trial and error is necessary.

If you correctly follow the steps in this chapter, you should get excellent results. The human eye detects very subtle movement, and it's usually easy to tell when motion doesn't look natural. The line between "acceptable" errors in the motion and what is just plain bad is up to you.

The footage you're about to work with was shot with the intention of adding the Jester character you created in Chapter 9, "Organic/Character Modeling Using the Patch Method for Broadcast/Film." We added trackable dots to the box and table in the scene, using small brightly colored tape dots and filling in a small black circle on the dot with a felt pen. We then recorded precise measurements of the scene, using a good old-fashioned measuring tape, to record where the dots were in relation to the lower-left edge of the table, as seen from a top-down view.

The scene was shot with a small handheld DV camera because we wanted the look and feel of a home video. Unfortunately, this can make extracting the camera movement more difficult. In this chapter, you get a sense of what it takes to complete one shot of camera tracking and gain a better appreciation for the teams of people it takes to do hundreds of shots for feature films.

Play the rendered video clip tracked_scene.avi to see a test render of the tracked footage with the animated Jester. This will give you an idea of the final result and what you're attempting to do in this chapter. A still image from the footage is shown in Figure 19.1.

Figure 19.1 A still image from the rendered video clip.

Exercise 19.1 Setting Up the Scene

First, you need to re-create the real scene in 3ds max. Camera Tracker relies on the measurements we took to accurately match the camera motion. We decided that the lower-left corner of the table (as seen from a top view) would be our zero mark for these measurements. It doesn't matter where the zero mark is, as long as we have one and record all the measurements based on that zero mark. That zero mark will be represented in 3ds max as coordinate 0,0,0 in world space.

Camera Tracker needs at least six features in the video to track to be able to extract the camera data. At least two of those features need to be non-coplanar with the others—for example, four on the ground and two elevated, or three on one wall and three on another. Tracking points can be intentional ones, such as the yellow dots we placed in the scene, or corners of tables and windows, and definable patterns on objects in your scene.

Note

For maximum match accuracy, you should use as many features as you can and select the features that are distributed as widely as possible over the scene. If you choose features that are too close together, you won't get a good track. Additionally, the tracker works best with features that have good contrast to their surroundings and are easily seen from frame to frame. This means you can get inaccurate motion data if a tracking feature in your scene is too similar in color or contrast to its surroundings, or is covered and cropped by camera movement.

We avoided problems with bad contrast in the scene by placing yellow dots on the table and on the present box. Some dots disappear behind other objects or are out of the frame, but it's all part of the challenge of creating this effect. These dots need to be painted out (roto-scoped) later using combustion, discreet's compositing and paint program, or another similar program.

1. Start a new max scene. Because we measured the points in the scene to track in inches, you need to set up the scene's units to feet with fractional inches.

2. From the Customize drop-down menu, select Units Setup. Check US Standard, select Feet w/Fractional Inches, and select ¼ for the fraction.

    Next, you're going to create CamPoints, which are helper objects, to represent the yellow dots in the footage.

3. To create CamPoints, select Create Panel/Helpers. In the pull-down menu, choose Camera Match, as seen in Figure 19.2. Place 10 CamPoints in the scene.

    It doesn't matter where you place the CamPoints because you'll be moving them to the exact coordinates specified in the grid reference later. You always need a zero point reference when you do your real-world measurements. CamPoint01 is your zero point, and guess where that point goes? If you said 0,0,0 you're on your way!

    This point is the leftmost point near the bottom of the table, if you were looking at it from the top view. Of course, it doesn't matter where your zero reference point is, just that you measure all the other points *relative* to that zero point. (Sorry for pounding this into your head, but it's one of the most important aspects of the camera tracking process.)

    We conveniently spaced the points on the table in a regular grid, and placed three dots on the birthday-present box to comply with the non-coplanar rule of tracking. (How else can the tracker determine the height of the camera?).

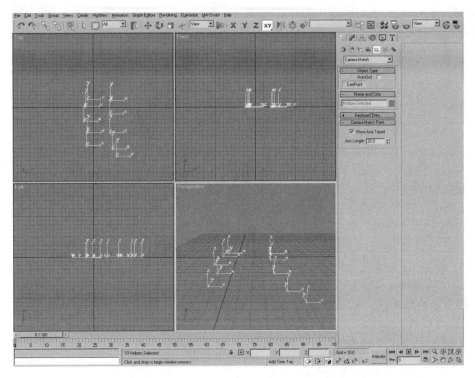

Figure 19.2   Camera Match, from the Create Panel/Helpers pull-down menu.

4. Use the new transform type—located at the bottom of the application, on the right side, just below the timeline—to position the CamPoints at the following locations:

Point	X	Y	Z
1	0	0	0
2	1' 0"	0	0
3	2' 0"	0	0
4	0	1' 0"	0
5	1' 0"	0' 10"	0
6	2' 0"	0' 10"	0
7	2' 0"	1' 8"	0
8	1' 7"	1' 5 ¾"	0' 5 ¾"
9	1' 4 ¾"	1' 9 ¾"	0' 5 ¾"
10	2'	1' 8"	0' 5 ¾"

Note

It might seem strange entering the fraction ¾, but because you're using fractional units of ¼, max expects each fraction to be entered with 4 in the denominator. If you type **1' 5 ½"**, it is converted to **1' 5 ¾"**. That throws out all the years of the "reduce that fraction" instruction from grade school, but if you're like me, most of that math stuff vacated your brain a long time ago.

Now you need to create the table and present box. These objects will be good visual indicators of how well the tracking is working, and they will work as matte/shadow objects so the character can cast realistic shadows onto the scene. Other objects, such as the cups and plates, should be modeled for even more realism of the shadows.

5. Create the table out of a Box primitive, with the following dimensions and location:

> length: **5' 0"**
>
> width: **2' 6 ¼"**
>
> height: **0' 1"**
>
> location: X **0' 11 ¾"**, Y **1' 6 ¾"**, Z **0' –1"**

6. Create the birthday present out of another Box primitive with the following dimensions and location:

> length: **0' 10"**
>
> width: **0' 8"**
>
> height: **0' 8"**
>
> location: **1' 7"**, **1' 5 ¼"**, **0**
>
> rotation: **Z 27.5**

7. Put an Edit Mesh modifier on the box and bevel the top for the final touch, as in Figure 19.3. In Poly Sub-Object mode, bevel the top face down to make it look like an open box without the lid.

If you don't have a lot of time, load the max file campoints_table.max, found on the accompanying CD-ROM. This file has all the CamPoints in place and the table and birthday present boxes inserted. Now you can continue with the next steps.

You need to load the footage into the viewport. I recommend copying the Footage folder from this chapter to your hard drive, because you'll get much better performance displaying the background images.

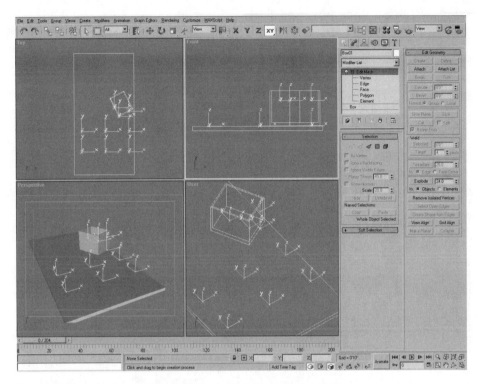

Figure 19.3   The box with an Edit Mesh modifier and a beveled top.

8. Create a free camera and position it in the scene to roughly match the view of the real camera. View one of the images from the Footage folder for a rough idea. (You can use the View Image File command from the File menu. It doesn't have to be perfect.) Make one viewport the active camera view.

9. With the camera viewport active, from the Views pull-down menu, choose Viewport Background (or use the keyboard shortcut Alt+B). Under Background Source, choose Files.

10. Navigate to the Footage folder on your hard drive and select the take01_000 .tga file. Check Sequence, and then choose Open. Match the Viewport Background settings to those shown in Figure 19.4.

Note

When the Image File List Control dialog box appears, click the Include Image Path check box. This adds the Windows path to your image path list in max, and you won't be prompted again for the location of these images.

Now you need to make sure the rendering output matches the footage size. Otherwise, the final render won't look right; more importantly, the Camera Tracker will fail to correctly analyze the motion.

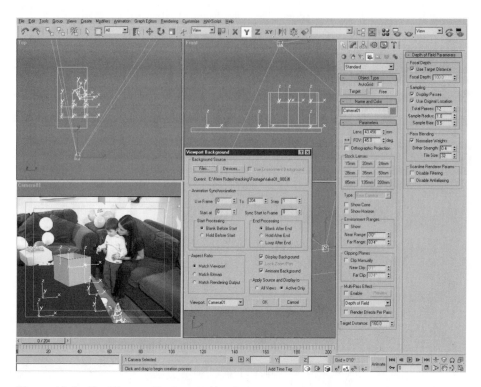

Figure 19.4   The Viewport Background settings.

11. Go to the Render Scene dialog box (or press F10). Choose the NTSC D-1 Video from the Output Size pull-down menu and click the 720×486 preset.

12. Right-click on the word Camera01 in the camera viewport and select Show Safe Frame. If it is already checked, leave it as is.

Try to position and rotate the camera to match the angle and field of view of the footage. Tough, isn't it? Imagine doing that for every frame of the animation. As much as you might think setting up tracking scenes like this is tedious and hard, it's much harder to do it by hand!

You're ready to jump into tracking. Be sure to save your work.

Exercise 19.2   Using the Camera Tracking Utility

In this exercise, you learn how the basic operations of the Camera Tracker work as you import the video footage and add motion tracking points that will read the motion of the pixels and generate the camera data.

1. In the Utilities panel, click More and select Camera Tracker from the list.

It's a good idea to add the Camera Tracker to the list of buttons in the Utility panel for easier access.

2. In the Move File rollout, click the None button and find the take01_001.ifl file that was created when you loaded the sequence into the background. Then click Display Movie.

3. Change the Deinterlace setting to Odd, as shown in Figure 19.5.

This setting blends one field of video into both fields and makes tracking fast-moving scenes more accurate.

Figure 19.5   Set Deinterlace to Odd .

4. Turn on Fade Display.

I like using the Fade Display option. This decreases the move image's opacity, which makes visualizing the motion trackers much easier.

 Note

If you haven't already done so, it's a good idea to expand the Command panel by 2 or 3 widths, because there are a lot of rollouts in the Camera Tracker. This great new feature in 3ds max 4 eases the pain of scrolling menus.

To expand the Command panel, grab the left edge of the panel (where it meets the viewports). Hold down the arrow cursor that appears and drag it to the left to increase the size of the panel.

5. Under the Motion Trackers rollout, choose New Tracker.

When you do, you'll get a set of two boxes, which represent the tracking gizmo. The inner box is the target feature image sampler. You generally want this box very tight around the feature image you're tracking, leaving just a few pixels surrounding it. The outer box represents the search bounds, or the furthest the feature image can travel on a per-frame basis. The max move/frame spinner also controls this setting. The search bounds box size can vary depending on the feature you're tracking, but the larger the search bounds, the more area the tracker has to search, and this can increase the calculation times.

6. Make sure Resample on Error is checked.

The implications of nonspherical tracking points that change their shape every frame with a change in camera perspective create the need to have error checking tools. Resampling on error means that when a motion tracker can't find a set of pixels similar enough to the previous frame, it resamples the pixels and uses that new sample to track to.

This enables the tracker to report errors, based on the values in the Error Thresholds rollout (to be discussed later). If it does find an error, the tracker backs up to the last good tracked frame and creates a keyframe. The tracker then samples a new feature image at that frame and uses it to track subsequent frames. If the feature image is changing drastically throughout the footage, the tracker can't always keep up and manual adjustments become necessary.

7. Set Subpixel Tracking to ⅛.

Note

You generally get a more accurate track when you use Subpixel sampling. Images can shift very subtly per frame, and when the tracker looks for pixel boundaries to lock onto, you can get noisy tracking data. The limited resolution and compression of video can create noisy data very easily when the trackers shift slightly per frame, even when there's no camera movement. By using Subpixel sampling, the software up-samples the image to add pixels within pixels. You can then position the tracker in the center of the pixel of the feature you're tracking, for improved accuracy. Be warned—this nice feature has a performance cost, so stick with ¼ or ⅛ for most tracking jobs.

8. Click in the Movie window and move tracker 1 to the leftmost dot on the present box, as shown in Figure 19.6.

9. Press the I key repeatedly to zoom all the way in to the image until it won't zoom anymore.

By pressing the I key repeatedly, you automatically zoom in to the tracker point that's active. Press the letter O key to zoom out.

Figure 19.6   The Movie Window clicked and tracker 1 moved to the leftmost dot on the present box.

 Tip

> If the keyboard controls don't seem to be responding, make sure you've clicked in the movie window and clicked on a tracking gizmo. If you're still not getting any response, close the window and reopen it.

10. Move the tracking gizmo and you'll see that you have eight snap points vertically and horizontally inside a single pixel.

11. Position the tracker in the center of the dot on the present box. Resize the feature image box (the inner gizmo) to closely encompass the dot. Shrink the search bounds box a bit.

12. Make sure the tracker is on, which is indicated by an X next to the name in the Motion Trackers rollout.

13. Open the Movie Stepper rollout. Turn Feature Tracking on by clicking the Off button, and click the >10 button.

    This analyzes forward 10 frames. You'll begin to see a trajectory line created (controlled by the Show track check box).

14. Click the >> button to analyze all the frames.

     You also can type a specific frame in the Movie Frame box to process to. To halt the process, press Esc or right-click the mouse.

     If all goes well, this point should track just fine to the end of the clip. You can even interactively zoom in and out of the movie frame as it's calculating the track, using the I and O keys .

Tip

If you're working on a slower machine, you can speed up the tracking solution by turning off the Show track check box or closing the movie window.

Now it's time to add two more trackers.

15. Make sure the settings for each new tracker match tracker 1 (subpixel tracking). Position tracker 2 on the center-tracking dot on the present box.

16. Position tracker 3 on the right side of the present box.

17. Scale the inner gizmo to tightly match the size of the tracking dots.

18. Turn the tracker 1 off in the Motion Trackers rollout and return to frame 0 in the Movie Stepper rollout.

19. Display the movie, if you closed it, and turn on the Show track option, as shown in Figure 19.7.

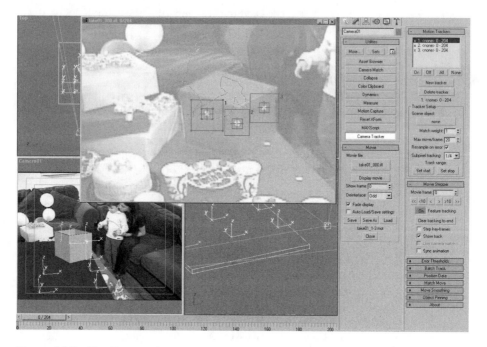

Figure 19.7   The Show track option turned on.

20. Now you can solve trackers 2 and 3. Make sure Feature Tracking is on and click the >> button.

You'll see little green boxes along the track path that's displayed. New keys are created when the tracker needs to update the feature image it's tracking—that is, when it detects a substantial change in that feature image. You can create keyframes manually just by resizing a gizmo or repositioning it.

Note

Tracker 3 will have some problems around frame 60, because the child's head covers the tracking mark. Tracker 2 might have jumped around frame 63, but could correct itself, depending on the size of your tracking gizmos. As mentioned before, you can get varying results depending on where you place your trackers and how big they are in relation to the pixels you're tracking, so your errors might be different than the ones I had.

21. Press Esc or right-click to halt the process.

22. Open the Batch Track rollout and click the Check Status button, which will give you an error report.

Note

The error report will show something like

```
3 @ 60, jd: 11.0
```

What is this computer mumbo-jumbo? It's quite simple—and helpful when you know how to read it.

The first number (3) is the tracker number, @ 60 is the frame in which the error occurred, and jd refers to the Jump Delta, which is the difference between the average movement of the feature being tracked for the preceding five frames and the jump in the current frame. If it's larger than the current threshold, you can get an error. Basically, the image is moving too fast for the tracker to keep up with the current Jump Delta settings. In the Error Thresholds rollout, you see the three rules that the tracker follows. Increase any of these numbers and it increases the slop factor when solving the track. The errors reported when you press Check Status are good guidelines for reducing errors while tracking. I had better luck increasing the Jump Delta to 7, but for these simple errors, adjust them manually.

Match Error (ME) refers to the percentage of difference in the feature image in the current frame and the image it's trying to match from the previous keyframe, so .05% is the difference allowed before it reports an error. Variance Delta (VD) works with Match Error to measure RGB variance in the target feature image and the current best match (at the current frame) as allowed by the Match Error threshold. If either of these values is too small, the tolerance for matching the ever-changing tracking dots will be too small and tracking will halt. I didn't adjust these values, because I never had any ME or VD errors. If you do, simply make these values one number higher than the one reported in the error and retrack the bad frames. If you have tracking features in other scenes that change RBG values greatly, increase these thresholds to compensate (adding more slop factor to the solution).

continues ▶

Tracker numbers in the Incompletes list of the Batch Track rollout means that all the frames for those trackers haven't been calculated. You can click the Complete Tracking button to track the remaining frames for all incomplete tracking points. If you click on an error in the error box, the movie frame jumps to that error and centers and selects the tracker in error.

23. Type **60** in the Movie Frame number box to go to the frame where the child's hand covers the tracking dot. Choose tracker 3 and click Clear Tracking to End.

This erases the bad data from this point.

24. Toggle back and forth between frames 59 and 60 to see how much the dot is moving (well, it's actually the camera that's moving). It's not much, but you still need to move the gizmo to compensate.

25. Click in the movie window and select tracker 3. Zoom in by pressing the I key and move the tracker into position, as shown in Figure 19.8.

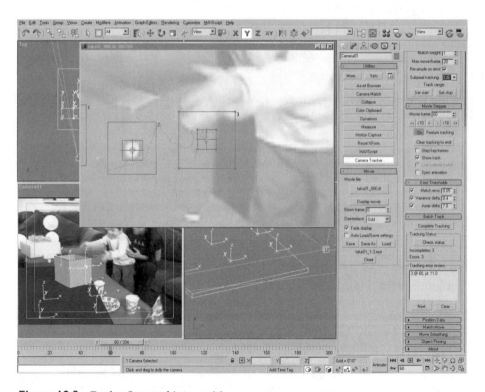

Figure 19.8   Tracker 3 moved into position.

Warning

Don't move a tracker when Feature Tracking is off. Doing so erases tracking data between the frame you move it to and the next keyframe, causing you to have to resolve that section.

26. Go to frame 61, and make another manual adjustment. Notice how you're adding keys (indicated by the green boxes).

27. Manually adjust frames 62 and 63. Now click the >10 button to solve the next 10 frames.

You still might see errors. Go back and move the tracker on those frames, and keep clicking the >10 button to test 10 frames at a time. At around 83, you should be able to click the >> button to solve to the end of the animation, as in Figure 19.9.

When manually adjusting trackers in the Movie window, it might be visually easier to have the Fade Display option off.

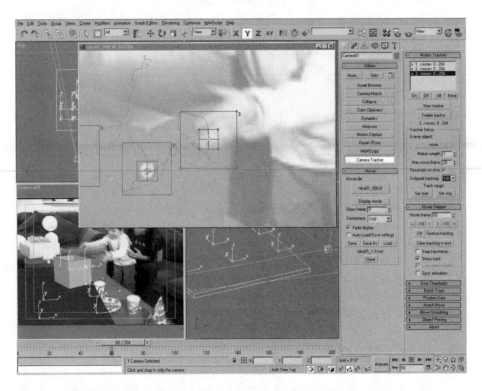

Figure 19.9   Click the >> button to solve to the end of the animation.

28. Check tracker 2 for errors that will have to be corrected by hand, repeating the procedures described in the previous steps.

Now would be a good time to save the tracking data.

29. In the Movie rollout, make sure Auto Load/Save Settings is checked, and click Save.

This names your motion data the same as your movie IFL file. When you load the IFL file again later, you'll get the tracking data associated with it automatically. You can always turn off this feature and save the data as a different name.

 Note

If you want to skip all these steps or start from a file that I created, load the take01_1-3.mot file from the accompanying CD-ROM, which contains the first three trackers and all the corrections made.

Now you're going to create three more trackers.

30. Put tracker 4 on the dot that's on the right edge of the table, tracker 5 on the dot in the middle of the table, and tracker 6 on the dot toward the middle bottom of the image, as shown in Figure 19.10.

You're going to track these one at a time to make error correction less confusing.

31. Turn off all trackers except tracker 4 in the Motion Trackers rollout.

32. Make sure Feature Tracking is on and the Movie Frame is set to 0. Click the >> button to solve. Press Esc as soon as you see an error.

I had errors from about 130 on, though very slight. I wanted to reduce the noise in the subtle motion by advancing frame by frame and making small adjustments to the tracking gizmo.

33. Click Check Status to see what kind of errors you have, if any, and adjust the thresholds accordingly before continuing to solve the track. You shouldn't have to do much tweaking of these numbers.

34. When you are satisfied with tracker 4, turn off that tracker, save your MOT file, and move on to tracker 5. Run the track and manually fix errors. Remember, you also can increase or decrease the tracking gizmo sizes, per frame if necessary.

35. Keep clicking the >10 button to see whether your adjustments allow the tracker to keep moving forward accurately.

This should speed you along without a ton of manual adjustments.

We've saved the best for last: tracker 6. If you've been watching it, you can see that it actually goes out of the frame at frames 50 and 84 (again, your errors might be different).

Figure 19.10   Trackers 4, 5, and 6 placed on the image.

36. Manually adjust the tracker for these errors. On the frames where the dot you're tracking goes off the screen, shrink the inner gizmo vertically and move the entire tracker lower in the frame (you can never move it off the movie image). Do your best to match the tracker frame by frame to the dot when it's offscreen.

37. When you think you're done, click Check Status in the Batch Track rollout again and correct any outstanding errors. If you have incompletes, click Complete Tracking to finish tracking over the range of frames. This could introduce more errors, so keep clicking Check Status to see.

    When you've corrected all the trackers, you might want to do one last visual check and play through the scene every frame or every 10 frames. Turn off Feature Tracking and click the > and >10 buttons to advance. If Step keyframes is checked, you'll jump between keyframes of the selected tracker. This is tedious, but it's the only way to ensure you have the best tracking data.

38. Save your MOT file again or load the take01_1-6.mot file from the accompanying CD-ROM, which is the data I generated.

Whew! You made it. That was definitely the toughest part of this whole process. To summarize, you learned how to create and assign motion trackers to the video footage, track them over time, interpret and correct errors, and manually adjust the trackers. This is a process that can be done over and over to generate more accurate data. Save new MOT files and they can be used in the following exercise to test different camera motions.

Exercise 19.3   Match Moving

The next stage in camera tracking is match moving, whereby the 3D camera motion is extracted from the tracking data and the CamPoints you placed in the scene.

First, you must link each tracker with its corresponding CamPoint. Do this in the Motion Trackers rollout.

1. Select the first tracker from the list, click the None button (in the Tracker Setup/Scene Object section), and select the corresponding CamPoint in the max viewport. Continue to do this for all five remaining trackers.

Note

If you need only 6 points in the video for generating the tracking data, why put 10 in the scene? You want to make sure there are enough trackable points visible in the scene for the duration of the clip. If a point you want to use had been obscured for half the clip, you could track that point, turn it off when it's obscured, and track a replacement point for the rest of the scene. Ideally, you want the same points tracked throughout the entire scene, but that's not always going to happen, so be sure you have placed and measured backup points. You also might want to try different camera moves and angles, so different tracking points will be used for different angles.

2. Open the Match Move rollout. This rollout contains the controls for generating the camera data.

   If you didn't create a camera earlier, now's the time.

3. In Create Panel/Cameras, select Free Camera. Place it anywhere in your scene.

   You need a free camera because Camera Tracker doesn't generate data for a camera target. A camera target is basically a node with a special look-at constraint built into the camera. Many people design custom camera rigs by using a target or free camera and linking it to other control nodes for special camera moves. In the case of Camera Tracking, the trackers are generating only position and rotation data for the camera and not a target, thus all we need is a free camera.

4. Go back to the Utility panel, and in the Match Move rollout, click the None button.

5. Select the camera in the scene. Make sure all the check boxes are checked under Match and that Frame count is set to **205**. Turn off Animate Displays (animating the max viewport displays can really slow down this process, so leave it off). Turn on Generate Keyframes, as shown in Figure 19.11.

Figure 19.11   Make sure Animate Displays is turned off and Generate Keyframes is turned on.

6. Finally, press Match Move and watch for any error windows that appear.

Note

If you get a constant error for every frame, there are a few things to check:

- Make sure the Render Output resolution is set to NTSC D-1 720X486 (adjust this if you're using video footage with a different size and aspect ratio).

- Under Batch Track, click Check Status again. If there are any incomplete trackers, click Complete Tracking. Other tracking errors are really irrelevant, unless you notice a tracker moving off its desired point in the footage.

- Double-check the trackers by turning them all on in the Motion Trackers rollout; and then under Movie Stepper, check each frame using the frame controls. Make sure Feature Tracking is off, unless you intend to make a manual tracker adjustment.

If you follow all the steps correctly, you shouldn't get any errors. If you still are having problems, do a test by loading the take01_1-6.mot file from the accompanying CD-ROM into the Motion Tracker; select the camera from the Match Move rollout and click Match Move.

Tip

Sometimes the motion tracker's display isn't correct, and after loading a MOT file you won't see the tracker names displayed. Toggling All and None in the Motion Trackers rollout can fix this.

Note

The reason we match-moved all the parameters for the camera is that we didn't have the camera on a tripod, and we didn't accurately measure any of the camera's lens settings, such as Field of View (FOV). If the camera had been on a tripod and just a panning move was shot, we could turn off everything but the FOV and Pan. The following is a technical description of the Match options:

FOV. Camera FOV (Field of View). This value changes depending on the lens you use or whether you zoom the lens.

Pan. Rotation about the local camera Y-axis.

Tilt. Rotation about the local camera X-axis.

Roll. Rotation about the local camera Z-axis.

Dolly. Movement along the local camera Z-axis.

Truck-H. Movement along the local camera X-axis.

Truck-V. Movement along the local camera Y-axis.

7. When the match move is complete, change your Perspective viewport to Camera01 and watch the animation. To have the background image update as you play, turn off Real Time in the Time Configuration dialog box, and make sure Update Background While Playing is checked on the Viewports tab of the Preference Settings dialog box, as shown in Figure 19.12.

   I also created a preview render of the background, geometry, and helpers (CamPoints) in wireframe rendering. To create your own, you must assign the footage to the Environment background.

8. In the Rendering pull-down menu, choose Environment. Click the None button under Environment map and choose Bitmap from the list. Locate the take01_000.ifl file in the Footage folder.

Now you're ready to make a preview or rendering. Cinepack compression is fine to use, and good enough for a rough preview. If you're not short on hard drive space and have a fast enough machine, use uncompressed. The new Divx codec is gaining popularity, because it's fast, produces good quality, and creates small files (not included on the accompanying CD-ROM).

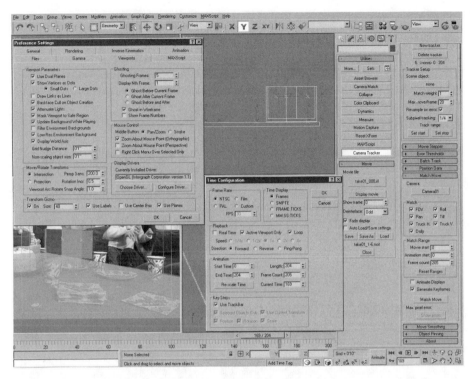

Figure 19.12   Make sure Update Background While Playing is checked on the Viewports tab of the Preference Settings dialog box.

The resulting camera move is a bit shaky and that's what a handheld camera is likely to produce. Camera Tracker has smoothing tools designed to massage the animation curves of the camera. In the next exercise, you learn how to smooth the animation. You don't want to smooth the camera's animation too much, because that will result in a worse match than you already have. The max file 8th_track.max on the accompanying CD-ROM has the scene full-tracked and ready for move smoothing.

Exercise 19.4   Move Smoothing

The first parameter we want to smooth, or rather lock, is the FOV. We want max to figure out the best average FOV setting for this tracking situation where there were no camera measurements.

If you look at the Track View animation curves for the camera, you see that the FOV is animated at one key per frame. There was no zooming involved when we shot the scene. If there were, we would most likely lock the FOV for the static frames using smoothing, and leave the zoom animated.

1. In the Move Smoothing rollout, click the FOV radio button. In the Smooth Type section, select Straight Line Average; in the Smooth Range section, select Match Move Range.

2. Check Re-match after smooth and click the Smooth button to begin the process. The Re-match after smooth option performs the camera match again, after the filter has been applied, and often results in a better match (see Figure 19.13).

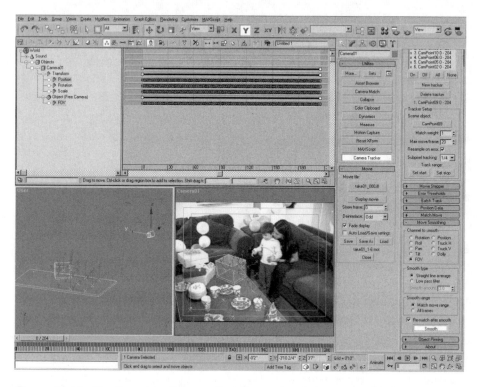

Figure 19.13   The Re-match after smooth option performs the camera match again, after the filter has been applied, and often results in a better match.

3. Create another preview and use the RAM Player (located in the Rendering pull-down menu) to compare the before and after smooth versions.

   Now you're going to smooth the Position channel.

4. First, duplicate Camera01 so you have a backup if the smoothing goes awry.

5. In the Move Smoothing rollout, check Position. In Smooth Type, check Low pass filter and set the amount to **3.0**.

This is a simple filter that will smooth out the position channel of the camera. The higher the smooth amount, the smoother the result. You don't want to smooth it too much, because the video is very shaky and an over-smooth camera wouldn't match.

6. Click the Smooth button. Figure 19.14 shows unsmoothed f-rotation curves, and Figure 19.15 shows over-smooth rotation curves, with a value of 50 used.

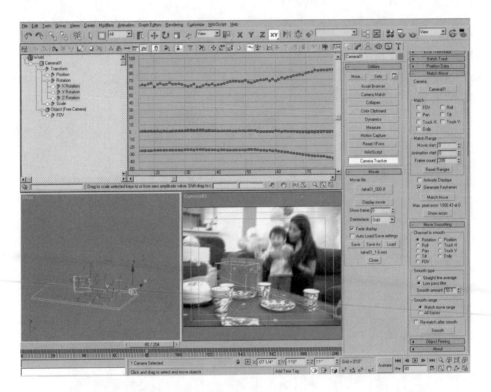

Figure 19.14   Unsmoothed f-rotation curves.

7. If you get an error for frame 0, click OK and continue.

   Frame 0 is altered and is now no good. You can copy the animation from the backup Camera02 or from frame 1 of Camera01.

8. Before creating another preview, change the color of the box and table geometry. This makes comparing the animations in the RAM Player easier.

   You can continue to experiment by copying cameras and applying additional smoothing to other channels, but I found the FOV and Position smoothing gave the best results—not perfect results, but good enough for this quick shot (see Figure 19.16).

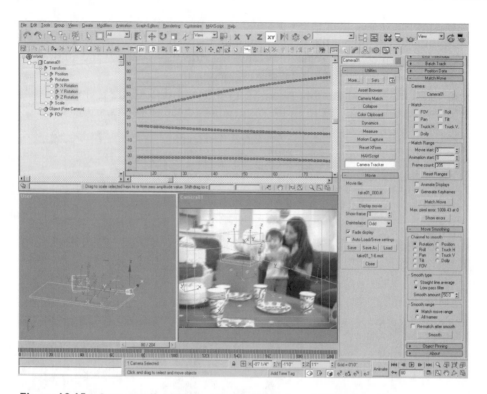

Figure 19.15   Over-smooth rotation curves, with a value of 50 used.

Figure 19.16   The final results.

Summary

This tracking exercise presented some challenges, and I hope you learned something about the complexities of this process. The next step is to pass this scene on to the animators and lighters so they can add to it. In the case of parallel workflow, I would create a separate max scene with an Xref Scene of the camera-tracked scene. That way no one could mess it up, and if I decided to change or modify the track, the animators and lighters could receive instant updates.

With the advent of digital video cameras and fire-wire, you should be excited at the possibilities of creating your own scenes with digital characters inserted.

Here are some tips to remember:

- A common mistake is moving the tracker while Feature tracking is off. A white dashed line appears between keyframes, wiping out the motion and causing you to retrack between those keyframes. Always have Feature tracking on when manually adjusting trackers.

- Use the Step keyframes mode to jump to the exact keys to retrack if you see a white dashed line in the tracking trajectory. Go to the first key in the retrack, turn on Feature tracking, and then type the last key number in the movie frame box to track to that exact frame.

- Other common mistakes include accidentally turning a tracker off, and trying to solve a track or recalculating a tracker by accidentally leaving it on. Double-check the trackers before you waste time calculating.

- Turning off Show track, zooming all the way out in the movie window, or closing the movie window speeds up the calculations.

 Tip

Sometimes the motion trackers display isn't correct, and after loading a MOT file you won't see the tracker names displayed. Toggling All and None in the Motion Tracker's rollout can fix this.

- Close and reopen the movie window if it's not responding to hotkeys or the display is funky.

- Make sure you have a tracker selected in order to move it or zoom in on it.

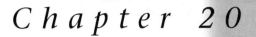

Chapter 20

Animation
Techniques

by Boris Ustaev

In this chapter you go through the steps

that I used to animate the Jester charac-

ter. You also explore some of the new

tools animators can use in 3ds max 4.

Specifically, by reading this chapter you learn the following:

- Working out the timing
- Animating with only the skeleton
- Using the animation tools in max 4
- Animating with the skeleton and the skinned Jester

Animating Is Practicing

Before you get into the details of this project, here are a few tips for experienced modelers who are just getting their feet wet in the art of animation. Animation is not something that can be explained easily in a manual. In fact, the only way that you can become a good animator is by constantly practicing.

The best way to practice is not to go straight into character animation. Start by animating simple things. Try animating inanimate objects and give them life. A good place to start would be with different types of balls—basketballs, tennis balls, golf balls, or bowling balls. Start by animating them rolling down the stairs or bouncing, and see if you can mimic the weight of each type of ball. If a person can recognize by the motion of the ball what type of ball it is, you have done a good job animating it.

Tip

Unfortunately, it is beyond the scope of this book to teach all the principles of the art of animation. For more information on animation techniques, check out the following books:

Cartoon Animation, by Preston Blair, presents the principles of animation as they are applied to traditional cel animation. It's a great book for beginners.

The Illusion of Life, by Frank Thomas and Ollie Johnston, is an in-depth account of the Disney way of animation. This book covers principles that are universal to all animation, whether traditional cel or 3D computer animation.

Timing

Your challenge for this project is to animate the Jester, who is mischievous and destructive. This project is challenging because of the minimal amount of frames available for animation. You have only 204 frames to work with, and out of those frames you can start animating only when the box opens up at around frame 60. This leaves roughly 140 frames, or less than six seconds to animate in. This is a short amount of time to have the character jump out of the box and do something destructive.

The best way to figure out timing is to create a 3D animatic or, if you're drawing, a boardamatic, which means roughly blocking out the animation. You can begin blocking out animation by creating key poses that define the character's motion, something usually done in traditional cel animation.

I began by blocking the animation out very roughly. To see just how rough the animation was, open the blocking.avi file and load it into the max Ram Player. Looking at the AVI file you can see that the motion is nothing fancy, but it is fine for the purposes of blocking out the animation. Using this technique gives a better time frame of what the character is capable of doing in less than six seconds.

For even better results, you can act out the motion and record it on a DV camera. This also helps to plan timing and can give good insight into the Jester's motion. (A MAX file of the animation with primitive motion is available on the CD-ROM that accompanies this book.)

Animating with Bones

The person who rigged the skeleton that I received did a very good job. I had all the control I needed to get the job done. This, of course, takes a little communication between the person who is rigging up the skeleton and the person who is animating it. Because the character was not skinned to the skeleton yet, (it was still being textured), I left the skeleton's initial pose at frame zero; this makes it hassle-free to skin the character afterward.

The next step was to take the rough timings and start animating. Animating with just the skeleton worked out well for two reasons. One reason was speed. All I animated was a set of bones; I had no deformation to slow down the system. The second reason it worked out well was that the bones in 3ds max 4 are three-dimensional and have adjustable wings, giving the animator a good representation of the Jester character. (See Figure 20.1.)

Figure 20.1   The new bones in 3ds max 4 provide a good representation of the Jester character.

Exercise 20.1   Animating the Skeleton with Bones

Start by animating the first foot plant. Keep in mind your animation will probably end up looking different from my animation. Just as in the art of painting, animation is an art where no two animations are alike.

In the file you're about to open, the only element that is animated is the Jester flipping out of the box. In this exercise, you lock the feet of the Jester to the ground as he lands.

1. Open the file named FootPlant.max from the accompanying CD-ROM.

2. Turn on the Animate button and move the time slider to frame 80.

Note

As you proceed with animating the Jester, you must keep in mind a few facts about the controls that were built in Chapter 14, "Organic/Character Model Rigging for Broadcast/ Film." The spline shapes located around the skeleton are used to control most of the movement on the Jester. In this project, you don't animate the skeleton directly. Any spline controls that are not bright yellow, such as the spline shapes named LAnkle and RAnkle and the COM spine shape, can be moved and rotated. The bright yellow spline shapes that look like spheres can only be rotated, with the exception of the ones that are on the wrists of the skeleton, which can be both moved and rotated.

3. Select the spline shape named LAnkle and move it so that it is located right under the skeleton's pelvis and is touching the top of the table on frame 80.

Note

You can use already existing animation on the spline shape named RAnkle for reference. Both of these shapes, LAnkle and RAnkle, control the position of the feet. If, for any reason, you are not sure where to place the feet, open the finishedAnimation.max file and look at it for reference.

After you place the feet in the desired location, you need to adjust the direction of the knee. The knee orientation is not controlled by the spline shapes; it is controlled by the Swivel Angle of the IK goal, which is considered a helper in max.

4. Go to the Display panel of the Command column, and in the Hide by Category rollout uncheck the Helpers check box. You should see all the helpers in the viewport now.

5. Click the new Select and Manipulator icon located to the right of the Select and Scale icon in the toolbar (see Figure 20.2).

Figure 20.2
The highlighted icon toggles the manipulators on and off.

   This invokes certain objects to display their green manipulators. One object you should look for in particular is the IK chain's green Swivel Angle manipulator.

6. Grab the green Swivel Angle manipulator, which looks like a handle located at the hip on either leg's IK chain, and move it.

   As it rotates, you can see that this will help you adjust the direction of the knee.

7. Repeat this procedure to adjust the elbow. The green manipulator for the elbow is located on the shoulder. You usually find green manipulator handles at the root of a given IK chain.

8. If you prefer to adjust the Swivel Angle value instead of the green manipulator, select the IK chain that you would like to modify—in this case, select the helper named IK Chain04. Go to the Motion panel, and under the heading IK Solver Properties, adjust and animate the direction of the knee by changing the value in the Swivel Angle spinner (see Figure 20.3).

Figure 20.3
In the IK Solver properties you can adjust and animate the direction of the knee.

9. Select the bright yellow spline shape named Spine_ control01, which is located on the skeleton's lower back. This spline control is meant only to be rotated. Moving it disturbs the Jester's height. Before you rotate any of the control splines, make sure your coordinate system is set to Local for Rotation. Rotating the

Spine_control01 adjusts the arc of the skeleton's back. Rotate it until his back is arched toward the ground on frame 89.

10. Select the spline control named Lwrist_control. This object enables you to control the position and rotation of the left hand. Move and rotate it at frame 89 until it is flat against the ground and looks like the opposite of the right hand. At this point, the skeleton should look as if it is on all fours (see Figure 20.4).

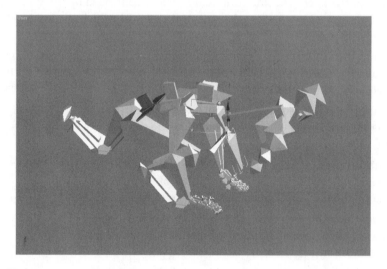

Figure 20.4   Here is what the skeleton looks like after it lands from the flip.

11. If you would like to adjust the fingers, make sure you have the RWrist_ control selected and go to the Modify panel. Using the newly added Custom Attributes, move the desired sliders to curl the fingers (see Figure 20.5).

12. Now you need to lock down the foot. Select the LAnkle object and go to the Mini Track view. Select the position key at frame 80 and, while holding down the Shift key, move the selected key to frame 95.

   This makes a copy of the key at frame 95. Between frames 80 and 95, the left foot should be locked down and should not move for those 15 frames.

13. Scrub the time slider from frame 80 to 95.

   Notice that the foot moves slightly. This is because the tangency curve on the position keys is set to Smooth and needs to be changed to Linear between frames 80 and 95.

   There are a few ways to change the In and Out tangency curves for those position keys. One method is to right-click in any viewport to bring up the Quad menu. Select Track View Selected, which brings up the Track view focused on the selected object. You can now change the position key's tangency curves in the usual manner.

Although this is a common approach, you also can use a MAXScript that comes with 3ds max 4.

14. Select Customize User Interface from the Customize drop-down menu. The Customize User Interface menu should appear. Make sure you have the Toolbars tab panel selected, and click the New button. Type **animation** as the name and click OK. You just created a new menu.

15. Under Category, select MAXScript Tools. Select and drag the Key Manager from the list to your new animation toolbar and exit the Customize User Interface menu. Click the newly created Key Tangent button to bring up the Key Manager (see Figure 20.6).

Figure 20.5
Use Custom Attributes to control the fingers.

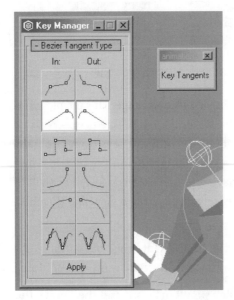

Figure 20.6   Bring up the Key Manager by clicking the Key Tangent button.

16. Select the two position keys in the Mini Track view. Click both the In and Out Linear buttons located second from the top of the Key Manager and click the Apply button. Scrub the time slider from frame 80 to 95 and you will notice that the foot is no longer moving. You just locked the foot for 15 frames.

17. Go to frame 107, select the LAnkle spline shape, and move it forward so the skeleton's foot appears to be sliding forward when you scrub the time slider.

18. Go back to frame 102 and move up the LAnkle spline shape in the Z-axis to animate a footstep. Remember, if you are not sure where to position any of the spline shapes, open the finishedAnimation.max file for reference.

Pat yourself on the back. You've just animated a foot plant. Everything after this is basically a repetition of these steps.

Using Animation Tools

In max 4, there are a number of new tools and interface changes that make it easier to animate. The Mini Track view is one of those, and is located under the time slider. You can control the parameter options of the Mini Track view by right-clicking the mouse button on the Mini Track view (see Figure 20.7).

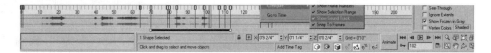

Figure 20.7 The Mini Track view simplifies the animation process.

The modifications include showing a selection range. This enables you to select any number of keys and create a solid bar under the selected keys. With this new selection range, not only can you move keys or move keys from one frame to another frame, but you can also scale the keys along the timeline by selecting either end of the bar. This works when you have multiple objects selected as well. In the past, to do the same thing meant having to go in the Track view and do a little more work for the same result.

During this project, I changed the In and Out range of frames in the Mini Track view via mouse and keyboard commands. Here are some tips on doing this:

- Press Ctrl+Alt and right-click simultaneously, and then move the mouse left or right to increase or decrease the number of frames toward the end of the timeline.

- Press Ctrl+Alt and left-click simultaneously, and then move the mouse left or right to increase or decrease the number of frames toward the beginning of the timeline.

- Press Ctrl+Alt and middle-click simultaneously, and then move the mouse left or right to move the entry frame left or right of the timeline.

It makes a lot more sense when you try it—trust me. Make sure you perform these commands under the time slider where you see the key animations of objects.

Another tool I used in the project was the newly modified Link constraint, formerly known as the Link controller. The nice thing about this tool is it enables you to link from one object to another during the course of your animation. The Link constraint enables you to inherit the position, rotation, and scale of the object you are linking to, usually called the *parent*. (For an example of this, load Link.avi in the max RAM Player and see how the fire truck links to the skeleton's right hand.)

I used this tool in a few places. The most obvious place is the toy fire truck. As the Jester comes closer to picking up the truck, you can tell on frame 142 the truck links to the Jester's right hand, and then on frame 185 it unlinks to be tossed away. Actually, it's not linked to the right hand on frame 186 but is linked to the world, a new option that was added in the Link constraint.

In the next exercise, you learn how to do this.

Exercise 20.2   Linking the Fire Truck

1. Open the file named linking.max and scrub the time slider. Notice that the skeleton is moving to pick up the fire truck but the truck does not move. Your job is to make the truck move when the Jester picks it up.

2. Turn on the Animate button and move the time slider to frame 141.

3. Select the green helper dummy named Master Point. This controls the fire truck's position and rotation. Then go to the Animation menu in the toolbar. Go to the Constraint list and select Link Constraint.

   You should see a dotted line coming out of the Master Point dummy.

4. Click the bright yellow spline shape named RWrist_control located on the right wrist. You just link-constrained the fire truck to the right wrist.

5. Make sure you have the Master Point dummy of the fire truck selected and go to the Motion panel. Scroll down the Command column until you reach Link Params. Go under the Key Nodes option and click the Child radio button.

6. Click the Delete Link button to remove the initial link to the RWrist object.

   You don't really want the link made between these two objects yet. However, when applying a Link constraint from the drop-down menu, max requires you to select an object.

7. Make sure you are still on frame 141 and click the Link to World button.

Using the Link Constraint

Before you go to the next step, examine the use of the Link constraint.

When the fire truck is linked to the world, it is no longer linked to any object in the scene. You can now animate the right hand and the fire truck will not follow. Before this version of max, you always had to be linked to some object in your scene. In the past, the Link constraint was tricky. You had to make sure you created position, rotation, and scale (PRS) keys for both objects—the child and parent—on the frame they were being linked on and off. If you didn't create these animation keys, a strange and unexpected result would take form as you continued animating the child and parent.

With the notion of resolving this unpredictable link problem, max 4 includes several options for the Link constraint. Three major ones are the radio buttons labeled No Key, Key Nodes Child or Parent, and Key Entire Hierarchy (see Figure 20.8). If you have No Key on, it acts like the previous version of max, and will not create any position, rotation, or scale for the parent or child. Toggling on the Key Nodes radio button automatically creates the PRS keys either on the parent or child object, depending on which key node option you selected.

The last radio button, Key Entire Hierarchy, does exactly what it says. It creates keys on the entire hierarchy of the parent or child object, depending on the radio button you selected. This does make it easier, but you still have to create keys manually for at least one of the objects. For example, if you picked the Key Nodes radio button and set it to Parent, any parent linked to the child will have keys created automatically. The child, on the other hand, has no keys unless you create them manually.

Figure 20.8
The No Key, Key Nodes Child or Parent, and Key Entire Hierarchy options help resolve problems of unpredictable links.

8. Go to frame 142 and click the Add Link button, and then select RWrist_control. Scrub the time slider.

   Now the skeleton picks up the fire truck. In the next step, it throws the truck away.

9. Go to frame 185 and click the Link to World button. Scrub the time slider.

   The fire truck stops moving on frame 185 and is suspended in midair.

10. Move the time slider to frame 192, select the master_point of the fire truck, and move it to the left of the screen until the fire truck disappears out of frame. Scrub the time slider.

    The truck is moving all over the place because the tangency curves for the position keys are set to Smooth. You need to change them to Linear as you did in the first exercise.

11. Select the appropriate position keys in the Mini Track view. Click both the In and Out Linear buttons, located second from the top of the Key Manager, and click the Apply button. Scrub the time slider.

The skeleton now throws the truck correctly.

Animating the Clothing

After the Jester was skinned, I realized some things needed to be finished for animation—his clothing, for example. I animated the bones in forward kinematics (FK) to simulate the swaying of cloth. I could have used the new Flex modifier, but for something this simple it wouldn't make any sense. Flex can be slow to work with and can give unpredictable results. For the Jester's face I used the morph targets that were created for me and animated them from the Morpher modifier panel, where I thought they would be appropriate for this project.

Seeing the Jester also helped me fix any objects that were intersecting the character throughout his motion. Just a reminder: Working with the skinned character makes it slow, so you can use the Optimize modifier to reduce the amount of geometry displayed. That up speeds procedures for your computer and you. Don't waste time doing high-resolution renders for motion tests. Do a preview render. It might not be pretty to look at, but it's fast and shows you the motion.

Summary

This chapter takes you through the most important technical steps of animating the Jester in this project, which include creating and editing keys and using the Link constraint. You should now be able to start from scratch with the skeleton and animate it on your own. Have fun with the animation. Don't forget that practice makes perfect.

The max file named FreshStart.max has the skeleton with no animation on it. Take this file and test some animation with the Jester.

Chapter 21

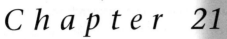

Particle Effects

by Brandon Davis

A *particle system* is a procedural animation tool in 3ds max 4 that enables users to animate large groups of objects by a series of rules and procedures. Unlike the traditional keyframe method of animating objects by interactively adjusting them from pose to pose, procedural animation is automated by the system and defined by a user set of parameters, such as velocity, mass, orientation, and so on. These parameters can be keyframed and are constantly evaluated by the system and applied to the objects or particles in this case. Particle systems are effective at replicating the motion of natural phenomena, such as rain, fire, and smoke. Confused? Think of it this way: Animating a stream of raindrops one by one would be very tedious. However, with a particle system, you can quickly animate hundreds of raindrops by just determining a few parameters and letting the system create the motion.

In this chapter, you explore the available particle tools in 3ds max 4 and how they work. Then you employ particle systems to create two effects: a turbulent, trailing pixie dust effect and a confetti effect. Specifically, this chapter discusses:

- The basic components of particle systems
- Particle classes
- Common particle parameters
- Simple Particles: Spray and Snow
- Super Particles: SuperSpray, Blizzard, PCloud, and PArray
- Special particle maps
- Space warps for particles

Note

One of the first, if not *the* first, uses of particle systems was for the Project Genesis formation shot in the 1982 film *Star Trek II: The Wrath of Khan*. This minute-long shot took the fledgling Industrial Light & Magic computer graphics group nearly six months to complete and was the first fully computer-generated sequence for a feature film. Bill Reeves contributed his particle system fire to the highly procedural project, which was led by Alvy Ray Smith and included other legendary CG pioneers, such as Loren Carpenter, Rob Cook, and Tom Duff. Incidentally, this is the group that would eventually split off in 1986 and become Pixar.

Basic Components of Particle Systems

At the base level, particle systems consist of three basic components: an emitter, particles, and fields. An *emitter* is often a nonrendering object that determines the space where particles are created or born. Some emitters are single points, and others are surfaces or volumes that contain particles. One of the main differences among the particle systems available in 3ds max 4 is the way they handle emitters.

Particles in their simplest form are actually just infinitely small points in space that contain only position and rotation information. Many particle systems offer particle primitives that are geometry types that can be automatically applied to particles. These often are simple shapes, such as spheres, cubes, tetrahedrons, and single polygons. At this level they are often employed for simple effects, such as sparks and rain. Some particle systems can reference complex geometry that is even hierarchically animated. This technique is often used for creating procedural animation for crowds or flocks of objects, such as birds.

Fields are an important component of particle systems that are used to influence a particle from the point of birth to death—essentially the entire lifetime of a particle. Examples of fields are Gravity, Wind, and Deflectors. Some fields' effects are localized to an area of influence, and others are global in scope. By using fields, particle systems can be made to act naturally (smoke and fire) or unnaturally (lasers and tractor beams).

All particles go through the following cycle: birth, life, and death. *Birth* is used to describe the formation of a particle in space. Birth is normally a function of time and quantity. In 3ds max, particles are born at either a variable rate per frame or from a set total. In the case of a total, a particle pool is created based on a value, and the particle count in the scene never exceeds that amount. All particles have a *life* value that determines how long they will be present in the simulation. When this value has been reached, *death* occurs and they are no longer a participant.

Although particles are alive, they can be influenced by fields. For example, Drag may be applied to particles to realistically dampen their motion over time. This is not applied at birth or death, but instead over the course of a particle's lifetime. All three stages can be controlled directly within the particle system. This is where many of the similarities end, however.

Particle Classes

In 3ds max 4, there are three classes of particle systems: Simple, Super, and Third-Party.

Simple Particles systems were the first ones included in Max 1 and these include Spray and Snow. They are considered simple because they contain only a few parameters and are designed for the most basic effects. Spray and Snow are still integrated and interactive, making them a big step up from their ancestors, the AXPs of 3d Studio DOS.

Super Particles systems were added in Max 2 by Yost Group members Eric and Audrey Petersen. This extended particles a bit further and in the process completely decentralized them. SuperSpray, Blizzard, and PCloud are nearly identical, except for the way they emit particles. SuperSpray emits particles from a point in space directionally in a stream that can be spread out conically or thin and wide like a fan. Blizzard emits from an invisible rectangular surface, and PCloud emits from within a geometric volume.

PArray is the only Super Particles system that differs more than any other. PArray emits particles from the geometry of objects and has the most options for determining what those particles are composed of. Unique to PArray is instanced geometry and fragments. Instanced geometry references an object in the scene to use for particles. Examples of such would be complex geometry such as detailed rocks or animated hierarchies such as a bird made up of several objects. Object fragments are created by placing particles on the surface of an emitter object, and then using that object's geometry to create fragments. A simple example would be to generate fragments from a cube. Each triangle polygon forming the cube is detached and becomes particle geometry. Where the particles move, the fragments move. This is a simple method that retains a few parameters to control how many fragments are created and how thick they are. Unfortunately, because they're working exclusively with triangle polygons, their results tend to be synthetic looking.

Third-Party particle systems are easily integrated into 3ds max 4 via its extensible architecture. Most Third-Party particle systems are specialized and operate uniquely compared to one another.

One common production add-on to the existing particle systems in 3ds max is Particle Studio from Digimation, an event-driven particle system that enables a non-linear and flexible particle workflow. In this method of working, particle systems are organized into blocks of events, the timing of which can be determined relatively, absolutely, or by particle age. Oleg Bayborodin (www.orbaztech.com), the developer of Particle Studio, has effectively balanced speed, ease of use, flexibility, and capability into a particle system for 3ds max 4.

Cebas Computer's (www.cebas.com) Matterwaves particle system is unique because it contains bitmap-driven parameters. Users can, for example, use a bitmap applied to emitter geometry to determine the rate of emission. This can be slow to work with, but has its merits. Cebas also recently released its flagship event-driven particle system, Thinking Particles. This is a highly procedural approach, building on the workflow method of Particle Studio—or Side Effects' Houdini, for that matter—but also greatly expanding upon it. My first impressions are that this is an overly complex particle solution, though, it's probably the most capable and flexible currently available to 3ds max users.

Next Limit's (www.realflow.com) RealFlow is a standalone computational fluid dynamics simulator that has hooks into 3ds max 4. Because it treats particles as fluids in a medium and allows for particle-to-particle interaction, RealFlow can simulate substances such as viscous fluids and gasses realistically.

Note

Prior to Max 1 in 1996, particle systems were rudimentary in 3d Studio DOS. Most (if not all) were third-party products, and only a few gave any sort of method of visualization or feedback. The AXP plug-ins tended to be in a small window with a few parameters to describe the particle system. Users had to render frames to see how the particles looked and moved.

Common Particle Parameters

Each class of particle system in 3ds max 4 has a common set of parameters that are used to control aspects of the particle system.

The following sections describe the parameters common to each class of particle system, both Simple and Super.

Simple Particles: Spray and Snow

Spray and Snow share most parameters; Snow particles have rotation parameters and Spray particles do not. The following are parameters for the Simple Particles:

- **Viewport and Render Count.** These parameters control the total number of particles that are emitted over time with regard to viewport display and render display. The main purpose for these related parameters being uncoupled is that the user can work faster in the viewports by displaying only a portion of the total particle count, while still rendering with a full quantity.

- **Drop Size.** This parameter controls the scale of the particle geometry.

- **Speed and Variation.** These are a bit misleading. Speed determines the velocity of the particles at birth, and Variation not only varies the speed value but also implements a sort of spreading pattern, with higher values increasing the spread.

- **Tumble and Tumble Rate.** These are rotational parameters added to Snow. Tumble controls the amount of rotation of the particles and Tumble Rate controls the speed at which the particles rotate.

- **Render Tetrahedron and Facings.** These parameters are the given particle primitives or predetermined geometry for the particles. Tetrahedrons are shaped like simple raindrops, and Facings are square polygons.

- **Start and Life.** These parameters control particle birth and death. Start determines the start frame of particle emission in absolute time, and Life is a relative value that determines how many frames a particle is "alive." Life is relative, because particles are constantly born and emitted, starting on the Start frame and continuing forever, so a particle born at frame 100 with a life of 60 dies at frame 160.

- **Birth Rate and Constant.** These parameters are used to pulse or burst emit particles, a simple method that is expanded by the Super Particles. Birth Rate determines the amount of particles emitted in a given round. When activated, the Constant check box disables the Birth Rate parameter.

Super Particles: SuperSpray, Blizzard, PCloud, and PArray

The Super Particles class of particle systems share many common parameters. In fact, SuperSpray, Blizzard, PCloud, and PArray are primarily differentiated by how they handle emitters. The following are parameters for the Super Particles:

- **Icon Size and Emitter Hidden.** These parameters are cosmetic values that control the size of the emitter icon and determine whether it is hidden or displayed.

- **Dots, Mesh, Ticks, and Bbox.** These parameters are the viewport display methods for particles. Dots vary depending on the viewport display method used (*Heidi dots* are single-pixel and OpenGL dots are much larger). Mesh displays the actual geometry to scale in the viewports, a method that tends to be computationally intensive but still useful. Ticks, like Dots, are constant in size with the exception of being shaped like crosses. Bbox displays the bounding box of the particle geometry. This is often faster than using the Mesh method.

- **Percentage of Particles.** This parameter controls the percentage of actual particles displayed in the viewports. This does not affect the quantity of particles at render time, but is used to speed up display by reducing the number of particles the display has to render.

Particle Generation

The Super Particles class was added in release 2 and builds on the previous particle systems, Spray and Snow. The main difference between the four Super Particle systems is the way in which they emit particles. Common particle generation parameters are as follows:

- **Use Rate and Use Total.** These parameters are the primary methods for controlling the amount of particles emitted. Use Rate determines a variable number of particles that are emitted at each frame. Use Total defines a total quantity of particles that the system can emit over time, the rate of which depends on the emission start and stop time.

- **Speed and Variation.** These parameters control the emission velocity of the particles. Variation controls the percentage at which Speed will be varied on a particle-by-particle basis. You use Variation as a common parameter with many particle systems because it's useful to break up the uniformity of values by adding some randomness to them.

- **Emit Start and Stop.** These parameters are the set frame numbers at which particles will start to be emitted and will stop.

- **Display Until and Life.** These parameters are used to determine when particles will die. Display Until is a rudimentary way of doing this absolutely so that on a given frame all particles will die. Life is like Spray, a relative value determining how many frames a particle will be present after it's been emitted.

- **Size, Grow For, and Fade For.** These parameters control particle geometry scale. Size is a multiplier of scale and has a Variation parameter tied to it to randomize the scale on a particle-by-particle basis. Grow For and Fade For are two parameters that cause particles to grow from a scale of zero to the full Size value and then fade to zero over a given set of frames.

- **Seed.** This parameter is an important random value that controls the uniqueness of particle systems. It's a random number that can be changed using the New button next to it. If multiple particle systems use the same Seed value, they emit particles identically. Use different Seed values to cause variation among particle systems.

Particle Types

The Super Particles class of particle systems shares three main types of geometric representations: Standard, MetaParticles, and instanced geometry. PArray contains a fourth type called Object Fragments.

Standard, MetaParticles, and instanced geometry determine the types of geometry the particles will be displayed as:

- **Standard.** This type offers several particle primitives, such as Triangle, Cube, Facing, and Sphere.

- **MetaParticles.** These are a special type of geometry primitive that is useful in creating amorphous liquid shapes. MetaParticles create spheres at each particle location, and then fuse the geometric surfaces together when their proximity to one another passes a user-defined threshold. When MetaParticles are sparsely spaced they appear as simple spheres, but when packed closely together they fuse into blob shapes. This is computationally expensive and should be used with extreme care.

- **Instanced Geometry.** This is a useful particle type that enables the user to reference separate objects in the scene as particle geometry. For example, a single teapot object can be referenced and will cause instances of the teapot to be emitted as particles. The instanced geometry can also be hierarchically animated, enabling effects such as swimming fish and flocking birds.

Rotation and Collision

All the Super Particles share the same set of Rotation and Collision controls, which specify the speed of rotation and starting angles. Collision is a bit misleading, because it has to do with particle-to-particle collisions only, not with objects in the scene. The following are Rotation and Collision controls:

- **Spin Time and Phase.** These control the amount of frames it takes for a particle to fully rotate, with low values causing faster spinning. Phase determines the starting angles of rotation.

- **Random, Direction of Travel, and User Defined.** These are three methods for controlling rotation. Random rotates the particles on varied axes. Direction of Travel forces the particles to orient themselves in the direction they are traveling, with an optional Stretch value to actually stretch the particle geometry based on velocity. User Defined sets an absolute rotational axis in X,Y, and Z.

- **Interparticle Collisions.** This is a set of parameters to test particle-to-particle collisions. This is computationally intensive and useful only in rare instances. Calc Intervals Per Frame is a parameter for controlling the rate at which the particle collisions are tested. *Bounce* is a percentage of force applied at collision.

Object Motion Inheritance

Object Motion Inheritance controls how much velocity is passed from the emitter to the particles. No motion inheritance causes the particle's speed to control velocity; 100% inheritance causes the full velocity of the emitter to be added to the particle emission speed. This is relevant only to a moving emitter. Object Motion Inheritance is a useful control for adding realism to particle motion. Unfortunately, the default value of 100% tends to confuse people. There are two controls:

- **Influence.** This determines what percentage of the particles is affected.
- **Multiplier.** This determines how much of the velocity is inherited from the emitter. A multiplier of 0 implies no inheritance, and 1.0 passes 100% of the emitter velocity to the particles.

Bubble Motion

Bubble Motion includes another set of parameters that are common to the Super Particles class of particle systems. These parameters are used to impart a wobbling motion to particles. Unfortunately, they aren't particularly intuitive and often require good viewport feedback to properly visualize. There are three main parameters to control Bubble Motion:

- **Amplitude.** This parameter controls the distance at which the particle will wobble away from its original direction.
- **Period.** This parameter controls the cycle time of particle oscillation, which is similar to waveform frequency.
- **Phase.** This parameter is used here similarly as it was with rotation, controlling the initial wobble offset.

Particle Spawn

All Super Particles have common controls for particle spawning. *Particle spawning* is the emission of particles from particles. There are several methods by which particles can be spawned over time:

- **None.** This method causes zero particle spawning.

- **Die after Collision.** This method causes particles to die when they collide with a Deflector space warp.

- **Spawn on Collision.** This method performs the opposite of the previous method, causing particles to be born on collision.

- **Spawn on Death.** This method causes a sort of fireworks effect by creating particle spawns when a particle dies.

- **Spawn Trails.** This method is pretty self-explanatory, causing particles to spawn trails of new particles behind them over their lifetime.

Each of the spawning controls has common parameters used to control the events and the spawned particles:

- **Spawns.** This parameter determines the number of particle spawns that happen over a particle's lifetime.

- **Affects.** This parameter determines the percentage of particles that will produce spawning.

- **Multiplier.** This parameter is a value that multiplies the number of particles spawned at a given event.

- **Directional Chaos.** This parameter is used to vary the direction at which particles are spawned.

- **Speed Chaos.** This parameter is similar to Directional Chaos, but instead varies the speed at which particles are spawned on a frame-by-frame basis.

- **Scale Chaos.** This parameter is similar to Directional Chaos and Speed Chaos, but varies the scale of spawned particles.

- **Lifespan Queue.** This parameter is used to determine several alternate lifetimes for spawned particles. Values are created and stored in the queue and then passed on to spawned particles on an event-by-event basis.

- **Object Mutation Queue.** This parameter works with instanced geometry and causes spawn particles to switch between instanced geometry types referenced in the queue on an event-by-event basis.

Parameters Unique Among Super Particles

As mentioned earlier, the main differences between the Super Particles are the methods used to emit particles. These unique features are described in the following sections.

Blizzard

Blizzard includes the following values:

- **Width and Length.** These are used to determine the size of the rectangular emitter object.

SuperSpray

SuperSpray includes the following values:

- **Off Axis and Spread.** These are two related values that control the angle of emission from a single point in space. Off Axis determines the angle off axis from Z (straight up through the emitter), similar to the elevation of a gun in a turret. Spread controls the angle at which particle emission is varied in a fan direction.

- **Off Plane and Spread.** These are two more related values to control the angle of emission from a point. Off Plane controls the angle of emission rotated around the plane of the emitter, similar to the azimuth of a gun in a turret. Spread controls the conical spread angle along the axis of emission. A value of 180 creates a complete cone shape.

PArray

PArray is unique because it uses geometry for emitters and can explode that geometry into fragments to use as particle geometry:

- **Object-Based Emitter.** This is a pickbutton used to determine which object will be used for emission.

There are several particle formation methods:

- **Over Entire Surface.** This method creates particles evenly over the surface of the emitter geometry. This is the most commonly useful method and thereby the default.

- **Along Visible Edges.** This method snaps particle emission to the visible edges of the emitter object.

- **At All Vertices.** This method restricts emission to the vertices of the emitter object.

- **At Distinct Points.** This method isolates particle emission to a given set of distinct points on the emitter's surface.

- **At Face Centers.** This method emits particles from the centers of all faces on the emitter object.
- **Use Selected Sub-Object.** This method is a check box that applies to all the previous methods. This enables the user to further restrict emission to only the selected sub-objects (faces, edges, verts) of the emitter geometry.

PArray has some unique parameters and methods for creating object fragments for particle geometry:

- **Thickness.** This parameter determines the size of the fragments' extrusion.

The following three methods determine how an object will fragment:

- **All Faces.** This method forces each face of the emitter geometry to be used as a polygonal fragment.
- **Number of Chunks.** This method sets a minimum number of fragments created.
- **Smoothing Angle.** This method controls the number of fragments created based on the angle of the surface normals of the emitter object. The higher the angle, the fewer the fragments created.

PCloud

PCloud is unique because it emits particles from within a volume instead of a surface. There are four methods to define the volume:

- **Box Emitter.** This method is a variable box shape controlled by length, width, and height.
- **Sphere Emitter.** This method is a variable spherical shape.
- **Cylinder Emitter.** This method is a variable cylindrical shape with parameters similar to Box Emitter.
- **Object-Based Emitter.** This method uses selected geometry from the scene to use as a volume emitter.

PCloud has unique particle motion methods:

- **Random Direction.** This method emits particles along random vectors.
- **Enter Vector.** This method uses X,Y, and Z vectors to determine the exact emission direction.

- **Reference Object.** This method uses a scene object's Z-axis as the target direction for particle emission.

Special Particle Maps

There are two special maps designed specifically for use with particles:

- **Particle Age.** This has three slots for maps or colors that can be blended based on particle age. It varies from particle to particle and is applied relatively.

- **Particle Mblur.** This changes the color of the leading and trailing edges of moving particles. It is most commonly used in the Opacity slot of the material, but can also be used in other slots.

Space Warps for Particles

There are lots of space warps that are used as fields to affect particle motion. They can be applied individually or globally—for example, a single space warp can affect several particle systems at once. Space warps for particles are divided into two groups: Forces and Deflectors. Forces affect the motion of particles during their lifetime and Deflectors work as collision objects for particles.

Forces

The Forces group of particle space warps includes the following:

- **Motor.** This is a dynamic force used to impart a torque effect on particles.

- **Push.** This is a simple repulsive force causing particles to push away along the space warp's direction.

- **Vortex.** This is new to 3ds max 4 and causes a special rotational-well effect similar to the vortex of a tornado.

- **Drag.** This is a useful motion dampener that causes particles to slow down a given percentage over time. This dampening effect can be isolated along certain axes.

- **Path Follow.** This forces particle motion to conform to a shape object in the scene.

- **PBomb.** This is another repulsive force but varies in shape. A repulsive force can be applied spherically, cylindrically, or from a plane.

- **Displace.** This is another useful space warp that uses an image or map to cause motion perturbation. It modulates the amplitude of the forces based on grayscale values, with white as full force and black as no force. The extents of the force depend on the shape of the gizmo being used.

- **Gravity.** This is a common variable force that uses Newtonian physics to cause an attraction or repulsion spherically or planar with acceleration.

- **Wind.** This is similar to gravity and works in both Spherical and Planar mode, but adds perturbation controls in the form of turbulence.

Deflectors

There are three basic categories of Deflectors, differentiated by their shape. All three categories include planar, spherical, and universal (object-based) shapes:

- **Deflector.** This is a standard Deflector that has bounce and friction controls, including Deflector, SDeflector, and UDeflector.

- **DynaFlect.** This is a special type of Deflector used in dynamics simulations. DynaFlect Deflectors have the added capability of enabling the user to include particle systems in dynamics simulations. They add physics-based parameters, such as mass, and include PDynaFlect, SDynaFlect, and UDynaFlect.

- **OmniFlect.** This is a variation of Deflectors that adds the capability of both reflecting and refracting particles. OmniFlect Deflectors include POmniFlect, SOmniFlect, and UOmniFlect.

The Project

Normally, particle systems are used in a subset of animation techniques called *effects animation*. With the exception of effects sequences, they are usually created later in the production pipeline when primary object animation has been completed. In the case of the ongoing project within this book they are being added when the camera has been tracked, the scene stand-in geometry has been matched, and the character and objects have been modeled and animated.

Effects animators are specialists similar to the way character animators are, focusing most of their attention on a complex aspect of animation as a whole. Effects animators tend to differ from character animators in their emphasis and approach to the technique of animation. Character animation focuses heavily on communication through motion and is hands-on, and effects animation tends to be more technical in nature. One isn't necessarily more difficult than the other, but their disciplines are different. There is definitely more art in character animation and more science in the production of effects animation. Thus many character animators are less package-specific, and effects animators are often married to their packages because they focus so strongly on their implementation of procedural tools.

The goals for effects animation in the project in this chapter are to create an exploding confetti effect when the box top blows off and the Jester character pops out. These will be instanced geometry particles that linger in the air and slowly fall to the ground, spinning along the way. Another effect will be a trailing pixie dust effect coming off the feet of the character as it leaps out of the box. This also will use space warps to help control the motion of the particles. All the effects will be tied together using Parameter Wiring and Custom Attributes to more easily adjust the effects in the scene.

Exercise 21.1   Setting Units

One of the first things to do with your scene when setting it up for work with particle effects is to adjust the units method. *Units* are the method used to represent values in parameters. This is important when modeling to scale, because you can set the values to real-world units such as decimal feet or meters. However, such units have no relevance to particle values, such as velocity and birth rate. You need to set the units of your scene to generic, which uses standard integer and floating-point values with no real correlation to real-world units.

  1. Select File/Customize/Units Setup. At the bottom of the resulting dialog box, set the radio button to Generic Units, as seen in Figure 21.1.

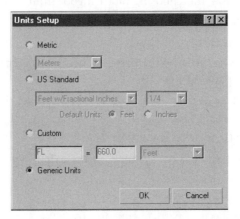

Figure 21.1   Select Generic Units in the dialog box.

Next you use PArray to create a trail of particles from the feet of the character.

2. In the Create panel, choose Particle Systems/PArray.

3. Click and drag anywhere in the Top viewport to create a PArray icon, as in Figure 21.2.

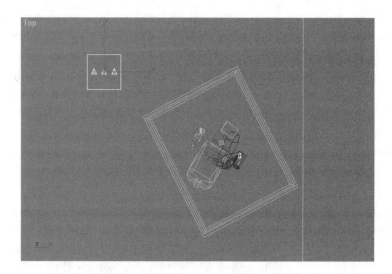

Figure 21.2   Add a PArray icon to the scene in the Top viewport.

There are a few PArray parameters you need to set up.

4. With the PArray selected, go to the Modify panel.

5. In the Basic Parameters rollout, set the Object Based Emitter by clicking the Pick Object button and choosing Bip01 R Foot from the list.

This sets the emitter to the biped's right foot.

6. Set the Viewport Display section to Dots.

This makes it easier to view the particles, because they are going to be represented by tiny pixie dust points.

7. Set the percentage of particles to **100%** so you can see the entire quantity for now.

8. In the Particle Generation rollout, set Speed to **0.1**.

The scale of this scene is pretty small, so the default value of 10 would be much too fast.

9. Set Variation to **25%**.

This varies the speed of particle emission by 25%.

10. Set Emit Start to **60**.

    This is the frame in which particles will first be emitted, when the character jumps out of the box.

11. Set Emit Stop to **96**.

    This is the frame in which particles will stop emitting and is the point when the character first reaches the surface of the table.

12. Set Display Until to **204**.

    This is the frame in which the particles disappear. This might seem pointless, because the particle emission ends at frame 96, but it's good practice to adjust this value from its default of 100 to at least one frame past the end of your animation. It's a common mistake to ignore this parameter, which results in all the particles disappearing at frame 100.

13. Set Life to **90**.

    This gives the particles a lifetime of 90 frames.

14. Set Variation to **5**.

    Unlike the other variation parameters, this one is in frames, not percentages. This causes the particle life value to vary plus or minus 5 frames. This reduces the uniformity of the effect by adding some randomness.

15. In the Particle Type rollout, set the standard Particles to Constant.

    This makes the particle geometry constantly scaled circular points that always face the camera.

16. In the Object Motion Inheritance rollout, set Multiplier to **0.2**.

    This causes the particles to receive 20% of the motion of the emitter—in this case the biped foot. This is important because in the real world when an object is ejected from a moving object, it begins its motion at the same speed as its parent.

17. Scrub the animation by clicking and dragging the time slider.

    You'll see a trail of particles emitting from the right foot of the biped object. Because of the motion inheritance, the particles aren't stationary but actually move with the foot as they're emitted. See Figure 21.3.

There is one problem, however. The particles are emitted too fast. There also needs to be a drag and gravity effect applied to them. This is done through space warps, which you tackle in the next exercise.

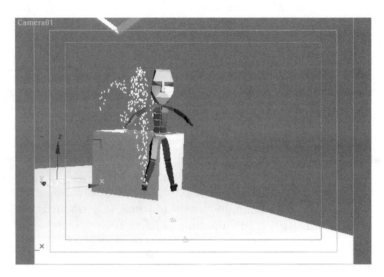

Figure 21.3   PArray particles trail from the right foot of the biped.

Exercise 21.2   Adding a Drag Effect

In this exercise, you add a Drag space warp to cause a dampening effect on the particles' velocity. *Space warps* are nonrendering objects that act as fields in the scene and are accessed through the Create panel like any other object.

1. Go to the Create panel and click the Space Warps button.

2. From the Forces drop-down list, choose Drag.

3. Click and drag a Drag icon into the Top viewport.

4. With the Drag space warp selected, go to the Modify panel.

   All the Drag parameters appear in the Modify panel. There are many for such a simple effect. The new Drag space warp offers much flexibility, including nonlinear and localized dampening, so the effect doesn't have to be uniform (on all axes) or affect the particles globally across the entire scene.

   You need to set a few parameters for this Drag space warp.

5. Set Time Off to **205**.

   Normally this is set to the default value of frame 100, which causes the Drag effect to end at frame 100, in the middle of the animation. It's generally good practice to change Time Off to match the end frame of your animation, which causes the Drag effect to continue until the end of the animation and not turn off inappropriately.

6. Set the Linear Dampening X-axis and Y-axis to **2.0**.

   This sets an equal amount of drag force along the X-axis and Y-axis.

7. Set the Linear Dampening Z-axis to **10.0**.

   This increases the Drag effect along the Z-axis, which prevents the particles from moving too much vertically as they are emitted. They also will be affected laterally in the X-axis and Y-axis, however, but much less. This gives them some freedom to wander. See Figure 21.4.

   The particle system is now bound to the space warp. If you go to the Modify panel with the Parray01 selected, you'll notice an entry in Stack View that shows a Drag Binding.

8. Play the animation by either scrubbing the time slider or clicking the Play button.

The particles are emitted from one of the feet of the biped, but slow down a bit and linger. There's still one more step to control the motion—adding turbulence—which you'll do in the next exercise. By using the Turbulence controls of a Wind space warp you can perturb the motion of the particles slightly as they linger in the air. This breaks up the uniformity of the effect, making it more realistic and natural.

Exercise 21.3   Adding a Wind Space Warp

You create a Wind space warp the same way you create a Drag warp. In fact, the Wind space warp is similar to the Gravity space warp because it has a directional icon showing the vector of the effect.

1. Go to the Create panel, choose Space Warps/Forces, and click Wind.

2. Click and drag in the Top viewport to create a Wind space warp.

3. Bind the particle system to the Wind space warp by selecting the Parray01 particle system.

4. Activate the Bind to Space Warp button with a single button-click.

5. Click and drag from the Parray01 particle system to the Wind space warp icon and release the mouse button.

6. Verify that the space warp is bound by checking Stack View for the Wind binding. Use Figure 21.5 as a reference.

Figure 21.4
Drag space warp parameters increase flexibility.

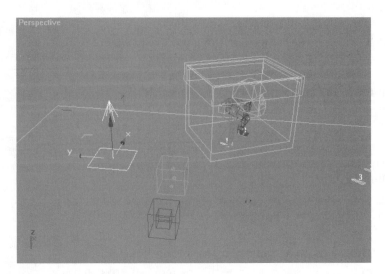

Figure 21.5 Wind space warp is added to the scene.

By default, Wind has a Strength value of 1.0. This is the amount of force in the direction of the Wind space warp icon's arrow—in this case, upward. If you scrub the animation at this point, you'll notice that too much force is applied to the particles and they are heavily displaced upward. If you select the Wind space warp, go to the Modify panel and look at the first two Turbulence parameters. Turbulence and Frequency are zero, which means that there is no perturbing effect on the particles. To create turbulence without forcing the particles in any given direction, you have to turn off the Strength value.

7. To turn off the Strength value, select the Wind space warp.

8. Go to the Modify panel and change the Strength value to **0**.

Now if you take a look at the animation, the particles don't launch upward in the direction of the Wind icon. No force is being applied in the Wind's direction. However, you still need to make adjustments to the Turbulence parameters to achieve the proper effect.

9. Adjust the Turbulence value to **0.02**.

10. Change the Frequency value to **0.15**.

11. Set the Scale value to **0.2**.

With those numbers plugged in, you should see some extra movement in the particle motion. Play with these numbers to experiment with the motion, but don't wander too far from these values because the effect can quickly become unrecognizable. At this point you leave the pixie dust effect for a bit and move on to a confetti effect.

Note

These might seem like arbitrary numbers, but I consider them default parameters for most scenes. These numbers are a good starting point for integrating turbulence into a scene. Many people often make the mistake of using higher numbers, such as 2.5 or 10. Unfortunately, this doesn't work because so much depends on the scale of your scene.

Keep the following in mind:

Turbulence controls the speed at which particles waver and curl or are perturbed from their normal paths. Lower amounts cause gentle motion, and higher values naturally cause excited motion.

Frequency is directly related to Turbulence. Frequency controls the amount of randomness in the motion over time. Higher numbers cause more variation.

Scale is probably the most important value to set correctly, because without matching this value to the scale of your scene, the effect is unnoticeable. The number values for this parameter might be misleading. Very low numbers—0.01, for example—cause large turbulent motion, and higher numbers cause tight motion. Turbulence is really just a fractal noise field applied to the particles. The Scale value controls the scale of the noise and therefore the visibility of the motion.

Exercise 21.4   Creating a Confetti Effect

In this exercise, you use a SuperSpray particle system emitting particles as instanced geometry to create a confetti effect. By using instanced geometry you'll be able to use a custom object as particle geometry. You'll also add some space warps to control the motion of the particles, and finally add some Custom Attributes and Wire Parameters to better control and automate both effects.

To start the confetti effect, you need to choose a particle system. SuperSpray is ideal in this case because it has similar parameters to the PArray particle system you used previously, but also has the capability of emitting particles from a single point outward in a controlled direction.

1. Go to the Create panel, choose Particle Systems, and click SuperSpray.

2. Click and drag in the Top viewport over the box01 object to create a SuperSpray icon, as seen in Figure 21.6.

Note

The SuperSpray icon is slightly different from the PArray particle system icon. SuperSpray emits particles in a direction determined by the icon, not by a geometric object in the scene. In this case, the location of the icon and the direction you point it in determine how particles are emitted. By creating the SuperSpray particle system in the Top viewport, you automatically create it pointing upward along the Z-axis. Notice there is an arrow built into the icon.

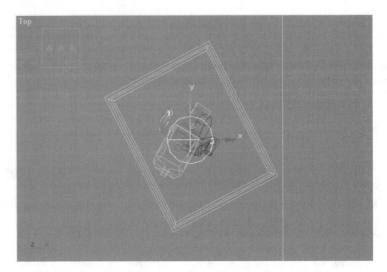

Figure 21.6   The SuperSpray particle system is located inside the gift box with the biped.

Before you go any further, there are a few parameters you need to adjust.

3. In the Basic Parameters rollout, set Percentage of Particles to **100%**.

This causes every particle emitted internally to be displayed in the viewports.

4. In the Particle Generation rollout, set Use Total to **100** by switching the radio button to activate this parameter and adjusting the total number of particles to be emitted to 100 particles.

5. In the Particle Motion subsection, set Speed and Variation to **2** units and **25%**, respectively.

These two values are related and therefore mentioned in the same space.

6. In the Particle Timing subsection, set Emit Start to **60**.

This defines the starting frame for particle emission.

7. Set Emit Stop to **65**.

This causes all particle emission to stop at frame 65. With these two start and stop values set accordingly, the total number of frames in which particles will be emitted is 5.

8. Set Display Until to **204**.

This should normally be a number beyond the final frame of your animation.

9. Set Life and Variation to **100** and **10**, respectively.

This defines the number of frames that particles will be "alive," give or take 10 frames. The Variation parameter is different from most others because it is defined in frames, not percentage. In this case when a particle is born its Life value is determined to be between 90 and 110.

If you take a look at the animation of the SuperSpray particles you see that they emit upward in a tight stream. This is a matter of adjusting some axis and spreading controls. You'll be able to better visualize these changes if you move the time slider to a frame where the particles are visible.

10. Go to frame 65 and select the SuperSpray particle system.

11. Go to the Modify panel and change the Off Axis Spread value to **80** and the Off Plane Spread value to **180**, as seen in Figure 21.7.

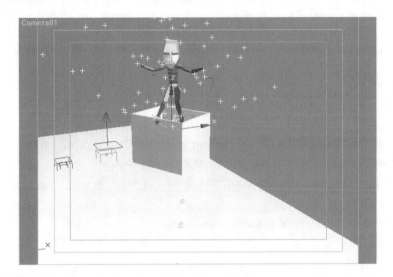

Figure 21.7   Adjust the Off Axis Spread and Off Plane Spread controls to create a more conical emission.

As you adjust these two values, notice what they do to the angle of the particle emission. When you adjust the first parameter, the emission is in the form of a flat fan. However, as soon as you adjust the second parameter, the shape of the spreading fan becomes conical. These are two powerful controls for shaping particle emission.

The next step is to assign instanced geometry to the SuperSpray particles. Recall that instanced geometry is a method of referencing an object in the scene to use as particle geometry. In this case, you need to make a confetti object to use as the instanced geometry in the particle system.

To create the confetti strip, you use a Plane primitive and apply a couple of modifiers to shape it. The modifiers will come in handy, because they enable you to edit the object's shape without destroying it.

12. Go to the Create panel, choose Standard Primitives, and click the Plane button.

13. In the Top viewport, click and drag to form a plane primitive in the scene.

The initial size of the plane primitive is irrelevant, because you'll adjust its parameters in the Modify panel.

14. With the plane primitive selected, go to the Modify panel.

15. Change the Length value to **2.0**, change the Width value to **0.5**, adjust the Length Segs value to **13**, and rename the plane primitive **ConfettiStrip**.

If you zoom in on the object, you'll see that it's a long, thin, single-sided object made up of evenly spaced polygons. The reason for adding more Length Segs past the default value of 4 is to make the polygons even. This becomes necessary when you're going to bend and twist the object, which you'll do next.

16. With the new ConfettiStrip object selected, go to the Modify panel.

17. Click Modifier List to open the drop-down list and choose Bend.

This adds a Bend modifier to the object, which enables you to warp the object on a specific axis a set amount of degrees. The motivation here is to skew the ConfettiStrip into a twisted piece of paper.

In the Bend parameters rollout, you make a few changes.

18. Set Angle to **–60**.

This bends the modifier gizmo –60 degrees.

19. Set Bend Axis to **X**.

This restricts the bending effect to the X-axis of the gizmo.

If you zoom in on the ConfettiStrip object in one of the side viewports, you can see the bending effect the modifier has on the object.

Next you add a Twist modifier, which is similar to a Bend modifier but has a more asymmetrical effect.

20. With the ConfettiStrip object selected in the Modify panel, click Modifier List to open the drop-down list and select Twist from the list.

This adds a second modifier onto the object's stack, visible in Stack View. As with the Bend modifier, there are two parameters you need to adjust.

21. Set Angle to **50**.

This increases the twist effect by 20 degrees.

22. Set Twist Axis to **Y**.

This isolates the effect to the Y-axis of the modifier's gizmo, as seen in Figure 21.8.

With these steps complete, you should have a long strip of polygons twisted and bent into a confetti shape. The next step is to tell the SuperSpray particle system to use this newly created shape as instanced geometry.

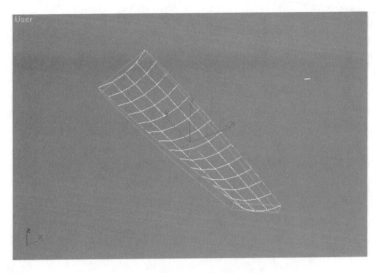

Figure 21.8   Apply Bend and Twist modifiers to ConfettiStrip.

23. Select the SuperSpray particle system. Go to the Modify panel to access its parameters.

24. In the Particle Type rollout, change the radio button to Instanced Geometry.

25. Click the Pick Object button below in the Instancing Parameters and choose the ConfettiStrip object.

    In your viewport, this doesn't make any immediate changes because the particles are still being displayed in their default manner as constant-sized Ticks. You can set the display option to show the actual geometry of the particles, though.

26. Go to the top rollout of the SuperSpray particle system and set the Viewport Display radio button to Mesh.

    Now you should see the ConfettiStrip object being instanced to each particle of the SuperSpray particle system. If your viewport display feedback is too slow, you can opt to set Viewport Display to Bbox. This reduces the detail of the instanced geometry displayed by showing only its bounding box. One problem does exist, though. The original ConfettiStrip object is still present in the scene and needs to be hidden.

27. To hide the original ConfettiStrip object, select it, go to the Display panel, and click Hide Selected, as shown in Figure 21.9.

    This doesn't delete the object, but hides it from view because you are not going to actually use it for anything other than reference for the SuperSpray particles.

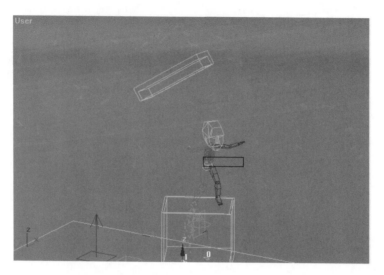

Figure 21.9 SuperSpray uses the ConfettiStrip object as instanced geometry.

Using instanced geometry is a useful way to extend the geometric representations of particles in 3ds max. You can use polygons, patches, and even NURBS as instanced geometry. Unfortunately, there are a few drawbacks. In particular you can instance only one particular object and its hierarchy, not a group of objects. For example, if you create geometry for coins—such as dimes, nickels, and quarters—you have to create a separate particle system to instance each type of object.

Exercise 21.5   Adding Drag, Wind, and Gravity

You now have the basic setup for the confetti effect. One of the problems at the moment is the unrealistic motion of the particles. They should explode out, slow down, and fall to the floor like flower petals. As you did previously with the PArray particle system, you can use space warps to control the motion of the SuperSpray particles. Drag and Wind space warps are present in the scene, but the only one you're going to reuse is the Wind space warp for its turbulence effect. Space warps can be used with multiple objects, and any changes in their parameters will affect those objects bound to it.

First you need to add a second Drag space warp with stronger, more uniform force.

1. Select the Drag01 space warp in your scene.

2. Switch to the Move tool by right-clicking the space warp and choosing Move from the quad menu.

3. Hold down the Shift key, drag the Drag space warp over so that it is separated from the original, and release the mouse.

4. In the resulting Clone Options dialog box, choose OK. Figure 21.10 shows the result.

You have just created a clone of your original Drag space warp. They have the same values in all parameters, with the exception of their names. This new Drag space warp needs to be stronger to slow down the exploding SuperSpray particles.

5. With the new Drag02 space warp selected, go to the Modify panel.

6. Change all three Linear Dampening X-, Y-, and Z-axis values to **5%**.

7. Select the SuperSpray particle system and bind it to the new Drag02 space warp using the Bind to Space Warp button.

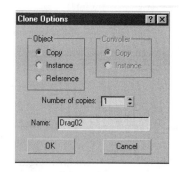

Figure 21.10
The Clone Options dialog box appears when you drag the Drag space warp while holding down the Shift key.

If you take a look at the animation now, at frame 60 the SuperSpray particles explode outward in a hemispherical pattern and quickly slow down so that they create a sort of confetti effect.

Two problems are obvious. First, the particles should look like little strips of paper, but they don't spin. Second, they don't fall downward toward the floor, essentially defying gravity. Both of these problems can easily be addressed.

First, rotation is merely a matter of adjusting a couple of parameters in the particles. Second, Gravity, like Wind and Drag, is a space warp that you add to the scene.

8. Select the SuperSpray particle system and go to the Modify panel.

9. In the Rotation and Collision rollout, set the Spin Time to **10** frames.

10. Set the Phase to **30.0** degrees.

Each of these parameters has a Variation parameter. This adds randomness to the values and breaks up the uniformity of the effect—something you should always strive for. It's also useful to use the Wind space warp's Turbulence values that are already in the scene to perturb the motion of the confetti particles.

11. Set both Spin Time Variation and Phase Variation values to **25.0**. Figure 21.11 shows the result.

12. Activate the Bind to Space Warp button and bind the SuperSpray particle system to the Wind01 space warp already in the scene.

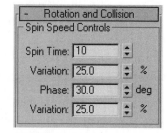

Figure 21.11
Set the Rotation and Collision parameters.

The only other force missing from this effect is Gravity, just another simple space warp to add to the system. Gravity works similarly to Wind because it is a planar directional effect by default. It can also be a spherical effect, as can Wind, but in this case the default setting works best to mimic the gravity of the sample scene.

13. In the Create panel, choose Space Warps/Forces and click Gravity.

14. In the Top viewport, click and drag a Gravity space warp icon into the scene.

15. Select the SuperSpray particle system and bind it to the new Gravity space warp. Figure 21.12 shows the result.

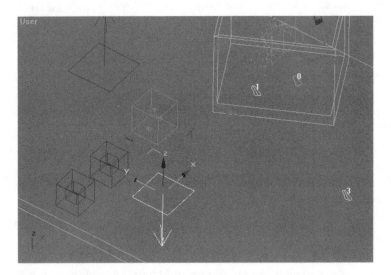

Figure 21.12   Add a Gravity space warp to the scene.

Now the SuperSpray particles explode outward, but fall downward too fast. You can fix this by reducing the strength of the Gravity effect. Instead of doing this immediately by modifying the value, do some parameter consolidation with Custom Attributes.

Exercise 21.6   Adding Custom Parameters Using Custom Attributes

Custom Attributes are a new feature in 3ds max 4 that enable you to add custom parameters to objects. Using Parameter Wiring, you can connect Custom Attributes to parameters in your scene, using them to drive animation or, in this case, to consolidate several parameters from different objects and store them in one easily accessible rollout. It might sound complicated, but it's actually pretty simple. Just follow the steps in this exercise.

You create a dummy object that will not render or participate in any way in the scene, other than to store several parameters that you can use to manipulate the scene.

1. In the Create panel, choose Helpers/Standard and click the Dummy button.

2. In the Top viewport, away from all the clutter in the scene, click and drag to create a Dummy object.

3. With the Dummy object selected, go to the Modify panel.

   The Dummy object has no parameters. You can use Custom Attributes to add parameters here that you define. Custom Attributes is accessed in the Animation menu at the top of the screen.

4. Select Animation/Add Custom Attribute.

   This causes a large floater to appear with lots of controls. This is sort of like a custom parameter construction set. First you add a Gravity Strength control.

   In the Add Parameter floater, the default parameter type is Float and the UI type is Spinner. Use these defaults.

5. Change the Name field to **Gravity**.

6. Open the Float UI rollout and set the Width value to **100.0**.

7. Set Range From to –1 and Range To to **1.0**.

8. In the Finish rollout, click the Add button. Figure 21.13 shows the result.

   A new parameter called Gravity appears in the dummy's Custom Attributes rollout. If you adjust this parameter, you'll see that it doesn't really do anything at the moment. The spinner field is 100 units wide, and the parameter's value range is from –1 to 1.0. You need to connect it to the Gravity space warp's Strength value by using Parameter Wiring.

9. Zoom out the Top viewport so you can clearly see both the Dummy object and the Gravity space warp.

10. Right-click on the Dummy object and select Wire Parameters from the Quad menu.

11. In the resulting pop-up menu, choose (in this order) Object(Dummy), Custom_Attributes, and Gravity.

12. Now click on the Gravity icon. Notice a line drawn from the dummy.

13. In the pop-up menu choose (in this order) Object(Gravity), and Strength. Figure 21.14 shows the result.

   This connects these two floating-point values internally via MAXScript. The resulting dialog box is the Wire Parameters dialog box where multiple wiring can be edited.

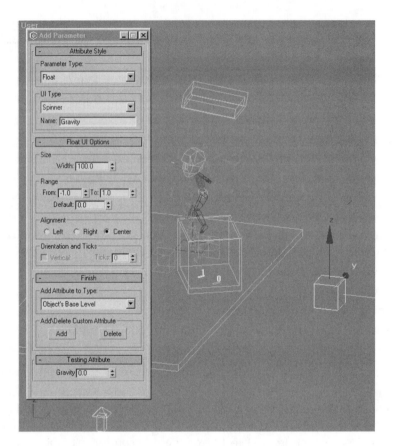

Figure 21.13   Set the controls in the Add Parameter dialog box.

The Gravity track is highlighted on the Dummy object on the left side of the box, and the right side shows the Strength track of the Gravity space warp. This identifies the two tracks that you are wiring together. Parameters can be wired in directions so that adjusting one track doesn't necessarily affect the other. Tracks can also be bidirectional, meaning that changing the values of either affects the opposite track. In the two lower boxes, there are text boxes with variables for the track values. This is actually an expression field and can be used to adjust how a track is interpreted. In the case of Custom Attributes that you're setting up, you want them to be bidirectional.

14. In the Parameter Wiring dialog box, click the Two-Way connection button. It's located at the top and looks like two opposing arrows.

15. Click the Connect button to create the connection. See Figure 21.15 for the result.

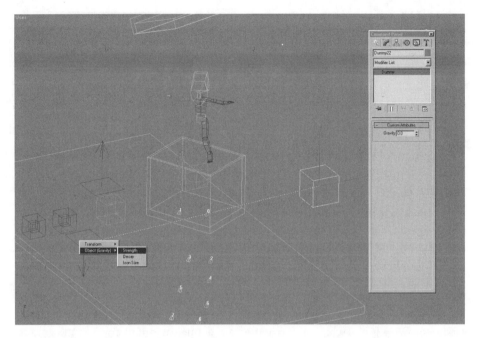

Figure 21.14   Wire the Custom Attribute to the Gravity's Strength value.

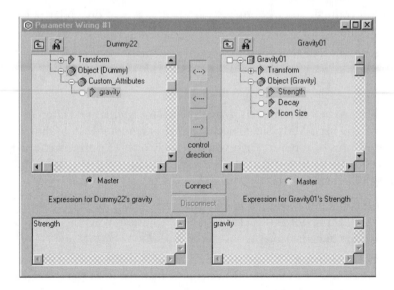

Figure 21.15   Complete the Parameter Wiring.

Now you've connected the Custom Attribute Gravity to the Strength value on the Gravity space warp. If you change the value of the Custom Attribute, the Gravity space warp's Strength value adjusts accordingly. Custom Attributes are fairly limitless, and using this method of storing them on a common object enables you to organize many parameters from several dissimilar objects into one consolidated interface.

The animation is nearly complete, but there still are a few tasks to do to complete the scene. Use the Custom Attribute you created to adjust the strength of the Gravity to a lesser amount more consistent with the scene.

16. Select the Dummy object and change the Gravity Custom Attribute value to **0.02**.

This will work with the Drag space warp to cause the confetti particles to linger in the air and slowly float downward. The confetti particles scale up quickly and then scale down as they die. This is a function of the Grow For and Fade For values in SuperSpray. The default parameters of 10 cause the particles to scale up from zero to their full size in 10 frames and fade out to nothing 10 frames before each dies.

Parameter Wiring and Custom Attributes are a huge windfall for 3ds max users. They extend the procedural tools to a new level by enabling you to easily set up and control complex interactions between parameters of dissimilar objects. With Custom Attributes, the user is free to add specialized parameters to objects or, as in this example, consolidate parameters in the scene to one object.

Exercise 21.7   Adding Materials and Effects

The last big step in this process is to assign special materials and effects to the particles. First, you use a Multi Sub-Object material to randomly assign different colors to different strips of confetti. Then you use the Render Effect Lens Effects to add a glow effect to the pixie dust particles. Finally, you adjust the properties of the particles to better integrate them into the scene.

1. Open the Material Editor and choose an empty slot, or make one by selecting an existing slot and clicking the Delete button, which looks like an X below the material slots).

If you are deleting a slot containing a material that exists in your scene, you are asked whether you want to delete the material from the scene (bad) or just remove it from this particular slot (good).

2. Create a Standard Material by clicking the Material Type button and choosing Standard from the list.

3. Change the Diffuse color swatch to a bright color, such as red.

4. Adjust the self-illumination value to **25**.

5. Click the 2-Sided check box.

6. Rename the material **Confetti** and drag it onto the SuperSpray particle system to assign it.

 Note

By adding a fraction of self-illumination, you fake translucency in the confetti strips, an effect common with thin paper. By clicking the 2-Sided check box, you define this material as an automatically two-sided one, regardless of the geometry it's assigned to. This is important because the ConfettiStrip object you created was initially created with a Plane primitive that has polygons facing in only one direction. This essentially makes it one-sided, and viewing from directly underneath the plane causes it to be invisible. By assigning a two-sided material to the object, you're automatically causing the object to be two-sided, overcoming the shortcoming of plane without adding geometry.

What if you want the confetti to be several different colors? With the tedious method, you create multiple copies of the confetti particle system. Controlling these separate systems could be a hassle. With the better method, you assign a Multi Sub-Object material, and the particles will cycle through the maps in the list on a frame-by-frame basis, assigning different materials to particles at the given frame in the cycle. This doesn't work when particles are emitted over the course of a single frame. Luckily, in this scene the particles emit over the course of five frames.

7. To change the Confetti material to a Multi Sub-Object material, select the Confetti material in the Material Editor.

8. Click the Material button (which should read Standard at the moment) and choose Multi Sub-Object from the list.

9. In the resulting Replace Material dialog box choose Keep Old Material as Sub-Material.

   This converts the Standard material into a Multi Sub-Object material with the default 10 entries. In the case of the confetti effect, you need only 5 entries.

10. Click the material's Delete button five times to remove materials 6 through 10 on the list.

    You've already defined one material with all its special parameters (the red one), so instead of going in and matching all the settings with the new materials, copy the red Confetti material slot into all the other slots. From there you can adjust the color for each without having to go into each material slot.

11. Click and drag the top material (the red Confetti material) slot to the next one below.

12. Set the radio button in the resulting Instance (Copy) Material dialog box to copy and press OK.

13. Repeat this until all five slots look the same.

In this sequence, you've copied the red Confetti material parameters to all the other slots in the Multi Sub-Object material. Now all you need to do is adjust the colors of the rest.

14. Click on the color swatch to the right of each submaterial and change it to a different color (try to stick to bright confetti-style colors, such as pink, aqua, and yellow). Figure 21.16 shows the result.

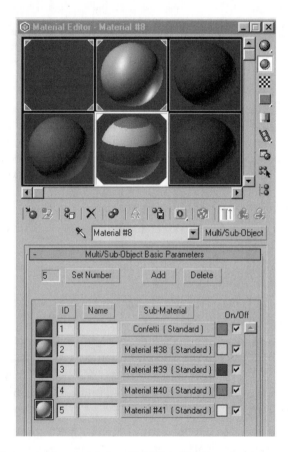

Figure 21.16 Store several materials in a Multi Sub-Object material.

When you look in the viewport, you won't notice any change in the color of the confetti particles, because, by default, the SuperSpray particles are getting their material from the instanced geometry and not the icon. This is easily changed in the SuperSpray parameters.

15. Select the SuperSpray particle system.

16. Go to the Modify panel. At the bottom of the Particle Type rollout, switch the Get Material From radio button to Icon.

17. Play the animation.

The colors of the confetti particles vary according to the list of materials stored in the Multi Sub-Object material. Figure 21.17 shows the result.

Figure 21.17   The confetti particles use a Multi Sub-Object material.

The next step is to assign a Glow effect to the PArray particles that are serving as pixie dust. At the moment they are rendering as tiny constant, or circular, geometry that always faces the camera. They have a default material attached to them that must be changed to make them more colorful. Luckily, you can use the same Multi Sub-Object material you created for the confetti particles.

18. Go back to the Material Editor and drag the Confetti material onto the PArray icon.

Note

There are a couple of ways to assign materials to objects, but this is one of the more direct. You can also use the Assign Material to Selection button in the Material Editor, but that requires a selection. The drag-and-drop method is quicker because it doesn't require any selections.

The viewport display of the PArray particles doesn't show multiple colors. Don't worry—currently the PArray particles are being displayed only as dots and not geometry. To verify that the assignment of multiple materials is working, try rendering out a frame to the virtual frame buffer.

Exercise 21.8   Using Render Effects

Render Effects are a post-process filter tool that was added in 3ds max r3. There are several kinds of Render Effects, but you work with an optical effects toolkit called Lens Effects in this exercise.

Lens Effects has tools for creating glows, highlights, sparkles, secondary reflections, and other optical anomalies via post-process. In the past, these kinds of filters resided only in Video Post and required much more time to work with. Moving Lens Effects to a Render Effect filter brings speed and flexibility to the workflow.

Render Effects can be added and edited with a single test render. Normally you have to re-render your scene to see any changes you make with a filter, but in the case of Render Effects, the filter is passed through a valid scene enumeration that can be stored in memory and applied to filter changes on-the-fly. This enables you to do much of your filter editing in near–real time.

In this exercise, you need a tiny subset of the Lens Effects toolkit: Glow.

1. From the top menu, choose Rendering/Effects.

2. Click the Add button and choose Lens Effects from the list.

3. Select the newly added Lens Effects entry.

   A few new rollups are added. One contains two windows with elements on the left, and one is empty on the right. The empty one is where you assign Lens Effects tools to the filter. The rollout below stores Lens Effects global variables that can be used to apply common parameter changes across several elements.

4. In the window on the left, choose Glow from the list and click the > arrow.

5. Select the Glow text in the right window. Figure 21.18 shows the result.

   Notice how a new set of rollouts is added below when you select the Glow element. These are the local controls for that tool. In the next steps, you adjust a series of parameters to create the pixie dust effect for your scene.

6. In the Parameters tab of the Lens Effects Globals rollout, change the Size value to **5.0**.

7. In the Parameters tab of the Glow Element rollout, adjust the size to **3**.

8. Change Use Source Color to **100**.

9. Click the Options tab.

10. In the Apply Element To field, click the Image Centers check box and clear the others.

11. In the Image Sources field, click Object ID and clear any others. Figure 21.19 shows the result.

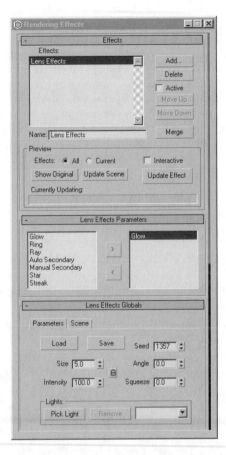

Figure 21.18   Select the Glow text in the Rendering Effects dialog box.

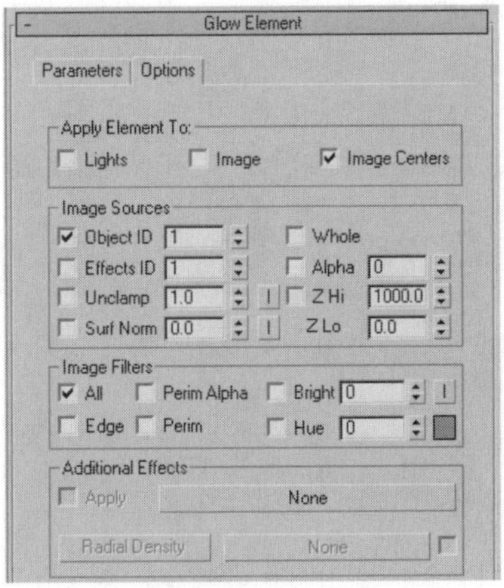

Figure 21.19   Adjust parameters for the Glow element.

Note

Here's a breakdown of what you just did. You adjusted the global scale of the Lens Effects filter. By default it's 100, which is too large for this scene. If you had multiple elements, you could use this global size value to adjust the scale of all elements equally at the same time. By setting the Use Source Color value to 100, you're telling the glow filter to glow the particles using each particle's material color 100%. This is a handy feature, though you can explicitly color Glow elements using different parameters in the filter. Finally, by setting Image Centers and Object ID 1, you're telling the filter to apply the Glow effect only to the center of nodes in the scene that carry an Object ID of 1. Currently, you have no objects with an Object ID of 1, so you need to set one.

12. Select the PArray particles and right-click directly over them.

13. Choose Properties from the Quad menu.

14. Set the Object Channel value to **1**.

15. Clear the Cast Shadows check box. Figure 21.20 shows the result.

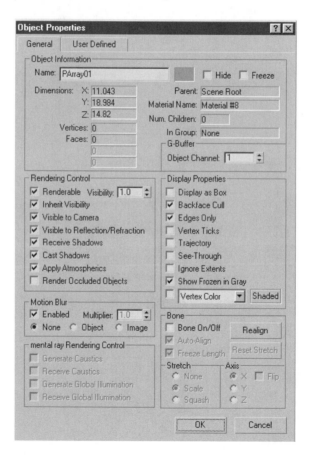

Figure 21.20   Set controls and properties in the PArray Object Properties dialog box.

Now if you render the Camera view, it first renders the entire scene, and then a Render Effects pass is processed. This can sometimes be very fast, but in the case of working with these particles it might be a bit slow.

The Render dialog box shows you the progress of the render effect, as seen in Figure 21.21. This glow effect is driven by Object ID 1 in the scene, so if any other objects in your scene were tagged with that ID they glow as well. You clear the Cast Shadows check box to force the PArray particles to not cast shadows onto other objects in the scene. Normally you'd think that this is important for integration into a live action shot, but in the case of these glowing particles they're appearing as a light source and therefore shouldn't cast any reasonable shadow.

Figure 21.21 The Glow effect is applied to particles.

The last thing you need to do with the PArray particles is to clone them so that you have a second stream that flows from the other foot of the biped. Instead of creating a second PArray particle system from scratch, use the Clone tool, because all the parameters are finalized in the original PArray.

16. Select the PArray particle system.

17. Choose Edit/Clone from the top menu.

18. In the Clone Options dialog box, accept the default name by clicking OK.

    This creates an exact duplicate of the previous PArray particle system and—more importantly—its particles have the same path. Why? They are being emitted from the same object and use the same Seed value. You need to adjust these two parameters to complete the effect.

19. With PArray02 selected, go to the Modify panel and change the Object-Based Emitter to Bip01 L Foot.

20. Scroll to the bottom of the Particle Generation rollout and click the New button next to Seed to create a new randomly generated Seed value.

Now if you play the animation you should have two sets of particles being emitted from the feet of the biped object. This concludes this section of the project.

Summary

As you can see from this chapter, particle systems are a useful, though specialized, tool in the 3ds max 4 tool set. They can easily and quickly animate lots of objects together, but they are specialized in their application and not always required in a project. Space warps go hand in hand with particle systems, often being required to integrate a system into a scene or to simply "wrangle" the particles in the direction you want them to go.

Chapter 22

Scripting Custom Animations

by Neil Blevins

The bane of all production animators is
doing the same boring, repetitive task
over and over again: "Dammit Jim, I'm
an artist, not a junior-level technician!"

This issue prompted me to start using MAXScript about a year ago, even though I have very little formal training in how to code. Why should you listen to a guy who doesn't have a computer science degree and has been doing this kind of stuff for only a year? Because you should realize that anyone with the will and a somewhat logical mind can do these things. You don't have to be a programming god to write simple scripts. You have to be frustrated with wasting time doing something that a computer should be doing for you.

I would not be programming today if it weren't for my need to get things done faster. That's the difference between a production programmer and a research programmer. I get to see my code applied instantly in a real-world environment, and as long as my programming either saves animators time or enables them to do something they couldn't do before, my job is done. It doesn't have to be pretty, and it might work in only a limited set of cases.

Here is a perfect example. I was busy working on a scene when I was approached by a supervisor who wanted me to go through all our old scene files, extract all the materials from them, and place them in a materials library that we could use in future projects. That task would probably involve 100–300 max scene files, and I started seeing the week disappear in a cloud of boredom. Instead of accepting that fate, I sat down and started programming. Two hours later, I had MaterialRipper, a script that automatically opens any max file in a directory (or series of subdirectories) and takes all scene materials and places them into a matlib file of the user's choosing. Problem solved, boredom evaded.

Every release of max enables us to script more and more items, and 3ds max 4 is no exception. With all its new options for customizable interfaces and more access to current max functions, the possibility for your scripts to change the way an animator works has never been stronger. So, dig in.

This Chapter's Exercise

The exercise in this chapter shows how a few simple requests given to me at Blur Studio (in Venice, California) resulted in LightUtilities, probably the most complex script I've ever written. Specifically, the exercise will do the following:

- Show you four stages of the script's evolution
- Explain the process behind doing what it does
- Explain some coding tricks along the way

This tutorial is not a replacement for the max manuals. Every effort has been made to make this chapter as accessible to everyone as possible, but you definitely need to know about a few basics, such as for loops, functions, and variables. Make sure you've looked through the max manual before proceeding. All the scripts mentioned in this tutorial can be found at `http://www.blur.com/blurmaxscripts/`, and the CD-ROM that comes with this book contains four zip files, revisions of LightUtilities, and the scripts that eventually became LightUtilities.

How Do I Start Coding?

Before getting into the specifics of my scripts, here are a few general tips and rules about coding:

1. Start small. My very first script was the following (called Sym):

```
instance $
about [0,0,0] scale $ [-1,1,1]
```

This code can be rewritten in pseudo-code as the following:

```
Make an instance of your selection
Mirror the selection
```

Pseudo-code is code that is not specific to any programming language. It is the set of instructions for a script. Pseudo-code is probably more important than the code itself; if you can see logically what you want a script to do, the rest is just translating that into the syntax that your particular scripting language understands. Think of it in artistic terms: After you've decided on the overall composition of the piece, you can then worry about putting the veins on the leaf.

2. Get a good text editor. Although you can use the text editor that exists inside max (MAXScript menu, New Script), this editor has a major disadvantage: If your script crashes max, the script is lost, and possibly a bunch of work with it. I tend to prefer editing my scripts in an outside text editor, such as Notepad or TextPad, which I now use exclusively (`http://www.textpad.com`). TextPad is cool because it enables you to search and replace in multiple documents at the same time. It also enables you to move from document to document quicker, which helps when you have multiple scripts that need editing at the same time.

3. Steal. Yes, I said steal. If you don't know how to do something, find someone else's script that does something similar and then adapt it until it does what you want it to do. This practice is common and will save you from rewriting

a lot of code that doesn't need to be reinvented. Remember, if a substantial part of your code belongs to someone else (or even just a function or two), it's good manners to credit the person somewhere in your script. Check the licensing agreement that comes with any script you're editing to make sure the author doesn't mind, or email the person and ask. Who knows, maybe the author can be even more help. For a good place to get scripts written by other users, try visiting `http://www.scriptspot.com`.

4. Use the MacroRecorder. Under the MAXScript menu is the MacroRecorder, which echoes commands you perform in the interface. For example, if you want to write a script that makes spheres, turn on the MacroRecorder, make a sphere in your interface, and a command like this appears in the MacroRecorder:

```
Sphere radius:31 smooth:on segs:32 chop:0 slice:off sliceFrom:0
sliceTo:0 transform:(matrix3 [1,0,0] [0,0,1] [0,-1,0] [100,200,200])
isSelected:on
```

If you want to create a sphere, you now have a good example of *how* to create a sphere. For simple scripts, you can record a series of events in this manner and then just drag the text from the MacroRecorder to any toolbar. A button will appear, and anytime you press that button, it will repeat the actions.

 Warning

The MacroRecorder does not echo everything that's scriptable. Something in max might be scriptable, but it doesn't appear in the MacroRecorder. In some instances, the MacroRecorder will give you false information. Use it for what it's worth, and if your action doesn't appear in the MacroRecorder, don't despair—it still might be possible to write your script.

5. Use the MAXScript online help. Not everything in max is scriptable. Unlike with Alias|Wavefront, which wrote a scripting language and then wrote a piece of 3D software (Maya) on top of it, max was written first and then MAXScript was put into max (in Max r2). This means there's a lot of stuff (much less in max 4) that still can't be done in MAXScript. That's why the MAXScript online help is so important. Frequently when someone asks me if something can be done in MAXScript, I first look to the online help, go to search, and search for some keywords to make sure I can actually write the script. I cannot recommend enough using the online help. When I'm scripting, I must refer to that document 20 times a day.

6. Write your script in pseudo-code first. As mentioned earlier, pseudo-code is good because it lets you work out how the script works before you have to code a single line. Get in the habit.

7. Try and generalize code when you feel it's worth it. In a production environment, often you make custom software to work only with the current situation. For example, suppose an animator has 10 objects he wants to move along a surface in a specific fashion. You could hard-code your script to work only with those 10 objects. This can be faster because you don't need to make a fancy interface and because you can make certain time-saving assumptions on how these objects will react to your script. It also means, however, that your code is now throwaway, useful only in this one instance; if another job comes up where you're doing something similar, you have to rewrite a whole lot of code. Learn when to generalize and when to be more specific.

8. Debug with the Print command. Although C++ programmers have complex programs to help them debug, the only thing that scripters have is the Print command. The best way to find bugs in a script, especially when the error messages are unhelpful, is to know the state of the script when the script goes down. If you know the values of all the variables when a script reaches an error, it might tell you where you've made a mistake.

The Print command prints something to the Listener. Use it in your code when trying to figure out why something should be happening, but isn't.

I was making a progress bar, which is one of those bars at the bottom of the screen that tells you how much longer until the script is finished. This is usually done by making a progress bar and then giving it a value. For example, a loop such as

```
progressStart "Progress Test"
for i = 1 to 10 do
    (
m = (i/10)*100
progressUpdate m
sleep 1
)
progressEnd()
```

creates a progress bar and then performs a loop that will update the progress bar 10 times. At `i = 1`, `m` is `10`, which updates the progress bar to 10% complete. The loop waits one second and then goes to `i = 2`, which updates the progress bar to 20%. This procedure continues to 100% complete.

But that's not what happened. Run the code. You'll notice that the progress bar won't update. So I placed the line

```
Print i/10
```

before line 4 of my code. I got 0 nine times, followed by 1 once. This totally confused me until I realized what was happening: At i = 1, you get 1/10, which should return a value of 0.1. Instead, it returned a value of 0. Because 1 is an integer and 10 is an integer, the answer returned was an integer, and the script converted decimal 0.1 to the integer 0. This is one problem with MAXScript. In other programming languages, you have to specify certain variables. For example, you have to define that i will be a float (a floating-point value), which includes decimals. MAXScript tries to guess the type of variable. In this case, it returned a rounded-down integer of 0 when what I wanted was the float 0.1. So by changing the code to

```
progressStart "Progress Test"
for i = 1 to 10 do
   (
m = ((i as float)/(10 as float))*(100 as float)
progressUpdate m
sleep 1
)
progressEnd()
```

I got a float value of 0.1, which when multiplied by 100 gave me 10. This made the progress dialog advance to 10%. I would have never known if I didn't know the stage of my variable, thanks to the Print command.

LightCleaner v1.00

Before LightUtilities was called LightUtilities, it started as a simpler script called LightCleaner. I was at Blur on a Saturday, and a supervisor told me that he had been given a MAX file from another animator (see Figure 22.1). The MAX file had about 50 lights, and all of them had Attenuation Display set to on. Imagine trying to deal with a scene that's so cluttered. He wanted a quick, automated way to turn them off because they were cluttering up his view.

Proof of Concept

Proof of concept means writing some really quick code to prove that what you're trying to do will work. For simple scripts it can be really easy. For example, a proof of concept for LightCleaner can be as easy as

```
$.showNearAtten = true
```

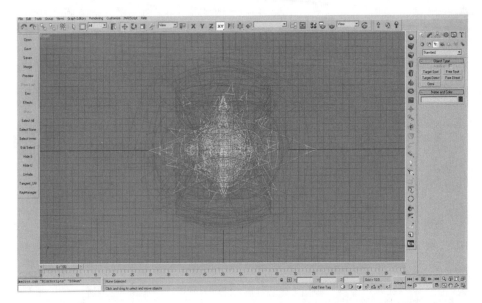

Figure 22.1   A scene with a lot of light; each light has Showcone, near and far attenuation
set to on.

If you type this into the MAXScript Listener, the selected light turns on its near attenuation display gizmo. If you do it the other way and click the check box in your light under Near Attenuation/Show, this command does not show up in the MacroRecorder. The only way to find out which command is needed to turn the near attenuation gizmo on and off is to look in the Online MAXScript Help files.

After you prove that you can do what you want through MAXScript, you can write the UI for the script, making the code pretty and foolproof.

On the CD-ROM, unzip the file LightCleaner_v100.zip. Unzip the file LightCleaner_ v100a.zip (the *a* on the end indicates this is not my original LightCleaner script; it has been slightly simplified for the purposes of this tutorial). Then view this file in a program such as Notepad or TextPad and follow along. Here's the code written out for you:

```
-- Functions

fn turn_on =
        (
        if $ == undefined then
        (MessageBoxi "Please select at least one object"
        ➥title:"LightCleaner")
        else
                (
                for i = 1 to selection.count do
```

```
                                (
                                if superclassof selection[i] == light then
                                        (
                                        selection[i].showNearAtten = true
                                        selection[i].showFarAtten = true
                                        if classof selection[i] == targetSpot or
                                        classof selection[i] == freeSpot or
                                        classof selection[i] ==
                                        ➥TargetDirectionallight or
                                        classof selection[i] == Directionallight
                                        ➥then
                                        selection[i].showCone = true
                                        )
                                )
                        )
                )

        fn turn_off =
                (
                if $ == undefined then
                (MessageBox "Please select at least one object"
                ➥title:"LightCleaner")
                else
                        (
                        for i = 1 to selection.count do
                                (
                                if superclassof selection[i] == light then
                                        (
                                        selection[i].showNearAtten = false
                                        selection[i].showFarAtten = false
                                        if classof selection[i] == targetSpot or
                                        classof selection[i] == freeSpot or
                                        classof selection[i] ==
                                        ➥TargetDirectionallight or
                                        classof selection[i] == Directionallight
                                        ➥then
                                        selection[i].showCone = false
                                        )
                                )
                        )
                )

-- Script

rollout lightcleaner_rollout "LightCleaner"
        (
        button button_on "On" width:150 align:#center toolTip:"On"
        button button_off "Off" width:150 align:#center toolTip:"Off"
        on button_on pressed do turn_on ()
        on button_off pressed do turn_off ()
        )

lightcleaner_floater = newRolloutFloater "LightCleaner v1.00" 230 123
addRollout lightcleaner_rollout lightcleaner_floater
```

Let's break this script into its various parts.

There are two functions, turn_off and turn_on. For the moment, forget about how these functions work; just accept that they do what you want them to do. There are several terms to describe this kind of thinking—for example, you are *abstracting* the code, or your function is now a Black Box. A *Black Box* is something that has inputs and outputs, but the mechanics inside the box are hidden from the user. As long as the user knows what information to give the box and the kind of answer he or she expects, the user doesn't need to know how it arrived at that answer. For the moment, know that running the function turn_off turns off all the attenuation range displays, and running the function turn_on turns them on again.

The rollout definition is next. A *rollout* is the interface that will appear in your floater. You define the rollout, which includes two buttons—button_on and button_off. Below those are two commands, specifying that pressing button_on performs the turn_on function and pressing button_off performs the turn_off function. Finally, the script ends with the floater definition. Remember, a rollout is just a set of buttons and other UI elements. A *floater* is a window that floats on your interface and can contain many rollouts. This example has one rollout, so first you define the floater and then you add the rollout to that floater. There it is—the script in a nutshell.

Pseudo-Code

In pseudo-code, the previous script might look something like this:

```
Function turn_off
Function turn_on
Rollout lightcleaner_rollout
        (
        button button_off
        button button_on
        when you press button_off do function turn_off
        when you press button_on do function turn_on
        )
Make a floater lightcleaner_floater
add lightcleaner_rollout to lightcleaner_floater
```

See how easy that is to read? When you stare at a complex bunch of code, it helps to see past the details and visualize the code as pseudo-code. Look at the basics of what the script does, and then go for the details.

Now look a little deeper into the turn_off and turn_on functions.

Functions

Functions are one of the most important parts of your script, and should be heavily abstracted. For example, suppose you have a function called ran_num. All you need to know about this code is that when you call this function, it gives you a random number. You don't have to worry about *how* it gives you this result. Here is an example:

```
fn ran_num =
        (
random 1 9999999
        )
```

Let's look at the turn_on function. When called, it turns on all the display gizmos for a set of lights. Here's the code again:

```
fn turn_on =
        (
        if $ == undefined then
        (MessageBox "Please select at least one object"
        ➥title:"LightCleaner")
        else
                (
                for i = 1 to selection.count do
                        (
                        if superclassof selection[i] == light then
                                (
                                selection[i].showNearAtten = true
                                selection[i].showFarAtten = true
                                if classof selection[i] == targetSpot or
                                classof selection[i] == freeSpot or
                                classof selection[i] ==
                                ➥TargetDirectionallight or
                                classof selection[i] == Directionallight
                                ➥then
                                selection[i].showCone = true
                                )
                        )
                )
        )
```

Let's convert this code to pseudo-code:

```
Function turn_on is
If no objects are selected, return an error message or else
Do the following code to each object you have selected
        (
        if the selected object is a light then
                (
                turn on its near attenuation range display gizmo
turn on its far attenuation range display gizmo
if the selected object is a targetspotlight, freespot, target
➥directional or directional light turn on its display cone
)
                )
```

Note

Notice within the function that I do a lot of testing to make sure that it performs only certain functions on certain types of objects. This process is usually called *filtering*. The first filtering asks whether any objects are selected. It's tough to perform operations on objects that are not selected. Don't expect the user to be smart enough to select objects and then run the script; you have to be ready for any eventuality. The next filter asks whether each object is a light. If it is a light, the filter does some things to it. Then because omnis don't have cones, the filter asks "are you an omni" by asking whether it is any of the other light types except omni. If it is not an omni, the light's cone is turned on. The same process occurs for `turn_off`.

Running the Script

Run the script by going to the MAXScript menu and choosing Run script. Choose LightCleaner_v100a.ms. You get the floater with your rollout, as shown in Figure 22.2.

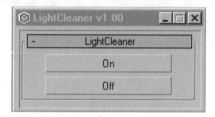

Figure 22.2   The LightCleaner script interface is a floater.

Select all the lights in the scene (and other objects, too—remember, thanks to filtering, the script won't perform the operations on any objects that aren't lights). Pressing the Off button turns off all the displayed lighting gizmos. This makes the scene a lot neater, as shown in Figure 22.3.

LightCleaner v1.10

After releasing the script free on the Internet, I got an email from someone saying he had modified my script to have it do some other tasks. Basically, he didn't want it to turn off all display gizmos immediately; he wanted to choose whether he wanted the cone on or off, the near attenuation on or off, and the far attenuation on or off. I liked the idea and made a variant on his variant. On the CD-ROM, unzip the file LightCleaner_v110.zip. You'll see the following code:

```
-- Variables

conevalue = 3
attnnvalue = 3
attnfvalue = 3
```

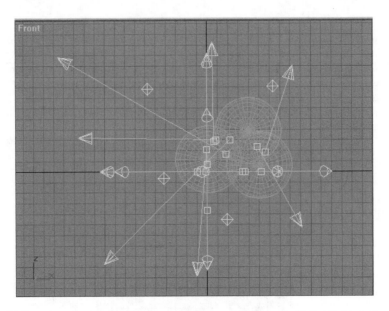

Figure 22.3   Notice how much cleaner your viewport is without all that light clutter.

```
-- Functions

fn turn_all_on =
        (
        for i = 1 to selection.count do
                (
                if superclassof selection[i] == light then
                        (
                        selection[i].showNearAtten = true
                        selection[i].showFarAtten = true
                        if classof selection[i] == targetSpot or
                        classof selection[i] == freeSpot or
                        classof selection[i] == TargetDirectionallight or
                        classof selection[i] == Directionallight then
                        selection[i].showCone = true
                        )
                )
        )

fn turn_all_off =
        (
        for i = 1 to selection.count do
                (
                if superclassof selection[i] == light then
                        (
                        selection[i].showNearAtten = false
                        selection[i].showFarAtten = false
                        if classof selection[i] == targetSpot or
                        classof selection[i] == freeSpot or
```

```
                              classof selection[i] == TargetDirectionallight or
                              classof selection[i] == Directionallight then
                              selection[i].showCone = false
                              )
                      )
              )

     fn cone_on_off =
              (
          for i = 1 to selection.count do
                  (
                  if superclassof selection[i] == light then
                          (
                          if classof selection[i] == targetSpot or
                          classof selection[i] == freeSpot or
                          classof selection[i] == TargetDirectionallight or
                          classof selection[i] == Directionallight then
                                  (
                                  if conevalue == 1 then
                                  ➥selection[i].showCone = true
                                  if conevalue == 2 then
                                  ➥selection[i].showCone = false
                                  )
                          )
                  )
              )

     fn attnn_on_off =
              (
          for i = 1 to selection.count do
                  (
                  if superclassof selection[i] == light then
                          (
                          if attnnvalue == 1 then
                          ➥selection[i].showNearAtten = true
                          if attnnvalue == 2 then
                          ➥selection[i].showNearAtten = false
                          )
                  )
              )

     fn attnf_on_off =
              (
          for i = 1 to selection.count do
                  (
                  if superclassof selection[i] == light then
                          (
                          if attnfvalue == 1 then selection[i].showFarAtten
                          ➥= true
                          if attnfvalue == 2 then selection[i].showFarAtten
                          ➥= false
                          )
                  )
              )
```

```
-- Script

rollout lightcleaner_rollout "LightCleaner"
        (
        group "What To Do"
        (
        label conelab "Cone" across:2 align:#left
        radiobuttons radcone labels:#("On", "Off", "—") columns:3
        ➥align:#right default:3
        label attn1lab "Near Atten" across:2 align:#left
        radiobuttons radattenn labels:#("On", "Off", "—") columns:3
        ➥align:#right default:3
        label attn2lab "Far Atten" across:2 align:#left
        radiobuttons radattenf labels:#("On", "Off", "—") columns:3
        ➥align:#right default:3
        )

        button button_apply "Apply" width:50 align:#center
        ➥tooltip:"Apply changes to lights" across:3
        button button_all_on "All On" width:50 align:#center
        ➥toolTip:"All On"
        button button_all_off "All Off" width:50 align:#center
        ➥toolTip:"All Off"

        on radcone changed chg do
                (
                conevalue = chg
                )

        on radattenn changed chg do
                (
                attnnvalue = chg
                )

        on radattenf changed chg do
                (
                attnfvalue = chg
                )

        on button_apply pressed do
                (
                if $ == undefined then
                (MessageBox "Please select at least one object"
                ➥title:"LightCleaner")
                else
                (
                if conevalue == 1 or conevalue == 2 then cone_on_off ()
                if attnnvalue == 1 or attnnvalue == 2 then attnn_on_off ()
                if attnfvalue == 1 or attnfvalue == 2 then attnf_on_off ()
                )
        )
        on button_all_on pressed do
                (
                if $ == undefined then
```

```
                    (MessageBox "Please select at least one object"
                    ➥title:"LightCleaner")
                    else turn_all_on ()
                    )
        on button_all_off pressed do
                    (
                    if $ == undefined then
                    (MessageBox "Please select at least one object"
                    ➥title:"LightCleaner")
                    else turn_all_off ()
                    )

        )

lightcleaner_floater = newRolloutFloater "LightCleaner v1.10" 250 180
addRollout lightcleaner_rollout lightcleaner_floater
```

This code creates the interface in Figure 22.4 for the user to operate.

This code is a little more complex than the code for LightCleaner v1.00, but it's still manageable. Just break it into pseudo-code:

Figure 22.4
The LightCleaner v1.10 interface.

```
Variable conevalue
Variable attnnvalue
Variable attnfvalue
Function turn_all_on (Turns NearAtten, FarAtten and
➥show cone on)
Function turn_all_off (Turns NearAtten, FarAtten and show cone off)
Function cone_on_off (Turns Cone on or off)
Function attnn_on_off (Turns NearAtten on or off)
Function attnf_on_off (Turns FarAtten on or off)
Rollout lightcleaner_rollout
        (
        Radiobuttons for cone, On off or unchanged
Radiobuttons for NearAtten, On off or unchanged
Radiobuttons for FarAtten, On off or unchanged
Button Apply
Button all_on
Button all_off

When you change the cone radiobutton, change the cone variable
When you change the NearAtten radiobutton, change the NearAtten
➥variable
When you change the FarAtten radiobutton, change the FarAtten variable
When you hit apply, do cone_on_off, attnn_on_off and attnf_on_off
➥functions
When you hit all_on, perform turn_all_on function
When you hit all_off, perform turn_all_off function
        )
Make a floater lightcleaner_floater
add lightcleaner_rollout to lightcleaner_floater
```

Variables

This script now has three *variables*—switches that tell the script what to do when performing functions. For example, you choose one of three positions for your cone radio button: on, off, or unchanged. When you change its position, you're actually affecting the variable conevalue, changing it from 1 to 2 to 3. 1 means you want to turn the cones on, 2 means you want to turn the cones off, 3 means don't do anything to it. Pressing Apply performs the cone_on_off function, which asks the question "do you want me to turn the cone on, off, or do nothing to it?" This question is answered by consulting your conevalue variable. A lot of script works this way: It gives the user some UI; the user changes values in that UI; those UI elements change values of variables; and then when a function is run, that function checks the states of those variables to decide what it's going to do. Notice at the beginning of the script conevalue = 3. If you look at the radio button it's attached to, the radio button defaults to 3.

LightViewer v1.00

The next light-related script I wrote was called LightViewer. The following production situation was given to me: I had a scene that showed a woman in a prison cell. The atmosphere was pretty dark, and yet for some reason, her teeth glowed bright white. I checked the teeth material and the material wasn't glowing, so I surmised that a light in the scene caused the teeth to glow for some reason. But which light? There were about 20 lights in my scene. I could turn off all the lights in the scene, turn on each light one at a time, render, and eventually find the light that was causing the problem. Rather than doing this the brute-force way, though, I wrote a script to do it for me. The script turned all the lights off, turned the first light on, rendered the view, turned it off, turned the second light on, rendered, and so forth, until I had 20 images. The image that had the glowing teeth was associated with the light I needed to fix.

Here is an example of the script at work—a scene with three lights (see Figure 22.5). The script shows the illumination of the first light on the scene (see Figure 22.6), the second light (see Figure 22.7), and the third light (see Figure 22.8).

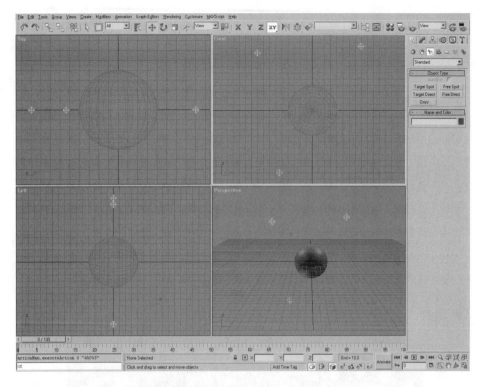

Figure 22.5   A simple scene with three lights.

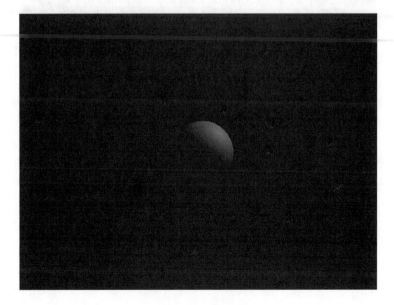

Figure 22.6   The scene as illuminated by the first light.

Figure 22.7   The scene as illuminated by the second light.

Figure 22.8   The scene as illuminated by the third light.

The file that contains this test scene is called maxscript_tut_01.max and is available on the CD-ROM. Here's the code, available in LightViewer_v100.zip:

```
-- Globals

global are_you_a_standard_light
global how_many_nonstandard_lights
global all_lights
global view_the_lights
global collect_the_lights
global view_1
global view_2
global view_3
global do_a_render
global put_it_back
global laststate = #()

global lv_rollout
global lv_floater

-- Variables

lv_type_value = 1
leave_t_value = false
no_t_value = false

-- Functions

fn are_you_a_standard_light s =
        (
        if \
        classof s == targetSpot or \
        classof s == Omnilight or \
        classof s == TargetDirectionallight or \
        classof s == Directionallight or \
        classof s == freeSpot \
        then true
        else false
        )

fn how_many_nonstandard_lights onwhat =
        (
        nsl = 0
        if onwhat == "scene" then
                (
                for s in lights do
                        (
                        if superclassof s != GeometryClass then
                                (
                                if are_you_a_standard_light s == false
                        ➥then nsl += 1
                                )
                        )
                )
```

```
        else if onwhat == "selected" then
                (
                for s in selection do
                        (
                        if superclassof s == light then
                                (
                                if superclassof s != GeometryClass then
                                        (
                                        if are_you_a_standard_light s ==
                                        ➥false then nsl += 1
                                        )
                                )
                        )
                )
        else (MessageBox "how_many_nonstandard_lights were called with
        ➥an improper parameter" title:"BSLib")
        nsl
        )

fn all_lights onwhat =
        (
        all_the_lights = #()
        if onwhat == "scene" then
                (
                for s in lights do
                        (
                        if are_you_a_standard_light s == true then append
                        ➥all_the_lights s
                        )
                )
        else if onwhat == "selected" then
                (
                for s in selection do
                        (
                        if are_you_a_standard_light s == true then append
                        ➥all_the_lights s
                        )
                )
        else (MessageBox "all_lights were called with an improper para
        ➥meter" title:"BSLib")
        all_the_lights
        )

fn view_the_lights =
        (
        if $ == undefined and lv_type_value != 3 then
        (MessageBox "Please select at least one light"
        ➥title:"LightViewer")
        else
                (
                freeSceneBitmaps()
                gc()
                collect_the_lights()
                if lv_type_value == 2 then view_2()
```

```
                              else if lv_type_value == 3 then view_3()
                                     else view_1()
                              put_it_back()
                          )
                      )

          fn collect_the_lights =
                      (
                      laststate = #()
                      for s in all_lights "scene" do
                              (
                              append laststate #(s, s.enabled)
                              )
                      if how_many_nonstandard_lights "scene" > 0 then
                      (MessageBox "At least one light in the scene is not a standard
                      ➥max light, and cannot be affected by this script."
          title:"LightViewer")
                      )

          fn view_1 =
                      (
                      for i = 1 to laststate.count do
                              (
                              if laststate[i][1].isselected == false then
                              ➥laststate[i][1].enabled = false
                              else laststate[i][1].enabled = true
                              )
                      do_a_render "SelectedLights"
                      )

          fn view_2 =
                      (
                      for w = 1 to laststate.count do
                              (
                              if laststate[w][1].isselected != false then
                                      (
                                      for i = 1 to laststate.count do
                                              (
                                              if i == w then laststate[i][1].enabled =
                                              ➥true
                                              else laststate[i][1].enabled = false
                                              )
                                      do_a_render laststate[w][1].name
                                      )
                              )
                      )

          fn view_3 =
                      (
                      for w = 1 to laststate.count do
                              (
                              for j = 1 to laststate.count do
                                      (
                                      if j == w then laststate[j][1].enabled = true
```

```
                            else laststate[j][1].enabled = false
                            )
                    do_a_render laststate[w][1].name
                    )
            )

    fn do_a_render thename =
            (
            outfile = (getdir #image) + "\\" + (thename as string) + ".tga"
            render vfb:off antiAliasing:false mapping:no_t_value
            ➥imageMotionBlur:false objectMotionBlur:false outputfile:outfile
            close (openbitmap outfile)
            display (openbitmap outfile)
            if leave_t_value == false then deleteFile outfile
            )

    fn put_it_back =
            (
            for i = 1 to laststate.count do laststate[i][1].enabled = last
            ➥state[i][2]
            )

    -- Script

    rollout lv_rollout "LightViewer"
            (
            dropdownlist lv_type "" items:#("Selected Together", "Selected
            ➥Separate", "All Separate")
            on lv_type selected i do lv_type_value = i

            checkbox leave_t "Leave Temporary Images" checked:false
            ➥align:#center
            on leave_t changed state do
                    (
                    if leave_t.checked == true then leave_t_value = true
                    else leave_t_value = false
                    )
            checkbox no_t "No Textures" checked:true align:#center
            on no_t changed state do
                    (
                    if no_t.checked == true then no_t_value = false
                    else no_t_value = true
                    )

            button view_b "View the influence" width:170 align:#center
            ➥toolTip:"View the influence of this light"
            on view_b pressed do view_the_lights()
            )

    lv_floater = newRolloutFloater "LightViewer v1.00" 230 163
    addRollout lv_rollout lv_floater
```

```
                    else laststate[j][1].enabled = false
                )
            do_a_render laststate[w][1].name
            )
        )

    fn do_a_render thename =
        (
        outfile = (getdir #image) + "\\" + (thename as string) + ".tga"
        render vfb:off antiAliasing:false mapping:no_t_value
        ➡imageMotionBlur:false objectMotionBlur:false outputfile:outfile
        close (openbitmap outfile)
        display (openbitmap outfile)
        if leave_t_value == false then deleteFile outfile
        )

    fn put_it_back =
        (
        for i = 1 to laststate.count do laststate[i][1].enabled = last
        ➡state[i][2]
        )

-- Script

rollout lv_rollout "LightViewer"
    (
    dropdownlist lv_type "" items:#("Selected Together", "Selected
    ➡Separate", "All Separate")
    on lv_type selected i do lv_type_value = i

    checkbox leave_t "Leave Temporary Images" checked:false
    ➡align:#center
    on leave_t changed state do
        (
        if leave_t.checked == true then leave_t_value = true
        else leave_t_value = false
        )
    checkbox no_t "No Textures" checked:true align:#center
    on no_t changed state do
        (
        if no_t.checked == true then no_t_value = false
        else no_t_value = true
        )

    button view_b "View the influence" width:170 align:#center
    ➡toolTip:"View the influence of this light"
    on view_b pressed do view_the_lights()
    )

lv_floater = newRolloutFloater "LightViewer v1.00" 230 163
addRollout lv_rollout lv_floater
```

The file that contains this test scene is called maxscript_tut_01.max and is available on the CD-ROM. Here's the code, available in LightViewer_v100.zip:

```
-- Globals

global are_you_a_standard_light
global how_many_nonstandard_lights
global all_lights
global view_the_lights
global collect_the_lights
global view_1
global view_2
global view_3
global do_a_render
global put_it_back
global laststate = #()

global lv_rollout
global lv_floater

-- Variables

lv_type_value = 1
leave_t_value = false
no_t_value = false

-- Functions

fn are_you_a_standard_light s =
    (
    if \
    classof s == targetSpot or \
    classof s == Omnilight or \
    classof s == TargetDirectionallight or \
    classof s == Directionallight or \
    classof s == freeSpot \
    then true
    else false
    )

fn how_many_nonstandard_lights onwhat =
    (
    nsl = 0
    if onwhat == "scene" then
        (
        for s in lights do
            (
            if superclassof s != GeometryClass then
                (
                if are_you_a_standard_light s == false
                ➡then nsl += 1
                )
            )
        )
```

```
        else if onwhat == "selected" then
            (
                for s in selection do
                    (
                        if superclassof s == light then
                            (
                                if superclassof s != GeometryClass then
                                    (
                                        if are_you_a_standard_light s ==
                                        ➥false then nsl += 1
                                    )
                            )
                    )
            )
        else (MessageBox "how_many_nonstandard_lights were called with
        ➥an improper parameter" title:"BSLib")
        nsl
    )

fn all_lights onwhat =
    (
        all_the_lights = #()
        if onwhat == "scene" then
            (
                for s in lights do
                    (
                        if are_you_a_standard_light s == true then append
                        ➥all_the_lights s
                    )
            )
        else if onwhat == "selected" then
            (
                for s in selection do
                    (
                        if are_you_a_standard_light s == true then append
                        ➥all_the_lights s
                    )
            )
        else (MessageBox "all_lights were called with an improper para
        ➥meter" title:"BSLib")
        all_the_lights
    )

fn view_the_lights =
    (
        if $ == undefined and lv_type_value != 3 then
        (MessageBox "Please select at least one light"
        ➥title:"LightViewer")
        else
            (
                freeSceneBitmaps()
                gc()
                collect_the_lights()
                if lv_type_value == 2 then view_2()
```

```
                else if lv_type_value == 3 then view_3()
                    else view_1()
                put_it_back()
            )
    )

fn collect_the_lights =
    (
        laststate = #()
        for s in all_lights "scene" do
            (
                append laststate #(s, s.enabled)
            )
        if how_many_nonstandard_lights "scene" > 0 then
        (MessageBox "At least one light in the scene is not a standard
        ➥max light, and cannot be affected by this script."
title:"LightViewer")
    )

fn view_1 =
    (
        for i = 1 to laststate.count do
            (
                if laststate[i][1].isselected == false then
                ➥laststate[i][1].enabled = false
                else laststate[i][1].enabled = true
            )
        do_a_render "SelectedLights"
    )

fn view_2 =
    (
        for w = 1 to laststate.count do
            (
                if laststate[w][1].isselected != false then
                    (
                        for i = 1 to laststate.count do
                            (
                                if i == w then laststate[i][1].enabled =
                                ➥true
                                else laststate[i][1].enabled = false
                            )
                        do_a_render laststate[w][1].name
                    )
            )
    )

fn view_3 =
    (
        for w = 1 to laststate.count do
            (
                for j = 1 to laststate.count do
                    (
                        if j == w then laststate[j][1].enabled = true
```

Globals

You have learned about variables, rollouts, floaters, and functions. Before you get into the pseudo-code, look at another element: globals. I started using globals not too long ago (that's why there are none in those previous two scripts). A *global* is a way of defining a variable, function, rollout, or floater that everything in a script will have access to. This also solves a problem that MAXScript has regarding functions: You need to define a function before being able to use it. Consider the following code:

```
fn test_function_1 =
        (
        a = 2
        test_function_2 a
        )

fn test_function_2 a_variable =
        (
        print a_variable
        )

test_function_1()
```

If you run this, you'll get an error saying that function `test_function_1` cannot run because it has no idea what `test_function_2` is. You define `test_function_2` after you define `test_function_1`. In order to use a function inside a function, you have to define the function ahead of time. To get it to work, you enter the following code:

```
fn test_function_2 a_variable =
        (
        print a_variable
        )

fn test_function_1 =
        (
        a = 2
        test_function_2 a
        )

test_function_1()
```

This seems as if you're going backward. You have to define something before using it. The key to solving this problem is globals. This code also works:

```
Global test_function_1
Global test_function_2

fn test_function_1 =
        (
```

```
        a = 2
        test_function_2 a
        )

fn test_function_2 a_variable =
        (
        print a_variable
        )

test_function_1()
```

This works because by defining a function globally at the beginning of the script, even though you have not defined what test_function_2 does until after you've defined what test_function_1 does, you tell MAXScript that there will be a function called test_function_2 defined elsewhere in the script. By defining functions, floaters, and rollouts at the beginning of your script, you can order your functions any way you want.

Pseudo-Code

Let's look at the pseudo-code for the script:

```
Define All Functions, rollouts and floaters globally
Make an Array called laststate
Variable lv_type_value = 1
Variable leave_t_value = false
Variable no_t_value = false
Function are_you_a_standard_light
Function how_many_nonstandard_lights
Function all_lights
Function view_the_lights
Function collect_the_lights
Function view_1
Function view_2
Function view_3
Function do_a_render
Function put_it_back
Rollout lv_rollout
        (
        Dropdown List to choose the type of view
Checkbox should I leave temporary images
Checkbox should I show textures in the vfbs.
When I change the dropdown, change the view type variable lv_type_value
When I check or uncheck the checkbox, change the state of the
➥leave_t_value variable
When I check or uncheck the checkbox, change the state of the
➥no_t_value variable
Button run the script
When you press the button have it run the script by executing the first
➥function view_the_lights
```

```
        )
Make a floater lb_floater
add lv_rollout to lv_floater
```

The interface is shown in Figure 22.9.

The following are more detailed explanations of each part of the pseudo-code script.

```
Variable lv_type_value
```

Figure 22.9
The interface for LightViewer v1.00.

This line explains the type of viewing you want to do—that is, whether you perform the function view_1, view_2, or view_3.

```
Variable leave_t_value
```

This line says to leave temporary image files true or false. To run, the script renders the different views and makes temporary image files in your max images directory. Then it displays all these images to the screen and deletes the temporary image. If this variable is set to true, it does not delete the images, allowing the user to later use them for other purposes.

```
Variable no_t_value
```

This line asks whether you want to have textures shown in your renderings, true or false.

```
Function are_you_a_standard_light
```

This function returns true or false, depending on whether the object given to it is a standard light (see next function for an explanation).

```
Function how_many_nonstandard_lights
```

This function returns the number of nonstandard lights. Now what does this mean exactly?

Consider this code:

```
For L in lights do print L
```

The word lights in the code refers to an array of all the lights in the scene. An *array* is a list of things, and MAXScript already has a list of all lights in the scene, which it calls lights. This code basically asks for all things in the list of scene lights (that is, for all lights in the list of lights) and prints the name of the light to the Listener.

The how_many_nonstandard_lights function exists because within the list of scene lights there could possibly be lights that have no MAXScript access. For example, if you own Shag:Hair from Digimation, you can create something called a *hair-enabled light*, which appears to be a light, but has no MAXScript access. If you perform a MAXScript operation on the light, it returns an error. The function `how_many_non-standard_lights` returns a number that represents the number of lights in the scene that have no MAXScript access.

This function requires the `are_you_a_standard` light function to operate. Notice how I broke what could be one function into two. There are probably plenty of points in my code where I might want to know whether the current selected object is a standard light. In my LightCleaner script, I performed this filtering within each function. Writing the filters repeatedly in this script, I create the filter function `are_you_a_standard_light` once and then call it from other functions.

Function all_lights

Using again the `are_you_a_standard_light` function, the `all_lights` function makes an array that is a list of lights in your scene or selection that have MAXScript access.

Function view_the_lights

This function is the heart of the script. When you click the View The Influence button, it runs this function, which merely calls a bunch of other functions. Think of it as the control to the script, a shopping list of things the script has to do.

Function collect_the_lights

This function is the first one called by `view_the_lights`. This function clears the array `laststate`, and then goes through all the lights in the scene and makes a new array whose members are the light itself and determines whether the light is on or off. Finally, it checks to see whether there are any nonstandard lights in the scene; if there are, `collect_the_lights` gives the user a dialog warning them that these lights will not be affected by the script.

What's inside the `laststate` array? Take, for example, a scene with two omnis. The first one is off, and the second is on:

```
laststate = #(#(Omni01, false), #(Omni02, true))
```

This line is an example of an array within an array. You have an array with two members, and each member is an array of two members. You access an array as follows: `laststate [1]` returns to you `#(Omni01, false)`, because you're asking for the first member of `laststate`. `laststate [1][2]` returns `false`, because you're asking for the second member of the first member of `laststate`. You collect this new array called `laststate` because when you finish turning lights on and off and rendering, you want to put everything back the way it was, which is performed by the `put_it_back` function, described later.

Function view_1

This line is the first possible viewing method. Notice that when you choose a viewing type in the drop-down list, it affects the variable `lv_type_value`. Then when the function `view_the_lights` is run, it decides which of the three view functions to invoke based on the value of this variable. `view_1` corresponds to `Selected Together`, which renders a single `vfb` that shows the effect of all currently selected lights. This function first turns off all the nonselected lights and then performs the render. Notice that the `do_a_render` function is a separate function, because it is called by `view_1`, `view_2`, and `view_3`. Instead of writing the code three times, it generalizes it as a separate function and calls it from within the three view functions.

Function view_2

This line corresponds to `Selected Seperate`. It has the same structure as `view_1`, but it contains two `for` loops. The first `for` loop iterates over each light in the selection. The second `for` loop turns off all the lights that need to be turned off and leaves on the first light in the array. Then it renders. It does the same thing for the second light in the group, and so forth. You get the results shown in Figures 22.6 through 22.8 shown earlier in this chapter.

Function view_3

This line is the same as `view_2`, except it checks all the lights in the scene, not just the selected lights.

Function do_a_render

This line is the render code. It takes the scene in its current state, renders the scene to a file—which it writes to the max default images directory—and then displays the file. It deletes the temporary file unless the user has chosen to leave temporary files by checking the Leave Temporary Files check box in the LightViewer interface. In the render command is the mapping parameter, which is the variable that is changed when the user checks or unchecks the Show Texture check box.

Function put_it_back

This code goes through all the lights in the scene and puts them back to the state they were before the script started. Remember, it has the information of which lights were on and off in the `laststate` array, so it uses that information to do its work.

The Script at Work

Remember my scene with the glowing teeth? Running the script on my original scene showed me the problem: One of the lights in the scene had cast off shadows, so the light was penetrating through the cheek and illuminating the teeth too much. Although this script took me a while to write, and I probably could have done it faster manually, I now know I will never have to do it again. Anytime any of the team is presented with the same problem, he or she can press a button to figure out the answer instead of doing a bunch of boring work.

The script isn't useful only for this particular problem. It's also useful for other purposes. For example, suppose you set up a scene with a number of lights and then decide, for speed purposes, that you should delete five lights from your scene. Which five lights do you pick? Being able to see exactly how much a particular light adds to the overall scene illumination can give you a better idea of where to cut. Maybe you'd like to see how much backlight your object is receiving from the backlight you added two weeks ago, now that the character and scene have undergone several hundred changes. Is it doing its job? Could it be doing its job better if you moved it a bit? Is that illumination you're seeing on the side of the face coming from Omni251 or Omni252? The possibilities are endless.

LightUtilities v2.50

As the months passed, I wanted to do a lot of things with lights. An animator gave me a request for a quick script that would enable him to take all selected lights and turn them on or off. I wanted to add more options to LightViewer, globally change parameters to a series of lights, and write a floater that enabled me to control a bunch of lights simultaneously.

Several years ago Blur Studio released a plug-in called LightBoy, which was a utility that listed all the lights in your scene and gave you some common parameters, such as multiplier, shadow map size, on and off, and shadows on and off. The interface for LightBoy is shown in Figure 22.10.

This was very useful because it enabled me to change the parameters on multiple lights quickly and efficiently. It also gave me the ability to compare lights to each other, and as anyone in deep production knows, we could easily have hundreds of lights in a scene. LightBoy had a few problems, however. For example, it was a utility and not a floater, so I had to keep going in and out of LightBoy if I wanted to modify something that LightBoy could not control. In addition, one of the animators complained that the lights in LightBoy were always ordered by creation order instead of alphabetically, making it harder to find my light.

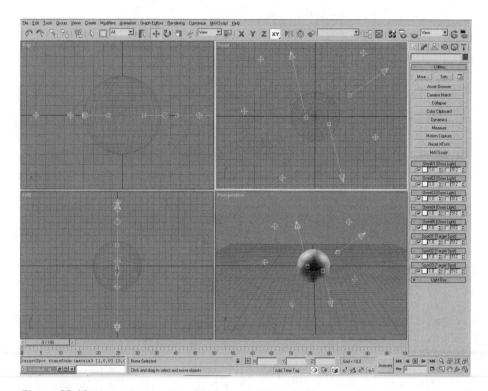

Figure 22.10   The LightBoy interface is on the right.

Others have tried tackling the LightBoy problem. 3ds max 4 ships with a script called LightLister (see Figure 22.11) that does the same thing LightBoy does, but it's a script *and* a floater. However, it also has disadvantages. An advantage is that you can affect more parameters with LightLister. A disadvantage is that it takes up too much screen space, and screen space for any production animator is always at a premium.

Seeing all the things that could be improved, I set out to make a new LightBoy-style script that tried to do everything the others did, without any of their inherent problems.

With all these scripts sort of converging, I decided to merge all the scripts into a single script called LightUtilities, shown in Figure 22.12.

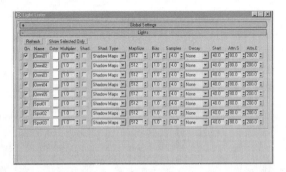

Figure 22.11   The interface for LightLister.

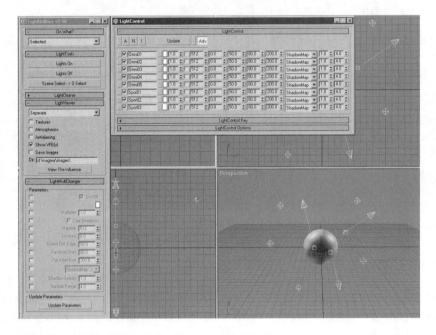

Figure 22.12   The LightUtilities interface.

I think I managed to cover all the ground that I needed to. It incorporates LightCleaner, LightViewer, and a MultiChanger to change multiple parameters. It has a LightLister interface, but notice the advanced (ADV) button, which is yellow. If you turn the ADV button off and minimize the LightUtilities floater, you get something compact and similar to the original LightBoy interface, but in floater form. If you don't need all those extra parameters, you don't have to have them cluttering your view. It also enables you to change the ordering of the LightControl panel from creation to alphabetical, under LightControl Options.

The script is available on the CD-ROM, and is actually a set of seven scripts. I started merging all the code into a single file, but I soon realized that trying to find anything in that file was difficult because of the sheer volume of text. So I split it up.

To install LightUtilities, unzip the LightUtilities_v250.zip file into your 3ds max 4 root directory and make sure you have recurse subdirectories on. This will place seven files into your max4\scripts\BlurScripts directory, scripts directory (found in your 3ds max 4 root directory). To run the script, run the file LightUtilities.ms, which is the main script. You'll see the following lines:

```
include "$scripts\BlurScripts\LightUtilities_Control.ms"
include "$scripts\BlurScripts\LightUtilities_Tools.ms"
include "$scripts\BlurScripts\LightUtilities_Cleaner.ms"
include "$scripts\BlurScripts\LightUtilities_Viewer.ms"
include "$scripts\BlurScripts\LightUtilities_Order.ms"
include "$scripts\BlurScripts\LightUtilities_MultiChanger.ms"
```

When you run the LightUtilities.ms file, it calls the other six files and includes their code in its own. It's easier to read when split into seven separate files.

Note

Notice the use of the token $scripts. This returns to the script the currently selected script directory for max 4. For example, my copy of max 4 is in my d:\magma directory. Someone else's could be in c:\3dsmax4. Because each of our installations writes a max INI file that specifies where the script directory is, you can access this information from MAXScript. As long as these six scripts are in a subdirectory of the current script directory called BlurScripts, they will be found by the main LightUtilities script.

Here's a more in-depth look at the six files that come with LightUtilities.ms:

- **LightUtilities_Control.** The LightBoy-type code.

- **LightUtilities_Tools.** Some random utilities, such as turning all lights on or off.

- **LightUtilities_Cleaner.** A more advanced form of my original LightCleaner script.

- **LightUtilities_Viewer.** A more advanced form of my old LightViewer script.

- **LightUtilities_Order.** Part of LightViewer. In one mode of LightViewer, you need to choose the order the lights will be viewed in; this code provides you a dialog to choose the order.

- **LightUtilities_MultiChanger**. A script that enables you to change parameters over many lights. For example, if you want the shadow map size of all selected lights to be 512, you can do this without having to change the parameter for each light.

As an exercise, start looking through the code. You might want to try replicating the code in pseudo-code to help you follow the action. The only part that might be confusing is how the LightControl interface code in LightUtilities_Control.ms works.

Code That Writes Code

When you create a rollout, you say "I want a radio button here, I want a button there." But what if you don't know how many buttons you'll need? That was the problem presented to me for LightControl. If I had 4 lights in the scene, I needed 4 light buttons; if I had 10 lights, I needed 10 buttons. I needed to define my rollout and then add as many UI elements as I had lights. I needed code that writes code, a series of commands that build code that is then run, defining my rollout. Although the code to do that in the LightControl script might seem daunting and complex, it's not that hard when you see how it's done.

Here's a simple example. Create a scene with four spheres. Make sure they are all selected and run the following code:

```
w=("Rollout w_rollout \"W\"\n")
w+="(\n"
for i = 1 to selection.count do
        (
        w+="label label" + (i as string)+ " \"" + (selection[i].name as
        ➥string) +"\"\n"
        )
w+=")\n"
execute w
w_floater = newRolloutFloater "" 250 400
addRollout w_rollout w_floater
```

The result is a rollout in a floater that contains the names of all four spheres. Now run it again with 3 spheres, 10 spheres, or any number you want. It always builds enough labels to accommodate the number of selected objects.

Let's take this one line at a time:

```
w=("Rollout w_rollout \"W\"\n")
```

The first obvious question is "what is w"? Is it a variable? It's actually a string. A *string* is a set of characters, letters, numbers, or so on. For example, `"hello"` is a string, and `"100"` is a string. You tell MAXScript that you're making a string by placing quotation marks around your collection of symbols. This example has a string called w. It looks similar to a rollout definition, but has backslashes (\) and extra quotation marks.

Look carefully at lines 1 through 7. The first line begins with w=, and three lines begin with w+=, which means "add to w." By line 8, we have a long string w that is a collection of many pieces. Let's take a closer look at what w becomes. Do this by typing `print` w before `execute` w. Select your four spheres and then run the script. The Listener returns the following:

```
"Rollout w_rollout "W"
(
label label1 "Sphere02"
label label2 "Sphere03"
label label3 "Sphere04"
label label4 "Sphere01"
)
"
```

Now you can start to see what's happening. Line 1 defines w as a string that produces the line `"Rollout w_rollout "W"`; line 2 produces the opening parenthesis; line 3 is a `for` loop that goes through all selected objects; and line 5 adds four lines to w, one for each object selected. Line 7 adds the closing parenthesis. The final line executes w. This code generates a string that contains code, and then by executing w, you execute the code that you have asked the script to write.

Once you've wrapped your head around that, the next question you might ask is "what are all those \n and extra quotes for?" Well, remember, a string is constructed by placing quotation marks to denote the string's beginning and end. How do you place a quotation mark inside a string, as in this example, when quotation marks usually end or begin a string? You use certain special characters, which are denoted by a backslash followed by a character. Here are some examples:

- \" means "No I don't want to end the string; I just want to place a quotation mark inside the string."
- \n means "Please give me a carriage return."

Look at line 5 at a value of i = 1:

```
w+="label label" + (i as string)+ " \"" + (selection[i].name as string)
+"\"\n"
```

This says the following: Add to w the words "label label", and then attach to label the number 1. (You have to type i as a string because i is a number, and you actually want the string "1", not the numeric value 1.) Then add to the string a quotation mark, add the name of the current selection as a string, add another quotation mark, and then add a carriage return. This produces the following line:

```
label label1 "Sphere02"
```

Take a close look at the LightControl code. A string called lrs has a lot of added characters. It creates a chunk of code that defines the LightControl rollout, which is then executed (defining the rollout) and placed in the LightControl floater.

Summary

In this chapter, you explored the thought process that goes into writing scripts for production use. Even a complex script such as LightUtilities starts with a few simple functions. The only way to avoid going crazy is by keeping things simple. Don't look at all the code at once, abstract it into basic functions, make sure the architecture of the script works first, and then the details are just a matter of hard work and a lot of bug fixing. Enjoy.

Part VII

Lighting

Chapter 23

Lighting Techniques for Broadcast/Film

by Ian Christie

In this chapter you use the Jester project

as your test-bed. Of course, one scene

cannot include all the possible lighting

scenarios you are likely to encounter as a

max artist. Some projects call for a stylized or non-naturalistic approach to lighting, and others strive for absolute realism. You might be asked to create whole CG worlds populated with animated characters or even humans shot against bluescreen.

In this chapter, however, you light a CG character and object against a photographic background, and if you're successful, the CG elements should look as though they were part of the original photography. It's a tall order—there are critical technical and aesthetic subtleties to creating convincing lighting. On the other hand, there are some audacious cheats that can really make your character spring to life.

Although you won't explore every type of lighting situation, you can build upon the essential techniques from this project and fit them to your needs. That's where your ingenuity and artistry take over. You should have access to the max manuals and be pretty familiar with its interface and 3D computer graphics in general—this chapter doesn't have much space for repeating the basics.

Note

There is rarely time to make everything perfect, so pick your battles. The eye will seize on some details immediately if they are not exactly right. Other things can be flawed without ever being noticed. The shot you've been working on for weeks will flash by in a second or two. Where will the viewers' eyes be focused? Don't put equal effort into a character's shoes as you do the face.

Following are some of the more important points you learn:

- Recognizing the differences between max lights and their real-world counterparts

- Executing your task, as a lighter, in relationship to the tasks of other team members and other parts of the scene creation process

- Using the properties of max lights that enable you to reach a higher level of depth and realism

- Using tools in max that help to make your life, as a lighting artist, a little easier and give you greater control

- Creating careful use of shading, color, highlights, and shadows that contribute to a convincingly realistic image

- Using artistic judgment to heighten both the realism and aesthetics of the scene

The Nature of max Lighting

Before you roll up your sleeves and start getting pixels under your fingernails, take a moment to think about how lighting in max works. If you have experience working with photographic lighting, you might have noticed that things work somewhat differently in the max universe. Although it uses a real-world studio as a paradigm, on closer inspection, the max world can be quite unnatural. In some cases that's a good thing. You have control over things that would be impractical or downright impossible in the real world. Unfortunately, there are many properties of light in nature that we take for granted but that are lacking from max lights. Often it takes some wrangling with max's more esoteric features to coax out a visually realistic image.

For instance, a subject can be adequately (if not attractively) lit by a single bare bulb in the real world. Light bounces off the walls, ceiling, and floor and illuminates the subject from all directions. Lights in max don't bounce. To simulate the real-world effect of surfaces lighting each other in max, you have to use several strategically placed lights. You might even have to use techniques such as light falloff or negative lights (like little black holes) to emulate the complex interactions of intersurface illumination and shading. Your best guide for this sort of thing is reference. Look at photographs of similar scenes and study them to see what makes real-world lighting look the way it does. Where two walls meet do they look brighter, darker, or unchanged? Notice colors. Does the color of a wall stay consistent across its entire surface? Probably not.

Some of the properties of real-world lights are missing from their max counterparts. One of those is size. 3ds max lights have no size—unlike real lights, which can range from pinpoint sparks to the entire sky. The reason for max's dimensionless lights is speed—one of max's primary virtues is its rendering speed, but max manages that performance by cheating. It simulates a light's size in a surface's material shader. Unfortunately, because max lights don't have a size, they are all treated the same when the object is evaluated by the renderer. A light representing a window appears the same as a light that is supposed to be a desk lamp. The color and intensity might differ, but the size is always the same (compare Figures 23.1a and 23.1b). Most of the time this really isn't much of a problem (as with the Jester project), but occasionally it's a killer.

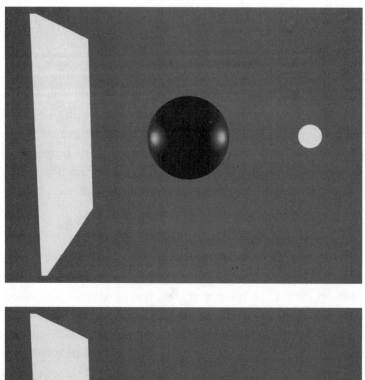

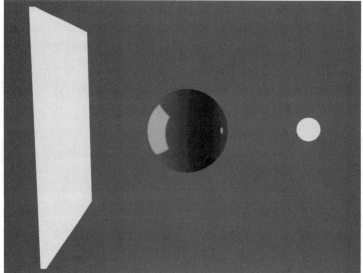

Figure 23.1   The rendering on top used raytracing and an array of lights to achieve more believable results than the out-of-the-box setup on the bottom.

Note

3ds max lights have two parameters that enable some individual control over a light's falloff across a surface—Contrast and Soften Diffuse Edge—and they are in the Affect Surfaces section of the Light rollout. These parameters *almost* work as a function to simulate light size. They both affect the transition between the diffuse and ambient components of a shaded surface. Unfortunately, neither of these parameters is based on physical properties of real lights, and it is difficult to control them in any meaningful way. Neither of these controls affects the specular components of materials. This would be a critical factor in simulating lights with dimension. After all, a specular highlight is really just the reflection of the light source.

Note

You might be surprised at how often professional photographers "light" objects with reflections. Highly reflective surfaces, such as bright metals, tend to be defined by their reflections; direct illumination becomes incidental. Take a look at some car ads. You'll see how the auto's contours are defined by big simple reflections. Or check out the product photos in the Sunday paper color inserts. No amount of direct light will make stainless pots and pans look right. Environments are created around the shiny subjects for them to reflect. The object's appearance is defined by the way it modulates its environment.

By this point you might feel as though max is rather primitive at simulating real-world lighting—and you'd be right. There are more sophisticated ways of lighting and rendering.

Renderers that attempt to model surface-to-surface illumination fall under the umbrella term *global illumination*. Although such rendering engines can sometimes produce uncannily photographic images, there is a price to be paid with speed and interactivity. Optimizations have made global illumination renders viable for applications such as architectural visualization, but at present, the capability of quickly tweaking and revising makes fast renderers such as max's more valuable for character animation.

You can't lay down lights in their theoretically correct positions and expect max to churn out beautiful, realistic images. Don't trust max—it won't necessarily give you the right thing. You have to think like an artist. Conjure the final image in your mind's eye and—with your knowledge of the max toolset—use whatever means necessary to reproduce your vision in the final image.

Preparing to Light

By now you're probably anxious to get going. But where do you start? If this were a real job you would, no doubt, have a meeting with your client or supervisor to get a sense of what is expected from your lighting and what the priorities are. It's essential, before you begin, to understand the intent of the shot and where in the frame the viewer should be focused.

Depending on the structure of your company, you need to coordinate with other members of the team responsible for this shot. If you are not doing your own animation, rigging, texturing, and so forth, you have to collect the necessary elements before you can begin. Even when you're part of a team, you probably still need to at least dabble in other disciplines. In the Jester project, for instance, you have to create stand-in geometry and a material to allow the Jester to cast shadows onto the background.

In an ideal world, everything you need would be perfect, complete, and ready to go by the time you started your lighting. As you might have noticed, this is *not* a perfect world. Due to scheduling constraints, you might be required to start lighting a shot before animation or materials have been completed. In this case, communication between artists is essential. Time is always a critical factor, so you do not want to get into a situation where hours of lighting work are rendered useless by a major change in animation. As you light, you might find that somebody else's work needs to be adjusted for the particular needs of your shot.

Suppose, for instance, you need tight little highlights in your character's eyes, but the material's highlight parameter is too soft for the right effect. It's usually acceptable, and often necessary, to tweak these kinds of things from shot to shot. Just make sure everyone is kept informed about your changes so that objectionable discontinuities don't develop between shots.

Exercise 23.1   Lighting the Jester

Enough theory—it's time to get to work. You have a CG Jester who jumps out of a live-action box and then picks up and tosses an equally CG toy truck. Except for the Jester and the truck, everything else in the shot is part of the photographed background image (known as the *plate*). Because the lighting in the plate is established and your elements must appear to be part of the scene, you have to match your lighting to that in the plate. So, look at the plate.

1. From the Rendering menu, select RAM Player. Click the little folder icon next to Channel A, and then find the background image sequence on the CD-ROM that came with this book (it's the sequence of Targa files titled take01*.tga).

Lighting Tips

The more information you have about how the plate was shot, the better. Indoors or out, almost every professionally photographed background plate involves some sort of supplementary lighting, whether a simple reflector card or two, or huge banks of arc lights.

It might be difficult to gauge exactly what is going on with the lighting in the plate without some sort of reference. Sometimes you might get written notes or a diagram describing the lights on the set. Often, plates are shot with some sort of reference. For instance, a gray sphere inserted in the shot gives accurate evidence of the colors and relative intensities of the lights in the scene as well as the softness or hardness of the illumination. The reflection in a mirrored ball also gives you a glimpse of the entire environment in which the plate was shot. It can even be used for generating environment maps.

If you're lucky, the film/video crew shot some frames of the plate with a reference model in place. This gives you a great starting point. Just make your CG model look like the one in the reference plate! If the photographer had a reference model on set, he or she probably lit the scene with the character in mind. This is not always the case. If there are actors in the shot—as there are in this case—and no reference model or stand-in was used, the lighting was probably set up solely for the actors. You probably have to add lights specifically for the character, as the photographer would have done had the character been in the set.

There are many styles of lighting for film and broadcast. Lighting for television tends to be brighter and more filled-in because the display settings of televisions can vary considerably. Producers want to create content that will look reasonably good on any set. Display environments for motion pictures (cinemas) are more controlled. In films, that technical freedom results in a wide range of lighting styles. Comedies and romances tend to be brightly lit, and dramas and horror flicks are usually darker and have more contrast. Whatever the style, the lighting is always carefully controlled.

Part of the challenge in lighting a CG character against a live-action plate is in producing the right dramatic effect while maintaining realism. There is a bit of a conflict here. The supplemental lighting on the set—that is, lights that have been added to enhance the subject but are not part of the natural environmental light—introduce a level of artifice. We tend to accept this without thinking much about it when live actors are the subjects. However, a CG character is already fighting an uphill battle toward believability. Basically, it's one of many situations that can be resolved only with your artistic judgment.

Note

Paul Debevec of the University of California at Berkeley has devised a fascinating method for deriving lighting information from a photographic plate. It involves making a high dynamic-range image of a mirrored sphere inserted into the scene. The sphere captures the lighting environment that is then used as the sole lighting source for the render. It reproduces the subtleties of the original environment with uncanny accuracy. Although this technology is not presently available for max, the mirrored sphere image alone makes a great visual reference for lighting artists trying to reproduce a photographic lighting environment with standard CG tools. Visit `http://graphics3.isi.edu/~debevec/Research/HDR/` or `debevec@cs.berkeley.edu` for more information.

Still have the background plate loaded into RAM Player? Good, because lacking reference materials, this is your sole source of information on how to light the shot.

Tip

If you don't have enough memory to keep the plate loaded, make a couple of reference AVI movies. Make one low-res movie of the entire frame range and another of a selected few high-res frames. Then you can see how the movie plays at speed, but you can also see the important fine details.

Luckily there are clues buried within the plate as to how the scene was shot. Can you find them? The best indicators of lighting in a plate are shadows and highlights in shiny objects.

Look at the balloons. It's pretty clear from the highlights that there are three strong bright sources. On the table, where the Jester will be, you can see strong shadows pointing in one direction. The highlights and shadows should tell you about the lights' colors, intensities, and size. The size of the lights determines how soft or hard the lights are. Broad lights wrap around objects and produce soft shadows, and small ones create crisp shading on objects and sharp shadows.

Note

The term *shadow* in computer graphics can be misleading. When you think of a shadow, you might picture the dark silhouette an object casts onto the ground by blocking a strong light source. You might also think of the side of an object darkened because it faces away from the light source and receives none of its illumination. In max, these two effects are created in completely different ways (see Figures 23.2a and 23.2b). In fact, the latter case works even when shadowing is turned off.

In CG parlance, this is shading; simply put, the area facing toward the light is illuminated, and the area facing away is not. Shadowing, in CG, occurs when a surface is facing a light but is still not lit (because something is between the surface and the light source, blocking the light). To accomplish this, max must render the scene from the point of view of each of the shadow-casting lights (creating the shadow texture). Rather than recording color or tone, max creates an image in which each pixel represents a distance from the light.

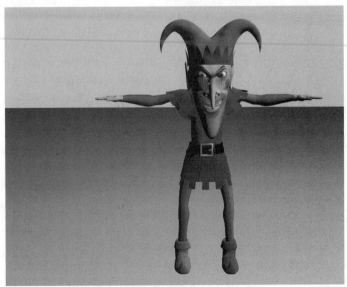

Figure 23.2 In the image on top, where shadows are turned off, the shading effect still creates a shadow side on the Jester.

To make the Jester look as though he is really in the scene, he should cast shadows onto objects in the plate and have plate objects cast shadows onto him. To do this, you need CG equivalents of those objects placed within your max scene file. Some of these objects might have already been created. The camera-match animator will have created at least some reference objects. Otherwise, neither you nor the character animator would know where to put anything. You might have to make some stand-in objects yourself. You can use these objects as aids in establishing your initial light positions.

2. To see what I mean, load scene file jester_scn_01.max from the *Inside 3ds max 4* CD-ROM.

This is a copy of the camera-match scene in which I've created some shadow geometry. Notice I also created a stand-in object for one of the balloons. This helps establish initial light positioning.

Note

I've created some scene files that you can find on this book's accompanying CD-ROM. The files might differ from similar scenes in other chapters, so be sure to use the files from the Chapter 23 section of the disk. (The example scenes are jester_scn_01.max to jester_scn_05.max. The scene file called jester_anim.max contains only the animated Jester and truck models.) You can, if you want, start with the initial scene and work along as you build the lighting for the Jester project. Versions of the scene at various stages of the process are on the CD-ROM in case you get unexpected results. If you simply want to browse through, I point out the appropriate file for each stage of the project development.

There are five light types listed in the creation panel of max 4: an omni light, two spots, and two directional lights. The lights are derived from one entity and each can be converted to any of the four types.

The two spots differ because one has an interest and the other does not (this is also true for the directional lights). The *interest* is a node toward which the light points. The interest is very useful in orienting the lights and can even be linked or constrained to an animated object so that the object always remains within the lights' field of view.

The direct lights are specialized; they emit light in parallel rays. Direct lights are used mostly to imitate sunlight, whose rays are effectively parallel because of the sun's great distance. Omni lights shoot light rays in every direction, which can be useful when you're rendering environments. They get a little dicey, though, if you want to cast shadows, because the shadow texture must cover the entire spherical region around the light; that stretches the shadow texture a bit thin (potentially leading to aliasing and other artifacts). By far, the most useful light for what you're doing here is the target spot.

Put some lights in the scene. You need to choose a frame within the sequence to begin lighting. As you can see from the plate, the camera swoops down from a high angle to a position more level with the table. The Jester isn't even visible at the beginning of the shot, so pick a frame closer to the end where you have a better view of the Jester.

3. Frame 202 appears to show the Jester in a fairly good pose. Start there and set the time slider to frame **202**.

To take advantage of the telltale highlights in the balloons, you use max's Place Highlight tool. This won't give you exactly what you need, but it'll be a good starting point.

4. In the Top viewport, create three target spots aimed and positioned roughly as you might guess from looking at the balloon highlights in the plate (see Figure 23.3). You can find the target spots either in the Lights pane of the Create panel or by choosing Create/Lights/Target Spotlight.

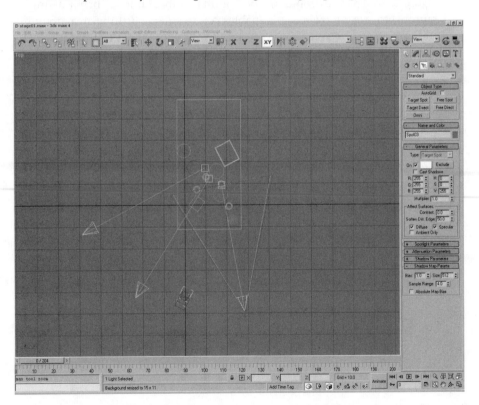

Figure 23.3   As a starting point, place the three main lights similar to this.

5. Select one of the lights. Make sure that Camera01 is the currently selected view (you might want to maximize it), and then click the Place Highlight icon on the toolbar (or from the Tools drop-down menu).

You'll see the cursor change to indicate that Place Highlight is active.

6. Position the cursor over one of the highlights on the reference balloon and click.

The light jumps to a location where it can mimic the plate highlight on the CG balloon.

7. Do the same for the other two lights and the other two highlights. Check your work by rendering the scene from the Camera view.

I've made a transparent material with red highlights for the CG balloon (named appropriately as red highlight). In the render, the red highlights should land fairly close to the highlights on the balloon in the plate (see Figure 23.4). Use the drop-down box on the toolbar (among the rendering buttons) to select Blowup. This enables you to enlarge just the area around the balloon to give you a more precise view of your render test (set it back to View when you're done). Don't worry about being too exact; you fine-tune the lights later.

Figure 23.4   The dark red highlights in the stand-in balloon's material show you how well-placed your spotlights are. The rendered red highlights should coincide with the highlights of the corresponding balloon in the plate.

Now all the lights are lighting the balloon nicely, but you want to light the Jester, not the balloon—and he's going to be on the table.

8. The toolbar has a drop-down list that enables you to restrict your selection to a particular class of object, the Selection Filter. From the Selection Filter, choose Lights, which makes it easier to select your lights from among the other objects in the scene.

9. From the Top view, draw a box around the lights' targets using the Select and Move tool (be sure to select *only* the targets, not the lights).

10. Reposition the targets to the middle of the table.

You can check your work by switching to each of the viewports (right-click the viewport's title, select Views, and then the name of the light) to look from the light's point of view (see Figure 23.5). Make sure the entire tabletop is within the light's field of view and pretty much centered. However, don't leave a lot of empty space around the area of interest; the light's shadow texture will be spread too thin, possibly leading to aliasing and other nasty artifacts. If you want to block certain areas from the light, you can screen-capture this view into a paint program and then use the image as a template for the slide map.

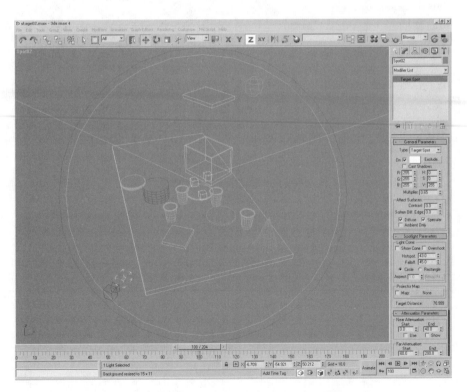

Figure 23.5   You can easily see the area of the scene covered by the light.

Keys, Fills, and Backlights

In traditional photography, there are terms for each light's role in the overall lighting scheme. The general categories of lights are key, fill, and backlight (or rimlight). These three lights form the basis for the traditional Hollywood beauty and portrait lighting. You might not necessarily need or want the Hollywood look, however the three-point lighting system is still useful as a point of departure and a frame of reference. For instance, you'll find the relationship between key and fill lights crucial to any lighting style.

The key is the main light, which is used to define the shape of the subject. (See Figure 23.6a.) Notice the border between the lit area of the subject and the dark. This contour is the critical element for giving the subject form and volume. The sharpness or softness of this border contributes to the overall mood of the lighting. In real-world lights, the size of the key light determines its softness; small lights produce hard edges, large lights are softer.

The fill generally does what it says. It fills the areas unlit by the key. Unless you are simulating a scene in outer space, you want at least some amount of illumination on the non key side (compare the key-only image, Figure 23.6a, with Figure 23.6b, where a fill light has been added). The fill intensity will be less than the key's intensity. The difference in their intensities is called the *key-fill ratio*. The degree of the ratio depends on the look you want to achieve. A high key-fill ratio, in which the key is much brighter than the fill, lends an intense, dramatic look to a scene, and a low ratio might be used for a brighter, more cheerful look.

The backlight is positioned behind the subject to create a bright edge to the subject (see Figure 23.6c). Two functions are served by the backlight. Like the key, the backlight can create an edge to help define the form of an object. It can also increase contrast between the subject and the background and provide some separation. If your subject is a similar tone to the background, the backlight can keep it from blending in.

Bounce is another category of light that isn't strictly a part of the real-world photography toolkit. *Bounce* light is the indirect light reflected from walls, ceilings, and so forth, that we usually take for granted in the real world. Although it's common for photographers to introduce reflective panels into a lighting setup, these fall under the umbrella term *fill light*. This is an arbitrary distinction, because fill lights are added to a set to act as, or enhance, naturally occurring bounce light. It's useful, however, to differentiate between incidental light and artificially introduced light sources.

Photographers often introduce specialized lights, for instance, to bring out the sheen in a subject's hair or to create highlights in the eyes.

In addition to using ratios of intensity for establishing the look of a lighting setup, you can use color to create contrast in a scene. Cool colors tend to visually recede, and warm tones jump forward. You can use this effect to accentuate volume and depth.

Figure 23.6   The key light creates a contour line dividing the face and enhancing the Jester's features. The backlight also helps bring out facial detail. The fill light and backlight give the face additional contrast and boost the dimensionality.

Other clues to light positions are the shadows cast across the table. These shadows are coming predominantly from one direction, thus from one light; this is your key light position.

Figure out which of the three lights is the one that would cast those shadows. The only way to tell is by rendering the scene three times, once with each light's shadow turned on.

In the next step, you use a great new feature in max 4 that speeds up the shadow test.

11. Make sure that Camera01 is the current view, and then click the little red teapot icon on the far right of the toolbar (or select ActiveShade Floater from the Rendering menu). *ActiveShade* is an interactive renderer that gives you quick feedback as you adjust parameters in max.

To make it easier, bring up another labor-saver. As you process lighting you switch from light to light, adjusting parameters and turning them on and off. This process gets tedious if you are constantly searching for lights in the scene. You need a lighting tool with all the relevant controls of all the relevant lights arranged in one neat panel. Fortunately, there is such a beast: LightLister, which can be found under the Tools menu. Being the lucky owner of this book, you have an even more powerful, feature-laden lighting arsenal with the Light Utilities scripts (found in Chapter 22, "Scripting Custom Animations)." If you haven't done so already, read the documentation and become familiar with your lighting panel.

12. In the ActiveShade window, you should see the camera-match stand-in objects rendered with a light gray material against the background plate. Turn off all but one of the lights and enable shadows (default settings are fine).

That lighting panel is showing its value already, isn't it? Do you see shadows in the ActiveShade window? If not, you have to force it to update.

13. Right-click in the ActiveShade window and select Initialize from the menu.

Are the shadows close to the ones in the BG plate (look at the Camera01 view)?

14. Try the same thing with the other two lights and make a note of which one is the closest. Select this light and rename it **Key**. While you're at it, give the other lights appropriate names, such as **Fill_Left** and **Fill_Right**.

Now that you have your key light identified and selected, you've probably noticed that the shadows don't *exactly* match those in the plate. Don't worry—with all the variability between the real world and the max world this is to be expected.

Let's bring the key light into line.

15. Set one viewport panel in max to show the view through the key light (see Figure 23.7), so you can see just where the shadows will fall. For instance, use the conical hat as a guide.

   Looking at the BG plate, note where the tip of the hat's shadow lands. At frame 75 it looks as if it's just behind the adjacent paper cup.

Figure 23.7 The Light view enables you to line up the tip of the hat to the point on the table where you want the shadow to fall, and the ActiveShade view gives you instant feedback.

16. Using the Orbit Light tool (the little Saturn icon in the lower-right of the max interface), rotate the view until the tip of the hat lines up with the point on the table where the shadow should fall. As you do this, you can see the results in the ActiveShade floater.

   If you like, compare your scene with jester_scn_02.max.

   You've done about all you can do without your star, the Jester. Let's bring him on stage along with his truck.

17. Choose File/Merge and find scene jester_anim.max from the Chapter 23 folder of the *Inside 3ds max 4* CD-ROM.

   This scene contains only the Jester and his truck.

18. Under the list of scene node, select All and click OK.

19. You don't need the camera-match stand-in geometry right now, so select and hide it. While you're at it, you can clean up some visual clutter by checking Shapes, Cameras, Helpers, and Space Warps in the Hide by Category section of the Display panel. Add a custom display filter to hide the bones (the Add button next to the list box in Hide by Category) .

If you prefer, you can skip the merging step and load scene jester_scn_03.max, which contains the Jester and the lighting steps thus far.

20. Make sure the time slide is on your reference frame, 202. Turn on all the lights and see how it looks in ActiveShade (you might have to close and restart the ActiveShade floater if you've made a lot of changes).

How's it look? Not too good? That's okay—you've got some work to do yet. You'll knock it into shape.

21. It's often helpful to work with one light at a time, so turn off everything but the key light.

The Jester still looks a little strange in the ActiveShade render. ActiveShade takes a lot of shortcuts for the sake of speed, so double-check it by doing a full max render.

22. Make sure that Camera01 is active and click the Quick Render icon on the toolbar (the little blue teapot). Still not sure? Use the drop-down list next to the render buttons on the toolbar to select Blowup.

23. Now when you click the Render button, you're presented with a crop box in the display window. Frame in tight on the little guy in tights and click OK.

The shadows just don't look right (see Figure 23.8a). The Jester has a great, long nose, but you can't see a shadow of the nose cast onto the face. Also, you'd expect there to be a little shadow between the edge of his hat and his forehead. Stranger still, the insides of his nostrils are lit.

Several factors create problems such as these, but let's start with the shadow map resolution, which isn't high enough. Because you're including the entire tabletop in your lights' fields of view, the shadow map textures are getting spread pretty thin.

24. To compensate, increase the shadow map size from the default 512 to **2048**. Render again. It's still not right.

The shadow bias is too high. The default settings for shadow bias are probably set high on the theory that slightly mismatched shadows are better than dark, buzzing surfaces (the curse of a bias set too low).

25. Set the bias to **.1** and re-render. That looks more like it (see Figure 23.8b)!

Figure 23.8   Several factors contribute to the shadow's effect in the top image. Some judicious twiddling of Shadow Map Size, Bias, and Sample Range produces the more desirable look on the bottom.

Note

The shadow map bias is a sort of fudge factor. The shadow map (also called a shadow buffer) is like a bitmap texture, but instead of colors or shades of gray, each pixel represents a measure of distance from the light: a z-buffer. When the renderer is shading a surface, it checks with each light to see whether that point is lit or shadowed. The light checks to see whether the surface point in question is nearer or farther than the pixel in the shadow map; nearer gets lit, farther does not (that is, it's shadowed).

A problem occurs when you evaluate the same surface in the renderer and in the shadow map. They are in exactly the same point in space (naturally) but, because of rounding errors, the points across the surface can register as—randomly—in or out of shadow. The truth is, you *never* want a point on a surface to shadow itself. To avoid the whole problem, you add a small offset to the shadow map values to guarantee no ambiguity at evaluation time: the shadow map bias. If the bias value is too small, you get the aforementioned nasty, noisy bogus shadowing problem. It's too large, and the shadow "pulls away" from the shadow casting object and some things don't get shadowed that should be. Or it might appear that an object that should be on a surface is floating above it.

Now you move on to the right fill light. Leave the key on, because you'll judge the brightness of the fill relative to the brightness of the key.

Many people set up a CG scene with one shadow-casting key light and several supplementary lights with shadows turned off. It's a mistake. All lights in the real world cast shadows, even indirect light bounced off surfaces. The problem, though, is not just that it is technically wrong, but that it looks wrong. Without shadows, lights illuminate surfaces that should not be lit.

It's a kiss-of-death, giveaway CG trademark to see creatures with the insides of their mouths glowing as if they had swallowed a flashlight. One of the reasons for the tradition of frugality with shadows is that, in the early days, shadows were expensive to render. That's no longer a problem. The other reason is that if you don't use shadows with care, multiple shadows can become busy-looking and unattractive. Study lights in the real world. Strong sources associated with key illumination tend to have well-defined shadows, and fill lights are often diffuse, with very soft shadows.

Note

Two parameters affect the sharpness of shadow: the size of the shadow map and the sample range. The smaller the shadow map, the more it has to be stretched to cover the area of the scene that the light is illuminating. As with any bitmap, the more you blow it up the blurrier it gets. Unfortunately, as with other bitmaps, the shadow map can exhibit stair-step aliasing. The other parameter, sample range, is like adding a blur filter to the shadow map; it's smooth, but at the expense of rendering speed. You could get the same look with a big shadow map and big sample range as you could with a small map and small sample range. It's a trade-off. You want to avoid aliasing without unnecessary over-rendering.

26. For the right fill, cut the map size in half and set the sample range to double that of the key light.

Judging by the paper cups in the plate, the light from the right is pretty bright. But the default levels for the right fill look too bright.

27. Reduce the multiplier of the right fill to .65.

You're into pretty subjective territory here, so feel free to use your own judgment.

28. Repeat the process for the left fill light.

I found that values similar to those of the right fill seemed pretty good. Don't spend too much time with this, because you still have to account for bounce light. Adding sources for these might cause you to want to revisit your decisions for the key and fills.

Notice that there are some unnaturally dark areas on the Jester (see Figure 23.9). All the objects on the table in the background plate receive indirect light from the ceiling, walls, and table surface. Because of the proximity, the table surface is a major contributor of indirect illumination to the objects sitting on it. To simulate the light reflected by the table, you add a light below the surface pointing up at the objects resting on the table (see Figure 23.10). Because you're not really interested in surfaces that face away from camera (you can't see them), you cheat the light slightly toward the front.

Figure 23.9 The Jester's main lighting is in place. However, he still has unnaturally dark areas in his face. Although you've replicated the set light sources, you still need to account for the ambient sources.

Figure 23.10 Our bounce lights make all the difference. The Jester has a natural appearance and avoids CG pitfalls like the over-reliance of the max ambient light
and shadowless lights.

29. Create another Target Spot pointing up from under the table and label it
TableBounce. The table bounce should be even softer than the fill lights,
so set the shadow texture size to half that of the fill lights' (**512**). Keep the
sample range the same (8).

You have to take the extra step of excluding the camera-match stand-in
geometry from the light or it'll be completely blocked by the table surface.

30. Click the Exclude button near the top of the table bounce light's rollout.
Select the camera-match stand-in geometry from the left list, and then click
the right-pointing double-arrow button to move the geometry to the list on
the right. The radio buttons should remain at their default settings of
Exclude and Both.

31. Set the color of the light to approximately the color of the tablecloth (I
used RGB 255, 214, 255). I set the multiplier to .35; set it to what looks good
to you.

32. Light that is as soft as bounce light from a table produces practically no
specular highlight in a surface. Therefore, in the table bounce light's rollout,
uncheck Specular in the Affect Surfaces box.

Although there is bounce light coming from all directions, you don't need to
account for all of it. The ambient light hitting a surface is obscured by the
much stronger direct light. You need to simulate bounce only in the areas

not receiving any direct illumination. Look at the CG model as it's lit so far (with the major sources accounted for); compare it to things in the background plate. The places where it seems unnaturally dark are where you need to add fill light. Creating additional bounce lights is an exercise for you (although I've added one more to the file jester_scn_05.max).

The file jester_scn_04.max contains all the steps to this point.

Note

As you know, light in a real-world scene bounces all around and gets everywhere. CG lights do not. To account for this level of ambient illumination, early CG pioneers devised the concept of ambient light. It's not really light at all, but adds a given value to every pixel in a rendered scene. It raises the lowest values in a scene so that there are no absolute blacks. This is not a wholly bad thing, because you probably never should see values of 0,0,0 in a scene. The problem is that so-called ambient light has no shape or direction; over-relied on (as it often is), it flattens a rendered scene and gives it an artificial look. I won't say never use it—it keeps your black levels from going to absolute zero—but *don't* use it as a substitute for indirect illumination. Create bounce lights instead.

What about other lights you might want in a scene? Often a backlight or rimlight is nice for adding some dimension and contrast to your CG element. It also helps separate it from the background. This can be good or bad. Remember, there's always a trade-off between making your character look great and making it look real. If you want to add some backlighting, find some motivation for it in the plate. You can often exaggerate what's in the plate to achieve the desired effect, but the further you depart from what's really there, the more artificial your shot becomes.

Note

Sometimes you'll find practical light sources in the plate. These are lights that are part of the scene such as table lamps, fireplaces, and flashlights. Obviously, you have to account for those if your character falls within their influence. Try to match color, intensity, and sharpness. You might have to account for changing values within the light. Light from a flickering fire, for example, might be simulated by adding a Noise Controller to the multiplier track. Projector maps in lights often are handy for simulating practical sources. If you'd like to create a realistic-looking flashlight beam, paint a bitmap with the pattern you always see projected by a flashlight's filament. Better yet, project a real flashlight onto a flat white surface and photograph the pattern it makes.

The eyes are windows to the soul, as the saying goes. If there's one feature of a character you want to pay special attention to, it's the eyes. A little sparkle in the eyes will go a long way, so you might need to create a special light just to get perfect little eye highlights. This is not unprecedented in photography. It is common to add a special light to get a nice eye glint. You can be far more precise, however.

33. Go to the frame with the most important key pose of the character. Let's stick with frame 202. Create a light and label it **EyeSpec**. It can be any type; you won't be using shadows or diffuse illumination.

34. Uncheck the Diffuse box in the Affect Surfaces group (Specular stays selected). You want to affect only the eyes, so open the Include/Exclude list for the EyeSpec light, move the eye geometry from the left pane to the right, and then change Exclude to Include (the radio buttons at the top of the dialog box). Click OK.

Now all you have to do is get the highlights in the right place. Sounds like a job for the Place Highlight tool!

35. Using the Place Highlight tool, click one of the eyes (in the Camera view) to place a nice glint somewhere within the iris area but without obscuring the pupil. Keep it on the same side as the key light.

It's time to bring the stand-in geometry back. As the Jester moves through the scene, he should have shadows falling on him from the surrounding objects. You would expect that, as he emerges from the box, he would be fairly shadowed.

36. Unhide the stand-in geometry. Make sure all the stand-in objects have the cm_default material (not the shadow/matte material). Select the tabletop, right-click with the mouse, and select Properties. The object's current material is listed near the top-right of the Properties panel.

37. Select all the stand-in geometry, right-click, and choose Properties from the Quad menu. Uncheck Visible to Camera.

Now when you render the stand-in, objects are absent but they still cast shadows onto the Jester.

You might have the light perfect for the last frame, but how will it look for the rest of the animation range?

38. Select a few keyframes for test renders and see how your lighting looks at various steps in the animation. For instance, you might want to make sure there aren't any weird shadows as the Jester picks up the truck. Does the Jester look appropriately shadowed as he jumps out of the box?

File jester_scn_05.max contains everything you've done to this point.

The lighting on the Jester looks pretty nice, but you're not quite done. Remember those shadows you lined up so carefully? You need to get the shadow of the Jester onto the background plate. You could accomplish this in the same render pass as the Jester, but creating a separate pass for the shadow allows more flexibility when it's time to composite the elements.

You want to hide the Jester and render the stand-in geometry with a matte/shadow material applied to it.

There are a couple of crucial points to consider. You can't actually hide the Jester, because then he wouldn't cast any shadows.

39. Select the Jester geometry (use the Selection Set), right-click to bring up the Properties dialog box, and then uncheck Visible to Camera.

The Jester will still be included in the shadows but not show up in the actual render.

40. Unhide the stand-in geometry if it is still hidden.

Even though you want to render the Jester's shadow, you don't want the stand-in objects to cast shadows in this pass. After all, the objects they are standing in for are already casting shadows in the plate.

41. Select all the stand-in geometry, and in the Properties dialog box, turn off Cast Shadows. Make sure Visible to Camera is on for the stand-in geometry. Keep the objects selected and open the Material Editor. Find the material called cm_shadow. (It should be easy to find; it's the pane without the texture sphere.) Apply it to the stand-ins. You won't see much when you render this pass until you view the Alpha Channel; this pass only creates a matte for later use in the composite. Take a look at Figures 23.11a, 23.11b, and 23.11c to see the main render frame, the shadow matte, and a final composite, respectively. (You might even want to render shadows from different lights, each in a separate pass. If needed, light arrays can be used where particularly soft shadows are needed.)

You can render the Jester and shadows in one pass. Leave the Jester's Visible to Camera property on. You'll probably want to fiddle with the Shadow Brightness level in the Matte/Shadow material, because the default, 0 brightness, is too dense to match the other shadows on the table. If you're compositing them separately you can worry about that later (or let the compositor worry about it).

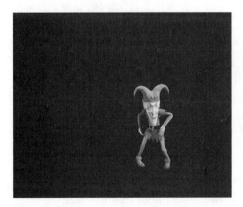

Figure 23.11a

Figure 23.11b

Figure 23.11c   Rendering the Jester's shadow in a separate pass permits more flexibility in the compositing stage.

Summary

This chapter presents a general methodology for lighting a CG scene and provides a taste of what it's like to troubleshoot a lighting job. Other philosophies of CG lighting might be considered equally valid. You should incorporate the suggestions in this chapter, other views, and your experience and devise your personal Tao of lighting.

This chapter only touches on some aspects of lighting. There are many good sources of information on lighting, including the following:

- *[digital] Lighting & Rendering* by Jeremy Birn, New Riders Publishing.

    In addition to lighting, Birn covers materials and rendering. This book covers many of the same principles as this chapter but in greater detail. Although not entirely max-specific, most of what you'll find in this book is readily applicable.

- *Film Lighting* by Kris Malkiewicz, Prentice Hall Press.

  This book is not about CG lighting; it is a series of interviews with motion picture photographers. Although many topics are irrelevant to CG lighting artists, such as techniques for chemically treating film, it is a great source for how masters of the art of lighting create their illusions.

- *Painting with Light*, by John Alton, University of California Press.

  This book is a reprint of a classic text on lighting techniques from Hollywood's golden years. Again, a lot of technical cinematography techniques won't apply much to max, but Alton presents some great insight into an aesthetic that should be understood by anyone lighting for film or broadcast.

Chapter 24

Lighting Techniques for Games/ Interactive Applications

by Sean Feely and Mike Hall

The process of lighting a scene for import

into a game engine is inevitably filled

with much guesswork. Those lighting

geometry for a final render have the

luxury of getting to check the actual look of their lighting at the touch of a button. Game people, however, have a longer and less clear path to travel before the final look is achieved.

There are many approaches to lighting an in-game scene, but you will focus on the techniques that use the tools found in the base 3ds max 4 package. These tools include the following:

- Max Standard Lights
- Assign Vertex Colors utility
- Vertex Paint utility

All these tools assign color values to vertices over a piece of geometry. This process is called *vertex lighting*.

In max, you light a scene in the same manner as you do for a render. This entails placing lights and giving them color and value properties. Then, using the Vertex Light tool, you can theoretically "burn" the effect of those lights into the vertices of your scene's geometry. Each vertex then remembers the parameters it was assigned from your scene lights, and it simulates the look of your renderable max scene in a game environment.

There are other tools, such as Vertex Paint, which enable you to adjust the effect of your lights after they have been burned in. Suppose, for instance, that you had an exterior shot of an apartment building at night. The scene has a cool, bluish lighting over it except for a few windows with yellow glows emanating from them. Maybe, after burning your lights into the scene, you found that the glow supposedly coming from the windows just wasn't strong enough. With Vertex Paint you could comb over those areas with a bright yellow brush, giving a strong accent to the areas that need it.

These techniques are not without their drawbacks. For instance, the amount of light detail is directly related to the number of vertices, so in certain cases tessellation of the mesh is required for a finer look. With some forethought and good judgment, the Vertex Paint and Assign Vertex Colors tools should be able to create the mood and feel you want.

Note

When I first started playing with lighting, I found that the render didn't look so good and it took too long to get it the way I wanted it. One afternoon a few months later I was watching a friend play some first-person shooter and noticed his monitor was displaying the game a little brighter than what I usually see. I realized my monitor wasn't calibrated. Before you start lighting, make sure you can see a full range of gray on your monitor. Some applications have their own color-correction controls that make an image appear lighter or darker when viewed inside that program. Turn off any feature like this so any images you see will be displayed as a constant.

Before you begin the following exercise, adjust the brightness and contrast of your monitor so you can see the full range of grays, as seen in Figure 24.1. An alternative to adjusting your display is to tweak the rendered image in an image-editing program, but after you adjust the monitor you won't need to do it again.

Model Preparation

In order for your model to take full advantage of the lights you place, you will probably have to tessellate the polys around the affected area of each light. This also applies to areas of the mesh that receive shadows. Now, place some lights.

Exercise 24.1   Placing Lights for an Interior Space

1. Open the file lighttut27.max from the accompanying CD-ROM.

2. In the Selection floater, you will see seven groups named ls_01-07. Select the groups and hide everything else.

   These objects represent the light sources, which illuminate the interior of the room.

3. Go to the Create tab and create an omni light in the Top view over one of the light sources, as seen in Figure 24.2.

4. If the omni is not still selected, do so and then go to the Modify tab. In the General Parameters rollout, set the omni's parameters to a color of white with a Multiplier of **1.0**.

5. In the Attenuation Parameters rollout under Decay Type, make the omni inverse square with a start of **6** units.

Figure 24.1
If your monitor is adjusted correctly, you should see the full range of grays in this image.

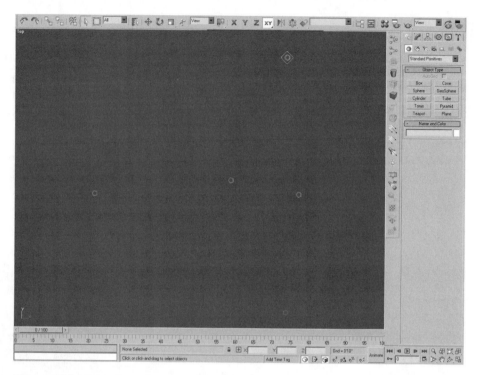

Figure 24.2   In the Top view, you should create an omni light.

6. Under the Shadow Parameters rollout, make sure the light is casting a shadow map by clicking on Object Shadows. Change the shadow color to black if it is not already.

You want this light to serve a purpose. You don't want it to affect the whole scene, so you use the Include/Exclude button under the General Parameters rollout.

7. Click the button to open the Include/Exclude floater. Select door01 through 04 and room01 from the Scene Objects list and click the arrow button that would direct the objects to the Include/Exclude list on the right.

In this case, you want to include the objects you just chose to be the only objects in the scene receiving light from this omni.

8. Now that the basic parameters are set and the light is localized, Instance the light to the other positions, as seen in Figure 24.3.

9. Switch to Perspective view and Instance the lights down to the light sources on the floor. Right-click on the View label and change your view to the camera named int_cam.

10. Go to the Display panel and unhide everything. Then render the view and compare it with Figure 24.4.

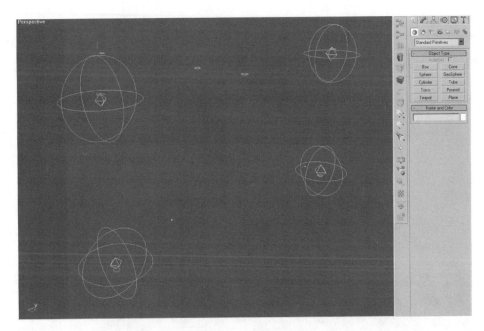

Figure 24.3   Instance the omni light to the other positions by holding down the Shift key and dragging along one of the XYZ gizmo axes.

Figure 24.4   You should see the corner of the room illuminated by the omni lights you just placed.

It's time to give some light to the hallway.

11. In the Front view, create a target spotlight so it shines down to the floor.

12. In the General Parameters rollout, give the spotlight a color value of RGB **240, 255, 238**. In the Spotlight Parameters rollout, change the hotspot and falloff to **9.6** and **41.6**, respectively.

13. This light will not cast shadows, because there are no obstructing objects in its way, so uncheck Cast Shadows if it's on. Set the Lights Multiplier to **0.8**.

14. Now copy, not Instance, one of the omnis to the other remaining light sources.

15. The only thing that needs adjusting is the Start field in Decay Type. Change it to **11** max units.

16. Move the two omnis you just copied so they are floating in the middle of the hallway. (See Figure 24.5.)

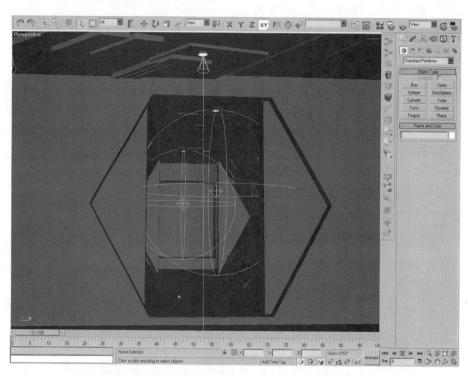

Figure 24.5   The two omni lights should be positioned in roughly the same location as shown here.

17. Change to the int_cam view and render the scene. Compare it with Figure 24.6. The decay set on these lights helps control the light from spilling into areas you don't want.

Figure 24.6   The hallway should now be receiving some light.

Everything in the camera's view is lit except the dark area at the end of the hallway.

18. Clone a copy of the target spot you made earlier and move it to the other end of the hallway. Move the spot along the X-axis 18'0" and the same distance along the Y-axis.

19. Go to the Display tab and unhide the objects named room01 and object01.

20. Position the target of the new spot so it's at the foot of the elevator, as demonstrated in Figure 24.7. Move the target of the light to the foot of the elevator and then move the light near the corner of the room.

21. Now select the spot and make a copy of it along the Y-axis 35'0", and then move its target so it's roughly above the previous spot's target. Adjust both lights so their hotspot and falloff are **13.3** and **85.5**. See Figure 24.8.

22. Change the view back to the int_cam and render the scene; and then compare it with Figure 24.9.

Add one more light for good measure. The area around the first set of doors is pretty dark, so add a fill light to remedy the problem.

Figure 24.7   Create a target spotlight near object 01.

Figure 24.8   Place the second light's target roughly above the previous spot's target.

Figure 24.9   Now you can see where the hallway ends and the second room begins.

23.   Copy an existing omni to the front of the hallway and move it in the Z-axis so it sits roughly in the same elevation as the omnis in the hallway. Change Decay Type to Inverse Square with a start of **09** max units.

24.   Render the scene from the int_cam camera. You should see the area around the doors lighten up quite nicely. The final render should look like something like Figure 24.10.

Figure 24.10   The omni you added should spill a little light onto the doors and floor of the room, giving a better contrast to the image.

Exercise 24.2   Placing Lights for an Exterior Scene

When lighting an exterior scene, less is more. Prior to placing lights, decide what time of day you want to represent. Use the image in Figure 24.11 to help pick a color value for the lights. I usually create a key light to represent a light source such as the sun, and then I make a few fill lights to emulate skylight.

11,000k	Skylight
6,000k	Strobe Light
5,000k	Daylight
1,900k	Candle Light

Figure 24.11   This Kelvin scale helps you choose a color value for your exterior lights.

If this is an environment that has an atmosphere like earth, not all is lost. You can still use this principal, but you might have to tweak the lights in your scene, which is what you'll do in this exercise.

1. Open the file lighttut28.max on the accompanying CD-ROM.

   You should see a file with a bunch of geometry and no lights.

2. Go to the Display tab, select everything, and freeze it.

3. In the Top view, create a Directional Target light.

4. Move the target of the light to roughly the same spot that you see in Figure 24.12.

5. Select the new light, and in the General Parameters rollout of the Modifiers panel, set the RGB value to **251, 238, 220**. Set the Multiplier to **1.0** and click the Cast Shadows check box.

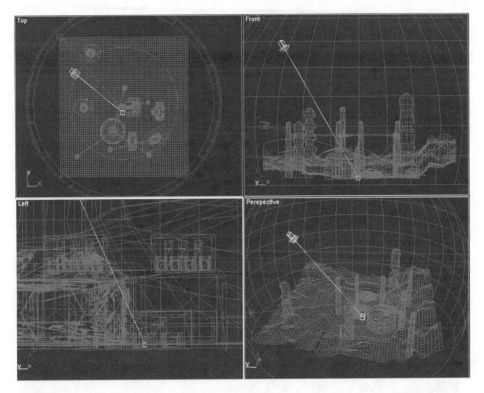

Figure 24.12   Place your Directional Target light as shown here.

In the Shadow Parameters rollout, click Ray Tracing Shadows, and in the Directional Parameters, click Overshoot and set the Falloff to **532** max units. Name this light **key01**.

Next you will create four new lights that will be used as fill lights.

7. In the Top view, create an omni light with an RGB value of **211**, **92**, **68**. Set the Multiplier to **0.3** and click Cast Shadows.

    It should default to Shadow Map with a shadow color of black.

8. Go to the Attenuation Parameters rollout and change Decay Type to Inverse Square with a Start of **274** max units. Name the light **fill01**.

9. Now copy the light three times and place it in roughly the same position as you see in Figure 24.13.

10. For the three new fill lights, change Decay Type to None.

11. In the Front view, move the fill lights up along the Y-axis in this order: fill01 up 286 max units and fill02, 03, and 04 up 163 max units.

12. Change your view to ext_cam, render, and compare it with Figure 24.14.

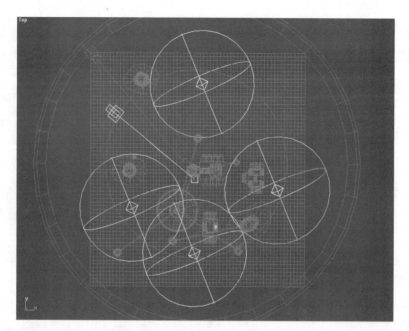

Figure 24.13   Place your three new omni lights as shown here.

Figure 24.14   The result of placing these exterior lights should look something like this.

Exercise 24.3   Applying Lights to the Geometry

Now that the lights have been placed in the scene, you begin the process of actually burning them in.

1. Open the file lightfinal.max from the accompanying CD-ROM.

2. Starting with the interior portion of the scene, hide everything except all the inside lights in the scene and the room01 piece of geometry.

3. Change the view to your interior camera, so it looks like Figure 24.15.

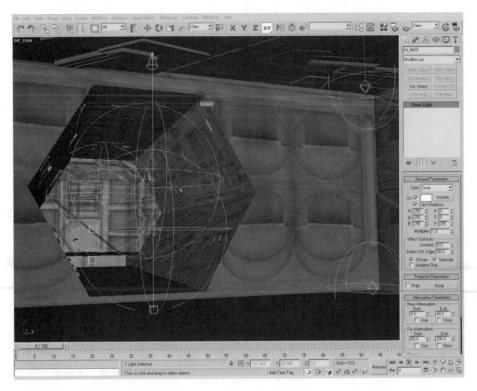

Figure 24.15   The interior room in the viewport prior to the vertex burn will look like this.

4. Select the room geo, and then go to the Max Display tab. At the bottom under the Display Properties rollout, click the box next to Vertex Colors and click the Shaded button.

This tells max to display the vertex coloring on an object in the viewport. The Shaded button enables you to see your vertex lighting in conjunction with the default scene lights. This should be something you toggle often, making sure that you're not mistaking the effect of a scene light for a vertex color.

5. Click the Utilities tab. Click the More button to find Assign Vertex Colors. Click the Mix Vertex Colors, Calculate Shadows, and Use Maps buttons.

Use Maps calculates the RGB values of a texture map on a poly with your scene lights to reach its value. This option is not always needed, and it pays to try your vertex burn with this option on and off; for this exercise, leave it on.

6. Click the Assign to Selected button at the bottom of the rollout. After it crunches through its processing, your viewport should look something like Figure 24.16.

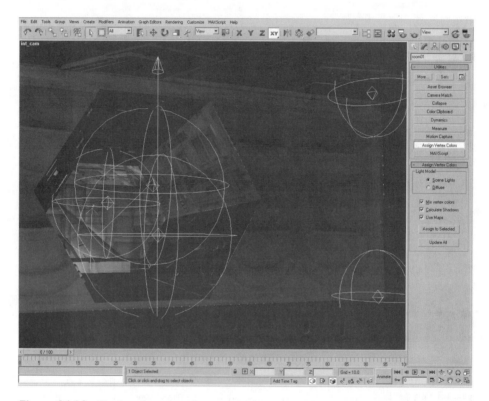

Figure 24.16   The interior room after an initial vertex color assignment still needs a little work.

Not too impressive, is it? As you can see, a bit of overcompensation is needed to get a significant burn on to the vertices. Now let's throw a little more firepower at them.

7. Take the multiplier of every unhidden light in your scene and crank it up to a value of **30**.

8. Reassign the lights to the room, and you should get something like Figure 24.17.

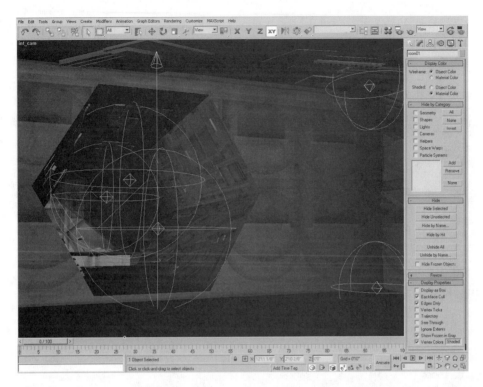

Figure 24.17   After pushing up the Multiplier value of your lights, you get a stronger effect on the room.

This is a little better. There is no real rule of thumb as to the exact values needed to get a significant level of color and brightness on to a vertex. It largely depends on the game engine that it will ultimately be going in to, as well as the number of actual game lights that will be affecting the scene. I generally find, though, that it doesn't hurt to push your light values way up.

Exercise 24.4   Using Vertex Paint

At this point you have a basic representation of the intended lighting scheme on the room. There are many more levels of control that you can delve into in order to get a striking look.

First, you'll collapse the Modifier Stack on your object.

1. Right-click under your Modifier List and select Collapse All.

    This allows access at an Editable Mesh level of more parameters than you would otherwise have.

2. Select Vertex mode on the room object, and then scroll down to the bottom of the rollout until you reach the Surface Properties area.

3. Switch to a Perspective view and pull out, as seen in Figure 24.18, so you can get a look at the entire piece of geometry.

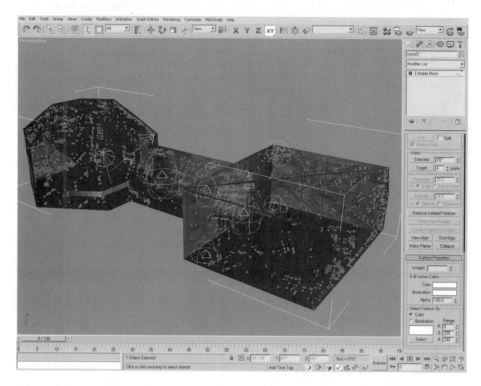

Figure 24.18   The room at an Editable Mesh level, now gives you access to more vertex color parameters.

It looks okay, but perhaps it could use a bit more contrast between the different rooms. Suppose you would like it to go from cold to warm, with the hallway staying neutral.

4. Switch to a Top view, and then center the room geo in the frame.

5. Select the vertices in the circular portion of the room, as seen in Figure 24.19.

6. Go back to the Smooth Shade Perspective view. Click the Zoom Extents All Selected button in the lower-right of the user interface to frame the vertices.

7. Under the Surface Properties/Edit Vertex Colors section, click the swatch next to Color. Give it an RGB value of **0, 100, 240**.

As you can see this gives it a complete blue wash. Maybe you would like something subtler.

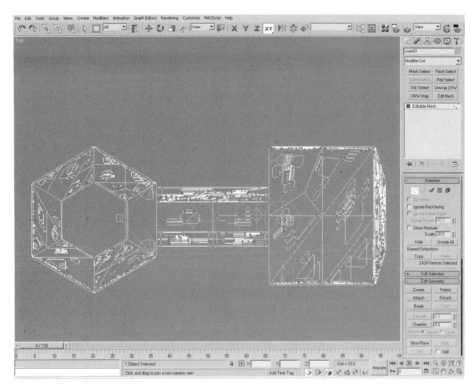

Figure 24.19   With this region of vertices selected, you can give the round portion of the
room a different tint than the rest of it.

8. Undo the Set Vertex Color command. Now try selecting just a few vertices
   around each corner on the hexagon and give those the same blue value that
   you previously gave to all the vertices in this part of the room.

   This should give you something like Figure 24.20.

   The room is no longer completely blue, but it could definitely use some
   polishing up.

9. Hide the lights in the scene so all that remains is the room. Take it out of
   Sub-Object mode, and then open its Modifiers rollout and select Vertex Paint
   under the Mesh Editing header.

10. Click the Paintbrush icon, and then give the brush an opacity of 30%.

    The brush is nice and sensitive from 1-30; after that, its touch can be heavy.

11. Select the blue swatch from the Color Palette, and then click the bigger swatch
    to the right of the eyedropper and desaturate your blue to around 145.

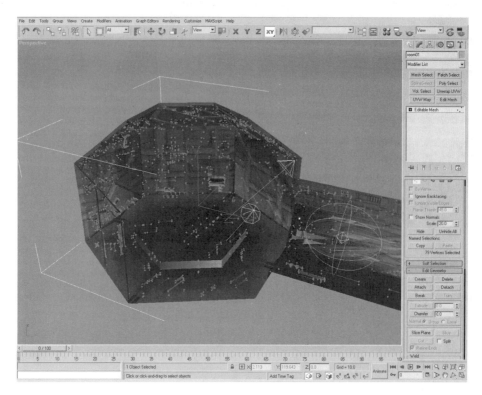

Figure 24.20   The complete blue tint has been lessened by giving only the corner vertices a blue value.

12. Now rotate around the model looking for areas that could use some smoothing.

   As you know, vertex coloring is directly tied to the vertices on the mesh, so larger polygons, which have a wider gap between verts, can shade awkwardly.

13. Using your Vertex Color paintbrush, begin clicking the areas of the model that could use some smoothing.

   You'll quickly get a feel for it. The brush continues to work for as long as you hold down the mouse button.

Experiment with different colors and opacity levels. When you're finished with the blue room, try giving the hallway a yellowish tint, maybe bringing some of the yellow over to the circular platform in the blue room. Now take a red brush and add some shadow detail to the darkest parts of the square room. When you're finished, your room should look something like Figure 24.21.

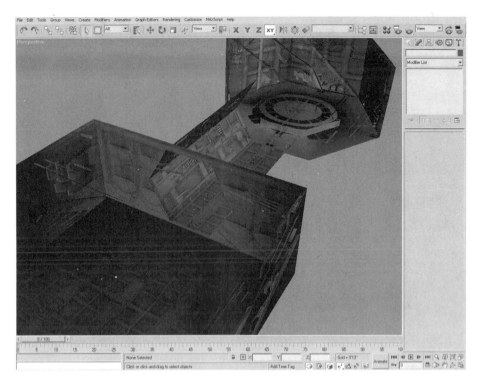

Figure 24.21 Adding a yellow glow and red shadows gives you a weathered, vertex-lit room, going from cool to warm tones.

Exercise 24.5 Burning Lights for the Exterior

Now that you have a sense of vertex lighting for a colorful interior environment, apply those same techniques for a sunlit exterior shot.

1. Hide or delete the vertex-lit room and its lights so that all that's left is what you see in Figure 24.22.

   Use a render of the exterior camera, as seen in Figure 24.23, as reference for the vertex-lit shot you want in your viewport.

   As you learned in the last exercise, the light brightness must be significantly bumped up from the values used for the render.

2. Give the Key01 directional light Multiplier a value of 35, and then give the fill lights values of around 20.

Figure 24.22   First hide the vertex-lit version of the exterior in the viewport.

Figure 24.23   Apply vertex lighting to achieve a nice raytraced render of the scene, which you are shooting to simulate with vertex colors.

Because of the rather long calculation time, I won't ask you to apply these lights to the scene's geometry. If you were to do this, however, it would look something like Figure 24.24.

Figure 24.24   The exterior loses the long shadows after burning in key and fill lights.

It's not terrible, but the long shadows from the render are lost. Subtle lighting techniques for render tend to just muddy up the desired effect.

3. To get the high-contrast Martian shadows that you want, delete all the fill lights so that only the key remains. Give the key an even stronger Multiplier value of around **50**, and then apply it to the objects in the scene. Figure 24.25 shows the effect.

   You have shadows now, but they could use some work. The shadows are completely black, bearing no detail on the texture beneath them.

4. Select only the main ground plane and hide everything else.

5. Collapse the Modifier Stack on this object and go into Vertex mode. Scroll to the bottom and expand the Surface Properties rollout, just as you did with the interior.

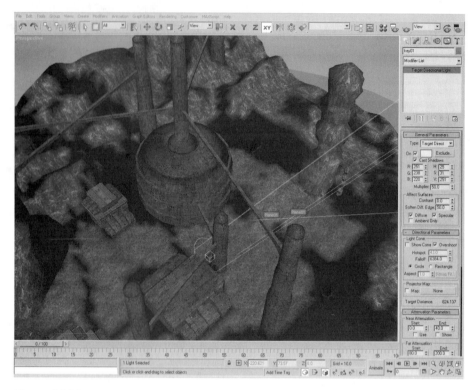

Figure 24.25   Using only a single key light, higher contrast is achieved.

6. Under the Select Vertices By section, click the color swatch, and then use your color picker to make it black. That's 0,0,0 black, to be sure. Click the Select button and all the shadow verts should select, as seen in Figure 24.26.

7. Drag the whiteness slider about a quarter of the way down in the color picker under Edit Vertex Colors.

   This makes the flat black shadow color a little more forgiving to the ground below.

   Depending on your polygon restrictions, it's possible to use this approach in conjunction with tessellation to get softer shadows. Let's try it.

8. With the same vertices in the shadowed areas selected, choose the Tessellate modifier from the drop-down list.

   Only the area around the selected verts should tessellate.

9. At this point, Update All from the Assign Vertex Color utility.

   This might be an excessive amount of tessellating for this scene, but it is a valuable technique, and when used sparingly and selectively, strong shadow effects can be achieved. Figure 24.27 shows the finished exterior with no max lights in the scene—only vertex lighting.

Figure 24.26   When selecting vertices by color, you can essentially select the shadows on your mesh.

Figure 24.27   Lit with only vertex colors, the exterior scene is ready for game import.

Note

It should also be noted that vertex color effects can be rendered with the use of a Vertex Color Map. This is achieved by simply picking a vertex color for the diffuse channel of a material assigned to your geometry. This, combined with a root Blend material, enables you to see both texture maps and vertex colors in a render.

A vertex can hold much more information than a simple point in world space. With the tools found in 3ds max 4, vertex lighting can be a powerful tool with many uses. It can be used by itself, as demonstrated in this chapter, or can be used on top of other methods, such as shadow maps, for that final sweetening pass.

Summary

Every game company has its own way of dealing with lighting, whether it's vertex lighting, a two-pass solution comprised of a diffused texture and a light map, or just a diffuse map with the light map burned into it. All these solutions have their good points, but the type of solution you will use depends on the type of game engine and platform you're developing for. Today, 3ds max 4 does not have a mesh-to-texture utility, so the two- and one-pass solutions have to be handled in another package. Let's hope this needed tool will be implemented in the near future.

Part VIII

Rendering and Compositing

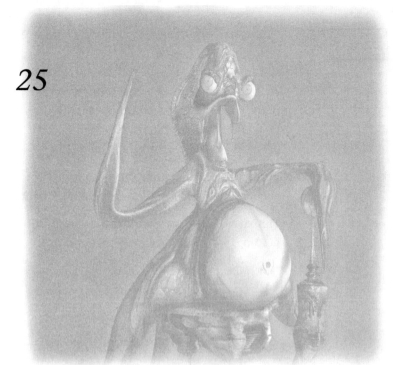

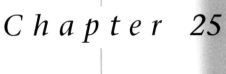

Chapter 25

Rendering for Compositing

by Max Ehrlich

Rendering is the point at which the piece

you are working on goes from a three-

dimensional environment to a two-

dimensional canvas of pixels—but it is

still an unfinished work. For this project, subtle touches of motion blur will help the computer-generated elements blend with the live-action backplate. Faint reflections of the animated character on the surface of the table in the backplate will help to ground this character in the real world.

The next step of the process is to prepare the render for compositing. The rendered image will be broken into passes that isolate specific image attributes to further enhance the match between the computer graphic elements and their environment.

This chapter discusses the steps involved in preparing a rendered scene for compositing. Specifically, it covers the following:

- Motion blur
- Matte objects
- Rendering in passes
- Network rendering

Motion Blur

Motion blur is an effect that simulates what happens when you film a moving object and the camera's shutter speed is not fast enough to freeze the action. Adding the motion blur effect can enhance the realism of an animation. It also helps smooth the strobe effect that occurs when an animated object travels across the screen quickly.

A new type of motion blur has been added to 3ds max 4, bringing the total number of motion blur effects to four. These are Image Motion Blur, Scene Motion Blur, Object Motion Blur, and the new one, Multi-Pass Motion Blur.

Image Motion Blur

Image Motion Blur, as seen in Figure 25.1, creates the blurring effect by smearing the rendered pixels in the direction of movement. The effect is fairly convincing, and it is quick because it is rendered in one pass. However, it blurs both the leading and the trailing edges of the object in motion, which is not what you would expect to see. Image Motion Blur also has problems when a moving object is occluded by another object that is moving more slowly or is not moving, because it is based on the changes in the pixels of an image. If you need to use Image Motion Blur with objects that become occluded, you can render the objects separately and composite them afterward. A helpful new addition to 3ds max 4 is access to Image Motion Blur through the Render Effects dialog box, which enables you to make changes to the blur settings interactively.

Figure 25.1   Here's an example of Image Motion Blur.

Scene Motion Blur

Scene Motion Blur, as seen in Figure 25.2, does not have the same problems with occluded objects that Image Motion Blur does. Scene Motion Blur takes considerably longer to render than Object and Image Motion Blurs because the effect is created by rendering multiple passes of the entire scene. Scene Motion Blur works well for creating special effects such as trails and exaggerated motion blur.

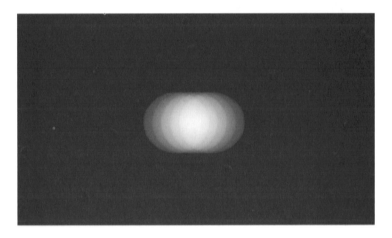

Figure 25.2   This is an example of Scene Motion Blur.

Object Motion Blur

Object Motion Blur renders copies of an object at the subframe level and merges them, creating a sort of stepped-looking effect (see Figure 25.3). Object Motion Blur does not take into account camera movement. Therefore, Object Motion Blur is the least effective at simulating camera motion blur. Object Motion Blur is not intended to simulate camera motion blur. It is better suited to smoothing the motion of fast-moving objects.

Figure 25.3   Object Motion Blur produces a stepped-looking effect.

Multi-Pass Motion Blur

Multi-Pass Motion Blur, as seen in Figure 25.4, looks very similar to Scene Motion Blur, but it has a couple of very important differences. Because it is one of the new Multi-Pass effects in 3ds max 4, it can be previewed in the Camera viewport. This can save a considerable number of trial-and-error renderings to get the parameters dialed in. Multi-Pass Motion Blur also has a Bias setting that is useful when you want the leading edge of the moving object to be blurred less than the trailing edge. Multi-Pass Motion Blur can also be time-consuming because it renders the entire scene for every pass that it makes.

 Warning

In 3ds max 4.02, there is a bug that does not render the Multi-Pass Motion Blur correctly when used with Render Elements. This bug creates trails of the object in your render. Discreet has acknowledged the problem and says that it will be fixed in one of the future 4.x releases.

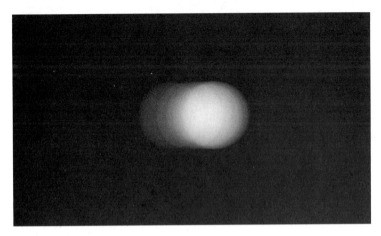

Figure 25.4   Here's an example of Multi-Pass Motion Blur.

 Tip

You can combine different types of motion blur to create more types of motion blur. For example, to take advantage of the Bias setting in Multi-Pass Motion Blur without the heavy rendering times caused by the number of passes needed to render the effect smoothly, you can lower the number of passes and use Image Motion Blur to smooth the stepped effect caused by the low number of passes.

Using Motion Blur

Applying motion blur to a render in 3ds max is a simple process. However, the four different types of motion blur have their controls in different areas of the interface in 3ds max. This can seem a little confusing at first.

The exact steps for applying motion blur to this project are covered in Exercise 25.1. The following list covers the location of the controls for all the types of motion blur offered in 3ds max:

- Image and Object Motion Blurs share control panels. These motion blur types must first be enabled in their respective objects properties, under the Motion Blur group. Settings in the properties also affect how the motion blur looks. These controls enable you to apply different motion blur settings for individual objects. Image and Object Motion Blurs must also be activated in the Render Scene dialog box under the MAX Default Scanline A-Buffer rollout. These settings enable you to activate and deactivate motion blur on a global basis for the whole scene. Global settings also govern the amount and duration of motion blur.

- New to 3ds max is an interactive version of the Image Motion Blur, mentioned previously. When you want to apply image motion as an interactive effect, you still need to access the properties and enable the effect under the Motion Blur group. However, you must add the motion blur to the list of effects in the Effects rollout of the Render Effects dialog box, and you must set the duration in the Motion Blur Parameters rollout of the Rendering Effects dialog box.

- Scene Motion Blur is activated entirely from the Edit Scene Event dialog box in video post under the Scene Options group. Scene Motion Blur is applied globally without any control over individual objects.

- Multi-Pass Motion Blur is activated from the Modify control panel in the Multi-Pass group when the camera is selected. Below the Multi-Pass group is the Motion Blur Parameters rollout, which contains all the controls for the Multi-Pass Motion Blur effect.

Exercise 25.1 demonstrates how to apply Image Motion Blur to the Jester and the toy truck. You will use the Render Effects version of motion blur to adjust the settings interactively.

Exercise 25.1   Applying Image Motion Blur to the Jester and Toy Truck

In this exercise, you will use the Image Motion Blur effect because this motion blur renders quickly and gives you a reasonably believable motion blur. The newly implemented version of Image Motion Blur in 3ds max's Render Effects also enables you to adjust the amount of motion blur and see the results immediately, without having to re-render the scene.

1. Load 25_01.max from the accompanying CD, and select the Jester.
2. Ctrl+right-click over the selection to display the Quad menu (see Figure 25.5).
3. Choose Properties from the Quad menu.
4. In the Motion Blur group, click Enabled and Image, set the multiplier to 0.5, and click OK (see Figure 25.6).

   As for the truck, you want to animate only the motion blur settings for the second half of the animation. If you left the motion blur on for the entire duration, the toy truck would be blurred by the camera movement, even when the truck is motionless on the table.

   If you look at the other objects on the table in the video backplate, you will see that the camera movement does not blur objects on the table. Animating the settings for the motion blur forces the truck to remain in focus while on the table and then to blur when the Jester picks it up and swings it.

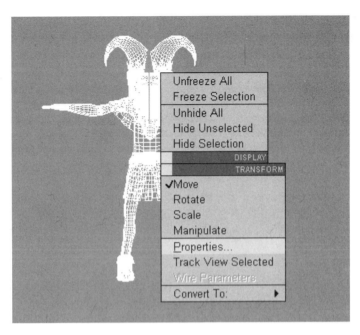

Figure 25.5   This is the Quad menu with Properties selected.

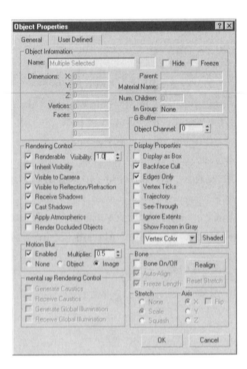

Figure 25.6   This is the Object Properties dialog box.

Tip

The Properties dialog box contains some very useful tools in the Rendering Control group that enable you to determine how individual objects in the scene render. This helps make rendering in 3ds max more productive.

For instance, the option Visible to Reflection/Refraction enables you to set whether an object appears in reflections. This can help improve rendering times in scenes using ray-traced reflections and refractions by allowing the user to prevent specific objects from being calculated by the ray-tracing process. Visible to Camera is very useful for creating reflection passes that show only the reflection of an object, not the object itself. The capability to turn off the Cast Shadows and Receive Shadows options also helps avoid unnecessary calculations by the renderer.

All the settings in the Rendering Control group are well documented in the manuals and in the online reference (see the Contents/Object Properties/Object Properties dialog boxes). It is recommended that you fully acquaint yourself with all the features of the Properties dialog box.

 5. Select all the parts of the toy truck.

   The following steps might seem a bit cumbersome, but this is the most direct way to force 3ds max to apply keyframes to the motion blur properties for multiple objects.

 6. Ctrl+right-click over the selection.

 7. Choose Properties from the Quad menu.

 8. In the Motion Blur group, click Enabled and Image, set the multiplier to **0**, and click OK.

 9. Go to the Customize menu and choose Preferences.

10. Press the Animation tab. Click Set Defaults in the Controller Defaults group (see Figure 25.7). Choose Bezier Float, and press the Set button.

11. Choose the Linear Tangent setting as the Bezier Default Key value, and close the dialog boxes.

12. Press the Animate button. Go to frame 140 and again bring up the properties for the toy truck.

   Next you want to create a key with a value of **0** at frame 140.

13. To do this, enter a new value (any value will do) in the multiplier, and set it back to **0**.

   This forces 3ds max 4 to create a key at frame 140 for all the selected objects.

14. Press the OK button. The settings take effect and the Properties dialog box closes.

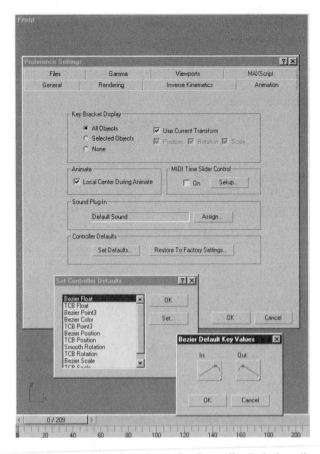

Figure 25.7   The Preferences dialog box shows the Controller Defaults rollout.

As you saw here, by turning on the Animate button and changing the settings for the duration of the motion blur to 0 and then back again, you forced 3ds max to create a key with a value of 0 at frame 140. The only other way to accomplish this (short of using MAXScript) would have been to set a key for each object's motion blur duration one at a time in the Track Editor.

> **15.** Go to frame 143 and in the Properties dialog set the Motion Blur multiplier to **0.5** with Animate on.

Matte Objects

Matte Shadow materials are used to help in compositing 3D elements with live action. Objects that have a Matte Shadow material assigned to them will not appear in the render. They also hide other objects that are inside of or behind them. These objects can be set to receive reflections and shadows cast by other objects in the scene.

Several objects in the scene have the same Matte Shadow material applied to them. In the next exercise, you will make two changes in the Matte Shadow material that is used.

Exercise 25.2   Matte Shadow Materials

1. Open the Material Editor. Use the Eyedropper tool to select the Shadow Matte material from the box that the jester jumps out of. The material is called cm_shadow.

2. In the Matte group of the Basic Parameters rollout, uncheck Opaque Alpha and checkReceive Shadows and Effect Alpha in the Shadow group. You will use only the Shadow options in the shadow pass. (See Figure 25.8.)

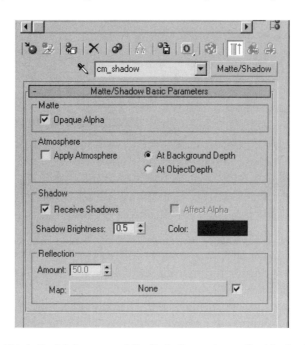

Figure 25.8   This is the Matte group of the Basic Parameters rollout in the Material Editor.

3. Go to the Rendering menu and select Environment. Load clean_Backplate 00000.jpg found in the Footage folder from the accompanying CD. Make sure that Use Map is checked, and close the dialog box.

4. Go to frame number 130. Make certain that the Jester, the toy truck, and all the Matte Shadow objects are visible. Render a test frame at 720×480 with Shadows enabled in the MAX Default Scanline Buffer rollout.

The resulting image should show the Jester standing on the table and casting a shadow on the backplate.

As you've seen here, it's not very difficult to use the Shadow Matte material to receive shadows, for the purpose of combining a CG character and elements with a live-action backplate.

Multi-Pass Rendering

The technique of rendering multiple passes comes from the world of film-based special effects, where elements of a live-action scene are filmed separately and assembled in a darkroom to create a composite image. This method has been adopted and expanded by digital media. Many 3D renders use a multitiered hierarchy of passes in which scenes are broken down and objects are rendered separately from one another and their environments. This process allows further adjustment to those elements independently of other objects in the scene.

To take this to the next level of quality, each of those passes can be further broken into elements. For instance, a single object in a scene might be composed of three or more passes: a diffuse pass, which contains color and shading; a specular pass, which has the object's specular highlights; and a reflection pass, which has reflections that appear on the surface of the object. The result of rendering those passes is a level of control over the final image quality that would be extremely difficult to achieve otherwise.

Figures 25.9 through 25.13 show examples of the passes that make up a typical multi-pass rendering.

Figure 25.9   The diffuse pass contains color and shading.

Figure 25.10   The reflection pass for the tray was rendered separately from other reflections in the scene, to allow it to be adjusted individually.

Figure 25.11   The cups were also rendered separately, to allow their reflections to be adjusted separate from the tray.

Figure 25.12   The shadow pass casts shadows where appropriate.

Figure 25.13   The passes have been combined to make a final composite. Note that the reflection and shadow passes were used at a fraction of their full strength.

Another benefit of rendering in passes is that if you need to make changes to specific characters or objects in an animation, you do not necessarily have to re-render the entire piece.

Multiple passes are also used to create the special effects for things such as iridescent and translucent objects. To create the effects in the movie *Hollow Man*, artists used many separately rendered layers of computer graphics to create a see-through character.

Rendering Multiple Passes

Previously, the way to render multiple-pass renders in 3ds max was to create a different MAX file for each pass and render each element separately. To say the least, this was tedious and time-consuming.

A new feature of 3ds max 4, called Render Elements, is aimed at making the process of creating multiple-pass renderings more efficient and easier. Render Elements renders a full image and breaks it into multiple passes that you can specify and customize to meet your rendering requirements.

In Exercise 25.3, you will use the Render Elements feature to set up multi-pass renders.

Note

Each rendering task is a different problem. The best way to begin is to render the Camera viewport and evaluate a frame or animated sequence to see whether the scene changes dramatically. In many instances, this also means working closely with the compositor to determine what elements he will need for the compositing process.

Here is a list of the different passes that you will need for compositing:

- You will render the diffuse passes for the Jester and truck as one pass. The diffuse pass will also contain the Alpha Channel, which will be used in compositing to matte the computer graphic elements over the video background.

- You will need a separate pass for the confetti particles so that they can be adjusted independently from the rest of the scene.

- You will need to render an effects pass of the particles emitted by the SuperSpray objects in the scene, to provide control over the level of the effect applied to the particles.

- You will need to render a shadow pass that will contain only the shadows cast by objects in the 3D scene. Because the lighting in the backplate is fairly uniform, you can render the shadows for all objects in the scene in one pass.

- You will need to render a reflection pass for the toy truck and a separate reflection pass for the tablecloth, providing individual control over the reflective properties of each object.

- You will need to render a specular pass, which will contain the scene object's highlights.

Diffuse Pass

The diffuse pass will contain the color information and shading for objects in the scene. Having color information as a separate pass is necessary to adjust color balance so that it blends with the background lighting. This is important when trying to match known colors such as skin tones with live-action backplates.

Sometimes, if the ambient lighting in a scene varies, it is helpful to render diffuse passes for each object or specific areas where the light is varied. In this scene, the ambient lighting is uniform throughout the scene, so you can render the diffuse pass for the entire scene.

In this next exercise, you set up the scene to render the individual passes needed to create the final composite.

Exercise 25.3   Setting Up the Passes

1. Open the file 25_01.max.

2. Go to frame 131. Render a single frame of the Camera viewport at 720×480 resolution with mapping, anti-aliasing, shadows, and the live-action backplate.

   The following steps require that your PC be either connected to a network or have the loopback adapter installed. For more information on this, refer to Chapter 4, "Changes in Rendering."

3. Go to the Display panel and check Particle Systems in the Hide by Category rollout. You will be creating separate diffuse passes for the particles.

4. Click the Render Scene button to open the Render Scene dialog box.

5. In the Render Scene dialog box under the Render Output group, click the Files button and select My Network Places (Network Neighborhood, if you are using Windows NT 4.0). Navigate to the name of the networked machine where you will be saving the renders (see Figure 25.14). Click the drive name where the project is stored, and create a new folder named Renders. This directory will hold the Render Elements.

Figure 25.14   The Render Output File dialog box is used to specify a UNC path.

Note

Regardless of whether you are connected to a network, you should use this method of choosing the destination for renders even when rendering to your local machine. This way, if you are working on a network and decide that you want to render on multiple machines, all the machines will be capable of accessing the destination. Even if you are working on a standalone PC, this is a good workflow habit to develop.

6. In the Render Scene dialog box, click the Render Elements rollout, as seen in Figure 25.15.

7. In the Material Editor, open the material called cm_shadow. These are Matte Shadow materials.

8. In the Matte group, make sure that Opaque Alpha is unchecked.

9. In the Shadow group, uncheck Receive Shadows and Affect Alpha.

10. Click on the Add button in Render Elements, choose Diffuse from the options presented, and press OK to close the dialog box.

   If you look in the Render Elements list, you can see that a diffuse pass has been added to it.

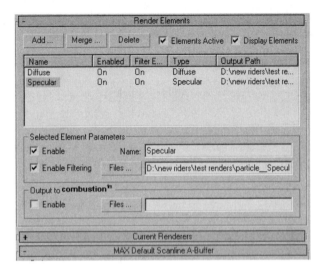

Figure 25.15   Here is the Render Elements rollout of the Render Scene dialog box.

11. Check to make sure that the pass has the Enabled option checked and that Display Elements is checked. Now render a single test frame from the Camera view.

The result should be two images: one labeled Camera01, and the other labeled Diffuse (as seen in Figure 25.16).

Figure 25.16   This is the diffuse pass.

12. Save the file as **25_render elements.max**.

Now that you've learned how to implement Render Elements to create a diffuse pass and how to save files using the Universal Naming Convention (UNC), you're ready to render passes for diffuse particles.

Exercise 25.4   Rendering Passes for Diffuse Particles

In this exercise, you will render separate passes for each of the two types of particles. The only thing you will be interested in doing with the particle passes is adjusting the color and compositing of each particle type separately. Both particle passes will be rendered without Render Elements because they do not have any specular or reflective properties that need to be adjusted.

1. Some of the passes will have to be set up in their own 3ds max file, so open the file 25_Render Elements.max. You will make changes to the previous file and save them under new names.

2. Go to frame 80, and select and hide the following objects: the particle systems called PArray01 and PArray02, the objects that make up the jester, and the toy truck.

3. Render a test frame to make sure that the only thing visible is the confetti particles (see Figure 25.17).

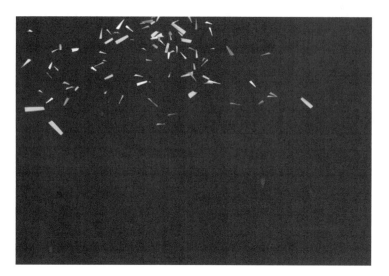

Figure 25.17   These are the confetti particles.

4. Save the MAX file as **confetti.max**.

5. Select and hide the particle system called SuperSpray01.

6. Unhide the particle systems called PArray01 and PArray02.

7. Render a test frame. Make certain that the Render Effect that was applied in Chapter 21, "Particle Effects," is enabled in the Render Effects dialog box. The result should be a rendering of only the pixie dust particles with a glow effect (see Figure 25.18).

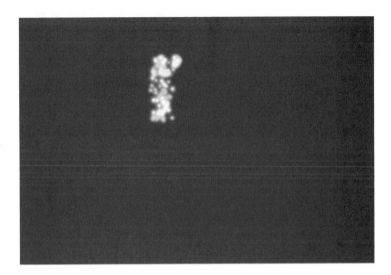

Figure 25.18   These are the pixie dust particles.

8. Go to the Render Scene dialog box and disable Render Elements. Name the rendered files **pixie.tga**.

9. Save the MAX file as **pixie.max**.

To recap, you saved two files—one with the confetti visible, and the other with the pixie dust visible—so that they can be rendered as separate passes. Now you're ready to apply specular highlights.

Exercise 25.4   Applying Specular Highlights

Specular highlights help you visually determine the smoothness of a surface. A highly polished or smooth surface such as glass will exhibit a highlight that is concentrated on a small area of the surface. This differs from a rough surface that is full of scratches or bumps that diffuse the highlights over a large area of the surface. Specular highlights respond less effectively to tweaking in the composite than the other layers, so you will render one specular pass for all the objects in the scene. Being able to make adjustments to the specular layer allows the levels and contrast of specular highlights to be adjusted to match the specular attributes of the backplate.

1. Open the file 25_Render Elements.max, and click the Render Scene button.

2. Click the Add button in the Render Elements area, and choose Specular.

3. Make sure that the specular element is enabled, and render the Camera 01 viewport at frame 130 (see Figure 25.19).

Figure 25.19   This is the specular pass.

Note

The resulting render will include a render of all elements in the scene together, and a render that has the specular attributes of the image separated from the rest. If any other Render Elements are enabled in the Render Elements queue, they will also be separated and displayed.

4. Save the file as **25_Render Elements.max**.

Now that you've added a specular pass to the Render Elements, you're ready to add a shadow pass.

Exercise 25.4   Creating a Shadow Pass

The shadow pass describes the areas of the scene in which a shadow-casting light is being blocked by an object with shadow-casting properties activated. Having the shadows isolated from the rest of the image enables you to adjust the density and sharpness of the shadows to match the characteristics of the shadows in the back-plate. As with the diffuse pass, when the scene is evenly illuminated, you can render one shadow pass for all the objects in the scene at once.

The procedure for creating the shadow pass is different from the previous passes you have set up. Because of a flaw in the Render Elements process, objects that use Shadow Matte material do not display shadows correctly when the Shadow Render Element is rendered.

You start by changing the Shadow Matte parameters so that the Shadow Matte material will display shadows that are cast on the matte objects in the scene.

1. In the Material Editor, use the Eyedropper tool to get the Matte Shadow material from any of the matte objects in the scene (these are objects with the cm_ prefix on their names). In the Basic parameters, check the Receive Shadows and Affect Alpha options.

2. Now open the Render Scene dialog box. Go to the Render Elements section and add a Shadow Render Element to the queue. Also disable the Specular Render Element. Render the scene.

    The scene will render a Camera View window and a Shadow window. The Shadow window appears empty because the information for the Shadow Render Element appears in the Alpha Channel of the shadow pass.

3. At the top of the Shadow window is a series of icons. Click the one that is a circle that is half black and half white to view the Alpha Channel.

    The image that you see is actually a negative of the shadows cast in the scene. Areas that are black are areas with no shadow, the white regions are fully in shadow, and gray areas are partially in shadow. You see that the Shadow Matte objects are not showing any shadow at all; that is the bug.

4. To see how the Shadow Matte objects should appear, click the Camera window and view its Alpha Channel. In the Camera window, you see the shadows projected correctly on the Matte Shadow objects.

    You will work around the bug with the following steps.

5. Go to the Display menu and select Unfreeze All.

6. Click the icon for the Material Editor.

7. Create a new material and call it **Shadow Receiver**. Set the ambient color to black and the diffuse color to white.

8. Activate one of the other slots in the Material Editor, and use the Eyedropper tool to select the material from the cm_table object in the scene. Use the Select By Material button to select all objects that use the cm_shadow material.

Note

Select By Material is a handy tool to use if you know what material the objects have but are not sure of the objects' names.

9. Go to the Material Editor, and make sure that the Shadow Receiver material is selected. From the Material Editor tool buttons, click the Assign Material to Selection button.

10. Open the Render Scene dialog box. Render the scene to see the result.

   The shadow pass information is visible in the Alpha Channel of the shadow window. The Matte Shadow objects should now have the shadows rendered on them. See Figure 25.20.

Figure 25.20   This is frame 130 of the shadow pass.

11. Save the scene as **Shadow Pass.max**.

Here you learned how to select by material and create a shadow pass without using Render Elements. Next, you'll apply a reflection pass.

Exercise 25.5   Applying the Reflection Pass

The reflection pass contains anything that is rendered as a reflection in the scene. Like specular passes, reflection passes tell you about the smoothness of a surface. Surfaces with scratches or pits diffuse and distort the scene reflected in them, and very smooth or polished surfaces reflect the scene more clearly. Because objects' surfaces can vary so greatly, it is very possible that you will need to break up the reflections for a scene into separate Render Elements for objects or areas of a scene that require different treatment.

When you look at the reflections in your scene, there are two major reflective objects. The truck has a glossy surface with defined reflections. In the backplate you see that the tablecloth reflects the objects that are sitting on top of it. The reflection is very subtle and reflects only the parts of the objects that are within half an inch of the tablecloth. As objects get farther away, the reflection quickly fades to nothing. Attention to how objects in the environment interact will help make your animation look as if it is really one with the backplate.

To make this reflection convincing, you will want to be able to adjust its intensity and softness later during the composite process without affecting the reflections on the Jester and the toy truck. To do this, you will create a reflection pass for the tablecloth that is separate from the other scene elements.

The first reflection pass will capture the reflections in the Jester and toy truck. You will render it as a straightforward Render Element pass.

1. Open the file 25_Render Elements.max, click the Render Scene button, and open the Render Elements section. Click Add and choose Reflection. Make sure that the reflection element is enabled, and render the Camera 01 viewport.

2. Render a test. It should be a render that has the reflection attributes of the image separated from the rest and the other Render Element passes that you have already set up. Save the file (see Figure 25.21) .

Figure 25.21   This is the Render Element reflection pass.

You will have to create a separate file that will contain the reflection on the tablecloth to create a reflection pass with the tablecloth only.

3. Open the Material Editor and create a new material called **Table Reflection**. Assign the material to the cm_table object.

4. Set the opacity and specular levels to 0.

You don't need to see the diffuse element of the object—just the reflections that it picks up.

5. Go to the Maps section of the Material Editor and click the Map button for reflection. Choose Raytrace from the Material/Map Browser. Open the Attenuation section (see Figure 25.22).

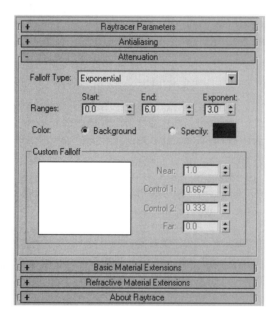

Figure 25.22   This is the Attenuation rollout.

Next you will set parameters that will cause the reflection to fade to 0 based on the distance of the geometry from the reflective surface.

6. Set the Fall-off Type to Exponential, and set the ranges to start at **0** and end at **6**, with the exponent set to **3**.

The Exponential Fall-off Type will cause a greater reduction in reflectivity for geometry that approaches the extent of the ranges. This simulates the effect of the reflection in the tablecloth in which you see only the parts of the objects that are in contact with or very close to the surface of the tablecloth.

7. Assign the material to the cm_table object.

In the second reflection pass, you will capture the reflections in the table-cloth. This will enable you to match the subtle effect of the reflections in the tablecloth in the video backplate.

8. Hide the toy truck.

The truck sits on top of a napkin in the backplate, so it will not show up in the reflections on the tablecloth.

9. Select the Jester and bring up Properties. In the Rendering Control group, uncheck the Visible to Camera property.

This causes only the reflection of the jester to appear in the rendering.

10. Open the Render Scene dialog box and go to the Render Elements section. Disable all but the Reflection Render Element.

11. Under the Selected Element parameters, click Files and set the output name to **tableclothref_.tga**. Close the Render Scene dialog box and save the file as **tableclothref.max**.

In this exercise you created two separate passes for the reflections in the scene to have control over individual parts of the scene's reflections. Now you're ready to render the output.

Exercise 25.6   Rendering Output

To set up the final renders for the project, you need to know several pieces of information:

- What frame range do you need to render?
- What is the format to which you are rendering?
- What type of files do you need to render?
- Does a special naming convention need to be followed?
- Are you rendering with fields?
- Will motion blur be applied to objects in the scene?

When you know the answers to these questions, you can set up the render.

1. To set up your render, open the Render Scene dialog box.

The first rollout, Common Parameters, is broken into four categories:

- Time Output
- Output Size
- Options
- Render Output

2. In Time Output, choose Active Segment to render the entire range of your animation.

In Output Size, you are matching a video backplate that has a pixel dimension of 720×480 and a pixel aspect ratio of 0.900000. You must match those dimensions so that your render will line up correctly when composited with the backplate.

3. Set the output size to match the size of the backplate.

   If you are creating an animation to be viewed on television, you might want to render using the Render to Fields option, found under the Options category. NTSC television monitors display video by breaking an image into numbered horizontal lines called scan lines. Each field represents one 60th of a second. The two fields are put together in one frame in a process called *interlacing*.

4. For passes that use Render Elements, open the Render Elements rollout. All the elements that you created are displayed.

5. Make sure that all the Render Elements are enabled. Then check the Enable box for the Output to Combustion option.

   The Output to Combustion option creates a combustion file that contains all the enabled Render Elements, precomposited and ready for tweaking.

6. Click the Files button to enter the output path for the combustion file xox.

   In the MAX Default Scanline A-Buffer rollout, you can define the parameters specific to the Default Max renderer.

7. In the Options group, check the Mapping and Shadows options.

   These options can be disabled when making test renders, but they should be enabled for any final renders.

8. In the Anti-Aliasing group, Anti-Aliasing and Filter Maps can be turned off to decrease test render times, but both should be checked for final rendering.

Note

Anti-aliasing reduces the jagged edges that result when you try to create a curved or diagonal line using pixels by blurring the edges of objects filtering scene geometry and its texture maps.

The Filter drop-down menu contains 12 different anti-aliasing methods that can be used. An in-depth description would require an entire chapter in itself. The different filters are representative of a wide range of filtering setups published in past SIGGRAPH papers. The differences between the filters are often subtle and can be affected by such variables as map detail and differences in geometry. A good starting point is the Sharp Quadratic filter, which is a very high-quality filter. The Blend filter enables you to combine the attributes of the Sharp Quadratic filters with softening. Cook Variable and Catmull Rom also produce good results.

In this exercise, we discussed the parameters that determine the duration and pixel dimensions of the rendered passes. We also discussed some of the items in the options groups that must be checked before initiating the final renders. These procedures need to be followed for each of the MAX files you created: render elements.max, confetti.max, pixie.max, shadow.max, and tableref.max.

Exercise 25.7   Network Rendering

Someone once said, "The best things in life are free." 3ds max's Network Rendering is easy to set up and use, and it can be installed on as many machines as you need, at no extra cost. This is great for users who are working at a company with networked PCs that are sitting idle on evenings and weekends.

But there are benefits for users who do not have a network, as well. Network Rendering can be used to queue up a number of files and render them one after another without any further interaction on your part. This is called *batch rendering* and is especially useful when rendering passes that are not created with Render Elements. Batch rendering is an aspect of Network Rendering that you can take advantage of, even if you have only one machine and no network.

Most of your passes will be created in one render using Render Elements. However, some passes that you are creating will not be rendered using Render Elements. These files were saved as separate MAX files and, as such, need to be loaded into 3ds max and rendered using the batch-rendering features of Network Rendering.

To use Network Rendering, you must have several computers connected by a TCP/IP network. Refer to Chapter 4, "Changes in Rendering," of this book and Chapter 13 of the *3ds max User Reference* for specific information.

During Network Rendering, it is important that all the files required for the render be available on the network in common directories that are accessible from the network. The destination directory must also be accessible from the network. Sometimes when a scene was first textured, the artist might not have used maps from a shared directory; it would be necessary to move the maps later. This also means reassigning the map paths in the Material Editor, which can be a lot of work if many maps are being used. The Utilities panel has a tool called the Map Path Editor that will move the files and reassign the map paths in a few steps.

To use the Map Path Editor, open the Utilities panel and load the Map Path Editor by clicking the More button and selecting it from the list.

In the Map Path Editor, select all maps in the list except the backplate. Click the Browse button and assign the map path through the network neighborhood.

Even if the maps are on a local drive this will map them using the UNC format for the paths, ensuring that all machines on the network will be capable of finding them.

Note

Another important consideration during network rendering is the amount of drive space available on the drive where the network server is installed. 3ds max's Network Renderer must be capable of creating a temporary version of the file being rendered on each network server. If there is not enough room on the drive where the server software is installed, the server will report an error and won't be capable of rendering the file.

Now, on to the exercise:

1. The first step in Network Rendering is to start the Network Manager software located in Programs/Discreet/3ds max/Network Rendering Manager of your Start menu.

   This distributes the jobs to the available servers and assigns which machine renders which frames.

2. When the Network Manager is running, start the Server application on all the machines that you want to render to.

   As the servers start up, they notify you that they are connected to the Network Manager. The notification states that the server is registered to the IP address of the machine on which the manager is running.

   When all servers are registered to the manager, you can start rendering.

3. Open 24_Render Elements.max. Before you render, make sure that the Use Map setting is not checked in the Common Parameters rollout of the Environment dialog box.

4. Click the Render Scene dialog box.

5. In the Time Output group, select Active Segment.

6. In the Output Size group, set the output to **720×480** with a pixel aspect ratio of **0.9**.

7. In the Options group, Effects should be the only option selected.

8. In the Render Output group, make sure that the output file path is set to your chosen renders directory and that Save File is checked. Click in the check box next to Net Render.

9. In the Render Elements rollout, make sure that Elements Active is checked, and then uncheck Display Elements.

   The Display Elements option is handy for test renders but is unnecessary for the final render and only uses up memory.

10. Make sure that all Render Elements are enabled.

11. In the Output to Combustion group, press the Files button and create a Combustion subdirectory in your chosen directory.

This creates a CWS file, which is a combustion workspace with the render elements already loaded and placed in a basic composition.

In the Max Default Scanline A-Buffer rollout, check the following settings:

12. In the Options rollout, check the Mapping and Shadows options—they might have been turned off to speed up test renders.

13. In the Anti-aliasing group, check Anti-aliasing and Filter Maps. Choose Cook Variable from the Filter options.

14. In the Image Motion Blur group, check Apply and set the duration to .25.

15. At the bottom of the Render Scene dialog box, make sure that ActiveShade is not checked and that you are rendering the Camera01 viewport.

16. Press the Render button.

    The Network Job Assignment dialog box opens. In the left side of the dialog box, you can edit the way the job is handled by the Network Renderer. You can make a number of edits, including the following:

    • You can enter a specific computer name or IP address. This feature is handy in a large shop in which several jobs using Network Rendering are running at the same time. In this situation, multiple versions of the Network Manager might be running on the same network. By entering a computer name or IP address, you can force the job to be assigned to the Network Manager of your choice.

    • The Priorities group enables you to choose Suspended. This option submits the job to the network but does not allow it to run until it is activated from the Queue Manager. This is especially useful when batch rendering on a single machine.

    • On the right side of the Network Job Assignment dialog box, you can view the available servers and jobs that are assigned via the manager to which you are currently connected. Here you can choose which network servers to use in your rendering. This is useful when you know that a certain machine does not have the resources to render your scene. In such cases, you can choose to exclude it from the Network Render.

17. After you have connected to a manager and have assigned your scene to the selected servers, press the Submit button.

    Your scene is sent to the Render Queue, where it is processed by the servers you specified.

18. Repeat the previous steps for the rest of the passes that are not rendered with Render Elements.

Note

To view the progress of Network Rendering, you can use the Queue Manager. This is the control tower of the network-rendering process. From the toolbar, you can connect or disconnect from managers that are running on the network.

The work area of the Queue Manager is divided into three sections. The upper-left section displays the jobs that are assigned to the current server. Right-clicking the jobs enables you to make a job active or inactive. You can also edit many of the render settings of jobs, such as ranges, file output settings, render options, and priorities.

When a job is selected, the upper-right section displays information about the selection. Here you can see who submitted a job, whether it has rendered, what the render settings were, render times for entire jobs and individual frames, and which network server rendered each frame.

The lower section displays information about the servers registered to a manager. Here you can view a server's statistics. This is very handy when you need to find out how much available workspace a particular server has. To view a server's statistics, right-click the server and choose Properties from the resulting menu. The right-click menu also allows the creation of server groups, which is a new feature that helps with resource management. In shops with render farms, this is a valuable tool for allocating render resources.

Summary

A render can be thought of as a painter's canvas. There is still a great deal of latitude for artistic expression, even after the models have been sculpted, the sets have been decorated, and the scenes have been composed and lit. Rendering can add subtle effects that blend 3D elements with live-action backgrounds. Rendering can also take a very prominent role in determining the look of a piece when used to render scenes in an illustrative style. Make use of every opportunity in the rendering process to add your input and make the piece the best that it can be.

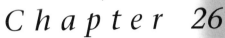

C h a p t e r 26

Compositing and Finishing in Combustion

by Max Ehrlich

This chapter discusses how to assemble rendered passes using Discreet's combustion. Specifically, you will learn how to do the following:

- Use combustion CWS workspace files created in 3ds max

- Combine additional rendered passes in the workspace

- Learn to use the transfer mode functions for compositing

- Render a final composite of the project

Why Combustion?

Most of what you will be doing in this chapter can be accomplished in any compositing package running on a personal computer. Combustion is used because of its tie-ins to 3ds max. 3ds max can render files directly to a combustion CWS file, doing the groundwork of setting up your composite for you. All you have to do is open the file in combustion and adjust the layers to your satisfaction. Combustion can also use the extended rendering features of the Rich Pixel Format (RPF files) that enable you to apply effects and make changes to a file after it has been rendered.

Finishing is the process of making adjustments to exposure, color correction, film grain, and more to the rendered output of a 3D animation. Many of these adjustments can be achieved in 3ds max itself, so why add another step to the process? The reason is simple: to save time.

You'll use tweaking exposure as an example. In your compositing program, you apply an effect that enables you to make changes to an image's histogram. You see the changes as you make them on a particular frame. Then you create a RAM preview to see the results on a range of frames. If you are satisfied, you are done. If not, you can further remove or tweak the settings without re-rendering the frames. The level of interactivity is also invaluable when combining 3D animation with live action. Being able to make adjustments to shadows, color balance, and reflections and to see the result immediately will help you create a more believable composite.

To get to the project at hand, you will have to make a couple of assumptions. The first is that you have combustion or the combustion demo installed on your computer. The second is that you have learned some basic tasks that all combustion projects require, one of which is how to open and save a workspace file. It is recommended that you at least complete Lesson 1 in the combustion tutorial to get the most out of the information in this chapter.

Exercise 26.1   Compositing in Combustion

1. Start combustion, go to the File/Open Workspace, and load the combustion workspace file render_elements.cws that was created by Render Elements in 3ds max, as seen in Figure 26.1.

Figure 26.1   This is how the render_elements.cws file looks as it was rendered from 3ds max.

In the lower-left area of the screen is the Workspace panel. The Workspace panel displays the footage that is being used in the composite and the order that the passes are composited in. Whether passes are in front of or in back of the other passes in the composite relates directly to the order in which they are placed in the workspace. Passes at the bottom of the workspace are behind passes that are higher up in the stack.

The workspace contains the diffuse pass, specular pass, and reflection pass. These are the Render Elements that were generated by 3ds max. Several render passes were rendered separately, and you will need to import these into the workspace as well.

2. In the Workspace panel, right-click the composite render_elements.cws and select Import Footage to bring up the Import menu.

3. Go to the directory where the files for this exercise are located, open the Backplate directory, and load the backplate.tga sequence.

Tip

Right-clicking in combustion activates context menus that enable you to perform actions and assign operators that you can also access through the menu bar at the top of the screen. Using the context menus will speed up your workflow.

When the backplate is loaded in combustion, the other layers in the composite disappear and all that you see is the newly imported layer.

Layers in a combustion composite are stacked on top of each other. Loading the backplate footage puts it at the top of the composite, which means that all other layers in the composite are behind it. You'll want to move the backplate behind all the layers in the composite.

4. In the Workspace panel, click and drag the backplate.tga footage to the bottom of the footage, just above the light and camera icons in the composite.

When moved to the rear of the composition, the backplate becomes partially obscured by the layers in front of it in the composition. There appears to be several black objects covering the table and the box that the Jester jumps out of. This is the Diffuse layer, and it does not have a correct Alpha Channel because of a bug in the Render Elements of 3ds max.

To work around this, you need a layer from which you can extract a correct Alpha Channel. When you rendered the max file, you anticipated this need and created the sequence alpha.tga.

5. Import the file alpha.tga into the workspace.

6. In the Workspace panel, click and drag the newly imported footage to the very bottom of the composite. Click the yellow icon next to alpha.tga.

This turns off the display of the footage. The icon turns gray to indicate that the footage is turned off. You never see this layer; you are using it as a matte to enable you to hide some of the objects in the Render Elements that are visible because of the bug in the process that creates the Render Elements Alpha Channels. You will use this layer to provide a correctly rendered Alpha Channel that will hide matte shadow objects.

7. In the Workspace panel, select the diffuse pass and right-click it. Select Channels/Set Matte from the Operators group of the right-click menu. Click on the gray arrow next to the layer's name to see the components of the layer.

The layer is made up of the footage diffuse.tga at the bottom and a Set Matte operator on top of it.

8. Click the Set Matte operator.

The controls for the operator are displayed in the area to the right of the Workspace panel.

9. Click the Layer button and select alpha.tga from the menu. Click the Input button and select Alpha.

Now the diffuse.tga layer uses the Alpha Channel from the alpha.tga footage as a mask. See Figure 26.2 for the result.

Figure 26.2 This is how the render_elements.cws file looks with backplate.tga inserted.

The reflections on the toy truck are more intense and defined than those on the other objects in the scene.

10. Lower the intensity by choosing the layer New riders_reflection. In the Composite Control panel, click the Opacity field and enter a value of **75**.

    You also want to lower the glossiness of the truck. You will do this with a Blur operator.

11. In the Workspace panel, right-click the layer New riders_reflection. Choose Box Blur from the Blur/Sharpen group. Click in the Radius field of the Box Blur controls and enter a value of **2**.

    The blur helps knock the hard edge off the reflections in the truck.

 Note

You can choose from two general-purpose Blur operators. Box Blur averages a pixel color based on pixels around it. It is fast and ideal for reflections on objects. Gaussian Blur is more realistic but takes longer to calculate, making it better for effects that are more noticeable.

The specular pass also needs to be turned down to make the specular high-lights on the trucks wheels less hot.

12. Do this by accessing the Composite Controls for the specular layer and entering a value of **70** in the Opacity field.

13. Next, import the tableclothref_.tga file into the workspace.

    This is the reflection of the Jester that appears in the tablecloth when he is standing on it.

14. Move the layer below the diffuse.tga layer.

    You want the reflection to be superimposed over the backplate.

    The Jester reflection also has no Alpha Channel. You will use Transfer modes to allow the layers below to show through.

15. Click the Surface button in the Composite Controls group. Click the Transfer Mode button and select Screen.

Note

When using Screen mode, pixels that are darker than the pixels over which the layer is being composited are not shown.

The reflection is too intense when compared with the reflections of other objects on the tablecloth.

16. Lower the opacity to 50% by clicking in the Opacity field and entering **50**.

    The reflection looks better but it is still too sharp. You will now add a blur operator to the tableclothref layer.

17. Right-click to bring up the Operator list and choose Blur/Sharpen/Gaussian Blur. In the Gaussian Blur controls, click in the Radius field and set the number to **2**. See Figure 26.3 for the result.

18. Import the shadows.tga pass into the workspace. Click and drag the shadow pass to be on top of the diffuse pass.

19. In the Composite Controls panel, set the Transfer mode to Multiply.

    This allows the shadow pass to affect only the areas that are in shadow.

    The shadows are too dark compared to the rest of the scene, so you need to adjust the opacity.

20. Set the opacity to **40** percent. Use an area of the real shadows on the table-cloth as a reference for the CG shadow.

21. The shadows in the scene are softer than the CG shadows, so apply a Gaussian Blur operator with a setting of **1** to soften them slightly (see Figure 26.4).

    The confetti was rendered as its own pass because you'll want to be able to color-correct it independently of the rest of the scene.

Figure 26.3   This is how render_elements.cws looks with reflections added.

Figure 26.4   This is how render_elements.cws looks with the shadows.tga pass added to it.

22. Import the confetti.tga layer into the workspace.

23. Adjust the saturation and the contrast by applying a Discreet CC Histogram operator from the Color Correction Operator group.

24. In the CC Histogram Controls panel (see Figure 26.5), click the Histogram button. Click the Master and RGB buttons to apply the adjustment to the entire range of the layer.

Figure 26.5   This is the combustion CC Histogram Controls panel.

The top set of sliders is called the Input Sliders. You will use the Input Sliders to adjust the contrast.

25. Click in the numeric field for the right Input Slider and enter 230.

The lower set of sliders is the Output Sliders. You will use them to adjust the saturation of the layer.

26. Enter 45 in the left Output Slider and 215 in the right Output Slider.

This moves the colors of the layer toward gray and reduces the saturation slightly. The effects are subtle, so do not expect to see a huge difference in the way the image appears. But it does help make the confetti look more realistic.

27. Now import the pixie.tga pass. In the Composite Controls, set the Transfer mode to Screen so that you can drop out the black background of the layer.

28. Click and drag the pixie.tga layer to the position just above the layer JesterRef.tga. You want the pixie dust to appear behind the Jester character. (See Figure 26.6.)

29. Save the Combustion workspace as **finalcomp.cws**.

Now that all the passes are in place, you can render the result.

30. Go to the finalcomp.cws file in the menu bar and choose Render.

The window that appears is the render queue. The combustion render queue provides much of the same functionality as the Render Scene dialog box in 3ds max, combined with the batch rendering of 3ds max's network rendering.

Figure 26.6   This is how render_elements.cws looks with confetti.tga and pixie.tga added.

31. In the Render Queue dialog box, choose Quick Setup.

This brings up a Render Queue Quick Setup dialog box, as seen in Figure 26.7.

32. Check the Use Preset option, and choose Targa Sequence (32-bit) Best as the output format.

33. Click the Render Folder button to select the folder where you want to render your project.

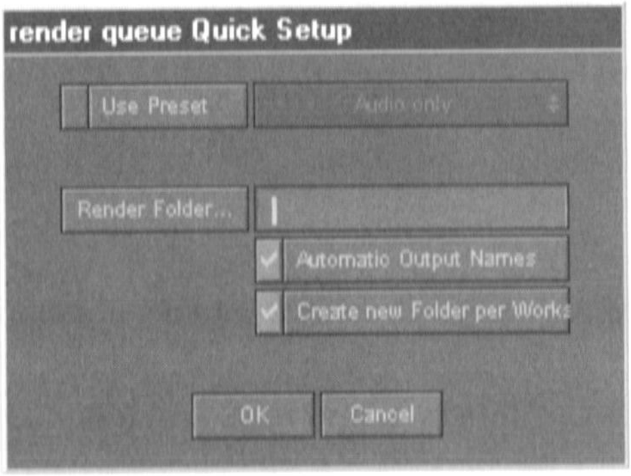

Figure 26.7   This is the Render Queue Quick Setup dialog box.

34. Uncheck the options Automatic Output Names and Create a New Folder Per Workspace; press OK.

35. In the Render Settings tab (see Figure 26.8), click the Filename button, choose a directory to render to, and save the rendered files as **finalcomp.tga**.

Figure 26.8   This is the Render Settings tab.

36. Press the Process button to start the rendering.

The Statistics tab appears and shows information regarding the progress of the render.

This concludes the compositing exercise. When the file is rendered, you can view the rendered files by importing them into a new combustion workspace or the 3ds max Ram Player.

Summary

This chapter focused on how the passes you created in 3ds max are reassembled in a compositing process to create a finished image. The information provided in this chapter is only an overview of what actually is done to composite a professionally produced video project. Almost all 3D work goes through a compositing program. It is necessary for people working in 3ds max to have some basic compositing skills and knowledge to help them to develop a strategy for how a project will be rendered, to understand the needs of the compositing process, and to even be able to assemble their own rendered passes to check their work before handing over the files.

Appendix A

What's on the CD-ROM

The accompanying CD-ROM is packed with all sorts of exercise files and products to help you work with this book and with 3ds max 4. The following sections contain detailed descriptions of the CD's contents.

For more information about the use of this CD, please review the [ReadMe.txt] file in the root directory. This file includes important disclaimer information as well as information about installation, system requirements, troubleshooting, and technical support.

> **Note**
>
> **Technical Support Issues**   If you have any difficulties with this CD, you can access our Web site at http://www.newriders.com.

System Requirements

This CD-ROM was configured for use on systems running Windows NT Workstation, Windows 95, Windows 98, or Windows 2000.

Loading the CD Files

To load the files from the CD, insert the disc into your CD-ROM drive. If autoplay is enabled on your machine, the CD-ROM setup program starts automatically the first time you insert the disc. You may copy the files to your hard drive, or use them right off the disc.

> **Note**
>
> This CD-ROM uses long and mixed-case filenames, requiring the use of a protected mode CD-ROM driver.

Exercise Files

This CD contains all the files you'll need to complete the exercises in *Inside 3ds max 4*. These files can be found in the root directory's Chapter Files folder. Please note, however, that you'll not find any folders for chapters 2, 4, 5, and 6; these chapters contain exercises for which you do not need to access any project files.

The CD also contains links to third-party programs talked about in this book.

Color Images

This CD also contains full-color screenshots of many of the images displayed in this book for use as reference. The images can be found in the Screenshots folder. Please note, however, that there are no images for chapters 5 and 6.

Read This Before Opening the Software

By opening the CD package, you agree to be bound by the following agreement:

You may not copy or redistribute the entire CD-ROM as a whole. Copying and redistribution of individual software programs on the CD-ROM is governed by terms set by individual copyright holders.

The installer, code, images, actions, and brushes from the author(s) are copyrighted by the publisher and the authors.

This software is sold as-is, without warranty of any kind, either expressed or implied, including but not limited to the implied warranties of merchantability and fitness for a particular purpose. Neither the publisher nor its dealers or distributors assumes any liability for any alleged or actual damages arising from the use of this program. (Some states do not allow for the exclusion of implied warranties, so the exclusion may not apply to you.)

Index

Q-R

S

T

U

V

W-Z